DRONE

Drones are the iconic military technology of many of today's most pressing conflicts, a lens through which US foreign policy is understood, and a means for discussing key issues regarding the laws of war and the changing nature of global politics. Drones have captured the public imagination, partly because they project lethal force in a manner that challenges accepted rules, norms, and moral understandings.

Drone Wars presents a series of essays by legal scholars, journalists, government officials, military analysts, social scientists, and foreign policy experts. It addresses drones' impact on the ground, how their use adheres to and challenges the laws of war, their relationship to complex policy issues regarding national security and foreign affairs, and the ways their deployment and development help us understand the future of war. The book is a diverse and comprehensive interdisciplinary perspective on drones that covers important debates on targeted killing and civilian casualties; presents key data on drone deployment; and offers new ideas on their historical development, significance, and impact on law and policy. *Drone Wars* documents the current state of the field at an important moment in history when new military technologies are transforming how war is practiced by the United States and, increasingly, by other states and by non-state actors around the world.

Peter L. Bergen is a journalist, documentary producer, and the author of four books about al-Qaeda, three of which were *New York Times* best-sellers and three of which were named among the best non-fiction books of the year by the *Washington Post*. He is Vice President, Director of Studies and of Fellows, and Director of the International Security Program at New America in Washington, DC; Professor of Practice in the School of Politics and Global Studies at Arizona State University and Co-Director of the Future of War Project; a Fellow at Fordham University's Center on National Security; editor of the South Asia Channel on Foreignpolicy.com; and a national security analyst at CNN. He has held teaching positions at Harvard University and Johns Hopkins University.

Daniel Rothenberg is Professor of Practice in the School of Politics and Global Studies and the Lincoln Fellow for Ethics and International Human Rights Law at Arizona State University, as well as a Fellow at New America and Co-Director of the Future of War Project. He was the founding Executive Director of the Center for Law and Global Affairs at the Sandra Day O'Connor College of Law. Previously, he worked at the International Human Rights Law Institute at DePaul University College of Law; was a Senior Fellow at the Orville H. Schell Jr. Center for International Human Rights at Yale Law School; and was an Assistant Professor at the University of Michigan and a Fellow in the Michigan Society of Fellows. From 2004 through 2010 he worked in Afghanistan and Iraq designing and managing human rights and rule of law projects.

Drone Wars

TRANSFORMING CONFLICT, LAW, AND POLICY

Edited by

PETER L. BERGEN

and

DANIEL ROTHENBERG

CAMBRIDGE
UNIVERSITY PRESS

CAMBRIDGE
UNIVERSITY PRESS

32 Avenue of the Americas, New York, NY 10013-2473, USA

Cambridge University Press is part of the University of Cambridge.

It furthers the University's mission by disseminating knowledge in the pursuit of
education, learning, and research at the highest international levels of excellence.

www.cambridge.org
Information on this title: www.cambridge.org/9781107663381

© Cambridge University Press 2015

First published 2015

Printed in the United States of America

A catalog record for this publication is available from the British Library.

Library of Congress Cataloging in Publication Data
Drone wars : transforming conflict, law, and policy /
Peter L. Bergen and Daniel Rothenberg, editors.
    pages   cm
Includes bibliographical references and index.
ISBN 978-1-107-02556-1 (Hardback) – ISBN 978-1-107-66338-1 (Paperback)
1. Air warfare (International law)   2. Uninhabited combat aerial vehicles   3. Aeronautics,
Military–Law and legislation.   4. Afghan War, 2001–Law and legislation.   5. Afghan War,
2001–Aerial operations.   I. Bergen, Peter L., 1962– editor.   II. Rothenberg, Daniel, editor.
KZ6680.D76 2014
358.4′14–dc23   2014020421

ISBN 978-1-107-02556-1 Hardback
ISBN 978-1-107-66338-1 Paperback

Contents

Contributors

Brad Allenby is the founding Director of the Center for Earth Systems Engineering and Management at Arizona State University, where he is a President's Professor and the Lincoln Professor of Engineering and Ethics. He is also the founding chair of the Consortium for Emerging Technologies, Military Operations, and National Security.

William C. Banks is the Director of the Institute for National Security and Counterterrorism at Syracuse University. He is also a Board of Advisors Distinguished Professor of Law at Syracuse University College of Law and has co-authored two leading texts in the field, *National Security Law* and *Counterterrorism Law*.

Peter L. Bergen is Vice President, Director of Studies and of Fellows, and Director of the International Security Program at New America in Washington, DC, as well as Professor of Practice in the School of Politics and Global Studies at Arizona State University. He is CNN's national security analyst and has authored several best-selling books on al-Qaeda, including *Manhunt: The Ten-Year Search for Bin Laden from 9/11 to Abbottabad.*

Charles Blanchard was the General Counsel of the United States Air Force and the chief legal officer and chief ethics official for the Air Force from 2009 through 2013. He was previously the General Counsel for the United States Army and Chief Legal Counsel for the White House Office of National Drug Control Policy; he is now a partner at Arnold & Porter LLP.

Megan Braun is a JD candidate at Yale Law School. A former Rhodes Scholar, she received an MPhil in International Relations from Oxford University, where she researched the evolution of US drone policy and the interaction between technology, law, and just war tradition.

Rosa Brooks is a Senior Advisor to the National Security Program at New America; a columnist for *Foreign Policy*; and a Professor at the Georgetown

University Law Center, where she teaches international law and constitutional law. She previously served as Counselor to Under Secretary of Defense for Policy Michele Flournoy.

Werner J. A. Dahm is the founding Director of the Security and Defense Systems Initiative at Arizona State University and Foundation Professor of Aerospace and Mechanical Engineering at Arizona State University. He previously served as the Chief Scientist of the United States Air Force.

Sarah Holewinski was Executive Director of the Center for Civilians in Conflict, which advises warring parties on preventing and responding to civilian harm. A former White House staffer, she is a Senior Fellow with the Truman National Security Project and contributes frequently to the *New York Times*, *Foreign Policy*, and the *Washington Post*.

Saba Imtiaz is a freelance journalist in Pakistan. Her work has appeared in the *Christian Science Monitor*, the *Guardian*, and the *Express Tribune*. She is the author of *Karachi, You're Killing Me!* and the forthcoming *No Team of Angels*.

Samuel Issacharoff is the Bonnie and Richard Reiss Professor of Constitutional Law at New York University School of Law. He specializes in civil procedure, law and economics, constitutional law, and employment law. He co-authored *Law and Democracy*, a casebook in the law of the political process, and he is a Fellow in the American Academy of Arts and Sciences.

Konstantin Kakaes is a journalist who writes about science and technology. From 2011 to 2014, he was a Fellow at New America. He was previously a Fellow of the International Reporting Project of Johns Hopkins University's School of Advanced International Studies and a Knight Science Journalism Fellow at the Massachusetts Institute of Technology.

Tara McKelvey is a features writer for the BBC and former correspondent for *Newsweek* and thedailybeast.com. She is the author of *Monstering: Inside America's Policy of Secret Interrogations and Torture in the Terror War* and was awarded a 2011 Guggenheim Fellowship in general non-fiction.

Richard Pildes is the Sudler Family Professor of Constitutional Law at New York University School of Law, where he focuses on democracy and law, constitutional law, and terrorism and law. He served as Co-Director of the NYU Center on Law and Security; co-authored *The Law of Democracy*, a casebook in the law of the political process; and is a Fellow of the American Academy of Arts and Sciences.

David Rohde is a columnist for Reuters, a former reporter for the *New York Times*, and a two-time recipient of the Pulitzer Prize for his reporting on the

Srebrenica massacre and the *New York Times*' reporting on Afghanistan and Pakistan. He is the author of *Beyond War: Reimagining American Influence in a New Middle East*.

Daniel Rothenberg is Professor of Practice at the School of Politics and Global Studies, the Lincoln Fellow for Ethics and International Human Rights Law at Arizona State University, and a Fellow at New America. From 2004 through 2010 he designed and managed human rights and rule of law projects in Afghanistan and Iraq.

Jennifer Rowland is a graduate student at Harvard University's Kennedy School of Government. Previously, she was a Program Associate for the National Security Program at New America. She has co-authored with Peter L. Bergen a number of columns published by CNN.com.

Naureen Shah is a human rights expert and frequent media commentator on US drone policy, as well as the former Associate Director at Columbia Law School's Human Rights Institute and Acting Director of the Columbia Law School's Human Rights Clinic.

Peter W. Singer is Strategist and Senior Fellow at New America. Previously, he was the Director of the Center for 21st Century Security and Intelligence and a Senior Fellow in the Foreign Policy program at the Brookings Institute. He is the author of numerous books on military issues, including the best-seller, *Wired for War: The Robotics Revolution and Conflict in the 21st Century*.

Christopher Swift is an Adjunct Professor of National Security Studies at Georgetown University and a Fellow at the University of Virginia Law School's Center for National Security Law. He is the author of the forthcoming book *The Fighting Vanguard: Local Insurgencies in the Global Jihad*. He is a practicing attorney in the field of arms control, counterproliferation, and counterterrorism.

David True is an Associate Professor of Religion at Wilson College in Pennsylvania. He is the managing editor of the journal *Political Theology* and is executive editor of its blog, *Political Theology Today*. He writes about the political theology in debates about issues such as immigration, torture, and drones.

Michael Waltz is a former counterterrorism advisor to Vice President Dick Cheney, a Special Forces officer in the reserves, and author of the forthcoming book *Warrior-Diplomat*. He is a Fellow at New America.

Acknowledgments

This book has grown out of a partnership between the two editors, Peter L. Bergen and Daniel Rothenberg, and between New America and Arizona State University (ASU). We decided to work on this book shortly after a joint ASU/New America conference organized in February 2011. Many of the essays collected here are versions of presentations from this event.

As the organizers of the conference and co-editors of this book, we are deeply indebted to the contributors, whose diverse opinions and intellectual perspectives are inspiring and whose patience and collegiality are much appreciated. It is striking what a kind, thoughtful, and generous group this has been, especially in light of the difficult nature of the subject matter and the challenges faced by addressing the ravages of war.

We are also very grateful for the extraordinary support and assistance of a number of dedicated colleagues.

At New America, thanks to Steve Coll, the former President, for the essential support he gave to the International Security Program under whose guidance we began our drone database and research. Thanks also to Anne-Marie Slaughter, the current President and CEO of New America, who has enthusiastically and expertly supported the program and our continued research on drones.

Jennifer Rowland, Bailey Cahall, and Emily Schneider all have made important contributions to our drone research and have assisted in various other ways to make this volume of essays a reality. Megan Braun helped to substantially improve our drone databases, as did Fatima Mustafa, Farhad Peikar, and Annie Osborne. They in turn built on the excellent work of Andrew Lebovich and Katherine Tiedemann. Thanks also to web production manager Nick McClellan, who built the database infrastructure.

In addition, many thanks to the advisory council for New America's International Security Program; its co-chairs Chip Kaye and Fareed Zakaria;

and its members, Rita Hauser, Tom Freston, Fred Hassan, and Bob Niehaus. Without their invaluable support we could not have maintained our drone databases or created projects such as this book. Thanks also to the foundations and program officers who have supported our work: Marin Strmecki of the Smith Richardson Foundation; Lisa Magarrell at the Open Society Foundation; and Stephen Del Rosso at the Carnegie Corporation.

At ASU, special thanks to President Michael Crow and Senior Vice President of University Affairs and Chief of Staff James O'Brien for providing exceptional institutional support for this initiative and for the Future of War project, a joint ASU/New America endeavor. Thanks also to Patrick Kenney, Vice Provost and Dean of the College of Liberal Arts and Sciences; Cameron Thies, Professor and Director of the School of Politics and Global Studies; and Christopher Callahan, founding Dean of the Walter Cronkite School of Journalism.

Thanks to former Dean Paul Berman of the Sandra Day O'Connor College of Law who played a key role in supporting the initial conference and promoting an interdisciplinary approach to international legal issues. In addition, Joel Garreau was essential in linking our two institutions; his enthusiasm for drones and the challenges of addressing technological innovation set the tone for our work. Special thanks to Laura Dickinson, who was instrumental in creating the Center for Law and Global Affairs and guiding many of the ideas that motivated the book; and to Emoline Fox, who provided extraordinary assistance in managing ASU's engagement with the initial conference and larger book project.

In addition, many thanks to key ASU colleagues at the College of Law working on international law and policy issues who provided guidance, support, and a productive and engaging intellectual community including: Kenneth Abbott, Daniel Bodansky, Charles Calleros, Aaron Fellmeth, David Gartner, and current Dean Douglas Sylvester. Also thanks to the drone conference co-sponsors Gary Marchant and Sandy Askland of the Center for Law, Science, and Innovation and Elizabeth Andersen, former Executive Director and Executive Vice President of the American Society of International Law.

In addition, a number of students at the College of Law and the Barrett Honors College provided significant background research, support, and assistance with different aspects of the book, including David Banko, Jason Burgoyne, Christopher Forbes, Christine Peters, Cruz Michael Ramirez, Evan Schechter, Sarah Ella Spears, and Andrew White. Special thanks to Alexa Magee, who devoted many hours transcribing interviews and researching drone policy; and to Major Michael Wilburn, USAF (Ret.), who provided essential review, research, and technical support.

We would also like to thank our editor, John Berger, for his exceptional guidance and support, David Jou and the others on the staff at Cambridge University Press, as well as Bindu Vinod, Sundararajan Rengarajan, and Lila Stromer for their assistance in making this book a reality.

Finally, Peter Bergen thanks his wife Tresha Mabile for all the essential support she has given him on this book project and others. Daniel Rothenberg thanks his wife Ilissa Lazar for her support, patience, and love.

Introduction

PETER L. BERGEN AND DANIEL ROTHENBERG

Drones are the iconic military technology of the current conflicts in Afghanistan, Pakistan, and Yemen. They have become a lens through which US foreign policy is understood, as well as a means for discussing key issues regarding the laws of war and the changing nature of global politics. In part, this is because drones involve new ways of projecting lethal force that challenge accepted rules, norms, and moral understandings. They enable strikes both within and outside of established war zones, highlighting divisions between the activities of military and intelligence services. They are controlled by pilots located half way around the world, which raises questions about the implications and possibilities of remote warfare. They engage in precision strikes yet harm civilians, opening discussions on the legitimacy, ethics, and legality of targeted killing.

Drones have also captured the public imagination. Stories about drones draw in viewers and readers interested in current affairs and foreign policy. They play a central role in defining conflicts that have continued for well over a decade, minimizing the risks of those that deploy them and expanding the reach of counterterrorism operations. Increasingly, drones appear in movies, television, and multiple forms of popular culture. Their sleek, stark appearance is visually striking. Their lack of an on-board pilot touches on deep-seated fears regarding the rapid advance of technology and a possible future of autonomous killing machines. These and other issues stimulate debates on drones that appear to reveal and heighten political divisions. Polls show that the American public largely supports the US deployment of armed drones abroad, even as significant majorities in other countries strongly object to these policies. Yet when Americans consider the possibility of domestic drone deployment, especially by the state, profound anxieties emerge.

This book addresses many of the issues raised by armed drones through a series of essays by legal scholars, journalists, government officials, social

1

scientists, foreign policy experts, and others. It is premised on the idea that today's drone wars provide an important opportunity for reflecting on global politics, technological innovation, and conflict within our rapidly changing world. The book is divided into four thematic sections that cover distinct though interrelated elements of drone use, policy, history, meaning, and impact. Each section begins with a personal narrative describing direct experiences with drones. This grounds larger policy discussions with a recognition that, in the end, drone deployment affects individuals and their communities on all sides of the conflict in significant and often transformative ways.

The first section reviews the impact of drones on the ground, with a focus on Afghanistan, Pakistan, and Yemen. It opens with an account by journalist David Rohde (formerly of the *New York Times*, now with Reuters) of a seven-month period when he was held by members of the Haqqani Network in Pakistan. He recounts his captors' fear of drones as well as their suspicions that local residents were spies secretly guiding attacks. This is followed by a chapter by Peter L. Bergen and Jennifer Rowland of New America, which discusses CIA drone strikes in Pakistan and Yemen from 2002 through 2013. The information they analyze has been gathered and cross-referenced from multiple news sources, revealing significant conclusions on drone strikes, civilian casualties, and the impact of these attacks on al-Qaeda and the Taliban. Next, Sarah Holewinski, former executive director of the Center for Civilians in Conflict, examines the impact of drone strikes on civilian populations, suggesting that current policies have serious and often poorly addressed consequences for local communities. She considers the secretive and often ambiguous process of targeting and highlights the need for greater transparency and accountability. Christopher Swift, a lawyer and fellow at the University of Virginia Law School's Center for National Security Law, writes about the drone campaign in Yemen based on fieldwork and interviews with tribal leaders, Islamist politicians, Salafi clerics, and others. He argues that understanding the impact of drone strikes in the country requires a contextually sensitive review of how al-Qaeda and its allies operate, using popular resentment as a key means of local recruiting. This approach reveals the political and operational limits of drone warfare in Yemen, with implications for drone use in other parts of the world. Finally, Saba Imtiaz, a Pakistani journalist, reviews what people in her country think about drones, outlining the history of local discussions and media reporting on US drone policy. She argues that the debate is more complicated than opinion polls suggest and is deeply entwined with local party politics, domestic divisions, and Pakistan's struggles to assert its sovereignty and define an inclusive national identity.

The second section considers how drone deployment engages the efficacy and value of the laws of war for regulating current conflicts. It begins with a narrative from a drone pilot operating out of Nellis Air Force Base in Las Vegas, Nevada. He describes the intimacy of drone warfare in which he surveils targets for long periods of time, following the lives of those he may later attack. He also discusses the complexity of modern warfare, in which just after completing a combat mission he might drive home to his family, shop at a mall, or attend a party or baseball game. Next, Charles Blanchard, former General Counsel for the US Air Force, critiques a series of common misunderstandings of drones, which he terms "remotely piloted aircraft," or RPA. He explains that drones are not unmanned in that they require large teams of professionals to perform their various functions, that they are deployed by the military in full accordance with domestic and international laws, and that their value comes from their role as one tool among many within a complex, integrated military strategy. In the next chapter, William C. Banks, of Syracuse University College of Law, uses the case of a drone strike in Yemen against Anwar al-Awlaki, a US citizen, to examine the legal basis for targeted killings. He reviews who can be targeted outside of traditional battle spaces and when, if ever, American citizens may be killed. Next, human rights expert Naureen Shah considers the role of the US military's Joint Special Operations Command (JSOC) in conducting drone strikes, arguing that there is no longer a marked separation between the military's actions in clearly defined war zones and the CIA's covert strikes in Pakistan, Yemen, and elsewhere. She suggests that JSOC's highly secretive nature raises questions as to the legality of the US military's drone operations and may signal a dangerous trend of blurring the traditional divisions between the military and intelligence services. Then journalist Tara McKelvey of the BBC profiles Harold Koh, a fierce opponent of George W. Bush administration's terrorism policies and the former Dean of the Yale Law School, who shifted his position from criticizing US drone strikes and counterinsurgency policies to affirming their legality during his time as the Legal Advisor at the US Department of State.

The third section reviews the implications of today's drone wars for larger policy debates. It opens with a narrative from Michael Waltz, a Special Forces officer who led missions in Afghanistan at a time when drone deployment there was expanding. He outlines the benefits of drones in providing real-time intelligence during combat while also suggesting that an overreliance on new technologies creates a more risk-averse military and may present obstacles to working with local populations. In the next chapter, P. W. Singer, an expert on national security based at New America, describes the "five deadly flaws" of addressing new military technologies. He argues that the transformative nature of drones and other emerging technologies, coupled with the extraordinary pace of their innovation, require that we openly confront the key legal, ethical, and policy issues they raise. Rosa Brooks, a Georgetown University law professor and former Pentagon official, questions the current fixation on drones over an assessment of the policies governing their use. She argues that current debates mask important questions regarding the ethics and efficacy of drone deployment and calls for a more open and honest policy discussion. Next, Rhodes Scholar Megan Braun writes that drones are not revolutionary but rather represent a particular technology that appeared at a unique moment when their capacities matched the needs of the US government, particularly the CIA. She sees the development of a program of targeted killing as more significant than the drones themselves and wonders about the nature of their future impact. David True, a professor of religion at Wilson College, argues that while drones provide new capabilities and powers, they also raise important ethical questions. He explores these issues by reviewing US drone policy in relation to just war theory and the realism of Reinhold Niebuhr. He argues that there has been inadequate clarity and care in developing an ethically engaged approach to drone deployment, suggesting that the costs of this failure are significant. Then, Peter L. Bergen and Jennifer Rowland consider the growing prevalence of drones around the world. Their chapter includes a detailed table, based on hundreds of news reports and government documents, which reveals that more than eighty countries currently operate drones. The chapter suggests that while the United States enjoys a relative monopoly on armed drones at present, this situation will not last long.

The fourth and final section considers what drone deployment teaches us about the future of war. It begins with the words of "Adam Khan," a pseudonym for a resident of Pakistan's tribal areas along the border with Afghanistan, who was interviewed by former *New York Times* reporter Pir Zubair Shah. Khan reflects on both the accuracy of drone attacks and the fear and uncertainty of living under their constant threat. In the next chapter, Werner J. A. Dahm, former Chief Scientist of the US Air Force, reviews the current and emerging technology of drones. He focuses on how drones present significant new capabilities for intelligence, surveillance, and reconnaissance; how there are no near-term plans to remove people from the "kill chain"; and why within a decade drones are likely to become many times more powerful with greater capacities, longer flight durations, and significantly expanded capabilities. Then Konstantin Kakaes, a journalist and former Fellow at New America, reviews the little-known history of drone development, from the early twentieth century through the present. He traces the testing and use of drones in the First and Second World Wars, multiple secret drone programs during the Cold War, their extensive use in the Vietnam War, and more recent deployment by Israel and the United States. By reflecting on past drone programs, those that failed and those that succeeded, he argues that significant future advances are inevitable, although they are likely to proceed at a slower pace and in a different manner than what is promised by many drone advocates. Samuel Issacharoff and Richard Pildes, both professors at New York University School of Law, describe how drone deployment reveals a fundamental transformation in the practice of war. They suggest that while traditional understandings of the laws of war define enemies based on status, emerging forms of war target opponents as individuals through a determination of personal responsibility within complex conflicts involving non-state actors operating in multiple locations. They argue that current understandings of the laws of war are inadequate for addressing these challenges and that we need to acknowledge this shift in order to design new and more appropriate military and legal regimes. Brad Allenby, a lawyer and engineering professor at Arizona State University, explores the degree to which drones represent a transformative technology that challenges established understandings of policy, strategy, and the laws of war. He argues that a deeper discussion of drones requires focusing attention away from the technology itself and toward an engagement with how innovations interact and co-evolve with society and its institutions. In the final chapter, Daniel Rothenberg, a professor at Arizona State University, argues that drones signal a shift in the nature of conflict toward "data-driven warfare." He suggests that this is seen most clearly in the use of signature strikes, which illustrate a newly invasive form of projecting lethal force linking substantive advances in information collection and analysis with remote killing. Facing these challenges requires rethinking the laws of war and developing, sooner rather than later, new rules for regulating conflict.

Taken together, the personal narratives and chapters presented here provide an overview of key legal, policy, and ethical issues associated with today's drone wars. The goal of this book is to encourage and enable an in-depth discussion of drone deployment and its broad implications for the changing nature of war and politics within a shifting global landscape. Some of the chapters provide insight into the current use of drones and their role within today's conflicts. Others focus on drone history, broad policy considerations, and the impact and legality of targeted killing. Still others suggest that drones are a useful way for understanding larger issues associated with the inadequacies of existing laws and norms and the profound challenges of facing a dangerous and rapidly changing world.

One thing is certain: the period during which the United States and a handful of other countries control the use of militarized drones is coming to an end. With increasing frequency and impact, drones will be deployed by an ever-larger number of states and may also be used by various non-state actors. In addition, the types of drones deployed will expand considerably, along with significant advances in their capabilities. For these reasons, it is important to reflect critically on today's drone wars as a means of preparing ourselves for the future. This is true as regards possible revisions to the laws of war, as well as serious reflections on the social and political impact of emerging technologies and changes in global policy and strategy. For these reasons, there is a pressing need to reflect critically on today's drone wars. This book is an effort to contribute to this process.

PART I
DRONES ON THE GROUND

My Guards Absolutely Feared Drones

Reflections on Being Held Captive
for Seven Months by the Taliban

DAVID ROHDE

I was kidnapped by the Haqqani Network and held captive for seven months, from November 2008 to June 2009, in North and South Waziristan.

My guards absolutely feared drones.

They would watch very closely whenever a drone was overhead and tracked how many drones appeared. They thought that when several drones gathered overhead, a strike was about to happen.

They avoided gathering in groups because they feared drone strikes. We were told not to hang our clothes on the walls to dry because they were afraid that it would appear as if a large number of people were there and this would attract the attention of the drones, which would lead to an attack.

However, in Miranshah, North Waziristan, they still managed to carry out trainings. Two of my guards would stay with me and two would go off and learn how to make roadside bombs. So, despite the fact that the drone strikes were being carried out, they did the trainings, just in much smaller numbers.

I would say that during the time I was in captivity there were two dozen drone strikes in North and South Waziristan. In February 2009 there was an attack in South Waziristan that reportedly killed thirty people. Among them were Uzbeks, who my guards said were known for teaching Afghani and Pakistani Taliban how to make bombs. In that case the strikes seemed accurate in terms of those targeted and killed. In general, the strikes angered my guards and the Taliban.

The closest drone strike to me was on March 25, 2009, in Makeen, South Waziristan, a stronghold of Biatullah Mehsud, the Pakistani Taliban leader. Two missiles struck two vehicles that were driving by the house where we were being held captive. The strikes were so close that pieces of shrapnel landed in the yard where we were and the explosion blew out the plastic sheeting over the windows. The attack killed seven militants, both Pakistani and foreign.

The guards were absolutely furious.

I saw on the ground what a terrifying situation the drones created among the Taliban. They were paranoid that all local people were spies and that they were secretly guiding the drone strikes. Once they blamed a local farmer for being an American spy. They thought that he somehow guided the strike on the two vehicles in Makeen and detained him. There were all these wild theories about secret GPS devices that enabled the attacks. They believed this farmer hid a GPS in the spare tire of his car.

He said he was innocent, but a group of foreign and Pakistani militants tortured him. First, they chopped off his leg and then disemboweled him, at which point he "confessed" to being a spy. I was told that they then decapitated him and hung his body in the market in Makeen as a warning to other villagers.

When we were held in Miranshah, North Waziristan, we were in the house of a local intelligence chief for the Haqqanis. He would come home at night and talk about how that day they had hung local people who were spies. They had the cell phones and other personal possessions of the people that they killed.

They were convinced that everyone who was not with them was against them.

I felt terrible for the locals because of what they were going through as a result of the drone strikes.

My captors complained about civilian casualties. Yet I had a general sense that the drone strikes were accurate. While at times there were civilians killed, they successfully targeted militants.

Nevertheless, I did not hear of senior militants being hit.

My main captor was Badruddin Haqqani, who is the younger brother of Siraj Haqqani. I met with Badruddin many times. He was very careful. He would often move around Miranshah on foot or sometimes drive around in his own vehicle. For some reason it took years for the Americans to target him. So, from my anecdotal evidence, it appears that the drones mainly target lower-level militants.

What also struck me was the level of hatred I found in North Waziristan toward President Obama, because the locals linked the increase in drone strikes to his administration. I watched one Taliban commander spit at a picture in the Pakistani newspaper of Barack and Michelle Obama dancing at an inaugural ball.

Overall, the Taliban saw the drones as a cowardly way to fight. They said, "Why don't the Americans come fight us on the ground?"

As someone who has done many embeds on the Afghan side of the border, I know that every member of the American military would love to cross the border into Pakistan. I understand how frustrating it must be for the American soldiers. Still, the Taliban interpreted the use of drones as a way to avoid a face-to-face fight.

As a result, my Afghani Taliban guards vowed to carry out revenge attacks in the United States. They could have been just talking. These could have been bluffs or idle threats. Still, they were very angry about the drone strikes and were eager to get back at the United States.

Overall, the drone strikes seemed to create a stalemate. They limited operations and killed some senior militants. However, they certainly did not stop these groups from being active in the tribal areas.

I was left with the impression that drone strikes are not a long-term solution. The only answer is to get the Pakistani military on the ground in North Waziristan and in key areas of South Waziristan. Drones alone will not solve the problem.

2

Decade of the Drone

Analyzing CIA Drone Attacks, Casualties, and Policy

PETER L. BERGEN AND JENNIFER ROWLAND

1. THE NEED FOR ACCURATE INFORMATION ABOUT DRONE STRIKES

The rise in the covert use of drones outside of traditional battlefields has come to define US counterterrorism efforts under President Obama. It serves as one of the core policies defining the transition from George W. Bush's "Global War on Terrorism" to what Obama has termed a "war with a specific network, al-Qaeda, and its terrorist affiliates who support efforts to attack the United States, our allies, and partners."[1]

The rapid increase in covert drone attacks managed by both the CIA and US Joint Special Operations Command outside of traditional war zones present multiple moral, legal, and strategic questions regarding new technologies and the changing nature of warfare.

While the debate on these issues is robust, if not highly divisive, substantively addressing drone policy requires establishing a firm factual foundation. Using reports from a variety of reliable news outlets, New America – a nonpartisan think tank in Washington, DC – has gathered material on drone strikes from 2002 to the present. The media outlets used by New America for its database of drone strikes are: the Associated Press, Reuters, *Agence France-Presse*; US newspapers: the *New York Times*, the *Washington Post*, the *Los Angeles Times*, and the *Wall Street Journal*; British newspapers: the *Telegraph* and the *Guardian*; and Pakistani news outlets: the *Express Tribune*, *Dawn*, the *Daily Times*, Geo TV, and the *News*; as well as the news outlets BBC and CNN.

This database provides a foundation for a reasoned review of the evolution of drone attacks on a number of key issues, including the number of strikes the CIA has carried out in Pakistan; the issue of civilian casualties and the less discussed number of militant leaders killed; the impact of the drone program on al-Qaeda and the Taliban; the development and expansion of drone strikes in Yemen; and the effects of these policies on public opinion in both Pakistan and the United States. Taken together, these issues allow for a reasoned assessment of the significance of what might be usefully termed "the decade of the drone," while also providing insight as to how to better manage the drone program in the future.[2]

Understanding the reality of the drone program also helps to ensure that conversations about its future are grounded in fact rather than based on ideology. Pakistan's former interior minister, Rehman Malik, claimed in 2012 that 80 percent of those killed in drone strikes in Pakistan were civilians, a wildly inaccurate estimate that served to intensify anger at what is perceived in Pakistan as an illegal and irresponsible war on a sovereign country's territory.[3] Meanwhile, implausibly low estimates from US officials regarding civilian casualties are unpersuasive, even to those that support the judicious use of drones. A productive discussion in which all sides understand the advantages and disadvantages of drone strikes requires referencing the best available data.

2. RAPID RISE IN DRONE STRIKES AND DEATHS

The CIA drone program began quietly under President George W. Bush with one strike in Yemen in 2002, and then a number of strikes in Pakistan between 2004 and 2007, before the start of a more sustained campaign in 2008. During his two terms in office, Bush authorized a total of forty-eight strikes in Pakistan.

Upon taking office in January 2009, President Barack Obama made drones one of his key national security tools. By December 2013, he had already authorized 322 strikes in Pakistan, six times more than the number of strikes carried out during President Bush's entire eight years in office (see Figure 1). Under Obama, the drone program accelerated from an average of one strike every forty days to one every four days by mid-2011.

New America's database reveals that 2,080 to 3,428 people were killed by drone strikes in Pakistan between 2004 and December 31, 2013. At this point, the number of estimated deaths from the Obama administration's drone strikes in Pakistan – somewhere between 1,702 and 2,871 – is more than four times what it was during the George W. Bush administration.[4] Interestingly, the lowest estimate of deaths from drone strikes in Pakistan under President Obama is around double the total number of detainees sent to Guantanamo by President Bush.

The year 2010, with a record 122 strikes in Pakistan, marked the most intense period of the Obama administration's drone campaign in Pakistan. This,

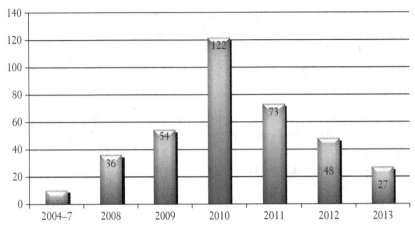

FIGURE 1. **Number of US Drone Strikes in Pakistan***
Note: Data from the New America, as of December 31, 2013

combined with the May 2011 raid on Osama bin Laden's compound in Abbottabad and the killing of twenty-four Pakistani soldiers in a NATO air strike in November 2011, severely damaged the relationship between the United States and Pakistan and resulted in the eviction of CIA-controlled drones from Shamsi Air Base in Balochistan.[5] At the same time, Cameron Munter, then-US Ambassador to Pakistan, was urging more judicious drone strike targeting as well as expanded consultation with the Pakistanis about these missions.[6]

In 2011, the number of drone strikes in Pakistan fell by 40 percent from the record number of strikes in 2010. A number of factors may have led to this sharp decline, including: US Department of State pushback, increased congressional oversight, the closure of the CIA drone base in Pakistan, a possible decline in the number of targets in the tribal regions, and a greater desire to pay attention to Pakistani sensitivities about drone attacks.

Meanwhile after the first drone attack in 2002 in Yemen, there were no reported strikes until President Obama took office in 2009. Obama vastly accelerated the drone campaign in Yemen, particularly in 2011 and 2012, just as drone strikes in Pakistan began to slow. At least forty-seven strikes took place in Yemen in 2012, marking the first time that the number of drone strikes in Yemen and Pakistan reached comparable levels. As of the end of December 2013, US air and drone strikes killed an estimated 719 to 929 people in Yemen, all but six of whom were killed under the Obama administration.

3. WHO ARE THE TARGETS?

Between 2004 and December 31, 2013, the drone campaign in Pakistan killed fifty-eight militant leaders whose deaths have been confirmed by at least two credible news sources. (A list of those al-Qaeda and Taliban leaders can be found in Appendix A, Appendix B, and Appendix C.) While this represents a significant blow to the militant chain of command, these fifty-eight deaths account for only 2 percent of all drone-related fatalities in Pakistan. Thirty-five leaders have been reported killed in Yemen, representing around 6 percent of the total casualties resulting from US strikes there.

This is a striking finding given that the CIA drone program began as a strategy to kill hard-to-capture al-Qaeda or Taliban leaders. In fact, the drone program has increasingly evolved into a more general counterinsurgency strategy that relies on this evolving air platform and in which victims are mostly lower-ranking members of the Taliban (Pakistan) and lower-level members of al-Qaeda and associated groups (Yemen). In 2010, a militant told a *New York Times* reporter, "It seems they really want to kill everyone, not just the leaders."[7]

In September 2012, President Obama told CNN that drone strikes were only used in "[situations] in which we can't capture the individual before they move forward on some sort of operational plot against the United States."[8] Clearly the threshold to launch drone strikes is far lower than this standard would suggest, given that the overwhelming percentage of those targeted are lower-level militants who do not have the capacity to plot effectively against the United States.

Under President Bush, about a third of all drone strikes in Pakistan killed a militant leader compared to less than 13 percent from the time Obama took office to December 2013. While Bush sought to decapitate the leadership ranks of al-Qaeda, Obama seems to be trying to destroy the entire network of allied groups, including the Tehrik-i-Taliban Pakistan (TTP) and Pakistani Taliban. As a result, so-called "signature strikes" have become a hallmark of Obama's drone war.[9] These are drone attacks that select targets based on patterns of suspicious activity rather than the identification of particular militants.

On July 1, 2012, a missile launched from a US drone struck a house in Pakistan's remote tribal agency of North Waziristan, killing eight suspected militants, most of whom were loyal to TTP commander Hafiz Gul Bahadur, who reportedly oversaw multiple attacks against NATO troops in Afghanistan.[10] The strike against Bahadur's fighters was part of a lesser-known campaign to target Pakistani militants less able to threaten the US homeland than the largely Arab members of al-Qaeda.

Some of these attacks were designed to help Pakistani interests. In the first eight months of 2009, the United States carried out nineteen drone strikes targeting affiliates of Baitullah Mehsud, the TTP leader who had carried out an extensive campaign of attacks against Pakistani police officers and soldiers, as well as ordinary civilians and politicians. Those targeted included former Prime Minister Benazir Bhutto, who was assassinated shortly after she returned to Pakistan in 2007 to run again for the post of prime minister.[11] Mehsud, who likely had the blood of hundreds, if not thousands, of Pakistanis on his hands, was finally killed on August 5, 2009, by a CIA drone strike.

During the Bush administration the drone campaign appeared to focus on killing al-Qaeda leaders, while under Obama the policies quietly and increasingly shifted to target Taliban foot soldiers. To the extent that it is possible to determine who has been killed in drone attacks, under Bush, al-Qaeda members appear to be the likely target in 25 percent of all drone strikes and Taliban members in just under 40 percent of attacks. Under Obama, only 10 percent of targets appear to be al-Qaeda militants, as compared to nearly 40 percent of Taliban targets.

Early in his administration, President Obama took it upon himself to act as the chief decision maker on which individuals would be added to the US drone "kill list." He would reportedly meet with a small group of top national security advisors every Tuesday to pour over intelligence gathered on suggested new targets. He was "determined to keep the tether [on the drone program] pretty short," according to National Security Advisor Thomas Donilon.[12] In October 2012, it was reported that the administration had been working for at least two years on a secret "disposition matrix" to replace the "kill list." With the matrix, officials sought to lay out all of the US resources being used to track down and build a case against terrorist suspects who might be either within the reach of drones or outside established drone theaters.[13]

4. WHERE ARE THE TARGETS?

Geographically speaking, of all the US drone strikes reported in Pakistan's tribal regions (see Figure 2), more than 70 percent have struck North Waziristan, home to factions of TTP and the Haqqani Network, which has launched multiple operations against civilian targets in Kabul.

Over a third of the strikes in North Waziristan have reportedly targeted members of the Taliban. At least ten of these strikes killed senior Taliban commanders, and others targeted hundreds of lower-level fighters.

It is interesting to note that of the 370 drone strikes that the CIA has mounted in Pakistan over the past 9 years, none have occurred outside of

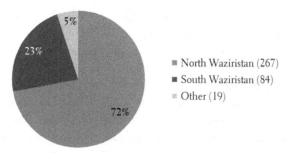

North Waziristan (267)
South Waziristan (84)
Other (19)

FIGURE 2. **Location of US Drone Strikes in Pakistan***
Note: Data from the New America, as of December 31, 2013

the tribal areas. The extension of the drone program to the "settled" areas of northwest Pakistan or to Balochistan is highly unlikely, as this would cause very significant problems for the ever-fragile US–Pakistan relationship.

5. CIVILIAN AND OTHER CASUALTIES

The US drone campaign became increasingly controversial and captured the public's interest as it expanded under Obama's administration. One of the main issues of contention has been the extent of civilian casualties resulting from drone attacks. Many human rights activists and organizations have claimed that a substantial number of civilians are killed in the attacks. Nevertheless, Obama administration officials, including the president's top counterterrorism advisor John Brennan, said publicly in 2011 that there were no civilian casualties as a result of the strikes.[14]

According to New America's database, by averaging the high and low casualty estimates of militant and non-militant deaths published in a wide range of reliable media outlets, the civilian death rate in US drone strikes in Pakistan has declined dramatically since the Bush administration to the low single digits in 2013.

It has been reported that the Obama administration considers any military-age male in the strike target area as a "militant."[15] The New America data is not based on the US official definition of a militant and does not rely on any US official counting of the strikes. Rather, it records as a militant only those identified in credible news reports as a "militant" or "suspected militant." The majority of the media outlets used in the database receive information on CIA drone strikes from Pakistani intelligence, security, and local government officials, as well as from local villagers. With such

Drone Wars

a range of sources, one can reasonably be sure that the data is not based on the official US government's definition of a militant.

New America's casualty counts also differentiate between individuals identified as "militants" and those identified as "civilians." The murkiness of some reporting in the tribal regions of Pakistan and in Yemen led New America researchers to designate another category for "unknown" casualties. If two or more media reports refer to those killed as militants, they are labeled as militants in the New America data. Similarly, if two or more media reports refer to those killed as civilians, they go under the civilian column in the New America database. And if the different media reports on a single strike are so contradictory that researchers do not feel comfortable placing either label on those killed, they are listed as "unknown."[16]

Often in areas controlled by the Taliban or other militant groups, armed men seal off the site of a drone attack immediately following a strike, preventing journalists, locals, and even officials from entering to see the destruction or victims for themselves. In other cases, bodies are incinerated or so badly dismembered that it is impossible for villagers to identify them with certainty. Because of this, claims may be based on knowledge of whether militants lived in the area, were known to be driving in a certain car, or similar information.

Over the life of the drone program through December 2013 in Pakistan, the estimated non-militant (civilian and unknown) death rate is 20 percent, referencing between 457 and 641 individuals, according to the New America database. Under President Bush, non-militant deaths represented 40 percent of those killed by drones, while under President Obama the numbers dropped to around 15 percent. In 2013, the proportion of total non-militants killed was around 5 percent, with 2.6 percent identified as civilians and 2.6 percent classified as unknowns (see Figure 3 and Tables 1 and 2).

TABLE 1. *Types of casualties per year* (Calculated using annual averages)*

Year	Militant	Unknown	Civilian
2013	95%	3%	3%
2012	88%	11%	2%
2011	81%	7%	12%
2010	93%	5%	2%
2009	61%	17%	13%
2008	75%	16%	9%
2004–2007	34%	9%	56%
TOTAL	80%	10%	10%

* As of December 31, 2013

TABLE 2. *Estimated total deaths from US drone strikes in Pakistan**

Year	Militant Low	Militant High	Unknown Low	Unknown High	Civilian Low	Civilian High	Total Low	Total High
2013	126	156	3	4	3	5	132	165
2012	194	317	23	39	5	5	222	361
2011	303	502	32	37	57	65	392	604
2010	555	960	40	50	14	17	609	1,027
2009	245	511	43	138	64	74	352	723
2008	157	265	42	48	20	34	219	347
2004–2007	43	76	16	18	95	107	154	201
Total	1,623	2,787	199	334	258	307	2,080	3,428

* As of December 31, 2013

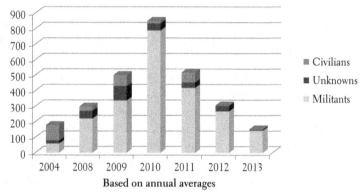

FIGURE 3. **Types of Deaths in US Drone Strikes in Pakistan***
Note: Data from the New America, as of December 31, 2013

The London-based Bureau of Investigative Journalism (BIJ) and the Washington, DC-based *Long War Journal* each maintains counts of drone casualties in Pakistan. BIJ reports that between 416 and 957 Pakistani civilians have been killed in US drone strikes from 2004 to 2013, representing 18 percent to 26 percent of the total casualties counted.[17] The *Long War Journal* reports that 156 Pakistani civilians have been killed, representing just 5.7 percent of the 2,730 deaths it has recorded over the life of the drone campaign.[18] All three databases report relatively low civilian casualty figures for 2013: New America reported between three and five civilian deaths (as well as three to four unknowns), BIJ reported between zero and four civilian deaths, and the *Long War Journal* reported fourteen civilian deaths.

In February 2012, the Associated Press conducted a rare on-the-ground investigation of ten of the deadliest US drone strikes carried out over the previous 18 months.[19] Reporters interviewed about 80 villagers from the areas affected by the strikes and found that of the 194 people reported killed in the attacks, at least 138 – about 71 percent – were identified as militants. The remaining 56 victims were either local tribesmen or police officers – about 29 percent of the total number – 38 of whom were reportedly killed in a single strike on March 17, 2011. If that single attack is excluded, the civilian casualty rate for the 10 deadliest strikes of 2010 and 2011 is 9 percent. This is within the range of the New America estimate of 13 percent non-militant casualties for all 141 strikes during the same time period.

In March 2013, following a visit to Pakistan, Ben Emmerson, the UN Special Rapporteur on human rights and counterterrorism, emailed the Associated Press that the Pakistani government told him it had confirmed at least 400 civilian deaths by US drones.[20] This number is in the range of the low estimate of 411 civilian deaths by the BIJ and is also in line with New America's estimate that between 258 and 307 civilians and a further 199 to 334 unknowns have been killed.

However, all of these figures are far below the civilian death rates reported by some Pakistani officials and private research groups, such as Pakistan Body Count. According to a 2010 report published in *Dawn*, one of Pakistan's leading English-language newspapers, Pakistani authorities estimated that for every militant killed in a drone strike in 2009, 140 Pakistani civilians also died. Pakistan Body Count's ongoing tally estimates the civilian casualty rate over the life of the drone campaign to be between 75 percent and 80 percent.[21]

In 2010, during background interviews with the *Washington Post*, Pakistani security officials acknowledged that improved technology, a deeper network of on-the-ground informants, and better coordination between US and Pakistani intelligence all contributed to a significant reduction in civilian deaths resulting from drone strikes.[22] Major General Ghayur Mahmood, a commander of Pakistani troops in North Waziristan, where the majority of drone strikes take place, conceded publicly in March 2011 that the "myths and rumors about US Predator strikes and the casualty figures are many, but it's a reality that many of those killed in these strikes are hardcore elements, a sizeable number of them foreigners."[23] The general went on to say that drone strikes had killed about one thousand militants in North Waziristan.

Beginning in 2012, Pakistani officials rarely based their criticism of US drone strikes on the incidence of civilian casualties. Instead, their critiques have pointed, quite reasonably, toward another objection: US violation of Pakistan's national sovereignty. Anger with the drone program led the Pakistani parliament to vote in April 2012 to end any authorization for the program, a vote the US government has so far ignored.[24]

Despite their public protests, some senior Pakistani officials appear to privately support the drone strikes. For example, in a 2008 State Department cable made public by WikiLeaks, President Asif Ali Zardari was reported to have approved the drone program in a discussion with US officials saying, "Kill the seniors. Collateral damage worries you Americans. It does not worry me."[25]

Further confirmation of official Pakistani support for the strikes came in April 2013 when Pakistan's former President Pervez Musharraf acknowledged to CNN that his government had secretly signed off on US drone strikes under the Bush administration. This was the first public admission by a senior Pakistani official of such a deal. However, Musharraf claimed that Pakistan's government agreed to drone strikes "only on a few occasions, when a target was absolutely isolated and no chance of collateral damage."[26]

An internal Pakistani government report on the strikes that was leaked in July 2013 finds that from 2006 through October 24, 2009, civilians made up a minority of those killed in drone strikes: 147 civilians in a total death toll of 742, or about 20 percent. That number is lower than the estimates of New America, BIJ, and *Long War Journal*. For example, New America estimates that during the same period up to 207 civilians were killed, along with up to 184 people who were not identified in reliable media reports to be either civilians or militants. In other words, the civilian casualty rates between 2004 and 2009 were quite high, though they decreased in subsequent years.

The drop in the number of civilian (and unknown) casualties in Pakistan since 2009 is the result of several developments, including a directive issued from the White House just days after President Obama took office, which clarified how the CIA could select targets and carry out strikes. Specifically, Obama wanted to evaluate and personally sign off on any strike where the agency did not have "near certainty" that it would produce no civilian casualties. In addition, the CIA began using smaller munitions for more pinpoint strikes,[27] and drones were able to circle over targets for longer periods of time than in the past, allowing attacks to be conducted when civilians were not in the target area.

Furthermore, the drone program has come under increasing congressional oversight. According to one former CIA official, this layer of accountability did not exist when he left the agency in 2009.[28] Since early 2010, members of the US House Permanent Select Committee on Intelligence and the US Senate Select Committee on Intelligence have held monthly meetings at CIA headquarters to watch video recordings of specific drone strikes and to review the intelligence used by CIA agents on the ground in Pakistan to select targets.

In a letter to the *Los Angeles Times* in May 2012, the chairwoman of the Senate Intelligence Committee, Senator Dianne Feinstein (D-California), wrote: "Committee staff has held 28 monthly in-depth oversight meetings to review strike records and question every aspect of the program including legality, effectiveness, precision, foreign policy implications and the care taken to minimize noncombatant casualties."[29] All of these factors have contributed to the steep decline in civilian deaths resulting from drone strikes.

Even though fewer civilians have been killed by drone strikes, the program remains deeply unpopular among the Pakistani public.[30] During summer 2010, New America sponsored one of the few public opinion polls ever to be conducted in Pakistan's Federally Administered Tribal Areas (FATA), finding that almost 90 percent of the respondents opposed US military operations in the region.[31] A Pew poll conducted in June 2012 found that just 17 percent of Pakistanis supported the US drone campaign as a means to help combat militancy in their country.

However, at the same time, only 32 percent expressed support for using the Pakistani army to fight militants.[32] Since 2002, the Pakistani army has waged a war against a number of militant groups, often with damaging effects on the civilian population. Amnesty International reported in 2010 that 1,363 civilians died in fighting between insurgents and Pakistani security forces in the tribal regions in 2009 (as compared with the New America data estimates of 64 to 74 civilians and 43 to 138 unknowns reportedly killed in US drone strikes during the same time period).[33]

There are many reports of civilian casualties at the hands of the Pakistani military. For example, on January 15, 2013, residents of Khyber Agency – a particularly restive region of FATA – reported that Pakistani soldiers killed eighteen civilians during house-to-house searches for militants, though the details of the raids remain murky.[34] The military has reportedly carried out reprisal attacks against villagers suspected of harboring or supporting militants. Just five days after the January 15 incident, a Pakistani helicopter reportedly fired on a home in Mir Ali, North Waziristan, killing five civilians. Locals said the attack was carried out intentionally in response to an improvised explosive device that had killed two Pakistani soldiers.[35]

In response, local leaders held a *jirga* – a tribal meeting – and threatened to march on the capital city of Islamabad to demand reparations and an end to the military's killing of civilians.[36] While the outrage that Pakistan's tribal population has expressed toward their country's own military is not often reported, even in the Pakistani press, it is comparable to the population's anger regarding US drone strikes.

Much of the world has expressed a similar opposition to the CIA drone program, according to a 2012 Pew poll of twenty-one countries. Muslim countries such as Egypt and Jordan expressed high levels of disapproval (89 percent and 85 percent, respectively), while non-Muslim countries that are close American allies also registered significant displeasure with the program – Germany and France respectively polled at 59 and 63 percent disapproval.[37]

Meanwhile, in the United States the drone program has enjoyed widespread support. In a February 2013 Pew poll, 56 percent of Americans said they approve of lethal drone attacks in countries such as Pakistan, Yemen, and Somalia.[38] This is hardly surprising as the human, financial, and political costs of the drone program for the United States are very low. These attacks require no American boots on the ground and a drone costs a fraction of the price of a fighter jet or bomber.

It is important to note that drones were widely used for years with only limited public awareness within the United States and with virtually no controversy. In fact it was not until early 2012, following the death of US citizen Anwar al-Awlaki in a drone strike, that debate in the United States over the legality and morality of covert drone attacks began to heat up. The issue only came to the fore of public political battles in early 2013, when continued media coverage of the strikes coincided with President Obama's nomination of John Brennan as director of the CIA. A 25-year veteran of the CIA, Brennan is one of the primary architects of Obama's drone campaign.

6. THE IMPACT OF DRONES ON MILITANT GROUPS

During the time of expanded CIA drone strikes, especially in Pakistan, there has been a significant reduction in the capacity of al-Qaeda. Dozens of al-Qaeda commanders have been killed by drones. The group has not been able to conduct a successful attack in the United States since 9/11 or in Europe since the attacks on the London transportation system in 2005. While it is not possible to determine with certainty how much of this decline is related to the use of drones, these shifts indicate some measure of success for overall US counterterrorism strategy, in which drones have played a significant role.

Osama bin Laden himself recognized the devastation that drones were inflicting on his organization, writing a lengthy memo about the issue that was recovered in the Abbottabad compound where he was killed. In the October 2010 memo to a lieutenant, bin Laden advised his men to leave the Pakistani tribal regions where the drone strikes had been overwhelmingly concentrated and head to a remote part of Afghanistan. He also suggested that his son Hamza decamp for the tiny, wealthy Persian Gulf kingdom of Qatar.[39]

The drone attacks in Pakistan have undoubtedly hindered some of the Taliban's operations and have killed hundreds of their lower-level fighters, as well as a number of top commanders. The strikes may even have contributed to a relative decrease in violence across Pakistan. For example, there were forty-one suicide attacks in Pakistan in 2011, down from forty-nine in 2010 and a record high of eighty-seven in 2009. While correlation is certainly not causation, it is interesting to note that the 122 drone strikes carried out in the tribal regions of Pakistan in 2010 coincided with an almost 50 percent drop in suicide attacks across the country, according to the Pakistan Institute for Peace Studies, which monitors Pakistani militant groups. Still, a more significant factor in the reduction of terrorism in Pakistan was likely the Pakistani military's own operations against the TTP, particularly its 2009 campaigns in Swat and South Waziristan. Some 1,600 Taliban fighters were killed during "Operation Rah-e-Rast" in Swat alone, while hundreds more surrendered to the government.[40]

Conversely, the CIA strikes may also be fueling terrorism. Faisal Shahzad, an American citizen of Pakistani descent trained by the Pakistani Taliban, tried to detonate a car bomb in Times Square on May 1, 2010. The plot failed, but Shahzad subsequently claimed that the drone program had motivated his anger against the United States.[41]

Drone strikes have the potential to reinforce a key motivator of terrorism: in order to effectively strike against a much stronger, seemingly impervious enemy, the weaker party must resort to spectacular acts of violence against civilians. The perpetrators of other recent terrorist attacks in the West have referenced the continued killing of Muslim civilians, though they have not pointed to drone strikes specifically. The man responsible for hacking a British soldier to death in broad daylight in May 2013 said in an amateur video taken after the attack: "The only reasons we killed this man ... is because Muslims are dying daily."[42] Tamerlan Tsarnaev, one of the two brothers behind the April 2013 Boston Marathon bombings, was found to have been in possession of material discussing civilian casualties caused by drone strikes.[43]

It is extremely difficult, if not impossible, to quantify how many acts of terrorism the drone program has prevented and how many it may have incited. And there is, of course, no acceptable justification for terrorism in any case. But if drone strikes are becoming a key part of the rhetoric that extremists use to recruit individuals to their cause, the US government should think carefully about their use moving forward.

7. DRONE CAMPAIGN IN YEMEN

On November 3, 2002, the CIA conducted its first drone strike in Yemen, on a vehicle in the province of Maarib, about 100 miles east of the capital city of Sana'a. It was also the first drone strike to kill an American citizen, Kamal Derwish, one of six al-Qaeda militants who died in the strike. Derwish was not the target, though. The target was Qaed Salim Sinan al-Harethi, al-Qaeda's top lieutenant in Yemen and the suspected mastermind of the bombing of the USS *Cole* off the Yemeni coast in 2000, which killed seventeen American sailors. The Yemeni government's official story was that a gas canister had exploded in Harethi's vehicle, killing everyone inside, but news quickly leaked in Washington that the strike had in fact been carried out by a US drone controlled by the CIA. Then-President Ali Abdullah Saleh was furious at being made to look like a liar and a puppet of the Americans, and put an end to the fledgling drone campaign in Yemen.

That program was not restarted again until early 2010, after a series of attempted terrorist attacks against the United States were traced back to al-Qaeda's Yemen-based affiliate, al-Qaeda in the Arabian Peninsula (AQAP). AQAP claimed responsibility for the would-be "underwear bomb" attack by Umar Farouk Abdulmutallab on a Detroit-bound flight on Christmas Day 2009. Fortunately for the 289 people on-board Northwest Airlines Flight 253 that day, Abdulmutallab's bomb was a dud, and he only succeeded in burning his pants rather than destroying a commercial airliner. Had his bomb exploded as intended, it would have been the most devastating terrorist attack on the United States since 9/11. This incident may have played a key role in the Obama administration's decision to resurrect the dormant drone campaign in Yemen. Less than a year later, AQAP plotted to blow up international cargo planes with two bombs hidden in printer cartridges that were mailed from Sana'a and addressed to two Jewish centers in Chicago. This time authorities in the United Kingdom were able to identify and seize the packages before their contents could be detonated, thanks to a tip from Saudi intelligence officials.

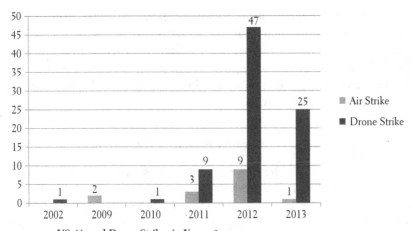

FIGURE 4. **US Air and Drone Strikes in Yemen***
Note: Data from the New America, as of December 31, 2013

Al-Qaeda's global strength and popularity was on the wane in 2010 and 2011. This shift was likely linked to a number of factors, including the drone campaign in Pakistan; the group's own violent, self-defeating tactics; and then the uprisings of the Arab Spring, in which al-Qaeda played no role. Indeed, in July 2011, then-Secretary of Defense Leon Panetta said the United States was "within reach of strategically defeating al-Qaeda," although Panetta was clear that al-Qaeda affiliates could still present a threat to the United States, particularly AQAP.

While there was a significant decrease in drone attacks in Pakistan from 2011 through 2013, there was a dramatic rise in strikes conducted in Yemen. In 2012 alone, Obama authorized at least forty-seven drone strikes and nine air strikes in Yemen. For the first time, the pace of the drone campaign in Yemen rivaled that of the campaign in Pakistan, according to data compiled by New America[44] (see Figure 4).

One explanation for this acceleration may have been President Obama's authorization in April 2012 of "signature strikes" that had been approved the previous year for use in Pakistan's tribal regions. In Yemen these were reportedly governed by stricter rules than in Pakistan and were given a different name – TADS, or Terrorist Attack Disruption Strikes.[45]

As of the end of December 2013, US air and drone strikes had killed an estimated 719 to 929 people in Yemen, 623 to 808 of whom were identified in media reports as militants, according to the New America database. Of these deaths, all but six occurred during Obama's presidency. The non-militant casualty rate from these strikes is estimated to be between 14 percent and 15 percent (109 to 134 people), roughly comparable with the civilian and unknown casualty rate from the US drone program in Pakistan, which averaged 11 percent in 2012.

Counting US strikes in Yemen, however, is perhaps more complicated than in Pakistan because it is often unclear whether attacks were launched from drones or from fighter jets, and villagers regularly provide conflicting accounts of the kinds of aircraft used. This is further complicated by diplomatic cables released by WikiLeaks, which have revealed that the Yemeni government has, on several occasions, taken credit for airstrikes carried out by the United States. According to one cable, then-Yemeni President Ali Abdullah Saleh told then-CENTCOM Commander General David Petraeus in January 2010, "We'll continue saying the bombs are ours, not yours." Deputy Prime Minister Rashad al-Alimi then joked that he had just "lied" to the Yemeni Parliament about the United States' role in such strikes.[46]

After more than thirty-three years in power, President Saleh was forced to step down in February 2012, giving the United States an opportunity to expand air and drone strikes in the country. From March through May that year, the United States launched an estimated thirty-one air and drone strikes in Yemen, as compared with just sixteen attacks in the previous two years. Unlike in Pakistan, where political leaders have almost universally – at least in public – condemned the strikes, current Yemeni President Abed Rabbo Mansour Hadi said during an interview with the *Washington Post* in September 2012 that he personally signs off on all US drone strikes in Yemen. Furthermore, he has said that they hit their targets accurately, asserting: "The drone technologically is more advanced than the human brain."[47]

During the Obama administration, US drones have killed at least thirty-five key al-Qaeda militants in Yemen, including the Yemeni-American cleric Anwar al-Awlaki and Fahd al-Quso, another suspect in the 2000 bombing of the USS *Cole*.[48] The group's senior leader, Said al-Shihri, reportedly died from wounds sustained in a US drone strike in November 2012.[49] (However, in April 2013, AQAP released an audio message purporting to be from al-Shihri, raising the possibility that the al-Qaeda leader had actually survived the attack.) AQAP has not attempted a plot against a Western target since trying to bring down US-bound cargo planes in October 2010.

Balanced against these issues is the fact that popular resentment toward the US drone campaign, similar to what has long festered in Pakistan, is beginning to emerge in Yemen, as evidenced by demonstrations by local tribesman. In addition, the drone program in Yemen is stirring some of the same international controversy as has been seen for years regarding the strikes in Pakistan. Human rights groups in the United States are particularly critical of the targeted killing of al-Awlaki, an American citizen who was killed by a drone on September 30, 2011, as was his teenage son.

On April 23, 2013, members of the Senate Judiciary Committee held the first public hearing focusing on the legal issues surrounding the US drone campaign. One of the six experts who testified that afternoon was Farea al-Muslimi, a young Yemeni activist who spent his high school years in the United States on a State Department scholarship. Al-Muslimi began his presentation by telling committee members that a drone strike had targeted a respected individual believed to have ties to al-Qaeda in his village of Wessab just six days prior. "What radicals had previously failed to achieve in my village," al-Muslimi told the senators, "one drone strike accomplished in an instant: There is now an intense anger and growing hatred of America."[50]

8. THE US GOVERNMENT OPENS UP ABOUT DRONES

For years after the United States instituted a robust and rapidly expanding drone program that relied heavily on covert actions, the Obama administration provided very little guidance on its design, legal justification, and operation. For this reason, New America and other organizations developed research programs to gather as much data as possible from public sources about the covert drone program.

In January 2012, President Obama made his first public comments about the secret drone program when he told participants of a Google+ Hangout that the United States only conducts "very precise, precision strikes against al-Qaeda and their affiliates, and we're very careful in terms of how it's been applied."[51] Many US officials have argued that the unprecedented precision of drones makes them by far the most effective weapon for striking a target and for avoiding civilian casualties. In addition, the Obama administration maintains that international law does not prohibit the use of lethal force against an active enemy "when the country involved consents or is unable or unwilling to take action against the threat."[52]

Critics of the drone program – both in the public and the government – have long called for the process of selecting drone targets to be more transparent, including making casualty counts public and ensuring that leaders are accountable for the strikes.[53] In mid-February 2013, Brennan himself explained in written responses to questions from Chairwoman Feinstein that he believed that the government should publicize civilian casualty counts from drone strikes. Brennan also stated that "in those rare instances in which civilians have been killed," the CIA conducts investigations and provides monetary compensation to the families of victims when appropriate.[54]

Additionally, there have been increased calls for the military to take control of the CIA's drone program. In an early February 2013 interview with NBC, then-Secretary of Defense Leon Panetta voiced support for this shift, which would allow for greater transparency regarding US procedures to identify targets and conduct strikes.[55] Officials close to Brennan said later that month that he also supported moving the majority of the program to the military.[56] Meanwhile, in early 2013, the Obama administration was expected to receive a draft of a "playbook" codifying the policies developed during its first term to govern the use of drones for targeted killing operations. Drone attacks in Pakistan would reportedly be exempt from this document, allowing the CIA to continue the current program without complying with any new requirements for at least another year.[57]

As media coverage and discussion of US drone strikes have proliferated, the US government has become increasingly candid about the program, its legal basis, and its procedures. Members of the Senate Intelligence Committee questioned Brennan about drone strikes at his confirmation hearing in February 2013, representing the first time officials had sparred publicly over the covert program. Just days before the hearing, a US Department of Justice memo summarizing the legal basis for killing US citizens in drone strikes abroad was leaked, sparking a flurry of discussion over the Obama administration's secret decisions and possible abuse of executive power.[58]

9. ASSESSING THE DECADE OF THE DRONE

By 2013, more than a decade after the CIA drone campaign began, the most significant changes have involved increased transparency regarding the program. Over the course of the previous two years, debates over the morality, legality, and efficacy of using drones to conduct targeted killing operations abroad have flooded the news media. The new Yemeni president publicly endorsed the strikes while Pakistani officials regularly denounced the strikes. Meanwhile, US officials quietly provided information to media outlets on conditions of anonymity. Finally, on February 4, 2013, NBC *News* obtained a copy of a classified memo that provided a summary of the legal justification for killing American citizens in drone strikes if they are believed to be high-level members in al-Qaeda.[59]

One notable aspect of the US debate has been widespread concern in Congress that drone attacks might violate the Fifth Amendment, which states: "no person shall ... be deprived of life, liberty, or property, without due process of law." For a time, the Senate held Brennan's confirmation hearings hostage, demanding that the White House release the full legal memoranda from which the leaked summary had been taken. In order to persuade the Senate to confirm Brennan as CIA director, the Obama administration eventually agreed to show the documents to both the House and Senate Intelligence Committees.[60] This occurred only after the Senate Intelligence Committee had a chance to question Brennan in a public, televised hearing about the CIA drone program that he helped create from within both the Bush and Obama administrations. Prior to that time, no member of Congress had publicly discussed the program, which the CIA and White House had kept covert even as news outlets, research organizations, and foreign governments openly discussed it. Still, as of early 2013, the drone campaign was no longer Washington's worst kept secret; it was, for all intents and purposes, out in the open.

There are several key questions surrounding the drone program that must be considered publicly. The first is whether the program has, in a sense, been "worth it." In the short term, drone strikes have undoubtedly taken dozens of dangerous individuals off the battlefield in Pakistan and Yemen. But have those tactical victories come at the detriment of longer-term US foreign policy objectives like building peace, stability, and good relations in the region? Thousands of militants have been killed in drone strikes, yet al-Qaeda remains an attractive brand to disenfranchised individuals all over the world. Meanwhile, anti-Americanism has skyrocketed in Pakistan, a nation of 180 million people, and is on the rise in much of the rest of South Asia and the Middle East.

The second question is whether the increased emphasis at the CIA on targeted killings hampered the agency's ability to understand and analyze important political developments in the Muslim world, such as the Arab Spring. As a senior Obama official has noted, "The CIA missed Tunisia. They missed Egypt. They missed Libya."[61] Even after the Egyptian revolution occurred, the CIA appeared to have failed to understand that fundamentalist Salafists would do very well in democratic elections, winning around one-quarter of the votes in the 2011 parliamentary election, to become the second largest political bloc in Egypt after the Muslim Brotherhood.

Third, is the United States setting a dangerous precedent for other nations with its aggressive and secretive drone programs in Pakistan and Yemen? Just as the US government justifies its drone strikes with the argument that it is at war with al-Qaeda and its affiliates, one could imagine a Chinese strike against Uighur separatists in western China or an Iranian attack on Baluchi national-ists along its border with Pakistan. The rules and regulations the US govern-ment places on its use of drones as targeted killing machines may well determine the degree to which future US leaders will be able to call on other countries to impose similar limitations. A failure to present a transparent, accountable structure within which drone targets are chosen, collateral damage decisions are made, and post-attack evaluations are managed could have important ramifications should countries like China and Russia cite US precedents for their own use of armed drones against individuals or groups they consider to be terrorists.

Related to this point, to what degree do the United States and its allies have an obligation to create an international framework governing the use of militarized drones? Perhaps the time has come for the develop-ment of an international legal mechanism to manage these emerging weapon systems, which promise to shape the future of warfare as much as tanks and aerial bombers did during the twentieth century. Yet so far, there has been limited substantive public discussion about drone deployment among policymakers at the international level.

And lastly, Washington needs to establish when and how it is going to transfer responsibility for the drones flying over Pakistan from the CIA to the US military. The Obama administration announced the planned shift in early 2013, but by August media reports indicated that it could be years before the change is implemented.[62] The CIA's control of the program in Pakistan is more a legacy of its longtime dominance of operations targeting al-Qaeda than a reflection of any special expertise in drone warfare, and military control would have several advantages. In Afghanistan, where US drone programs are already controlled by the Pentagon, US military lawyers ensure that the strikes conform to the laws of war. In Pakistan, whatever review process the CIA uses remains largely opaque. In Afghanistan, the US military also tends to pay compensation for accidental civilian deaths, whereas Pakistani civilians in the tribal areas have virtually no mechanism to seek legal or material responses from the United States when their relatives are killed or injured. Overall, what is needed is greater openness and transparency about the covert US drone program around which many myths have sprung up. As US Supreme Court Justice Louis Brandeis observed a century ago, "Sunlight is the best disinfectant."

APPENDIX A

This is a list of the thirty-five al-Qaeda and affiliated group leaders who have been killed, as of December 31, 2013, in the CIA drone campaign in Pakistan.

May 18, 2005: Haitham al-Yemeni, an al-Qaeda explosives expert

December 1, 2005: Abu Hamza Rabia, a top al-Qaeda official

January 29, 2008: Abu Laith al-Libi, described as the then-"Number Three" man in al-Qaeda, who orchestrated a 2007 suicide attack targeting then-Vice President Dick Cheney while he was visiting Bagram Airfield

May 14, 2008: Abu Sulayman Jazairi, an Algerian al-Qaeda planner

July 28, 2008: Abu Khabab al-Masri, al-Qaeda's WMD expert

September 4, 2008: Abu Wafa Al Saudi, an al-Qaeda commander and logistician

September 8, 2008: Abu Haris, al-Qaeda's chief in Pakistan

October 2008 (exact date unknown): Abu Hassan al-Rimi, an al-Qaeda "emir" who led cross-border operations against coalition forces in Afghanistan

October 16, 2008: Khalib Habib, a senior member of al-Qaeda

October 31, 2008: Mohammad Hasan Khalil al-Hakim – also known as Abu Jihad al-Masri – al-Qaeda's propaganda chief

November 19, 2008: Abdullah Azzam Al Saudi, a senior member of al-Qaeda, liaison between al-Qaeda and the Taliban operating in Pakistan's northwest, facilitator of al-Qaeda's external operations network responsible for plotting attacks against the West

November 22, 2008: Abu Zubair al-Masri, a senior member of al-Qaeda and an explosives expert

2009 (exact date unknown): Saad bin Laden, bin Laden's second eldest son, whose death was confirmed by documents found in the Abbottabad compound

January 1, 2009: Osama al-Kini, al-Qaeda's then-chief of operations in Pakistan, who also played a central role in the 1998 bombings of US embassies in Kenya and Tanzania

January 1, 2009: Sheikh Ahmed Salim Swedan, al-Kini's lieutenant, who also played a role in the 1998 embassy bombings

April 29, 2009: Abu Sulayman al-Jazairi, an Algerian al-Qaeda planner who American intelligence officials believe helped train operatives for attacks in Europe and the United States (no relation to the Abu Sulayman al-Jazairi killed on May 14, 2008)

September 14, 2009: Nazimuddin Zalalov – also known as Yahyo – a leader of the Islamic Jihad Union and a bin Laden lieutenant

December 8, 2009: Saleh al-Somali, al-Qaeda's external operations chief and the link between al-Qaeda in Afghanistan and Pakistan and al-Qaeda abroad

December 17, 2009: Zuhaib al-Zahibi, a well-known al-Qaeda commander in North Waziristan

February 15, 2010: Abdul Haq al-Turkistani, an al-Qaeda-linked leader of the Turkistani Islamic Party

February 17, 2010: Sheikh Mansoor, an Egyptian-Canadian al-Qaeda leader

March 8, 2010: Sadam Hussein Al Hussami – also known as Ghazwan al-Yemeni – an al-Qaeda planner and explosives expert with contacts in AQAP, the Afghan Taliban, and TTP

May 21, 2010: Mustafa Abu al-Yazid, al-Qaeda's then-"Number Three" and the group's commander in Afghanistan

September 26, 2010: Sheikh al-Fateh, an al-Qaeda chief in Afghanistan and Pakistan

June 3, 2011: Ilyas Kasmiri, a senior al-Qaeda commander in Pakistan associated with the 2008 Mumbai attacks

August 22, 2011: Atiyah Abd al-Rahman, al-Qaeda's then-"Number Two"

September 11, 2011: Abu Hafs al-Shahri, then-al-Qaeda's chief of operations in Pakistan

January 10, 2012: Aslam Awan, a senior al-Qaeda operations organizer in Abbottabad

February 9, 2012: Badar Mansoor, thought to be al-Qaeda's most senior leader in Pakistan

June 4, 2012: Abu Yahya al-Libi, al-Qaeda's then-"Number Two"

September 24, 2012: Abu Akash al-Iraqi, a senior al-Qaeda operative

September 24, 2012: Seleh al-Turki, a mid-level al-Qaeda operative

December 1, 2012: Abdul Rehman al-Zaman Yemeni, an al-Qaeda operative said to have had links to bin Laden

December 6, 2012: Abdel Rehman al-Hussainan – also known as Abu Zaid al-Kuwaiti – a senior member of al-Qaeda

July 2, 2013: Abu Saif al-Jazeri, senior al-Qaeda operative

APPENDIX B

This is a list of the twenty-three Taliban and other Pakistan-based leaders who have been killed, as of December 31, 2013, in the CIA drone campaign in Pakistan.

June 18, 2004: Nek Mohammad, a Taliban leader

August 13, 2008: Abdul Rehman, a Taliban commander in South Waziristan

October 26, 2008: Mohammad Omar, a close associate of Nek Mohammad

August 5, 2009: Baitullah Mehsud, the overall leader of TTP

December 31, 2009: Haji Omar, a key Taliban commander in North Waziristan

January 2010 (exact date unknown): Mahmud Mahdi Zeidan, a Taliban commander from Jordan

February 24, 2010: Mohammad Qari Zafar, a Taliban commander wanted in connection with the March 2006 bombing of the US Consulate in Karachi

December 17, 2010: Ali Marjan, a local commander of Lashkar-e-Islam

October 27, 2011: Khan Mohammad, one of TTP commander Maulvi Nazir's deputies

October 27, 2011: Hazrat Omar, Maulvi Nazir's younger brother

October 27, 2011: Ashfaq Wazir, a Taliban commander

October 27, 2011: Miraj Wazir, a Taliban commander

March 13, 2012: Amir Hamza Toji Khel, one of Maulvi Nazir's senior commanders

March 13, 2012: Shamsullah, one of Maulvi Nazir's senior commanders

August 21, 2012: Badruddin Haqqani, commander of military operations and third-in-command for the Haqqani Network

October 11, 2012: Maulana Shakirullah, the commander of TTP's Hafiz Gul Bahadur group

October 11, 2012: Umar Haqqani, a Taliban commander in the Punjab region of Pakistan

January 2, 2013: Maulvi Nazir – also known as Maulvi Nazir Wazir – the TTP leader in South Waziristan

January 2, 2013: Ratta Khan, one of Maulvi Nazir's deputies

January 3, 2013: Shah Faisal, a militant commander under current TTP leader Hakimullah Mehsud

January 6, 2013: Wali Mohammad Toofan, head of the TTP's suicide wing

May 29, 2013: Waliur Rehman, second-in-command of the TTP

November 1, 2013: Hakimullah Mehsud, commander of the TTP

This is a list of the thirty-five key al-Qaeda militants who have been killed as of December 31, 2013, in US air strikes and drone attacks in Yemen starting in 2002.

November 3, 2002: Qaed Salim Sunian al-Harethi, al-Qaeda's chief operative in Yemen and a suspect in the October 2000 bombing of the USS *Cole*

July 14, 2011: Hadi Mohammad Ali, a militant commander in Abyan Province

August 1, 2011: Naser al-Shadadi, a leading al-Qaeda militant

September 30, 2011: Anwar al-Awlaki, a radical Yemeni-American cleric

September 30, 2011: Samir Khan, the Pakistani-American founder and editor of AQAP's English-language magazine *Inspire*

October 14, 2011: Ibrahim al-Bana – also known as Abu Ayman al Masri – AQAP's media chief

December 23, 2011: Abdulrahman al-Wuhayshi, a brother of AQAP leader Nasser al-Wuhayshi

January 30, 2012: Abdel-Munem al-Fatahani, a local militant leader who was linked to the bombing of the USS *Cole* and the 2002 Limburg oil tanker attack

March 9, 2012: Abdulwahhab al-Homaiqani, a local AQAP leader in Bayda Province

March 13, 2012: Nasser al-Zafari, a local AQAP leader in Bayda Province

April 22, 2012: Mohammed al-Umda, the fourth most-wanted al-Qaeda militant in Yemen; he was convicted in 2005 of a 2002 attack on the Limburg oil tanker

May 6, 2012: Fahd al-Quso, who was on the FBI's most-wanted list for his role in the 2000 bombing of the USS *Cole*

May 10, 2012: "Jallad," who was in charge of armaments for AQAP fighters

July 3, 2012: Fahd Saleh al-Anjaf al-Harethi, a senior al-Qaeda operative

July 3, 2012: Hassan Ali al-Ishaqi, a senior al-Qaeda operative

August 6, 2012: Abdullah Awad al-Masri – also known as Abou Osama al Maribi – a top AQAP bomb maker

August 31, 2012: Khaled Batis, a top al-Qaeda militant wanted for his role in the 2002 attack on the Limburg oil tanker

September 5, 2012: Murad Ben Salem, a senior al-Qaeda operative

September 8, 2012: Abdulraoof Ahmad Nasser al-Thahab, the brother of Tariq; al-Qaeda's leader in the Radaa' District of al-Baidha Province

October 18, 2012: Nader Al-Shadadi, al-Qaeda's leader in Jaar, a city in Abyan Province

October 21, 2012: Sanad Abdulla al-Aqili, an al-Qaeda operative

October 28, 2012: Said al-Shihri, AQAP's "Number Two," was wounded in this strike. It was reported that he died on January 22, 2013, but that was disputed by April 2013 in AQAP statements purporting to be from him. Al-Shihri's status remains unknown at this time.

November 7, 2012: Adnan al-Qadi, an al-Qaeda operative previously detained in relation to the 2008 bombing of the US Embassy in Sana'a

December 24, 2012: Abdel-Raouf Naseeb, a mid-level al-Qaeda operative

December 28, 2012: Abdullah Bawazir, an al-Qaeda operative who was the chief architect behind a mass prison break in Yemen

December 29, 2012: Saleh Mohammed al-Ameri, a prominent local fighter in the Radaa' District of al-Baidha Province

January 3, 2013: Moqbel Ebad Al Zawbah, a senior al-Qaeda figure

January 19, 2013: Ismaeel Bin Saeed Bin Jameel, a local al-Qaeda operative

January 21, 2013: Ahmed al-Ziadi, an al-Qaeda leader in Marib Province

January 21, 2013: Qasem Naser Tuaiman, an al-Qaeda operative who had been freed from detention by Yemeni authorities

January 21, 2013: Ali Saleh Tuaiman, an al-Qaeda operative who had been freed from detention by Yemeni authorities

April 17, 2013: Hamid al Radmi, a local AQAP leader

May 20, 2013: Abd Rabbo Mokbal Mohammed Jarallah al-Zouba, a local al-Qaeda operative

May 20, 2013: Abbad Mossad Abbad Khobzi, a local al-Qaeda operative

June 9, 2013: Saleh Hassan Huraydan, a senior al-Qaeda leader

August 30, 2013: Qaid Ahmad Nasser Al Dhahab, a local senior al-Qaeda leader

NOTES

1 Harnden, Toby, "Barack Obama declares the 'war on terror' is over," *Telegraph*, May 27, 2010.

2 New America, Drones database. http://securitydata.newamerica.net/drones/pakistan/analysis.

3 *Pakistan Observer*, "Drone attacks kill 80% innocent people: Malik," October 18, 2012.

4 New America, Counterterrorism Strategy Initiative, "The year of the drone: An analysis of U.S. drone strikes in Pakistan, 2004–2013." Unless specifically cited, all numbers regarding drone strikes and casualty rates in Pakistan come from this database.

5 Masood, Salman, "C.I.A. leaves base in Pakistan used for drone strikes," *New York Times*, December 11, 2011.

6 Entous, Adam, Siobhan Gorman, and Julian E. Barnes, "U.S. tightens drone rules," *Wall Street Journal*, November 4, 2011.

7 Perlez, Jane, and Pir Zubair Shah, "Drones batter Al Qaeda and its allies inside Pakistan," *New York Times*, April 4, 2010.

8 CNN, "Drone strikes kill, maim and traumatize too many civilians, U.S. study says," September 25, 2012.

9 Schmitt, Eric, "U.S. to step up drone strikes in Yemen," *New York Times*, April 25, 2012.

10 *Nation*, "Drone strike kills 8 in N. Waziristan," July 1, 2012.

11 CNN, "U.S. suspects Taliban leader behind Bhutto plot," December 29, 2007.

12 Becker, Jo, and Scott Shane, "Secret 'kill list' proves a test of Obama's principles and will," *New York Times*, May 29, 2012.

13 Miller, Greg, "Plan for hunting terrorists signals U.S. intends to keep adding names to kill lists," *Washington Post*, October 23, 2012.

14 Shane, Scott, "C.I.A. is disputed on civilian toll in drone strikes," *New York Times*, August 11, 2011.

15 Becker and Shane, "Secret 'kill list' proves a test of Obama's principles and will."

16 New America, "Drone wars methodology." http://natsec.newamerica.net/drones/methodology.

17 Bureau of Investigative Journalism, "Get the data: Drone wars." www.thebureauinvestigates.com/category/projects/drones/drones-graphs/.

18 *Long War Journal*, "Charting the data for US airstrikes in Pakistan 2004–2014."

19 Abbott, Sebastian, "AP Impact: New light on drone war's death toll," Associated Press, February 26, 2012.

20 Abbott, Sebastian, "UN says US drones violate Pakistan's sovereignty," Associated Press, March 15, 2013.

21 Pakistan Body Count, "Pakistan body count: Drone attacks." http://pakistanbodycount.org/drone_attack. Last modified April 17, 2013.

22 Warrick, Joby, and Peter Finn, "Amid outrage over civilian deaths in Pakistan, CIA turns to smaller missiles," *Washington Post*, April 26, 2010.

23 Sherazi, Zahir Shah, "Most of those killed in drone attacks were terrorists: Military," *Dawn*, March 9, 2011.

24 Leiby, Richard, "Pakistan calls for end to U.S. drone attacks," *Washington Post*, April 12, 2012.

25 Bhutto, Fatima, "What Wikileaks tells us about how Washington runs Pakistan," *Mother Jones*, December 9, 2010.

26 Robertson, Nic, and Greg Botelho, "Ex-Pakistani President Musharraf admits secret deal with U.S. on drone strikes," CNN, April 12, 2013.

27 Becker and Shane, "Secret 'kill list' proves a test of Obama's principles and will."

28 Dilanian, Kevin, "Congress zooms in on drone killings," *Los Angeles Times*, June 25, 2012.

29 Feinstein, Dianne, "Letters: Sen. Feinstein on drone strikes," *Los Angeles Times*, May 17, 2012.

30 Mahsood, Salman, and Declan Walsh, "Pakistan give U.S. a list of demands, including an end to C.I.A. drone strikes," *New York Times*, April 12, 2012.

31 New America, "FATA: Inside Pakistan's tribal regions." http://pakistansurvey.org/.

32 Pew Research Center, "Pakistani public opinion ever more critical of U.S.," *Global Attitudes Project*, June 27, 2012.

33 Amnesty International, "'As if hell fell on me': The human rights crisis in northwest Pakistan," June 2010.

34 Khan, Riaz, "Pakistani villagers protest 18 killed in northeast," Yahoo News, January 16, 2013.

35 Gul, Pazir, "Five killed in Mirali shelling," *Dawn*, January 18, 2013.

36 Farooq, Umar, "Civilians bear brunt of Pakistan's war in the northwest," *Foreign Policy*, February 11, 2013.

37 Pew Research Center, "Global opinion of Obama Slips, international policies faulted: Drones strikes widely opposed," *Global Attitudes Project*, June 13, 2012.

38 Pew Research Center for the People and the Press, "Continued support for U.S. drone strikes: Civilian casualties a concern, even among supporters," February 11, 2013.

39 Bergen, Peter, "Bin Laden's final days – big plans, deep fears," CNN, March 19, 2012.

40 Tighe, Paul, and Khaleeq Ahmed, "Pakistan must fight extremism through education, Gilani says," *Bloomberg*, July 12, 2009.

41 Johnston, Patrick B., "Drone strikes keep pressure on al-Qaida," RAND Corporation, August 22, 2012.

42 Smith-Spark, Laura, and Victoria Eastwood, "Trial begins for 2 men accused of 'callous murder' of UK soldier Lee Rigby," CNN, December 1, 2013.

43 Andersson, Hilary, "Tamerlan Tsarnaev had right-wing extremist literature," BBC, August 5, 2013.

44 New America, "Drone wars Yemen: Analysis." http://natsec.newamerica.net/drones/yemen/analysis. Unless specifically cited, all numbers regarding drone strikes and casualty rates in Yemen come from this database.

45 Becker and Shane, "Secret 'kill list' proves a test of Obama's principles and will."

46 Booth, Robert, and Ian Black, "WikiLeaks cables: Yemen offered US 'open door,'" *Guardian*, December 3, 2010.

47 Miller, Greg, "Yemeni president acknowledges approving U.S. drone strikes," *Washington Post*, September 29, 2012.

48 Lister, Tim, and Paul Cruickshank, "Anwar al-Awlaki: al Qaeda's rock star no more," CNN, September 30, 2011.

49 Al Haj, Ahmed, "Saeed Al Shiri: Top Al Qaeda leader in Yemen reportedly killed," *Huffington Post*, January 24, 2013.

50 Londoño, Ernesto, "Drones cause 'growing hatred of America,' bipartisan Senate panel told," *Washington Post*, April 23, 2013.

51 Jackson, David, "Obama defends drone strikes," *USA Today*, January 31, 2012.

52 Jansen, Lesa, "Obama to release document on targeted killings to Congress," CNN, February 7, 2013.

53 Associated Press, "Lawmakers in both parties urge oversight of US drone program," *Fox News*, February 10, 2013.

54 Zakaria, Tabassum, "Nominee for CIA chief says casualties from drones should be public," Reuters, February 15, 2013.

55 "Press pass: Leon Panetta," *Meet the Press Blog*, NBC News, February 3, 2013.

56 Dilanian, Ken, "CIA's covert drone program may shift further onto Pentagon," *Los Angeles Times*, February 17, 2013.

57 Miller, Greg, Ellen Nakashima, and Karen DeYoung, "CIA drone strikes will get a pass in counterterrorism 'playbook,' officials say," *Washington Post*, January 19, 2013.

58 Isikoff, Michael, "Justice Department memo reveals legal case for drone strikes on Americans," NBC News, February 4, 2013.

59 Ibid.

60 Shear, Michael D., and Scott Shane, "Congress to see memo backing drone attacks on Americans," *New York Times*, February 6, 2013.

61 Mazzetti, Mark, *The way of the knife: The CIA, a secret army, and a war at the ends of the Earth* (New York, NY: Penguin Press, 2013), p. 253.

62 Dilanian, Ken, "Drone strike campaign in Yemen shows U.S. standards are elastic," *Los Angeles Times*, August 17, 2013.

3

Just Trust Us

The Need to Know More About the Civilian
Impact of US Drone Strikes

SARAH HOLEWINSKI

As a general proposition ... I want to make sure that people understand that actually, drones have not caused a huge number of civilian casualties. For the most part they have been precise, precision strikes against al-Qaeda and their affiliates and we are very careful in terms of how it's been applied.[1]

President Barack Obama, January 2012

1. THE IMPORTANCE OF THE CIVILIAN IMPACT
OF US DRONE STRIKES

The US government claims that its covert drone program has little impact on the civilian populations in Pakistan, Yemen, and Somalia, where unmanned aerial vehicles are used to strike al-Qaeda and its affiliates. There is reason to believe this may not be true. While the Obama administration began publicly acknowledging in 2009 the use of drones outside of the Afghanistan combat theater, many elements of the program remain secret, leaving serious questions about the impact of the program on civilians.

For many Americans, drones make all the sense in the world. The public is tired of its sons and daughters being killed in faraway places for seemingly abstract reasons. For policymakers, drones may appear like the antidote to the expense, exhaustion, and dubious results of US military actions in Afghanistan and Iraq. For military strategists, drones may be preferable to other weapons. They can stay in the air for far longer than fighter jets and other aircraft and gather information that may assist in accurate targeting, helping to distinguish between civilians and combatants. This is especially true where drones' around-the-clock video surveillance is supported by good ground intelligence.

In Washington's war on terror, drones are being used for secret attacks against unspecified targets, without public scrutiny, based on questionable intelligence, and with unknown outcomes. This type of warfare raises red flags about how these tactics affect civilians.

It is important to note that nobody fully understands the impact of US drone use yet – not even the president of the United States. Publicly available government statistics on civilian casualties from drone attacks are consistently low compared with estimates from human rights groups. A recent Pentagon-sponsored report by the Center for Naval Analysis casts doubt on drones' much acclaimed potential to limit civilian harm, finding that unmanned aerial vehicles in Afghanistan were ten times more likely to cause civilian harm as compared with traditional manned aircraft during the same period.[2] While it is difficult to calculate, there is strong evidence that psychological trauma, loss of livelihood, and rampant fear and suspicion related to drone use are severely detrimental to civilians. These effects must be considered along-side deaths and injuries from drone strikes to gain a full understanding of the impact of US drone deployment.

It is particularly striking how the official US response to civilian drone casualties differs from the response to casualties caused by combat operations in Iraq and Afghanistan. While the administration has become significantly more adept at addressing civilian harm during military operations – engaging in thorough investigations of allegations of civilian casualties, tracking and analyzing civilian casualty rates over time, and providing amends to survivors – no such policies are in effect for drone attacks in Pakistan, Yemen, Somalia, and elsewhere.

The most obvious improvement in US recognition of civilian harm has occurred in Afghanistan, where officials have seriously engaged the issue and publicly responded to multiple incidents. For example, in May 2009, US Ambassador Karl Eikenberry stood before a thousand people at a mosque in Farah, Afghanistan, and offered his condolences after an American airstrike killed several dozen civilians, saying: "I assure the people of Afghanistan that the United States will work tirelessly with your Government, Army, and Police, to find ways to reduce the price paid by civilians, and avoid tragedies like what occurred in Bala Baluk."[3]

The attack had previously led to protests and anger among the local population. Eikenberry's visit to honor the dead soothed tensions while investigators worked to unravel what went wrong and the military developed policies to assist victims.

Similar acts of strategic diplomacy and the acceptance of responsibility do not occur in Pakistan, Somalia, or Yemen. There are no military staff on the ground to investigate the aftermath of drone strikes, nor is anyone responsible for addressing the potential harm to civilians in communities subjected to attack. In fact, in these contexts it is even unclear how the United States defines a civilian, meaning that civilians may be killed because they are erroneously considered to be combatants. In this confusion of identities, attempts to accurately count civilian casualties and track them over time to improve operations will produce dubious results. In the unlikely event that civilian casualties are identified after a covert drone strike, their families will be left to mourn the victims and rebuild their lives in the absence of any official US response or aid.

These negative consequences deserve attention. With some notable exceptions in the post-Vietnam era, American policymakers have sought to avoid killing or traumatizing civilians where the US military is deployed. This has been done out of respect for ethical principles, adherence to the law of armed conflict, and because of a general acceptance of the strategic value of this approach. As history has shown, causing unintended harm to civilians and then ignoring these actions can erode support for a war at home, abroad, and within the war zone itself. In addition, accurately assessing strategic risks depends on Washington's ability to collect and analyze the data of the short- and long-term implications of specific policies. A significant amount of this information should be made public to meet reasonable commitments to ethical principles and legal obligations. This will help the US government avoid the widely held perception that it is engaging in illegal activities and has a great deal to hide, as has occurred with today's drone policies.

Because so much of drone deployment remains secret, it has been difficult to accurately evaluate the program. In fact, most of what we know about who is targeted and who is doing the targeting have been communicated through vague statements by US officials. The more recent attempt by President Obama himself to explain the drone program at the National Defense University in May 2013 seems to boil down to some version of "just trust us."

Weaponized drones are neither inherently good nor bad for reducing civilian harm, but should be judged solely on how they are used. The problem with the US counterterrorism drone program is that it is conducted in secret in remote areas with limited public accountability. As a first step, a responsible and ultimately more effective drone program requires open public discussion about who is targeted, when, under what circumstances, and by whom. This discussion must include an honest assessment of the impact drone operations are having on civilian populations. Only then can reasonable policies be developed that both respect fundamental rights and minimize negative responses that are damaging to US interests.

2. THE TARGETS: PERSONALITY STRIKES AND SIGNATURE STRIKES

Drone targeting in the war on terror fall into two categories: "personality strikes" and "signature strikes."[4] Although the two categories have recognizable labels, they are both shrouded in secrecy.

"Personality strikes," in which the identities of targeted individuals are known, are not unique to drones. They have been used in military operations going back centuries, and the United States is not the only country currently involved in this form of targeting. These attacks are likely based on some type of "kill list," a collection of preselected, named targets. Such lists are used in many conflicts and by many nations to identify specific, high-value individuals who can be targeted. While the idea of a "kill list" has made headlines because of its ominous name, using such lists is far better than striking indiscriminately in the hope that multiple attacks will strike known valuable targets. For example, in Iraq, in the early stages of the war, US forces had a deck of playing cards that identified high-level targets in the regime, all with names and faces.[5] The cards were readily available to anyone who wanted to see them and were even used by the US government in press conferences as a means of highlighting purported progress in the war.

In contrast, Washington's drone kill list is a closely guarded secret. While some amount of secrecy surrounding military targets is justified, in this case the level of concealment is excessive. Not only are the names and faces hidden, but even general descriptions of the criteria for being placed on the list remains unknown outside a tiny circle of US officials, who essentially expect the public to trust them in choosing and vetting targets.

Yet this situation may well be exposing civilians living under the constant threat of drone attacks to an untenable situation. That is, they have no way of knowing what type of behavior might get them killed. A shopkeeper in Waziristan cannot determine whether offering a ride to a customer, who turns out to be a low-ranking militant, might identify him as a target. Similarly, civilians associating with those they know to be militants, including friends, neighbors, and relatives, may be at risk of being killed. This danger could extend to a doctor who treats those wounded in combat, a cook who prepares food for militants, or a financier who assists someone linked to an al-Qaeda cell. While these individuals might be subjected to targeting under US policy, they are protected civilians under international law.

The second type of strike used by the United States in its covert drone program are "signature strikes," a practice that began in 2008 under President George W. Bush, and increased significantly under President Obama. An unnamed US official in 2011 said that the United States killed twice as many "wanted terrorists" through signature strikes as through personality strikes,[6] and these strikes are especially significant in Yemen.[7] In signature strikes, attacks are not directed against specific individuals identified as threats to US national security, but rather are based on a set of observed actions and indicators understood to be significant enough to warrant lethal action. The United States does not disclose what behaviors justify a signature strike, nor does it provide any guidance on this issue.

Many lawyers argue that targeting an individual based on a set of activities that suggest some form of allegiance but are not linked to actual participation in hostilities may violate international law.[8] Young men with weapons driving around in convoys may appear suspicious and such behavior might meet the guidelines for a signature strike. However, in the tribal regions of Pakistan, that behavior may not imply either illegal activity or actions that threaten the United States or its allies. While drone operators have the ability to track such movements over time, this may not provide adequate clarity as to whether the individuals are members of al-Qaeda or associated organizations.

In fact, with little to no ground-based intelligence, how are US analysts to determine whether men targeted in signature strikes are not armed shepherds on their way to a market or locals patrolling their land? Many men in the areas where the drone strikes are concentrated carry guns as an ordinary part of their daily lives. They often travel in groups and may engage in actions that meet hidden criteria for targeting, yet have no relationship to any genuine threat. And the same is true in Yemen. As one official there said: "Every Yemeni is armed ... so how can they differentiate between suspected militants and armed Yemenis?"[9] Former intelligence analyst Marc Garlasco noted how difficult it was to develop "signatures" even in Iraq, where American forces had an enormous military presence on the ground and a substantial intelligence infrastructure. With this in mind, he argues that it is unlikely that the United States could develop accurate analyses for signature strikes in places such as rural Pakistan, where there are limited legitimate intelligence sources.[10]

Measuring the impact of remote drone use on civilians, whether for personality strikes or signature strikes, has not been a US policy priority. Drone operators have little way of knowing if those they have killed were actually combatants, especially where there are few trustworthy local contacts, limited ground-based intelligence, and no conventional troops or related forces available to investigate and corroborate the accuracy of targeting process. In addition, civilians have no useful way of notifying officials about drone attacks, and local governments may have limited interest or ability to respond, especially given the covert nature of these missions. Unlike in Afghanistan, where the US military has commissioned studies on civilian casualties and has adjusted operations to reduce such harm, no such efforts exist in Pakistan, Yemen, or Somalia.

On March 17, 2011, in Shiga, Pakistan, a signature strike targeted a group of heavily armed men.[11] The United States claimed it killed twenty combatants associated with al-Qaeda.[12] However, locals and Pakistani officials said the missiles hit a tribal meeting held to resolve a mining dispute.[13] They claimed that four Pakistani Taliban fighters and thirty-eight civilians and tribal police were killed.[14] A farmer, Gul Ahmed, explained: "The militants were there because they controlled the area and any decision made would need their approval."[15] American officials contended that all the people killed were insurgents, one official stating: "These people weren't gathering for a bake sale. They were terrorists."[16]

In fact, it is hard to know what the truth is. The local account seems plausible and Pakistani officials support that version.[17] Yet in this case, did the United States determine that the civilian casualties were acceptable based on a clear interpretation of the laws of war (assuming they apply in Pakistan and that the CIA understands its actions as bound by them)? If this is the case, on what basis was this decision made?

Interestingly, getting accurate information about a drone strike may be easier to obtain by consulting a Pakistani farmer than by questioning the US government. In early 2013, a federal court dismissed a lawsuit brought by the American Civil Liberties Union and the *New York Times* to get the United States to release records about the process for designating targets.[18] The US government's ongoing effort to impede public inquiry and oversight into drone attacks has thwarted accountability.

3. THE TARGETERS: CIA AND JSOC

Compounding the general secrecy of the program, the government has tasked two clandestine entities – the CIA and the Defense Department's Joint Special Operations Command (JSOC) – with carrying out the drone program outside of traditional battle spaces. To some degree, this is to be expected. Every nation engages in clandestine activities to protect national security. However, assigning a clandestine agency to take the lead on or even to participate in a lethal global campaign – a task usually reserved for the military, which is bound by law and appropriately subjected to greater public debate – is deeply problematic.

In early 2013 the Obama administration appeared to be shifting some CIA drone operations to the Department of Defense, following a pledge by the president to be more transparent.[19] This is a shift human rights groups have been advocating for years because Pentagon operations are under far greater congressional oversight. The timeline for transferring operations and just what percentage of drone operations will reside with the Pentagon, however, is not public.

For the moment, drone operations outside of Afghanistan are conducted by either the CIA or the JSOC, and sometimes jointly. Although the JSOC is part of the US military, and might reasonably be expected to uphold a commensurate level of transparency and adherence to the law of armed conflict, the JSOC operates in a black hole of accountability. Secrecy pervades all aspects of the JSOC, from its structure, to its size, to its budget.

Despite being a part of the Defense Department, the JSOC may or may not follow the same protocols as the conventional military in minimizing civilian harms in drone strikes and other lethal operations. A former counterinsurgency adviser to General David Petraeus described the JSOC as "an almost industrial-scale counterterrorism killing machine."[20]

When it comes to the CIA, administration officials repeatedly offer assurances that the agency complies with the law and tries to avoid civilian casualties. Such a general assurance – with no supporting evidence – would be viewed as unacceptable by most objective standards. In fact, this is precisely the sort of statement that the US government would not accept from most other nations in the world, particularly those facing reasonable criticism from established human rights groups, UN agencies, and others.

When US officials call international law a set of "principles" rather than rules, there is cause to question whether the CIA sees itself as bound by them. At a speech ironically titled "The CIA and the Rule of Law" at Harvard Law School, delivered in April 2012, CIA lawyer Stephen Preston noted:

> [T]he Agency would implement its authorities in a manner consistent with the four basic principles in the law of armed conflict governing the use of force: Necessity, Distinction, Proportionality, and Humanity. Great care would be taken in the planning and execution of actions to satisfy these four principles and, in the process, to minimize civilian casualties.[21]

Human Rights Watch responded that "the laws of war are not mere principles but legally binding restrictions on all forces of the parties to an armed conflict."[22]

Beyond concerns about adherence to international law, there is no indication that the CIA has an ethos that would motivate it to reduce civilian harm. The agency does not have an institutional history of analyzing and understanding global, or even US, norms and values in using force. By contrast, the US military is relatively good at this, with a range of efforts to think critically, as evidenced in military handbooks, rules of engagement, and best practices documents. Many of these recent outputs discuss civilian protection and both past failures and lessons learned in an effort to improve over time. The CIA has no parallel process, or if it does that process is entirely and unnecessarily classified.

Joint CIA–JSOC drone operations may not even be considered "military operations" by the US government, which means US Army, Navy, and Marine directives on civilian protection or law of war compliance might not apply.[23] It is just as likely drone operations are governed by the CIA's procedures, or some set of procedures established specifically for such joint operations. What civilian protection planning and precautions are included in those procedures is a mystery, subject neither to public review, open analysis, nor clear accountability standards.

As noted, the administration goes out of its way to reassure critics that it is being careful. President Obama and counterterrorism adviser John Brennan demanded the CIA make changes after a spike in civilian casualties in Pakistan during the first half of 2010.[24] In a key address in April 2012, Brennan provided a rare public defense of the policy stating that a target would only be authorized if there was a "high degree of confidence" that civilians would not be injured or killed "except in the rarest of circumstances."[25] These are important reassurances, but they are too general to responsibly combat the perception that the United States is doing what it wants without any accountability to civilians, the American public, or international law.

A fact as simple as whether or not the CIA and JSOC drone operators are trained in civilian protection best practices remains unknown. Certainly there is no reason to keep secrets regarding this type of issue. Even members of the congressional committees tasked with overseeing the CIA and the military have voiced concerns. In 2010, the House Permanent Select Committee on Intelligence criticized the Pentagon's tendency to classify its clandestine intelligence gathering activities because it prevents relevant members from assessing those operations.[26]

4. THE CIVILIAN TOLL

There is evidence that US drone operations have profound negative consequences for civilian populations. While headlines focus on putting a hard number to militant versus civilian deaths, drone strikes also cause other types of harm. These may be understood as second- or third-order impacts, and they are often overlooked or underestimated as part of support for the drone program's apparent efficacy in killing targeted individuals.

It is important to note that nobody has accurately measured the true extent of civilian harm caused by drones or the related harm done to America's reputation. In fact, the potential costs of the program are almost impossible to measure, whether in dollars, deaths, or reputation. Nevertheless, seriously considering these costs is an important element of ensuring that the United States is balancing the strategic effectiveness of the drone program with its broader impact in order to assess whether it may, in the end, be counter-productive to key strategic goals and legal commitments.

To be sure, there may be cases in which civilians have been spared in a drone strike that might otherwise have died in a bombing raid or ground troop action. Yet this is difficult to ascertain as there is no clear way to calculate the potential of "civilians not harmed." More to the point, the oft-repeated precision of drones has almost certainly been overstated. For example, Brennan likened drone strikes to surgery, saying they could remove the "cancer" of al-Qaeda without affecting the surrounding "tissue" of civilians in the area.[27] Brennan's analogy, however, ignores the harms to civilians that we already know about, to say nothing of the impact of unreported strikes. In reality, civilians in drone zones are living through the brutality of a secret war, and the "surgery" Brennan references may be a far blunter instrument than the government acknowledges.

Civilian deaths and injuries – Drones may kill civilians when an individual or group is near an intended target or where they are mistaken for militants. There are also reports of civilians killed when a drone strikes again after an initial strike, including when rescuers come to the aid of those harmed in the first attack.[28] This is believed to have occurred in both Pakistan and Yemen.[29]

The truth of civilian deaths and injuries remains unknown because, to date, there have been no large-scale on-the-ground studies of civilian casualties caused by covert drone strikes in Pakistan, Yemen, or Somalia. Most drone strikes occur in areas inaccessible to foreigners, although several organizations have investigated incidents of civilian harm in Pakistan and have aggregated reports of strikes that appear in the media.[30] While findings from these groups vary on the total numbers of civilian deaths, they consistently point to signifi-cantly higher civilian casualties than those suggested by the US government.

Statistics shift depending on the definitions used by journalists, analysts, and governments to differentiate between "civilians" and "combatants." While technically these terms are at the core of the law of armed conflict, the ways

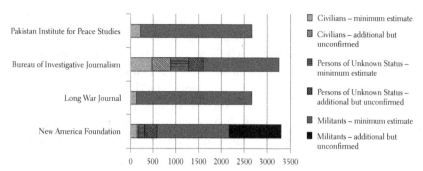

FIGURE 5. Estimated number of Deaths by US Drone Strikes in Pakistan
Source: Center for Civilians in Conflict and Human Rights Clinic, Columbia Law School.
"The Civilian Impact of Drones: Unexamined Costs, Unanswered Questions", p. 20.

they are used vary, allowing for distinct and even confusing claims regarding who has been harmed. Media reports routinely cite unnamed Pakistani government officials as confirming the identity of the individuals killed as "militants," but these claims are rarely corroborated. A former senior official in the Obama administration, John Boyle, in a 2013 study for Chatham House, said the administration has been "so successful in spinning the number of civilian casualties is that it has adopted a controversial method for tracking casualties which inflates the totals of 'militants' killed and systematically underestimates civilian casualties."[31] A sampling of estimates is seen in Figure 5.

Aside from a debate about the numbers of those killed, a single civilian death or injury is enough to dramatically alter families' lives. In Pakistan, families are often large and their well-being depends on intricate connections among many members. The death of one person in a family can create long-lasting instability, particularly if the individual killed is the primary breadwinner.

In regions most often targeted by drones, women typically have a limited earning capacity, few families have significant savings, and insurance is non-existent. This leaves the wives and dependents of those severely injured and extremely vulnerable. A single drone attack may force a family into poverty. It may lead sons to drop out of school to provide for their family and prevent daughters from pursuing educational opportunities because they may have to take on the role of caretakers.[32] Similar familial dynamics exist in Somalia and Yemen.

While the missiles used by the United States can hit precise targets and are thus more likely to kill than to injure, injuries in drone attacks occur. Hakeem

Khan, from Mohmand Agency in the Federally Administered Tribal Areas of Pakistan, lost his leg to flying debris after a drone struck his neighbor's house. He told the Center for Civilians in Conflict: "I am living a very painful life ... I use a stick to support my body and find it too difficult to move from place to place. I need compensation for the loss of my leg."[33]

Given that serious injuries can devastate a family for generations, civilian casualty statistics indicate an affected population many times greater than the numbers of those directly killed or wounded, highlighting the broad social impact of drone attacks.

Psychological impact – Civilian deaths, injuries, displacement, and property loss caused by conflict are traumatic for the local population. Covert drone strikes take a particular toll, striking unannounced and without any clear public understanding of who is – and importantly, who is not – a target. For victims, there is no one to turn to for formal recognition, apologies, or explanations to mitigate their sorrow. And for communities living under the constant watch of drones, there is no one to hold accountable for their fear or suffering. Drone strikes not only produce civilian death and injury, but also create long-term, unseen impact that tear at the fabric of communities.

In places such as the tribal areas of northwestern Pakistan, where drones often buzz overhead for 24 hours a day, people live in constant fear of being attacked.[34] Michael Kugelman of the Woodrow Wilson International Center for Scholars notes: "I have heard Pakistanis speak about children in the tribal areas who become hysterical when they hear the characteristic buzz of a drone ... Imagine the effect this has on psyches, and particularly on young ones already scarred by war and displacement."[35]

Unlike deaths and property loss, which may affect one or more families, the fear associated with covert drone strikes affects nearly everyone in the communities under drone surveillance. One victim told the Center for Civilians in Conflict: "We fear that the drones will strike us again ... my aged parents are often in a state of fear. We are depressed, anxious, and constantly remembering our deceased family members ... it often compels me to leave this place."[36] Another man described the anguish of his sister-in-law, who lost her husband and two sons in a US drone strike in Pakistan: "After their death she is mentally upset ... she is always screaming and shouting at night and demanding me to take her to their graves."[37]

An investigator at the UK advocacy group Reprieve met a young man named Tariq Aziz shortly before he was killed in strike on March 17, 2011, reporting:

I asked him, "Have you seen a drone," and I expected him to say, "Yes, I see one a week." But he said they saw 10 or 15 every day. And he was saying at nighttime, it was making him crazy, because he couldn't sleep. All he was thinking about at home was whether everyone was okay. I could see it in his face. He looked absolutely terrified.[38]

With US targeting criteria classified, civilians in Pakistan, Yemen, and Somalia do not know when, where, or against whom drones will strike. The US policy of signature strikes compounds these fears because family members might be unexpectedly and suddenly killed without realizing that they were acting in a way that defined them as a target. Finally, civilian victims of drone strikes have been assumed by their communities to be connected to militant actions. In this way, victims may face the double burden of dealing with the aftermath of an attack as well as with the stigma associated with having been targeted.

Property loss, displacement, development, and poverty – A house is often a family's greatest financial asset and its destruction can be financially and socially devastating. In Pakistan's tribal areas, homes are often shared by multiple families, compounding the suffering and hardship caused when a house is damaged or destroyed.

Remote drone operations have struck many homes, including those of individuals and families that pose no threat to the United States. For example, Usman Wazir of northwest Pakistan is now homeless and sleeps either at the local mosque or with relatives since a drone destroyed his home and killed his brother, his sister-in-law, and their two teenage children. Shakeel Khan, also of northwest Pakistan, and his elderly parents survived a drone attack on their home, which killed his brother, his sister-in-law, and their children. He explained: "We don't have enough to reconstruct our house and fear that the drones will strike us again."[39] Daud Khan and the surviving members of his family were forced to move from their village in Waziristan when they could not afford to rebuild their home destroyed in a drone strike.[40]

Drone strikes have also hit homes in Yemen, adding to the displacement of the population caused by local and national conflicts.[41] An airstrike in Jaar in southern Yemen reduced an entire block to rubble in two consecutive explosions. Because of the secret nature of these missions, it remains unclear whether the attack was the responsibility of the US or Yemeni government, compounding a sense of frustration and the impossibility of accountability or recognition for victims.[42]

Some Somali civilians have fled their homes out of fear of drone attacks targeting al-Shabaab. In January 2012, citizens of the small town of Elasha Biyaha on the outskirts of Mogadishu fled to the main city to seek refuge after strikes killed a senior rebel leader there.[43] Lisa Schirch of 3P Human Security explains the impact of these attacks: "[D]rone-related displacement disrupts long-term stability by decreasing the capacity of local people to respond through civil society initiatives that foster stability, democracy and moderation and increase displaced people's vulnerability to insurgent recruitment."[44]

The threat of drone strikes in Yemen and Pakistan and the resulting fear of random or at least unpredictable targeting have led parents to prevent their children from attending schools.[45] And, in Pakistan there have been several reports of drone strikes that have damaged or destroyed local schools.[46]

Many within the US administration justify the drone program because it produces minimal damage to civilians. This claim, however, is too often made from places far from where drones actually strike and may appear as a benefit too seductive to seriously question. Nevertheless, the use of lethal force always involves tough policy decisions, and managing these issues in a responsible manner requires fully reflecting on their consequences.

5. QUESTIONING THE MAGIC OF DRONES

The American people and the politicians they elect commonly make three blanket assumptions about drones: first, very few civilians are killed by them; second, they collect high-quality intelligence that ultimately reduces the risk to civilians; and third, their attacks are extremely precise. However comforting these assumptions may be, they do not necessarily hold up under scrutiny. Even within the more traditional combat theater of Afghanistan, where drone strikes are supported by ground intelligence, a study by the Center for Naval Analysis found that they were ten times more likely to cause civilian casualties than attacks by manned aircraft.[47] This statistic alone shows why the seemingly intuitive argument that drones are better at avoiding civilians should never take the place of hard facts.

This is not to say that drones are unethical or necessarily strategically damaging. Rather, smart policymaking and a commitment to humanitarian values requires that we question the assumptions that drones represent an unproblematic, if not magical, tool to combat terrorism. In fact, many lives, as well as the long-term success of counterterrorism, are at stake in this debate.

"Extremely low" civilian casualties – There are practical obstacles in any effort by the United States to determine exactly how many civilians are killed or injured by drone attacks. These strikes often occur in remote areas and in countries with no conventional US or allied forces on the ground to conduct investigations or talk to witnesses. Even in Afghanistan, military investigations following drone attacks are often limited to overhead surveillance rather than

fieldwork-based reviews involving witness statements and forensic evidence. These systems may not identify actual civilian casualties, such as children, and they cannot see whether there are bodies, such as infants or individuals that might be homebound, inside structures that are destroyed.

Still, US officials stand by their assessment that drone strikes cause "extremely low" civilian casualties, and at times they have claimed that drone attacks have produced no civilian deaths. When US officials provide data, what they present is often so confusing that it defies credibility. In June 2010, officials estimated that drone strikes had caused a total of fifty civilian casualties. Early in 2011, that estimate was revised downward to thirty.[48] By June 2011 Brennan claimed: "There hasn't been a single collateral death because of the exceptional proficiency, precision of the capabilities we've been able to develop."[49]

A former senior legal adviser to the US Army Special Forces told Reuters: "[B]ased on my military experience, there's simply no way so few civilians have been killed. For one bad guy you kill, you'd expect 1.5 civilian deaths, because killing from that high above, there's always the 'oops' factor."[50]

The United States might also overlook or undercount civilians harmed by covert drone strikes because, in those cases, everyone harmed might be presumed to be a militant. According to an unnamed Obama administration official, the United States "in effect counts all military-age males in a strike zone as combatants ... unless there is explicit intelligence posthumously proving them innocent."[51] In response, one presidential aide called this a "wild oversimplification," but a more nuanced statement about how combatants are defined might be problematic.[52] Either way, families of civilians killed by drones have no venue in which to prove that their loved one was not a combatant.

Signature strikes present a particularly significant challenge to US civilian casualty statistics. As the identity of the dead may never have been known to begin with, combatants can be easily confused with civilians. Whether one explains this through the misidentification of a target or the "'oops' factor," journalists, human rights advocates, and investigators do not have regular access to the places where drones are commonly deployed in order to determine whether the government's claims are correct. This means that the covert drone program is not subject to the sort of serious public scrutiny that is essential for an effective and humane management of war and its consequences.

Despite the obstacles to understanding the aftermath of a drone strike, this process is essential for analyzing the program's effectiveness. In fact, not being able to investigate may prevent the United States from knowing whether a strike succeeded or whether subsequent attacks may be necessary.

Failure to examine the aftermath of a particular strike may also obscure the long-term, strategic costs of alienating the local population. Failing to acknowledge harm to civilians can cause the same kind of popular anger and resentment that has plagued US actions in Iraq and Afghanistan, and now may be spreading around the world. Whether in Pakistan, Yemen, or Somalia, if the United States does not know how many civilians have been harmed, it cannot offer appropriate amends – in the form of aid or perhaps even monetary payments – for the losses suffered. Finally, only an accurate assessment of civilian casualties and an ongoing consideration of lessons learned can lead to more effective operations that cause less harm in the future.

Smarter intelligence needed – Because drones offer unparalleled surveillance capabilities, they are assumed to enable extremely accurate intelligence. Round-the-clock video footage before, during, and after strikes helps operators keep track of those on the ground and can enable accurate targeting.

However, for operations in remote locations such as in the tribal regions of northern Pakistan, there are often systematic flaws in the intelligence used for targeting decisions. Where intelligence and analysis is faulty or unsubstantiated by trusted intelligence assets on the ground, drone strikes can result in significant unintended civilian casualties.

The fundamental problem is that the capabilities of the machines deployed are outpacing the capacities of those operating them. Drone development, particularly video surveillance capability, has increased at a very rapid rate and operators are unable to properly analyze incoming data. This risks mistakes in targeting and, ultimately, increased civilian casualties. Drones currently capture far more data than can be effectively reviewed and this problem is only increasing as the capabilities of drone technology advance and as their use proliferates. In April 2012, Secretary of the Air Force Michael Donley said that it would be "years" before Air Force personnel would be able to sift through the "unsustainable" amounts of video and still imagery collected by its drones.[53]

The problem of too much data and not enough analysis will only worsen. The newly developed "Gorgon Stare" surveillance system, for example, will have at least nine cameras capable of watching and recording the activities of an entire small town. To keep pace with so much data, new technologies are being developed to analyze the massive amounts of information being collected. However appealing the solution – matching advances in technology with other advanced technologies – it may not enable the critical thinking necessary to make the best and most appropriate decisions.

Some drone cameras can identify minute details, such as whether an individual is missing an arm or wearing a hat. However, those sorts of details are not always very clear at 20,000 feet. And even where descriptive information can be gained with some level of accuracy, this data may not allow operators to distinguish civilians from combatants. The problem is especially difficult in communities, large and small, where militants co-mingle; dress as civilians; and may even engage in acts that draw the attention of drone operators, such as carrying assault weapons. Marc Garlasco has pointed out the difficulty of using video in densely populated or thickly forested areas, as are found in parts of northern Pakistan.[54] Even in relatively barren environments in Afghanistan, a Predator was "unable to discriminate the highly distinctive outline of two Marines (with full battle equipment) from the irregular enemy" as recently as April 2011.[55]

Even if the battlefield is relatively clear and the drone operator knows the affiliation of those watched from afar, missions remain subject to multiple technological constraints. For example, drone actions involve what is known as the "soda straw effect," in which as the drone zooms in on a target, it loses a wider picture of the area – like viewing a small area through a soda straw. While zoomed in, a civilian may enter the vicinity of the strike without being noticed and therefore will not be considered within the targeting analysis.

In the book *Predator: The Remote-Control Air War Over Iraq And Afghanistan*, a drone pilot described targeting a truck in Afghanistan. Viewed through Predator video, the truck appeared to be far enough away from surrounding houses and pedestrians for the strike to be given the go-ahead.[56] The ground commander, who was also monitoring the Predator footage, gave clearance to take the shot. After the missile had been fired, when the focus was no longer zoomed in, two young boys riding bicycles appeared on the operator's screen. The pilot cried "Oh, God! Not again!" as he powerlessly watched as the missile killed the two boys, together with the occupants of the truck, and thought about his daughter back home.[57] Had there been a wider field of vision or real-time ground intelligence, the two boys would likely have been noticed and the attack could have been delayed until they had passed.

The technological limitations of drones highlight the importance of linking them with other forms of data collection and intelligence to avoid critical errors, including killing civilians. While US forces cross-reference video surveillance with electronic signals intelligence, the latter may be limited to intercepting and tracking phones because drone strikes so often occur in low-tech environments where no other types of signals exist. In fact, armed groups are often aware of this challenge and have manipulated intelligence gathering to mislead US drone operators.[58] In Mali, an al-Qaeda affiliated militant group left behind a sheet of twenty-two tips on how to avoid being struck by a drone: Tip 2 is to broadcast frequencies that disrupt the drone's operations, Tips 5 and 6 involve jamming electronic communications by using old equipment, and Tip 12 is to "maintain complete silence of all wireless contacts."[59]

In some cases, phone intercepts are used to locate a target using the identifiers of particular phones, such as SIM cards. However, armed groups know this and can swap SIM cards from one phone to another. As a result, individuals killed based on tracking cell phones may not be the intended targets but may simply be a relative or friend who has been given the device. The accuracy of a strike may also be subject to the quality of the cell phone network and whether the location can be accurately triangulated.[60]

Without its own robust intelligence gathering operation on the ground, the United States may be forced to rely on a variety of uncertain local sources for human intelligence. This raises obvious questions about the quality, motivation, and vetting of sources. In desperately poor regions, cash payments for information are likely to turn up people willing to provide whatever information they think US intelligence groups want to hear.[61] This was the case in the early stages of the US invasion of Afghanistan. Many of those detained, including significant numbers of those flown half-way around the world to be held at the base in Guantanamo Bay, were individuals turned in for rewards or as a means of settling local disputes.

Stories abound in northwest Pakistan of families and rival groups using locator chips to have their enemies targeted.[62] In addition, actual informants or those believed to be informants often endanger their families and their communities. The International Crisis Group reported that militants in Federally Administered Tribal Areas have tortured suspected informants and released video footage of their executions as warnings to locals not to collaborate with the United States.[63] An al-Qaeda affiliated group's leader in Mali noted in a missive given to operatives that anyone helping the Americans locate targets should be "hanged in the public places with a sign hanging from his neck identifying him as an 'American spy.'"[64]

US intelligence sometimes uses information provided by other governments for targeting decisions. However, this information may also be inaccurate, either because the intelligence is false, poorly gathered, or purposefully manipulated. Even in circumstances where US forces are working in close cooperation with local or national leaders, they may find themselves being urged to strike targets that have more to do with the local balance of power than the war on terrorism, and potentially with little concern for protecting civilians. For example, some US officials believe that in 2010 they were manipulated by the Yemeni government, when it called for a drone strike that killed Jabir Shabwani, a political rival of then-President Abdullah Saleh.[65]

Precision – The official US narrative about drones is that they are able to deliver weapons that are uniquely "precise" and among the most accurate in the history of warfare. In this way, drones are believed to be more capable of minimizing civilian harm than other weapons systems. In fact, whether or not ordinance launched from a drone actually hits its target and avoids civilian harm when doing so depends not only on the "precision" of the weapon deployed, but also on information about the target and the possible presence of civilians in the strike area. The combination of questionable intelligence, the limitations of video surveillance, and the lack of granular human intelligence from the ground call into question US claims of precision drone attacks.

The US narrative on "precision" has been taken for granted by the American public and many senior policymakers. In part, this is because it is so appealing. And, in part, it is because there are limited counternarratives in situations where operations are covert and the truth about what is actually going on remains hidden. That is, the idea that drones target with great precision is largely based on trust in US government claims, while a serious assessment of the actual impact and effectiveness of drones requires facts and objective independent review.

John Brennan's April 2012 speech on drones defended the legality of their use by focusing on their precision:

> Targeted strikes conform to the principle of distinction, the idea that only military objectives may be intentionally targeted and that civilians are protected from being intentionally targeted. With the unprecedented ability of remotely piloted aircraft to precisely target a military objective, while minimizing collateral damage, one could argue that never before has there been a weapon that allows us to distinguish more effectively between an al-Qaida terrorist and innocent civilians.[66]

This statement is misleading in several ways. As noted, drone strikes can indeed precisely target a military objective. But "minimizing collateral damage" is possible only if the operator knows whom he or she is targeting. Without trusted intelligence fed from the ground to the operations center, drone operators in a given strike may not be able to correctly distinguish between civilians and combatants in a manner as accurately as we would like to believe.

Signature strikes make distinguishing between civilians and combatants particularly challenging. In fact, this method of targeting cannot be considered precise under any circumstances. Brennan continued:

Targeted strikes conform to the *principle of proportionality*, the notion that
the anticipated collateral damage of an action cannot be excessive in relation
to the anticipated military advantage. By targeting an individual terrorist or a
small number of terrorists with ordinance that can be adapted to avoid
harming others in the immediate vicinity, it is hard to imagine a tool that
can better minimize the risk to civilians than remotely piloted aircraft.[67]

It is technically true that, as Brennan suggests, a drone can shoot a missile that
destroys a house thought to have militants meeting inside and not damage the
house next door. However, a fighter jet can do the same thing, and there
are several ways in which drones may produce less precise attacks than
conventional airstrikes. Visual feeds from the air are limited in fidelity,
especially when there are obstructions, such as buildings. Because there
may be more people involved in targeting using drones, there are greater risks
of miscommunication and confusion among multiple parties.

To ensure the right person is targeted and that there is minimal civilian
harm, the military locates a target, tracks it, and "engages" it – meaning killing
the person targeted. The effectiveness of this process has little to do with
the drone itself and far more to do with the availability of accurate and
verifiable intelligence.

6. WHAT IS TO BE DONE?

The US drone campaign is unlikely to stop. However, given the problems with
the current covert drone program, a pause is warranted to assess what might
be going wrong and to make key corrections at this relatively early stage in
drone deployment. After all, drone strikes may not be the answer to global
terrorism that the administration and the American public appear to believe
they are. In 2013, General Stanley McChrystal, former commander of international forces in Afghanistan, said: "What scares me about drone strikes is
how they are perceived around the world ... [t]he resentment created by
American use of unmanned strikes ... is much greater than the average
American appreciates. They are hated on a visceral level, even by people
who've never seen one or seen the effects of one."[68]

Whatever benefits drone attacks may provide, their widespread use involves
substantial strategic costs that deserve careful scrutiny. Instead of constantly
repeating claims about precision, effectiveness, and low levels of civilian
harm, US policymakers should develop a well-reasoned policy with a full
and open acknowledgment of the complex and often unintended consequences of drone deployment. There is a pressing need for a more open
and conscious drone policy. Policymakers must remember that their decisions

are likely to be copied by other countries, as both allies and enemies will soon be deploying multiple types of drones in a variety of places.

It is important that the United States responsibly manage its current position as a leader and innovator in the use of militarized drones so that widespread use of these new technologies does not make it easier to use lethal force in ways that violate established international norms or threaten US security. At a minimum, this process should involve the following five steps.

More transparency – Few outside a tight circle of policymakers know enough about the process and rules for making targeting decisions in drone attacks. It is important that there exist greater oversight regarding the policies used to determine who is targeted, why they are targeted, how they are targeted, and what measures are put in place to protect civilians. In defending national security, some degree of secrecy is justified. However, the details of the drone program and decisions made to use drones to kill people abroad should be more transparent, at the very least to Congress. If the US government does not control the drone program and the narrative about it, its enemies will.

The American people cannot be simply asked to trust their leaders to conduct a lethal program of this scale free from meaningful oversight. This is especially clear in light of the dark and often embarrassing history of CIA assassination operations. The administration should develop express mechanisms of rational, rule-based reviews in line with domestic and international law. To the degree that these systems are already in place, it is essential that there exist greater transparency regarding elements of the targeting process, application of the laws of war, and human rights training for drone operators.

The administration should engage in discussion about how it defines civilians and combatants and how it tracks and assesses civilian casualties, both after individual strikes and over time. If drone operators are properly trained in civilian harm-mitigation tactics, non-classified details of such training should be shared. Similarly, some amount of transparency on who can be targeted and why is important, so that civilians can protect themselves from behavior that might subject them to being targeted. Given that the US military has become relatively open about similar protocols of conventional strikes, there is no reason the CIA and JSOC could not better explain their procedures as well.[69]

Department of Defense, not the CIA – An intelligence agency should not be managing large-scale military operations. The entire drone program should be run by the Department of Defense. America's armed services have a transparent chain of command and a stated commitment to respect the rule of law. They train troops in civilian protection practices and closely adhere to the law of armed conflict. They study operations to learn lessons from past activities and to improve future operations. Perhaps most importantly, they have a far higher level of accountability to Congress. This issue is critical because the American public has a right to know that what is being done overseas in its name is reviewed by their representatives. This process should include as much open, public review of policies as possible.

However, placing the drone program under military command will not necessarily ensure thorough transparency. The JSOC, which currently runs part of the program in cooperation with the CIA, may operate outside of conventional military protocols and operate with minimal congressional oversight or public scrutiny.[70] With this in mind, to the degree that the Department of Defense's control over the drone program is managed by the JSOC, it is essential that accountability be expanded to meet the existing standards of conventional military operations.

Alternatives to lethal action – The use of lethal force is always a significant and grave decision that almost always puts civilians in danger. Under the covert drone program, an ever-greater number of individuals are vulnerable to lethal targeting, which increases the risk that civilians will be killed in a strike against a legitimate target or mistakenly considered to be a target.

In addition, the US drone program currently targets and kills individuals who otherwise might be detained and interrogated. Drones deny these individuals any opportunity to surrender. While interrogations and detentions carry their own risks of human rights abuses, they provide the United States and its allies with the potential to better assess actual threats posed by the detainee. As we know from the many thousands of detainees in Afghanistan, Iraq, and elsewhere, many of those questioned for potential connection to al-Qaeda and other groups are subsequently released when their cases are reviewed and it is determined that they pose a minimal threat to national security. Once lethal action is taken, there is, of course, no going back.

While the Obama administration has repeatedly stated a preference for capturing insurgents over killing them, it commonly claims that capture is impractical for multiple reasons, from logistical difficulties to the limited availability of appropriate detention facilities.[71] This position helps justify the use of lethal force in the drone program while at the same time abdicating the responsibilities that arise in non-lethal actions. A fearful and war-weary American electorate appears to be convinced, and has not demanded alternatives to systematic use of lethal counterterrorism tactics.

In October 2013, US Special Operations Forces carried out a capture mission in both Libya and Somalia. Media commentators suggested these missions might signal a decreased reliance on drones, as did a senior congressional aid: "I think this goes along with this policy that they are trying to move counter-terrorism operations from CIA to Defense [Department], and trying to operate less with drones."[72] However, two missions alone do not define a trend, and "capture" might have been preferable to "kill" in these cases because of the value of the intelligence that these individuals might offer.

Recognizing civilian harm – Monitoring, tabulating, and responding to incidents of civilian harm caused by the drone program is both ethically correct and strategically imperative. It reflects America's stated commitment to humanity even in times of war, and it may simultaneously ease some of the anger building in the civilian population.

To find proof that recognizing civilian harm works, one need look no further than Iraq and Afghanistan, where the US military and USAID have successfully addressed civilian losses through the media; consultations with local leaders and village elders; and through amends including formal apologies, monetary payments, and livelihood assistance.[73] However, in Pakistan, Yemen, and Somalia – sites of covert drone strikes – recognition and amends for civilian harm do not exist. During his Senate confirmation hearings in February 2013, Brennan said: "Where possible, we also work with local governments to gather facts and, if appropriate, provide condolence payments to families of those killed."[74] However, there is no known evidence to prove that this is true. The refusal of the United States to acknowledge the seriousness of civilian harm may well have profound and long-term consequences.

Research in Iraq, Afghanistan,[75] and Pakistan[76] shows that when civilians are known to suffer losses, even more than money, most victims simply want an explanation of why they were harmed.[77] Clearly nothing can bring back someone who has been killed or adequately compensate for the loss of a loved one, yet explanations have great significance for victims, their families, and their communities. They can answer unanswered questions, dignify loss, and, in cases where the explanation is public, can remove local suspicion that families victimized in a strike must by definition have been up to no good.

In Afghanistan, US military officials found that focusing on reducing and recognizing civilian casualties can benefit all sides by limiting local anger and increasing operational effectiveness.[78] The lack of conventional American ground forces in areas where covert drone programs are conducted does not absolve the United States from responsibility to investigate incidents of civilian harm and, where appropriate, to recognize and assist victims.

Similar activities in Pakistan and Somalia would be undoubtedly complicated but by no means impossible. The United States can use the combined data of video feeds, other forms of electronic intelligence, trusted local interlocutors, local government officials, civil society, and media to get a picture of what civilian harm occurred following a strike. Washington could initiate a claims process by working in concert with personnel on the ground, either through USAID programs, civilian officials in-country, or, when trusted, connections to the local government.[79] Apologies for harm in Somalia, as one example, could be made through local clan leaders, and any financial amends could be made through mobile phones, which are used extensively for everything from communications to receiving remittances from relatives working overseas.

Distinguish between civilians and combatants – The US military has rigorous procedures to ensure that targets are selected responsibly –procedures that help avoid killing the wrong people, including civilians. However, little of Washington's rhetoric about the need to avoid civilian casualties matters unless the United States acknowledges that unidentifiable targets might also be "civilians."

The CIA's track record in this regard is, perhaps not surprisingly, opaque. However, there are reports of instances where the agency has declined to conduct strikes based on the presence of civilians.[80] What is missing is public information about the standard procedures that the CIA targeters and drone operators use for selecting and striking targets.

The ongoing secrecy surrounding drones is unnecessary and unjustified. Both the CIA and JSOC should be made to publicize their civilian protection protocols, at least in broad enough terms to provide confirmation that they adhere to domestic and international law. The American public has the right to know how and why people are being put on kill lists, and Congress should be provided with relevant details to ensure that targeting and attacks are managed in an appropriate manner.

Part of this review process should be the end of signature strikes. Washington must acknowledge that many men in countries such as Yemen and Pakistan routinely and legally engage in activities that may define them as suspicious. Under the law of armed conflict, as well as international law, the mere fact that people interact with known targets does make them legitimate targets.

For many people around the world, drones have become synonymous with US counterterrorism strategy. However, unlike in conventional wars, US policymakers often fail to ask the difficult questions about the impact of drone deployment on civilians, including whether civilian harm and related public anger around drone operations does more harm than good.

Congress should better exercise its oversight, and any US agency or department engaging in drone strikes should track and investigate any civilian harm that may be caused, develop proper responses to substantive claims, and address victims' needs. In addition, any president – whether Barack Obama or a future elected leader – should be as transparent as possible with the American people about the use of lethal force. As with any other weapon, proper drone use does not depend only on technical capabilities, but also on how they are used. It is time to treat drones like other weapons systems: as military tools used to enable a rational, humane strategy, not as a solution in and of themselves.

NOTES

1 Brief of *Amici Curiae*: The Bureau of Investigative Journalism, Campaign for Innocent Victims in Conflict, Center for Constitutional Rights, Center on National Security at Fordham Law, The Constitution Project, First Amendment Coalition, Human Rights Watch, International Commission of Jurists, and National Security Archive in Support of Plaintiffs–Appellants Seeking Reversal. www.constitutionproject.org/wp-content/uploads/2012/10/20120322ciafoiaamicusfinal filed.pdf.

2 Lewis, Larry, and Sarah Holewinski, "Changing of the guard: Protection for an Evolving Military," *Prism* 4(2): 57–65. The unclassified summary study can be found at http://cna.org/research/2013/drone-strikes-civilian-casualty-consideration.

3 Embassy of the United States to Afghanistan, "U.S. Ambassador Karl W. Eikenberry," transcripts and remarks, May 19, 2009.

4 Center for Civilians in Conflict and Human Rights Clinic, Columbia Law School, "The Civilian Impact of Drones: Unexamined Costs, Unanswered Questions," 2012.

5 *Guardian*, "US shows off new card trick," April 11, 2003.

6 Ibid.

7 Entous, Adam, Siobhan Gorman, and Julian E. Barnes, "US tightens drone rules," *Wall Street Journal*, November 4, 2011.

8 Zenko, Micah, "Reforming the U.S. drone strike policies," *Council on Foreign Relations*, January 2013, p. 12: "Human rights advocates, international legal experts, and current and former U.S. officials dispute whether this post hoc methodology [i.e., signature strikes] meets the principle of distinction for the use of lethal force."

9 Entous, Adam, Siobhan Gorman, and Julian E. Barnes, "US relaxes drone rules: Obama gives CIA, military greater leeway in use against militants in Yemen," *Wall Street Journal*, April 26, 2012.

10 Columbia Human Rights Clinic, interview with Marc Garlasco, Pentagon former senior intelligence analyst, New York City, April 11, 2012.

11 Abbott, Sebastian, "AP Impact: New light on drone war's death toll," Associated Press, February 26, 2012.

12 Rhode, David, "The Obama doctrine: How the president's drone war is backfiring," *Foreign Policy*, March/April 2012, p. 65.

13 Abbott, "AP Impact."

14 Ibid.

15 Ibid.

16 Masood, Salman, and Pir Zubair Shah, "C.I.A. drones kill civilians in Pakistan," *New York Times*, March 7, 2011.

17 Inter Services Public Relations, press release, March 17, 2011. Woods, Chris, and Christina Lamb, "CIA tactics in Pakistan include targeting rescuers and funerals," Bureau of Investigative Journalism, February 4, 2012.

18 Kravetz, David, "'Alice in Wonderland' ruling lets feds keep mum on targeted-killing legal rationale," *Wired*, January 2, 2013.

19 Zakaria, Tabassum, and Mark Hosenball, "Pentagon to take over some CIA drone operations: Sources," Reuters, May 20, 2013.

20 Lt. Col. John Nagl, quoted in Gavett, Gretchen, "What is the secretive US 'kill/capture' campaign?" PBS, *Frontline*, June 17, 2011.

21 Wittes, Benjamin, "Remarks of CIA counsel Stephen Preston at Harvard Law School," *Lawfare*, April 10, 2012.

22 Human Rights Watch, "US: Transfer CIA drone strikes to military," April 20, 2012.

23 Department of Defense, "Directive 2311.01E: DoD law of war program," May 9, 2006, section 4.1.

24 DeYoung, Karen, "Secrecy defines Obama's drone war," *Washington Post*, December 20, 2011.

25 John Brennan, "The ethics and efficacy of the president's counterterrorism strategy," speech given at the Woodrow Wilson International Center for Scholars (hereafter Woodrow Wilson Center), Washington, DC, April 30, 2012.

26 The committee did not take any legislative action to rectify the situation, relying instead on discussions it had with the Pentagon. It did, however, issue an ultimatum. House of Representatives No. 111–186, June 24, 2009, p. 49: "[I]f [the] DOD does not meet its obligations to inform the Committee of Intelligence activities, the Committee will consider legislative action clarifying the Department's obligation to do so."

27 Brennan, "The ethics and efficacy of US counterterrorism strategy."

28 Matulich, Peter, "Why COIN principles don't fly with drones," *Small War Journal*, February 24, 2012: "[K]ill-boxes follow-up attacks [that] often occur after the initial strike" and where "rescuers are targeted in an attempt to score a windfall of extra militants killed." BBC, June 4, 2012: "US drone strike 'kills 15' in Pakistan," in which it was reported that a "second missile killed 12 more militants who arrived at the scene." *Express Tribune*, "Within 24 hours: Three suspected militants killed in drone attacks," May 29, 2012, which reported successive strikes within a one-hour period.

29 Almasmari, Hakim, "Two suspected US drone strikes reported in Yemen," CNN, May 15, 2012, reporting that "Jaar district residents said civilians were killed after

they rushed to the site of the first strike." Woods, Chris, and Christina Lamb, "CIA tactics in Pakistan include targeting rescuers and funerals."

30 Center for Civilians in Conflict and Human Rights Clinic, Columbia Law School, "The Civilian Impact of Drones: Unexamined Costs, Unanswered Questions."

31 Boyle, Michael J., "The costs and consequences of drone warfare," *International Affairs* 89 (1): 1–29, p. 7.

32 Rogers, Christopher, "Civilians in armed conflict: Civilian harm and conflict in northwest Pakistan," Center for Civilians in Conflict (2010), p. 26.

33 Ibid., p. 81.

34 Woodrow Wilson Center, interview with Pakistani civilian (name withheld), interview no. 59, Northwest Pakistan, 2010. Center for Civilians in Conflict and Human Rights Clinic, Columbia Law School, "The civilian impact of drones: Unexamined costs, Unanswered questions."

35 Kugelman, Michael, "In Pakistan, death is only one of the civilian costs of drone strikes," *Huffington Post*, May 2, 2012.

36 Center for Civilians in Conflict and Human Rights Clinic, Columbia Law School, "The civilian impact of drones: Unexamined costs, Unanswered questions," p. 24.

37 Ibid.

38 Schifrin, Nick, "Was teen killed by CIA drone a militant – or innocent victim?" ABC *News*, December 30, 2011.

39 Rogers, "Civilians in armed conflict," pp. 60–62.

40 Ibid.

41 International Committee of the Red Cross, June 6, 2012: "Yemen: Tens of thousands in Abyan in need of urgent help," which reported "fierce fighting, sometimes involving air strikes, has led to a severe deterioration of the humanitarian situation" in parts of southern Yemen. Office of the UN High Commissioner for Refugees, March 9, 2012: "Briefing Notes: Internal displacement grows in Yemeni," in which it was estimated that there were 150,000 internally displaced people in the south.

42 McEvers, Kelly, "Yemen airstrikes punish militants, and civilians," NPR, July 6, 2012.

43 Radio Bar Kulan, "Locals flee their homes in Elasha Biyaha," January 22, 2012.

44 Schirch, Lisa, "9 costs of drone strikes," *Huffington Post*, June 28, 2012.

45 Gelling, Peter, "Obama's counterterrorism strategy: New York Times buries the lead," Global Post, May 29, 2012.

46 BNO News, "Three US drone strikes kill at least 12 in NW Pakistan," May 28, 2012.

47 Lewis, Lawrence, "Drone strikes: Civilian casualty considerations," CNA, June 18, 2013.

48 See Cloud, David S., "UN report faults prolific use of drone strikes by US," *Los Angeles Times*, June 3, 2010, in which it was suggested that fewer than fifty civilians had been killed in strikes since summer 2008. Dilanian, Ken, "CIA drones may be

avoiding Pakistani civilians," *Los Angeles Times*, February 22, 2011, in which it was reported that a few months later that only thirty civilians had been killed in strikes since June 2008.

49 Shane, Scott, "C.I.A. is disputed on civilian toll in drone strikes," *New York Times*, August 11, 2011.

50 Entous, Adam, "Special report: How the White House learned to love the drone," Reuters, May 18, 2010.

51 Becker, Jo, and Scott Shane, "Secret 'kill list' proves a test of Obama's principles and will," *New York Times*, May 29, 2012.

52 Rosen, James, "Obama aides defend claim of low civilian casualties after drone 'kill list' report," Fox *News*, May 30, 2012.

53 Ackerman, Spencer, "Air force chief: It'll be 'years' before we catch up on drone data," *Wired*, April 5, 2012. Aid, Matthew M., *Intel wars: The secret history of the fight against terror* (New York, NY: Bloomsbury Press, 2012), p. 55.

54 Columbia Human Rights Clinic, interview with Marc Garlasco.

55 Wheeler, Winslow, "Finding the right targets," *Time*, February 29, 2012. Rogers, Keith, "Predator strike that killed sailor angers father," *Las Vegas Review-Journal*, April 1, 2012, which describes the Central Command Investigation report that the newspaper received through a *Freedom of Information Act* request.

56 Martin, Matt J., with Charles W. Sasser, *Predator: The remote-control air war over Iraq and Afghanistan: A pilot's story* (Minneapolis, MN: Zenith Press, 2010), pp. 211–212.

57 Ibid.

58 Fitsanakis, Joseph, and Ian Allen, "Cell wars: The changing landscape of communications intelligence," *Research Institute for European and American Studies*, Research Paper No. 131, May 2009. Scarborough, Rowan, "Taliban taunts US eavesdroppers," *Human Events*, February 11, 2009.

59 Ferran, Lee, "Al Qaeda's tips for avoiding drones: Russian tech, decoys, trees," ABC *News*, February 21, 2013.

60 Ibid.

61 Rodriguez, Alex, "Pakistani death squads go after informants to US drone program," *Los Angeles Times*, December 28, 2011. Mayer, Jane, "The Predator war: What are the risks of the C.I.A.'s covert drone program?" *New Yorker*, October 26, 2009. Nawaz, Shuja, "Drone attacks inside Pakistan: wayang or willing suspension of disbelief?" *Georgetown Journal of International Affairs* 12 (Summer/Fall 2011): 79–87. Rogers, "Civilians in armed conflict," p. 22.

62 Rogers, "Civilians in armed conflict," p. 61.

63 International Crisis Group, "Drones: Myths and reality in Pakistan," May 21, 2013.

64 Ferran, "Al Qaeda's tips for avoiding drones."

65 Entous, Adam, and Julian E. Barnes, "US doubts intelligence that led to Yemen strike," *Wall Street Journal*, December 29, 2011.

66 Brennan, "The ethics and efficacy of the president's counterterrorism strategy."

67 Ibid.

68 Alexander, David, "Retired general cautions against overuse of 'hated' drones," Reuters, January 7, 2013.

69 Sewall, Sarah, and Larry Lewis, "Joint civilian casualty study," CNA, August 2010.

70 Scahill, Jeremy, *Dirty wars: The world is a battlefield* (New York, NY: Nation Books, 2013). In an interview on MSNBC's *NOW With Alex Wagner*, on June 4, 2013, Scahill noted: "The [JSOC] are used to operating in the shadows with very little or minimal effective congressional oversight and they also have a streamlined pipe right to the commander-in-chief."

71 Entous, Adam, "Special report: How the White House learned to love the drone," quoting an unnamed administration official. Priest, Dana, and William M. Arkin, *Top secret America: The rise of the new American security state* (New York, NY: Little, Brown, and Company, 2011), p. 211: "[Drone strikes became] popular [because] there was really nowhere to put captives if the CIA didn't want to hand them over to the military and if the military didn't want to keep them in the politically unpopular prison on Guantanamo in Cuba."

72 Sorcher, Sarah, "Obama is changing the way he fights the war on terrorism," *National Journal*, October 7, 2013. Wolverton II, Joe, "Do the Libyan and Somali raids signal a drone drawdown?" *New American*, October 8, 2013.

73 "Amends" is the emerging practice of warring parties providing recognition and assistance to civilians they harm within the lawful parameters of their combat operations. At its core, the practice of making amends to civilians suffering combat losses is a gesture of respect to victims. Amends can take a variety of forms but must be culturally appropriate. They can include public apologies, monetary payments, livelihood assistance programs, and other offerings in accordance with victims" needs and preferences. See Center for Civilians in Conflict, "Amends and Post-Harm Assistance."

74 "Questions for the record: Mr. John Brennan," *Open Hearing: Nomination of John O. Brennan to be the director of the Central Intelligence Agency*, United States Senate Select Committee on Intelligence, 113th Cong., February 7, 2013, p. 1.

75 Center for Civilians in Conflict, "Caring for their own: A stronger Afghan response to civilian harm" (2013).

76 Rogers, "Civilians in armed conflict."

77 This conclusion is based on many years of work by the Center for Civilians in Conflict, formerly the Campaign for Innocent Victims in Conflict, a Washington, DC-based non-profit organization founded in 2003 by Marla Ruzicka. It has worked for many years in Iraq, Afghanistan, and elsewhere conducting hundreds of extensive discussions with war victims.

78 Sewall and Lewis, "Joint civilian casualty study."

79 Holewinski, Sarah, "Do less harm: Protecting and compensating civilians in war," *Foreign Affairs*, January/February 2013.

80 Dilanian, "CIA drones may be avoiding Pakistani civilians": "The CIA passed up a chance last year to kill Sirajuddin Haqqani, the head of an anti-American insurgent

network in Pakistan that is closely linked to al-Qaeda and the Afghan Taliban, when it chose not to fire a missile at him from a Predator drone because women and children were nearby, US and Pakistani officials say. The incident was one of at least three occasions in the last six months when a militant was identified on video and a shot was available, but US officials decided not to fire in order to avoid civilian casualties, said a senior Pakistani official familiar with the drone program."

4

The Boundaries of War?

Assessing the Impact of Drone Strikes in Yemen

CHRISTOPHER SWIFT

1. MAKING SENSE OF DRONE DEPLOYMENT IN YEMEN

Abd Rabbuh Mansur Hadi is an unlikely advocate for American power. Born during the heady days of Arab nationalism, Yemen's president came of age in an era and region shaped by anti-colonial sentiment. His political party advocates Arab unity in the face of Western imperialism. His tribal and religious allies threaten *jihad* against foreign intervention. His predecessor even went so far as to support Saddam Hussein in the 1991 Persian Gulf War, casting it as a war against the Arab Nation. Confronted with a restive population and complex political transition, Hadi had every incentive to conceal or condemn US counterterrorism operations on Yemeni soil.

Yet advocate he did. Appearing before the UN General Assembly on September 28, 2012, Hadi urged the international community to bolster his fragile government's campaign against al-Qaeda in the Arabian Peninsula (AQAP) and Ansar al-Shari'ah, its local auxiliary: "We invite our international partners in combating terrorism to provide more logistical and technical support to [Yemen's] security forces and counter-terrorism units."[1] Two days later, Hadi endorsed covert US operations in Yemen during remarks at the Woodrow Wilson Center in Washington, DC. Speaking through a translator he publicly acknowledged that the United States was using unmanned aerial vehicles (UAVs), or drones, to augment the Yemeni Air Force's strikes on terrorist targets.[2]

UAVs are now a permanent feature in Yemen's counterinsurgency campaign. With al-Qaeda's center of gravity shifting from Pakistan to the Arabian Peninsula, the CIA sought authority to conduct so-called "signature strikes" on suspected militants throughout this arid, sparsely populated country.[3] The frequency and intensity of drone strikes in Yemen swiftly eclipsed similar operations in Pakistan, with the CIA and Joint Special Operations

Command (JSOC), each conducting their own independent campaign.[4] By the end of 2012, the United States had conducted an estimated fifty-six air and drone strikes across Yemen – a figure nearly three times greater than the total from the three preceding years.[5]

These developments led to contentious debates within Yemen, pitting President Hadi and his security apparatus against an unlikely coalition of conservative Islamic clerics and liberal youth activists. For the former, drones offer a tactical edge in a protracted counterinsurgency campaign. For the latter, drones signify government collusion with Western powers – collaboration that supports a corrupt regime, threatens Yemen's sovereignty, and undermines the population's right to national self-determination.[6]

Similar controversies shape US policy discourse. Where counterterrorism officials view drones as an essential tool in defending against an irreconcilable adversary that plans attacks from regions difficult to access, many legal scholars perceive this strategy as a threat to the sovereignty of foreign nations and a violation of principles of non-aggression and core human rights norms.[7] While military commanders emphasize the efficacy and necessity of targeted strikes, civil libertarians cast them as part of an inexorable march toward unconstitutional wars, unaccountable leaders, and unchecked executive power.[8] In this sense, drones have become a proxy for US debates over the War on Terror in much the same way that they reflect the frustrations manifest in the Arab Spring.

Although these differences reveal deep conceptual and ideological divisions in the debate over drones, neither approach offers pragmatic solutions. By recycling familiar narratives, these normative struggles obscure the scope and character of Yemen's internal crisis. In reducing liberty and security to immutable absolutes, they animate activists with no common language and even less common ground. Divorced from developments in the field, they offer little insight into the ways in which the conflict in Yemen transcends the legal and policy boundaries commonly used to understand war.

Making sense of these issues involves three elements. First, it is essential to view the conflict using the logic of attritional warfare, which provides the rationale for US policy of conducting remote aerial strikes. Second, it is important to understand the structure and strategy of AQAP's campaign in Yemen, especially its efforts to co-opt indigenous tribal structures. Third, there is a need for a more contextually sensitive review of the links between US drone operations and AQAP's burgeoning ranks, distinguishing discrete patterns of local recruitment from a general sense of popular resentment. Working from these foundations there are clear political and operational limits of drone warfare in counterinsurgency operations in Yemen, and perhaps elsewhere.

This analysis draws on extensive published and unpublished source reviews, as well as forty structured interviews conducted in Sana'a and Aden between May and June 2012. This cohort included tribal leaders, Islamist politicians, Salafi clerics, and other indigenous sources from fourteen of Yemen's twenty-one provinces. As a group, these men were older, more religious, and far more skeptical of Western influence than the Arab Spring activists that inspire international acclaim. Yet they also offered unique insight into Yemen's internal struggles. Many faced insurgent infiltration in their own districts and most viewed drone strikes with a degree of nuance and pragmatism absent in broader public debate. In this way, an analysis of these discussions illustrates the need for a more focused, context-sensitive engagement with the social and political dynamics driving armed conflict on the ground.

2. THE LOGIC OF ATTRITIONAL WARFARE

The May 21, 2012, suicide bombing in Yemen's capitol bore all the hallmarks of an al-Qaeda operation. Clad in a Yemeni Army uniform, the perpetrator infiltrated the long columns of marching soldiers from a nearby park, briefly falling into step before detonating his weapon. The blast tore through the ranks like fire through a stand of birch trees, killing nearly 100 soldiers and injuring 300 more.[9] As men lay dead and dying in Sabeen Square, a second assailant rushed through the carnage to attack the reviewing stand with a rocket-propelled grenade. According to a senior army spokesperson, Yemeni Defense Minister Mohamed Nasser Ahmed was the intended victim.[10]

The perpetrators swiftly confirmed that claim. "The primary target of this blessed operation was the Defense Minister of the Sana'a regime and his corrupt entourage," explained an Ansar al-Shari'ah communiqué.[11] Casting the attack as a "response to the unjust war launched by the Sana'a regime's forces in cooperation with the American and Saudi forces," the al-Qaeda front organization justified the indiscriminate slaughter of ordinary soldiers as vengeance for "the demonstrators and all Muslims who tasted the scourge of the Yemeni central security forces" during the Arab Spring protests.[12]

This unlikely combination of indiscriminate slaughter and targeted assassination offers insight into Yemen's simmering insurgency. Cognizant of their relative weakness, AQAP and Ansar al-Shari'ah target key commanders in an effort to disrupt Yemeni counterinsurgency operations. By attacking junior officers and military cadets parading in Sabeen Square, the assailants sought to degrade the Yemeni government's ability to field an effective fighting force.[13] The July 18, 2012, assassination of Major General Salim Ali Qatn in Aden followed a similar logic. Coming just days after the seizure of terrorist strongholds in Abyan Province, the operation demonstrated AQAP's capacity to target and successfully attack the army's leadership structure in the midst of a major counteroffensive against their own positions.[14]

A similar attritional logic also informs US counterterrorism operations in Yemen, albeit in very different ways. By locating and eliminating terrorist leaders, targeted killings aim to disrupt AQAP's operations, degrade its strength, and destroy its command structure. The goal is to achieve a rate of systemic organizational collapse that exceeds the terrorist network's capacity to recover and adapt. In this sense, drone strikes are no different from any other kinetic operation. While the specific tactics and instruments may vary, the ultimate purpose is to compel the adversary to change its behavior by inflicting pain and eroding its capacity to resist.[15]

However, there are important distinctions between conventional attacks and drone strikes. Designed with light airframes and low profiles, drones can remain on station and conduct covert surveillance for extended periods. Telescopic cameras and satellite uplinks allow decision makers to track and engage discrete targets in real time. These technologies increase tactical reach and enhance battlefield reconnaissance while substantially reducing the risks to military personnel. The result is a distinct competitive advantage for those countries with drones, particularly when fighting irregular units that disperse their forces in rough or otherwise inaccessible terrain.

Drones also reduce the transaction costs associated with foreign military interventions. Launched from regional installations and piloted by satellite, drones provide a real-time presence without the need to establish forward-operating bases, secure supply routes, or win local hearts and minds. They can operate covertly, overtly, or as auxiliaries to other units. Most significantly, they enable targeted attacks on discrete individuals. In this manner, drones transcend some of the legal and political boundaries that distinguish societies at peace from those engaged in war.

These boundaries can be difficult to discern in Yemen. Beset with weak institutions, endemic corruption, and persistent political turmoil, the government has been unable to extend its writ to the sparsely populated rural areas where 73 percent of the population lives.[16] Social and political dynamics also diminish the government's reach. With 34 percent of the population unemployed[17] and 45 percent living below the United Nations' poverty line,[18] Yemen is one of the poorest countries in the Arab world. It also has among the youngest populations, with three-quarters below age thirty and 46 percent below age fifteen.[19] The result is a country that is difficult to govern, hard to secure, and where a volatile mixture of institutional collapse and structural poverty fosters conditions where insurgents thrive.

Al-Qaeda's efforts to integrate itself with indigenous Yemeni society permeate these conventional boundaries. Unlike al-Qaeda cells in Afghanistan, Pakistan, and other areas in the periphery of the Arab world, AQAP operates at its core. Its Yemeni leaders speak the local dialect, understand local culture, and shelter within local communities. Rooted in tribal society, these targets are difficult to reach and destroy without undertaking costly operations that would likely incur significant local casualties and mobilize ongoing indigenous resistance.

These conditions inform the growing preference for drones. Chastened by similar circumstances in Iraq and Afghanistan, US policymakers have become increasingly reluctant to engage in protracted counterinsurgency campaigns across the greater Middle East. Rather than commit blood and treasure in weak states and hostile societies, the drone campaign allows the United States to support the Yemeni government's local counterinsurgency operations while simultaneously reducing its own risk exposure. Working from this basis, the increasing reliance on drones helps US policymakers seriously engage an adversary in Yemen while maintaining a lighter, less invasive operational footprint. While on their own drones cannot defeat AQAP, they provide an effective tool for confronting a dangerous, adaptive, and increasingly resilient adversary.

3. INDIGENOUS DYNAMICS AND AL-QAEDA IN YEMEN

AQAP is a conglomerate. Forged in a January 2009 merger between al-Qaeda cells operating in Saudi Arabia and Yemen, the movement incorporates militants with different experiences, perspectives, and priorities. Its leader, Nasir al-Wuhayshi, served with Osama bin Laden in Afghanistan.[20] Two of its Saudi commanders, Said Ali Al-Shiri and Mohamed Atiq Awayd al-Harbi, were former Guantanamo Bay detainees.[21] Other founding members fought in Algeria, Bosnia, and Chechnya.[22] Proven in war and hardened by prison, these globalized, delocalized *jihadis* sought a new sanctuary in Yemen's turbulent tribal society.[23]

Adapting to Yemeni society demanded a significant shift in al-Qaeda's modus operandi. Unlike its counterpart in Iraq, AQAP rejected a strategy based on tribal coercion and domination and instead developed a more nuanced approach aimed at building – and ultimately sustaining – indigenous support.[24] It courted local leaders with longstanding grievances and encouraged conservative clerics like Abdul Majeed al-Zindani to challenge the

Yemeni regime.[25] It convinced prominent sheikhs like Tariq al-Fadhli to turn
against the Yemeni government.[26] Most significantly, AQAP built its
movement from the ground up rather than the top down. Anxious to avoid
an indigenous uprising similar to the Sunni Awakening in Iraq, al-Wuhayshi
approached Yemen's tribes as allies with the goal of building a more
authentic, self-sustaining base of support.

Much of this engagement now occurs through Ansar al-Shari'ah. Operating
under its own banner, this front organization issues communiqués, operates
media outlets, and generates propaganda aimed at Yemen's Sunni
tribesmen.[27] In doing so, Ansar al-Shari'ah has rejected some of the elitist,
globalized rhetoric espoused by *salafi-jihadi* ideologues in favor of a more
parochial, locally resonant message.[28] In doing so, this front organization
gave its al-Qaeda parent a measure of authenticity that it otherwise lacked.
As senior AQAP official Abu Zubayr Adel Al-Abab observed: "[T]he
name Ansar al-Shari'ah is what we use to introduce ourselves in areas
where we work, to tell people about our work and goals, and [to show] that
we are on the path of Allah."[29]

However, this strategy masks factional divisions within AQAP. Dominated
by Saudi nationals, the movement's foreign fighters tend to view jihad as an
ethical rather than political struggle. Preoccupied by lofty rhetoric and high
drama, they tend to embrace Osama bin Laden's emphasis on provocative
operations against Western targets. These sentiments are particularly strong
among the movement's Somali contingent. Despite the notional alliance
between AQAP and al-Shabaab,[30] al-Qaeda's affiliate in Somalia, many of
these foreign fighters rejected the clan-based struggles that inform jihadi
movements in their homeland.[31] They view themselves as part of a global
vanguard rather than as reinforcements from a sympathetic ally.[32]

AQAP's Yemeni faction, by comparison, is composed of political pragma-
tists. Though no less virulent in ideology, leaders like al-Wuhayshi seek
concrete, incremental gains that expand their influence, undermine their
adversaries, and consolidate their power. The result is a different, and
sometimes conflicting, outlook. Where ideological purists revere bin Laden
and emphasize global operations, al-Wuhayshi and his Yemeni lieutenants
model their campaign on the Taliban and seek deeper indigenous traction.[33]
Latent nationalism may also inform their outlook. Although some members of
AQAP's Yemeni leadership were born or educated in Saudi Arabia, and thus
removed from the rigors, demands, and allegiances of tribal life, these
militants still share the belief that Yemen is a prize to be won in its own right.[34]

Ansar al-Shari'ah bolsters this Yemeni faction. Some, like Tariq al-Fadhli,
are veterans of the Soviet–Afghan War with lingering personal and political

grievances.[35] Others are holdovers from the 1994 Yemeni Civil War and, to a lesser extent, the now-defunct Aden Abyan Islamic Army.[36] Ansar al-Shari'ah's numbers also include younger Yemenis, including graduates of al-Zindani's Imam University outside Sana'a.[37] Energized by public protects and radicalized by government crackdowns, a new generation of *salafi* activists has reportedly left the university during the midst of the Arab Spring and joined the insurgency's ranks.[38]

Each of these trends reflects the localization of global *jihad*. Although AQAP remains loyal to al-Qaeda's senior leadership, and is now ensconced within that leadership, this franchise frames its objectives, organization, and operations in a fashion consistent with indigenous insurgencies. And despite occasional attacks on US and Saudi targets, its current objective is establishing an Islamic emirate within Yemen itself.[39]

Creating that emirate entails a three-pronged strategy. First, AQAP actively exploits the prospect of inter-tribal conflict. Emulating a tactic used by the Taliban, it recruits members from one tribe and deploys them within the territory of another, thus guaranteeing that any action against its own forces will be met with retaliation from the victims' own tribesmen.[40] That prospect makes weaker tribes less likely to challenge AQAP's presence in their traditional sphere of influence.[41] Fearful of provoking their stronger neighbors, some are shifting the burden of securing remote regions to Yemen's fractious transitional government.[42] Others simply accept AQAP's encroachment and adopt a strategy of passive accommodation. Working from this basis, AQAP and Ansar al-Shari'ah have extended their reach into twelve of Yemen's twenty-one provinces, including the capital.[43]

Second, AQAP uses this accommodation to secure sanctuaries, build training camps, and establish limited territorial control.[44] In some regions it actively governs, using armed militias and shari'ah courts to prosecute criminals, protect private property, and establish a brutal yet predictable sense of order.[45] In others it adopts a territorial exclusion strategy, briefly capturing and looting cities to signal their presence and then to replenish supplies.[46] Together, these tactics reveal an incremental approach that has more in common with the Taliban insurgency in Afghanistan than it does with al-Qaeda's global terrorist strikes.[47] Working village by village and district by district, they seek a self-sustaining insurrection.

The third prong involves indoctrination and popular mobilization. Anxious to capitalize on Yemen's internal turmoil, AQAP reframes and redirects indigenous grievances in a fashion that resonates with its own interests and ideology. In 2009, al-Wuhayshi publicly endorsed the South's secession and the establishment of an independent state – a proposal at odds with al-Qaeda's dream of uniting all Muslims under a reinvigorated Caliphate.[48] In 2010, he temporarily abandoned al-Qaeda's wholesale condemnation of Arab Socialism in a short-lived attempt to co-opt secessionist forces in Yemen's southern provinces.[49] AQAP has even appealed to the Shi'a rebels in northern Yemen, emphasizing the historical and political commonalities between Sunni and Zaidi Islam in an equally transparent attempt to destabilize the Yemeni government.[50]

These appeals were a ploy, to be sure. Aggregating these disparate opposition groups into a coherent opposition movement is highly problematic. Spanning Sunni and Shi'a, secular and religion, north and south, they do not have a shared view of the political future. Despite a lack of credibility, al-Wuhayshi's propositions reflect a broader effort to identify and exploit grievances across Yemeni society. In doing so, they underscore the corrosive effects public resentment can have on the legitimacy – and viability – of an unpopular regime.

4. POPULAR RESENTMENT AND AQAP RECRUITMENT

Many critics of US counterterrorism operations argue that the military benefits obtained through drone remote strikes are offset by the local resentment they engender. As Gregory Johnsen has observed, the accidental death of some forty civilians in Majala during a December 2009 cruise missile attack enraged tribal leaders and gave AQAP an unexpected propaganda coup.[51] Other Yemenis point to the targeted killings of US-born cleric Anwar al-Awlaki and his seventeen-year-old son as evidence of ruthless American imperialism.[52] Drones even feature in AQAP propaganda films, which offer accounts from militants that survived these covert attacks.[53] By lionizing their own fighters and condemning civilian casualties, these narratives stoke public anger with the goal of building popular support and delegitimizing the regime.

Like all effective information operations, AQAP propaganda has a basis in truth. According to research compiled by New America as of the end of December 2013, drone strikes killed some 77 to 83 civilians in Yemen since US operations began.[54] A similar count by the *Long War Journal* found 99 Yemenis killed, or approximately 20 percent of the total casualties since 2002.[55] The United Kingdom's Bureau of Investigative Journalism places the tally higher, with an estimated 122 civilians out of 724 drone victims.[56]

Some of these figures may underreport actual civilian casualties, in part because of the challenges of collecting credible reports from an active conflict zone. Official US tallies are also problematic given the covert nature of drone operations.[57] Other sources overestimate the numbers of those killed. As drone strike have become more common, they have come to be associated with covert air strikes conducted by the Saudi Air Force,[58] and even bombing campaigns by Yemen's own armed forces. In addition, there is evidence that some Yemeni officials purposefully conceal civilian deaths from US drone strikes in order to avoid a public backlash.[59]

Faced with that concealment and frustrated by unresponsive institutions, a growing number of Yemeni activists and opposition figures view the ongoing drone campaign as prima facie evidence of their own government's collusion in a Western imperialist conspiracy.[60]

Working from this basis, the late Ibrahim Mothana alleged that the US "drone program is leading to the Talibanization of vast tribal areas and the radicalization of people who would otherwise be America's allies."[61] Some journalists paint a darker picture, with the *Washington Post* reporting that the United States' escalating drone campaign "is stirring increasing sympathy for al Qaeda-linked militants and driving tribesmen to join a network linked to terrorist plots against the United States."[62] The fact that AQAP ranks swelled to nearly 1,000 fighters between 2009 and 2012 strengthens claims about the connection between drone strikes and indigenous radicalization.[63]

However, a reflection on local reality provides a much more complex picture. Despite Yemenis' growing antipathy toward drones, AQAP typically recruits through economic inducement rather than popular resentment. According to tribal leaders from al-Jowf, Lakij, and Marib, Ansar al-Shari'ah attracts members with the promise of a new rifle, a new car, and monthly salaries between two hundred and four hundred dollars.[64] For unemployed teenagers with little education and low social status, joining the insurgency offers the material and symbolic trappings of manhood.[65] For underemployed adults, membership provides a means of lifting their families out of permanent structural poverty. The result is a set of powerful local and highly personal incentives. As one Islamist parliamentarian from Hadramout observed, "The driving issue is development ... some rural districts are so poor that joining al-Qaeda represents the best of several bad options."[66]

These incentives can carry even greater value in isolated, resource-scarce communities. With nearly half of Yemen's population subsisting on less than two dollars per day,[67] an Ansar al-Shari'ah salary offers a level of security and sustenance that few tribal leaders can provide.[68] Weak and marginalized sheikhs also benefit, with AQAP providing the money and manpower necessary to revive a local leader's prestige and enforce his writ. This trend reveals the depth of local desperation and breath of insurgent infiltration. In communities plagued by chronic drought or hunger, tribal elders have reportedly recruited fighters for Ansar al-Shari'ah in exchange for new wells, new irrigation systems, and even food.[69]

These economic inducements build tribal networks based on mutual dependency. By conditioning the provision of salaries, public services, and other benefits on loyalty, the syndicate discourages its partners from pursuing alternative sources of patronage.[70] The same incentives operate on a tribal level. By identifying and empowering weak sheikhs in isolated communities, AQAP is able to operate *through* indigenous social structures without resorting to the overt coercion practiced by its counterparts in Iraq.[71] More significantly, it uses the possible loss of personal status, family resources, and social influence to cement new alliances and deter potential defectors.[72] As the leader of one tribal confederation observed, "Al-Qaeda attracts those who can't afford to turn away."[73]

In some instances, these networks of mutual dependency may even replace traditional forms of tribal patronage. Supported by generous stipends from Saudi Arabia and enriched by their commercial ties to the Gulf States, tribal confederation leaders and paramount sheikhs are increasingly abandoning their local base for greater proximity to the seat of power in Sana'a.[74] This migration fosters isolation and fragmentation in some districts, effectively removing sheikhs from their traditional role as local benefactors and mediators.[75] It also creates resentment, sidelining lesser sheikhs while forcing them to contend with levels of drought, poverty, and population growth that often exceed their own limited resources.[76] The result is a radical shift in local influence and, consequently, personal allegiances.

Drones play no discernable role in these dynamics. While resentment or revenge may strengthen existing relationships, none of the subjects interviewed for this study believed that targeted strikes were the proximate cause for AQAP's growing ranks. Nor were they a necessary condition. Even if drone strikes were to cease, noted one tribal militia commander, the economic and social conditions that facilitate terrorist recruiting in Yemen would still remain.[77] "Those who fight do so because of the [economic] injustice in this country," explained a Salafi cleric with ties to AQAP. "A few in the north are driven by ideology, but in the south it is mostly about poverty and corruption."[78]

None of these observations detract from the scope or significance of Yemeni anger. Nor do they alter the growing perception that every airstrike – including airstrikes conducted by the Saudi Air Force[79] – is launched by a US drone. Instead, they distinguish generalized resentment from the specific pathways that bring individuals, families, and villages into AQAP's domain. While civilian deaths may increase sympathy for al-Qaeda in a nominal sense, only two of the forty subjects interviewed for this study believed that the fury these tragedies engender is systemic, sustained, or sufficient to produce the kind of broad popular radicalization presumed by many outside observers. In short, the evidence of a direct causal linkage between drone strikes and terrorist recruiting appears anecdotal at best.

However, widespread public anger highlights another challenge. Though enraged by civilian casualties (and the perception of civilian casualties), Yemenis view drones as an affront to their national pride. As a member of the Yemeni Socialist Party observed: "Drones remind us that we don't have the ability to solve our problems by ourselves. If these were Yemeni drones, rather than American drones, there would be no issue at all."[80] Islamist politicians offered similar observations. "No one resents a drone strike if the target was a terrorist," explained a member of the Muslim Brotherhood. "What we resent is the fact that outsiders are involved."[81]

These perceptions have a direct impact on Yemen's political transition. To the extent that US drone strikes undermined public support for Hadi's transitional government, they complicated international efforts to convene a national dialogue, draft a new constitution, and hold legitimate parliamentary elections before 2014. A leader from the Zaydi community framed these challenges in stark terms. "The problem is not killing people like [Anwar] al-Awlaki," he explained. "The problem is when the US ambassador goes on television and takes credit for it."[82]

5. GROUNDING POLICY IN INTERNATIONAL LAW AND LOCAL CONTEXT

Such statements reveal a schism between means and ends. Viewed in exclusively military terms, drone campaigns are a logical means of mitigating the risks of protracted attritional war. These risks, in turn, flow from AQAP's unique ability to balance the ideological dictates of global *jihad* with the practical realities of local insurgency. Nevertheless, military intervention still carries significant political consequences. Although there is no evidence that drone strikes drive Yemenis into al-Qaeda's ranks, they may still be undermining other policy objectives.

Chief among them is Yemen's fragile political transition. Although US counterterrorism operations in Yemen involve a much lighter footprint than the protracted counterinsurgency campaigns of Afghanistan and Iraq, local reaction to foreign military intervention still resonates in counterproductive ways. This is particularly true when covert action and civilian casualties are involved. By animating anti-imperial sentiments and aggravating long-standing conspiracy theories, US drone strikes may generate population resentment and jeopardize political reform, even as they mitigate a growing terrorist threat.

Part of this disconnect is inherent in war itself. Violence and the perception of violence shape social and political relationships in profound and often transformative ways.[83] Gaining and sustaining public support are always the most important objectives in armed conflict.[84] In this sense, the efficacy of any military campaign – including covert counterterrorism operations – must ultimately "be judged not in military but in political terms."[85]

The ability to conduct remote aerial strikes at comparative low cost and limited risk does not alter war's immutable nature. While targeted killings are more discriminating and proportional than other kinetic approaches, the use of force still invites unintended social and political consequences. In this sense, an overemphasis on drone *operations* in Yemen risks undermining the broader political and economic *strategies* necessary to disrupt AQAP recruiting and degrade the syndicate's base of support. Technological innovation does not trump policy; it merely provides new tools for policymakers to use.

Legal norms can play a central role in aligning short-term security imperatives with long-term policy objectives. By setting boundaries on the use of force, principles like distinction, proportionality, and military necessity can limit the indiscriminate use of force and temper war's tendency to escalate violence and discontent. Following these principles also curbs civilian casualties, thus mitigating the grievances, outrage, and insurgent propaganda that exacerbate Yemen's political turmoil. This is particularly true in the context of targeted killings. By developing objective targeting criteria and marrying them to better intelligence, decision makers will be in a stronger position to conduct the type of "surgical" operations that properly distinguish belligerents from civilian bystanders.

Clearer adherence to the principle of distinction resonates within Yemeni society. Despite Yemenis' general antipathy toward drones, those living in active conflict zones draw clear distinctions between less discriminating operations, such as the 2009 cruise missile strike at Majala, and targeted killings of senior AQAP figures. "Things were very bad in 2009," observed a tribal militia commander from Abyan Province, "but now the drones are seen as helping us ... we can accept them as long as there are no more civilian casualties."[86] Islamists affiliated with Yemen's separatist al-Harak movement expressed similar views. AQAP's growing strength had made local leaders "very practical about drones," he explained. "If the United States focuses on the [terrorist] leaders and civilians aren't killed, then drone strikes will hurt al-Qaeda more than they help them."[87]

A similar degree of pragmatism was also evident among former drone opponents. Separatists in Aden who publicly derided AQAP as a ruse created by Yemen's recently deposed president, Ali Abdullah Saleh, privately acknowledged the utility of the US drone campaign. For example, a former official from the now-defunct People's Democratic Republic of Yemen claimed, "Saleh created this crisis in order to steal from America and stay in power ... [but] now it is our crisis and we need every tool to solve it."[88] A Yemeni journalist who interviewed commanders in AQAP training camps expressed similar views: "I was opposed to the US drone campaign until I saw what al-Qaeda was doing in Jaar and Zinjibar," he explained. "Al-Qaeda hates the drones, they're absolutely terrified of the drones ... and that is why we need them."[89]

These observations resonate with longstanding principles of the laws of war. Although insurgencies tend to collapse the traditional boundaries of war, concepts like distinction, proportionality, and necessity should be used to regulate the use of drones and other emerging military technologies. They also provide a legal basis justifying drone strikes.

Domestic reactions to drone targeting in Yemen rest on the sense that the technology is used to target legitimate targets and, more precisely, the perception that the United States adheres to the principle of discrimination. As long as drones target members of actual insurgencies, a significant number of Yemenis will grudgingly accept their utility. And to the degree these operations minimize collateral damage, it will be the easier to diminish generalized resentment and assist local leaders in addressing the threats emerging in their own communities. Respecting the laws of war and clarifying drone use through clear rules of engagement is central to a more effective balance between short-term military operations and long-term strategic objective. Indeed, the more that ordinary Yemenis perceive the United States as a credible, responsible partner, the more officials from both countries will be able to effectively address the perceptions and presumptions that threaten the success of Yemen's political transition.

Policymakers must also pursue indirect strategies that undermine AQAP's traction in Yemen's tribal society. To that end, the United States should support Yemeni efforts to mediate tribal disputes through local religious leaders and NGOs. Such mediation would limit AQAP's ability to exploit local grievances while reducing the prospect of inter-tribal conflict. These confidence-building measures might also encourage sheiks to withdraw customary protections for tribesmen who join Ansar al-Shari'ah, thus enabling neighboring tribes to expel insurgents from their territory without fear of retaliation.

Developing indigenous sources of resistance is crucial for undermining AQAP. Rather than simply increasing the frequency and intensity of US drone strikes and Saudi airstrikes, policymakers should identify and support tribal militias fighting to restore their traditional sphere of influence. Such efforts would hedge against AQAP's attempts to infiltrate and undermine the Yemeni security services. More significantly, they would provide a means of repairing the fragmented relationships between local leaders and Yemen's central government. Properly conceived and executed, these measures would go a long way toward building the transitional government's popular legitimacy – the very legitimacy that AQAP systematically attacks. However, in the absence of such measures, US policymakers risk viewing the Yemeni public "only as agents or patients in [their] own strategic plan."[90]

Finally, US counterterrorism officials must give their Yemeni counterparts a meaningful stake in the country's complex and contested political transition. For diplomats, this means facilitating a productive dialogue between Hadi's transitional government and Islamist, secessionist, and tribal leaders. For development specialists, it means transitioning from aid-based assistance programs to economic partnerships designed to alleviate chronic structural poverty. And for covert operators, it means recognizing and adapting to the risks of waging war by remote control.

None of these measures require the prolonged deployments and enormous investments witnessed in Afghanistan or Iraq. Nor do they demand a fundamental reevaluation of the relationship between our values and interests. What they do require is a willingness to subordinate the practical instruments of war to effective, long-term policy objectives grounded in an understanding of the local context. To the extent that drones upset this balance in Yemen, their short-term military utility may engender long-term political instability.

NOTES

1 Reuters, "Yemeni president calls for more support to fight al-Qaeda," September 26, 2012.
2 Hadi, Abd Rabbo Mansur, "Yemen's transition: The way forward," speech given at the Woodrow Wilson International Center for Scholars (hereafter Woodrow Wilson Center), Washington, DC, September 28, 2012, p. 11.
3 Miller, Greg, "CIA seeks new authority to expand Yemen drone campaign," *Washington Post*, April 18, 2012.
4 Schachtman, Noah, and Spencer Ackerman, "Let's admit it: The U.S. is at war in Yemen, too," *Wired*, June 14, 2012.

5 New America, "Drone wars Yemen: Analysis." http://securitydata.newamerica.net/drones/yemen/analysis.

6 Personal interview, Yemeni human rights activist, Washington, DC, October 2, 2012.

7 Bowcott, Owen, "Drone strikes threaten 50 years of international law, says UN rapporteur," *Guardian*, June 21, 2012.

8 Vanden Heuvel, Katrina, "Obama's 'kill list' is unchecked presidential power," *Washington Post*, June 12, 2012.

9 Personal interview, Yemeni Army lieutenant, Sana'a, Yemen, May 29, 2012.

10 Personal interview, Yemeni Army colonel, Sana'a, Yemen, May 28, 2012.

11 Madad News Agency (Azzan), "Statement on the Sabeen Square bombing," May 21, 2012.

12 Ibid.

13 Personal interview, Yemeni Army lieutenant, Sana'a, Yemen, May 29, 2012.

14 Kasinof, Laura, "Yemeni commander killed in suicide bombing," *New York Times*, June 18, 2012.

15 Clausewitz, Karl von, *On War*, Michael Howard and Peter Paret (eds. and trans.) (Princeton University Press, 1976), p. 75.

16 *Sabanews* (Sana'a), "World Bank launches report on poverty in rural areas of Yemen," January 16, 2010.

17 Assamiee, Mahmoud, "Yemen asks for USD 44 billion from friends of Yemen," *Yemen Times* (Sana'a), April 6, 2010.

18 *Al Jazeera* (Doha), "Yemen: Country profile," March 3, 2010.

19 Madsen, Elizabeth Leahy, "The effects of a very young age structure in Yemen: Country case study," *Population Action International* (2010): 1–20, p. 2.

20 Raghavan, Sudarsan, "Al-Qaeda group in Yemen gaining prominence," *Washington Post*, December 28, 2009.

21 Al-Oraifij, Abdullah, and Khaled Al-Shalahi, "Al-Oufi, Al-Shihiri betrayed our trust: Families, friends," *Saudi Gazette*, January 28, 2009.

22 Wanger, Rob L., "Bitter school dropout who became a flamboyant killer," *Saudi Gazette* (Riyadh), June 20, 2004.

23 Johnsen, Gregory D., testimony before the Senate Foreign Relations Committee, January 20, 2010, p. 13.

24 Barfi, Barak, "AQAP's soft power strategy in Yemen," *Combating Terrorism Center Sentinel* 3 (November 2010): 1–5. Evans, Ryan, "From Iraq to Yemen: Al-Qai'da's shifting strategies," *Combating Terrorism Center Sentinel* 3 (October 2010): 11–15.

25 Personal interview, senior sheikh, Bakhil Tribal Confederation, Sana'a, Yemen, May 27, 2012.

26 Personal interview, senior provincial security official, Aden, Yemen, May 28, 2012.

27 Personal interviews: tribal mediator from Marib Province, Sana'a, Yemen, May 30, 2012; tribal leader from Al-Jawf Province, Sana'a, Yemen, June 1, 2012.

28 Personal interview, director of Yemeni NGO, Sana'a, Yemen, June 2, 2012.

29 International Center for the Study of Radicalization and Political Violence, "Online question and answer session with Abu Zubayr Adel Al-Abab, Shari'ah official for al-Qaeda in the Arabian Peninsula," April 18, 2012, trans. Amany Soliman.

30 Zarif, Maseh, "Terror partnership: AQAP and Shaba'ab," American Enterprise Institute, *Critical Threats*, July 2, 2011.

31 Personal interview, director of Yemeni think tank, Sana'a, Yemen, June 2, 2012.

32 Personal interview, independent Yemeni journalist, Aden, Yemen, May 29, 2012.

33 Personal interview, director of Yemeni think tank, Sana'a, Yemen, June 1, 2012.

34 Swift, Christopher, "From periphery to core: Foreign fighters and the evolution of Al-Qaeda in the Arabian Peninsula" in Michael Noonan (ed.), *The foreign fighter problem: Recent trends and case studies* (Philadelphia, PA: Foreign Policy Research Institute), pp. 55–68.

35 Personal interviews: Yemeni political analyst and opposition activist, Sana'a, Yemen, May 27, 2012; Yemeni researcher and Al-Islah Party activist, Sana'a, Yemen, May 31, 2012.

36 Personal interview, senior Yemeni Socialist Party official, Aden, Yemen, May 28, 2012.

37 Personal interview, independent Yemeni youth leader, Sana'a, Yemen, May 31, 2012.

38 Ibid.

39 Madayash, Arafat, and Sawsan Abu-Husain, "Al-Qaeda call for Islamic state in Southern Yemen," *Asarq al-Awsat* (London), May 14, 2009.

40 Personal interview, tribal leader from Dhamar Province, Sana'a, Yemen, May 30, 2012.

41 Ibid.

42 Personal interviews: senior provincial security official, Aden, Yemen, May 28, 2012; Popular Committee commander from Abyan Province, Sana'a, Yemen, May 31, 2012.

43 *Al Jazeera* (Doha), "Yemeni troops target al-Qaeda," January 5, 2010.

44 Personal interview, director of Yemeni think tank, Sana'a, Yemen, June 2, 2012.

45 Personal interview, Al-Islah Party official from Hadramout Province, Aden, Yemen, May 28, 2021.

46 Al-Haj, Ahmed, "Al-Qaeda in Yemen captures town south of capital," Associated Press, January 16, 2012.

47 For more on this imitation and idealization of the Taliban regime, see Abd Illah Haydar Sha'a (Yemeni journalist), interview with Narir Al-Wuhayshi, www.abdulela.maktoobblog.com.

48 Madayash and Abu-Husain, "Al-Qaeda calls for Islamic state in southern Yemen."

49 *Sasa al-Malahim* (Azzan), "The southern issue: Secession or unity. Is there another option?" May 13, 2010.

50 Al-Sanai'ani, Abu'l-Bara'a'. "The Houthis are Rafidis in the guise of the Zaydis," *Sasa al-Malahim* (Azzan), February 12, 2010.

51 Khan, Azmat, "Study suggests Yemen strikes are radicalizing population," PBS, *Frontline*, May 30, 2012.

52 Personal interview, tribal leader from Lakji Province, Sana'a, Yemen, June 1, 2012.

53 Abdul-Ahad, Gaith, "Al-Qaida's wretched utopia and the battle for hearts and minds," *Guardian*, April 30, 2012.

54 New America, "Drone wars Yemen: Analysis."

55 Roggio, Bill, and Bob Barry, "Charting the data for US air strikes in Yemen, 2002–2014," *Long War Journal*.

56 Ibid.

57 Columbia University Law School, Human Rights Clinic, "Counting drone strike deaths," October 2012, p. 9.

58 Craig, Iona, "Saudi jets join American's secret war in Yemen," *Times*, January 4, 2013.

59 Raghavan, Sudarsan, "When U.S. drones kill civilians, Yemen's government tries to conceal it," *Washington Post*, December 24, 2012.

60 Personal interview, Yemeni researcher and Al-Islah Party activist, Sana'a, Yemen, May 31, 2012.

61 Mothana, Ibrihim, "How drones help Al-Qaeda," *New York Times*, June 12, 2012.

62 Raghavan, Sudarsan, "In Yemen, U.S. airstrikes breed anger, and sympathy for al-Qaeda," *Washington Post*, May 29, 2012.

63 Khan, Azmat, "Understanding Yemen's al-Qaeda threat," PBS, *Frontline*, May 29, 2012.

64 Personal interviews: tribal leader from Al-Jawf Province, Sana'a, Yemen, May 30, 2012; tribal mediator from Marib Province, Sana'a, Yemen, May 30, 2012; tribal leader from Lakji Province, Sana'a, Yemen, June 1, 2012. Sources from Abyan, Hadramout, and Shabwah Provinces also gave similar accounts of Ansar al-Shari'ah's local recruiting techniques.

65 Personal interview, tribal leader from Dhamar Province, Sana'a, Yemen, May 30, 2012.

66 Personal interview, Al-Islah Party official from Hadramout Province, Aden, Yemen, May 28, 2012.

67 World Bank, *Yemen country brief*, April. 2012.

68 Personal interview, tribal leader from Abyan Province, Aden, May 28, 2012.

69 Personal interviews: tribal mediator from Marib Province, Sana'a, Yemen, May 30, 2012; Popular Committee commander from Abyan Province, Sana'a, Yemen, May 31, 2012.

70 Personal interview, tribal leader from Lakji Province, Sana'a, Yemen, June 1, 2012.

71 Personal interview, tribal leader from Al-Hudaydah Province, Sana'a, Yemen, May 31, 2012.

72 Personal interview, independent Yemeni researcher, Sana'a, Yemen, June 2, 2012.

73 Personal interview, Yemeni tribal confederation chief, Sana'a, Yemen, May 27, 2012.

74 Personal interview, director of Yemeni NGO, Sana'a, Yemen, June 2, 2012.

75 Ibid.

76 Personal interviews: tribal leader from al-Hudaydah Province, Sana'a, Yemen, May 27, 2012; tribal leader from Shabwa Province, Aden, Yemen, May 28, 2012.

77 Personal interview, Popular Committee commander from Abyan Province, Sana'a, Yemen, May 31, 2012.

78 Personal interview, Salafi cleric from Lahij Province, Sana'a, Yemen, June 2, 2012.

79 Craig, "Saudi jets join America's secret war in Yemen."

80 Personal interview, senior Yemeni Socialist Party official, Aden, Yemen, May 28, 2012.

81 Personal interview, Al-Islah Party official from Hadramawt Province, Aden, Yemen, May 28, 2012.

82 Personal interview, senior Al-Haqq Party official, Sana'a, Yemen, May 27, 2012.

83 Barkawi, Tarak, "On the pedagogy of 'small wars,'" *International Affairs* 80 (2004): 19–38.

84 Clausewitz, *On War*, p. 45.

85 Howard, Michael, *Clausewitz* (Oxford University Press, 1983), p. 37.

86 Personal interview, Popular Committee commander from Abyan Province, Sana'a, Yemen, May 31, 2012.

87 Personal interview, Islamist politician and Al-Harak activist, Aden, Yemen, May 28, 2012.

88 Personal interview, former senior official from the People's Democratic Republic of Yemen, Aden, Yemen, May 28, 2012.

89 Personal interview, independent Yemeni journalist, Aden, Yemen, May 29, 2012.

90 Howard, *Clausewitz*, p. 46.

5

What Do Pakistanis Really Think About Drones?

SABA IMTIAZ

1. PAKISTANI RESPONSES TO DRONE ATTACKS

In the nine years since US drone strikes began in Pakistan, the once-secretive program has been discussed and debated extensively. While there has been considerable reporting on the mechanics of the drone program – how strikes are conducted, their legality, and their impact on foreign policy – there is little understanding, especially in the United States, of how the public debate in Pakistan has shaped the perceptions of its citizens.

What do Pakistanis really think about drones? Opinion polls over the last number of years suggest massive opposition to US drone deployment in the country. A widely referenced poll by Al Jazeera/Gallup in 2009 put support for drone strikes at 6 percent.[1] Other polls, as well as data on drone strikes, are repeated by politicians and journalists and provide the main reference point for Pakistani opinions on drones.[2] In fact, virtually all current polling and writing on the subject shows overwhelming opposition to the use of drones in Pakistan by US forces.

Nevertheless, what Pakistanis actually think about drones may well be more complicated than is commonly reported. While at present the opinions of Pakistanis on drones are polarized, the discussion of drones has evolved over almost a decade and has become a complex lens through which multiple issues are understood. And while the question of US drone deployment has taken center stage within reflections of national and international politics, there are significant differences as to what motivates the debate, including humanitarian concerns, questions as to the legality of surveillance and attacks, and the larger question of Pakistan's sovereignty. What is perhaps most significant is how, over a number of years and in the face of a shifting debate and a general lack of accurate information, the use of drones in Pakistan has become the face of US foreign policy in the country and, as such, is profoundly influencing national politics.

Despite the enormous significance of drones in contemporary Pakistani politics, there is still limited understanding of what is actually occurring in the areas where drones are deployed. There is almost no independent reporting from the tribal areas, and most information, analysis, and commentary comes from urban areas. In fact, the polls that describe Pakistani opinions on drones largely report data from cities and regions far from where drones are deployed, failing to document the experiences of those living in the affected regions. The same is true of the thousands of opinion pieces, essays, and other reflections on drone surveillance and attacks in the country. Overall, despite extensive reporting, campaigns, and protests, very little has been heard from those directly affected by drone strikes.

To understand the Pakistani discourse on drones, it is essential to look at how the messaging and reporting on these attacks has evolved. Since Pakistanis first learned about drone strikes, these programs have been shrouded in secrecy, confusion, and contradictory statements. This inevitably set the tone for how the discourse on drones developed and how public perceptions have been formed. Whereas drone attacks are now widely criticized throughout the country, the current position has developed over years in relation to the positions of the Pakistani and US governments, shifts in national politics, and the influence of a number of key events.

2. EARLY DEBATE – THE "MYSTERIOUS" DEATH OF NEK MOHAMMAD, GOVERNMENT DENIALS, AND LOCAL MEDIA INVESTIGATIONS

The first US drone strike in Pakistan took place in 2004 in South Waziristan, killing militant Nek Mohammad.[3] Initially, the Pakistan Army claimed responsibility for the attack. At the time, the Pakistan Army's spokesperson claimed: "We have various means and a full array of weapons at our disposal. We have artillery that can fire with precision and we have helicopters with night vision capability, which can fire guided missiles. But I am not going to give out operational secrets on how he was killed." The spokesperson went on to say that it was "absolutely absurd" to suggest that Nek Mohammad had "been killed with US assistance." Despite these claims, Pakistani publications suggested that the US government might have been involved, repeating rumors that there was more to this attack than was publicly revealed.[4]

At that time, there was little understanding of drones, including limited knowledge of what kind of missiles could have been used in such an attack. This made rumors of American involvement difficult to address.

In December 2005, Pakistani officials, including President Pervez Musharraf, told the press that Abu Hamza Rabia, an al-Qaeda commander, was killed at his home. The Pakistani government claimed that he died while "working with explosives."[5]

However, Hayatullah Khan, a freelance journalist, had filed a story and photos of the December attack, including of Hellfire missile debris, suggesting that the United States had conducted the strike. The story appeared in the Urdu newspaper *Ausaf,* and the photos were distributed by the European *Pressphoto Agency.* Soon after, Khan was abducted. His death was confirmed six months later through a phone call to his family by a man who identified himself as a Pakistani intelligence officer.[6] Later, in 2007, his widow was killed.[7]

During this time, the government, led by Army Chief General Pervez Musharraf, continued to deny that the United States, a key ally, was deploying drones in Pakistan. After a drone strike in January 2007, then-military spokesperson Shaukat Sultan told the Reuters news agency that the report was incorrect. "We have already denied it. This is usual that such things are said on such occasions but these are wrong."[8] In April 2007, a senior military official told the Associated Press that those killed in an alleged strike had died in an explosion that occurred while they were trying to make bombs.[9] In addition, the US military also issued ongoing denials that it was responsible for attacks in Pakistan.[10]

For the first few years of the program, Pakistani media outlets commonly referred to these attacks as "suspected drone strikes" in which "suspected militants" were killed. This was partly because neither the United States nor Pakistan officially acknowledged that these strikes had taken place.[11]

The lack of clarity about drone attacks also indicated how little on-the-ground reporting was possible in the regions where drones were being deployed. In general, local journalists had to rely on occasional accounts of those from the affected areas who could be interviewed in other, safer parts of the country. "Initially, there was only anecdotal evidence," recalls Iftikhar Firdous, a Peshawar-based journalist: "If someone from the area came to the main bus station of the district headquarters (for example, Miramshah in North Waziristan), they would tell people there that something had happened in their area."[12]

As the drone strikes continued from 2004 to 2007, the discourse largely comprised a back-and-forth of denials, which set the tone for how the drone program was initially perceived in Pakistan. In this way public understanding of the drone program began to emerge: shadowy, subversive, not under the control of the Pakistani government, but with clear signs of complicity on the part of that nation's military.

3. DRONE DISCUSSIONS MATURE – PAKISTANI GOVERNMENT COLLUSION WITH US FORCES

Since 2001 Pakistan had helped the United States in its war against al-Qaeda. Its cooperation ranged from detaining and handing over hundreds of men suspected of militancy, to organizing raids, to capturing high-value targets such as alleged 9/11 plotter Khalid Shaikh Mohammad and al-Qaeda leader Abu Faraj al Libi.[13]

As more drone attacks occurred, it became increasingly clear to many Pakistanis that drone strikes were an extension of Musharraf's support of US policies. The refusal of the Pakistani government to openly acknowledge cooperation on the drone program seemed partly a function of their understanding that neither the political parties nor the public would support these actions. As former Pakistani ambassador to the United States, Sherry Rehman explained: "The US drone program in Pakistan has always been criticized in Pakistan, for multiple reasons, and by multiple players. Whatever agreements General Musharraf made with the Americans on flight boxes and bases, there was no parliamentary or public buy-in for that."[14]

In November 2007, both the Pakistan Army and the Pentagon denied responsibility for a drone strike near a seminary in North Waziristan. The Pentagon spokesperson stated that it was not conducted by a "US military asset," but did not comment on whether it could have been carried out by a non-military US agency, such as the CIA. In a story reported by Reuters, the Pakistan Army's spokesperson said, "I have heard there was an explosion in a house, but we didn't carry out any action." Reuters noted: "[T]he U.S. does not usually acknowledge making any strikes in order not to embarrass its ally. Pakistani security forces are bearing the brunt of a suicide bomb campaign because of President Pervez Musharraf's support for the war on terrorism."[15]

However, many years later the link between Musharraf and US attacks became public knowledge. For example, in April 2013 Musharraf admitted that his government approved drone strikes, although he qualified the claim by stating that this occurred "only on a few occasions, when a target was absolutely isolated and [there was] no chance of collateral damage."[16]

While the Pakistani government continued to deny the US role in drone strikes, growing numbers of casualties shifted the public debate. When government officials began publicly condemning the attacks as the drone strikes continued, it was increasingly clear that these were not being conducted by the Pakistani government.

In January 2006 a drone strike that killed eighteen people led to public complaints by the Pakistani government. An Inter-Services Intelligence agency official told the UK's *Telegraph* newspaper, "All those killed in the airstrike are innocent civilians. They [the United States] are now trying to cover this up by leaking faulty information to the media."[17]

This was followed by the October 2006 strike on a seminary in Bajaur Agency that killed more than eighty people. This attack represented a turning point in the drone discourse in Pakistan as it prompted protests in the tribal areas and condemnation by the country's parliament of the military, which claimed that it had carried out the attack against militants.[18] Nevertheless, there was still very limited information publicly available on the drone strikes and the military continued to avoid serious discussions of these attacks.[19]

The final two years of Musharraf's term in power was highly turbulent. In March 2007 he deposed the chief justice, sparking a popular movement for his restoration. Then in June the siege of the Red Mosque in Islamabad served to polarize opinions in Pakistan regarding both the military and fundamentalist groups. And in November Musharraf imposed a state of emergency.

Within this context, there was growing resentment against the central government. This was partly influenced by Musharraf's positioning of Pakistan as a significant non-NATO ally in the war against al-Qaeda. Over time, anger increased over the government's role in allowing US drones to operate in Pakistan, as well as its past support of the arrest and rendition of hundreds of suspects from Pakistani territory to American custody.

After the 2008 parliamentary elections in Pakistan, the Pakistan People's Party (PPP) – reeling from the assassination of its chairperson Benazir Bhutto – formed a government with the Nawaz Sharif – led Pakistan Muslim League and the Awami National Party.[20] The election was followed by the resignation of former Army General Musharraf as president in August that year. This marked a significant shift in Pakistani politics after nine years of military rule.[21] While exactly how the Musharraf government's relations with the United States impacted the election remains unclear, voters were clearly influenced by these issues.

The transition to a popularly elected government was an important initial step for Pakistan's return to democratic rule and a changing role for the military. Nevertheless, the military continued to take the lead on foreign policy issues and remained a powerful force in domestic politics.

The PPP-led government was keen to build strong relations with the United States and to form a partnership on fronts other than "cooperation in the war on terror." Nevertheless, the government was weak in several ways: it was distrusted by the military; the Pakistan Muslim League-Nawaz quit in August 2008; and the global economic recession led to a crisis for the cash-strapped country. Moreover, militancy was on the rise in the country, with insurgent movements in Balochistan; the rise of the Tehrik-e-Taliban Pakistan (TTP) and other militant groups in the tribal areas and the Khyber Pakhtunkhwa Province; and sectarian and religious violence in the urban areas, including in the cities of Lahore and Karachi.

The government – embroiled in a battle with militants in the Swat and Malakand districts of Khyber Pakhtunkhwa Province, as well as in the tribal areas, a financial crisis, and a host of governance issues – did not initially focus on the drone strikes.[22] Still, by this time the Pakistani military began objecting to the strikes, although its criticism remained fairly muted.[23]

That May, TTP leader Baitullah Mehsud was killed in a drone strike.[24] *Dawn* – a leading English-language Pakistani newspaper that ran a front-page story on the strike – headlined "Good riddance, killer Baitullah" – reported: "It is understood that the strike to take out Baitullah was the outcome of a joint Pakistan–U.S. intelligence operation that may, according to some officials, indicate a new level of trust between the often mutually suspicious intelligence agencies of the two countries."[25] While the drone strike that killed Mehsud may have appeased the Pakistani government, it also fueled the public's perception that their government was working with the CIA to carry out drone strikes.

The drone program escalated in 2008. Despite the lack of transparency on these attacks, information on the CIA drone program began to emerge. This included disclosures on how the program was conducted, as well revelations about the Pakistani government's involvement.[26] In fact, by 2008, it was evident that the 2004 missile strike that killed Nek Mohammed and initiated national concern regarding drones was conducted by the United States, as were several other attacks in prior years that the Pakistan Army had claimed were its own missions.[27]

By this time, the official Pakistani position was that drone strikes were a violation of the country's sovereignty, even as government officials tried to receive technological support to conduct its own drone program.[28] Yet at the same time, Pakistan was conducting air operations in the tribal areas: deadly missions that have generated far less attention than the American drone strikes.[29]

According to Madiha Tahir, a journalist and doctoral candidate at Columbia University in New York, the idea of "faux secrecy" allowed the

US government to control the narrative domestically.[30] That is, it presented the program's secret nature as central to its success and ultimately as a legitimate aspect of protecting national security. In Pakistan, however, the narrative on drones was built on arguments and counterarguments that reflected on core debates within national politics. In this way, the discussion of drones within Pakistan engaged deep-rooted internal political struggles. Joshua Foust explains:

> The initial deal between the CIA and ISI over drones – first clandestine, then an arrangement whereby CIA can strike in exchange for ISI's [Inter-Services Intelligence] publicly complaining about them – set a dangerous precedent ... Even now, where Pakistan is using the drones program to directly hurt American interests, they can say they're operating within the bounds of the program. It set a horrible tone.[31]

Ambassador Rehman describes the confusion:

> No democratically-elected government can afford to sanction drone strikes. What General Musharraf agreed to had no consent from parliament, so it generated more resentment as the strikes picked up momentum. The perception or contention that Pakistan continues to sanction drone strikes is a self-serving one for a U.S. foreign policy establishment that now has to answer to its own civil society on the use of this covert instrument.[32]

The inability of either side to officially acknowledge the drone strikes skewed the reporting of the subject. "The end result is like talking to a brick wall," says Foust, "where one side double-talks while the other refuses to."[33]

While in the United States criticism of the drone program has centered on the legality of conducting the strikes, the perception of the CIA's drone operations in Pakistan has largely revolved around the notion of sovereignty. The lack of transparency on the program, which has continued since its inception, has led these attacks to be viewed very differently in the United States and Pakistan. As Rehman explains: "So the program that is on the frontlines of how the U.S. projects its power remains largely covert in America, while in Pakistan, instead of the anti-terror instrument it is seen as in the U.S., it becomes the visual, tangible embodiment of an unremitting public challenge to the state and people of Pakistan."[34] Over time, the Pakistani government's approach to drone strikes metastasized into considerable political opposition, especially from the conservative politician Imran Khan and religious–political parties.

The idea of Pakistani sovereignty and protecting the country's borders has long been a unifying notion, even at the cost of sanctions and global censure. This has been true from its war-time messaging in 1971 to its testing of nuclear missiles in 1999. Claims of sovereignty have come to define Pakistani perceptions of drone strikes, and this issue is considered to be the strongest point in the case against drones. Political parties, religious groups, and journalists have used this theme to critique the US drone strikes.[35] Those opposed to this position argue that foreign militants are also violating Pakistan's sovereignty by using the country's tribal areas as a base.[36]

The democratically elected government that followed Musharraf's regime in 2008 took the position that drone strikes were a violation of the country's sovereignty. The government would routinely lodge official protests of the strikes with US officials.[37] In November 2008 then-US ambassador to Pakistan Anne Patterson was summoned to the Foreign Office after a drone strike in the Khyber Pakhtunkhwa Province, which was an atypical site for a Predator attack.[38] Pakistan Army Chief General Ashfaq Parvez Kayani also echoed his opposition, calling for an end to the use of "unmanned combat aerial vehicle within Pakistan territory" in a speech to NATO's military committee in November 2008.[39] This led to the impression that the United States was continuing to act unilaterally against Pakistan. According to a 2009 Pew survey, 58 percent of Pakistani respondents said they believed drone strikes were being carried out without their government's approval.[40]

4. DRONE CRISIS — FIVE KEY EVENTS

The debate on drone strikes, their legality, utility, and discussions of who sanctioned them, continued in Pakistan for several years. Then in 2010 and 2011, a succession of events occurred that shaped the debate and redefined the issue as a political crisis. During this time, Pakistanis not only faced the reality of unmanned drones in the country's airspace that killed individuals within the nation's borders, but they also confronted multiple examples of what was widely perceived to be American aggression. These high-profile events served to strengthen the widespread interpretation of the United States as part ally and part enemy. While some of these events were not directly linked to drone strikes, they further supported the perception that the US government's intentions in Pakistan were not above board. Moreover, they helped strengthen the opposition to drones and American unilateral action in Pakistan.

WikiLeaks – The first blow to the perception that drone strikes were opposed by the Pakistani government and military came with the 2010 WikiLeaks release of classified US diplomatic cables. The publication of leaked cables was extraordinary in that it revealed how the Pakistani government dealt with US officials. In particular, the documents showed how closely the United States was involved in Pakistani politics and revealed the specific types of demands and requests made by Pakistani officials and politicians to US officials.

While the documents revealed many salacious tidbits – such as what Saudi Arabia thought of President Asif Ali Zardari[41] – issues of national security formed a large part of the public discourse. The English and Urdu press reported extensively on the cables. Previously, it had been impossible to get a candid look at the Pakistani civilian government and military establishment's national security policies. With their release, consistent Pakistani government acquiescence to US demands for permission to begin the drone program were revealed,[42] as well as what appeared to be active requests for drone coverage in South Waziristan.[43]

Although the government and military denied the information outlined in the leaked cables, direct quotes from this material made headlines.[44] One of the most telling remarks that laid bare the Pakistani government's stance on drones was by then-Prime Minister Yousaf Raza Gilani. He was cited saying, "I don't care if they do it [drone strikes] as long as they get the right people. We'll protest in the National Assembly and then ignore it."[45] The statement was widely seen as a sign of the Pakistani government's duplicity regarding drone strikes. *Dawn* partnered with WikiLeaks for the release of all leaked cables on Pakistan in 2011 and put Kayani's request for drone support on its front page.

The remarks continued to dog the government throughout its five-year term, and military and political opponents used excerpts from the cables to highlight the government's support for US drone strikes.

Karim Khan – While there had been protests in Peshawar and Miramshah over drone strikes, none made as strong an impact as one man's lawsuit. In late 2010, Karim Khan – who identified himself as a journalist – threatened to sue the CIA's station chief in Islamabad after his brother and son were reportedly killed in a drone strike in North Waziristan.

This event alone might not have had as significant an impact had it not been marked by the disclosure of the CIA station chief's identity in local newspapers by a journalist known for his strong ties to the military establishment.[46] The agency pulled the station chief from the country, and US officials said at the time that they were investigating whether the ISI had leaked the name.[47] The Karim Khan case received widespread coverage and marked a turn in the discourse on drone strikes because it involved someone who had been directly impacted by drone strikes, as opposed to general criticism of the program from politicians, activists, and religious leaders.

Raymond Davis – One of the most significant events that shaped the Pakistani government's stance on drones occurred in 2011 when Raymond

Davis, a CIA contractor, was detained on charges of killing two people in Lahore.[48] Davis's act, along with the disclosure that he was working for the CIA and was not a consular staff member as the United States had claimed, drove US–Pakistan relations to a new low. There were protests around the country that called for Davis to be executed. Foreign Minister Shah Mehmood Qureshi publicly disagreed with the US government that Davis had diplomatic immunity. As a sign of the serious nature of the dispute, Senator John Kerry flew to Pakistan negotiate for Davis's freedom.[49]

Two months later, after the US government provided the victims' families with compensatory payments under Pakistan's Islamic laws, Davis was released. But the resolution of the crisis did not mark an immediate change in relations between the two countries.

The Raymond Davis episode highlighted how contentious the role of the United States had become in Pakistan. For many Pakistanis, the legal issues associated with the case – from the question of diplomatic immunity to the payment of "blood money" – revealed a selective implementation of international and domestic law when it came to the US government's actions in Pakistan.

North Waziristan drone strike – On March 17, 2011, a drone strike killed more than forty people believed to be tribesmen gathered for a *jirga* near Miranshah, North Waziristan. The high number of casualties caused by the strike brought up comparisons to the contentious 2006 strike in Bajaur that had played a role in shifting the Pakistani government's stance on drone strikes.[50]

The strike occurred a day after the release of Raymond Davis and solidified outrage at the United States and the role of the CIA in Pakistan. The decision to launch a strike so soon after a serious diplomatic crisis signaled to the press and the public that the United States was back to business-as-usual in Pakistan. There were even reports that the then-US ambassador to Pakistan, Cameron Munter, had disagreed with the timing of the strike.[51]

Journalist Rahimullah Yusufzai noted then that the strike had "exposed the myth," espoused by the Pakistani military, that drone strikes were largely targeting militants.[52] It was not just that a drone strike had taken place, but that a jirga meeting of civilians was the target.

The Pakistani tolerance for drone strikes was steadily decreasing. As the numbers of attacks grew and reports were released on drone strike casualties, it was becoming evident that civilians were being killed.[53] This was in stark contrast to the descriptions of the drone program in earlier years when it was suggested that only high-profile militants such as Baitullah Mehsud were being targeted. According to Yusufzai: "By killing 45 innocent tribesmen including children at a *jirga* convened in the open in keeping with tradition to discuss local issues, the U.S. not only overstepped the mandate apparently given to it by Pakistan's fearful ruling elite but also did something that exposed the myth that the drones are always on target."[54]

The March 17 strike even changed the way that the military reacted to the drone program. A statement by the military's publicity wing, attributed to Kayani, offered one of the strongest criticisms made by a military officer on drone strikes: "It is highly regrettable that a *jirga* of peaceful citizens including elders of the area was carelessly and callously targeted with complete disregard to human life. In complete violation of human rights, such acts of violence take us away from our objective of elimination of terrorism."[55]

The bin Laden raid and "friendly fire" – The May 2, 2011, US Navy SEAL team raid that killed al-Qaeda leader Osama bin Laden, and the NATO/ International Security Assistance Force (ISAF) airstrike on November 26, 2011, which killed twenty-four Pakistani soldiers at the military's Salala check posts in Mohmand Agency, effectively ended the days of confusing statements by Pakistan's government and army on drone strikes and US operations in the country.[56]

These two events strengthened support for the narrative about the importance of defending Pakistani sovereignty against repeated violations by the United States. Regarding criticisms of the attack on bin Laden, the Pakistani government and military failed to explain how he managed to live in the country undetected, focusing instead on the violation of national sovereignty by US forces in organizing a raid and killing individuals on Pakistani territory.

In a closed-door briefing by the military and the ISI to Pakistani legislators – details of which were leaked to reporters in Islamabad almost simultaneously – there was an intense barrage of questions aimed at the intelligence operatives. ISI chief Ahmad Shuja Pasha was quoted as having told the legislators: "We are at a point in our history where we have to decide whether to stand up to America now or have [following] generations come to deride us."[57]

The November 26 strike on the twenty-four Pakistani soldiers became another outlet for the government to express its anger at the United States for repeated violations of the country's sovereignty. The event was initially described as a "firefight," which enraged the Pakistani government, military, and the public.[58] While a US investigation found that the Pakistan Army had fired first at an Afghan–American patrol,[59] the Pakistan Army said that the attack was unprovoked and did not fall in the ambit of "self-defense." In addition, the Pakistanis claimed that the Salala incident was not the first of its kind and that its soldiers had been targeted by NATO/ISAF forces in the past.[60]

After the Salala attack, the government blocked NATO's supply routes through Pakistan and asked the United States to vacate the Shamsi airbase in Balochistan, which had been used to launch CIA drones.[61]

5. DRONES: SHAPING PERCEPTIONS OF THE UNITED STATES

The CIA-run drone program has significantly impacted Pakistani's perceptions of the United States at every level, from the general public to high-level diplomats and other government officials.

In March 2012, Pakistan's parliament set out to redefine its relationship with the United States, calling for a review of its presence in the country.[62] This reflected the mood of the Pakistani people; a Pew Global Attitudes survey in 2011 found that of the 56 percent of the respondents who had heard of drone strikes, 89 percent thought they were killing too many innocent people.[63]

Ambassador Rehman noted that drone strikes had become the "foreign policy face" of the United States in Pakistan, and were delegitimizing "much of the good the US government does in Pakistan."[64]

However, it is important to note that drones are not the sole cause of anti-US sentiment in the country and that many Pakistanis were opposed to the United States well before the drone program began. In fact, drones are not the core problem in US–Pakistan relations, but rather a symbol, for many, of what is wrong with American interventionism in general.

After the drone strike on March 17, 2011, and during the two years leading up to the 2013 parliamentary election in Pakistan, the issue of drone strikes took center stage in Pakistan. Imran Khan's Pakistan Tehreek-e-Insaf (PTI) party focused its messaging on key themes that gained traction in both urban and rural Pakistan, including corruption, the rule of law, and Pakistan's relationship with the United States, an issue intimately bound to drone strikes.[65]

The PTI had long been opposed to American intervention in Pakistan, and from 2011 on, the party's campaign against drone strikes and for banning NATO from shipping supplies through Pakistan gained critical mass. The PTI's appeal, however, was not only based on its critical stance toward the United States. Khan was a well-known figure whose career as a cricketer and a philanthropist had won him broad public support, although his party remained untested in government. Nevertheless, the PTI's ascendancy was boosted between 2011 and 2013 by the rising anger regarding drone attacks and other US policies.[66] The party's messages, combined with the existing opposition to these issues from right-wing religious–political parties and pressure groups had a direct impact on the discourse on drones.

The PTI organized a widely publicized march to South Waziristan in October 2012 to show its solidarity with the people of the region. The event was attended by representatives of Code Pink, a US-based advocacy group that had taken a strong anti-drone stance, and by Reprieve, a UK-based activist and human rights group.[67] Khan's increasing popularity ensured that he received exceptional amounts of media coverage – both in the local and foreign press – and a platform for his campaign against drones.[68] The drone march was termed an "unprecedented gesture" by a mainstream politician, even if it had the feel of an election campaign.[69]

The PTI went on to win a majority in Khyber Pakhtunkhwa Province in the 2013 election, wiping out the secularist Pashtun Awami National Party, which it had accused of being "pro-American."[70] Given that Khyber Pakhtunkhwa has an established trend of voting out incumbent parties, it would be inaccurate to suggest that the PTI won solely because of its stance on drones. However, the party's popularity and electoral success underscored the importance of its messaging in urban Pakistan and its attraction for those opposing US drone strikes, even if they disagreed with the party's other views.[71] The imagery of the PTI's events – the crowds of thousands, the press coverage, and the symbolism – has played a significant role in building the perception that people opposed any unilateral action by the United States.

Bushra Gohar, the Awami National Party's senior vice president, pointed out that while the presence of foreign militants is of great concern, drones have become an "easy source of building anti-US sentiments by the largely right-wing pro-Taliban groups."[72] Foust echoes this idea by suggesting that politicians often use anti-US sentiments to avoid other serious issues: "I don't doubt that Imran Khan dislikes drone strikes, for example, but I also think he cynically uses drones to distract from the much more difficult job of confronting the terrorist groups in the FATA [Federally Administered Tribal Areas] while avoiding asking too many hard questions of his military sponsors."[73]

The victories of the PTI in Pakistan's parliamentary elections and the importance accorded to the drone program during the campaign show that the issue has become a core component of Pakistan's national security and domestic policy debate. It has also served to strengthen the image of the United States as an aggressor and not an ally; a perception that has prevailed for decades in Pakistan and has been exacerbated by the wars in Iraq and Afghanistan. For many Pakistanis, it is hard to accept the idea of the United States as an ally that provides aid and support at the same time as the CIA is raining down missiles on its territory – even if these attacks are killing militants. In this way, drone strikes are perceived as part of a war against Muslims being waged by the United States. This impression will likely continue while there is a US presence in Afghanistan and in the Middle East.

6. BEHIND THE DEBATE

While the military and the government have tried to influence the debate, the Pakistani media has played the core role in shaping views of the drone program. Nevertheless, the media has not been able to report on drones in a transparent manner based on direct verifiable reporting. Over the past nine years, journalists have rarely been able to report directly from the sites where the drone strikes occur. This makes gaining information from the strike sites a challenge, and confirmation of a drone strike is a complicated process involving shreds of reporting from locals, tribal leaders, the political administration of the area, and the military.

The Peshawar-based journalist Iftikha Firdous explained, "No (news) organization wants to spend money on tribal journalists, and these people are living in conflict zones. There are meager resources." He claimed: "These areas are informational black holes. This is *ilaqa ghair* [an out-of-bounds territory]. If someone gives me a quote today, how will I go back and find him tomorrow?"[74]

However, the inability to accurately report on what is actually occurring in the places where drones are deployed has not deterred the media from influencing the debate. Talk show hosts and English and Urdu newspaper columnists have discussed drone strikes – making the case for and against these attacks – for years. Foreign journalists relying on the arguments made in the English press – which one critic says is "largely pro-bombing"[75] – feed into the narrative of how Pakistanis perceive the drone strikes. Others say the security establishment has manufactured its own drone narrative to create acceptance of the Taliban.[76]

"There are two factions – one that is against drones, and one that is not," Firdous said. "There is the Pashtun civil society who issued a declaration that drone strikes are good, and there are political forces like the PTI."[77]

Interestingly, there is anecdotal evidence to suggest that the US drone program has some support in Pakistan, particularly in the tribal areas most affected by the conflict.[78] In February 2010 some members of Pashtun civil society issued the Peshawar Declaration, which stated, somewhat implausibly: "If the people of the war-affected areas are satisfied with any counter militancy strategy, it is the Drone attacks which they support the most. According to the people of Waziristan, 'Drones have never killed civilians.'"[79]

On the other hand, Ahmad Shuja Pasha, the former head of the ISI, admitted to a judicial commission that drone strikes had their utility, but said they were a violation of the country's sovereignty.[80]

In this way, the debate on drones in Pakistan is often characterized by polarization. Over the past couple of years, politicians, talk show hosts, and columnists have managed to stereotype those commenting on drones. As a result of these divisions, after nine years of drone strikes in Pakistan, there is no independent figure that can lead or influence the debate, or build a clear picture of what is happening in the tribal areas.

What is interesting to look at is where either side of the divide is gathering its information. For political parties, they often turn to their own members and representatives; others rely on a combination of local sources, rumor, and hearsay. Each group portrays the perspectives of those living in the tribal areas in ways that serve their particular agenda.

It is remarkable, in retrospect that the highly divisive discourse on drones has developed alongside a marked absence of direct information about the individuals and communities who have experienced the strikes directly. Pakistani journalist Madiha Tahir notes:

> Both in Pakistan and beyond, what is interesting is that the voices of the people most directly impacted by drones – survivors and families of the dead – are fairly tangential to the debate around drones. It is almost as if what they've got to say, for instance about the aftereffects is beside the point. It's not "useful" information in that, this information is not going to help a pundit or a lawyer, etc. decide whether those who died in this bombing or that bombing were a "civilian" or a "militant." But that is the stuff that is going to stick around long after the pundits are done categorizing people. It will live in the public memory of the communities that are under attack. It's a series of messy and tangled consequences that don't fit into the neat columns designating the number of drone attacks, the numbers of dead, the numbers of civilians or militants etc. Databases are instrumental, but [are] actually a fairly terrible way to apprehend life.[81]

Over the past nine years – since that first missile felled Nek Mohammad – the flip-flops of the Pakistani government and military have helped build the perception that the drone war is "America's war," and has nothing to do with Pakistan's own fight against militancy. The debate has now reached a point where drone strikes alone are widely believed to be one of the major causes of militancy in Pakistan.

This theory has been discussed incessantly in the media and among political leaders for the past five years, and reached fever pitch levels during the 2013 election campaign. If the Americans were the ones raining down missiles, how could these acts be seen as serving Pakistan's national security needs? Furthermore, were drone strikes counterproductive to Pakistan's own fight against militancy? Were militants only attacking Pakistani targets because of the government's support for the drone program?[82]

In a 2009 interview then-Prime Minister Yousaf Raza Gilani explained:

> Once there is American interference, as with the drones, the public starts thinking that it is a proxy war. At times, the public sentiment is quite anti-American. The political and the military leadership have been very successful in isolating the militants from the local tribes. But once there is a drone attack in their home region, they get united again. This is a dangerous trend, and it is my concern and the concern of the army.[83]

Ambassador Rehman said: "Rejecting U.S. drone strikes should not be seen as an endorsement for coddling terrorists or extremists. Today, a U.S.-led drone strike triggers an ultra-nationalist public response in Pakistan, which leeches away crucial space for building a consensus against terrorism at home."[84]

Religious–political parties such as the PTI, the Jamaat-ud-Dawa, and Jamiat Ulema-e-Islam (led by Fazlur Rehman) have latched onto the theme that drones are to blame for militancy in Pakistan, and that if drone strikes were to stop Pakistan could "own" the war on militancy instead of fighting "America's war."[85] In January 2013, the Jamaat-ud-Dawa's Chief Hafiz Saeed said that allowing the CIA to carry out drone strikes was part of a plot by the United States and India to target Pakistan's nuclear weapon arsenal.[86]

This claim is backed by the fact that the TTP has pointed to drone strikes as its motivation for carrying out militant acts, including as responses to drone strikes that have targeted its leadership.[87] The growing perception that drones are the "sole" cause for TTP's activities is a byproduct of the TTP's own statements, as well as the fact that these drone-related statements get more coverage, given that they have often been connected to attacks on highly prominent targets – including the murders of soldiers and civilians in a military camp in Lakki Marwat on February 2, 2013, and nine foreign mountaineers in Gilgit-Baltistan on June 23, 2013.[88]

However, this perception, which is getting increasing attention in Pakistan, ignores two other distinct factors: first, the TTP is engaged in a full-fledged war against the state and is driven by multiple motivations, and second, the TTP is not the only militant group in the country. Sectarian organizations such as Lashkar-e-Jhangvi, which is credited with organizing large-scale massacres of Shi'ite Muslims around the country, are thriving in Pakistan in regions completely unaffected by drone strikes. There are numerous other groups in Pakistan involved in inciting and carrying out attacks against religious minorities such as Ahmadis, Christians, and Hindus.

Nevertheless, drones do not factor in to these militant groups. Even if one ignores the sectarian conflict in Pakistan and focuses on the theory that "drones are fueling the TTP," it is highly unlikely that the TTP will end its attacks if US drone strikes were to stop. In fact, the TTP – itself a fragmented movement – has used other pretexts to carry out attacks.[89] In other words, ending US drone strikes in Pakistan may have little to do with stopping militant groups.

The Pakistani government, led by Prime Minister Nawaz Sharif, has strongly advocated ending drone strikes. But it remains unclear whether a new government – eager to build a strong relationship with the United States – will push this through. As the perception that drone strikes drive the TTP to engage in terrorist acts continues to have substantial public support, the Sharif administration and the military will have to rethink their overall counter-terrorism strategy. Over the past decade, there has been little clarity on Pakistani government's efforts to end militant movements and eliminate the causes of radicalization. Calls for transparency on the drone program have been made by all political parties, even Sharif's rival PTI. But whether Sharif and the military can respond now, while the Predators buzz overhead in the tribal areas, remains to be seen.

In his first speech after being elected prime minister, Sharif called for an end to drone strikes and for finding a way to "resolve the issue."[90] His government followed up on those statements a few days later and issued a demarche to the US ambassador to Pakistan over a June 7 drone strike.[91] The demarche emphasized the importance of ending drone strikes, which the government said were counterproductive and had a negative impact on US–Pakistan ties.

The Sharif administration has also faced several challenges from the insurgency since assuming power in June 2013, including attacks on foreign tourists, on the Shi'ite community in Balochistan, and in Sharif's home-town of Lahore. Drone strikes have slowed considerably since 2008, as has the average death count.[92] However, a drone strike on July 3, 2013, appeared to have reversed this trend – with a reported death toll of sixteen – and provoked the usual reaction of condemnation from the Pakistani government.[93] The Sharif administration is set to introduce a new counter-terrorism policy.[94] It has also gained consensus from political parties on opening negotiations with militants. But it is unlikely that the process will kick-start while militants continue to attack the Pakistan Army and civilians.[95] Moreover, the TTP has demanded that drone strikes end as a precursor to negotiations, a step that the Pakistani government is unable to take itself.[96]

Pakistan's stance on drones is likely to remain consistent, especially given the internal political dynamics of the country that have made this an issue of national importance, and the Pakistani people are unlikely to build consensus on the use or utility of drone strikes. With no compelling evidence that drone strikes have stemmed militancy in Pakistan, and increasing public outrage over drone strikes and American policy, it is evident that drones remain highly unpopular with the government, military, and the public and will continue to impact the US–Pakistan relationship.

NOTES

1 *Al Jazeera*, "Pakistan: State of the nation," August 13, 2009.

2 International Human Rights and Conflict Resolution Clinic, Stanford Law School and Global Justice Clinic, New York University School of Law, "Living under drones: Death, injury, and trauma to civilians from US drone practices in Pakistan," September 2012. Aryana Institute for Regional Research and Advocacy, "Drone attacks – a survey" (opinion polls), March 5, 2009. New America Foundation and Terror Free Tomorrow, "Public opinion in Pakistan's tribal regions," September 28, 2010. Orakzai, Rifatullah, "No easy answers after Bajaur raid," BBC, May 19, 2008.

3 Khan, Ismail, and Dilawar Khan Wazir, "Night raid kills Nek Muhammad, four other militants: Wana operation," *Dawn*, June 19, 2004.

4 Ibid.

5 CNN, "Al Qaeda No. 3 dead, but how?" December 4, 2005.

6 Dietz, Bob, "The last story: Hayatullah Khan," Committee to Protect Journalists, September 20, 2006.

7 Reporters Without Borders, "Slain tribal area journalist's widow murdered," November 17, 2007.

8 Reuters, "U.S. drone attack? It was us, says Pakistan army," January 19, 2007.

9 Bashirullah, Khan, "Missile strike in Pakistan kills 4," Associated Press, April 27, 2007.

10 Witte, Griff, "Blast kills at least 20 in Pakistan," *Washington Post*, June 20, 2007.

11 Khan, Ismail, "Missile attack, possibly by NATO, kills 8 in Pakistan," *New York Times*, February 29, 2008.

12 Interview with Iftikhar Firdous, July 2013.

13 BBC, "Pakistan 'catches al-Qaeda chief," May 4, 2005.

14 Interview with Sherry Rehman, July 2013.

15 Cameron-Moore, Simon, "Drone kills 5 in Pakistan, Pentagon denies hand," Reuters, November 2, 2007.

16 Robertson, Nic, and Greg Botelho, "Ex-Pakistani leader admits secret deal with U.S. on drone strikes," CNN, April 12, 2013.

17 Ali, Imtiaz, and Massoud Ansari, "Pakistan fury as CIA airstrike on village kills 18," *Telegraph,* January 15, 2006.

18 Woods, Chris, "The day 69 children died," *Express Tribune,* August 12, 2011. Wasim, Amir, "Commotion in senate ahead of Bajaur debate," *Dawn,* November 25, 2006

19 *International Herald Tribune,* "15,000 armed Pakistanis protest deadly airstrike," October 31, 2006.

20 Laskar, Rezaul H., "PPP stakes claim to form new government," Press Trust of India, February 24, 2008.

21 Musharraf seized power in a military coup on October 12, 1999.

22 Associated Press, "Pakistan: Next U.S. leader must stop attacks," April 4, 2008.

23 Reuters, "Pakistan army takes issue over US missile attack," May 18, 2008.

24 Walsh, Declan, "Pakistan's top Taliban leader Baitullah Mehsud killed in US drone attack," *Guardian,* August 7, 2009.

25 Khan, Ismail, "Good riddance, killer Baitullah," *Dawn,* August 8, 2009.

26 Khan, Mohammad, "Pakistan says U.S. planes crossed border and killed 18," *New York Times,* January 13, 2006. Coghlan, Tom, Zahid Hussain, and Jeremy Page, "Secrecy and denial as Pakistan lets CIA use airbase to strike militants," *Times,* February 17, 2009.

27 Priest, Dana, "Surveillance operation in Pakistan located and killed Al Qaeda official," *Washington Post,* May 15, 2005.

28 Barnes, Julian E., and Greg Miller, "Pakistan gets a say in drone attacks on militants," *Los Angeles Times,* May 13, 2009.

29 Scahill, Jeremy, "Pakistan's two air wars," *Nation,* May 12, 2010.

30 Interview with Madiha Tahir, June 2013.

31 Interview with Joshua Foust, June 2013.

32 Interview with Sherry Rehman, July 2013.

33 Interview with Joshua Foust, June 2013.

34 Interview with Sherry Rehman, July 2013.

35 Associated Press, "Pakistan summons US ambassador to protest against latest drone killings," June 8, 2013. Javaid-ur-Rahman, "JUI-F stays joining N," *Nation,* May 19, 2013.

36 Interview with Bushra Gohar, June 2013.

37 Perlez, Jane, "Pakistan protests U.S. missile strikes," *New York Times,* October 29, 2008.

38 BBC, "Pakistan protest to US ambassador," November 20, 2008.

39 Reuters, "Pakistani general calls for halt to missile strikes," November 20, 2008.

40 Pew Research Center, "Pakistani public opinion: Growing concerns about extremism, continuing discontent with U.S.," August 13, 2009.

41 Imtiaz, Saba, "Pakistan: WikiWreaks havoc," *Express Tribune,* December 2, 2010.

42 Woods, Chris, "Drone strikes rise to one every four days," Bureau of Investigative Journalism, July 18, 2011.

43 Zaidi, Hasan, "Army chief wanted more drone support," *Dawn,* May 20, 2011.

44 *News,* "No drone attack support ever sought: ISPR," May 21, 2011.

45 *Guardian*, "US embassy cables: Pakistan backs US drone attacks on tribal areas," November 30, 2010.

46 Abbasi, Ansar, "Local CIA chief may face case against drone attacks," *News*, December 1, 2010.

47 Entous, Adam, "CIA station chief, his cover blown, departs Pakistan," *Wall Street Journal*, December 18, 2010.

48 Reuters, "Raymond Davis, U.S. embassy official, detained in Pakistan on murder charges," February 11, 2011.

49 Traub, James, "The all-American," *New York Times Magazine*, July 4, 2011.

50 BBC, "US drone strike 'kills 40' in Pakistani tribal region," March 17, 2011.

51 Gannon, Kathy, Kimberly Dozier, and Sebastian Abbot, "Timing of US drone strike questioned," Associated Press, August 2, 2011.

52 Yusufzai, Rahimullah, "Getting serious about drones," *News*, April 27, 2011.

53 International Human Rights and Conflict Resolution Clinic, Stanford Law School and Global Justice Clinic, New York University School of Law, "Living under drones: Death, injury, and trauma to civilians from US drone practices in Pakistan."

54 Yusufzai, "Getting serious about drones."

55 Associated Press, "Pakistan army chief condemns drone attack that killed 38 people," *Guardian*, March 17, 2011.

56 Perlez, Jane, "Pakistan army chief warns U.S. on another raid," *New York Times*, May 5, 2011.

57 Waraich, Omar, "Berating General Pasha: Pakistan's spy chief gets a tongue-lashing," *Time*, May 13, 2011.

58 Masood, Salman, and Eric Schmitt, "Tensions flare between U.S. and Pakistan after strike," *New York Times*, November 26, 2011.

59 Schmitt, Eric, and Matthew Rosenberg, "U.S. report faults two sides in deadly Pakistan strike," *New York Times*, December 22, 2011.

60 Inter-Services Public Relations, "Pakistan's perspective on investigation report conducted by BG Stephen Clark into 26th November 2011 US led ISAF/NATO forces attack on Pakistani Volcano and Boulder posts in Mohmand Agency," January 23, 2012.

61 Masood, Salman, "C.I.A. leaves base in Pakistan used for drone strikes," *New York Times*, December 11, 2011.

62 Asghar, Raja, "Parliament sets out to reorder US ties," *Dawn*, March 20, 2012.

63 Pew Research Center, "U.S. image in Pakistan falls no further following bin Laden killing," *Global Attitudes Project*, June 21, 2011.

64 Interview with Sherry Rehman, July 2013.

65 Coll, Steve, "Sporting Chance," *New Yorker*, August 13, 2012.

66 Based on the number of seats, the PTI now holds in the lower house of parliament.

67 Wake, Damon, "Khan leads march against drone killings," *Agence France-Presse*, October 7, 2012.

68 Burke, Jason, "Imran Khan: The man who would be Pakistan's next prime minister," *Observer*, March 4, 2012.

69 *Agence France-Presse,* "Imran Khan: From cricket star to political kingmaker," October 9, 2012.

70 *News,* "US drones to be shot down after May 11: Imran," May 5, 2013.

71 Interview with Madiha Tahir, June 2013.

72 Interview with Bushra Gohar, June, 2013.

73 Interview with Joshua Foust, June 2013.

74 Interview with Iftikhar Firdous, July 2013.

75 Interview with Madiha Tahir, June 2013.

76 Interview with Bushra Gohar, June 2013.

77 Interview with Iftikhar Firdous, July 2013. See also Ali, M. "Arithmetic on the frontier," *Friday Times,* April 22, 2011.

78 International Human Rights and Conflict Resolution Clinic, Stanford Law School and Global Justice Clinic, New York University School of Law, "Living under drones: Death, injury, and trauma to civilians from US drone practices in Pakistan," p. 16.

79 Khan, Behroz, and Ben Arnoldy, "Pakistan Taliban: US drone strikes forcing militants underground," *Christian Science Monitor,* March 15, 2010.

80 *Agence France-Presse.* "Report reveals Pasha's admission of Pak–US 'understanding' on drones," July 9, 2013.

81 Interview with Madiha Tahir, June 2013.

82 Ali, Manzoor, "Lawmakers unable to forge consensus on terrorism, other core issues," *Express Tribune,* July 2, 2013.

83 Kazim, Hasnain, "Spiegel interview with Pakistan's Prime Minister: 'American drone attacks are counterproductive,'" *Der Spiegel,* December 1, 2009.

84 Interview with Sherry Rehman, July 2013.

85 Ali, "Lawmakers unable to forge consensus on terrorism, other core issues."

86 The Jamaat-ud-Dawa Party, press release, January 21, 2013.

87 *Tribune Express,* "TTP claims responsibility for attack on Bannu police station," December 10, 2012. *Daily Times,* "TTP claims responsibility for Nangarhar bombing," June 15, 2008.

88 Masood, Salman, and Ismail Khan, "Taliban militants attack Pakistan base," *New York Times,* February 2, 2013. Khan, Tahir, "TTP claims responsibility for killing tourists in Gilgit-Baltistan," *Express Tribune,* June 23, 2013.

89 Imtiaz, Saba, "Defending militancy: Why they kill civilians, attack the state," *Express Tribune,* August 20, 2011.

90 BBC, "Pakistan PM Nawaz Sharif urges end to drone strikes," June 5, 2013.

91 Laskar, Rezaul H., "Pakistan summons US envoy over drone strike," Press Trust of India, June 8, 2013.

92 Serle, Jack, and Chris Woods, "Six-month update: US covert actions in Pakistan, Yemen and Somalia," Bureau of Investigative Journalism, July 1, 2013.

93 Ross, Alice K., and Jack Serle, "Deadliest drone strike in nine months bucks recent trend," Bureau of Investigative Journalism, July 5, 2013.

94 Ghauri, Irfan, "Fighting terror: Draft policy aims to dismantle terror networks," *Express Tribune*, August 13, 2013. Khan, Iftikhar Ahmad, and Baqir Sajjad Syed, "No radical shift in new anti-terror policy," *Dawn*, July 6, 2013.

95 Shah, Saeed, "Taliban claim killing of Pakistan general," *Wall Street Journal*, September 15, 2013.

96 Shah, Saeed, "U.S. drone strikes cloud peace overtures with the Taliban," *Wall Street Journal*, September 13, 2013.

PART II
DRONES AND THE LAWS OF WAR

6

It Is War at a Very Intimate Level

DRONE PILOT

NELLIS AIR FORCE BASE, LAS VEGAS, NV*

There's an insatiable appetite for RPAs [Remotely Piloted Aircraft] right now. When RPAs were first deployed they were so new that the leadership did not realize how popular and successful they would become. Initially, RPAs did not draw in a cadre of fighter pilots. But then things began to change and you saw fighter pilots, bomber pilots, and others who brought with them a lot of experience flying RPAs. Now we're at the point where RPA pilots are getting the most combat experience of anyone. In my opinion, a lot of the most significant work is being done in the RPA community and that is drawing in the top-tier guys. There is pride associated with flying RPAs.

The important thing for me is the twenty-year-old with the rifle on the ground, sleeping in a ditch. That is why we do this job. If I can be more successful supporting that soldier, then that is what I want to do, day in and day out. Would I like to be flying an F-22 around and doing loops and rolls and things? Sure, absolutely. But I find what I do now to be more meaningful than anything else I could think of.

The RPA is remotely operated, but it is very much a manned aircraft. There are a lot of people involved in the operation of an RPA, in fact more than for a regular airplane. You need classic pilot training to fly an RPA. Absolutely. We have a stick, we have a rudder; you're flying an airplane, you are just doing it remotely. All the same skills are necessary. You have to worry about the traditional things that concern pilots, like altitude de-confliction and airspace de-confliction. In addition, you need the ability to manage and disseminate information and deal with different scenarios with other individuals and other aircraft. You also need to know who needs information "X" and who needs information "Y" and how do I get it to them? How do I make sure

---

* This interview was conducted, edited, and prepared for publication by Daniel Rothenberg.

they understand what they need to know? And, how do I give it to them in the simplest form?

Flying an RPA is more like being a manager than flying a traditional manned aircraft, where a lot of times your focus is on keeping the shiny side up, keeping the wings level, putting the aircraft where it needs to be to accomplish the mission. In the RPA world, you're managing multiple assets and you are involved with the other platforms using the information coming off of your aircraft.

You could use the term "orchestrating"; you are helping to orchestrate an operation.

We have several different communication pieces that we use to talk to those on the ground, just like with a regular aircraft. In addition, there are other systems that we use to talk to other aircraft and to network with other individuals. We do what we call CRM, Cockpit Resource Management. That is the ability to take in a lot of information and disseminate it to where it needs to go. There could be fifteen to twenty people that are using the information that is coming off an RPA at any given time, live while we're flying.

People talk about RPAs as if they are like a videogame. We hear that all the time, "You play videogames for a living." Well, people do not die in videogames. And you're not able to save people's lives in videogames. I cannot cause an aircraft to have a collision with another aircraft in a videogame. Flying RPAs is simply not a videogame.

Physically, you don't have the sensation of flying. I think that is pretty obvious to most people, but then many people assume that to fly airplanes we need to look outside, to see the world around us. And, most of the time, that's not really the case.

We use the same navigation system to fly RPAs as with traditional aircraft. However, RPA missions can extend far longer, which is one of the major benefits of using these systems. In an F-16, a mission is around two hours, but with an RPA you're flying twenty plus hours. You can't argue with those efficiencies. Still, it is exhausting. And there are often multiple pilots for a mission. It's odd because you have several different pilots flying one RPA on any given mission. For a pilot, this is a paradigm shift.

Because of the length of time that you fly over a certain area you're able to engage in lengthy communications with individuals on the ground. You build relationships. Things are a little more personal with an RPA than with an aircraft that is up for just a few hours. When you're talking to that twenty-year-old with the rifle for twenty plus hours at a time, maybe for weeks, you build a relationship. And you develop an emotional attachment to those individuals.

You see them on the screen. That can only happen because of the amount of time you are on station. I have a buddy who was actually able to make contact with his son's friend over in the AOR [Area of Responsibility]. If you don't think that is going to make you focus, than I don't know what will.

Many individuals that have been over there have said, "You know we were really happy to see you show up"; "We knew that you were going to keep us from being flanked"; "We felt confident in our ability to move this convoy from 'A' to 'B' because you were there." The guy on the ground and the woman on the ground see how effective we are. And it gives them more confidence.

Sometimes, by chance, we meet face-to-face with the individuals who were on the ground while we were in the air. Somebody will start talking about where they were or what operation they were involved with, and I'll say, "Really? What time were you there?" And then through the conversation, I'll find out that the person was part of the same operation.

Sometimes we'll meet someone whose life we saved.

Once, I met someone like that at a Little League baseball game. We just started talking about the geographical area and the time and then we pieced together that I was there and I was providing overwatch for the person while he was on the ground. And he said, "Thank you."

When you see a person who is at a baseball game now because you were doing your job, well, words cannot describe the feeling. It is uplifting. Every day I leave work with a sense of accomplishment, a sense of pride.

This is a strange dynamic in RPA operations. I think it makes people more focused on the mission. Does it cause you to be more emotionally invested? Absolutely. That's the human aspect of it. That is the man-in-the-loop aspect of it. In some ways drone use is more human from the pilot's perspective, which is kind of ironic.

Flying an RPA, you start to understand people in other countries based on their day-to-day patterns of life. A person wakes up, they do this, they greet their friends this way, etc. You become immersed in their life. You feel like you are a part of what they're doing every single day. So, even if you're not emotionally engaged with those individuals, you become a little bit attached. I have learned about Afghan culture this way. As an RPA pilot, you see their interactions. You study them. You see everything.

In a traditional manned aircraft you drop ordinance and leave. You know that there was a big bang, but that is it. With an RPA you see these individuals and their interactions with people prior to an engagement and after the engagement. We see the aftermath. We see what happens next. That more than anything draws an emotional response.

They are human beings, right? That is the bottom line, so it affects you to watch the impact of a kinetic strike. You have to provide the battle damage assessment. We do that quite often and it can take a long time. You might even watch the burial and see the ceremony. We're not disconnected from what is happening. We're not playing videogames. With RPAs, you grasp your enormous level of responsibility. You witness it all.

Targeting with RPAs is more intimate. It is war at a very intimate level.

Someone might ask, "How could you not be upset by that?" But you have to step back from and say, "There's a reason these individuals were targeted." The strike may be a response to the fact that many twenty-year-olds have died. The person targeted may have been involved in building IEDs [improvised explosive device] or suicide vests. Whatever the case may be, there was a reason that person was targeted. I think it is important to keep that in mind. So, do I feel sorry for that person? No. But, we're dealing with human beings. Just because you are separated by technology does not mean you are separated emotionally.

The biggest misunderstanding within the military about being a RPA pilot is that it's not stressful. Probably the lack of personal risk for the pilot has a lot to do with that attitude.

However, there are unique stresses to flying an RPA, especially the lack of transition time between a mission and regular life. When I deploy in a manned aircraft, I am on a base for months. And when I'm there, that's my world. I go fly a mission, I come back to the base, I talk about the mission, and then I plan for the next mission. Then I go fly that mission, come back, and talk about it. Every once in a while I'll get on the phone with my wife or kids and try to stay in touch with what is going on at home. But for the most part my world is the mission and the war.

When you're doing RPA operations, you're mentally there, wherever there is. You're flying the mission. You're talking to folks on the ground. You're involved in kinetic strikes. Then you step out of the Ground Control Station [GCS] and you're not there anymore.

One of the strangest sensations I have is when I step out of the GCS and realize, "Ok, I am not there."

I'll go meet my wife for lunch.

I'll step out from doing a mission and go off to my child's soccer game.

Those are two very, very different worlds. And you're in and out of those worlds daily. I have to combine these two worlds. Every single day. Multiple times a day. So, I am there and then I am not there and then I am there again. The time between leaving the GCS and, say, having lunch with my wife could be as little as ten minutes. It's really that fast.

So, how do I – as an individual, as a human being – operate in these two very different worlds on a daily basis? You learn to deal with it. You learn to compartmentalize. You learn to take that mission and put it away to revisit it at a later time.

Inevitably, RPAs will change war. What we will have ten years from now is going to make things that we are doing today seem almost primitive. What we call pilots today will change. The skillsets necessary to be a pilot will be vastly different ten years from now. Maybe we won't even continue to call them pilots. And what is going to happen twenty years from now? It's going to be dramatically different.

However, there will always be a need for the man in the loop. There are always going to be people involved, making decisions for all of this to work. You have got to bring it back down to what we are trying to accomplish. If we're talking about war, just war, then the bottom line is that we're trying to support the twenty-year-old with the rifle on the ground. That is what matters.

Personally, I am excited to see what the future holds. I am very proud to be part of the most technologically advanced air force in the world.

We do not take it lightly.

We do not take the application of firepower lightly.

7

This Is Not War by Machine

CHARLES BLANCHARD

1. ADDRESSING MISCONCEPTIONS ABOUT RPAS

There are a number of misconceptions about the use of remotely piloted aircraft (RPAs) as a weapons system by the US military. Some commentators focus excessively on RPAs' role in attacking targets when, in fact, this is a less critical element of the platform's innovation and value. Others suggest that RPAs place humans outside of the conflict and lead us toward "push-button warfare," some new machine-driven vision of combat, when their actual use involves large teams of professionals engaged with the impact of war in a very direct and detailed manner. Still others suggest that the use of RPAs is illegal and runs counter to established domestic and international norms. These and other positions are based on core misunderstandings about the main value of RPAs, their complex role within integrated military actions, and the ways in which these platforms are transforming conflict.

The United States Air Force (USAF) use of RPAs has been largely confined to the conflicts in Afghanistan and Iraq. Despite the fact that many RPA pilots are not themselves in Afghanistan or Iraq, it is important to note that these RPAs are always utilized in a manner that integrates into a broader military strategy. In the major theaters of operation, the US Army, Marines, Navy, and Air Force are engaged in a joint fight under a joint commander running the fight plan. Every day, the air operation plan, which addresses use of the MQ-1 (the Predator) and MQ-9 (the Reaper) as part of a larger set of air assets, is in turn integrated with the larger joint fight. RPA capabilities are factored into the overarching theater campaign plan, and, as with other assets, RPA support is provided in response to requests by land and sea forces to achieve campaign objectives.

Over the past few years, RPA use has increased substantially.[1] And it is certain that the current generation of RPAs, as well as future, more advanced models, will play significant roles within the US military, as well as the militaries of other nations. For this reason, reasoned public debate and discussion of RPAs is important for our society, as well as for our military services. At present, the innovative qualities of these new technologies are often masked by the nature of current public debate, which would benefit from a clearer understanding of what RPAs actually do, what roles they serve, and how they are impacting military activity and strategy.

2. UNDERSTANDING THE REAL BENEFIT OF RPAS

Contrary to popular belief, the primary benefit of RPAs is not their utility as an attack platform – although RPAs have indeed become an important attack option for commanders. To date, their main value has been that they can stay over a target for a very long period of time – almost 24 hours for the Predator and a little less for the Reaper.[2]

They also can fly at a very high altitude. The Predator performs at a maximum altitude of 20,000 feet; the Reaper up to 30,000 feet.[3] As a result, their main benefit for the USAF is as an intelligence, surveillance, and reconnaissance asset. By having the capacity to gather information about a target persistently for long periods of time, they provide an especially valuable understanding of what is occurring on the ground. In addition, they can follow friendly troops and offer them battlefield intelligence in real time so the troops know what is ahead of them and can prepare accordingly. They can also provide surveillance of transportation routes to look for IEDs (improvised explosive device) and otherwise help minimize military casualties.[4] The contribution of RPAs – as well as their primary use – is as a tool for gathering intelligence and engaging in sustained surveillance and reconnaissance.

Most of the airstrikes that are occurring in Afghanistan right now are *not* Predator or Reaper RPAs employing weapons. Instead, the strikes are being done by other air platforms, such as fighter jets like the F-16 or attack aircraft like the A-10, and bombers such as the B-2.[5] That said, it is very likely that the reconnaissance, intelligence, and surveillance assets of the Reaper and/or the Predator are instrumental in virtually every one of these strikes.

Of course, RPAs also carry weapons and are used to conduct strike missions. The Reaper, which is the more recently developed of the RPAs in use, actually carries a lot of ordinance. A fully armed Reaper can stay in the air as long as fourteen hours (and considerably longer unarmed) and has a total payload of 3,000 pounds.[6] Factoring in the weight of fuel tanks, this means a combat-ready Reaper can carry either sixteen Hellfire missiles or four 500-pound laser guided bombs. The Predator's offensive capabilities are considerably more modest; with fuel, it has a payload of 450 pounds, or two Hellfire missiles.[7] It is important to note that this is a fraction of what traditional aircraft can carry. For instance, in addition to its powerful GAU-8 cannons, an A-10 can carry a payload of 16,000 pounds of ordinance.[8] As such, an A-10 has the air-to-ground attack capability greater than five Reapers and more than thirty-five Predators.[9]

3. RPAS ARE NEITHER "DRONES" NOR "UNMANNED"

Despite its prevalence in the media and public conversation, the word "drone" is not just misleading but, in fact, incorrect. Similarly, the term "unmanned vehicle" fails to capture the staffing demands of these technologies or the degree to which their operation requires the substantial involvement of many people. Contrary to commonly held perceptions, there are more than one hundred human beings involved in a Reaper or Predator mission.[10] In addition to the launch and recovery team, which can be several dozen people, there is the pilot who operates the vehicle, the sensor operator who manages the sensors, and rooms full of intelligence analysts across the country, often in multiple locations, who look at the intelligence feeds. And there are command teams at the Combined Air Operations Center (CAOC) in Doha, Qatar, who look at the video feeds and make real-time decisions regarding targeting and missions.

Along with these professionals, there are feeds that connect to ground units, linking RPAs with military forces engaged in patrols, direct combat, and other operations. In other words, using RPAs requires intense coordination among many groups operating in multiple locations, sometimes separated by thousands of miles. In this way, these operations are anything but "unmanned."

The chain of communication for an RPA operation involves multiple links and networks connecting many levels of command. These groups are in constant conversation with specific issues and shifting information based on the particular mission.

For example, an RPA operation in southern Afghanistan might begin with a request from ground forces for aerial support. This would be passed on to the CAOC, located about a thousand miles away in the Gulf. Commanders at the CAOC review the request and might approve the operation based on consultations with military lawyers, who are on duty 24 hours a day.[11]

The CAOC would then relay instructions to US-based RPA operators. The vehicle's operator might be stationed some 7,000 miles from the site in Afghanistan and many thousands of miles from the CAOC at Hancock Field Air National Guard Base in New York,[12] or more than 8,000 miles away from the Creech Air Force Base in Nevada.[13] Because of the signal delay between operators in the United States and the vehicle in Afghanistan, crews in Afghanistan would control the vehicle during takeoff and landing.[14]

Once in the air, the US-based team would then control the RPA via satellite links and fly the vehicle to assist the troops requesting support, sometimes providing assistance from as high as 50,000 feet above the site.[15] While these different actors start operating in distinct sites around the world, they are in constant communication.[16]

The complex link between information gathering, analysis, and global control and contact is not only what defines RPAs as substantively distinct in the management of conflict, but is also what demonstrates that this is war waged by human beings making decisions.[17]

This is not war by machine.

4. RPAS DO NOT CREATE PUSH-BUTTON WARFARE

Perhaps what is most troubling and disconnected from the reality of the use of RPAs is the idea that they enable push-button warfare. Many people believe that these vehicles create a context that is similar to a video game. They suggest that RPAs are changing war so that it becomes automated and mechanical, such that those involved engage in destructive activities more easily. There are allegations that pilots – those that actually "push the button" to initiate an attack – are desensitized through their use of remotely piloted vehicles in warfare.

In fact, my experience is quite different. RPA pilots usually have more and sustained contact with the realities of warfare than fighter and bomber pilots. I recently spoke to an F-16 pilot who flew combat missions over Afghanistan and Iraq earlier in his career and is now a Reaper pilot. His observation was the opposite of what many people say about RPAs. He explained that as an F-16 pilot, you would feel all the sensations of a jet fighter; you would direct your plane to the target, fire your weapon, and feel the g-forces of flying fast and pulling away. Yet he also explained that as an F-16 pilot, you have far less engagement with the impact of an attack than as a Reaper pilot, while the Reaper pilot's perspective is far more personal.[18]

Jet fighter planes fly quickly, maneuver extremely well, and are highly sophisticated aircraft. In an attack, they can be engaged quickly and then be flown back to base. Given that F-16s can only be flown a couple of hours without refueling, they do not have the capacity to remain over targeting sites for half a day, or even many hours.[19] Even with aerial refueling, F-16 missions rarely are flown long periods of time.

As a result, fighter pilots – as well as pilots of other key assets like the A-10, and even more so for high-altitude bombers – have limited direct engagement with the impact of the attacks with which they are involved. A Reaper pilot, however, commonly stays over a target for many hours. He does not leave after the bomb strikes like an F-16 pilot, but instead he remains overhead and immediately goes into battle damage assessment mode, including assessing collateral damage.

A Reaper pilot spends substantial time reviewing, with significant visual detail, the results of a mission. In this way, Reaper pilots actually deal much more with the human impact of an attack than other pilots. For this reason, we have Reaper pilots who have had to receive mental health counseling because of the stresses and strains of being in a war environment. The idea that RPA pilots are psychologically remote from the battlefield is incorrect.

5. RPAS DO NOT VIOLATE THE LAW OF ARMED CONFLICT

There are some who suggest that the use of RPAs by the US military is unlawful. This is not true. President Obama said unequivocally in his recent speech at the National Defense University, "America's actions are legal."[20] The USAF complies with all law, domestic and international, in the deployment and use of military assets. This applies to the use of RPAs, as well as F-16s, A-10s, and B-52s.

Regardless of the asset, the US military applied the Law of Armed Conflict (LOAC). In fact, the USAF Rules of Engagement in a counterinsurgency (COIN) environment, as in Afghanistan, are often much more careful and conservative than what is allowed under LOAC.

The main legal concepts that guide the decision making in the CAOC by military lawyers are the principles of necessity, distinction, and proportionality. These three ideas define the core of LOAC. Primarily, they seek to ensure that the use of military force is only directed against legitimate military targets and in a manner designed to minimize collateral damage. USAF cadets have long been trained in international law and it is an institutionalized part of USAF's ethos.[21]

The principle of "necessity" requires that all potential targets have military value. The principle of distinction is motivated primarily by a desire "to shield those who are not directly participating in the conflict from its effects."[22] In other words, military force cannot be directed at those not participating in the conflict and those employing force have an affirmative responsibility to identify and distinguish between combatants and non-combatants. A target that does not satisfy the principle of distinction cannot be deliberately attacked.[23] This is a gatekeeping principle, because even if a target is identified as a combatant, other principles may limit the ability to engage the target.

The principle of proportionality means that in an attack against a military target, we are required to make efforts to avoid or minimize the incidental loss of civilian life or injury, as well as possible harm to civilian property or other civilian objects.[24] Thus, even if a target satisfies the principles of necessity and distinction, it may not satisfy the principle of proportionality if the collateral damage is expected to be excessive in relation to the anticipated military value in attacking the target.[25]

Proportionality defines an obligation – a legal obligation – to minimize civilian casualties. And more importantly, the value of the military target has to justify the possibility of civilian casualties that might result from an attack. Where there is a high-value target, the principle of proportionality allows some risk to civilian populations, but more routine military targets would hardly ever justify the endangerment of civilian life. This has a major impact on how force is used in combat.

Some have suggested that targeting specific individuals constitutes unlawful extrajudicial killing. That is, if we target an individual without giving them due process, that would constitute a violation of US domestic law. In the context of Afghanistan, this issue does not really arise. The country is a conflict zone in which the laws of armed combat apply, allowing for individual combatants to be targeted.[26]

Although modern conflicts against transnational terrorist organizations pose difficult questions concerning the scope of the battlefield, the present action in Afghanistan falls squarely within the traditional concept in that it is primarily a conflict between a national government and a readily identifiable insurgency movement: the Taliban.[27] This is the sort of conflict anticipated by Geneva Common Article III, which governs LOAC for conflicts "occurring in the territory of one [state]."[28]

In this way targeting a particular individual, or leader, or individual in a military force, as is sometimes done with RPAs, does not violate LOAC. We have targeted individuals in the past, and where those individuals are legitimate military targets and fall under the principles of distinction, proportionality, and other elements of the laws of war, these actions are legal. The most famous example is Admiral Yamamoto, who planned the attack on Pearl Harbor in World War II.[29] Similarly, during many other conflicts the United States has attacked particular leaders or particular high-value targets to the extent they were legitimate military targets.

However, it is important to note that there are cases where targeting individuals could occur in ways that might raise legal questions. There are a number of possible scenarios where targeting an American citizen would raise substantial legal questions. At one extreme there could be an American member of a foreign military engaged in hostilities against the United States in a traditional, foreign war zone. In such a scenario, targeting the American citizen would likely be consistent with constitutional due process.[30]

On the other extreme, however, there might be an American member of an international terrorist organization, located in a remote corner of the United States. Targeting that citizen may raise stronger constitutional concerns and present policy suggests that, unless that citizen were directly engaged in combat against the United States, targeting them would not be acceptable.[31] However, as long as we are engaged in armed conflict and as long as our forces are authorized to use military force, targeting individuals does not constitute unlawful extrajudicial killing.[32]

Uniforms have long been recognized as a key indicator of the difference between combatants and non-combatants and are enormously useful for respecting the principle of distinction. The Geneva Conventions require combatants to have a "fixed distinctive insignia recognizable at a distance" in order distinguish themselves from non-combatants.[33] And the US Supreme Court has ruled that combatants without uniforms are "unlawful combatants" who are not entitled to prisoner of war status.[34]

However, in many modern conflicts, including in Afghanistan, our enemies are often difficult to distinguish from the civilian population. This poses a serious challenge for using the principle of distinction. Similarly, in a COIN environment, as in many current conflict zones, it is especially important to use focused, specific targeting to avoid civilian casualties both to respect the principle of proportionality and to meet strategic needs.

RPAs, with their ability to loiter over targets for extended periods of time and to gather extensive intelligence through surveillance and reconnaissance, are particularly well suited to meet this legal requirement. In fact, RPAs are better able to provide the information necessary to avoid civilian casualties than what we have used in the past. As it was described to me, our RPA pilots can monitor the activities of individuals over time, to select the moment when we know that individual is engaged in setting up an improvised explosive device, or, potentially to deflect an attack if innocent civilians come on the scene. In this way, RPAs and other emerging technologies have raised the bar for military leaders on when they can authorize strikes and when they cannot.

The advanced intelligence and surveillance capabilities of RPAs have increased our capacity to successfully engage in warfare in a manner that is consistent with the laws of war. The more we have used these new technologies, the better we have become at focused targeting that minimizes civilian casualties.

However, to best understand how information gathered by RPAs allows for the more effective application of LOAC, as well as conditions where targeting occurs under stressful conditions, it is useful to distinguish between three different types of attacks.[35] Planned attacks are where a target is identified in advance and the mission can be timed for when the individual is away from potential civilian casualties. This allows for careful and coordinated action; in these cases we rarely have civilian casualties.

Dynamic targeting attacks involve decisions during missions where there is some ability to make determinations as to when and how to strike. In these cases, we also do quite well in limiting collateral damage. Then there are troops in contact situations. This is where our military units are engaged in actions and require immediate assistance and rapid decision making regarding targeting. This is where the fog of war enters the situation. It is in these cases that we tend to see civilian casualties.[36]

RPAs play an increasingly important and diverse role in the USAF. They help to save the lives not only of our troops on the ground, but also of civilians caught in conflict areas. They enable us to better comply with our international legal obligations. They neither remove humans from the decision to take a life, nor do they constitute our primary mode of aerial attack. Overall, it is important that we address and move beyond the many misconceptions surrounding RPAs, especially as they are an increasingly instrumental, effective, and, ultimately, more humane tool within our nation's system of national security.

It is essential that we continue to discuss RPAs and the role they play in our national security. However, it is important that this conversation be informed by facts and not be prejudiced by the novelty of the platform at issue.

NOTES

1 US Department of Defense, *Unmanned Systems Integrated Roadmap, FY2011–2036*, 2011, p. 22, in which the rapid increase of unmanned aircraft system flight hours from 1996 to 2011 is noted.
2 US Air Force, *Unmanned Aircraft Systems Flight Plan 2009–2047*, 2009, pp. 26–27.
3 Ibid.

4 Vanden Brook, Tom, "Spy planes help detect roadside bombs in Afghanistan," *USA Today*, July 15, 2012.

5 Between 2010 and January 2013, 1,109 weapons were released from remotely piloted aircraft, out of a total of 14,785 weapon releases. Even in spite of the recent increased use of remotely piloted vehicles, they still constitute a minority of weapon releases. For instance, in January 2013, out of 192 weapon releases, only 44 came from remotely piloted vehicles. US Air Force, *Combined Forces Air Component Commander 2008–2013 Airpower Statistics* (on record with author).

6 US Air Force, *Fact sheets: MQ-9 Reaper*, March 29, 2013.

7 US Air Force, *Fact sheets: MQ-1B Predator*, March 29, 2013. Winslow, Wheeler, "Revisiting the Reaper revolution," *Time*, February 27, 2012.

8 US Air Force, *Fact sheets: A-10 Thunderbolt II*, September 10, 2012.

9 Wheeler, Winslow, "The MQ-9's cost and performance," *Time*, February 28, 2012.

10 One 24-hour combat air patrol requires 174 service members and 4 RPAs, requiring pilots, maintenance crews, sensor operators, mission coordinators, and administrative personnel. Hoffman, Michael, "Army, air force answer critics of UAV progress," *Army Times*, June 19, 2010. The military has, in fact, had to recruit intensively in order to ensure proper staffing for the use of RPAs. Thompson, Mark, "Manning unmanned systems," *Time*, September 10, 2012.

11 Zenko, Micah, and Emma Welch, "Where the drones are," *Foreign Policy*, May 29, 2012.

12 Bumiller, Elisabeth, "A day job waiting for a kill shot a world away," *New York Times*, July 29, 2012.

13 Zucchino, David, "Drone pilots have a front-row seat on war, from half a world away," *Los Angeles Times*, February 21, 2010.

14 US Air Force, *Air force instruction 11-2mq-1&9, vol. 3, Flying operations, MQ-1 and MQ-9 — operations procedures 32*, November 1, 2012, which describes Mission Control Elements operating MQ-1 and MQ-9 from "a geographically separated location" as responsible for taking an aircraft from a Launch and Recovery Element (LRE) after takeoff, executing the mission, and then handing the aircraft back to the LRE for recovery and landing. Blackhurst, Rob, "The air force men who fly drones in Afghanistan by remote control," *Telegraph*, September 24, 2012.

15 Wheeler, "The MQ-9's cost and performance."

16 Bumiller, Elisabeth, "Air force drone operators report high levels of stress," *New York Times*, December 18, 2011.

17 US Department of Defense, *Unmanned Systems Integrated Roadmap, FY2011–2036*, p. 27: Given the huge cost of supporting RPA missions, the Department of Defense (DoD) will likely use technology to reduce the number of airmen required for RPA missions. This will mean more true autonomy. US Department of Defense, *Department of Defense directive 3000.09, autonomy in weapon systems*, November 21, 2012, p. 2: Critically, it is DoD policy that "[a]utonomous and semi-autonomous weapon systems shall be designed to allow commanders and operators to exercise appropriate levels of human judgment over the use of force." Given the

requirements of the law of armed conflict, it is highly likely that humans must remain "in the kill chain" for the foreseeable future. Nonetheless, there is a robust debate about whether there should be an international agreement banning all fully autonomous weapon systems. See, e.g., Human Rights Watch, *Losing humanity*, 2012. Anderson, Kenneth, and Matthew Waxman, "Law and ethics for robot soldiers," *Policy Review*, December 1, 2012.

18 US Department of Defense, *Department of Defense directive 3000.09, autonomy in weapon systems*, p. 2: An air force study in 2011 found that nearly half of RPA operators had high levels of job-related stress. One particularly high-stress inducing part of working as an RPA pilot was "watching hours of close-up video of people killed in drone strikes."

19 Axe, David, "Upgrades to killer drone could make it fly for 2 days straight," *Wired*, April 19, 2012.

20 *New York Times*, "Obama's speech on drone policy," May 23, 2013.

21 See, e.g., Cunningham, Ernest D., "International law: An enrichment course," *Air Force Law Review* 7 (1965): 17–20, in which it is described why international law is a required part of a cadet's curriculum. Maj. Dennis W. Shepherd, USAF, "A bias-free LOAC approach aimed at instilling battle health in our airmen," *Air Force Law Review*, 37 (1994): 25–40, which details how all USAF trainees are taught basic international law and how JAGs are responsible for institutionalizing and routinizing its application throughout the branch. US Air Force, *Air force policy directive (AFPD) 51-4, compliance with the law of armed conflict*, August 4, 2011, p. 3, which describes the requirement that the air force ensure personnel comply with the LOAC during all armed conflicts and in all other military operations through systematic training, and by making legal advisers available "at all levels of command to provide advice about law of war compliance during the planning and execution of exercises and operations."

22 Schmitt, Michael N., "The principle of discrimination in 21st century warfare," *Yale Human Rights & Development Law Journal* 2 (1999): 143–182, p. 145.

23 Swiney, Gabriel, "Saving lives: The principle of distinction and the realities of modern war," *International Law* 39 (2005): 733–758, p. 734.

24 Ibid.

25 Schmitt, "The principle of discrimination in 21st century warfare," p. 150.

26 *Authorization for Use of Military Force*, Pub. L. No. 107-40, 115 Stat. 224 (2001), which allows the president to use "all necessary and appropriate force against those nations, organizations, or *persons* he determines planned, authorized, committed, or aided the terrorist attacks that occurred on September 11, 2001, or harbored such organizations or persons, in order to prevent any future acts of international terrorism against the United States by such nations, organizations or persons" (emphasis added).

27 Blank, Laurie R., "Defining the battlefield in contemporary conflict and counter-terrorism: Understanding the parameters of the zone of combat," *Georgia Journal of International & Comparative Law* 39 (2010): 1–38, p.3.

28 Geneva Convention Relative to the Treatment of Prisoners of War, art. 129, August 12, 1949, 6 U.S.T. 3316, 75 U.N.T.S. 135.

29 Admiral Yamamoto's plane was shot down over Bougainville in the Solomon Islands, approximately 450 miles from the closest military installation, a US air base. Despite that vast distance from the "front lines," such strict geographic limitations on defining the battlefield have no basis in practice or law. Lewis, Michael W., "Drones and the boundaries of the battlefield," *Texas International Law Journal* 47 (2012): 293–315, p. 303.

30 See *Hamdi* v. *Rumsfeld*, 542 U.S. 507, 518 (2004) (Plurality Op); *id.* at 587, 597 (Thomas, J., dissenting).

31 Weiner, Rachel, "Eric Holder responds to Rand Paul with 'no,' Paul satisfied," *Washington Post*, March 7, 2013.

32 US Department of Justice, White Paper, *Lawfulness of a lethal operation directed against a U.S. citizen who is a senior operational leader of Al-Qaida or an associated force*, November 8, 2011.

33 Geneva Convention Relative to the Treatment of Prisons of War art. 4, August 12, 1949.

34 Ex parte Quirin, 317 U.S. 1, 31–32 (1942).

35 USAF-targeting doctrine explicitly recognizes two forms of targeting: deliberate (or planned) and dynamic. It defines deliberate targeting as "the procedure for prosecuting targets that are detected, identified, and developed in sufficient time to schedule actions against them in tasking cycle products such as the air and space tasking order (ATO). Targets prosecuted as part of deliberate targeting are known to exist in an operating area and have missions or actions scheduled against them." Conversely, dynamic targeting consists of "the procedure for prosecuting targets that are not detected, identified, or developed in time to be included in deliberate targeting, and therefore have not had actions scheduled against them. Targets prosecuted as part of dynamic targeting are previously unanticipated, unplanned, or newly detected and are generally of such importance to a component, the CFC, or higher authority that they warrant prosecution within the current execution period." Targets that are not high priority are typically not suitable for dynamic targeting and are "developed for prosecution during a later execution period." US Air Force, Targeting: Air force Doctrine (Document 2-1.9), June 8, 2006, p. 18. A third type of attack here is not a form of affirmative targeting, but rather is typical air–ground interdiction on behalf of endangered ground troops.

36 Saletan, William, "In defense of drones," *Slate*, February 19, 2013, in which a 2008 Human Rights Watch report is quoted as emphasizing: "High civilian loss of life during airstrikes has almost always occurred during the fluid, rapid-response strikes, often carried out in support of ground troops after they came under insurgent attack."

8

Regulating Drones

Are Targeted Killings by Drones Outside Traditional Battlefields Legal?

WILLIAM C. BANKS

1. LAW AND TARGETED KILLINGS

Targeted killing is nasty business, however carried out. For the US government, the pace of targeted drone strikes has quickened dramatically in the early years of the Obama administration. If the use of sophisticated armed drone technology has become the contemporary weapon of choice for responding to terrorists and insurgents who wantonly cause civilian deaths, US policymakers, as well as society at large, have an obligation to see to it that the weapons and their use are subject to a tightly managed and accountable set of legal controls that are as transparent as possible.

After the George W. Bush administration deployed drones in the Afghanistan and Iraq wars and introduced cross-border strikes in Pakistan as an adjunct to the Afghan campaign, the Obama administration accelerated their use. Central to this process was the role of targeted killing as a key element of counterterrorism and counterinsurgency campaigns against al-Qaeda, the Taliban, and associated groups. As early as 2009, commenting on the use of drones for targeting killings in Pakistan, the former director of the CIA, Leon Panetta, said, "It's the only game in town in terms of confronting or trying to disrupt the al Qaeda leadership."[1] Meanwhile, public support for the policy was strong. A January 2012 ABC News–*Washington Post* poll found that 83 percent of Americans approved of the administration's use of drones for targeted killing of terrorist suspects.[2]

There are signs that drone strikes and targeted killing will remain a prominent US policy in the near term. Even as it prepared to absorb $487 billion in cuts over the next decade, the US Department of Defense (DoD) requested a substantial increase in its fiscal 2013 budget to Congress to fund a 30 percent expansion of its worldwide fleet of drones.[3] In February 2012, the Obama administration announced that it was teaming with the new government in Yemen to kill or capture about two dozen of al-Qaeda's most dangerous operatives, including those focused on attacking America and its interests.[4]

The decision to target specific individuals with lethal force after September 11 was neither unprecedented nor surprising. In fact, the United States has engaged in targeted killing since at least 1916, when it was first used during a border war with Mexican bandits.[5] In a time of war, subjecting individual combatants to lethal force has been a permitted and lawful instrument of waging war. Nevertheless, there are questions as to the elements of a lawful targeted killing policy that operates outside of a declared war, such as the military campaign against non-state enemies – al-Qaeda, the Taliban, and associated forces – outside the battle spaces of Iraq and Afghanistan, Pakistan, Yemen, Somalia, Libya, and elsewhere. Who may be legally targeted in these new battlefields, under what circumstances, and subject to which conditions? When, if ever, may a US citizen be targeted with lethal force in such contexts? These questions require answers backed up by established law and managed through appropriate policy.

2. DRONES AND TARGETED KILLING: NEW STRATEGIES FOR A NEW TYPE OF WAR

Predator drones were introduced to the Afghan battlefield in late 2001. However, the significance of their deployment changed dramatically on November 3, 2002, when a drone fired a Hellfire missile at a car in a remote part of the Yemeni desert.[6] This was the first use of an armed Predator outside Afghanistan or Iraq, and it killed Qaed Salim Sinan al-Harethi, a senior al-Qaeda leader.

Al-Harethi was described as among the most significant al-Qaeda figures in Yemen, one of the top ten to twelve al-Qaeda operatives in the world, and a suspect in the October 2000 suicide bombing at a Yemeni port of the destroyer USS *Cole* that killed seventeen US Navy personnel. US intelligence and law enforcement officials had been tracking his movements for months before the attack. During the strike against al-Harethi, five other al-Qaeda operatives were killed, including Kamal Derwish, an American citizen of Yemeni descent, who, according to FBI intelligence, recruited American Muslims to attend al-Qaeda training camps.[7]

Over the next decade, targeted killing operations employing drones operated by the CIA and US military became an integral part of the government's counterterrorism strategy. Over time, first in the Bush administration and then in an expanded and more aggressive strategy under the Obama administration, the United States has been conducting what the *New York Times* described as a "shadow war against al Qaeda and its allies": "In roughly a dozen countries – from the deserts of North Africa, to the mountains of Pakistan, to former Soviet republics crippled by ethnic and religious strife – the United States has significantly increased military and intelligence operations, pursuing the enemy using robotic drones and commando teams, paying contractors to spy and training local operatives to chase terrorists."[8]

As more details have emerged, the scale and dimensions of this shadow war have come into sharper, albeit still murky, focus. Unprecedented cooperation between military and CIA personnel has spurred a campaign to use missile-armed drones in multiple sites. Outside the Afghan battlefield, the US military has expanded its activities in part through drone bases in Djibouti, Ethiopia, the Seychelles, and at a secret location in the Arabian Peninsula.[9]

In a May 2010 speech, President Obama's top counterterrorism adviser, John O. Brennan, said that the administration favored using "a scalpel, not a hammer" in a "multigenerational" campaign against al-Qaeda and its affiliates.[10] In September 2011, several weeks after the Special Forces operation in Pakistan killed Osama bin Laden, Brennan stated:

> [T]he United States does not view our authority to use military force against al Qaeda as being restricted solely to "hot" battlefields like Afghanistan ... [W]e have the authority to take action against al Qaeda and its associated forces without doing a separate self-defense analysis each time ... That does not mean we can use military force whenever we want, wherever we want. International law principles, including respect for a state's sovereignty and the laws of war, impose important constraints on our ability to act unilaterally – and on the way in which we can use force – in foreign territories.[11]

Through the first three years of the Obama presidency, the administration built its targeted killing program through an extensive apparatus of secret facilities and operational hubs in the United States and at bases in at least six countries on two continents. By early 2012, nearly 800 Predators, Reapers, and other drones were in the US arsenal; more than 30 of them believed to be operated by the CIA.[12]

From late 2001 through the end of the Bush presidency, the United States launched 44 strikes, nearly all of them in Iraq, Afghanistan, and northwest Pakistan.[13] Since taking office, President Obama has authorized more than four times as many drone strikes as did the Bush administration throughout its two terms, many of them in Pakistan and some in Yemen, Somalia, and Libya.[14] In Yemen alone, the CIA and Special Forces have carried out nearly a dozen drone strikes against al-Qaeda operatives since May 2011.[15] Given the rise in drone use, what is the legal basis for targeted killing operations, especially those in the shadows outside the "hot" battlefields? To answer this question, it is useful to examine the lawfulness of a particularly complex case, the September 2011 strike in Yemen that killed US citizen Anwar al-Awlaki.

Under US law, the Obama administration has made a persuasive case that the president's constitutional defensive war powers and the 2001 Authorization for the Use of Military Force (AUMF) permit remote targeting where there is convincing evidence that the target is affiliated with al-Qaeda, is committed to carrying out terrorist attacks against Americans, and where an arrest or capture is not a feasible alternative to the use of lethal force. Furthermore, the administration does not believe that a longstanding executive order and its prohibition on assassination apply to a strike that meets the conditions identified above. However, are these legally valid claims? Does the killing of al-Awlaki raise additional legal issues given the constitutional protections accorded to him as a US citizen?

One of the murkiest legal areas concerning drone strikes in the shadow war is cooperation among the CIA, the military, and the role of Congress in providing oversight of this relationship. May the CIA lawfully engage in targeted killing? To what extent must the congressional intelligence oversight committees be informed about the shadow war operations? Do CIA paramilitary operations in Yemen require presidential authorization and/or notice to the intelligence committees? Do these requirements apply to secret military operations? What rules apply where CIA and military units coordinate their actions in a common operation?

Finally, from the perspective of international law, do relevant treaties and customary law on self-defense, international humanitarian law, and human rights law define these acts as illegal?

While there remain sharp disagreements among experts about the legality of these actions, drone strikes outside traditional battlefields may well be lawful under domestic and international law. Context and facts are decisive. Some critics claim that the United States is developing a policy that legitimizes killing anyone it wants, anywhere it wants.[16] While such a targeting policy would be unlawful, a careful assessment of US policy reveals a narrower approach that that is legally justifiable under national and international law. Nevertheless, to ensure that drone strikes are fully legal, they should be enabled and limited by formal authorization and controls within the government and structured in relation to the legitimate questions raised by both domestic critics and the international community.

3. COUNTERING TERRORISM IN THE SHADOWS: TARGETING ANWAR AL-AWLAKI

Anwar al-Awlaki was a Yemeni-American citizen who emerged in recent years as a leading English-language proponent of violent *jihad*, including explicit calls for the indiscriminate murder of Americans. The FBI first investigated al-Awlaki in 1999 in connection with his position in an Islamic charity suspected of siphoning funds to extremists, and because he had been indirectly connected to Osama bin Laden and Sheik Omar Abdel Rahman.

According to the United States, since 2006, al-Awlaki assumed an operational leadership role with al-Qaeda in the Arabian Peninsula (AQAP), recruiting and directing individuals to engage in the indiscriminate murder of Americans and others.[17] US officials later learned that al-Awlaki communicated from Yemen with Fort Hood shooter Major Nadal Malik Hassan. According to a Justice Department memorandum, al-Awlaki was also believed to be the principal operational planner in the unsuccessful 2009 Christmas day attempt by Umar Farouk Abdulmutallab to set off a bomb hidden in his underwear on a flight bound for Detroit.[18] In 2010 al-Awlaki publicly supported violence against American civilians.[19]

Between 2002, with the targeted killing of al-Harethi and his colleagues, and late 2009 there are no records of US drone strikes in Yemen. However, during this time journalists reported that the Yemeni government, supported by the United States, carried out attacks on AQAP targets

News reports indicate that al-Awlaki was added to a list of al-Qaeda-linked terrorists that the CIA was authorized to capture or kill. Administration officials asserted that every name on the list was carefully vetted to ensure clear evidence of responsibility for terrorist activities, and, as such, those on the list could be legitimately targeted under US law. Because al-Awlaki was a US citizen, placing him on the CIA list was also approved by the National Security Council.[20]

By summer 2010 CIA analysts rated the threat from AQAP as more grave and urgent than the dangers from the core al-Qaeda group based in Pakistan. Although the United States did not immediately then transfer its drones to Yemen from the war zones in Afghanistan and Iraq, a US airstrike in May 2010 targeted militants in the Marib Province.[21]

In recent years, the CIA and military Joint Special Operations Command (JSOC) have shared the airspace over Yemen, flying nearly identical aircraft and alternating on taking the lead in drone strikes. CIA and JSOC teams share intelligence and coordinate their attacks. When the CIA determined that al-Awlaki was in Yemen, it moved drones from Pakistan to Yemen.

Yemen's President Salah secretly granted the United States permission for the mission. On September 30, 2011, the CIA deployed two Predator drones, which pointed lasers at al-Awlaki's car, while a third circled over the target area to be certain that no civilians were in the area. Then one of the drones fired a missile that killed al-Awlaki.

The attack on al-Awlaki also killed a second US citizen, Samir Kahn, the editor of *Inspire*, the AQAP English-language online magazine. In addition, two weeks later, al-Awlaki's sixteen-year-old son was killed unintentionally when he was within a strike area where a suspected Egyptian terrorist was hit by a JSOC-fired drone.[22]

4. US LAW AND TARGETED KILLINGS OUTSIDE TRADITIONAL BATTLEFIELDS

The policy efficacy of drone strikes does not make them legal. For drone strikes to be acceptable, they must be supported by the law, not simply defined by the absence of clear legal violations, but through positive legal authority. Indeed, where the subject is intentional, premeditated killing by the government, the need for clear legal authority is paramount. After all, it is legal authority that distinguishes murder from lawful policy. While much of the debate about targeted killing has focused on international law, domestic law may supersede incorporated international law for understanding US policy and should be at least the starting point for legal analysis.[23]

Targeted killings – Under the Constitution, the president may order targeted killing to defend the United States in war. The president's authority as commander in chief to "repel sudden attacks"[24] has traditionally been interpreted as having a real-time dimension, a sort of imminence requirement that may be analogous to the doctrine of self-defense within international law. However, a terrorist attack is usually over before it can be repelled; and when there is a suicide attack, it is impossible to respond to those involved in the actual action. In addition, the United States has learned to expect terrorists to pursue a course of continuing attacks as part of a broad multiyear strategy. As such, over time the United States has developed domestic law of anticipatory self-defense that permits the president to use deadly force against a positively identified terrorist if other means of apprehension have been exhausted.[25] Congress has the legal authority to regulate this use of force and, in fact, has done so.[26]

Of course, the United States, like other governments, has long engaged in secret operations. The use of secret agents for gathering intelligence is a key element of foreign affairs and has often proved essential for the success of policy. There is no evidence, however, that the United States used targeted killing as an instrument of foreign policy until the early twentieth century. The first recorded instance was in 1916, when someone within Army General John Pershing's staff hired four Mexicans to kill revolutionary leader Francisco "Pancho" Villa by dropping poisoned tablets into his coffee. The attempt failed and Pershing hid the news of the mission, even from the president. The cover up lasted until the 1980s, when historians uncovered the story.[27]

Immediately after World War II, establishing legal controls on intelligence functions was a low priority in the larger wrangling over establishing a peacetime military and defining the role of the DoD. When the Cold War began to define security concerns in Europe and elsewhere, presidential directives and eventual legislation established the country's first publicly acknowledged peacetime intelligence functions. Although the National Security Act of 1947[28] authorized the newly created CIA to "perform such other functions and duties related to intelligence affecting the national security as the President or National Security Council may direct,"[29] it did not spell out in any detail the role of the intelligence agency or restrictions on its activities.

The law was designed to enable dynamic authority that would be shaped by practice and necessity. Over time, the agency's practices came to include targeted killing, especially of foreign leaders and others opposing or believed to be opposing US policy and threatening national security.[30] After the Church Committee investigation reported assassination plots by the CIA or its agents during the 1960s and early 1970s, President Ford issued an executive order prohibiting CIA involvement in assassinations (but notably not restricting targeted killing).[31]

Around the same time, Congress enacted intelligence oversight legislation that continues to require reporting by the president of significant anticipated intelligence operations, implicitly including those involving targeted killing or support for such acts. For example, the Hughes–Ryan Amendment to the Foreign Assistance Act of 1974 provided that no funds could be expended by the CIA on "operations in foreign countries, other than activities intended solely for obtaining necessary intelligence, unless and until"[32] the president finds that each operation is important to US national security. Furthermore, the law requires that where these cases may occur, a report including "a description and scope of such operation" must be presented to the intelligence committees. In other words, any use of targeted killing must include a finding containing the factual and policy predicates for the proposed act and must be personally approved by the president.[33] This law established for the first time in US history an explicit congressional role in reviewing covert actions by the CIA, including targeted killing, and it also linked the president directly to these actions, defining that position as personally accountable.[34]

Did Hughes–Ryan Amendment provide a sort of backhanded authorization for covert actions, including targeted killings? The historical record suggests that it is reasonable to understand that congressional knowledge and approval of CIA involvement in these operations, whether open or through the lack of critical response, might extend to targeted killing and thus broaden the statutory authority under the 1947 act.[35] With this in mind, the Hughes–Ryan Amendment allows CIA covert operations to be understood as operating with government authorization if findings are prepared and delivered to select members of Congress before the operation described, or in a "timely fashion" thereafter. That is, as long as the intelligence committees are kept "fully and currently informed," the law permits the president broad discretion to use the nation's intelligence agencies to carry out national security operations, arguably including targeted killing.[36]

The 1975 Ford Executive Order provided that "no employee of the United States government shall engage in, or conspire to engage in, political assassin-ation."[37] Although the record shows that President Ford opposed political assassination, the likely impetus for his executive order was an attempt to stop the then-building momentum in Congress to enact legislation following the Church Committee report that would have categorically banned assassin-ations. The record also makes clear that insertion of the "political" modifier was intended to limit application of the ban to officials of foreign govern-ments. In addition, like its successor orders, President Ford's order did not ban assassination absolutely, but instead insisted that it could not be lawfully undertaken without the president's approval.[38] By their nature, executive orders bind the president and others at whom their provisions are directed, until changed or revoked by either the president issuing the order or a subsequent president. The president could lift the ban or make exceptions, as long as doing so does not violate some other law.[39]

As modified by later presidents to eliminate the "political" qualifier on assassination, and to extend the prohibition to any person "acting on behalf of" the US government, Executive Order 12,333 continues to forbid direct or indirect US involvement in assassination. The order forbids US officials from encouraging any person "employed by or acting on behalf of" the United States to "directly or indirectly" carry out an assassination.[40]

The executive order is of limited utility in setting the domestic law framework for targeted killing. First, the order does not define "assassination" and there is no agreed-upon definition of the term. Some commentators assert that all assassination is murder and therefore unlawful.[41] Yet defining assassination as murder makes short work of analyzing its legality, and is logically circular in rendering lawful killings as "non-assassination." For this reason, some legal experts have attempted to carve out categories of lawful assassination, although without much success. The problem is heightened by our colloquial understanding of assassination as negative, destructive, and clearly illegal, conjuring up images of the murders of leaders such as Abraham Lincoln or John F. Kennedy. For this reason, it may be useful to reserve the term "assassination" for unlawful killing and to use the term "targeted killing" – the premeditated killing of an individual by a government or its agents – which may, in fact, be permitted under US law.

The answer to the question of when a premeditated killing of an individual by a government or its agents is assassination and when it is targeted killing depends on which legal framework applies. During wartime, the framework is the Constitution and international humanitarian law (IHL), understood by the US military as the Law of Armed Conflict (LOAC). Under these bodies of law, many examples of targeted killing are lawful, so long as they meet a set of standards that have wide global acceptance. Nevertheless, even in war, killing by treacherous means is not permitted. During peacetime the framework is, again, the Constitution coupled with a well-defined body of domestic criminal law. Under this body of law, an extra-judicial killing by a government agent would only be lawful if undertaken in self-defense or for the defense of others.

However, neither of these frameworks provide adequate guidance for addressing the demands of countering terrorists and insurgents. This leaves the United States with a number of vexing questions. What legal framework applies when the country is under threat of continuing terrorist attack? When is targeted killing lawful in the shadows between war and peace, and when is it unlawful and therefore assassination?

Applying the domestic legal framework to terrorists and insurgents in the post-9/11 context depends on whether the target falls within a group of persons positively identified as operational participants in actual or planned attacks against the United States and whether the targeted killing takes place in an armed conflict or war authorized by declaration, statute, or attack upon the United States. In addition, it is necessary to consider whether the target was selected to defend against continuing, imminent, or impossible-to-repel attacks. Finally, even if the executive order banning assassination would otherwise apply, it is important to know whether it has been waived or rescinded by the president.

The legality of decisions to engage in targeted killing may also be supported by Congress's September 14, 2001, AUMF, providing the president with the authority to use "all necessary and appropriate force" against "persons he determines planned, authorized, committed, or aided the terrorist attacks" of September 11.[42] The sweeping authority granted in the resolution is neither time-limited, nor does it have a geographic constraint. In addition, the AUMF does not limit the president's discretion on selecting targets as long as they are connected to the September 11 attack and to al-Qaeda.

For example, the targeted killing of Osama bin Laden was lawful through the clear application of the AUMF. He and other al-Qaeda leaders demonstrated their intentions to engage in ongoing and imminent threats against the United States that could not be effectively addressed in a different, less aggressive, and less lethal manner. Every president in the last three decades has made secret presidential findings authorizing targeted killings, including Ronald Reagan against Muamar Qaddafi prior to an air strike on Libya in 1984; William Clinton against bin Laden before targeting a terrorist training camp in Afghanistan in 1998; George W. Bush against bin Laden and his associates after 9/11; and Barack Obama in multiple cases involving al-Qaeda operatives and others, including those killed by drones.

The targeting of "terrorists" was first explicitly mentioned in 1995 in an executive order by President Clinton, which introduced a category of "specially designated terrorists" on a list maintained by the Secretary of State and the Treasury Office of Foreign Assets Control.[43] The CIA has been authorized since 1998 to use covert means to disrupt and preempt terrorist operations planned by bin Laden, and to use lethal force against a short list of named targets, but only if capture was not feasible.[44] The Clinton administration directive was affirmed by President George W. Bush before September 11 based on evidence linking al-Qaeda to the August 1998 bombings of US embassies in Africa. Following the September 11 attacks, the Bush administration amended the finding a second time, expanding CIA discretion by omitting the list of named targets and removing the feasibility of capture as a condition.[45] In addition, the 2001 finding was apparently modified in 2006 by President Bush to broaden the class of potential targets beyond bin Laden and his inner circle, and also extend the boundaries beyond Afghanistan.[46]

Reportedly, President Obama did not change the CIA authority to choose targets and launch drone strikes in Pakistan. Outside Afghanistan and Pakistan, all drone strikes to date have required White House approval, whether executed by the CIA or the military.[47] The authority given in these presidential findings is surely the most sweeping and most lethal since the founding of the CIA. These findings contemplate a high and unprecedented degree of cooperation among the CIA, Special Forces, and other military units.

Targeting US citizens – Under what conditions could a US citizen lawfully be subject to a drone attack, conducted by the CIA or the military? Before September 11, the government's authority to kill a citizen outside the judicial process was generally restricted to situations where the individual is directly threatening the lives of other Americans or their allies.[48] However, President Obama's intelligence finding specifically listed US citizen targets. In addition, the AUMF authorizes strikes against al-Qaeda operatives. There may thus be two sources of statutory authority to use lethal force against an American.

There is no doubt that the Constitution prohibits targeted killing of US citizens inside the United States. But why? The due process clause protects "any person" from being "deprived of life ... without due process of law." Capital punishment is not unlawful because it is imposed with the full judicial process of criminal law. However, extra-judicial killing ordinarily lacks such process. In addition, the Fourth Amendment protection against unreasonable seizures would foreclose killing a suspect when apprehension is possible unless there is a risk of serious harm to the arresting officers or others.

How does the constitutional framework apply abroad? The Supreme Court has held that "the people" protected by the Fourth Amendment do not include aliens outside the United States who lack "substantial connections with this country."[49] Clearly, however, US citizens enjoy Fourth and Fifth Amendments protections abroad. In addition, whether or not persons abroad may invoke constitutional rights, US officials are required by the Constitution to find positive legal authority to conduct targeted killing.[50] While no court approved the targeting of al-Awlaki, it is not clear that he was necessarily denied due process protection. That is, context has driven the demands of due process for a long time and, as this targeted killing was ordered during an ongoing conflict against al-Qaeda and its affiliates, it is reasonable that the targeting decision would be left to the president and Congress according to their own internal and often secret processes. To support this claim it is useful to note that the congressional intelligence committees were informed that al-Awlaki had been placed on a list of potential targets.

Reportedly multiple intelligence sources concluded that al-Awlaki was a dangerous and continuing threat to the United States, and lawyers from various government agencies reviewed the intelligence and targeting criteria and agreed with the determination that no capture or arrest option was available.

The Obama administration developed a legal memorandum more than a year before al-Awlaki was targeted.[51] This was in response to a 2010 lawsuit filed by al-Awlaki's father, who sought to enjoin the anticipated targeting.[52]

The legal memorandum concluded that al-Awlaki was within the range of targets contemplated by the AUMF, based on intelligence indicating that he had become an operational leader within AQAP, was planning to attack the United States, and that capturing him alive or arresting him was not feasible. The memorandum asserted that the United States remained in an armed conflict with al-Qaeda and its affiliates, which had attacked the country or were planning attacks.[53] According to the memorandum, the executive order banning assassinations would not apply to the killing of a lawful target in an armed conflict. Similarly, the federal criminal law prohibiting the government from killing US citizens would not apply when the individual is targeted in a manner consistent with IHL. The memorandum also maintained that it would not matter for adherence to IHL or domestic law, if the drone operator who fired the missile at al-Awlaki worked for the CIA.

In a March 2012 speech, Attorney General Eric Holder highlighted the administration's positions on its legal authority to use lethal force for targeted killing generally and against a US citizen consistent with the Fifth Amendment.[54] He noted that the amendment's due process clause has no "one-size-fits-all requirements, but instead mandates procedural safeguards that depend on specific circumstances." Nor does the Fifth Amendment require that the president obtain targeting permission from a federal court. Taking contextual factors into account, Attorney General Holder affirmed that under US law targeting "authority is not limited to the battlefields of Afghanistan," and that a citizen abroad could be targeted if he has a senior operational role with al-Qaeda or an associated force, is involved in plotting focused on killing Americans, the threat of an attack is imminent, capture is not feasible, and the strike complies with IHL principles. Concerning the critical question of what is meant by the "imminence" of a threat, Attorney General Holder said that relevant considerations include "the possible harm that missing the window would cause to civilians, and the likelihood of heading off future disastrous attacks against the United States." He explained that the Constitution "does not require the President to delay action until some theoretical end-stage of planning – when the precise time, place, and manner of an attack becomes clear" and that such a requirement would subject the country to "an unacceptably high risk."[55]

In this way, Attorney General Holder made a strong case for targeting in general and as applied specifically to al-Awlaki. However, missing from the attorney general's analysis is any description of the internal review procedures employed by the military or CIA personnel in targeting, and how, given a particular set of circumstances, the feasibility of capture is determined. If due process protections are to be satisfied by something other than a judicial procedure, the administration's legal posture would be strengthened if the processes used by the executive were clearly defined and more fundamentally transparent.

The statutory framework for intelligence operations is open-ended, complex, and textured, and oversight by Congress is far from perfect. Still, the evolving legislative framework encourages a considerable amount of information sharing within the intelligence committees. As amended several times since 1980, oversight legislation requires that the president keep the intelligence committees "fully and currently informed" of "significant anticipated intelligence activities." A targeted killing abroad carried out by the CIA would require that the president submit a finding and report to the intelligence committees.[56] By 1991, the first statutory definition of "covert action" also made it clear that a targeted killing by the CIA would fall within the definition.

In his findings, the president must determine that a covert action is "necessary to support identifiable foreign policy objectives of the United States, and is important to the national security of the United States," and he must specify which US agencies or third-party elements not part of the US government are authorized to participate in any significant way in the covert action.[57] No US funds may be expended for a covert action "unless and until a Presidential finding" has been made in accordance with the oversight act. The 1991 amendments preserve the option for the president to limit notice to a small group of congressional leaders in "extraordinary circumstances," and presumably to withhold it altogether in rare cases, subject to subsequent reporting "in a timely fashion."[58]

It is also true that the conventional constitutional understanding of "war" does not fit the al-Awlaki targeted killing very well. Though it is legal to target soldiers with lethal force during wartime, including US citizens serving with the enemy armed forces, the al-Awlaki case is legally different. The scope and nature of the battlefield outside Afghanistan is not clearly marked or agreed upon; who counts as the "enemy" is likewise a matter of dispute; and the overlap between such a targeted killing and criminal law enforcement requires a careful evaluation of the factual context before legally authorizing a drone strike. In this way, the term "war" may obscure rather than clarify the pertinent legal authorities.

Still, the combination of the authority given by Congress to the president as commander in chief in the AUMF and the intelligence oversight legislation, along with the president's defensive war powers, provide adequate domestic legal authority for targeted killing in the shadows and outside of hot battlefields. However, this is only true provided that the factual predicates emphasized by the Department of State and Department of Justice exist in the individual case under review. For a case of targeted killing to be legally acceptable, the government must identify the target as an operational partici-pant in terrorist attacks against the United States, there must be an imminent threat of continuing attacks, and officials must determine that capture or arrest is not feasible. Since these pre-conditions were met in the al-Awlaki case, it is reasonable to conclude that he was lawfully targeted.

5. INTERNATIONAL LAW AND TARGETED KILLING OUTSIDE TRADITIONAL BATTLEFIELDS

Within international law, targeted killings by drones outside of conventional wars and armed conflicts remain very controversial. These counterterrorism and counterinsurgency operations in the shadows may be conducted at least partly outside the UN Charter-based regime and established IHL. In addition, some opponents of the US targeted killing policy assert that the drone strikes violate international Human Rights Law (HRL) and that capture, arrest, and prosecution of the terrorists or insurgents should follow implementation of law enforcement mechanisms and processes.[59] Former UN Special Rapporteur Philip Alston asserted "outside the context of armed conflict, the use of drones for targeted killing is almost never likely to be legal."[60]

In a March 2010 speech, State Department Legal Adviser Harold Koh offered a vigorous defense of the use of force against terrorists under international law, including the targeting of persons "such as high-level al Qaeda leaders who are planning attacks."[61] Koh indicated that each such strike is analyzed beforehand based on "considerations specific to each case, including those related to the imminence of the threat, the sovereignty of the states involved, [and] the willingness and ability of those states to suppress the threat the target poses." Koh stated that, because we are in an armed conflict with al-Qaeda, the Taliban, and associated forces, the United States "may use force consistent with its inherent right of self-defense under inter-national law."[62]

According to Koh, al-Qaeda continues to present an imminent threat to the United States such that "the United States has the authority under international law, and the responsibility to its citizens, to use force, including lethal force, to defend itself." Accordingly, targeting decisions are made case-by-case, based on "the imminence of the threat"; "the sovereignty of the other states involved"; and "the willingness and ability of those states to suppress the threat the target poses."[63] Koh added that IHL principles must be followed in any such targeting, including the core principles of distinction and proportionality. The IHL principle of military necessity is also ascertained by virtue of the imminence criterion noted above.

Attorney General Holder reiterated Legal Advisor Koh's description of the international law justification for targeting in his March 2012 address. Holder agreed that the United States has international law authority "to target specific senior operational leaders of al Qaeda and associated forces."[64] The attorney general summarized the pertinent IHL principles that apply, including the requirement to avoid using weapons that cause unnecessary suffering. In fact, Holder suggested that advanced weaponry might well minimize the risk of civilian casualties.

International Humanitarian Law – The international law directly relevant to targeted killing includes the UN Charter, and treaty-based and customary IHL, especially *jus ad bellum* (the law regulating how parties can engage in war) and *jus in bello* (the law regulating how parties should act during war). Articles 2 and 51 of the UN Charter protect national borders and sovereign prerogatives when it comes to the use of force, while preserving states legal right of self-defense. The *jus ad bellum* requirements are normative, and in the context of drone strikes, they focus largely on whether the host state has consented to the incursion, as well as issues of military necessity and proportionality. As a subset of international law, the *jus in bello* element of IHL applies only when an armed conflict exists and limits drone strikes in ways that are identical to well-accepted restrictions on other weapons.

The right of states to employ force in self-defense has long been understood to be a core element of customary international law. Self-defense was codified in Article 51 of the UN Charter, which provides: "Nothing in the present Charter shall impair the inherent right of individual or collective self-defense if an armed attack occurs against a Member of the United Nations, until the Security Council has taken measures necessary to maintain international peace and security."[65]

Although the United States relies on Article 51 to justify its drone strikes, the clause must be read alongside the parallel provision in Article 2, which obligates all members states to "refrain ... from the threat or use of force against the territorial integrity or political independence of any state."[66]

In practice, following an attack by a suspect who is at large in another state, states must and generally do follow a regularized process, through diplomatic channels, where a victimized state asks the sanctuary state to remove the threat by arrest or other means. If the state meets its obligation, no self-defense right to use military force in the sanctuary state exists. If the state is unable or unwilling to take action necessary to remove the threat against the victim state, that state may use military force (including drone strikes) in self-defense.[67]

Resembling an exhaustion of remedies requirement, the obligation by the victimized state to determine whether the host state can and will remove the threat plays out in dynamic circumstances, especially in today's shadow wars.

An additional complicating factor in assessing the international legality of drone strikes is the non-state identity of the enemies in the shadow wars. The charter, IHL, and customary international law was developed to control the use of force by states, and self-defense was thought by many to be available only in response to armed attacks by states on states.[68] Yet the text of Article 51 does not specify the source of the armed attack that gives rise to the right of self-defense. Since 9/11, state practice has recognized a right of self-defense against non-state actors. There have been non-state actor attacks on states throughout history, of course, but international law conventionally left them for control by law enforcement and domestic laws. The 9/11 attacks changed the law in this critical respect; if not overnight, soon thereafter. The UN Security Council, NATO, and several states acted in self-defense against terrorists thereafter, including the United States in Afghanistan and Israel responding to Hezbollah in Lebanon.

The defensive use of force – targeted at a known al-Qaeda leader, for example – also has firm legal roots in customary international law. In making operational decisions like the ones made to strike with the Predator in Afghanistan, Yemen, or Pakistan, international and US laws concerning self-defense permits targeting al-Qaeda combatants, although carrying out the strike in Yemen rather than on a traditional battlefield complicates the international legal issues. Whether waged against the United States by a state or a non-state terrorist organization, war is defined by what it does, not by the identity of the perpetrator. Still, the law has not yet evolved to account adequately for the twilight zone between conventional war and conventional peace, when nations are subject to the continuing threat of terrorist attack.

In the particular context of targeted strikes against individuals, the self-defense justification has matured and sharpened, as articulated by the Obama administration, to focus on the imminence of the continuing threat posed by the target. Combining self-defense and IHL principles, a targeted strike must be militarily necessary, demonstrated by the host state being unwilling or unable to remove the threat and by the victimized state showing that the strike will likely prevent further attacks.[69] In Pakistan, consent may be as much a matter of domestic and international politics as tactical and strategic considerations on the ground. In Yemen, consent may or not be realistically obtainable depending on the region of Yemen under consideration.[70]

In Yemen, one alternative to the drone strikes in 2002 and 2011 was a "snatch and grab" operation conducted by a squad of commandos, deployed by helicopters from ships in the Red Sea. In discussions with Yemeni officials, that option was rejected because it was feared that a ground operation could ignite a guerrilla war. Armed Predator drones had been flying over Yemen for some time, awaiting targets of opportunity. According to US officials, Yemeni government officials were aware of the surveillance and of potential strikes against al-Qaeda.

In fact, the Yemeni government increased its cooperation with the US effort in the months before the November 2002 strike. This occurred after US officials complained of a lack of cooperation in investigating the USS *Cole* bombing and other terrorist attacks where suspects hiding in Yemen were potentially involved. Although Yemen sought to conduct its own counterterrorism operations near its remote and largely lawless border with Saudi Arabia, a principal sanctuary for al-Qaeda operatives, a December 2001 operation led to heavy Yemeni casualties.[71]

If Yemen consented to the al-Awlaki strike, the legal analysis under international law is simplified, because Article 2 is satisfied and the Article 51 self-defense argument is no longer necessary. The 2002 Yemen strike was conducted after considerable cooperation between US and Yemeni officials, including a joint US–Yemen intelligence team.[72] Although it is impossible to find definitive evidence of Yemeni government consent on the public record, there are reports of Yemeni President Saleh agreeing to give US military and CIA personnel a green light to attack al Qaeda targets in Yemen.[73] The agreement pre-dates the 2002 al-Harethi drone strike, and the continuation of a cooperative venture by US and Yemeni officials and their forces (from the end of 2009 into 2011) has been documented by journalists. Because Yemen has attempted to keep its cooperation with the United States quiet, details are hard to come by, including any specific indication that Yemen approved the al-Awlaki strike.

If the evidence of Yemen's consent is insufficient legally, the international law right of self-defense recognized in Article 51 nonetheless supports the strike. Focusing on the narrow question of whether the United States may use force targeted at an individual in Yemen based on self-defense against AQAP, the case is strong as applied to the al-Awlaki attack. Treating AQAP as a stand-alone entity, the case for self-defense begins with the bombing of the USS *Cole* in Yemen in 2000, and mortar attacks and car bombing of the US embassy in Yemen by AQAP in 2008. More recently, AQAP attempted to destroy passenger and cargo jets bound to the United States in 2009 and 2010, and al-Awlaki's conspiring with "the underwear bomber" Abdulmutallab and Major Hasan at Fort Hood strengthen the case.[74]

Because Yemen has a duty to ensure that its territory is not used as a base for attacks against others, the victim state must only demand that the host state remove the threat and give some reasonable time for it to respond before exercising the self-defense use of force. There is also debate concerning the legal authority to use self-defense against a non-state target in a sanctuary state, but there is a strong argument by those who support what we might call the "host state responsibility" position that victim states may use force in self-defense against non-state targets if the host state is simply unable to control the threat – what has been called the "failed or impotent state" exception.[75] The exception has direct bearing on AQAP and some parts of Yemen.[76]

Like Article 51, IHL limits the exercise of self-defense against non-state actors. Whether the Article 51 understandings of necessity, proportionality, and distinction are substantively different than their IHL contents is unclear, yet these can also be used to evaluate the al-Awlaki strike. Under IHL, the principles of distinction, necessity, and proportionality would certainly limit drone strikes, as they do any other use of force, in an armed conflict. However, instead of the threshold requirement that there be an "armed attack" for invoking Article 51, uses of force against a state that do not meet the conditions of an armed conflict are regulated by customary international law, HRL, and domestic law. Although it is debatable whether transnational terrorism and al-Qaeda's attacks emanating from Yemen constitute an armed conflict, emerging state practice, and the view of many scholars, is that non-state transnational terrorism may rise to the level of an international armed conflict (IAC) or non-international armed conflict (NIAC) under IHL. The United States appears to consider transnational terrorism a form of NIAC and, as such, IHL and its principles apply.[77]

One of the most vexing challenges in IHL that extends to drone use is identifying lawful targets, an essential component in complying with the principle of distinction. Legitimate targets under IHL include combatants, members of organized armed groups, and civilians directly participating in hostilities. If a legitimate target is identified, he may be struck without any evidence of a threat to the attacking force.[78] Terrorists and insurgents do not wear uniforms, are not part of an identifiable state army, and often intentionally mingle with and carry out their attacks from within civilian areas.

Within the shadowy zone of terrorist threats, it is not clear exactly what distinguishes a combatant, and thus a proper target, from a civilian who may not be targeted. Nor has it been settled what evidence is adequate to warrant targeting with lethal force against someone who does not wear a uniform and who does not fight for a sovereign state, yet is implicated in terrorist activities. Since 9/11, the view of the United States and its allies is that someone who is positively identified as an al-Qaeda operative may be targeted on the basis of membership in an organized armed group as defined by IHL.[79]

Outside an armed conflict, an individual may be targeted with lethal force by a state acting in self-defense only when the state credibly maintains that the target poses an imminent threat of future attacks. Some have worried that the IHL status-based targeting and self-defense conduct-based targeting may have merged in the legal justifications offered by the United States for its drone strikes. A careful review of the Obama administration statements, however, shows that the administration has maintained the distinctions between the two regimes. Even though both IHL and self-defense may support the al-Awlaki targeting and other strikes in the shadow wars, the administration has identified who the enemy is in its armed conflict and it has stated that only individuals meeting strict requirements would be targeted and only if the three factors mentioned above are met: positive identification as a terrorist threat, imminence of the continuing threat, and unwillingness or inability of the host state to remove the threat.

An evolving understanding of what it means to be a civilian who is involved in the "direct participation in hostilities" (DPH) focuses attention on the status of the target. Under IHL, such persons may be targeted "during and for such time" as they are engaged in DPH.[80] As with application of the principle of distinction more generally, targeting such a civilian must be tied to an armed conflict. According to the law of self-defense, the criterion for targeting is imminence of the threat, not status of the target, and the United States has offered clear justifications for targeting under the DPH standard as well. Some assert that the US government's adoption of the International Committee of the Red Cross (ICRC) interpretive guidance that allows targeting civilians who are members of an armed group when they have a "continuous combat function" (CCF) enables substituting a status determination for the factual questions required by the "for such time" portion of DPH.[81]

However, the United States has continued to make both status and conduct determinations on a case-by-case basis in its targeting. The CCF concept allows for the targeting of a terrorist operative who, for example, carries out his attack and then begins his shift at the local bakery. According to the ICRC, a person becomes part of an "armed group" by virtue of his "continuous function for the group involving his or her direct participation in hostilities."[82] This approach allows terrorists and insurgents to be viewed as combatants as a matter of law.

Does it matter under international law that the target of an American drone strike is a US citizen? The short answer is: not in this case. As an operational leader of AQAP, al-Awlaki was a combatant or a civilian taking direct part in hostilities in an ongoing armed conflict with al-Qaeda or AQAP. Thus, he could be targeted on the basis of his status or his conduct. Self-defense law also permits the use of lethal force against any target that presents an imminent threat of continuing attacks against the United States. Like the US citizen who was part of the World War II German saboteur team in Ex Parte Quirin,[83] US citizenship did not stand in the way of the prosecution of persons as "enemies who have violated the law of war."[84]

Regarding proportionality, targeting an individual – al-Awlaki or someone else – is certainly proportionate to the attacks AQAP has attempted against the United States. The IHL principle requires that parties refrain from attacks where the expected civilian casualties will be excessive in relation to the anticipated military advantage. By their nature, drone strikes afford greater precision than conventional air strikes. In addition, the IHL rule requires balancing civilian losses against the military advantage expected to be gained by the attack, as determined by the military commander. The more common objection is that the drone strikes may generate more sympathy for AQAP and anger and resentment toward the United States and the Yemeni government. This may well present a powerful critique, but it is a criticism of a policy decision, not evidence of a failure to respect existing law.

What does international law in general, or IHL in particular, have to say about the status of individuals operating drones? The question focuses on the CIA most prominently, yet could also be asked of civilian contractors. The answer is, not much. For the CIA, international law does not forbid those who are not members of the armed forces from participating in armed conflict.[85] Instead, those who operate drones become "unprivileged belligerents." This means that, despite being civilians, they lose their protected status by participating in hostilities.[86] As such, CIA or contractor personnel can be lawfully targeted by the enemy, and if captured they would not be entitled to POW status or immunity from prosecution. In addition, both CIA personnel and contractors could be prosecuted under the domestic law of any country from which they conduct drone strikes, and could also be prosecuted for violating US laws.

As outlined above, the CIA has the domestic legal authority to carry out targeted killing by drone strikes. Nevertheless, the legitimacy of these policies would be heightened with greater public clarity as to the substantive and procedural aspects of their involvement in these controversial strikes. The CIA may be in the process of improving training for those involved in the drone program and may have rigorous guidelines for the processes and criteria for targeting. However, at present, it is impossible to find confirmation of these developments in the public domain. Executive branch and congressional oversight has not been transparent, and, in fact, there is little detailed guidance on just what oversight is required.

Doctrines of avoidance have practically foreclosed a role for the courts in reviewing the CIA role (or the role of the military in targeted killing, for that matter),[87] and occasionally lucid and helpful media reports must rely on leaks from the CIA or elsewhere inside the classified environment. Even if most of us accept that secrecy is a necessary element of intelligence gathering in modern governance, licensing the CIA to use lethal force under an open-ended statutory or executive order rubric is ill advised.

Related to the concerns about the CIA operating in violation of international law is the tendency of the United States to mount many of its drone strikes as joint CIA–DoD operations. To be sure, domestic law questions at the heart of the so-called "Title 10/Title 50 debate" (the two titles of the US Code where military and intelligence activities are authorized and regulated by Congress) are complex and understudied, at least until recently.[88] Still, to the extent that United States targeted killing operations have converted spies into soldiers and soldiers into intelligence operatives, the bases for assessing accountability are further blurred, leading to the erosion of the international legal credibility of the operations.

International Human Rights Law – How does human rights law apply to drone strikes in the shadow wars? During an armed conflict, force may be used as a first resort against individuals identified as the enemy. Under HRL, the dominant international law framework where there is no armed conflict, armed force is permitted only as a last resort. Whereas an individual who is part of the enemy in an armed conflict may be targeted under IHL, the use of lethal force under HRL is permitted only when the individual poses a direct threat to others at the time of targeting. While IHL tolerates the incidental loss of life as long as the losses are proportionate to the military objective, under HRL no incidental casualties are permitted. As noted above, since the 9/11 attacks, the United States has considered itself engaged in an armed conflict with al-Qaeda, the Taliban, and associated forces wherever their operatives may be found and it has maintained that self-defense principles support the use of military force against those targets.

To the extent that the shadow wars occur where there is an armed conflict – and this is a reasonable conclusion as regards AQAP at the time of al-Awlaki's death – the United States does not believe that HRL applies. This is because IHL is regarded as *lex specialis*, special law, used for managing state power and other issues within a "special" context: in this case, war. So, HRL would apply to the al-Awlaki drone strike and other attacks in the shadow wars only where there is no armed conflict or based on the understanding that HRL may apply alongside IHL. That is, even within armed conflicts, HRL supplies an important set of general rules and limitations relevant to state action, such as drone strikes.

For example, the foundational idea of HRL is the right to life, which imposes the necessity requirement on the use of deadly force.[89] HRL concepts also inform ideas such as a preference for the use of non-lethal means and issues of imminence.[90] In other words, as long as the United States had substantial reason to believe that al-Awlaki was continuing to play a leadership role in planning attacks against the country and that he could not realistically be captured or arrested, he could be killed consistent with HRL.

However, US legal advisers did not choose to select either IHL or HRL in analyzing drone strikes in general or the al-Awlaki attack in particular. Perhaps following the lead of the Israeli Supreme Court in the 2006 *Targeted Killings* decision, the US position combines IHL and HRL considerations. The US government applies IHL based on the determination that there is an ongoing armed conflict against al-Qaeda, the Taliban, and associated groups in which terrorist operatives are understood to be members of an armed group within IHL, thus permitting targeting at any time upon positive identification. The United States also applies HRL concepts of reviewing whether arrest or capture is possible before deciding to use a lethal strike. Although an interest in arrest or capture may be viewed as an element of IHL proportionality, it also expresses core HRL commitments to respecting the right to life and due process protections, illustrating a convergence of frameworks that is occurring in the post-9/11 world of terrorist and insurgent violence.

Overreliance on international law in analyzing drone strikes – Most of the criticism leveled by legal experts at the US targeted killing policy in general, and at the al-Awlaki strike in particular, allege violations of international law. Unsurprisingly, the substantial energy that has been invested by US legal advisers in offering a legal rationale for targeted killing and drone use, including targeting US citizens, has also focused on international law. Though understandable given the international controversy generated by the policy, it is unfortunate that the legal picture has focused largely on inter-national law. In part this is because, as mentioned above, US domestic law may supersede inconsistent international law, whatever its contents and sources. In addition, the focus on international law may draw attention away from the need for significant reform of domestic law and institutions for addressing the issues raised in drone strikes.

In any case, the defense of targeting offered by State Department Legal Adviser Harold Koh is persuasive, leaving only a few unsettled international law questions. Outside the "hot" battlefields, drone strikes in the shadow wars may or may not be amenable to the *jus in bello* principles of IHL and to HRL. The evolving customary understanding of self-defense permits drone strikes against a non-state target in the shadows, based on host-state consent, an impotent state, and an imminent threat posed by the target. The United States has, as a matter of policy, followed the IHL *jus in bello* principles of military necessity, distinction, and proportionality in assessing targeting decisions prior to each drone strike.

Regarding Yemen and the al-Awlaki attack, it is likely that the Yemeni government consented to the September 2011 strike, as it had to the 2002 targeting. If Yemen consented, the UN Charter requirements were met and the self-defense argument is superfluous. If the evidence of consent is insufficient, the case for self-defense against al-Awlaki is strongly based on the US government's presentation of evidence of his personal leadership role in operations between 2009 and 2010. In this sense, al-Awlaki was lawfully targeted based on his positive identification as a terrorist threat, the imminence of his continuing threat, and the unwillingness or inability of Yemen to remove the threat. Although the United States and some other nations view IHL as *lex specialis* when an armed conflict is ongoing, the United States also seriously considered HRL in its assessment of targeted drone strikes. The right to life protection in HRL may be subordinated in al-Awlaki's case on the basis of the imminence of the threat he posed and the unrealistic prospects for his capture or arrest.

However, from an international law perspective, the significant shortcoming in the US policy is its lack of transparency. Particularly when implemented by the CIA, but only slightly less so when carried out by JSOC, drone strikes are secretive, both legally and practically. As a consequence, the international legal obligation of the United States to ensure that its use of force is accountable cannot at present be met, under IHL or HRL.[91] If the United States does nothing to remediate its domestic law rules and processes along these lines, this international legal precedent will likely open the door for other states to pursue the use of drone strikes untethered by legal constraints.

6. DRONE STRIKES AND NEW BATTLEFIELDS: THE NEED FOR MORE EFFECTIVE LAW AND POLICY

The wars of the foreseeable future are not likely to be conventional state-on-state military conflicts. Irregular wars will be fought across a spectrum of battlefields – some physical and some virtual – and by a mind-numbing array of means, from traditional military hardware, to pilotless drones, to other semi-autonomous or even autonomous machines with directed energy weapons systems, and to cyber and electronic warfare. There is no question that the use of lethal drones has become the counterterrorism weapon of choice for the United States in recent years, for use in hot battlefields as well as in the shadow wars that are and will continue to take place in weak or failing states where local governments are either unwilling or unable to address serious threats on their own. The legal questions surrounding drone use outside traditional battlefields are complex and unsettled, though tentative answers are being developed through largely US state practice, one drone strike at a time.

Apart from the law, are the drone strikes in the shadows efficacious? A senior US military official said that among the surviving leaders and foot soldiers in al-Qaeda: "[The death of al-Awlaki] sets a sense of doom for the rest of them ... [the strike] increases the sense of fear. It's hard for them to attack when they're trying to protect their own backside ... Bottom line, they've taken a severe impact."[92]

But others, such as Audrey Kurth Cronin, argue that the drones program may be tactically successful in the short-term but not helpful in defeating al-Qaeda in the longer term. She maintains that drones "may be creating sworn enemies out of a sea of local insurgents."[93] So, regardless of the legality of targeted killing with drones, there are many complex policy and ethical considerations, such as whether drone strikes are, in fact, effective or counter-productive in addressing global terrorism; whether there are core ethical failures in a policy that kills persons not wearing enemy uniforms without any transparent judicial process; and whether there are broad implications for warfare practiced by civilian or military "pilots" operating unmanned vehicle from thousands of miles away.

Throughout history the law has failed to keep up with changes in the dynamics of military conflicts. In domestic law, no law specifically author-izes or controls lethal targeting by drones, whether operated by the military, the CIA, or contractors. When Congress reacted to the gravity of the 9/11 attacks by enacting the AUMF, they understandably authorized the broadest authority for the president as commander in chief to attack those connected to the responsible parties. Yet more than a decade later, no revisions of the AUMF have been enacted, and there has been no recogni-tion by Congress that the United States is now fighting irregular wars in the shadows. Nowhere is the weakness of the legal regime more glaring than in its treatment of targeted killing. The relevant spheres of authority overlap – the laws of the United States (constitutional, statutory, and executive) and international laws (treaty-based and customary, IHL, and HRL).

The relationship of these spheres of authority to one another and their application as binding law remains unclear and contentious.

In at least one respect, the emerging shadow wars call into question the role of Congress. After enacting the AUMF and giving President George W. Bush expansive authority to invade Iraq, Congress learned that the expanding involvement in the shadow wars – including lethal targeting with drones in Pakistan, Yemen, and Somalia – bore little risk of US casualties. Despite the hundreds of drone strikes that have been carried out in these states since 2004, there has been no debate and not a single vote in Congress either in favor of or in opposition to the targeted killing policy outside traditional battlefields.

These new battlefields require adaptations of old laws, both domestic and international.[94] The authority for targeted killing may be found within the existing domestic and international law. However, the foundational authorities are not well formed, and there has been little deliberative attention toward modernizing the law to reflect the modern battlefield. Congress should enact policies and set legal criteria for the use of force against non-state enemies that operate in the shadows. In addition, the pertinent executive order continues to use the term "assassination" without definition or limitation, creating ambiguity and misunderstandings of its impact and policy significance. Congress and the president should supply definitions distinguishing assassination and targeted killing, and Congress should revisit its intelligence oversight legislation to make explicit the inclusion of targeted killing within the scope of the legislation's presidential finding and notice requirements.

In terms of specific targeting authority, Congress should replace the AUMF with a more fine-grained authorization for the use of military force against terrorists. This should involve supplying clear criteria for the use of force in self-defense, including targeted killings, within and outside what are regarded as traditional battlefields. In addition, Congress should establish processes that must be followed before carrying out a strike. Is functional membership in al-Qaeda or a related group sufficient? Must the target be taking a direct part in hostilities? Does this mean the he must be engaged in preparing for an imminent attack against the United States? Or is providing financial or logistical support to terrorists enough to permit targeting with lethal force? To what extent should the consent of a sovereign state be required before military force is used against terrorists who seek refuge in that state? These refinements would improve the legal framework for targeted killing and they would divide the labor more appropriately and more in line with constitutional provisions on the proper relationship between the distinct branches of government. These revised laws would then define the nasty business of targeted killing as they should be understood: as a permissible but tightly managed and fully accountable means of national self-defense in an era of terrorist and insurgent attacks on the United States.

In addition, the international community should consider a multilateral treaty on the uses of drone technologies, including lethal targeting. In particular, a UN-initiated convention and subsequent treaty could engage questions of target identification and targeting criteria, host-state consent, distinction, and proportionality standards. Customary international law is being developed now through state practice. Yet much of it is quite literally in the shadows – in the form of unconfirmed or only barely acknowledged strikes by the CIA. Secret strikes cannot inform customary law because they are not publicly known or acknowledged. The publicly confirmed drone strikes that have occurred in the shadow wars – in Pakistan, Yemen, and Somalia – raise contentious issues at the intersection of IHL and HRL, not to mention *jus ad bellum* questions that likewise would benefit from airing in the process of shaping an international agreement. Continuing efforts by the United States and other states, along with the ICRC and other NGOs, can work toward more refined understandings of the answers to the issues.

A recently disclosed Iranian Quds Force plot to kill the Saudi ambassador to the United States by blowing up a fashionable Georgetown restaurant provides further evidence that the shadow war is evolving, perhaps in unpredictable and dangerous new ways. Instead of a conventional military operation to attack Iranian facilities, the United States (and its likely partner Israel) have used covert means – including the Stuxnet computer worm and bomb attacks against Iranian nuclear scientists – to attack and at least slow down Iran's efforts to construct nuclear weapons.[95] The Iranian government fully understands, of course, the source or sources of the covert operations against it.

As we learned during the Cold War, both sides can operate in the shadow war. That the Georgetown plot against the Saudi ambassador was discovered and thwarted does not mean that the next one will end the same way. Nor will smaller and less powerful states or non-state actors necessarily be deterred by US military superiority when fighting the shadow war. Drone strikes may be carried out relatively cheaply, whether in retaliation for US incursions or to further some other aim in the shadows.

Although only the United States, Israel, and United Kingdom have used drones for lethal targeting so far, our near monopoly on weaponized drones is coming to an end.[96] Around eighty countries have built or purchased drone technology and the number continues to increase. Private groups may acquire them too, as is illustrated by their reported presence in the arsenal of Hezbollah.

If for no other reason, the inevitability that other states and non-state actors will use drones to hit targets that the United States wishes to protect – our own people or allies – should cause us all to think long and hard toward establishing durable, transparent, legal criteria for lethal drone strikes.

The practice of the United States is generally supported by international and domestic law, but there are no detailed substantive criteria for drone use outside of hot battlefields. As such, current US drone policy provides an easy template for other empowered actors to deploy drones for targeted killing in multiple contexts with limited adherence to core legal principles and perhaps with even less transparency.

NOTES

1 CNN, "U.S. airstrikes in Pakistan called 'very effective,'" May 18, 2009.
2 ABC *News–Washington Post* poll, "Drones, Gitmo and drawdown give Obama foreign policy cred," February 8, 2012.
3 *National Journal*, "Report: Military alignment to emphasize drones and Special Forces," January 26, 2012. Kessler, Glenn, "President Obama and the defense budget," *Washington Post*, February 14, 2012.
4 Schmitt, Eric, "U.S. teaming with new Yemen government on strategy to combat Al Qaeda," *New York Times*, February 27, 2012.
5 Banks, William C., and Peter Raven-Hansen, "Targeted killing and assassination: The U.S. legal framework," *University of Richmond Law Review* 37 (2003): 667–749, p. 688.
6 Lumpkin, John J., "Al-Qaida suspects die in U.S. missile strike," Associated Press, November 5, 2002.
7 Banks, William C., "The Predator" in Volker Franke (ed.), *Terrorism and peacekeeping: New security challenges* (Westport, CT: Greenwood Press, 2004), pp. 142–157.
8 Shane, Scott, Mark Mazzetti, and Robert F. Worth, "Secret assault on terrorism widens on two continents," *New York Times*, August 14, 2010.
9 Miller, Greg, "Under Obama, an emerging global apparatus for drone killing, *Washington Post*, December 27, 2011.
10 John Brennan, "Securing the homeland by renewing American strength, resilience and values," speech given at the Center for Strategic & International Studies Statemen's Forum, May 26, 2010.
11 John Brennan, "Strengthening our security by adhering to our values and laws," speech given at the Harvard Law School Program on Law and Security, Cambridge, MA, September 16, 2011.
12 Miller, "Under Obama, an emerging global apparatus for drone killing."
13 Rhode, David, "The Obama doctrine: How Obama's drone war is backfiring," *Foreign Policy*, March/April 2012.

14 Bergen, Peter, and Katherine Tiedemann, "Washington's phantom war," *Foreign Affairs*, July/August 2011.

15 Schmit, "U.S. teaming with new Yemen government on strategy to combat Al Qaeda."

16 Kamiya, Gary, "Hypnotized into an endless dirty war," *Salon*, February 20, 2012.

17 Fishman, Brian, "Anwar al-Awlaki, the infidel," *Jihadica*, November 20, 2009.

18 Finn, Peter, "Awlaki directed Christmas 'underwear bomber' plot, Justice Department memo says," *Washington Post*, February 10, 2012.

19 Ibid.

20 Shane, Scott, "Judging a long, deadly reach," *New York Times*, September 30, 2011.

21 Miller, Greg, and Peter Finn, "CIA sees increased threat from al-Qaeda in Yemen," *Washington Post*, August 24, 2010.

22 Finn, Peter, "Secret U.S. memo sanctioned killing of Aulaqi," *Washington Post*, September 30, 2011.

23 See US Const. art. VI.

24 Farrand, Max, (ed.) *The records of the federal convention of 1787*, vol. 2 (rev. ed. 1937), p. 318.

25 Banks and Raven-Hansen, "Targeted killing and assassination," pp. 677–681.

26 Ibid., p. 679.

27 Ibid., p. 689.

28 *National Security Act of 1947*, Pub. L. No. 80-253, 61 Stat. 495 (1947) (codified as amended at 50 U.S.C. secs. 401–442 (2010)).

29 Ibid., sec. 102(d)(5) (codified as amended at 50 U.S.C. sec. 403–4a(d)(4) (2010)).

30 Banks and Raven-Hansen, "Targeted killing and assassination," pp. 702–705.

31 Exec. Order (hereafter EXORD) No. 11,905, 3 C.F.R. 90 (1976).

32 *Foreign Assistance Act of 1974*, Pub. L. No. 93-559, sec. 32, 88 Stat. 1804 (1974).

33 The military use operations orders, and are thus neither given authority nor restricted by the findings.

34 Banks and Raven-Hansen, "Targeted killing and assassination," pp. 711–712.

35 Ibid., pp. 712–713.

36 *Foreign Assistance Act of 1974*: "No funds appropriated under the authority of this or any other Act may be expended by or on behalf of the Central Intelligence Agency for operations in foreign countries, other than activities intended solely for obtaining necessary intelligence, unless and until the President finds that each such operation is important to the national security of the United States and reports, in a timely fashion, a description and scope of such operation to the appropriate committees of the Congress."

37 EXORD No. 11,905, 3 C.F.R. 90 (1976).

38 Banks and Raven-Hansen, "Targeted killing and assassination," pp. 717–721.

39 Ibid., p. 720 n377.

40 EXORD No. 12,333, 3 C.F.R. 200 (1981) as amended by EXORD 13,470 (2008).

41 Banks and Raven-Hansen, "Targeted killing and assassination," p. 670.

42 *Authorization for the Use of Military Force*, Pub. L. No. 107-40, 115 Stat. 224 (2001).

43 Gellman, Barton, "CIA weighs 'targeted killing' missions," *Washington Post*, October 28, 2001.

44 DeYoung, Karen, "Secrecy defines Obama's drone war," *Washington Post*, December 19, 2011.

45 Ibid.

46 Johnston, David, and David E. Sanger, "Fatal strike in Yemen was based on rules set out by Bush," *New York Times*, November 6, 2002, p. A16.

47 Priest, Dana, and William M. Arkin, *Top secret America: The rise of the New American security state* (New York, NY: Little, Brown and Company, 2011). DeYoung, Karen, "Secrecy defines Obama's drone war."

48 Lumpkin, John J., "U.S. Can Target American Al-Qaida Agents," Associated Press, December 3, 2002.

49 *United States v. Verdugo-Urquidez*, 494 U.S. 259 (1990).

50 Banks and Raven-Hansen, "Targeted killing and assassination," p. 677.

51 Savage, Charlie, "Secret U.S. memo made legal case to kill a citizen," *New York Times*, October 8, 2011.

52 *Al-Aulaqi v. Obama*, 727 F. Supp. 2d 1 (E.D.N.Y. 2010).

53 DeYoung, "Secrecy defines Obama's drone war," p. 44.

54 Eric Holder, address at Northwestern University School of Law, Chicago, IL., March 5, 2012.

55 Ibid.

56 Banks and Raven-Hansen, "Targeted killing and assassination," p. 727.

57 *Intelligence Authorization Act*, Pub. L. No. 102-88, 105 Stat. 441 (1991).

58 *Intelligence Authorization Act Fiscal Year 1991*, as amended, 50 U.S.C. secs. 413–414.

59 Pedrozo, Raul A., "Use of unmanned systems to combat terrorism." *International Law Studies* 87 (2011): 217–269.

60 Alston Report, *Extrajudicial, Summary or Arbitrary Executions, Study on Targeted Killings: Rep. of the Special Rapporteur*, para. 85, UN Doc. A/HRC/14/24/Add.6 (May 8, 2010).

61 Harold Koh, "The Obama administration and international law," keynote address at the annual meeting of the American Society of International Law, Washington, DC, March 25, 2010.

62 Ibid.

63 Ibid.

64 Holder, address at Northwestern University School of Law.

65 For the full text of all articles, see www.un.org/en/documents/charter/.

66 Ibid.

67 Schmitt, Michael N., "Drone attacks under the jus ad bellum and jus in bello: Clearing the 'fog of war,'" *Yearbook International Human Law* 13 (2010): 311–326, p. 316.

68 Cassese, Antonio, "The international community's 'legal' response to terrorism," *International and Comparative Law Quarterly* 38 (1989): 589–608, p. 597.

69 Chesney, Robert, "Who may be killed? Anwar al-Awlaki as a case study in the international regulation of lethal force," *Yearbook of International Humanitarian Law* 13 (2010): 3–60.

70 In Somalia, which is essentially a failed state, consent is not a realistic criterion.

71 Risen, James, and David Johnston, "Threats and responses: Hunt for Al Qaeda; Bush has widened authority of CIA to kill terrorists," *New York Times*, December 15, 2002. Risen, James, and Judith Miller, "CIA kills a leader of Qaeda in Yemen," *International Herald Tribune*, November 5, 2002.

72 Hersh, Seymour, "Manhunt," *New Yorker*, December 23 and 30, 2002, p. 66.

73 Chesney, "Who may be killed?" pp. 15–18.

74 Schmitt, "U.S. teaming with new Yemen government on strategy to combat Al Qaeda."

75 O'Connell, Mary Ellen, "Lawful self-defense to terrorism," *University of Pittsburgh Law Review* 63 (2002): 889–908.

76 Deeks, Ashley S., "Unwilling or unable: Toward a normative framework for extra-territorial self-defense," *Virginia Journal of International Law* 52 (2012): 484–550.

77 Schmitt, "U.S. teaming with new Yemen government on strategy to combat Al Qaeda," p. 319 n32.

78 Corn, Geoffrey S., "Self-defense targeting: Conflict classification or willful blindness?" *International Law Studies* 88 (2012): 57–92.

79 Corn, Geoffrey S., and Chris Jenks, "Two sides of the combatant coin: Untangling direct participation in hostilities from belligerent states in non-international armed conflicts," *University of Pennsylvania Journal of International Law* 33 (2011): 313–362.

80 Protocol Additional to the Geneva Conventions Relative to the Protection of Victims of International Armed Conflicts art. 51(3), August 12, 1949 [hereafter Additional Protocol I].

81 Alston Report, para. 65.

82 Melzer, Nils, "Interpretive guidance on the notion of direct participation in hostilities under international humanitarian law," *International Review Red Cross* 90 (2008): 991–1047, p. 1007.

83 317 U.S. 1, 20 (1942).

84 Ibid.

85 Alston Report, paras. 70–71.

86 Additional Protocol I, art. 51(3).

87 See *Auluqi v. Obama*.

88 Chesney, Robert M., "Military-intelligence convergence and the law of the Title 10/Title 50 debate," *Journal of National Security Law and Policy* 5 (2012): 539–629. Alston, Philip, "The CIA and targeted killing beyond borders," *Harvard National Security Law Journal* 2 (2011): 283–446.

89 See, e.g., International Covenant on Civil and Political Rights art. 6, December 16, 1966.

90 See Pub. Comm. Against Torture in *Israel* v. *Gov't of Israel*, HCJ 769/02, Judgment, para. 40 (December 13, 2006).

91 Alston Report, paras. 87–92.

92 Kasinof, Laura, Mark Mazzetti, and Alan Cowell, "U.S.-born Qaeda leader killed in Yemen," *New York Times*, September 30, 2011.

93 Cronin, Audrey Kurth, "Why drones fail: When tactics drive strategy," *Foreign Affairs*, July/August 2013, p. 44.

94 Banks, William C. (ed.), "New battlefields/old laws: From The Hague conventions to asymmetric warfare" (Columbia University Press, 2011).

95 Sanger, David E., "America's deadly dynamics with Iran," *New York Times*, November 6, 2011.

96 Shane, Scott, "Coming soon: The drones arms race," *New York Times*, October 8, 2011.

9

A Move Within the Shadows

Will JSOC's Control of Drones Improve Policy?

NAUREEN SHAH

1. JSOC AND DRONE OPERATIONS

Lethal drone operations have become a staple of US counterterrorism, and some US policymakers and observers believe that this strategy is likely to increase over the next decade. While much of the criticism of the drone campaign has focused on the covert and possibly illegal actions of the CIA, there has been very little public discussion of the significant and complex role of the Joint Special Operations Command (JSOC) in targeted killings. This is significant because a common misconception presents the US drone strategy as falling into two distinct programs: the conventional military's overt drone strikes in Afghanistan, and the CIA's covert strikes in Pakistan and Yemen.[1] In fact, JSOC has worked alongside the CIA in Yemen and perhaps in Pakistan, although the character of their cooperation appears to depend on the particular theater and perhaps even the specific operations. What is clear from limited US government disclosures – mostly in the form of leaks to the press – is that JSOC has been involved in lethal targeting operations across the globe.

This is very significant in that JSOC is a military organization that works alongside the CIA. Yet it is neither part of the conventional military nor wholly akin to the CIA. It is a highly secretive military organization with a record of human rights abuses, possibly resulting from a distinctive culture and dubious relationship to international humanitarian law (also known as the Law of Armed Conflict, or LOAC), which defines clear rules governing the conventional military. Understanding US policy regarding drones requires a deeper consideration of JSOC and its role in these programs. This is because this element of the US military enjoys expansive authority, is increasingly convergent with the CIA, apparently lacks adherence to LOAC, and suggests a new less legally bound projection of military force that creates a variety of ethical and policy concerns.

The president has suggested that drone operations will increasingly be managed by the Department of Defense (DoD) rather than the CIA. Observers hope this change will bring greater transparency and respect for the law to the drone program. However, within this possible shift, a key issue remains: the role of JSOC. This is particularly significant as limited government disclosures suggest that JSOC has conducted drone strikes in parallel and cooperation with the CIA and may be unlikely to reform its approach to these missions to address core problems with the current program.

Not nearly enough is publicly known about JSOC to know for certain whether it would be more responsible and accountable than the CIA in preventing civilian casualties and complying with the LOAC. For this reason, removing the CIA from the drone program will not necessarily address the program's controversial nature. Assuming this shift occurs, the significant scrutiny applied to the CIA's drone strikes should be equally applied to the DoD–JSOC drone deployment.

2. JSOC: A SECRET GROUP WITHIN THE US MILITARY

The public and policymakers know little about the extent and scope of JSOC operations. What is most familiar are its successes, mostly notably their operational role in the Abbottabad, Pakistan raid that killed Osama bin Laden. This and other capture/kill missions have led to a remarkable level of political support for JSOC, as well as widespread tolerance of its extreme secrecy. One former military general described JSOC with admiration as composed of "the most dangerous people on the face of the Earth."[2] With political support, JSOC has evolved into what a former counterinsurgency adviser to General David Petraeus describes as "an almost industrial-scale counterterrorism killing machine."[3] Indeed, JSOC has tripled in size since 9/11, to more than 4,000 soldiers and civilians, and a budget of more than $1 billion.[4] It has "all of the pieces of a self-sustaining secret army," including its own intelligence division and its own drones.[5]

From a human rights perspective, these are dubious accolades. Yet it is hard to dispute that JSOC is an exceptionally effective and significant element of the US military. The current JSOC is a creature born of post-9/11 counter-terrorism strategies and related real and imagined needs. It is segregated from the regular military and its bureaucratic entanglements, highly special-ized through its focus on counterterrorism, and extremely secretive. It may be even more shadowy than the CIA in that it lacks the stigma or notoriety of the agency.

JSOC is a part of the US military, yet it stands apart. It is part of the far larger Special Operations Command (SOCOM). Termed by one observer "the military's secret military," SOCOM deals with a universe of US military activity that occurs almost completely outside of the view of the American public.[6] SOCOM operates in at least seventy-five countries, with missions as varied as foreign troop training and counterproliferation of weapons of mass destruction.[7]

SOCOM and JSOC were created in the early 1980s during a period that saw a resurgence of US military expansion. Military failures – including the unsuccessful attempt to rescue American hostages from Iran, the terrorist bombing attack in Lebanon, and higher-than-expected military casualties during the invasion of Grenada – led to increased congressional concern about the post-Vietnam deterioration of US Special Operations Forces (SOF). In 1986, Congress mandated the creation of a unified command headed by a four-star general for all SOCOM.[8] It was composed of units from all the service branches, including the Army's Green Berets and Navy SEALs. JSOC was reportedly created through a classified charter around the same time.[9] It was officially subordinated to the newly established SOCOM, which provided support to regional commands.[10]

Particularly since 9/11, JSOC has functioned separately from the rest of the US military. In 2003, then-Secretary of Defense Donald Rumsfeld grew frustrated at the CIA's better capacity to operate on the ground in Afghanistan as compared with the SOF.[11] He made SOCOM a "supported command" – allowing it to plan and execute its own missions apart from regional combatant commanders.[12] Moreover, administration officials have reportedly bypassed SOCOM and issued orders directly to JSOC, treating it as the "President's Army."[13]

At the direction of the executive branch, JSOC became a specialized counterterrorism unit with nearly worldwide authority to kill or capture al-Qaeda operatives. A September 2003 Executive Order (EXORD), known as the al-Qaeda EXORD, or AQN EXORD, authorized JSOC operations in Afghanistan, Iraq, and a dozen other countries, reportedly including Pakistan and Somalia.

Though the AQN EXORD has never been made public, some details are known. It granted authority for lethal actions in Iraq and Afghanistan without additional presidential approval, while activities in other countries were subject to various rules imposed by the National Security Council. It reportedly included detailed rules of engagement, requiring higher levels of approval for actions, for example, that might result in a large number of civilian casualties.[14]

Under the Obama administration, the AQN EXORD and other Executive Orders have reportedly been rewritten to require more vetting by the White House.[15] There are also reports that General David Petraeus, as head of the military's Central Command, expanded and updated the order in 2009.[16]

Despite JSOC's size, it has been able to maintain a degree of secrecy exceeding any other US organization wielding force, including the CIA.[17] As retired General Barry McCaffrey testified to Congress, JSOC has "run [as] a parallel universe" that "publicly we don't talk too much about."[18] JSOC "camouflages itself with cover names, black budget mechanisms, and bureaucratic parlor tricks" to maintain its secrecy.[19] Indeed, the official description of JSOC still mentions a host of roles: "to study Special Operations requirements"; ensure "interoperability and equipment standardization"; develop "joint Special Operations plans and tactics"; and conduct "joint Special Operations exercises and training."[20] None of this mentions JSOC's targeting or drone operations.[21] Moreover, a lack of clear oversight structures has enabled JSOC "to slip out of the grip" of Washington bureaucracy, as General Stanley McChrystal put it when he was commander of JSOC.[22]

3. JSOC AND CIA: ISSUES OF ACCOUNTABILITY

Perhaps due to JSOC's secrecy, its involvement in drone strikes has drawn far less attention – and criticism – than the CIA's. Although US officials have leaked information about particular drone strikes involving both JSOC and the CIA, they have declined to delineate the particular roles of the two entities. Most of what we know comes from reports by journalists and scholars.

The catalogue of reporting contains information that is at times conflicting and ambiguous, but overall suggests two kinds of CIA–JSOC cooperation. First, some operations are parallel, meaning that JSOC and the CIA conduct separate campaigns of strikes in the same region. In these parallel operations, the CIA and JSOC may exchange information and provide each other with operational support. Second, the CIA and JSOC conduct joint operations. In these cases, it appears that cooperation is significant but bifurcated, for example, with JSOC taking a lead on operations that are conducted under the CIA's legal authority. This has various implications, including allowing JSOC to escape the scrutiny of the congressional committees charged with oversight of the military. While public information on its activities remains limited and difficult to obtain, it is clear that JSOC has played a significant role in drone strikes in Pakistan, Yemen, and Somalia, all sites outside of traditional legally defined conflict zones, such as Afghanistan and Iraq.

Pakistan – The vast majority of US drone strikes have occurred in Pakistan, and US officials have credited these actions with severely diminishing al-Qaeda's capacity in the region. In Pakistan, the CIA began conducting strikes in 2004. President George W. Bush ordered an increase late in his term, in 2008.[23] While the CIA's campaign is well known and US officials have repeatedly alluded to it, there are also reports of parallel JSOC operations in the same region.[24] A WikiLeaks cable from October 2009 appears to confirm US Special Forces involvement in drone strikes, with the knowledge and consent of the Pakistani Army.[25] A military intelligence official told the *Nation* in 2009: "Some of these strikes are attributed to . . . [the CIA], but in reality it's JSOC and their parallel program of UAVs strikes."[26]

According to one account, JSOC carried out three drone strikes in Pakistan under the George W. Bush administration before being pulled out in response to public outcry and the concerns of the US ambassador.[27] Other reports suggest that JSOC's role in Pakistan has been limited to providing intelligence for drone strikes conducted under CIA authority. US officials maintain that SOF in Pakistan have been present only to train Pakistani forces.[28]

Yemen – In Yemen, the CIA and JSOC both operate drones and have repeatedly conducted strikes since 2011.[29] US officials have leaked details about particular drone strikes, but declined to clarify which agency takes operational lead or under which agency's legal authority the operations are conducted.[30] Accordingly, it is unclear whether current drone strikes are conducted jointly by JSOC and the CIA, or are run as parallel but distinct campaigns.

In 2011, unnamed administration officials described JSOC and CIA operations as "closely coordinated" but separate campaigns.[31] Some 2011 media accounts described US operations as run by JSOC, but with CIA assistance.[32] According to one account, JSOC and CIA alternate Predator missions in Yemen and borrow each other's resources."[33] JSOC commanders even "appear on videoconference calls alongside CIA station chiefs."[34]

JSOC has conducted ground operations in Yemen, as well as drone strikes. According to one report, in 2010 President Obama sent several dozen JSOC troops to Yemen to kill "scores of people on JSOC's hit list" over a six-month period, including six of the fifteen individuals US intelligence had identified as top regional commanders.[35]

Some operations in 2011 may have been conducted under the CIA's legal authority rather than JSOC's. According to unnamed US officials, the CIA took a more dominant role in Yemen in 2011 due to uncertainty about continuing Yemeni government consent in light of the political uprising against then-leader and US ally Ali Abdullah Saleh. US officials believed that if Saleh's regime failed and they lost the consent of the Yemeni government, the CIA could still carry out the strikes as "covert actions."[36]

Perhaps the most well-known drone strike in Yemen occurred in September 2011, when the US killed US citizen Anwar al-Awlaki in Yemen. Anonymous US officials described the CIA as "in control of all the aircraft, as well as the decisions to fire." However, the officials did not know "whether a drone supplied by the CIA or the military fired the missile that ended the al-Qaeda leader's life" because the "operations were so seamless."[37]

Somalia – JSOC and the CIA have conducted operations in East Africa since 9/11, and there are indications that JSOC is expanding its ability to conduct targeting and surveillance.[38] The CIA, US air force, and American security contractors are reported to be operating air bases in East Africa, as well as the Seychelles,[39] and the US military is building "a constellation of bases in the Horn of Africa and the Arabian Peninsula."[40] The three known American bases operating drones[41] in the region are said to be operating as many as twelve Predators and Reapers at a time.[42]

The first reported US drone strike in Somalia occurred on June 23, 2011.[43] While most reports attributed the strike to JSOC[44] or SOCOM,[45] CNN described the strike as "part of new secret joint Pentagon and CIA war" against the Somali-based al-Shabaab, based on a statement by Leon Panetta that the Pentagon denied as indicating JSOC involvement in Somalia.[46] As *Wired* reported, "the military rarely confirms drone operations over Somalia – and the CIA *never* does,"[47] while some news reports attribute strikes only to "the United States."[48]

The CIA and JSOC's convergence in drone strikes manifests a broader trend signaling their cooperation in counterterrorism operations generally.[49] Indeed, Admiral William McRaven, former commander of JSOC and current head of SOCOM, has described the two agencies as having spent "a decade in bed together."[50] Robert Gates, then-secretary of Department of Defense, heralded JSOC–CIA cooperation after the joint raid that killed Osama bin Laden, calling it "an extraordinary coming together" that is "unique in anybody's history."[51]

Whatever the advantages of CIA–JSOC convergence, it necessarily belies the hope that in the near future the DoD will take full ownership of the drone program away from the CIA. Years of integration and interdependence may make it very difficult to disentangle the CIA and JSOC as regards drone missions and may be unattractive to policymakers impressed with these actions to date. According to journalists Marc Ambinder and D. B. Grady, after some early turf conflicts between the organizations, "the integration" in Yemen at least "is almost seamless," "JSOC and the CIA [are] alternating Predator missions and borrowing each other's resources, such as satellite bandwidth."[52]

CIA-JSOC convergence also bodes poorly for increasing the transparency and accountability of US drone operations. Government secrecy about the delineation of responsibilities between JSOC and the CIA in drone strikes has institutionalized both organizations' avoidance of accountability. As a practical matter, at times even government officials do not have a clear understanding of which organization is responsible for a strike or for particular conduct. In 2011, the *Washington Post* reported: "[C]omingling at remote bases is so complete that U.S. officials ranging from congressional staffers to high-ranking CIA officers said they often find it difficult to distinguish agency from military personnel."[53]

According to another report: "American military and intelligence operatives are virtually indistinguishable from each other as they carry out classified operations in the Middle East and Central Asia."[54] And during the drone strike in Yemen that killed Anwar al-Awlaki, which reportedly involved both JSOC and CIA drones: "[T]he operation was so seamless that even hours later, it remained unclear whether a drone supplied by the CIA or the military fired the missile that ended the al-Qaeda leader's life."[55]

Being unable to identify which agency carried out an operation could make it difficult to assign responsibility in the event of abuses or mistakes. The blurring could create a gap in which no congressional committee has clear jurisdiction to exercise oversight over a particular operation.[56]

Moreover, congressional oversight is compromised when JSOC conducts operations under the CIA's statutory authority.[57] These joint operations have been characterized as Title 50 operations,[58] referring to the section of the US Code that governs the CIA, as compared to Title 10 operations, which govern military activities. In fact, Title 10 and Title 50 of the US Code provide various and often mutually supporting authorities for the military and intelligence services. Nevertheless, insofar as congressional oversight is organized around the strict delineation between Title 50 operations that are overseen by the intelligence committees, and Title 10 military operations that are overseen by the armed services committees, joint operations between the CIA and JSOC significantly challenge effective oversight.

Indeed, members of Congress have expressed concern that operations conducted under JSOC's authority escape proper review.[59] While the CIA generally reports on some aspects of its operations to Congress's intelligence oversight committees, JSOC's joint operations with the CIA may avoid scrutiny by the armed services committees, which do not traditionally exercise over military operations.[60]

Another danger is that some joint missions could be reported to the intelligence committees, while others are reported to the armed services committees, meaning that while there may be oversight of particular missions, no committee would have a comprehensive understanding of joint operations generally or the ability to exercise complete and robust oversight over the drone program as a whole.[61]

While some commentators suggest that joint CIA–military operations are subject to double scrutiny – reporting to both the congressional committees that oversee the CIA and those that oversee the military – members of those committees themselves have voiced concerns.[62] In a report accompanying the House of Representatives' version of the 2010 intelligence authorization bill, the House Permanent Select Committee on Intelligence criticized the Pentagon's tendency to classify its clandestine intelligence gathering activities such that: "[They] often escape the scrutiny of the intelligence committees, and the congressional defense committees cannot be expected to exercise oversight outside of their jurisdiction."[63]

During a March 2012 hearing, Representative Hank Johnson, a member of the House Armed Services Committee, questioned military officials about oversight of special operations forces operating under the CIA. Pointing out a disconnect between funding and reporting requirements, Johnson noted that although the House Armed Services Committee has budgetary authority over SOCOM, when special operations forces act under CIA authority, the Pentagon is not required to report back to the committee about its activities.[64]

4. JSOC PRACTICE AS DISTINCT FROM US MILITARY ETHOS

A transfer of drone strikes from the CIA to JSOC, even if likely, might not improve the drone program in terms of transparency, accountability, or compliance with the law. JSOC has an ethos and relationship to LOAC that is unique – it neither approaches the law in the same manner as the conventional military nor in the same way as the CIA. JSOC's record should be considered as a cautionary tale of potential problems with a DoD takeover of US drone operations.

Over time and in response to public pressure, conventional US military forces have developed and implemented systems of substantive legal accountability. Though not without serious flaws, the conventional military's practices provide a stark counterpoint to JSOC's secrecy and evasion of accountability. US conventional military forces are required to follow LOAC in all operations.[65] These legal requirements are not merely a matter of regulation, but are also a key component of the military's institutional culture.

One of the major symbolic moments in the military's cultural transformation toward greater sensitivity to the importance of LOAC was the 1968 My Lai massacre.[66] Chilling accounts of the deliberate and sustained killings of an estimated five hundred unarmed men, women, and children over the course of four hours in a small Vietnamese village highlighted serious problems with the military's capacity to comply with established law and minimize civilian harm.[67] As military leaders and policymakers evaluated what went wrong at My Lai, and in other Vietnam-era war crimes, they identified soldiers' inadequate knowledge of the law as a central contributing factor. Enemy fighters in the Vietcong were not only "indistinguishable from the local population, but also refused to abide by the established principles of the laws of war," circumstances that led soldiers to view the limitations of the law as irrelevant.[68] As two judge advocates wrote on the occasion of the twenty-fifth anniversary of the My Lai massacre in 1993: "This is the first lesson of My Lai; soldiers not only must know the law of war, but also must be able to understand the necessity and rationale for having a law of war."[69] In response to these abuses, the Department of Defense designed a comprehensive program to effectively implement the laws of war by educating soldiers and encouraging a shift in attitudes from one of reluctant tolerance for legal limitations to a robust engagement and internalization of LOAC's norms and rules.

In 1974, the DoD promulgated a directive mandating that every member of the military had to be trained in the laws of war, and assigned primary responsibility for training and law compliance to unit commanders. The directive mandated the reporting of war crimes and of timely and proper investigations.[70] A version of the 1974 directive is still in place today. It unequivocally requires that all Department of Defense organizations "comply with the law of war during all armed conflicts, however such conflicts are characterized, and in all other military operations."[71]

Post-Vietnam law of war training emphasized the rationale and foundation of the laws of war. W. Hays Park, former chief of the Law of War branch of the Navy's Office of Judge Advocate, described this mandatory training as "marrying" law of war obligations "to military effectiveness, professionalism and good leadership."[72]

In fact, US military actions in conflicts and operations after Vietnam have showed that implementation of the laws of war required more than good training, or a distributed manual. According to Hays Park, "It requires an ethos. It requires comprehensive implementation, in peace and war, at all levels of armed forces."[73]

Today, there are dozens of rules, mechanisms, and guidelines created by the US military to implement the laws of war, defining a superstructure that serves not only to motivate legal compliance, but also to integrate law of war norms into the core ethos of the armed services. Indeed, several of the services explicitly describe law of war compliance as part of the "warrior ethos," having "the honor to comply with the Laws of War, the courage to report all violations, and the commitment to discipline the violators."[74]

One result of this institutional shift is that when significant abuses against detainees occurred during military operations in Iraq and Afghanistan, military personnel themselves took leading roles in reporting those violations up the chain of command and to the media, even though they risked retaliation from other soldiers, disciplinary actions for their involvement, and potential prosecution.[75] As a general matter, military personnel are motivated by the threat of punishment, as well as scrutiny by Congress and the public. Nevertheless, they are also compelled to act by the norms and ethos of their organizations. Indeed, some military practitioners and scholars viewed abuses at Abu Ghraib prison in Iraq not merely as violations committed by a few individuals that damaged the Army's reputation, but as violations of the US military's core values, such that those acts undermined the institution. As one military scholar put it: "Army ethos requires the strict adherence to all laws governing the conduct of war. And since the Army ethos is a fundamental attribute of Army professionalism, if [sic] follows that the abuses that occurred at Abu Ghraib directly undermined the foundations of Army professionalism."[76]

Another result of the post-Vietnam transformation of the military is its greater acceptance of international law and a related sensitivity and engagement with the domestic and international public. The military has created institutions to foster learning and development regarding how the law of war applies in complex and novel situations. For example, judge advocates receive intensive law of war training at the Judge Advocate General's School and similar schools administered by the navy and air force. In 1988, the army established a Center for Law and Military Operations, which publishes the *Law of War Deskbook*, a database for judge advocates around the world.[77] Judge advocates are actively involved in practical training operations at four Combat Training Centers, where training units engage in simulated combat and peace operations.[78]

This system of linking classroom teaching with study of the practical application of the law of war has led to a greater openness and pluralism within the military at an intellectual level and has helped to foster the emergence of a culture of critique and debate around difficult legal and moral questions. For example, members of the armed forces have published many constructive reviews of the effectiveness of the military's systems for investigating civilian deaths and assessing battle damage after targeting.[79]

Equally significant are the roles of military lawyers and scholars in aggressively engaging with debates about interpretations of the law in novel and complex circumstances, not only within their own institutions, but also among academics and policymakers. For example, the Naval War College hosts an annual symposium on international law that brings together leading military practitioners, scholars, human rights lawyers, and government attorneys from the United States and other countries to debate and discuss key issues within the field. At outside conferences on international law, military lawyers regularly participate in public lectures and debates on the law of war, including its relationship to international human rights. Such engagement by the military allows the institution's views and policies to be effectively informed by the perspectives of outsiders. Similarly, the military's public engagement with legal issues aids debates within the broader society and among policymakers.

The US military's commitment to LOAC as interpreted through specific rules and procedures, such as its rules of engagement and elaborate pre- and post-strike targeting processes, often reflect not only the strict and uncontroversial requirements of the law, but also an interest in preventing or mitigating civilian harm. These policies and practices are motivated by the internalization of norms described above, as well as the military's concern for public opinion both at home and abroad.

Rules of engagement have, for example, restricted the number of civilian casualties that are acceptable in targeting operations, beyond what is be required by international law.[80] For some operations, the military uses a "collateral damage methodology" to estimate likely civilian harm from an operation and consider ways to reduce it, based on "empirical data, probability, historical observations from the battlefield, and physics-based computerized models."[81] Collateral damage estimates draw from frequently updated reference tables that are subject to "physics-based computer modeling" and "supplemented by weapons testing data and direct combat observations."[82] The collateral damage mitigation process and attendant rules have a cultural effect. For example, according to a 2010 government study, the rules in Afghanistan bolstered the ability of air force pilots "not to engage because they perceived risks of civilian casualties."[83]

The conventional military also sometimes conducts "battle damage assessments" after strikes and, when civilian harm has occurred, they have in some cases led the military to provide medical aid or initiate a condolences process.[84]

The military's rules also reflect counterinsurgency strategies that require the military to engage with local communities so as to gain a level of legitimacy.

In Afghanistan, a 2010 tactical directive issued by General David Petraeus emphasized, "every Afghan civilian death diminishes our cause."[85]

The conventional military's rules and procedures are a response to the high visibility of civilian casualties. In an era of cell phone cameras and YouTube as a platform for global dissemination, allegations of civilian casualties, backed up by images and other data, have perhaps never before posed such a significant issue for military leaders. More generally, as Jack Goldsmith has noted, the growth of global television and the Internet have "made war observable anywhere, practically in real time." As a result the "[l]awful action – and also important, the perception of lawful action – had become more than a demand of honor or morality or something to abide legal scrutiny; it had become a military imperative."[86]

Indeed, a July 2012 US Army manual on civilian casualty mitigation emphasizes that even unavoidable or lawful civilian casualties "will be publicized by the news media and critically viewed by the American people, the local population, and the international community"; it cautions that "operations against insurgents may have to be postponed or modified if [civilian casualties] and other collateral damage would undercut mission goals or political support."[87]

In contrast to the firm US military ethos to fully respect LOAC, bolstered by sensitivity to public pressure, CIA and JSOC drone strikes have limited visibility and are less impacted by the demands of public pressure. Because both the CIA and JSOC routinely operate secretly, the structures and procedures that the military has built up around legal compliance and a concern for civilian harm may be lacking, notwithstanding the organization's claims to ensure formal compliance with the law.

5. JSOC'S RELATIONSHIP TO MILITARY RULES AND RECORD OF ABUSE

As part of the military, JSOC is fully bound by LOAC and the DoD's policies on legal compliance. Insofar as JSOC's leading officers are drawn from the regular military, the organization should also benefit from the ethos of abiding by the law and reporting abuse. Yet JSOC has a far more complex relationship to these norms and a troubling and ambiguous relationship to DoD rules.

Considering the military's structure, DoD policies should apply fully to JSOC. SOCOM provides SOF units to geographic commands, like US Central Command. As a SOCOM officer explained: "Once those forces are in a geographic combatant commander's area of responsibility, they work for that commander ... under the same rules as other forces."[88]

However, when JSOC conducts operations under CIA authority, it may fall under CIA rules and processes, which use a more flexible interpretation of the use of armed force in comparison with the conventional military. Most notably, in contrast to the DoD, the CIA has never clarified whether and to what degree it considers itself legally bound by international law.[89]

Moreover, it is unclear whether JSOC operations are reviewed by military lawyers or CIA lawyers. This is relevant because for all their good faith efforts, CIA lawyers lack the experience and training of their military counterparts.[90] Indeed, military lawyers may have the potential to provide greater checks on potential abuses than CIA lawyers. In part this is because military lawyers are a key element of an independent chain of command that emphasizes independence and enables greater objectivity of legal review.[91] A judge advocate described the military lawyer's role as standing for "integrity and to be the commander's conscience ... not like an inspector general but rather an internal conscience."[92]

While CIA lawyers may be effective at clarifying law of war constraints to agency decision makers, it is unclear whether they have internalized these rules and perceive their position as ensuring that operations conform with the law's underlying values. In light of the legal complexities of current drone operations, there is a risk that decision makers at the CIA might conduct strikes justified by gaps or ambiguities in the law, as their lawyers are either unable or unwilling to exert countervailing pressure.

If CIA interpretations of the law guide JSOC when it conducts operations under the agency's authority, concerns about the CIA culture become relevant to an evaluation of whether or not JSOC is the appropriate entity for managing drone strikes. The CIA's relationship to legal compliance is often formalistic; and even in accounts favorable to the agency, it is viewed as engaging the law largely as a means of avoiding liability and political repercussions for actions that, if revealed, might be perceived as illegal, even if technically legal. In these accounts, there is a possibility that even if interpretations are technically legal, they might nevertheless offend the purposes and values of the law, or so severely test the limits of the law as to be inappropriate.

JSOC's operations under CIA authority complicate its relationship to the conventional military's rules and procedures, particularly those designed to prevent and mitigate civilian harm. It is possible that joint JSOC–CIA operations are governed by the military's rules of engagement, set by Central Command and other geographic commands, and that targeting operations are subject to the military's pre-strike and post-strike assessment and investigation processes. However, it is also possible that these joint operations are governed by the CIA's operating procedures, or some set of procedures established specifically for such joint operations. Adding to the confusion is a third possibility: JSOC–CIA operations may take place within a *sui generis* framework that breaks from traditional rules and procedures and fails to draw lessons from the military's decades of experience in mitigating and accounting for civilian harm.

With limited public information about the rules and procedures guiding these missions, it is impossible to clearly analyze JSOC's relationship to the law in joint drone operations with the CIA. However, JSOC's practices in other contexts provide some cause for concern.

Although JSOC is part of the US military, its record suggests that it does not share the same ethos and relationship to LOAC and international law as the conventional military. In fact, accounts of JSOC operations describe the organization as highly independent and often not subjected to the scrutiny and oversight of regional military commands. According to one report, "JSOC's missions are highly classified and compartmentalized" and sometimes, "JSOC operators have conducted operations without informing the combatant commanders of their presence."[93]

Moreover, there are indications that JSOC has its own rules of engagement.[94] This is unsurprising as policymakers designed JSOC to function as the "president's army," in part to evade bureaucratic and legal impediments to rapid deployment and operation.

JSOC's independence from oversight rules and military rules vary and may have improved over time in response to allegations of abuse. For example, in Afghanistan, even if JSOC may not be formally bound by the rules of engagement of the regional command, it appears to follow them in practice. JSOC is primarily responsible for nighttime kill and capture operations. These have become quite controversial, leading to multiple complaints from the Afghan government, human rights groups, the United Nations, and others. Yet these raids increased dramatically in 2009 and 2010 to, on average, nineteen raids per night.[95] International Security Assistance Force tactical directives set strict limits on nighttime raids in an effort to reduce civilian harm. Because of JSOC's command structure, it is unclear whether these directives necessarily apply to their operations, although military officials say that, in practice, JSOC follows these guidelines.[96]

In contrast, in Iraq, JSOC apparently operated according to unique procedures and rules that sometimes resulted in serious abuses. JSOC, "unlike other military groups," was "authorized to work from raw intelligence and did not need to wait for authorization for follow-on strikes based on the acquired information" and conducted lethal operations "without consulting ·

higher-ranking officials, a circumvention of the chain of command authority."[97] Commentators have heralded JSOC's lethal operations in Iraq as critical to supporting US strategic goals and possibly reducing violence. Nevertheless, human rights groups, journalists, and others have reported that their actions resulted in many potentially illegal killings and the improper detention of thousands of innocent civilians.[98]

JSOC's interrogation and detention of prisoners in Iraq was also run as a parallel operation and reportedly led to multiple cases of torture and inhumane treatment of detainees.[99] At Camp Nama, a site run jointly by the CIA and JSOC's Task Force 6–26 at Baghdad International Airport, a poster advised "No Blood No Foul" and the slogan reportedly reflected an adage adopted by JSOC's task force: "If you don't make them bleed, they can't prosecute for it," suggesting brutal actions were used that were designed to leave no open wounds.[100] Problems were so severe that the CIA and FBI barred their own personnel from participating in JSOC interrogations, and the Defense Intelligence Agency withdrew its personnel from a JSOC-run detention site.[101]

While JSOC was subject to military investigations for its conduct in Iraq, it succeeded in keeping details about its abuses and formal responses to complaints secret. Some abuses led to official military investigations, but the results remain classified.[102] About thirty members of JSOC were disciplined, with some forced to leave the military or were transferred to other units. Nevertheless, for the most part, "JSOC prefers to keep its record of accountability in-house" and has not made the results of investigations public.[103]

General Stanley McChrystal reportedly initiated reforms that required JSOC to use the rules for interrogation laid out in the Army Field Manual. However, even after these reforms were instituted, JSOC interrogators were still allowed to hold detainees for up to ninety days without seeking approval from superiors or DoD lawyers.[104] Moreover, according to Human Rights Watch, even after a military investigation in 2003, abuses continued to occur.[105] According to media reports, General McChrystal ordered that JSOC–CIA prison Camp Nama would not provide access to the International Committee of the Red Cross for inspection – in contravention of the laws of war.[106]

In sum, while there are indications that JSOC has operated independently and followed rules divergent from that of the conventional military forces, there is so much secrecy about their actions that is difficult to evaluate whether, and to what extent, JSOC's respects LOAC and takes concerted actions to reduce civilian harm. JSOC has not made public the specific reforms it has adopted to prevent further abuses, and its secrecy about past accountability processes makes it difficult to assess the effectiveness of internal oversight.

6. SECRECY LIMITS ABILITY TO DRAW CONCLUSIONS

Congressional scrutiny is a necessary check to the expansive authority delegated to JSOC to conduct operations after 9/11. JSOC is relatively new and accordingly remains unencumbered by many of the oversight processes and reporting requirements that developed, over time and in response to scandals and public pressure, for the CIA and conventional military forces. The result is that policymakers are relatively uninformed about JSOC. Many US intelligence officials, for example, did not learn of JSOC's new intelligence fusion center in Washington, DC, until an Associated Press revealed its existence in a 2011 article.[107]

Even as congressional oversight of JSOC has been frustrated, and despite the organization's secrecy, JSOC enjoys wide political support. In congressional hearings, JSOC has been credited with several successes,[108] including eradicating al-Qaeda Iraq in urban Baghdad[109] and the killing of Osama bin Laden.[110] Congressional committees have praised JSOC's flexibility and "unique interagency authorities" as an example for other military forces.[111] The Senate Armed Services Committee has praised and encouraged the spread of JSOC "man-hunting" tactics to other branches of the military.[112] Congressional enthusiasm can be traced to JSOC's 2006 killing of Abu Musab al-Zarqawi, after which Senator Evan Bayh reportedly requested and received "an unprecedented (and secret) billion-dollar earmark for intelligence, surveillance, and reconnaissance assets on the basis of a battlefield conversation" with JSOC personnel.[113]

These successes threaten to obscure the need for scrutiny of JSOC's record. As journalist Marc Ambinder noted: "[M]any in Congress who'd be very sensitive to CIA operations almost treat JSOC as an entity that doesn't have to submit to oversight."[114] Congress has a crucial role to play in balancing the secrecy of JSOC's operations. As scholar Robert Chesney noted: "[Congressional oversight is crucial to] reconcile the need for secrecy and discretion in the pursuit of national security aims, on the one hand, with the need to subject the resulting powers as much as possible to mechanisms that enhance accountability and compliance with the rule of law, on the other."[115] The gaps and ambiguity in congressional oversight jurisdiction over joint CIA and JSOC operations may require changes to governing US law on oversight.[116]

Congressional scrutiny would serve the crucial function of clarifying basic details about JSOC's operations. Public uncertainty over who makes key decisions regarding JSOC operations and what rules apply adds a layer of obscurity to programs that are already secret. An unidentified military intelligence source told a reporter in 2009: "When you see some of these hits [that are attributed to the CIA], especially the ones with high civilian casualties, those are almost always JSOC strikes."[117]

CIA–JSOC convergence threatens the substance and vision of efforts to reform the US drone program. Because JSOC involvement is not generally acknowledged, a drone strike outside of a traditional war zone with high civilian casualties will likely be blamed on the CIA, even though it may well have been conducted by JSOC, or possibly some other entity.

It appears that US drone operations will continue and may well expand to other sites around the world. In general, the US public understands US drone policy as neatly divided between military deployment in conventional war zones, such as Iraq and Afghanistan, where attacks are managed under rigorous LOAC standards, and CIA drone actions in places such as Pakistan, Yemen, and Somalia, where the principles used for targeting decisions are far less clear. Policy plans to move the entire lethal drone program to the DoD are presented as a means of ensuring greater legal rigor and reducing civilian casualties and addressing other criticisms of the program. However, if drone deployment continues to be managed by JSOC based on its secretive operation, there may be no significant improvements in transparency and adherence to established law for regulating the use of force.

NOTES

1 Mayer, Jane, "The Predator war: What are the risks of the C.I.A.'s covert drone program?" *New Yorker*, October 26, 2009, in which it was reported: "The U.S. government runs two drone programs. The military's version, which is publicly acknowledged, operates in the recognized war zones of Afghanistan and Iraq, and targets enemies of U.S. troops stationed there. As such, it is an extension of conventional warfare. The C.I.A.'s program is aimed at terror suspects around the world, including in countries where U.S. troops are not based." Radsan, John Afsheen and Richard Murphy, "Measure twice, shoot once: Higher care for CIA targeted killing," *University of Illinois Law Review* 4 (2011): 1202–1241.

2 Statement of Gen. Barry McCaffrey, USA (Ret.), House Hearing of the Committee on Armed Services, Oversight and Investigations Subcommittee, "Afghanistan and

Iraq: Perspectives on U.S. Strategy, Part 1," H.A.S.C. No. 111–103, at 2, October 22, 2009.

3 Lt. Col. John Nagl, quoted in Gavett, Gretchen, "What is the secretive US 'kill/capture' campaign?" PBS, *Frontline*, June 17, 2011.

4 Ambinder, Marc, "The secret team that killed bin Laden," *National Journal*, May 2, 2011.

5 Priest, Dana, and William M. Arkin, *Top secret America: The rise of the new American security state* (New York, NY: Little, Brown, and Company, 2011), p. 225.

6 Turse, Nick, "The U.S. military's secret military," *Al Jazeera* (in English), August 8, 2010.

7 DeYoung, Karen, and Greg Jaffe, "U.S. 'secret war' expands globally as special operations forces take larger role," *Washington Post*, June 4, 2010.

8 US Department of Defense, "U.S. Special Operations Command: A History" (6th ed., March 2008).

9 US Government Accountability Office, "Special Operations Forces: Structure and readiness issues (chapter report)," GAO/NSIAD-84-105, April 24, 1994. Kibbe, Jennifer D., "Covert action and the Pentagon," *Intelligence and National Security* 22 (2007): 57–74, p. 58. Ambinder, Marc, and D. B. Grady, *The command: Deep inside the president's secret army* (Hoboken, NJ: John Wiley and Sons, 2012, Kindle edition).

10 Kibbe, "Covert action and the Pentagon," p. 59.

11 Turse, Nick, "A secret war in 120 Countries: The Pentagon's new power elite," *TomDispatch*, August 3, 2011.

12 US Department of Defense, news transcript, "DoD news briefing: Secretary Rumsfeld and Gen. Meyers," January 7, 2003, which announced steps to strengthen US Special Operations Command.

13 Scahill, Jeremy, "The secret US war in Pakistan," *Nation*, November 23, 2009, quoting Col. Lawrence Wilkerson, chief of staff to Secretary of State Colin Powell from 2002 to 2005: "I think Cheney and Rumsfeld went directly into JSOC. I think they went into JSOC at times, perhaps most frequently, without the SOCOM [Special Operations] commander at the time even knowing it. The receptivity in JSOC was quite good." Black, Eric, "Investigative reporter Seymour Hersh describes 'executive assassination ring,'" *MinnPost*, March 11, 2009, in which Hersh said of JSOC: "They do not report to anybody, except in the Bush-Cheney days, they reported directly to the Cheney office."

14 Priest and Arkin, *Top secret America*, pp. 236–237, which describes the rules of engagement under the EXORD. Ambinder and Grady, *The command*, in which they write: "JSOC could not set foot in Iran; it had to jump through hoops to chase terrorists in Pakistan; Somalia was an open zone."

15 Ignatius, David, "Rewriting Rumsfeld's rules," *Washington Post*, June 3, 2011.

16 Scahill, Jeremy, "Osama's assassins," *Nation*, June 8, 2011.

17 Alston, Philip, "The CIA and targeted killings beyond borders," *Harvard National Security Law Journal* 2 (2011): 283–446.

18 Statement of Gen. Barry McCaffrey, USA (Ret.), House Hearing of the Committee on Armed Services, at 2.

19 Ambinder and Grady, *The command.*

20 US Special Operations Command, www.socom.mil/Pages/JointSpecialOperations Command.aspx.

21 US Special Operations Command, *Factbook 2012*, p. 22, which offers the official description of JSOC. However, the *Factbook* does list the MQ-1 Predator and MQ-9 Reaper drones as Special Forces "inventory" (p. 29).

22 Priest and Arkin, *Top secret America*, p. 238.

23 Ghosh, Bobby, and Mark Thompson, "The CIA's silent war in Pakistan," *Time*, June 1, 2009, which describes President Bush's order during the final months of his presidency, and that the CIA greatly increased drone strikes in Pakistan. Bergen, Peter, and Katherine Tiedemann, "Washington's phantom war," *Foreign Affairs*, July/August 2011.

24 Scahill, "The secret US war in Pakistan."

25 *Guardian*, "Pakistan Army GHQ again approves embedding," October 9, 2009.

26 Scahill, Jeremy, "The CIA's secret sites in Somalia," *Nation*, July 12, 2011.

27 Priest and Arkin, *Top secret America*, p. 227.

28 US Department of Defense, news transcript, "DoD news briefing with Geoff Morrell from the Pentagon," November 24, 2009: "[Special Operations Forces] have been for months, if not years now, training Pakistani forces so that they can in turn train other Pakistani military on how to – on certain skills and operational techniques. And that's the extent of our – our, you know, military boots on the ground in Pakistan."

29 A CIA drone strike in 2002 killed a US citizen suspected of ties to al-Qaeda, but the United States reportedly did not begin strikes again until May 2011. Boone, Jeb, and Greg Miller, "U.S. drone strike in Yemen is first since 2002," *Washington Post*, May 5, 2011.

30 Miller, Greg, and Karen DeYoung, "U.S. launches airstrike in Yemen as new details surface about bomb plot," *Washington Post*, May 10, 2012: "U.S. officials said it was too early to determine whether any high-value targets had been killed in the Thursday attack and declined to say whether it had been carried out by the CIA or the U.S. Joint Special Operations Command, which also patrols Yemen with armed drones and conventional aircraft."

31 Entous, Adam, Siobhan Gorman, and Julian E. Barnes, "U.S. relaxes drone rules," *Wall Street Journal*, April 26, 2012: "Both the CIA and U.S. military's Joint Special Operations Command, or JSOC, conduct parallel drone campaigns in Yemen." Miller, Greg, "CIA to operate drones over Yemen," *Washington Post*, June 14, 2011. Mazzetti, Mark, "U.S. is intensifying a secret campaign of Yemen airstrikes," *New York Times*, June 8, 2011.

32 Mazzetti, Mark, "C.I.A. building base for strikes in Yemen," *New York Times*, June 14, 2011.

33 Ambinder and Grady, *The command.*

34 Ibid.

35 Priest and Arkin, *Top secret America*, p. 251.

36 Gorman, Siobhan, and Adam Entous, "CIA plans Yemen drone strikes," *Wall Street Journal*, June 14, 2011. Miller, Greg, and Julie Tate, "CIA shifts focus to killing targets," *Washington Post*, September 1, 2011. Mazzetti, "C.I.A. building base for strikes in Yemen." Miller, "CIA to operate drones over Yemen."

37 Miller, Greg, "Strike on Aulaqi demonstrates collaboration between CIA and military," *Washington Post*, September 30, 2011.

38 Ambinder and Grady, *The command*, which notes that with JSOC expansion, Africa is transitioning "from a CIA to a wider Department of Defense theater."

39 Axe, David, "Hidden history: America's secret drone war in Africa," *Wired*, August 13, 2012.

40 Whitlock, Craig, and Greg Miller, "U.S. assembling secret drone bases in Africa, Arabian Peninsula, officials say," *Washington Post*, September 20, 2011. Barnes, Julian E., "U.S. expands drone flights to take aim at East Africa," *Wall St. Journal*, September 21, 2011.

41 Lemonnier in Djibouti; Arba Minch in Ethiopia; and Seychelles; see http://publicintelligence.net/us-drones-in-africa/.

42 Axe, "Hidden history."

43 Cadde, Aweys, and Mohamed Ahmed, "Airstrikes hit Al-Shabaab camp near Kismayo," Somalia Report, June 24, 2011. Jaffe, Greg, and Karen DeYoung, "U.S. drone targets two leaders of Somali group allied with al-Qaeda, official says," *Washington Post*, June 29, 2011. Mazzetti, Mark, and Eric Schmitt, "U.S. expands its drone war into Somalia," *New York Times*, July 1, 2011. Al Jazeera, "US extends drone strikes to Somalia," July 1, 2011. Guled, Abdi, and Malkhdir M. Muhumed, "'Partner' airstrike hits Somali militants' convoy," Associated Press, June 24, 2011, referring to strike by "military aircraft" from a "partner country."

44 DeYoung, Karen, "CIA idles drone flights from base in Pakistan." *Washington Post*, July 1, 2011.

45 Jaffe and DeYoung, "U.S. drone targets two leaders of Somali group allied with al-Qaeda, official says." Mazzetti and Schmitt, "U.S. expands its drone war Into Somalia."

46 Starr, Barbara, "U.S. strikes al Qaeda affiliate in Somalia," CNN, June 28, 2011.

47 Axe, "Hidden history."

48 Aweys Cadde, "Suspected U.S. drone down in Kismayo," Somalia Report, September 25, 2011. Cobain, Ian, "British 'al-Qaida member' killed in US drone attack in Somalia," *Guardian*, January 22, 2012. Ibrahim, Mohammed, "U.S. drone strike kills foreign commander fighting for militants in Somalia," *New York Times*, January 23, 2012. Pflanz, Mike, "US drone strike in Somalia kills Britain-linked al-Qaeda agent," *Telegraph*, January 22, 2012. Sheikh, Abdi and Feisal Omar, "Somalia's Shabaab says air strike kills foreign fighter," Reuters, January 21, 2012. allAfrica, "Somalia: Drone crashes in Al Shabaab controlled town of southern Somalia," September 25, 2011. *Nation*, "US drones kill 9 civilians in Somalia,"

September 15, 2011. BBC, "Somali militants in key port 'attacked by US drones,'" September 25, 2011. *Al Jazeera*, "Deaths in US drone strike in Somalia," February 25, 2012, which refers to a US military strike.

49 Priest and Arkin, *Top secret America*, p. 222, which notes that when the CIA "needs help, or when the president decides to send agency operatives on a covert mission into a foreign country, it often borrows troops from JSOC." Ambinder and Grady, *The command*, which notes that the JSOC's Mission Support Activity unit has "gathered intelligence directly, technically reporting to the CIA."

50 Allison, Graham, "How it went down," *Time*, May 7, 2012.

51 Schmitt, Eric, and Thom Shanker, *Counterstrike: The untold story of America's secret campaign against Al Qaeda* (New York, NY: Times Books, 2011), p. 259.

52 Ambinder and Grady, *The command*.

53 Miller and Tate, "CIA shifts focus to killing targets."

54 Schmitt and Shanker, *Counterstrike*, p. 245.

55 Miller, "Strike on Aulaqi demonstrates collaboration between CIA and military."

56 Kibbe, Jennifer D. "Conducting Shadow Wars," *Journal of Law and National Security Policy* 5 (2012): 373–392, pp. 382–386.

57 Entous, Adam, "Special Report: How the White House learned to love the drone," Reuters, May 18, 2010: "A former U.S. intelligence official said the CIA was conducting the drone strikes instead of the U.S. military because the covert nature of the program gives Islamabad the 'fig leaf of deniability.'" Ignatius, "Rewriting Rumsfeld's rules," reporting that the "coordination process is often informal" with the CIA director and military commander calling each other "to sort out which activities should be done by the military under Title10 and which should be CIA Title 50 'covert' activities."

58 Peretz, Aki, and Eric Rosenbach, *Find, fix, finish: Inside the counterterrorism campaigns that killed bin Laden and devastated Al Qaeda* (New York, NY: Public Affairs), p. 215: It is described that in the raid that killed Osama bin Laden, JSOC operators were reportedly tasked to "work under CIA direction, which under US law allowed them to pursue covert actions within Pakistan."

59 Ignatius, "Rewriting Rumsfeld's Rules."

60 Chesney, Robert, "Military-intelligence convergence and the law of Title 10/Title 50 debate," *Journal of National Security Law and Policy* 5 (2012): 539–629. Kibbe, "Conducting Shadow Wars," pp. 382–386.

61 Miller and Tate, "CIA shifts focus to killing targets."

62 Wall, Andru E., "Demystifying the Title 10–Title 50 debate: Distinguishing military operations, intelligence activities & covert action," *Harvard National Security Journal* 3 (2011): 85–141, p. 103: includes a Venn diagram of congressional oversight of military and intelligence activities.

63 The committee did not take any legislative action to rectify the situation, relying instead on discussions it had had with the Pentagon. It did, however, issue an ultimatum. House of Representatives No. 111-186, p. 49 (2009): "[I]f DOD does not meet its obligations to inform the Committee of intelligence activities, the

Committee will consider legislative action clarifying the Department's obligation to do so."

64 Hearing Before the H. Armed Servs. Comm. on Central-Special Operations-Transportation Command's Budget, 112th Cong. (2012).

65 US Department of Defense, Directive 2311.01E, "DoD Law of War Program," May 9, 2006, certified current as of February 22, 2011, sec. 4.1.

66 Hays Parks, W., "The United States and the law of war: Inculcating an ethos," *Social Research* 69 (Winter 2002): 981–1015, p. 985.

67 Linder, Douglas, "The My Lai massacre trial," *Jurist* (March 2000).

68 Maj. Jeffrey F. Addicott and Maj. William A. Hudson, Jr., "Twenty-fifth anniversary of My Lai: A time to inculcate the lessons," *Military Law Review* 139 (1993): 153–185, p. 165.

69 Ibid.

70 US Department of Defense Directive 5100.77 (November 5, 1974).

71 US Department of Defense, Directive 2311.01E, "DoD Law of War Program."

72 Hays Park, "The United States and the law of war."

73 Ibid.

74 US Marine Corps, "War Crimes," MCRP 4-11.8B, September 5, 2005: "America is trusted by the world to do the right thing, and so must be the United States Marines. Following the rules, including the rules in warfare, must be a part of our warrior ethos. The application of honor, courage, and commitment in the conduct of military operations means: the honor to comply with the Laws of War, the courage to report all violations, and the commitment to discipline the violators." US Army, *Field Manual* 3-21.75, secs. 1–5, January 2008: in "Warrior Ethos," it is noted that "[e]very Soldier adheres to these laws, and ensures that his subordinates adhere to them as well, during the conduct of their duties. Soldiers must also seek clarification from their superiors of any unclear or apparently illegal order."

75 Human Rights Watch, "'No blood, no foul' soldiers' accounts of detainee abuse in Iraq," 18 (July 2006): 1–53, p. 25, which notes that the report is based primarily on "firsthand accounts by military personnel station in Iraq … from soldiers who witnessed and in some cases participated in abuses." Phillips, Joshua E. S., "Inside the detainee abuse task force," *Nation*, May 13, 2011, which reported that military whistle-blowers faced retaliation from fellow soldiers and internal discipline, factors which can deter them from reporting violations.

76 Lt. Col. Dean Bland, "The Abu Ghraib scandal: Impact on the army profession and the intelligence process," US Army War College Strategy Research Project 8, March 18, 2005.

77 Hays Parks, "The United States and the law of war," pp. 994–995.

78 Ibid., 995.

79 Groves, Brendan, "Civil-military cooperation in civilian casualty investigations: Lessons learned from the Azizabad attack," *Air Force Law Review* 65 (2010): 1–49, p. 33. Diehl, James G., and Charles E. Sloan, "Battle damage assessment: The ground truth," *Joint Force Quarterly* 37 (April 2005): 59–64, p. 63.

80 Center for Law and Military Operations, *The judge advocate general's operational law handbook* (Charlottes, VA, 2011), see p. 78: Rules of Engagement (RoE) are directives issued by a competent military authority that delineate the circumstances and limitations under which US forces will initiate and/or continue combat engagement with other forces encountered. They differ according to the conflict. There are standing rules of engagement that are adapted by combatant command- ers for particular wars. RoE are the most specific sort of instruction for troops, and are based on the broader instruction given in tactical directives.

81 McNeal, Gregory S., "U.S. practice of collateral damage estimation and mitiga- tion," Pepperdine Working Paper (2011), quoting the Joint Civilian Casualty Study.

82 Ibid.

83 Ibid.

84 Joint Publication 3-60, "Joint Targeting," April 13, 2007: Battle damage assessments are often mandated as a matter of policy or regulation, but are not a legal obligation. US military manuals indicate that assessment is an integral part of the targeting cycle. International Security Assistance Force, "COMISAF's Tactical Directive," November 30, 2011: describes a tactical directive issued by Gen. John Allen that requires "ground battle damage assessments in all situations where there is a potential loss of life or injury to insurgents or Afghan civilians, except when an assessment would put ISAF personnel at greater risk."

85 See NATO/International Security and Assistance Force (ISAF) Unclassified Tactical Directive, August 1, 2010. A counterinsurgency guidance released at the same time adopts similar reasoning. COMISAF Counterinsurgency Guidance, August 1, 2010 "If we kill civilians or damage their property in the course of our operations, we will create more enemies than our operations eliminate." This policy has continued since General John Allen took command of the ISAF. General John R. Allen, COMISAF Letter to the Troops, dated July 18, 2011: "We are here to protect the population as we subdue the insurgency, and I expect every member of ISAF to be seized with the intent to eliminate civilian casualties caused by ISAF." Likewise, in NATO/ISAF Unclassified Tactical Directive, July 6, 2009, General Stanley McChrystal stated: "[T]here is a struggle for support and will of the population. Gaining and maintaining that support must be our overriding operational imperative – and the ultimate objective of every action we take."

86 Goldsmith, Jack, *Power and constraint: The accountable presidency after 9/11* (New York, NY: W. W. Norton and Co., 2012), p. 131.

87 US Department of the Army, "Civilian Casualty Mitigation," ATTP 3-37.31, July 2012, pp. 1–5, where it notes that "even unavoidable and lawful CIVCASs [civilian casualties] will be publicized by the news media and critically viewed by the American people, the local population, and the international community."

88 Email from Kenneth S. McGraw, deputy public affairs officer, US Special Operations Command, March 26, 2012 (on file with Columbia Human Rights Clinic).

89 For a discussion of the CIA's statements about whether international law is binding, see Center for Civilians in Conflict and Human Rights Clinic, Columbia Law

School, "The civilian impact of drones: Unexamined costs, Unanswered questions," pp. 57–58.

90 Ibid.

91 Dickinson, Laura A., "Military lawyers, private contractors, and the problem of international law compliance," *International Law and Politics* 42 (2010): 355–388, pp. 367–370.

92 Ibid., p. 367.

93 Scahill, "Osama's assassins."

94 The Al Qaeda EXORD sets rules of engagement for JSOC.

95 Open Society Foundations and The Liaison Office, "The cost of kill/capture: The impact of the night raid surge on Afghan civilians," September 19, 2011, p. 2.

96 Ibid., pp. 20–21: "Despite repeated inquiries, international military officials were not able to confirm that the ISAF [International Security Assistance Force] tactical directives applied to these forces, given their different command structure," though "ISAF officials noted that these forces follow all of the tactical directives in practice, including reporting incidents like suspected civilian casualties immediately."

97 Peretz and Rosenbach, *Find, fix, finish*, p. 128.

98 Porter, Gareth, "How McChrystal and Petraeus built an indiscriminate 'killing machine,'" *Truthout*, September 26, 2011.

99 JSOC stationed task forces in Iraq that were responsible for detention, sometimes in joint operations with the CIA. Human Rights Watch, "'No blood, no foul' soldiers' accounts of detainee abuse in Iraq." Heffernan, Tim, "Who the hell is Stanley McChrystal?" *Esquire*, May 19, 2006.

100 Schmitt, Eric, and Carolyn Marshall. "In secret unit's 'black room,' a grim portrait of U.S. abuse," *New York Times*, March 19, 2006.

101 Priest and Arkin. *Top secret America*, pp. 247–249. Schmitt and Shanker, *Counterstrike*, p. 71.

102 White, Josh, "U.S. generals in Iraq were told of abuse early, inquiry finds, *Washington Post*, December 1, 2004.

103 Ackerman, Spencer, "How the Pentagon's top killers became (unaccountable) spies" (interview with Marc Ambinder), *Wired*, February 13, 2012.

104 Priest and Arkin. *Top secret America*, p. 249.

105 Human Rights Watch, "'No blood, no foul' soldiers' accounts of detainee abuse in Iraq."

106 Heffernan, "Who the hell is Stanley McChrystal?"

107 Ambinder and Grady, *The command*, pp. 997–998: "At the time when McRaven christened the center, its existence was a secret to many U.S intelligence officials, who learned about it by way of an Associated Press newsbreak in early 2011." Dozier, Kimberly, "Building a network to hit militants," Associated Press, January 6, 2011.

108 Opening Statement of Hon. Adam Smith, House Hearing of the Committee on Armed Services, Unconventional Threats and Capabilities Subcommittee,

"Lessons for countering Al Qaeda and the way ahead," H.A.S.C. No. 111-114 September 18, 2008, pp. 1–2.

109 Prepared Statement of Gen. Barry McCaffrey, USA (Ret.), Senate Hearing before the Foreign Relations Committee, "Iraq after the surge," S. HRG. 110–757, April 2, 2008, pp. 10, 33–34. Statement of General Barry McCaffrey, USA (Ret.), House Hearing before the Committee on Armed Services, Oversight and Investigations Committee, "A continuing dialogue: Post-surge alternatives for Iraq (Part 1 and 2)," H.A.S.C. 110–106, January 16, 2008, p. 9.

110 Following the Osama bin Laden killing, the House proposed a resolution commending the men and women of the military and intelligence agencies, and explicitly named JSOC House Resolution, "Commending President Barack Obama and the men and women of the military and intelligence agencies...," H. Res. 240, May 2, 2011, p. 1.

111 House Report of the Committee on Armed Services, "To accompany H.R. 2647, *National Defense Authorization Act for Fiscal Year 2010*," House Report 111–166, June 18, 2009, pp. 364–365: the House Committee on Armed Services urged the USSOCOM Commander to "utilize to the fullest extent the unique interagency authorities available to the Joint Special Operations Command (JSOC) and incorporate guidance and direction from the Director, Center for Special Operations (CSO), in relation to interagency matters and concerns." In fact, Congressional leaders have long touted the interagency coordination strength of JSOC. See, e.g., Statement of Hon. Adam Smith, House Hearing of the Committee on Armed Services, Unconventional Threats and Capabilities Subcommittee, "Irregular warfare and stability operations: Approaches to interagency integration," H.A.S.C. No. 111–118, February 26, 2008, p. 2.

112 Senate Report of the Committee on Armed Services, "To accompany S. 3001, *National Defense Authorization Act for Fiscal Year 2009*," Senate Report 110–335, May 12, 2008, pp. 100–101.

113 Ambinder and Grady, *The command*, p. 638.

114 Ackerman, "How the Pentagon's top killers became (unaccountable) spies."

115 Chesney, "Military-intelligence convergence and the law of Title 10/Title 50 debate," p. 629.

116 Kibbe, "Conducting Shadow Wars," p. 373.

117 Scahill, "The secret US war in Pakistan."

10

Defending the Drones
Harold Koh and the Evolution of US Policy

TARA MCKELVEY

1. OBAMA, KOH, AND THE "BUSINESS OF SECRET KILLINGS"

Harold Hongju Koh, dean of Yale Law School and one of the most highly regarded experts on international human rights, became the legal advisor to the State Department shortly after President Obama was inaugurated. He was one of the most vocal critics of the George W. Bush administration's policies on detention, "enhanced interrogations," and other issues relating to the global war on terror, as the conflict was known at the time. In fact, he was so outraged by US government actions and their questionable legal justification that he was one of the leading members in a movement of academics and international-law experts publicly opposed to the White House officials and their policies. In a hearing before the Senate Judiciary Committee in January 2005, Koh spoke about the legal memos written by the George W. Bush administration lawyers that defended the use of harsh interrogation methods on detainees. Koh described the memo as "perhaps the most clearly erroneous legal opinion I have ever read," claiming that it "grossly over-reads the president's constitutional power."[1] Yet as a high-level adviser to the President Obama and Secretary of State Clinton, he provided legal and policy support for the US government's substantial expansion of the use of armed drones.

When Barack Obama was elected president, liberals in the United States were thrilled that a former community activist – one of their own, they thought – would take control of the White House. They believed that he would roll back the counterterrorism excesses of the Bush administration and would restore the reputation of the United States around the world. Obama promised his supporters that he would engage in many corrective policies, from closing the detention center in Guantanamo Bay to outlawing the use of harsh interrogation methods and torture. In addition, he said that he would hold his deputies to the highest standards and would work hard to make amends with those in other countries who were appalled by US policies under the Bush White House, often viewing them as both morally reprehensible and illegal.

In the early months of the administration, academics, liberals, and others who had supported Obama during the presidential campaign expected major changes. Among the shifts they expected was the appointment of a new group of high-level administration officials and government lawyers who would no longer be as dismissive of international law and human rights as the team working under the Bush White House. In addition, liberals expected the new administration officials to ensure that there was proper legal justification for government policies.

As part of his reformist pledge, Obama named Koh to the position of Legal Advisor at the Department of State, one of the most important jobs in the government, and a central post for ensuring that US policy respected international law. In spring 2009, Koh stepped down from his job as dean of Yale Law School to join the Obama administration as head of "L," as the Office of the Legal Advisor at the Department of State is commonly known.

Koh understood the challenges of the job, at least in theory. He admired others who had previously held the position, yet he had also seen them struggle with many difficult decisions. Mainly, though, he was excited about the possibility of taking a post that he described in a speech as "the most fascinating legal job in the U.S. government."[2]

Many in the legal academy who had known Koh for years believed that he would shake things up in the State Department. They also believed that now that he was in the White House, Obama would make wholesale changes in government policy that would substantially increase respect for international human rights law.

However, the Obama administration did not end up changing US policy as expected – certainly not in the way that legal academics and liberal supporters had both hoped and expected. While some changes were quickly implemented, they were often managed in a manner that exhibited minimal substantive shifts in policy. For example, Obama closed the so-called "black sites," where prisoners were held in secret and interrogated by the Bush administration. By the time the policy was implemented, however, no one was being detained in these sites because these facilities had already been emptied.

In addition, Obama and his deputies formally announced an end to torture, potentially representing a profound change in US policy. However, the administration continued to use rendition to transport prisoners. For example, a so-called "dirty" team of American interrogators questioned a terrorism suspect, Mohamed Ibrahim Ahmed, in a jail in Nigeria, and refused to allow him to retain a lawyer, according to proceedings in a US federal court following his transfer to New York to face charges.[3] In this way Obama administration officials appeared to outsource illicit counterterrorism activities, or to allow actions to unfold secretly in other countries, rather than taking a clear stand to prevent such policies.

Meanwhile, the prison at Guantanamo Bay remained open. This was an issue that Obama and his deputies had initially thought would be easy to resolve, yet it turned out to be an intractable problem, partly because they had underestimated the importance of working with members of Congress on the issue in the early stages of his administration.

While Obama White House officials and government lawyers approached international law and human rights in a serious way, they accepted nearly all of the counterterrorism policies of the second Bush term. This meant that even as White House officials used soaring rhetoric about the importance of human rights and adherence to international legal norms, they chose not to change key policies in a substantive way. Indeed, the Obama White House officials adopted some of the counterterrorism policies, such as a reliance on remotely piloted vehicles, or drones, to target and kill terrorism suspects, with an enthusiasm that surprised even insiders that had worked in the Bush administration.

According to General James Cartwright, the former Vice Chairman of the Joint Chiefs of Staff, when Koh assumed his new position he described drone strikes as "extrajudicial killings." Yet over time, he became an ally of Cartwright and others who supported an expanded covert drone program.

Koh became one of the only administration officials who spoke publicly about the legal basis for the US drone program, defending policies that represented a startling reversal of his prior position. He publicly defended the process of placing people on lists of those who could be targeted and explained that the legal procedures for these actions were "extremely robust."[4] How did Harold Koh, a leading international law expert, and one of the most revered US legal scholars, who spent decades promoting human rights around the globe as a core part of US foreign policy, get into the business of secret killings?

2. A "LIBERAL ICON"

By his own account, Koh had a special appreciation for the liberal values that were woven into the fabric of US society and legal culture, a contrast to the authoritarian regime that he had experienced as a child. Koh was six years old when a military coup toppled the government in South Korea in 1961. His father, Kwang Lim Koh, was acting ambassador to the United States, and soon afterwards resigned from his diplomatic post. Based in Washington, Kwang Lim Koh was concerned about the fate of the political leaders who remained in South Korea – the deposed prime minister had been placed under house arrest – and turned to deputy national security advisor Walt W. Rostow for help. Rostow assured him that American officials knew where the prime minister was and that he would be safe. "Rostow's words stunned my father, who simply could not believe that any country could have such global power and reach," wrote Koh, explaining that his parents told him the story repeatedly when he was growing up, "as proof of the goodness of American power."[5]

Koh's father was offered a teaching position at Yale University, and over the years his son would excel academically and reach the highest levels of success. A graduate of Harvard University and Harvard Law School, Koh served in 1981 as a law clerk for Supreme Court Justice Harry A. Blackmun and was deeply influenced by the classic liberal legal values of his boss. Justice Blackmun was perhaps best known as the author of the majority opinion in *Roe* v. *Wade* and a major voice of classic twentieth-century liberal jurisprudence. He had a modest, unassuming style. He drove a Volkswagen to work and ate breakfast with the law clerks. As Koh wrote:

> In law school, we had learned to revere the larger-than-life Justices – Holmes, Frankfurter, Douglas – brilliant, arrogant men (always men) with slashing pens, free of indecision and self-doubt. Harry Blackmun hardly fit that mold. During the Term I clerked, he never gave an order. He worked constantly, arriving at seven, leaving at seven, and reading at home until midnight. He never cut corners. He never pretended that decision was effortless. No case was beneath his dignity, nor any task so trivial that it could be done carelessly. "This is the end of the line," he often said, and everything we did mattered.[6]

Koh went on to explain how seriously Blackmun understood the gravity of his role and its impact on ordinary people: "In dissents read from the bench, he would mention litigants' names and how the cases affected their aspirations," Koh wrote. "'How will this affect real people?' he would ask, in tiny, perfect handwriting in the margins of cert pool memos."[7]

Koh's ideas, commitment to the law, and sense of social responsibility were shaped by both his father's view of the United States and his own experience as a clerk for Justice Blackmun, one of the most powerful men in the country who acted with a sense of humility even as he reviewed cases before the Supreme Court. His father's lessons about the positive influence of US global power and its role in the world, and Justice Blackmun's thoughtful approach to decision making on the Supreme Court, helped define Koh's career as a law professor and expert in international law. These experiences continued to guide him during years spent in public service in public service as he faced his own difficult choices and grappled with the repercussions that government's policies would have on individuals in the United States and abroad.

In 1985, Koh started teaching at Yale Law School, following in the footsteps of his father, who had taught a course called East Asian Law and Society in the early 1960s. Koh is the author or co-author of eight books, has published more than 180 articles, and is revered as a brilliant scholar. Yale was Koh's home, a place that he would occasionally leave in order to work in Washington, but where he would always return. (In January 2013, he left the State Department to go back to Yale Law School, becoming the Sterling Professor of International Law.)

In the 1990s, President Bill Clinton reached out to liberals and academics and offered them a chance to shape law and policy, rather than simply write about the issues from within the academy. Koh was appointed Assistant Secretary of State for Democracy, Human Rights and Labor. He served for three years and then returned to Yale in 2001. Also, Koh created the Orville H. Schell Jr. Center for International Human Rights at Yale Law School and was the driving force behind major lawsuits against the US government when it used Guantanamo as a holding facility for Haitian immigrants seeking asylum.

After the terrorist attacks in September 2001, Bush White House officials struggled with the challenge of combating al-Qaeda and other terrorist groups that were operating as rogue agents, unaligned with a particular state or government. To do this, they formulated a new kind of counterterrorism strategy for the United States based on a set of creative legal arguments that ran counter to dominant understandings of international law. White House officials believed that al-Qaeda represented a security risk that was so different from prior threats that new, more ambitious policies were required. Koh and other legal scholars, especially those with a strong background in international law and human rights, were deeply troubled by these policies and their justifications. They were particularly worried about how a response to the legitimate threat of terrorism would be used to expand of the legal authority of the president to authorize aggressive tactics that violated established principles of domestic and international law.

As part of the evolving Bush-era US counterterrorism policy, John Yoo, a lawyer in the Justice Department's Office of Legal Counsel, wrote a number of influential legal memos. These opinions reinterpreted the Geneva Conventions, the core international treaties that define state responsibilities and limit state actions during wartime, arguing that the president had a broad mandate to fight terrorists. Within this new paradigm, Americans were allowed to use "enhanced interrogation methods" on detainees, techniques that were widely recognized as torture and clearly prohibited by international law. President Bush also authorized a CIA-targeting program to hunt down and kill suspected terrorists in countries around the world.

Koh told a *New York Times* reporter in December 2002 that he found President Bush's targeted-killing program unsettling and believed that it violated the government's long-standing domestic legal ban on assassination. He wondered aloud how government officials would determine which individuals would be hunted down and killed: "The question is, what factual showing will demonstrate that they had warlike intentions against us and who sees that evidence before any action is taken?"[8]

Koh and other legal scholars were uneasy with the Bush White House policies because they believed they violated international law. In addition, they were especially concerned with secret government activities out of sensitivity to recent American history and the prior activities of the CIA.

In the mid-1970s, after the journalist Seymour Hersh published an exposé about the CIA abuses in the *New York Times*, the US Congress created a special investigative committee to look into the scope of covert intelligence operations. The committee was led by Senator Frank Church, who reviewed decades of secret actions by CIA operatives in the United States and around the world. Members of the Church committee, as it became known, gained access to a great deal of classified information and uncovered agency plots to assassinate Castro, the South Vietnamese president, and a Chilean general. The revelations of the Church committee helped to convince congressional leaders that independent actions to target and kill enemies on the part of both the CIA and the executive branch should be ended. In 1976 President Gerald R. Ford signed Executive Order 11905, a rule that has the force of law, banning the CIA from carrying out assassinations.

Between 2002 and 2009, Koh was one of the harshest critics of the Bush administration. He joined other academics and international legal scholars, including some who had previously worked in government, to criticize Bush White House policies, expressing their views in op-eds, journal articles, and interviews with journalists. Martin S. Lederman, who served in the Justice Department's Office of Legal Counsel (OLC), told a *Time* magazine reporter that he believed Yoo's work would "be seen as one of the most extreme deviations from the rule of law and from the President's obligation to take care that the law is faithfully executed."[9] Lederman and David J. Barron criticized the writings of Bush administration officials in a 2008 article published in *Harvard Law Review*, stating that their "bold claims of preclusive war powers are clearly rooted in an overarching view of executive authority."[10]

Koh echoed these ideas in his writings and public lectures. For example, in testimony presented to members of the Senate Judiciary Committee's Subcommittee on the Constitution on Restoring the Rule of Law in 2008 he wrote, "The Bush Administration has consistently asserted a constitutional theory of unfettered executive power."[11]

Koh continued stating that officials in the Bush White House had rejected the universalism of human rights in favor of executive efforts to create law-free zones, such as Guantanamo; executive courts, such as military commissions; extralegal persons, who are labeled enemy combatants; and law-free practices, such as extraordinary rendition, all of which it claimed were exempt from judicial review.[12]

In his testimony, Koh also expressed the belief that the United States embodied the highest standards in human rights and international law:

> From World War II until September 11, ours was universally regarded as a nation that valued human rights and the rule of law, that spoke out against injustice and dictatorship in other countries, and that tried to practice what we preached. Of course, we were never perfect, but we were usually thought to be sincere . . . Other countries would listen to what Americans had to say because we were powerful, but they thought us powerful in part because they thought us principled.[13]

For his long-standing commitment to international law and his efforts over the years to promote liberal values, journalist and author Paul Starobin heralded Koh: "[He is] the inspiration for a generation of human rights activists and lawyers passionately committed to a vision of a post-imperial America as a model of constitutional restraint." He went on to state, "[H]is colleagues viewed him as not only a brilliant scholar but a 'liberal icon.'"[14]

Koh was not the only one who opposed President Bush's counterterrorism strategy. For example, William H. Taft, IV, who had previously served as Deputy Secretary of Defense in the Reagan administration and served as Legal Advisor for the US State Department under George W. Bush, opposed the president's efforts to expand the authority of the executive branch.

Years later, Taft recalled how he felt when he saw one of John Yoo's memos in early January 2002 and realized that Yoo and other lawyers in the Justice Department did not believe the president had to respect or abide by the Geneva Conventions. "I was surprised," Taft said. "Actually, I have to say maybe it sounds a little silly, but I thought they were wrong and didn't think we would have too much trouble persuading them they were wrong. It turned out we could not persuade them."[15]

Two days after he read Yoo's memo, Taft sent a response: "In previous conflicts, the United States has dealt with tens of thousands of detainees without repudiating its obligations under the Conventions. I have no doubt we can do so here, where a relative handful of persons are involved."[16]

His memo came to light sometime after it was written. In fact, Koh referenced the document, which represented a significant effort to convince Yoo and other Justice Department lawyers that they should reconsider their position. In a speech in Washington, Koh stated, "Taft ended on this memorable and poignant note,"[17] which he then quoted from the memo's closing paragraph: "Your draft acknowledges that several of its conclusions are close questions. The attached draft comments will, I expect, show you that they are actually incorrect as well as incomplete. We should talk."[18]

3. SPEAKING LAW TO POWER

After Barack Obama was sworn in as president, liberal scholars and academics such as Koh and Lederman were offered positions in the government, mirroring Clinton's nominations a decade earlier. Writing an article for *Slate*, "And then they came for Koh," legal correspondent Dahlia Lithwick said that President Obama could have chosen "mild-mannered tax attorneys to these high government positions." Instead, she explained, "he opted to pick precisely the sorts of people we most need there: fierce advocates who care deeply about these agencies and the law as it applies to them."[19]

As the State Department's Legal Adviser, Koh was given a chance to correct the course that Bush White House officials had embarked on during their years in Washington and to re-establish the moral ground that the United States had once claimed. Koh understood the limits of the position of legal adviser in a bureaucracy such as the State Department, but he embraced the chance to oversee an office of international lawyers and to help shape the thinking of the secretary of state and the president as they forged a new path for the nation.

In a speech at Georgetown University in March 2011, he said:

Ideally, the legal adviser should act as an independent, nonpartisan expert on and scholar of international law, with a wide-ranging remit across the department's entire workload, always giving legal advice that is sensitive to the clients' policy objectives, takes the long view, and seeks to advance the best long-term interests of the State Department as an institution rather than the interests of any particular individual or administration. These competing commitments require the legal adviser to balance the concerns of politics and the law, to report directly to the secretary (with career lawyers in turn reporting directly to the legal adviser), and to run an office of professional international lawyers that is kept in the loop with regard to all departmental matters.[20]

At the 2010 Annual Meeting of the American Society for International Law (ASIL) he said: "We also serve as a conscience for the U.S. government with regard to international law. The Legal Advisor, along with many others in policy as well as legal positions, offers opinions on both the wisdom and morality of proposed international actions."[21]

He went on to quote the legal scholar Richard B. Bilder, who co-authored a 2004 paper that was subtitled "Lawyers and Torture," which described the role of the State Department Legal Adviser as one who engaged in "speaking law to power."[22] Koh said, "In this role, the Legal Advisor must serve not only as a source of black-letter advice to his clients, but more fundamentally as a source of good judgment. That means that one of the most important roles of the legal advisor is to advise the secretary when a policy option being proposed is 'lawful but awful.'"[23]

Koh's day as the State Department's Legal Adviser started with an 8:45 a.m. meeting with Secretary Hillary Rodham Clinton and other high-level officials. When he walked into the room, he carried an ASIL coffee mug. He was proud of his three-decade-long affiliation with ASIL and wanted to stay close to the organization and its principles during his tenure at the State Department. ASIL was founded in 1906 and is the premier US organization that promotes international relations based on a respect for the norms and principles of international law. He began attending the annual ASIL conferences in the late 1970s and later recalled what it was like to see prominent experts and scholars at the conference: "For international lawyers, that is as close as we get to watching the Hollywood stars stroll the red carpet at the Oscars."[24]

However, by many accounts, from both inside and outside the government, his allegiances to ASIL were tested by what happened while he was working in the Obama administration.

The State Department's Office of the Legal Adviser has a staff of roughly 180 lawyers, all of whom, explained Koh, have "a finely tuned sense of humor and irony." Having a sense of humor was helpful in a place where debates about Libya, drone strikes, and other issues of global importance were discussed often under tight deadlines and within a tense political climate. The work was difficult and they often faced mundane obstacles and challenges; the printing machine reserved for classified documents was frequently on the blink and Koh recounted how he and his staff often found themselves "eating out of vending machines."[25]

Many of the issues they faced were complex and multilayered, and Office of the Legal Advisor staff commonly worked with lawyers and others from multiple federal agencies. At times, State Department lawyers were at odds with OLC lawyers, precisely the sort of conflict that former Legal Adviser William Taft experienced under the Bush administration. The OLC remains the primary office for government legal opinions and its lawyers often see themselves as the ultimate arbiters of the most authoritative and correct interpretations of domestic and international law. Nevertheless, State Department lawyers believe that they had the final word on international law issues within the executive branch. According to John Bellinger, another former Legal Advisor, which agency's positions are authoritative is "an issue that has still not been sorted out."[26] Presidents theoretically can ignore legal opinions written by lawyers in the OLC, but in practice that almost never happens.

4. FROM AN "IN-HOUSE SCOLD" TO KEY SUPPORTER OF EXPANDED DRONE STRIKES

Koh initially had trouble with Obama White House officials, who rejected the harsh interrogation methods that were sanctioned under the Bush administration, but otherwise adopted most of the counterterrorism policies that were formulated in President Bush's second term. "He was so far out there, and so convinced that everything the previous administration had done was wrong," General Cartwright said.[27] In addition, some things seemed to bother Koh more. He was "a little queasier about the whole killing enterprise" than others who worked for the government, explained journalist Daniel Klaidman in his book, *Kill or Capture: The War on Terror and the Soul of the Obama Presidency*.[28] A *Wall Street Journal* editorial described Koh as an "in-house scold."[29]

Koh modeled his actions with the care and commitment of his mentor Justice Blackmun, who cautiously considered abstract notions of justice as well as the practical impact of his judgments. Koh faced his own tough decisions and approached each matter in a personal manner, with sensitivity toward those individuals affected by his actions. While he was the dean at Yale, Koh spent hours poring over files of law school applicants. As Legal Advisor, he spent roughly the same number of hours examining the files of young people who were also at a pivotal moment in their lives, though the outcome was more significant: they might be killed by American forces. "Often I know their backgrounds as intimately as I know those students," Koh explained.[30]

Nevertheless, Koh was savagely critical during policy debates about drones in the early days of the Obama White House. "Everybody hated him," said General James Cartwright, the former vice chairman of the Joint Chiefs of Staff. He described how Koh would rip into him and others. "He would say, 'Oh, you military guys, you're just so stupid.'"[31] Koh got so worked up during the meetings in which he failed to win people over that he would often rant about his colleagues. At the time Koh described drone strikes as "extrajudicial killings," referencing a major violation of international law.

Even the most diplomatic interlocutors, such as a former UN legal counsel who tussled with Koh recently when he was on a panel in Washington, said that he could be "a little bit impolite." Cartwright is less diplomatic: "Just as a personality – he's annoying."[32]

During this time, the administration was committed to a substantial increase in drone operations. In fact, from Obama's inauguration in 2009 to the end of 2013, American forces carried out more than 370 drone strikes in Pakistan, according to the Washington-based think tank New America. This is roughly six times more drone attacks than were conducted during eight years of President George W. Bush's administration.

These strikes have killed fearsome enemies, such as Taliban leader Baitullah Mehsud, who was hit by a CIA-directed drone strike in Pakistan in August 2009; radical cleric and US citizen Anwar al-Awlaki, who was killed in Yemen in September 2011; and scores of other al-Qaeda and Taliban commanders in multiple sites around the world. The strikes also have killed people who got in the way, including women and children. The expansion of the targeted killing program has been fueled by a complicated set of factors ranging from national security concerns, to economic savings, to political efficacy.

When Obama entered the White House in January 2009, the outlook for the country was dire. Unemployment was alarmingly high at 7.5 percent, up from 5 percent during the previous spring; the real estate market was in steep decline; and the gross domestic product was sinking. President Obama and his advisers were deeply concerned about the faltering economy and were trying to wind down the wars in Iraq and Afghanistan as a way to spare American lives, address declining public support, and save money. Within this context, administration officials saw the political advantages in the drone program: "A UAV doesn't have a mom," a retired military officer explained, using an acronym for an unmanned aerial vehicle. "If a UAV is destroyed, no one cares."[33]

Some Washington officials questioned the wisdom of the strategy. For example, Mike McConnell, the director of National Intelligence, worried that the allure of covert action would be too strong for the president to stop once he began. Moreover, he believed that the battle against al-Qaeda was best addressed by requiring not a strategy of targeted strikes but a nuanced approach that linked military action with political and economic support for counterterrorism. In the end, however, McConnell had less influence than key advisers who were more familiar with domestic politics, such as Chief of Staff Rahm Emanuel; Vice President Joe Biden; and White House National Security Advisor Tom Donilon (who had previously worked as a lobbyist for mortgage giant Fannie Mae and was a key figure in Biden's 2008 presidential campaign). Emanuel was especially keen on the drone program and he would call CIA Director Leon Panetta, who was in charge of drone strikes in Pakistan, and ask: "Who did we get today?"[34]

Other critics, including many academics and legal experts, echoed Koh's criticisms of Bush administration policy, suggesting that the US drone program violated international law and the sovereignty of other nations. They also claimed that these policies ran counter to core liberal and democratic principles, the very ideas that Koh used to define his personal and professional identity.

Nevertheless, over time, the drone program gained support among the US public. By February 2012, 83 percent of Americans said they were in favor of using drones against al-Qaeda and other terrorists.[35] Meanwhile, the program was reviled in Pakistan and other countries where the strikes were carried out, defining targeted killing by drones as a key subject for growing tensions and demonstrations. In this way, the drone program came to define Obama administration foreign policy in a way that was perceived internationally as heavy-handed, disrespectful of national sovereignty, and in clear violation of international law.

It was within this context that Harold Koh, as Legal Advisor to the Department of State, was charged with developing legal arguments to support government policies that appeared much like those he had previously criticized.

One of the most important cases arose in spring 2010, less than a year after Koh started his job. At the time, lawyers in OLC were examining the question of whether or not the CIA could kill an American citizen. President Obama's advisers and CIA analysts believed that a cleric named Anwar al-Awlaki, who was originally from New Mexico, was a threat to national security. An eloquent speaker, al-Awlaki wrote for a slickly designed al-Qaeda magazine, *Inspire*. In one piece, they published a close-up of a black handgun with a photo caption about a military officer, Major Nidal Malik Hasan, who had shot and killed thirteen people in Fort Hood, Texas, with text by al-Awlaki, "How can there be any dispute about the virtue of what he has done?"[36] In fact, al-Awlaki had corresponded with Major Hasan before the Fort Hood shootings, and since 2007, was linked by email correspondence, either directly or indirectly, to instigators of many other terrorist plots in the United States. However, because he was an American citizen, marking him for targeting raised complex legal and constitutional questions.

Aside from the legal issues, Koh was not sure that al-Awlaki was as bad as others said. Koh knew that al-Awlaki would not have a chance to appear in court and defend himself against charges of terrorism, so he wanted to make sure the case was as solid as possible. Koh retreated to a "crappy little room" at the State Department where officials with high-level security clearances could read classified documents. He spent five hours in the small room and reviewed the material that had been compiled about al-Awlaki's life and activities as a member of al-Qaeda. "There were plans to poison Western water and food supplies with botulinum tox, as well as attack Americans with ricin and cyanide," Klaidman wrote. "Koh was shaken when he left the room. Awlaki was not just evil, he was satanic."[37]

For many, that was beside the point. Jameel Jaffer, the deputy legal director of the American Civil Liberties Union, an organization that filed a lawsuit against the Obama administration on behalf of the father of the cleric explained, "The government's power to use lethal force against its own citizens should be strictly limited to circumstances where the threat of life is concrete and specific, and also imminent."[38]

"It's an important question," said former Legal Adviser William Taft. "And I think a fairly close one."[39]

A federal statute, the Foreign Murder of United States Nationals,[40] states that an American who "kills or attempts to kill a national of the United States while such national is outside the United States" may be prosecuted. In addition, the Fourth Amendment provides protections against forcible state seizure, stating that the government cannot detain a person without justification, and the Fifth Amendment states that citizens shall not be "deprived of life, liberty, or property, without due process of law."

In fact, Georgetown University's Gary Solis, a former military prosecutor and judge who was involved in more than 700 courts martial, argued in an op-ed for the *Washington Post* that as civilians were running the CIA's lethal operations, they could be classified as unlawful combatants. This meant that they would not be protected by key provisions within the law of armed conflict that prevented military personnel from being prosecuted for legitimate wartime activity. So, if civilian CIA officers or contractors killed al-Awlaki, they could be potentially charged with murder.[41]

Nevertheless, government lawyers stated that al-Awlaki was an enemy combatant and that his current home, Yemen, was a battleground in the global war against al-Qaeda and allied groups. Therefore, the lethal operation could be justified an act of self-defense for the United States, a means of protecting Americans from harm. The argument was based on the Authorization for the Use of Military Force, which was adopted by Congress shortly after the 2001 terrorist attacks, which allowed the president to use force against "those nations, organizations or persons he determines planned, authorized, committed or aided" the 9/11 attacks.[42] For Obama administration lawyers, this provided a key justification for determining that killing al-Awlaki was legal and therefore could not be considered murder. On September 30, 2011, a missile attack from a drone killed al-Awlaki in Yemen. Some of the most vocal supporters of this lethal operation were lawyers who served in the Bush White House, who had previously defended the use of harsh interrogations, arguably acts that constituted torture, against detainees. For example, in a piece for the *Wall Street Journal*, John Yoo applauded the way that Obama White House officials "embraced the legal theories of the Bush administration."[43]

Critics of the Obama administration accused Koh of overseeing a program of "extrajudicial killing." He believed that these critics were misguided. The clearest public expression of this position came in March 2012 at the Fairmont Hotel in Washington when Koh presented a major address at the ASIL annual meeting. It was 8:45 in the morning and Koh already had a five o'clock shadow. His dark jacket was wrinkled in the back. Working for the government is hell on your looks, and he looked even more rumpled and jowly than usual.

Like Supreme Court Justice Harry A. Blackmun, Koh has a simple, unassuming style. He carries his belongings in a worn tote bag from Labyrinth Books, an independent bookseller, and usually has a can of Diet Coke near him. Even with a disheveled appearance, or perhaps because of it, Koh inspired deep affection among people in Washington, judging by the number of women who approached him that morning at the hotel, patting his arms and shoulders and whispering to him. Women – and men, too – were drawn to him because of his brilliance and also because he wore his scholarship lightly, making allusions to UN Security Council resolutions and *Star Trek* with equal ease. ("Thank you, Captain Kirk," said the moderator of a State Department panel on Libya in 2012 "Sulu, please," Koh replied dryly.[44])

Speaking before many of his academic colleagues at one of the country's most important international law gatherings, he described the legal justification for the Obama administration's drone program: "The principles of distinction and proportionality that the United States applies are not just recited at meetings. This administration is committed to ensuring that the targeting practices that I have described are lawful."[45]

In other words, one of the world's foremost authorities on international law and human rights, and the top State Department legal official, explained that the US government's expanded use of drones for targeted killing was completely lawful.

In this and other public forums, Koh clarified the position that individuals can be slated for death if they are senior members of al-Qaeda and are planning to attack Americans, regardless of whether they are fighting in Afghanistan, a country where the United States is officially at war and therefore allowed to kill its enemies, or on a desert road in Yemen, a sovereign country where the United States is not at war.

General Cartwright said that Koh had undergone a difficult process while he was wrestling with the legal and ethical questions of the targeted killing program, one that had encompassed many of meetings and discussions. "It's like going through these five stages of grief," Cartwright explained, joking about how Koh experienced the policy debate within the government.

Afterwards, Cartwright said, he reassured Koh that the process, however arduous, had been valuable. "I told him, 'Now you have conviction,'" Cartwright said.[46]

"If you had told anybody who knew Harold Koh that he would someday be making this argument, they would have snickered at you," said Benjamin Wittes, a senior fellow at the Brookings Institution and author of *Law and the Long War: The Future of Justice in the Age of Terror*. Wittes supports the targeted killing program, but he believes that Koh and others have not gone far enough in outlining the legal framework for these operations. "The answer can't be, 'It's okay if Obama does it,'" he said. "That's not the position of a morally serious person."[47]

Koh's friends and colleagues have theories about why he changed his views about targeted warfare since coming to Washington. W. Michael Reisman, a Yale professor of international law, and the author of a 1995 paper, "Covert action," said, tartly, "I guess he understood it better."[48]

Many, like Reisman, were not surprised by Koh's arguments in support of targeted killing by drones. "I think when you join the government, you get access to other kinds of information and also hear the opinions of other professional staff," said Charles J. Dunlap Jr. a retired Air Force general who is now executive director of Duke University's Center on Law, Ethics, and National Security. He said that he generally agreed with Koh's position, though he would like to know more about its legal basis.[49]

To gain access to information about the drone program, lawyers at media organizations and civil liberties groups have filed *Freedom of Information Act* requests and lawsuits. In 2011, the *New York Times* went to court claiming that government officials have refused to release information about the program. These actions have stalled in the courts or been thrown out and officials have yet to release additional information.

5. STATESMAN FOR THE OBAMA ADMINISTRATION'S DRONE PROGRAM

Less than a month after Anwar al-Awlaki was killed, Abdulrahman al-Awlaki, the 16-year-old Denver native and the son of Anwar, was also killed in a drone strike in Yemen. American officials said later that Abdulrahman died because of a targeting mistake. "Not even the White House knows who it's killing with drone strikes – civilian or militant," said Naureen Shah, the lead author of a September 2012 report about the drone program from Columbia Law School.[50]

Philip Alston, the former United Nations Special Rapporteur on extrajudicial, summary, or arbitrary executions wrote: "Assertions by Obama administration officials, as well as by many scholars, that these operations comply with international standards are undermined by the total absence of any forms of credibly transparency or verifiable accountability."[51]

Reviewing the government's own systems for ensuring compliance with the law, he continued:

> The CIA's internal control mechanism, including its Inspector General, have had no discernible impact; executive control mechanisms have either not been activated at all or have ignored the issue; congressional oversight has given a "free pass" to the CIA in this area; judicial review has been effectively precluded; and external oversight has been reduced to media coverage which is all too often dependent on information leaked by the CIA itself. As a result, there is no meaningful domestic accountability for a burgeoning program of international killing.[52]

For many in the international law community, Koh's arguments in favor of Obama administration policies were especially disturbing, particularly following two terms of the Bush administration's legal claims. As Harvard Law School Professor Noah Feldman explained:

> People were not angry at the Bush policies because the Bush administration offered a mediocre legal justification, but because the policies were wrong. It was not, "We should be mad at John Yoo because he was bad at his job."

We should be mad at Yoo because he said torture is okay ... Most of the world understands that laws are tools that we use to try and get the government to do the right thing. The idea that the government can do the wrong thing but it can be legally justified makes it OK – that is a very, very confused position.[53]

Yet as Feldman wrote in *Bloomberg News*, "Killing terrorists with drones is great politics."[54] It means that Obama White House officials can avoid legal questions of detention and interrogation.

Moreover, as American University's Kenneth Anderson explained in an essay widely read in Washington, unmanned aircraft provide a politically compelling policy because "if one intends to kill, the incentive is to do so from a standoff position, because it removes potentially messy questions of surrender."[55]

Nevertheless, Koh's transition from international law scholar to State Department statesman for the drone program has been a surprise for many. "In the Bush administration, we had leading academics who fell from grace after responding to the allure of power," said Jonathan Turley, a law professor at George Washington University, "and what has been unnerving to many law professors is that Obama seems to have the same corrupting influence on lawyers that Bush had."[56]

Bruce Ackerman, a professor at Yale Law School said: "Why did he get involved? It's quite inconsistent with his general work before. Koh's claim to fame as a law professor has to do with the notion that the way international law and human rights become effective is through internalization in people like the Legal Advisor at the State Department."

He continued, "To put it gently, targeted killings are not acceptable under international law."[57]

Nevertheless, Koh says that he has felt little tension between his previous life in the academy and the position that he held in the State Department. He explained:

[B]ecause my job is simply to provide the President and the Secretary of State with the very best legal advice that I can give them, I have felt little conflict with my past roles as a law professor, dean, and human rights lawyer because as my old professor, former Legal Advisor Abram Chayes, once put it, "There's nothing wrong with a lawyer holding the United States to its own best standards and principles."[58]

He believes that he and other officials have addressed legal issues appropriately within the framework of domestic and international law:

If it ever came to the point where I thought those rules were being violated, I would resign. Frankly, I'm someone who has both served in Democratic and Republic administrations, and I have sued both Democratic and Republican administrations for violations of the rules of war. To me, obedience with the law is why I'm here, and if I ever believed that this administration was not obeying the law, I would leave. So since I'm still here you can draw your own conclusions.[59]

One of Koh's favorite jokes is about a man who is traveling near Galway, Ireland. He gets lost and implores someone for directions: "So how do you get to Dublin?" he asks. The other person says, "I wouldn't start from here." After becoming the State Department's Legal Adviser, Koh told the joke frequently in Washington as a way to illustrate the challenges that he and other officials were facing in the government, though the story might also be used to describe his own journey.

At the 2012 annual meeting of ASIL, a journalist asked Koh why he had seemed conflicted – and eventually changed his mind – about the legality of drone strikes, referring to the way that General Cartwright described his change of heart. Standing near a coffee table, Koh was quiet for a moment. "If that's what Cartwright remembers, he's wrong. I never used that phrase. If you look at the speech I gave at the ASIL conference," he said, referring to a prior meeting in March 2010, "you'll see that I said they were not 'extrajudicial killings.'"[60]

Koh brushed off a question about the 2002 *New York Times* interview in which he criticized targeted killings and claimed his views on the subject have remained the same, "I have never changed my mind," he says. "Not from before I was in the government – or after."[61]

When a journalist asked former Legal Advisor William Taft why the law matters when everyone thinks something is okay, Taft took a moment to respond. "That is actually a deep question. When a human life is at stake, there needs to be a process for determining that a person can be executed or shot in an armed conflict," he says. "Otherwise, we will have an individual just deciding that he wants to kill someone."

"What if it's the president?" someone asked.

"Especially," said Taft. "He's the main person who might possibly have this authority, and you've got to watch it."[62]

Koh has not publicly expressed doubts about the drone program.

However, some former officials, even the program's strongest supporters, have done so. For example General James Cartwright, now retired, sitting in his office at the Center for Strategic and International Studies said: "To me, the weakness in the drone activity is that if there's no one on the ground, and the person puts his hands out – he can't surrender. I have to have the authority to go after you – or not. I can't be an assassin. What makes it worse with a Predator is you're actually watching it. You know when he puts his hands up."[63]

Koh speaks with conviction about the drone program, just as Cartwright once said he would. At a 2012 panel at the US Holocaust Memorial Museum, "In Search of Accountability: Justice After Nuremberg," Koh asked, "How do we deliver justice to the enemy?" He answered, "I think there are different ways. It can be delivered through trials. Drones also deliver."[64] He spoke in measured tones, with a mastery of complex legal and ethical issues, an ideal spokesman for one of the administration's most controversial policies.

NOTES

1 Harold Koh, testimony before the Subcommittee on the Constitution on the Restoring the Rule of Law, Senate Judiciary Committee, September 16, 2008.

2 Harold Koh, "The Obama administration and international law," keynote address at the annual meeting of the American Society of International Law, Washington, DC, March 25, 2010.

3 Whitlock, Craig. "Renditions continue under Obama, despite due-process concerns," *Washington Post*, January 1, 2013.

4 Koh, "The Obama administration and international law."

5 Koh, Harold, "On American exceptionalism," Yale Faculty Scholarship Series, 2003.

6 Koh, Harold, "A tribute to Justice Harry A Blackmun," Yale Faculty Scholarship Series, 1994.

7 Ibid.

8 Risen, James, and David Johnston, "Threats and responses: Hunt for Al Qaeda; Bush has widened authority of CIA to kill terrorists" *New York Times*, December 15, 2002.

9 Dwyer, Johnny, "Bush torture memo slapped down by court," *Time*, November 3, 2008.

10 Barron, David J., and Martin S. Lederman, "The commander in chief at the lowest ebb – framing the problem, doctrine, and original understanding," *Harvard Law Review* 121 (2008): 692–800, p 712.

11 Koh, testimony before the Subcommittee on the Constitution on the Restoring the Rule of Law.

12 Ibid.

13 Ibid.

14 Starobin, Paul, "A moral flip-flop?" *New York Times*, August 7, 2011.

15 McKelvey. Tara, "Interview with Harold Koh, Obama's defender of drone strikes," *Daily Beast*, April 8, 2012.

16 Memorandum from Taft to John C. Yoo, January 11, 2002; available through the National Security Archive Project at The George Washington University.

17 Harold Koh, keynote address, "Law and U.S. foreign policy," Washington, DC, March 30, 2011.

18 Ibid.

19 Lithwick, Dahlia, "And then they came for Koh," *Slate*, March 26, 2012.

20 Koh, keynote address, "Law and U.S. foreign policy."

21 Koh, "The Obama administration and international law."

22 Bilder, Richard B., and Detlev F. Vagts, "Speaking law to power: Lawyers and torture," *American Journal of International Law* 98 (2004): 689–695.

23 Koh, "The Obama administration and international law."

24 Koh, Harold, "The role of the Legal Adviser," Yale Faculty Scholarship Series, 2010.

25 McKelvey, "Interview with Harold Koh, Obama's defender of drone strikes."

26 Dahl, Dick, "Bellinger, former state department legal adviser, offers advice to Harvard Law School students," Harvard Law School, September 30, 2010.

27 McKelvey, "Interview with Harold Koh, Obama's defender of drone strikes."

28 Klaidman. Daniel, *Kill or Capture: The war on terror and the soul of the Obama presidency* (New York, NY: Houghton Mifflin Harcourt, 2012).

29 *Wall Street Journal*, "Killing Awlaki: The drone campaign is legal and a national security success," October 3, 2011.

30 McKelvey, "Interview with Harold Koh, Obama's defender of drone strikes."

31 Ibid.

32 Ibid.

33 McKelvey, "Viewpoint: US media lax on drones" BBC *News*, February 6, 2013.

34 Woodward, Bob, *Obama's Wars* (New York, NY: Simon & Schuster, 2011).

35 ABC *News*–*Washington Post* poll, "Drones, Gitmo and drawdown give Obama foreign policy cred," February 8, 2012. .

36 MacEoin, Denis, "Anwar al-Awlaki: 'I pray that Allah destroys America,'" *Middle East Quarterly* Spring (2010): 13–19.

37 Klaidman, *Kill or Capture*.

38 PBS, *Need to Know*, interview with Jameel Jaffer, September 30, 2011.

39 McKelvey, "Interview with Harold Koh, Obama's defender of drone strikes."

40 18 U.S. Code, sec. 1119 – Foreign murder of United States nationals.

41 Solis, Gary, "CIA drone attacks produce America's own unlawful combatants," *Washington Post*, March 12, 2010.

42 *Authorization for Use of Military Force (AUMF)*, Pub. L. 107-40, codified at 115 Stat. 224, and passed as S. J. Res. 23 by the United States Congress on September 14, 2001.

43 Yoo, John, "The good and bad in Eric Holder's drone defense," *Wall Street Journal*, March 12, 2012.

44 McKelvey, "Interview with Harold Koh, Obama's defender of drone strikes."

45 Koh, "The Obama administration and international law."

46 McKelvey, Tara, "Lethal drone program flourishes under Obama," Investigative Reporting Workshop, American University, April 8, 2012.

47 Interview with Benjamin Wittes.

48 McKelvey, "Interview with Harold Koh, Obama's defender of drone strikes."

49 Ibid.

50 Center for Civilians in Conflict and Human Rights Clinic, Columbia Law School, "The Civilian Impact of Drones: Unexamined Costs, Unanswered Questions," 2012.

51 Alston, Philip, "The CIA and targeted killings beyond borders," *Harvard National Security Law Journal* 2 (2011): 283–446.

52 Ibid.

53 Author telephone interview with Noah Feldman, December 7, 2011.

54 Feldman, Noah, "Obama team's Al-Awlaki memo furthered Bush legacy," *Bloomberg News*, October 16, 2011.

55 Anderson, Kenneth, "Targeted killing in U.S. counterterrorism strategy and law," Brookings Institution, May 11, 2009.

56 McKelvey, "Interview with Harold Koh, Obama's defender of drone strikes."

57 Ibid.

58 Koh, "The Obama administration and international law."

59 Ibid.

60 McKelvey, "Interview with Harold Koh, Obama's defender of drone strikes."

61 Zenko, Michael, "Talking in Circles: Why Harold Koh's big speech on targeted killings is just more of the same, intentional Obama muddle," *Foreign Policy*, May 9, 2013.

62 McKelvey, "Interview with Harold Koh, Obama's defender of drone strikes."

63 Ibid.

64 Ibid.

PART III
DRONES AND POLICY

11

"Bring on the Magic"
Using Drones in Afghanistan

MICHAEL WALTZ[*]

As a Special Forces commander in Afghanistan, I used drones in a variety of ways – from the Raven, literally a small device you throw in the air and use to view the surrounding area, to the ubiquitous Predator and the intelligence and the imagery that comes from the strategic-level UAVs (unmanned aerial vehicles). In my time in Afghanistan, I saw drone use progress from the early part of the decade when there was very limited reliance on drones at the tactical operational level to now when almost every squad leader demands to have one.

In 2005, drones were a rare commodity, particularly in Afghanistan. This is because they were being fielded in Iraq as fast as they could be deployed. Back then, the only time we had drones was for what we call a TIC, a "troops in contact" situation. There was only a small Coalition (Forces) presence in the south then and we were very isolated, far from any type of support. We were using drones as kind of a force protection, a mode of survival.

It was not until 2009 and 2010 that we had enough assets to use drones for what we call "pattern of life" operations, continuously watching certain areas day and night until a certain event led to night raids to capture insurgent leaders. Even then there was a constant competition between military head-quarters for who was able to use those assets. If we were lucky we would get drone coverage for a day or a day and a half at most. It was only JSOC [Joint Special Operations Command] that had dedicated assets that could watch areas literally for days. The rest of us – the Green Berets, SEALs, and conventional forces – we were all scrambling to gain access to drones.

Drones enable great precision, especially if one compares current capabil-ities to the Vietnam-era arc-like bombings or World War II with the massive B-17 and B-24 strikes. The precision targeting of drones and other technologies

* This interview was conducted, edited, and prepared for publication by Daniel Rothenberg.

provide a tremendous advantage on the battlefield, especially to a commander in a counterinsurgency environment where the careful and proportionate use of force to avoid civilian casualties is particularly important.

I remember a conversation with an elder in Eastern Afghanistan who was amazed by the precision of our strikes. He had seen numerous cases where we were able to hit different commanders – whether they were Haqqani, Taliban, or HIG (Hezb-e-Islami Gulbuddin) – who would come across the border from Pakistan. The attacks would strike exactly where the insurgents were sleeping. People would see a room literally explode and then those individuals would no longer be there.

That elder, as well as others, called these strikes "the magic."

He much preferred drone attacks to the impact of platoons of armored coalition vehicles that would engage in fire fights and possibly catch his village in the cross fire. Culverts would be blown up, roads destroyed, and fields damaged. And there were often civilian casualties when Coalition Forces responded to a Taliban ambush.

A group of Haqqani Network fighters had come into his area and they were truly bad actors. One of them had machine-gunned a girls' school with the girls in it. Another one hung a seven-year-old boy that had American dollars in his pocket. The atrocities went on and on. The people wanted to get rid of these commanders and their fighters, but they were afraid. They asked for the precision of drones.

I remember him telling me, "Bring on the magic."

Of course, because of their scarcity back then, we could not always get a drone when we wanted one. So, if you were in a unit deemed to be a lower priority, then you would not get access to a drone and you might not be able to conduct the mission.

There were times when elders facing insurgent abuses and intimidation would ask me, "Why can't you give us the magic?"

Those situations were really hard.

There was one particular village on the border that became a way station for insurgent commanders coming into the Khost Province from their sanctuaries in Pakistan and then going up to training camps in the mountains or on into the villages. We received a call from an elder with whom we had been working. He was an influential leader of his tribe. Several of his sons worked on our base. Members of his extended family were well educated and worked as interpreters for NGOs and the Coalition.

He told us that two Haqqani commanders were coming through his village that evening, and sure enough they did. They gathered the village together and said, "You're going to give us five of your sons or we'll kill one. And you're also going to give us the money you received from the Nation Solidarity Program for development projects."

They gave up the money and then the village held a *jirga* to try to decide which of the sons they would provide to become Haqqani fighters. They called us. The elder was a proud Afghan man who was almost in tears begging us to come help.

"Don't come capture them," he said. "Come kill them. Because if you capture them, they'll eventually be released and come back after us."

All that afternoon and evening we were trying desperately to put together a mission to kill or capture these men. At the end of the day, we were not allowed to go because we did not have access to a Predator drone. The helicopter unit transporting us insisted on having a Predator clear the landing zone of potential attackers before conducting the mission. But, at the time, all the drone assets were supporting another attack and so none were available to us.

So the village gave up their five sons.

However, they did not only provide the young men to the insurgency, the tribe also told all of the men working with the Coalition to come home. They said that they were no longer going to work with us. The elders cut off contact completely.

That had a serious impact on our counterinsurgency campaign. We basically lost the cooperation of an important tribe and all of our links with this significant village along the Pakistani border. And all of this happened just because on that one day we were unable to access a drone and were told that we could not conduct the mission without one.

Still, when we did get a drone, it was a fantastic asset.

You could be in the field, facing a series of compounds, which are complex mazes of homes and additions behind five-foot thick mud walls that have been built up over literally hundreds of years. With a drone overhead we would have an aerial view of these compounds. We could see who was coming and going. We knew where the women and children tended to congregate. This real-time information allowed us to better understand our environment right up to the point where we were entering an Afghan home. We knew exactly where the civilians would be moving within the compound so that when we went in we were better able to avoid civilian casualties.

Drones brought a tremendous capability for us to see things and make decisions that were impossible only a few years ago. In 2005, if I called in an airstrike as a response to someone firing at me from a compound, they would probably have destroyed the entire compound. Now, if I have access to a drone I can see that, even though we're being attacked from that compound, there are also seven women inside. That information allows for a different decision and a different way of managing the threat.

Drones also help protect our troops. I remember a time when my team was in a three-sided ambush. As the ground force commander, I was determined to press on to the objective. At this point we had lost guys and we thought that we had fought through the worst of it. But my decision was overridden by the command at Bagram, who were watching images of the ground from drones. They saw that there were several hundred more armed fighters waiting for us. So, that time, drones saved my life.

Still, we have to be careful as a military force of taking drone use too far and becoming overly dependent on them. Over the past decade, the increasing use of drones has been a significant factor contributing to risk aversion in tactical operations and counterinsurgency strategy.

I remember one day when a PRT (Provincial Reconstruction Team) was not allowed to go through a narrow pass in order to get to a valley and visit a series of villages controlled by an influential tribe that we wanted to access. I talked to the lieutenant in charge of the mission and he said, "I have been told by headquarters that I am not allowed to go through this pass until a drone comes overhead and checks it out for us."

In the meantime, I asked my interpreter to call down to one of the villages on the other side of the pass where I knew he had a cousin. The cousin rode his motorcycle up into the pass, looked around and said that there were no problems. So our team went through.

When we got to the main village, I saw that there were kids everywhere. That is a key indicator that things are safe. We know that every time we had a problem here in this area, there would be no kids outside. I contacted the lieutenant and told him this. He called headquarters and told them that our team went through the pass with no problem and that we were in the village. But they still were not allowed to proceed. Those were their orders. Drones enable that type of mentality.

I spoke with the elders who had been sitting there waiting for the PRT. They were insulted and said, "Don't they know that we invited them here? Don't they trust us? Don't they understand that we want to work with them?"

The PRT was charged with bringing development aid and projects to various communities. But the elders saw that there was not a level of trust. Under their code, *pashtunwali*, an invitation by the elders, meant that the PRT would be protected. They understood the failure of the PRT to arrive as an insult. That day an overdependence on drones stood in the way of a commonsense approach and prevented the PRT from accomplishing its mission and assisting the Afghan people.

Drones have also changed the management of missions. Now, literally, anyone up the chain of command can watch a mission as it occurs. From literally thousands of miles away, you can see individual soldiers making decisions regarding specific objectives. Once I ran into a general in the White House and we were talking about our time overseas. For some reason we began talking about Helmand Province in Southern Afghanistan. Then we progressed to talking about a pretty significant battle that happened outside a town called Musa Qala.

He asked, "Was that you?"

I told him yes and described what happened.

Then he said, "I remember. I watched the whole thing from beginning to end in Tampa, Florida, in the conference room." And he described how everybody was talking about what should be done and asking questions about why certain decisions were being made.

I told him, "While you guys were talking among yourselves, I had four chains of command on the radio also watching what was going on and asking me personally about specific issues." Drones and related technology enable a type of micromanagement that was never possible in the past.

What is odd about this is that there are many people who describe the use of unmanned systems as extrajudicial or outside of the laws of land warfare. Let me assure you that there are multiple layers of checks and balances on how and when they are used. First, there is someone like myself on the ground. And I have my bosses looking over my shoulder. In addition, I am talking to the pilot of the UAV, wherever he may be, who also has his bosses looking over his shoulder. And these bosses have their lawyers standing next to them reviewing everything before an action is taken. They are constantly considering the rules of engagement and risk mitigation for civilian casualties.

Why is this a potential problem? Well, it stifles initiative on the battlefield. It stifles the ingenuity of junior commanders that are out there and are most in touch with the human dynamic. Drones have helped support an "era of investigations" because now every move you make, for better or for worse, whether you make mistakes or not, is watched, recorded, and often times investigated. I do not think that this is necessarily a good use of the system or a positive step forward for our military culture.

Drones can encourage a negative cycle where the default reaction is inaction. After all, if you have a bad outcome – a base overrun or heavy casualties – that has tremendous ramifications for one's career. Deciding not to conduct a raid and not to take a risk is safer.

Also an overreliance on unmanned or robotic systems may remove the personal touch of dealing firsthand with the population on their terms. That is something we need to be concerned about. In this way, drones have redefined the way we do things in the field. There's an element of my profession in Special Forces that involves building relationships, developing cultural understanding, being a teacher, and training others to be a force enabler. Those needs will never go away, especially in a counterinsurgency environment. Unmanned technology cannot replace those very human skills.

There is now an expectation that we will not conduct missions unless we have drones. This trend is likely to increase as drones redefine warfare.

I think I am among the last of the pre-drone combat generation.

12

The Five Deadly Flaws of Talking About Emerging Military Technologies and the Need for New Approaches to Law, Ethics, and War

P. W. SINGER

1. WE LIVE IN A WORLD OF "KILLER APPLICATIONS"

It used to be that every so often a new technology would come along and change the rules of the game. These were technologies like the printing press, gunpowder, the steam engine, or the atomic bomb. Such technological innovations were rare in history and occurred over the course of generations.

What is different today, and so challenging to policy, law, and ethics, is the incredible pace of the emergence of new technologies. It was once commonplace for entire generations to pass without a single technological breakthrough that significantly altered the way people worked, communicated, fought, or played. By the so-called "age of invention" in the late 1800s, transformative innovations were appearing around once every decade or so. Today, with the ever-accelerating pace of technological development (best illustrated by Moore's Law, the finding that, over the last forty years, microchips – and related developments in computers – double their power and capability every eighteen months), wave after wave of new inventions and technologies that are literally rewriting the rules of the game are bursting onto the scene with an ever-increasing pace. From robotic planes that strike targets 7,000 miles away to man-made cells assembled from DNA created out of chemicals in a laboratory, the types of technologies that are being developed now are astounding, yet they are appearing with such regularity that we are almost numb to their historic importance.

Looking ahead, the range of military technologies that are currently at the prototype stage – not off in the fictional distance but already being researched and developed – cover everything from: directed energy weapons, also known as lasers; precision-guided munitions, also known as smart improvised explosive devices (IED); nanotechnology and microrobotics; bioagents and genetic weaponry, also known as DNA bombs; space weaponry; and human performance modifications, chemical and hardware enhancements to the human body, basically the real-world version of the science fiction narratives, a situation in which Iron Man meets Captain America. These advances include taking a present game-changer – unmanned systems – a great leap forward. While increasingly autonomous armed robotics may cause deep concern for international humanitarian law and the weapons clearance process (indeed, sparking the so-called "Stop Killer Robots" campaign), they are currently in development in a number of countries and many are already at the prototype stage.

The point is that there are all sorts of very real technological innovations today that appear straight from science fiction, even as they are on track to being deployable before many of us pay off our mortgages. Such advances are often misunderstood, especially because they are frequently presented as "silver bullet" solutions.

These technologies can be viewed as a type of "killer application," or "killer app," that is, a "revolutionary" or "disruptive" technology that rocks an existing understanding back on its fundamentals. A prototypical example from a non-military domain is what the iPod has done to the music industry. While iPods have not ended the commercial production, sale, and enjoyment of music, they have changed these activities forever.

It is not just the capabilities that these innovations offer that matter. It is also the tough questions they force us to ask. Questions about things that are now possible that were never possible before; questions about what is proper that we never had to wrestle with before.

These issues are not just intellectually fascinating as regards their proper use and in terms of ethical and legal discussions. The challenges and disputes that arise in addressing emerging military technologies have immense consequences in terms of international security. In fact, they can start wars.

For example, the science fiction image of a boat that can go under the sea – what we now call a submarine – and attack civilian shipping on the surface was first conceptualized by the writer Jules Verne. Once submarines were created some years later, it was a political and legal dispute over when and how they could operate that was partly responsible for the decision by the United States to enter World War I. Basically, the American position view was that the new technology should operate under the old mores, which would ban attacks on shipping without having the submarine first reveal itself and board its targets. The Germans held a different position, feeling that old mores defeated the very value of the new technology.

Another example of how ideas that first appeared in science fiction influenced actual practice is seen in H. G. Wells's concept of what he called "the atomic bomb." His ideas inspired the real-world scientists of the Manhattan Project. Nuclear war technology kept the Cold War cold, but continues to haunt the world today through its own set of complex legal and ethical questions.

Why are these questions of ethics and technology so difficult, especially in the realm of war? At the dawn of the nuclear era, in a speech on the eve of Armistice Day in November 1948, General Omar Bradley said: "The world has achieved brilliance without wisdom, power without conscience. Ours is a world of nuclear giants and ethical infants. We know more about war than we know about peace, more about killing than we know about living."[1]

Why is it that we are "giants" when it comes to the technology of battle, yet at the same time "ethical infants"? Answering this question requires engaging effectively with the five deadly flaws of thinking and talking about new killer applications.[2]

2. FIRST DEADLY FLAW — DISCONNECTED FIELDS

The first flaw involves a disconnect between different professional and technical fields. When issues cross from one field into another, it is often like crossing from one's own nation into a foreign country. The paths and even key norms of behavior may be familiar but the language and terms are foreign.

For example, consider cyber security, which is literally a world in which the operative language is composed of zeroes and ones. Recently a virtual world company discovered that somebody was carrying out an act of cybercrime within its system. They were stealing virtual currency that they were then able to convert into actual currency. The company discovered what was going on and contacted the FBI. After an hour of discussion, the FBI agent responded, "So, um, this is on the Internet, right?"[3] That is, you have a law enforcement agent who is being asked to investigate a crime in a technologic realm but who barely understands the very basics of the technology on which the crime took place.

This situation is particularly difficult for those wrestling with the law, ethics, and the science of war. As daunting as it is for someone who is trained in the fields of law, politics, or philosophy to talk about the design parameters of the MQ-9 Reaper, it is equally difficult for the scientists and engineers who are conversant with technical issues to enter into discussions about ethical dilemmas.

As one robotics expert told me, "Having a discussion about ethics is very difficult because it requires me to put on a philosopher's hat, which I don't own." The result is that we usually engage with the fields within which we work and do not speak with those working in other areas. This is true even when it is precisely this sort of dialogue that is required for understanding the problems we face.

The Association of Unmanned Vehicles and Systems International, the industry trade group dealing with drones, conducted a survey of some of the most influential twenty-five technologists and experts in the field. They asked them if they found "social, ethical or moral problems with the continued development of unmanned systems" – any problems at all. Sixty percent answered with the simple response of, "no."[4] So, while philosophers and academics of various types almost always see problems with emerging technologies (although they may disagree as to the core issues), those working on these questions are often profoundly disengaged from these issues and this way of thinking.

The result is that we have a rather ostrich-like approach when we come to these discussions of law, morality, and technology. Those who carry out the policy and ethical discussions, especially on the topic of unmanned systems, are often uninformed or, even worse, guided by those who do not have scientific facts on their side. In turn, scientists and engineers who have actual ethical and legal dilemmas to resolve are left outside of these discussions, creating a situation that makes developing real solutions almost impossible.

Today a young robotics graduate student working on the next generation of these systems might ask himself or herself such questions as: From what individual or organization can I ethically accept research and development money? What type of autonomy can my system have and still meet basic legal and moral standards? Who should be allowed to buy the systems I am developing? Who should be allowed to use these systems? Who should have access to the information that my system is constantly gathering about the world around us?

However, a young researcher asking such questions would currently have no focused, coherent ethical code to use for guidance. Nor is there a formal institution to consult for reasonable answers to these questions. This presents a situation quite distinct from a young student in medicine, law, or most other professional fields. At present, those developing drones, military robots, and other emerging technologies lack agreed-upon standards to guide them, and they have no professional body to approach for assistance when facing some of the most important questions associated with their work.

The key is not simply recognizing a gap between practice and established legal and ethical norms, which is to be expected in any cutting-edge field, but rather engaging what is and is not being done to address these issues. For example, the scientists working in the Human Genome Project set aside

5 percent of their annual budget to engage in discussions on the "ethical, legal, and social implications" of their work.[5] While this has not resolved the tough issues related to the field of genetics, the effort signals an engagement with the necessity of linking the technological innovations of genetic research with a consideration of core social questions. This has helped create awareness among scientists and the broader public about the important implications and challenges of advances in genetics, helping us manage these debates in a more nuanced and useful manner.

However, this is the exception that proves the rule. The prevalent attitude we find in the field of emerging military technologies is perhaps best encapsulated by a response from a professor after I presented a speech about the future of robotics at an engineering school. His department receives most of its research funding from the Department of Defense, and he wrote to chastise me for "troubling his students by asking them to think about the ethics of their work." Isaac Asimov and perhaps even Socrates may well be laughing at us right now.

3. SECOND DEADLY FLAW – APPLIED ETHICS AND THE REVENGE OF THE REAL WORLD

New technologies in war are often described as a way to reduce the cost of war, mitigate its passions, and limit the possibility of excessive acts or crimes. This is nothing new. For example, in 1621, the poet John Donne foretold how the invention of better cannons would mean that wars would come to "quicker ends heretofore and the great expense of blood be avoided."[6] Yet this is clearly not what occurred; as we know, more powerful cannons have created more devastating conflicts.

Four hundred years later we are having similar discussions when it comes to the current generation of remotely piloted vehicles, as well as future versions that will be autonomous. The media has frequently published discussions about Pentagon-funded projects on "ethical governors," the supposed software packages that would be applied to unmanned systems to ensure that the use of weapons would automatically adhere to the laws of war. The argument in favor of these mechanisms is that, because the machines are programmed and therefore unable to deviate from rule-based commands, they will always follow the law as compared to humans, who are inherently unreliable. Ron Arkin, a professor of computer science at Georgia Tech who is working on these issues explained: "Ultimately these systems could have more information to make wiser decisions than a human could make. Some robots are already stronger, faster and smarter than humans. We want to do better than people, to ultimately save more lives."[7]

That is a noble sentiment and it echoes the vision expressed by Donne so long ago. However, an easy confidence in ethical governors ignores the seamy underside of war and the multiple ways in which a technology that promises a more humane outcome may, in fact, lead to just the opposite result.

Too frequently innovative technologies and discussions about them are presented (particularly by the technophile thinkers who once surrounded former Secretary of Defense Donald Rumsfeld) as mechanisms through which "the fog of war can be lifted."[8] They imply that either the perfection of our technology or the perfection of our souls, or some combination of the two, will prove to be a "silver bullet" solution to the problems of war.

However, the reality is that war in the twenty-first century has many of the exact same characteristics as war in prior centuries. It is a terrible, awful mess, although maybe now it has become an even more complicated mess. When people assert that a new military technology will reduce bloodshed or improve compliance with established moral principles, they may want to consider these issues through the dirty lens of modern warfare. This might encourage a reflection on the growing role of global private military industries and the influence of money and greed in war. Or, they might consider the sad reality of child soldiers and the fact that in contemporary conflicts, one of every ten combatants is a child.[9]

When we own up to the reality of contemporary war, rather than how we wish it would operate, we see the double-edged sword of technology. We see that, for example, while human enhancement research takes us beyond the existing limitations of the human body, these improvements do not take us past our all too human limitations and inherent flaws such as our capacity for arrogance, greed, and hate. Similarly, just as a fork can be a tool for eating as well as plucking out eyeballs, a "non-lethal weapon" can chase away Somali pirates, be used by Japanese fisherman to repel environmentalists protesting the illegal slaughter of endangered whales, or be deployed by an autocratic regime to torture prisoners.

Beyond this, there are two additional problems. First, the promises of morally perfected technology and ethical governors are usually false because the technology is actually what we call "vaporware," that is, it does not yet exist and is largely imagined. Second, an enduring part of war is that no matter how novel the technology, the enemy is unlikely to act as predicted and will almost certainly present new challenges that will prove such promises to be empty. For instance, many wars now involve adversaries that know about the laws of war and then violate those laws as an element of their military strategy. This is what Charles Dunlap, former US Air Force general and now a law professor at Duke University has termed "lawfare."[10] For example, in Somalia, a US

Ranger described how he was shot at by a gunman using an AK-47 propped up between the knees of two women kneeling front of him while four children lay across his back.[11] The shooter had literally created a suit of non-combatant armor around him. When I worked for the Office of the Secretary of Defense during the Kosovo conflict, one of the challenges we faced in selecting targets was a case where there was a tank parked in a schoolyard. In another case, a tank that was carrying out an ethnic cleansing mission had children riding on top. In the recent Lebanon war, there were instances of civilians forced to launch rockets from their farms, while in Syria at a time of possible US air strikes, the regime openly moved civilians into military facilities and placed soldiers in civilian areas.

There are thousands of such cases, each of which challenge the careful calculation of acceptable targeting under the laws of war. Well-intentioned experts, lawyers, and military officers often find themselves discussing these cases, which are difficult to resolve and require a degree of sensitivity and contextual grounding that far exceeds the domain of ethical governors. So, imagining that a computer that speaks in the language of ones and zeroes will be capable of addressing these types of issues is not realistic now or any time soon.

4. THIRD DEADLY FLAW – DIVERGENT IDEAS, OR "YOUR ETHICS ARE NOT MY ETHICS"

It is our luck that we live in a diverse world. As Gene Roddenberry, futurist and creator of *Star Trek* once said: "If man is to survive he will have to learn to take delight in the simple differences between cultures. He will learn that differences in ideas and attitudes are a delight, part of life's exciting variety, not something to fear."[12]

While we may delight in our different cultures and beliefs, they have a real impact on how we look at technology, as well as the ways we understand the need to regulate new and emerging weapons systems.

Take the example of autonomous drones and other robots. In Western culture, going back to the first use of the world "robot" in a 1920s play titled *RUR*, autonomous machines have consistently been portrayed as mechanical servants that wise up and then rise up against human society. Whether inspired by early science fiction movies or more recent evocations, such as the *Terminator* or *RoboCop* movies, there is something in Western culture that views robots as dangerous tools destined to grow intelligent and come after us.

However, this is not a universal view. "The machine is a friend of humans in Japan. A robot is a friend, basically," says Shuji Hasimoto, a robotics professor at Waseda University in Tokyo.[13] In Asian cultures, robots are commonly understood in a different manner arising from different contexts. The robot first appears in Asian science fiction after World War II in a positive light. Perhaps this is because in the wake of Hiroshima, it is humans who are seen as the ultimate villains. In Asia, robots are not necessarily bad, as in Western fiction, but often appear as heroes, such as Astro Boy. While our moral understandings of technology are not driven solely by popular culture, this domain illustrates how our engagement with emerging technologies represents a complex reflection and expression of social reality.

Indeed, the divide on robotics may also draw from religion and different conceptions of the division between the living and the dead. While Christianity sees a strict divide between what is alive and what is not, within Shintoism, for example, both animate and inanimate objects can be endowed with a spirit. A stream has a spirit, a rock has a spirit, and a robot also may have a spirit. In fact, there are robots in Toyota factories that receive Shinto rites.

The point here is that there are fundamentally different perceptions of what is acceptable when it comes to technology. In Asia, companion robots for the elderly and babysitter robots for children are marketed with very little controversy. By contrast, Rodney Brooks, an MIT professor and the chief technical officer of the iRobot company, explains that these types of machines would not be accepted in the United States for the simple reason that Americans find them "too artificial and icky."[14]

"Icky" is an interesting term because it matters in both law and ethics. In international relations, we felt the need to develop a response for weapons systems that may appear to be technically legal, but their possible use is troubling to the "public conscience" in some other way. Within international law this is seen in the Martens clause from the original 1899 Hague Conventions.[15] Interestingly, there are multiple examples involving new technologies that raise these issues in different contexts and cultures. For example, while heart transplants are completely acceptable in the West, in Japan the first surgeon to carry out the operation was prosecuted for murder.

Arming autonomous weapons systems is currently hugely controversial and plays off of these differences of social understanding. In the West it is a matter of deep concern, but Korea deployed two robotic snipers to Iraq in 2004 with little public debate. Indeed, Samsung manufactures the autonomous sentry gun, which is a 5.5 millimeter machine with two cameras, infrared and zooming capabilities, and pattern recognition software processors that allow it to identify, classify, and destroy moving human targets from one and a quarter miles away. Not only does the company produce these weapons, but it also markets and sells them and has a promotional video that one can watch online.[16] The images, set to rousing jazzy music, celebrate the invention and its technological possibilities.

Another related issue is designer hubris: the assumption that just because one party is the first to develop a new technology that means that they will always be in control of the innovation, and their views and mores will be used to manage and guide its use forever. The hubris of the United States after developing the atomic bomb applied not only to the government at the time but also to the designers. Members of the Manhattan Project honestly thought that they would have control over targeting decisions. They expressed frustration and anger that they were not allowed into the White House during the decisions to bomb Japan, leading to the strikes on Hiroshima or Nagasaki, and that these actions were out of their hands.

In 2013, the US State Department organized a meeting on how long the country should expect to maintain a monopoly over emerging military technologies and how it could prevent their proliferation. Simply put, no such monopoly exists. Right now there are at least eighty-seven other nations building, buying, and using military robotics.[17] This group represents a diverse collection of nations, from US allies like Great Britain, Israel, France, and Germany, to others countries such as Pakistan, China, Russia, and Iran. Of course, there are also multiple non-state actors gaining access to innovative military technologies.

One of the key differences with new generations of military technologies as compared with prior revolutionary military advances is that they often rely on open-source innovations. My own unintentional role in the defense industrial complex presents an illustration of this issue. Working as a consultant for the *Call of Duty* video game, I was part of a team that conceived of what the next generation of soldiers might want in a tactical-level drone. We took our inspiration from the strengths and weaknesses of the current generation of military systems and what was becoming available on the civilian side of the market. The concept melded a nimble "quadrotor" that could move rapidly but also perch and stare into urban canyons, be armed with a machine gun and explosives, and take on roles that ranged from scout to overhead watch to sniper. It had to not only be easily controlled by a single soldier with minimal training, but also be able to take on certain roles autonomously. And it had to be cheap enough to be purchased in sufficient numbers such that they could conceivably be deployed at the squad or platoon level to be distributed across the battlefield.

The concept itself is appealing, but what happened next is fascinating. For a commercial for the video game release in 2012, Activision built "Charlene." It was a kind of prototype – not the final version but a working version of the system with the various key attributes. It cost less than $5,000. Notably, when the video of Charlene went viral on YouTube (showing a quadrotor, controlled by a tablet computer, shooting up various targets with an Uzi equivalent and then taking out a car in a fiery explosion), offices in the Pentagon began to wonder why some crazy Russian (actually an actor) had a better drone today than the US military.[18] At the 2013 weapons trade shows, various defense contractors began to display their early knockoffs of Charlene (but always at a much higher price). This illustrates profound social, legal, and ethical changes. To make a World War II parallel, Hitler's Luftwaffe was unable to strike the United States. It simply could not fly aircraft across the Atlantic, yet a 77-year-old blind man built his own drone and flew it across the Atlantic using GPS guidance.[19]

Complications also occur as one moves outside the context of conflict. The US Department of Homeland Security uses Predator-class drones for border security. Meanwhile, a private militia on the Arizona border has used unmanned drones, including ones it purchased for $25,000 each, which is a fraction of the cost of the military-grade drones used by the federal government. There are multiple domestic and legal issues that arise from using emerging military technologies for law enforcement purposes, and there is the general question: What does it mean to have an all-seeing eye in the sky? And specifically, how does the deployment of this technology affect constitutional rights? What limitations should be placed on private use and how will these be managed and enforced? This is not a theoretical issue, but represents the opening of a huge area of public debate and law as civilian airspace opens up to the use of unmanned systems in roles that range from policing to journalism to crop-dusting.[20]

What we are seeing is the beginning of a mass proliferation of new technologies, and with this change come many policy questions that will notably play out in very different contexts. As these machines are developed and deployed in multiple social and cultural environments, different understandings of their proper use will hinder efforts to control their availability on a global scale.

5. FOURTH DEADLY FLAW – SUSPICION OF ETHICS AND LAW

In the spring of 2010, I had the honor of sharing a panel with two US military JAG officers at a session hosted by the Institute for Ethics and Public Affairs at Old Dominion University. The session's focus was on the ethical questions of using new robotic technologies in war. A member of the audience stood up and asked a question more fundamental than what any of us on the panel had discussed: "What would you tell a mother who has lost her son to one of these terrorists in Iraq as to why we should even care about something like ethics or the laws of war? Why should we even bother?"

That question cuts to the heart of the complex nature of wrestling with the nuances of right and wrong when people – our sons, daughters, parents, spouses – are risking their lives in complex and difficult contexts. That is, why should we even care about right or wrong and technical legal issues in a realm of unconventional war where there is already so much wrong, harm, and illegality? Why should we care about ethics and morality in war?

For me there are two answers to this issue that are relevant for a discussion of emerging technologies. First, the son who was killed was a serviceman. That service distinguishes him and defines what, how, and why he and his comrades are fighting. That is, they did not fight out of anger or hate. They served something beyond themselves. They took an oath of service. They served the US Constitution. And that is a distinguishing factor because not only do they believe that they are on the right side in these wars (which every side believes itself to be), but also that they are committed to adhering to a set of rules and values. The sense of service is not just why we fight, but it is why our way of fighting is bound by laws and therefore made just.

The second factor is something that we do not like to talk about in ethics, but matters a great deal: raw self-interest (a motivating force that we may sometimes sugarcoat by terming it "pragmatism"). In fact, the facts show that violating the laws of war does not provide a strategic advantage. In the history of war, the side that has fought with a sense of ethics, respected the laws, and operated as "professionals" has tended to win more often than not. That is, over thousands of years of warfare, professionals almost always triumph over barbarians.

Indeed, this distinction was found to be essential in Iraq, where the woman's son was killed. Even though the US forces in Al Anbar Province were unfamiliar with local society in comparison with members of al-Qaeda and others fighting there, and many in the media complained that our forces were stymied by an intricate web of laws and lawyers, US forces ultimately won and they did so because of, not in spite of, an adherence to the laws of war. Al-Qaeda extremists and the twenty-first-century version of barbarians carry the seeds of their own downfall as a result of their wanton use of violence, including purposefully targeting civilians. Eventually, it was these factors that persuaded local Sunni tribes to turn on them, which was a key factor in the success of the "surge."

Nevertheless, while the facts may not support the position, the narrative that ethics is a hindrance to success in war remains powerful and popular. Those who care about morality and norms must acknowledge that they face a basic problem of convincing people both inside and outside the military that ethics in warfare is essential, not because the position is morally praiseworthy but because we are self-interested and want to win.

6. FIFTH DEADLY FLAW – MAGIC, OR WE FEAR WHAT WE DO NOT UNDERSTAND

When the warriors of the Hehe tribe in Tanzania surrounded a single German colonist in 1891, they seemingly had little to worry about. But he had strong magic, a box that spat out bullets (what we call a machine gun). Armed with such seemingly mystical power, he killed almost a thousand warriors carrying spears.[21]

As English physicist and science fiction author Arthur C. Clarke famously put it, "Any sufficiently advanced technology is indistinguishable from magic."[22] And there is no realm where this is truer than in war, where we not only view advanced technology as magical but we fear it for that very reason. We fear what we do not understand.

Some people would say that in the twenty-first century we have put such ideas behind us, that we no longer suffer the confusions of magic. However, that is not true; we are actually facing the challenge of magic in all sorts of ways.

For example, the discussion over the impact of unmanned systems strikes in Pakistan is not just a narrative of the relative value of targeted killings and the numbers of civilian casualties. It is also a debate regarding technologies that appear magical and inspire fear. A member of the US Joint Special Operations Command told me about a meeting that he had with a set of elders in the Federally Administered Tribal Authority region in Pakistan. He described that they served tea and cookies. One of the elders was enamored with the sweet bread-like food that he had never tasted before. That same elder went on say that he believed that the Americans had to be working with the forces of evil because of the way that their enemies' homes were blowing up even though US forces were not present.

He did not talk about the issue of civilian casualties, but instead illustrated a gap in understanding as to the mechanisms of modern war. The elder went on to acknowledge that the United States might be targeting bad guys, but that they "must have the power of the devil" behind them. The officer said, "You have a guy who has never eaten a cookie before. Of course he is going to see a drone as like the devil, as like black magic."

The point is that the elder thought that the United States was doing
something very bad – evil – not because of the actions but because of the
way of acting, a reliance on magical forces that he did not understand and
feared. As Marian Anderson once put it, "Fear is a disease that eats away at
logic."[23]

But this suspicion of advanced technologies is not limited to distant tribal
regions. It is something that increasingly plays out here in the United States,
and harming our ability to have effective discussions on policy and ethics in
the twenty-first century. We are seeing what CNN has characterized as a
growing American "fear of science," or what writer Michael Specter explored
in his book, *Denialism*. As Specter puts it, the problem now when it comes to
discussions that involve the intersection of science and public policy is that
"when people don't like facts, they ignore them."[24]

We see this in all sorts of areas, from the widespread fear of vaccines, to the
useless trust placed in the multibillion-dollar industry of dietary supplements,
to the climate change debate. Indeed, a major political party nominated a
candidate for US vice president who described the scientific method as "snake
oil."[25] However, we should not use such facts to disparage a particular political
campaign because this is simply a reflection of the opinions and attitudes of the
American people, of whom 11 percent believe that Elvis is still alive and nearly
one in five think that the sun revolves around the earth.[26] Applied to the realm
of war, we see how Hollywood notions of the "Terminator" have clouded the
reality of what is and is not possible with drones and other advanced military
technologies, indeed fueling a very debate over the term itself.[27]

This is the context in which our society engages with transformative
technologies. Our challenge, then, is to make sure that policymakers and
the larger public not only understand the ethical issues of emerging technologies, but that they also accept the scientific principles and related limitations
underlying these technologies.

7. CONFRONTING DIFFICULT QUESTIONS

These challenges are certainly daunting, but by no means do they imply that
discussions of morality and technology are hopeless. In fact, the difficulties of
managing these issues highlight the importance of thinking, speaking, and
acting ethically when it comes to emerging military technologies. The complex nature of this process makes it all the more important and efforts to solve
these issues all the more worthy.

Our success or failure in navigating the moral dilemmas of a world of
killer apps will depend on recognizing that these very problems are part

and parcel of the discussion. We must own up to the challenges presented by these five deadly flaws. We must face them head on and learn to overcome them. Otherwise we will spin in circles and fail to face important social issues, and this may have disastrous consequences. And we had better act soon. What unites the complex moral and policy issues associated with transformative military technologies and killer applications is how the rapid rate of innovation makes it difficult for our all too-human institutions, including those involved in managing ethics and law, to keep pace.

NOTES

1 Bradley, General Omar N., "An Armistice Day Address: 10 November 1948" in *The Collected Writings of General Omar N. Bradley*, Vol. I (Washington, DC: Government Printing Office, 1967): 584–589, p. 588.

2 In fact, there are seven "deadly sins" in dealing with these issues that I have explored elsewhere, but this chapter addresses five. The two not addressed are first, the role that money plays – not just in terms of what people build but also what people talk about, research, and write about; and, second, the issue of geographical and chronological dislocation.

3 Author interview with Linden Lab executive, March 27, 2010.

4 Survey released at AUVSI-San Diego, conducted by Kendall Haven, October 27, 2009.

5 Moore, Julia A. "The future dances on a pin's head: Nanotechnology: Will it be a boon – or kill us all?" *Los Angeles Times*, November 26, 2002.

6 Dunlap, Jr., Charles J., *Technology and the 21st century battlefield: Re-complicating moral life for the statesman and the soldier* (Carlisle, PA: Strategic Studies Institute, Army War College, 1999).

7 Bland, Eric. "Robot warriors will get a guide to ethics," *Discovery News*, May 18, 2009.

8 See, for example, Owen, William, *Lifting the fog of war* (The Johns Hopkins University Press, 2001). Cebrowski, Arthur K., and John J. Garstka, "Network-centric warfare: Its origin and future" in *United States Naval Institute Proceedings* 124 (1998), p. 28. Risen, Clay, "War-mart: So long, Clausewitz. Hello, Tom Peters," *New Republic*, April 3, 2006, p. 20.

9 These issues are discussed in depth in Singer, P. W., *Corporate warriors: The rise of the privatized military industry* (Cornell University Press, 2003), and Singer, P. W., *Children at war* (New York, NY: Pantheon, 2005).

10 Dunlap, Charles, "Law and military interventions: Preserving humanitarian values in 21st century conflicts," prepared for the Humanitarian Challenges in Military Intervention Conference, Harvard University, Carr Center for Human Rights Policy, Washington, DC, November 29, 2001.

11 Edwards, Sean J. A., *Swarming and the future of warfare*, PhD dissertation, Pardee Rand Graduate School, RAND, 2005. p. 288.

12 Quotation of *Star Trek* creator and producer Eugene W. Roddenberry, recorded in Santa Barbara, CA (1971). http://memory-alpha.org/wiki/Template: Gene_Roddenberry_quotes.

13 Jacob, Mark, "Japan's robots stride into future," *Chicago Tribune*, July 15, 2006, p. 7.

14 Singer, P. W., *Wired for war: The robotics revolution and conflict in the 21st century* (New York, NY: Penguin Press, 2009), p. 168.

15 Laws and Customs of War on Land (Hague II), July 29, 1899. Meron, Theodor, "The Humanization of humanitarian law," *American Journal of International Law* 94 (January 2000): 239–278.

16 Available at www.youtube.com/watch?v=v5YftEAbmMQ.

17 Singer, P. W., "The global swarm," *Foreign Policy*, March 11, 2013.

18 Available at www.youtube.com/watch?v=SNPJMk2fgJU.

19 Brown, Emma, "Model airplane history-maker Maynard Hill dies at the age of 85," *Washington Post*, June 9, 2011.

20 Brookings Policy Paper, "The Predator comes home: A primer on domestic drones, their huge business opportunities, and their deep political, legal and moral challenges," March 13, 2013.

21 Ellis, John, *The social history of the machine gun* (The Johns Hopkins University Press, 1975), p. 89.

22 This is known widely as Clarke's Third Law. Clarke, Arthur C., *Profiles of the Future: An Inquiry into the limits of the possible* (New York, NY: Harper & Row, 1962); see www.quotationspage.com/quotes/Arthur_C._Clarke/.

23 Johnson Lewis, Jone, "Marian Anderson Quotes," http://womenshistory.about.com/od/quotes/a/marian_anderson.htm.

24 Specter, Michael, *Denialism: How irrational thinking hinders scientific progress, harms the planet and threatens our lives* (New York, NY: Penguin, 2009).

25 *CBS* News, "Palin: Global warning just 'snake oil,'" February 9, 2010.

26 Specter, *Denialism*.

27 *Slate*, "Banishing the term drone won't solve the UAV Industry's problems," August 16, 2013.

13

Drones and Cognitive Dissonance

ROSA BROOKS

1. WHAT IS IT ABOUT DRONES?

There is something about drones that makes sane people crazy. Is it those lean, futurist profiles? The activities drone technologies enable? Or perhaps, it is just the word itself – *drone* – a mindless, unpleasant, dissonant thrum. Whatever the cause, drones seem to produce an unusual kind of cognitive dissonance in many people.

Some demonize drones, denouncing them for causing civilian deaths or enabling long-distance killing, even as they ignore the fact that the same (or worse) could be said of many other weapons delivery systems. Others glorify them as a low-cost way to "take out terrorists," despite the strategic vacuum in which most drone strikes occur. Still others insist that US drone policy is just "business as usual," despite the fact that these attacks may undermine US foreign policy goals while creating an array of new problems.

It is worth taking a closer look at what is and is not new and noteworthy about drone technologies and the activities they enable. Ultimately, "drones," as such, present few new issues – but the manner in which the United States has been using them raises grave questions about their strategic efficacy and unintended consequences. In fact, the legal theories used to justify many US drone strikes risk dangerously hollowing out the rule of law itself.

2. DEMONIZING DRONES

For many on the political Left (and more than a few in the middle), drone strikes are the paradigmatic example of US militarism run amok. But many of the most common objections to drones do not hold up well under serious scrutiny – or, at any rate, there is nothing uniquely different or worse about drones, as compared to other military technologies.

Consider the most common anti-drone argument: *drone strikes kill innocent civilians*. This is undoubtedly true, but it is not an argument against drone strikes, as such. After all, *war* kills innocent civilians. And there are some means and methods of warfare that tend to cause more unintended civilian deaths than others.

The website for CodePink, a women's peace group, states: "Drones scout over [Afghanistan and Pakistan] launching Hellfire missiles into the region missing their intended targets, resulting in the deaths of many innocent people."[1]

Similarly, the Anti-War Committee asserts "the physical distance between the drone and its shooter makes lack of precision unavoidable."[2]

But to paraphrase the National Rifle Association, "Drones don't kill people, people kill people." At any rate, drone strikes kill civilians at no higher a rate, and almost certainly at a lower rate, than most other common means of warfare. In fact, drones actually permit far greater precision in targeting. Today's unmanned aerial vehicles (UAVs) carry highly accurate ordinance that generally produce far less widespread damage that other munitions. UAVs' low profile and relative fuel efficiency permit them to spend more "time on target" than any manned aircraft. And unlike pilots of manned aircraft, pilots of unmanned vehicles can regularly be replaced while on a mission both to avoid fatigue and ensure greater accuracy.

Drones can engage in "persistent surveillance." That means they do not just swoop in, fire missiles, and fly off. Instead, they can spend hours, days, weeks, or even months monitoring a potential target. Equipped with imaging technologies that enable operators who may be thousands of miles away to see details as fine as individual faces, modern drone technologies allow their operators to distinguish between civilians and combatants far more effectively than most other weapons systems.

That does not mean that civilians are not killed in drone strikes. They are. But how many civilians are killed in these actions, and are these casualties greater than if other weapons systems had been used? The numbers are not completely clear. The British Bureau of Investigative Journalism (BIJ) analyzed reports by "government, military, and intelligence officials, and by credible media, academic, and other sources."[3] The BIJ determined that of the 383 known drone strikes in Pakistan from 2004 to 2012, between 2,296 and 3,718 people were killed, of whom they estimated between 416 and 960 were civilians (the numbers for Yemen and Somalia are less accurate).[4] New America came up with slightly lower numbers, estimating that in roughly the same time period, between 2,080 to 3,428 people were killed in Pakistan, of whom between 258 and 307 were reported to be civilians (and an additional 199 to 334 were difficult to categorize as either civilians or militants).[5]

Behind the numbers, regardless of which data set is right, lie the mangled bodies of human beings. And whether drones strikes cause "a lot" or "only a few" civilian casualties depends on what we regard as the right point of comparison. Compared to the mass bombing campaigns of the Vietnam era or the Second World War (to say nothing of the use of atomic weapons), drone strikes involve relatively few civilian casualties. Yet these comparisons may not tell us anything useful.

Should we compare the civilian deaths caused by drone strikes to the civilian deaths caused by large-scale armed conflicts? One study by the International Committee for the Red Cross found that on average, ten civilians died for every combatant killed during the armed conflicts of the twentieth century.[6] For the Iraq War, estimates vary widely; different studies place the ratio of civilian deaths to combatant deaths anywhere between 10 to 1 and 2 to 1.[7]

The most meaningful point of comparison for drones is probably manned aircraft. It is difficult to get solid numbers here, but one analysis published in the *Small Wars Journal* suggested that in 2007 the ratio of civilian deaths due to Coalition air attacks in Afghanistan may have been as high as 15 to 1.[8] More recent UN figures suggest a far lower rate, with as few as 1 civilian killed for every 10 airstrikes in Afghanistan.[9]

It is also important to note that drone strikes have become far less lethal for civilians in the last few years. New America concludes that between 89 to 102 civilians or "unknowns" were killed by 73 US drone strikes in 2011, for instance.[10] Reductions in civilian casualties are due to technological advances in drones, surveillance and targeting systems, and far more stringent rules for when drones can release weapons.

Pacifists that condemn all forms of armed conflict can condemn drone strikes without a trace of cognitive dissonance. However, for non-pacifists, a per se condemnation of drone strikes makes little sense. While it is reasonable to condemn a particular war or particular policy, why fixate on a specific method of ordinance delivery? Why focus special attention on drone strikes, which cause relatively low numbers of civilian deaths, and largely ignore the many civilian deaths that occur during raids by ground troops, at vehicle checkpoints, or as a result of close air support?

Drones strikes are bad because killing at a distance is unsavory – If killing from a safe distance is somehow "wrong," what should be our preferred alternative? Should we set aside the technological advantages that protect soldiers, stripping troops of body armor, taking away guns that allow attacks from far away, and requiring troops to engage in hand-to-hand combat?

Here again, it requires more than a little cognitive dissonance to condemn drone strikes for allowing us to kill from a safe distance. If drone strikes enable us to kill enemies without exposing our own personnel, this presumably should be considered a good thing, not a bad thing. Maybe no one should be killed, or maybe we are killing the wrong people, but these are assertions about ethics, intelligence, and strategy, not about drones.

And drones are hardly the only technology that has facilitated killing from a distance. Drones do not present any "new" issues not already presented by aerial bombing, or by guns or bows and arrows, for that matter. In the early 1600s, Cervantes called artillery a "devilish invention" allowing "a base cowardly hand to take the life of the bravest gentleman," with bullets "coming nobody knows how or from whence."[11] Much like drones, the longbow and crossbow were also once considered immoral, or at any rate distinctly unchivalrous. In 1139, the Second Lateran Council of Pope Innocent II is said to have "prohibit[ed] under anathema that murderous art of crossbowmen and archers, which is hateful to God" – at least when used against Christians.[12]

Historically, virtually every significant advance in distance killing has caused anxiety, but there is no reason to regard drones as presenting fundamentally new issues.

Drones turn killing into a video game – Writing in the *Guardian*, Phillip Alston, the United Nations Special Rapporteur on extrajudicial, summary, or arbitrary executions, and Hina Shamsi, of the American Civil Liberties Union, criticized "the PlayStation mentality" created by drone technologies: "Young military personnel raised on a diet of video games now kill real people remotely using joysticks. Far removed from the human consequences of their actions, how will this generation of fighters value the right to life?"[13]

But are drones any more "video game-like" than other modern military technologies, such as laser-guided munitions, remote sensing, satellite imaging, or placing cameras in the noses of cruise missiles? Those old enough to remember the First Gulf War will recall the once-shocking novelty of images taken by cameras inside Tomahawk missiles, the jolting, grainy images in the crosshairs before everything went ominously black.

Regardless, there is little evidence that drone technologies "reduce" their operators' awareness of human suffering. If anything, drone operators may have a far greater sense of the harm they help inflict than snipers or bomber pilots, precisely because the technology enables such clear and long-term visual monitoring.

Journalist Daniel Klaidman reports the words of one CIA drone operator, a former air force pilot: "I used to fly my own air missions ... I dropped bombs, hit my target load, but had no idea who I hit." With drones, it was a different story: "I can look at their faces ... see these guys playing with their kids and wives ... After the strike, I see the bodies being carried out of the house. I see the women weeping and in positions of mourning. That's not PlayStation; that's real."[14]

Increasingly, there is evidence that drone pilots, just like combat troops, can suffer from post-traumatic stress disorder. They watch a man play with his children and live his life, sometimes for extended periods of time. And then they drop ordinance on the man and see his mangled body. Surely this takes a psychological toll. A recent air force study found that 29 percent of drone pilots suffered from "burnout," with 17 percent "clinically distressed."[15]

Targeted killings are creepy – Many critics of drone strikes also express discomfort with "targeted killings," viewing them as little more than assassinations or simple murder. In targeted killings, lethal force is aimed at specific, named individuals. Note, not all targeted killings involve drone strikes – some may involve bombs dropped from manned aircraft, or missiles fired from an aircraft carrier, or a boots-on-the-ground raid – just as not all drone strikes are targeted killings.

But assuming the law of war applies, or that the right to national self-defense has legitimately been triggered, it is hard to see any inherent problem with targeted killing. Should we prefer *untargeted* killing? Is it not better to strike only those named individuals about whom we have specific evidence of terrorist activities than target unnamed individuals about whom we know far less?

3. GLORIFYING DRONES

For every critic who demonizes drones while ignoring their similarities to other less-demonized technologies, there are twice as many people who seem to regard drones as a near-panacea – an almost magical new technology that will allow us to economically stave off foreign threats from the safety of home.

The notion that we can kill bad guys with a cheap, replaceable, unmanned vehicle in a manner that allows us to minimize unintended casualties, without risking American lives, is appealing. Indeed, this is vastly more appealing than, say, sending scores of thousands of troops off to war. Had it not been for the availability of drone technologies, it is not clear that the United States would have intervened in Libya. In fact, once Libya's air defenses had been eliminated by US missiles (many launched by old-fashioned manned aircraft), the intervention in Libya became, to a great extent, a drone war. In that case, the United States was able to reduce the risk to human pilots by sending in drones to attack targets on the ground.

However, the advantages of drones are often as overstated and misunderstood as the problems they pose. In some ways, the perceived advantages of drones cause new problems, which are generally ignored by their proponents. In particular, drone technologies temptingly lower or disguise the costs of lethal force. In this way, their apparent benefits may mask their potentially dangerous, longer-term impact and the broader strategic consequences of an increasing reliance on drones.

Armed drones lower the perceived costs of using lethal force in at least three ways. First, drones reduce the financial cost of projecting force in foreign countries. Most drones are substantially less expensive than the available alternatives. For example, manned aircraft are quite costly: Lockheed Martin's F-22 fighter jets cost around $400 million each,[16] F-35s are $130 million,[17] and F-16s are $47 million.[18] But the 2011 price of a Reaper drone was $28 million,[19] while Predator drones cost only about $4.5 million.[20]

Some assert that the true costs of drones are (or will soon be) far higher, both because the United States is in the process of developing more sophisticated and expensive drones and because production costs do not reflect the expenses of the underlying research and development. As with so many things, putting a dollar figure on drones is difficult, as it depends on what costs are counted and what time frame is used. However, the issue here is not only whether drones are truly less expensive than alternative technologies, but also the degree to which they are *perceived* as cheaper by government decision makers.

Second, relying on drone attacks unquestionably reduces the domestic political costs of using lethal force. Sending Special Operations Forces after a suspected terrorist places the lives of US personnel at risk, and full-scale invasions and occupations endanger even more American lives. In contrast, using armed drones eliminates all short-term risks to the lives of US personnel involved in the operations. Because drone attacks do not involve "sustained fighting . . . active exchanges of fire . . . [or] US ground troops,"[21] any need for congressional notification and approval under the War Powers Resolution can conveniently be avoided.[22] It is no coincidence that while Americans generally view the Iraq and Afghanistan wars as costly mistakes, substantial majorities approve of President Obama's drone policies.

Third, by reducing accidental civilian casualties, precision drone technologies reduce the perceived moral and reputational costs of using lethal force.[23] Most US officials care greatly about avoiding civilian casualties, and even those who might be willing to discount the moral cost of civilian deaths understand the reputational costs. Dead civilians upset local populations and host-country governments, alienate the international community, and sometimes even disturb the sleep of American voters.[24]

Government officials are extremely sensitive to financial, political, and reputational costs. Thus, when new technologies appear to reduce the costs of using lethal force, their threshold for deciding to use lethal force correspondingly drops. If killing a suspected terrorist based in Yemen or Somalia will endanger expensive manned aircraft, the lives of US troops, or the lives of many innocent civilians, US officials will reserve such killings for situations of extreme urgency and gravity (for example, stopping another 9/11 or targeting a significant enemy such as Osama bin Laden). However, if all that appears to be at risk is an easily replaceable drone, officials will be tempted to use lethal force more often and more casually.

The trouble with drones is that they make it a little too tempting and perhaps too easy to use force.[25] If a government has a tool that allows it to target potential bad guys with very little risk, it makes sense that it would use it ever more frequently. Thus, we have seen drone strikes evolve in the last decade from a technology with limited deployment used to target specifically identified high-ranking al-Qaeda officials to a tool used in an increasing number of countries to attack an apparently endlessly lengthening list of supposed bad guys, some identified by name, others targeted on the basis of suspicious behavior patterns, with an increasingly tenuous link to grave or imminent threats to the United States.

As their use has grown, drones strikes have targeted militants who appear to be lower and lower down the terrorist hierarchy,[26] so that rather than a focus on terrorist masterminds, attacks now focus on low-level insurgents.[27] Although drone strikes are believed to have killed more than 3,300 people since 2004,[28] by most accounts only a small fraction of those successfully targeted have been so-called "high-value targets."[29] In addition, drone strikes have spread ever further away from "hot" battlefields such as Afghanistan and northern Pakistan, to Yemen, to Somalia (and perhaps to Mali[30] and the Philippines[31] as well).

While drone technologies enable the United States to reduce some of the costs of using lethal force inside the borders of other states, an increasing reliance on drones, justified partly on their "reduced costs," may have potentially devastating consequences.

For one thing, drones encourage a "short-term fix" approach to counterterrorism that relies excessively on eliminating specific individuals deemed to be a threat, with limited discussion of whether this strategy is likely to produce long-term security gains. Most counterterrorism experts agree that in the long-term, terrorist organizations are rarely defeated through military action. After all, terrorists hold no territory and often lack centralized command structures; you cannot "invade" al-Qaeda or force its parliament to accept a peace treaty. Instead, terrorist groups tend to fade away when they lose the support of the populations where they operate. They die out when their ideological underpinnings come undone: when new recruits stop appearing, when local communities stop providing active or passive assistance, when respected leaders speak out against them, and residents report their activities and identities to the authorities.

For these reasons an effective, comprehensive counterterrorist strategy requires activities that undermine terrorist credibility within populations, as well as on activities designed to disrupt terrorist communications and financing. This is not to deny the role for military actions such as targeted killings, but rather to emphasize the fact that a strategy that emphasizes kinetic force is unlikely to dismantle these types of organizations. As we have already seen, killing "al-Qaeda's #3" does not do much good when a #4 stands ready to take his place (after all, as several political commentators have claimed, the United States has supposedly killed al-Qaeda's "#3 official" dozens of times).[32]

Meanwhile, drone strikes – lawful or not, justifiable or not – may well increase both regional instability and anti-American sentiment. Drone strikes sow fear among the "guilty" and the innocent alike, and the use of drones in Pakistan and Yemen has increasingly been met with popular resentment and – in Pakistan at least – diplomatic and political protests.[33] As the Obama administration increases its reliance on drone strikes as the counterterrorism tool of choice, it is quite possible that we are trading short-term tactical gains for long-term strategic losses.

What impact will US drone strikes ultimately have on the stability of Pakistan, Yemen, or Somalia?[34] To what degree are we actually creating new grievances within the local population, especially as we reach further and further down the terrorist command structure, killing lower-level operatives who may be motivated less by ideology than economic need?[35] As Defense Secretary Donald Rumsfeld asked during the Iraq War, are we creating terrorists faster than we kill them?[36]

It is not hard to imagine hypothetical situations in which drone strikes would be both lawful and strategically effective. Yet even if these conditions are met, many drone strike supporters seem unable to acknowledge that there is little persuasive evidence that current US drone policy will benefit us in the long term.

4. LEGALIZING DRONES

There is nothing mystical about drones. They are neither inherently "evil" nor the answer to US national security concerns. Drone strikes are just another tactic in America's lethal toolkit, simply another means of delivering death, not inherently any worse or any better than any other way of killing people.

From a narrow legal perspective, drones are also "business as usual." Both the United States and the international community have long had rules governing armed conflicts and the use of force in national self-defense. These rules apply whether the lethal force involves knives, assault weapons, grenades, tank-mounted machine guns, or weaponized drones. When drone technologies are used in traditional armed conflicts – on "hot battlefields" such as those in Afghanistan, Iraq, or Libya, for instance – they pose no new legal challenges, and can and should be regulated using the existing laws of war.

But if drones used in traditional armed conflicts present no "new" legal issues, some of the activities and policies enabled and facilitated by drones pose enormous challenges to existing legal frameworks. For example, as discussed above, the availability of drone technologies makes it far easier for the United States to "expand the battlefield," striking targets in places where it would be too dangerous or too politically controversial to send troops. Often this expansion challenges existing legal frameworks.

For example, drones enable the United States to strike targets inside foreign states, and to do so quickly, efficiently, and deniably.[37] As a result, drones have become the tool of choice for so-called "targeted killing" – the deliberate targeting of an individual or group of individuals, whether known by name or targeted based on patterns of activity, inside the borders of a foreign country. It is when drones are used in targeted killings outside of recognized armed conflicts that their use challenges existing legal frameworks.

Law is almost always out of date: We make legal rules based on existing conditions and technologies, perhaps with a small nod in the direction of predicted future changes. As societies and technologies change, law increasingly becomes an exercise of jamming square pegs into round holes. Eventually, that process begins to do damage to existing law: it gets stretched out of shape, or broken. Ideally, we update the laws before too much damage is done. Right now, US drone policy is on the verge of doing irreparable damage to the rule of law – and it is not clear that either the president, Congress, or the public cares enough to address the issue.

Understanding how US drone policy challenges existing legal ideas, systems, and norms requires a consideration of the concept of "rule of law," as well as a review of the relationship between the laws of war and "ordinary" law.

The rule of law – A lot of ink has been spilled defining the rule of law. At root, the concept is fairly simple. The rule of law requires that governments follow transparent, universally applicable, and clearly defined laws and procedures. The goals of the rule of law are to ensure predictability and stability and to prevent the arbitrary exercise of power. When you have the rule of law, a government cannot fine you, lock you up, or kill you on a whim; it can only exercise its authority in accordance with pre-established rules that reflect basic notions of humanity and fairness through fair processes.

Precisely what constitutes a fair process is open to debate. Nevertheless, most would agree that, at a minimum, fairness requires that individuals have reasonable notice of what the law is, reasonable notice that they are suspected of violating the law, reasonable opportunity to respond to allegations against them, and reasonable opportunity to have the outcome of any procedures be reviewed by an objective individual or body.

In the domestic US context, for instance, respect for the rule of law means that the government cannot detain people on a mere hunch or harm or kill citizens solely based on a suspicion of wrongdoing. For the police to arrest and detain someone, they must demonstrate that "probable cause" exists to suspect someone of a crime, and conviction and punishment (whether imprisonment or death) requires the state to prove – in court – guilt "beyond a reasonable doubt." The accused is entitled to legal representation, to confront the evidence against him or her, and to appeal an adverse ruling to a higher court.

International law recognizes the same core rights recognized within the US constitutional system. These rights are enshrined in the Universal Declaration of Human Rights, the International Covenant on Civil and Political Rights, and other treaties and declarations endorsed by the United States and vast majority of states around the globe.

Normally, these universally acknowledged rights (together with international law principles of sovereignty) make it clearly unlawful for one state to target and kill an individual inside the borders of another state. In 1976, for instance, when the Pinochet regime in Chile killed Chilean dissident Orlando Letelier in Washington, DC, using a car bomb, it was understood as an unlawful political assassination; a case of murder.[38]

The laws of war – However, during times of war, the "ordinary" legal rules do not apply. Certain state-sponsored actions that are considered illegal (as well as immoral) under "ordinary" circumstances are legally permissible in the context of an armed conflict. To start with the obvious, in war, the willful killing of human beings is permitted, regardless of whether the act is committed with a gun, a bomb, or a long-distance drone strike.

The same is true for a wide range of other acts. In war, it is legal for a combatant to knowingly inflict injury and death on others as long as they are enemy combatants or otherwise participating in hostilities. In fact, it is lawful for such acts to be committed against ordinary civilians as long as the actions are consistent with core principles of international humanitarian law, such as proportionality, necessity,[39] and distinction.[40] It is also legal to destroy property and engage in various restrictions on individual liberties provided that these acts are conducted in accordance with the law. For example, in war, enemy combatants can be detained with little or no due process for the duration of the conflict, not because they have committed crimes but to keep them from returning to the battlefield (although they must be treated humanely as defined by a detailed set of rules). In addition, civilians may also be detained if they pose specific threats.

While this is a radical oversimplification of a very complex body of law,[41] as with the rule of law, the basic idea is relatively simple. When there is no war – when ordinary, peacetime law applies – agents of the state are not supposed to lock you up, take your things, or kill you unless they have first engaged in multiple formal legal processes. In other words, under ordinary circumstances you are protected both by domestic law and (in theory) by international human rights law.[42]

However, when there is a war, everything changes. While war, as managed by law, is not a free-for-all – actions such as torture, rape, and killing that is willful, wanton, and "not justified by military necessity"[43] remain crimes[44] under the law of war – there are far fewer constraints on state behavior.

Technically, the law of war is referred to using the Latin term *lex specialis*, special law. It is applicable in and *only* in special circumstances, and in those cases it supersedes *lex generalis*, general law, that prevails in peacetime. We have one set of laws for "normal" situations and another more flexible set of laws for "extraordinary" situations, such as armed conflicts.

Of course, the *lex specialis* of the law of war does not pose any inherent problem for the rule of law. The rule of law is as much a set of moral commitments as a specific body of rules, and it is that bundle of rules, institutions, and norms that we rely on to ensure fairness and predictability and prevent the abuse of power. Having one body of rules that tightly restricts the use of force and another body of rules that is far more permissive does not fundamentally undermine these commitments, as long as we have a reasonable degree of consensus on what circumstances trigger this "special" law.

In other words, the different rules of war do not challenge ordinary law as long as war is the exception and not the norm. In addition, it is essential that there is general agreement as to what constitutes war, clarity as to when war begins and ends, and rules that discriminate between combatants and civilians and between those places where there is war and places where there is peace.

Now, how does this discussion relate to drones and targeted killings? Where these distinctions are clear, the use of drones for targeted killings does not necessarily present a legal or policy problem. For example, in Libya, a state of armed conflict clearly existed inside the borders of the country and between Libyan government and NATO states. In that context, the use of drones to strike Libyan military targets was no more controversial than the use of manned aircraft for similar attacks.

This is because our core rule of law concerns have generally been satisfied. We know that there is an armed conflict because all parties to it agree that this is the case; because we can objectively verify the presence of uniformed military personnel engaged in using force; because the violence is, from an objective perspective, widespread and sustained – it is not a mere skirmish or riot or criminal law enforcement situation that got out of control. We know *who* the "enemy" is: Libyan government forces. We know *where* the conflict is and is not: It is in Libya, but not in neighboring Algeria or Egypt. We know *when* the conflict began. We know who authorized the use of force (the Security Council, which is legally empowered under the UN Charter to authorize such actions) and we know whom to hold accountable in the event of error or abuse (the various governments involved).

Another recent example is Afghanistan. Here, the enemy is not another state's organized, uniformed armed services, but rather a loosely knit network of allied insurgent forces. Nevertheless, the existence of an armed conflict in Afghanistan is not disputed and can be objectively verified by journalists, observers, or international monitors. Large numbers of US, NATO nation, and Afghan troops are visibly engaged in an armed conflict. Taliban and other armed groups are organized, can be identified by local informants, and are openly engaged in an armed conflict. Afghans understand that there is a war in their country. When large-scale violence occurs, it does not come as a surprise and almost all groups involved in the country have a reasonably clear understanding of what does and does not constitute "participating in hostilities."

To be sure, there are mistakes and abuses and cases in which civilians are killed. However, it is appropriate to call these situations what they are: mistakes and abuses within an armed conflict that are defined and regulated by the laws of war. Where there are specific violations of the laws of war, these are war crimes and can and should be prosecuted using existing legal mechanisms.

War causes terrible suffering, but as long as war is the exception and not the norm, it does not fundamentally challenge the *lex generalis* or the rule of law. In fact, it is partly the *lex specialis* of the laws of war that allows a law-abiding society the capacity to engage in the devastating practice of armed conflict in a manner that creates a set of clear and enforceable limits on possible actions, thereby respecting both the spirit and principles of the rule of law.

Targeted killings and the laws of war – Once one takes targeted killings outside of formal battlefields, the story changes. The Obama administration is using drones to strike terror suspects in Pakistan, Somalia, Yemen, and perhaps Mali and the Philippines. Defenders of the administration's increasing reliance on drone strikes in such places assert that the United States is in an armed conflict with "al-Qaeda and its associates," and on that basis they claim that the laws of war are applicable – in any place and at any time – as regards whomever the government deems a combatant.

The trouble is that no one outside a small group within the US executive branch has the ability to evaluate who is and who is not a combatant. The campaign against al-Qaeda and its associates is not like World War II or even the wars in Libya or Afghanistan: It is an open-ended conflict with an inchoate, ill-defined adversary. After all, what does it mean to be one of al-Qaeda's "associates"?

What's more, targeting decisions within this nebulous "war" are based largely on classified intelligence. As a result, the administration's assertions about who is a combatant and what constitutes a threat are entirely non-falsifiable because they are based on secret and undisclosed evidence. Added to this complex situation is still another problem, which is that most of these strikes are considered covert actions. Although the United States sometimes takes public credit for the deaths of alleged terrorist leaders, most of the time the administration will not officially acknowledge the targeted killings that are part of this expansive vision of armed conflict.

The US government has not yet offered clear, full, and consistent answers to any of the key rule of law questions related to the ongoing war against al-Qaeda and its "associates."[45] If this is an armed conflict, what changes will indicate that the war is over? Is there a future point at which the war will end, thereby allowing those detained to be released, fulfilling a key criteria of the laws of war? Based on what measure might someone be considered a combatant or someone "directly participating in hostilities"? Is serving as Osama bin Laden's cook enough evidence to be designated for a targeted killing? What about an elderly Somali woman in Detroit who unwittingly gives money to an Islamic charity that serves as a front, or even a partial front, for a terrorist organization? Can she be targeted? What constitutes "hostilities" and what does it mean to participate in them?

It is also unclear just where this war is located. Does the war (and thus the relevant application of the laws of war) somehow travel with combatants as they move from one place to another? That is, if a suspected al-Qaeda operative goes to Pakistan, Yemen, or Somalia, do the laws of war apply to all US actions in those countries? Or does this body of law only apply to some actions in some situations? Does the United States have a "right" to target enemy combatants anywhere on earth, or do such actions require the consent of the state where the attack occurs?

These questions matter. What if, for example, the CIA uses an unmanned aerial vehicle to kill a US citizen whom it suspects is a member of Mali's Ansar Dine, a militant Islamist group alleged to be allied with al-Qaeda?[46] If being a suspected member of Ansar Dine makes someone a combatant in a war on al-Qaeda, and the laws of war apply with regard to combatants regardless of the sovereign state within which they operate, then the hypothetical drone strike is perfectly lawful, US citizenship notwithstanding. Where there is a war, the laws of war apply; enemy combatants can be targeted and killed, and such actions are legal and above board.

But if there is no war, or if the suspected Ansar Dine member is neither a combatant nor a civilian engaged in hostilities, or if there *is* a war, somewhere, but not in Mali, then the hypothetical drone strike would be state-sanctioned murder (of a US citizen, no less).[47]

The rule of law problem here should be obvious: We have no principled basis for deciding how to categorize such targeted killings. Are these actions, as the US government argues, legal under the laws of war? Or, are they cases of unlawful murder?

The laws of war were developed in a different era, with a different set of realities in mind. The world has changed since these principles were developed and codified. When it comes to terrorism, we are stuck today trying to make legal arguments based on once-clear categories that no longer have much value. The result? Neither law nor political institutions now offer any limiting principles on state use of coercion and force.

This murky context requires a substantial capacity for cognitive dissonance to assert that US drone strikes are "obviously" legal under the laws of war and to leave it at that. Every individual detained, targeted, and killed by the US government may well deserve his or her fate. However, when a government claims for itself the unreviewable power to kill anyone, anywhere on earth, at any time based on secret criteria and secret information discussed in a secret process by largely unnamed individuals, it has blown a gaping hole in the rule of law.

Self-defense – When faced with criticisms of the laws of war framework as a justification for targeted killing, the US administration and its supporters often shift their position, arguing that international law rules on national self-defense provide an additional or alternative legal justification for targeted killing. Here, their argument is that if a person located in a foreign state poses an "imminent threat of violent attack" against the United States, then it can lawfully use force in self-defense, provided that the defensive force used is otherwise consistent with core principles of the laws of war.

In fact, this general principle is uncontroversial. For example, if an individual overseas is about to launch a nuclear weapon at New York City, the United States has the right – and the president has a constitutional duty – to use force to prevent the attack, regardless of the attacker's nationality, location, or other similar factor.

But once again, the devil is in the details. First of all, what action or actions constitute an "imminent" threat? Traditionally, both international law and domestic criminal law understand that concept quite narrowly: for a threat to be "imminent" it cannot be distant or speculative.[48] However, for the Obama administration, "distant and speculative" are apparently perfectly consistent with "imminent." According to a 2011 Justice Department White Paper, the most detailed legal justification that is publicly available, the principle of imminence "does not require the United States to have clear evidence that a specific attack on US persons and interests will take place in the immediate future."[49] In other words, "imminence" as defined by the administration does not require actual *imminence*.

On the contrary, the United States can, in effect, target anyone deemed to be an operational leader of al-Qaeda or its "associated forces" because "certain members of al Qaeda are continually plotting attacks ... and would engage in such attacks regularly [if] they were able to do so, [and] the US government may not be aware of all ... plots as they are developing and thus cannot be confident that none is about to occur."[50]

In effect, the concept of "imminent threat" becomes conflated with status or identity. Under this definition, any "operational leader" of al-Qaeda or its "associates" is, by definition, *always* presenting an imminent threat and can, under this argument, be subjected to a targeted killing by a drone or other military action.

This concept of imminence is as loose, ill defined, and self-serving as might be imagined. Although the Justice Department White Paper notes that the use of force to prevent imminent threats of violent attacks must comply with general principles of the laws of war, including proportionality and discrimination, it offers no guidance on how these principles might, in practice, guide decisions on whether a particular proposed strike would be permissible.

From a traditional international law perspective, necessity relates to the imminence and gravity of a threat itself. In the example of a terrorist group about to launch a nuclear weapon aimed at the United States, few would question the "necessity" of a drone strike to prevent such an act. However, there are many examples of potential acts by individual terrorists and their affiliates that might meet the general definition of imminence as outlined by the Justice Department, but would hardly seem legitimate, legal, or necessary. For example, how would the administration view a highly successful fundraising effort for an armed group, an angry mob of youths throwing rocks at a US embassy, or a vitriolic lecture on the evils of American society by someone ideologically supportive of a terrorist group?

Here again, the Justice Department document leaves many of the most important questions unanswered: Is any threat of "violent attack" sufficient to justify killing someone in a foreign country? What if the individual is a US citizen? Is every potential suicide bomber a legitimate target? At what point would he or she be a legitimate target? Are we justified in drone strikes against targets who might, if given a chance at some unspecified future point, place an IED that could, if successful, kill one person? Two people? Twenty? Two thousand? How grave a threat must there be to justify the use of lethal force against an individual abroad?

Defenders of the administration's policies acknowledge that the criteria for determining how to answer these questions have not been made public. However, they insist that this should not cause concern. Insiders[51] consistently reassure critics and the public in general that executive branch officials go through an elaborate process in which they carefully consider every possible issue before determining that a drone strike is lawful.[52] While this may be true, formal processes tend to further normalize once-exceptional activities – and the claim to "trust us" is a shaky foundation for the rule of law.

After raising and quickly rejecting potential constitutional arguments against the targeting of US citizens overseas, the Justice Department White Paper concludes that the determination of whether an American citizen overseas can be killed can be made by "an informed, high-level official of the US government,"[53] and that neither Congress nor any court can countermand or question this decision. The document explains that this is because "matters intimately related to foreign policy are rarely proper subjects for judicial interventions," and such matters "frequently turn on standards that defy judicial application."[54]

This restates the problem nicely: Generally speaking, standards that would "defy judicial application" are effectively no standards at all. They consist of sweeping generalizations about legality, but offer no criteria for actually determining legality (or necessity, or strategic wisdom). This is not a reason to *reject* any notion of judicial review. Rather this is the very reason one might consider a review outside the executive branch as essential.

As with law of war arguments, stating that US targeted killings are obviously legal under traditional self-defense principles requires more than a little cognitive dissonance. Law exists to restrain untrammeled power. Certainly, it is possible to make a plausible legal argument justifying each and every US drone strike, but this merely suggests that we are working with a legal framework that has begun to outlive its usefulness.

The real question is not whether US drone strikes are "legal." The real question is: Do we really want to live in a world in which the US government's justification for killing is so malleable?

The example we set – Another reason to worry about the US government's overreliance on drone strikes is that if other states were to follow America's example, the results might be quite disturbing. Consider the Letelier murder previously referenced. In 1976, this was an international scandal; it significantly delegitimized the Chilean government (and later led to a number of civil and criminal legal cases). If the Letelier assassination took place today, you can imagine that Chilean authorities would insist on their national right to engage in "targeted killings" of individuals deemed to pose imminent threats to Chilean national security. They would justify such killings based on the same legal theories that the United States currently uses to support targeted killings in Yemen or Somalia.

Right now, the United States has a decided technological advantage when it comes to armed drones. However, this situation will not last long. Rather than continue on the present path, our government should use this window to advance a robust legal and normative framework that will help protect against abuses by those states whose leaders can rarely be trusted.

Unfortunately, we are doing exactly the opposite. Instead of articulating norms based on transparency and accountability, the United States is effectively legitimizing the sorts of policies that have traditionally been used by authoritarian regimes, handing other countries – perhaps China, Russia, Iran, or North Korea – a playbook for how to use legal arguments to foment instability and get away with murder.

Take the issue of sovereignty. Sovereignty has long been a core concept of the Westphalian international legal order.[55] The basic idea is that within the international arena, all states are formally considered equal and possessed of the right to control their own internal affairs free from the interference of other states. One expression of this idea is the principle of non-intervention, which means, among other things, it is generally a fundamental violation of international law for one sovereign state to use force inside the borders of another sovereign state.[56]

There are some well-established exceptions to this principle, but these are few in number. For example, a state can lawfully use force inside another sovereign state with that state's invitation or consent, in self-defense "in the event of an armed attack,"[57] or when force is authorized by the Security Council, pursuant to the UN Charter.[58]

The principle of sovereignty might appear to pose substantial problems for current drone policy. After all, how can the United States lawfully use force to kill suspected terrorists inside Pakistan, Somalia, or Yemen, or in other states in the future? The United States does not have Security Council authorization for drone strikes in those states, so the justification has to rest either on consent or on some theory of self-defense. Thus, the Justice Department White Paper blithely asserts that targeted killings carried out by the United States do not violate another state's sovereignty, provided that state either consents or is "unwilling or unable to suppress the threat posed by the individual being targeted."

Superficially, this position appears plausible. However, woven into this argument is an idea of American exceptionalism, in which the United States views itself as the sole arbiter of whether a state is "unwilling or unable" to suppress a threat. This presents a circular logic: the United States, using its own infinitely malleable definition of "imminent," decides that a person residing in a sovereign state poses a threat to the United States such that removing this threat requires that he or she must be killed. Once the United States decides that this person must be killed, the principle of sovereignty presents no barriers, because either: the state will *consent* to the US use of force inside its borders, or the state will *not* consent to the US use of force inside its borders, in which case the United States will deem the state to be "unwilling or unable to suppress the threat" posed by this person. That is, regardless of the position taken by the sovereign state, the use of force by the US government will be interpreted as lawful, at least by the United States.

To the degree that this is the logic of US drone activity, it more or less eviscerates traditional notions of sovereignty and has the potential to significantly destabilize the already shaky collective security regime created by the UN Charter. If the United States declares itself the sole arbiter of whether and when force can lawfully be used inside the borders of another state, why should other strong states not make similar claims?

Of course, if the US executive branch is the sole arbiter of what constitutes an imminent threat and who constitutes a targetable enemy combatant in an ill-defined war, what prevents other states from making identical arguments and then using them to justify the killing of dissidents, rivals, or unwanted minorities?

Consider Russia, in which dissidents, investigative journalists, and unwanted political rivals are commonly arrested, jailed, and sometimes killed.[59] At the moment, the Russian government disclaims responsibility when a troublesome citizen is conveniently murdered in a foreign country. But with the United States presenting a highly flexible interpretation of the laws of war and the scope of self-defense, why should Russia bother to deny targeted killings of its enemies in the future?

Perhaps soon, the Russian government will explain the next dissident's death (whether by drone strike in Belarus or radioactive sushi in London)[60] with a dignified news release. The murdered "dissident": a combatant in Russia's war with terrorists and an imminent threat to Russian national security. The evidence: classified, but all actions taken have been lawful and subject to a rigorous internal Kremlin review process. If US officials are skeptical, Russian officials can always approvingly quote President Obama: "There are classified issues, and a lot of what you read in the press ... isn't always accurate ... My most sacred duty ... is to keep the ... people safe."[61]

5. DEALING OPENLY WITH DRONES

We need to stop relying on a questionable, often ad-hoc defense of US drone policy and start talking honestly about the use of these emerging technologies, the activities they enable, and the strategic and legal frameworks in which these activities take place. Those who criticize the deployment of drones should end their irrational insistence on viewing drones as somehow inherently more "immoral" than other military technologies. But drone strike boosters also need to engage in a more honest conversation, and grapple with the argument that although drone strikes appear to offer a cheap, low-risk, "quick-fix" approach to counterterrorism, they may well be doing the United States as much harm as good.

By far the most egregious form of cognitive dissonance afflicts those who deny that the US policy of targeted killings presents rule of law problems. Is it possible to argue that current US drone policy is entirely lawful? Certainly, if you are willing to accept virtually everything that the government says about the strikes on faith and you do not mind jamming square pegs into round holes. But "legality" is not the same as morality or common sense. Current US drone policy is largely secret, offers no safeguards against abuse or error, and sets a dangerous precedent that other states are sure to exploit.

There is nothing pre-ordained about how we deploy new technologies. However, by lowering the perceived costs of using lethal force, drone technologies enable a particularly invidious sort of mission creep. When covert killings are the rare exception, they do not pose a fundamental challenge to the legal, moral, and political framework in which we live. But when covert killings become a routine and ubiquitous tool of US foreign policy, we cannot afford to let them remain in the legal and moral shadows. Our nation, and the world, needs an honest conversation about how to bring targeted killings under a rule of law umbrella by creating more transparent rules and more robust checks and balances.

"Tell me how this ends," said General David Petraeus in 2003.[62] He was speaking of the war in Iraq, which was born out of faulty intelligence and faultier strategic logic, leading the mission to spiral rapidly out of control. Today we know the answer to Petraeus's question: The war ended with tenuous stability for Iraq won at the price of some 4,500 dead Americans,[63] hundreds of thousands of dead Iraqis,[64] millions of displaced people, and roughly a trillion dollars in direct costs,[65] as well as incalculable damage to the United States' global reputation. By 2012, two-thirds of Americans were convinced the war in Iraq had not been worth it.[66]

Petraeus's famous question about Iraq might equally be asked of America's covert drone war. In this shadowy domain, we know the US government claims the legal right to kill any person, anywhere on earth, at any time based on secret evidence collected and reviewed by unnamed officials, without any form of prior or subsequent external review or investigation. And though most covert drone strikes are not officially acknowledged, we know from media and NGO reporting that between 3,000 and 5,000 people have been killed by US drone strikes in Pakistan and Yemen.

There is still a great deal that we do not know about US drone policy. We do not know if this shadow war has any limits, what these limits may be, or how they are reviewed and enforced. We do not know if there are any meaningful mechanisms to prevent mistakes and abuses, and we do not know how many of the deaths so far were the result of such errors or abuses. We do not know if we will be expanding our shadow war into additional foreign states; and if we do, what those states might be. We do not know if our government believes there are any limits on whom we can target, when they can be targeted, or where such targeting may occur. We do not know the objectives of this shadowy war. Is the goal to end the operational effectiveness of al-Qaeda and its affiliates? To end global terrorism? To reduce anti-American violence? We have no clear idea as to how or when we will know if our policies are effective and enable us to achieve our objectives. Above all, we do not know if our shadow war is making us safer, or simply making our world less stable.

How does this end?

NOTES

1 CodePink, "Take Action!" www.codepinkalert.org.

2 Schmidt, Harrison, Jennie Eisert, and Meredith Aby, "Stop drone warfare!" Anti-War Committee, June 20, 2012.

3 Bureau of Investigate Journalism, "Obama 2013 Pakistan drone strikes," January 3, 2013.

4 Ibid.

5 New America, "Drone wars Pakistan: Analysis." http://securitydata.newamerica.net/drones/pakistan/analysis.

6 Tavernise, Sabrina, and Andrew W. Lehren, "A grim portrait of civilian deaths in Iraq," *New York Times*, October 23, 2010.

7 Wikipedia, "Casualties of the Iraq War," which compares statistics compiled by various reporting organizations.

8 Dadkhah, Lara M., "Close air support and civilian casualties in Afghanistan," *Small Wars Journal*, December 30, 2008.

9 United Nations Assistance Mission in Afghanistan and UN Office of the High Commissioner on Human Rights, *Afghanistan Annual Report 2011: Protection of Civilians in Armed Conflict*, February 2012.

10 New America, "Drone wars Pakistan: Analysis."

11 Fuller, J. F. C., *Armament & history: The influence of armament of history from the dawn of classical warfare to the end of the Second World War* (New York, NY: First Da Capo Press, 1998), pp. 91–92.

12 Eternal World Television Network, "Second Lateran Council (1139)." www.ewtn.com/library/councils/lateran2.HTM.

13 Alston, Philip, and Hina Shamsi, "A killer above the law?" *Guardian*, February 8, 2010.

14 Klaidman, Daniel, "Daniel Klaidman on the mind of a drone strike operator," *Daily Beast*, June 8, 2012.

15 Martin, Rachel, "Report: High level of 'burnout' in US drone pilots," NPR, December 18, 2011.

16 Hennigan, W. J., "Sky-high overruns, safety ills plague jet," *Los Angeles Times*, August 7, 2011.

17 Abramson, Larry, "At $130 million a plane, critics question the cost of the F-34," NPR, January 2, 2013.

18 Aircraftcompare, "Lockheed Martin F16 Flying Falcon." www.aircraftcompare.com/helicopter-airplane/Lockheed-Martin-F16-Fighting-Falcon/169.

19 Benjamin, Medea, *Drone warfare; Killing by remote control* (London: Verso Books, 2013), ch. 2.

20 Deloitte, "Disruptive innovation; case study: Unmanned aerial vehicles (UAVs)," 2012.

21 *New York Times*, "White House report on US actions in Libya," June 15, 2011.

22 Savage, Charlie, and Mark Landler, "White House defends continuing US role in Libya operation," *New York Times*, June 15, 2011.

23 Shane, Scott, "The moral case for drones," *New York Times*, June 14, 2012.

24 Drum, Kevin, "Do Americans care about civilian deaths in drone attacks?" *Mother Jones*, August 28, 2012.

25 Brooks, Rosa, "Take two drones and call me in the morning," *Foreign Policy*, September 12, 2012.

26 Bergen, Peter, and Megan Braun, "Drone is Obama's weapon of choice," CNN, September 19, 2012.

27 Miller, Greg, "Increase US drone strikes in Pakistan killing few high-value militants," *Washington Post*, February 21, 2011.

28 New America, "Drone wars Pakistan: Analysis."

29 Miller, "Increase US drone strikes in Pakistan killing few high-value militants."

30 Roggio, Bill, and Lisa Lundquist, "Did the US launch a drone strike on AQIM in northern Mali?" *Long War Journal*, June 24, 2012.

31 Ahmed, Akbar, and Frankie Martin, "Deadly drone strikes on Muslims in the southern Philippines," Brookings Institution, March 5, 2012.

32 Mackey, Robert, "Eliminating Al Qaeda's No. 3, again," *New York Times*, June 1, 2010.

33 *Economist*, "Don't drone on," September 1, 2012.

34 Harris, Paul, "Drone attacks create terrorist safe haven, warns former CIA official," *Guardian*, June 5, 2012.

35 Raghavan, Sudarsan, "In Yemen, US airstrikes breed anger, and sympathy for al-Qaeda," *Washington Post*, May 29, 2012.

36 *USA Today*, "Rumsfeld's war-on-terror memo," October 16, 2003.

37 Granted, existing technological limitations make drone strikes an effective tool only in states that either consent to their use or that lack sophisticated anti-aircraft technologies, as today's drones are relatively vulnerable to attack.

38 Rohter, Larry, "Chile seeks US files on 1976 assassination," *New York Times*, September 21, 2006.

39 International Committee of the Red Cross, "Customary IHL: Rule 14."

40 Ibid., "Customary IHL: Practice relating to Rule 1. The principle of distinction between civilians and combatants."

41 International Humanitarian Law Research Initiative, "IHL primer #1 – what is IHL?"

42 Koh, Harold Hongju, "How Is International Human Rights Law enforced?" *Indiana Law Journal* 74 (1999): 1397–1477.

43 International Criminal Court, Elements of Crimes, UN Doc. PCNICC/2000/1/Add.2 (November 2, 2000), art. 8(2)(a)(iv).

44 *The War Crimes Act of 1996*, Pub. L. No. 104-192, 110 Stat. 2104 (codified in part at 18 USC. sec. 2441).

45 Human Rights Watch, "Q&A: US targeted killings and international law," December 19, 2011.

46 Polgreen, Lydia, "Faction splits from Islamist group in northern Mali," *New York Times*, January 24, 2013.

47 Khaki, Ategah, and Hannah Mercuris, "Why targeted killing is "unlawful and dangerous," American Civil Liberties Union, June 13, 2012.

48 Arend, Anthony Clark, "International law and the preemptive use of military force," *Washington Quarterly* 26 (2003): 89–103, pp. 90–91, which discusses the *Caroline* incident.

49 US Department of Justice, "Department of Justice White Paper: Lawfulness of a lethal operation directed against a US citizen who is a senior operational leader of Al-Qaida or an associated force," released February 4, 2013.

50 Ibid. p. 8.

51 Harold Koh, "The Obama administration and international law," keynote address at the annual meeting of the American Society of International Law, Washington, DC, March 25, 2010.

52 Becker, Jo, and Scott Shane, "Secret 'kill list' proves a test of Obama's principles and will," *New York Times*, May 29 2012.

53 US Department of Justice, "Department of Justice White Paper: Lawfulness of a lethal operation directed against a US citizen who is a senior operational leader of Al-Qaida or an associated force," p. 16.

54 Ibid., p. 10, quoting *Haig v. Agee*, 453 US 280, 292 (1981) and *Baker v. Carr*, 369 US 186, 211 (1962).

55 Jackson, John H., "Sovereignty-modern: A new approach to an outdated concept," *American Journal of International Law* 97 (2003): 782–802.

56 Vlasic, Mark V., "Assassination and targeted killing: A historical and post-Bin Laden legal analysis," *Georgetown Journal of Internal Law* 43 (2012): 259–333, p. 318, citing UN Charter art. 2, paras. 1 and 4.

57 Ibid.

58 United Nations, Charter of the United Nations, October 24, 1945, 1 UNTS XVI UN Charter art. 42.

59 Freedom House, "Russia 2012: Increased repression, rampant corruption, assisting rogue regimes," March 21, 2012.

60 *Fox* News, "Traces of radioactive material found in sushi restaurant, home of dead spy," November 25, 2006.

61 Woods, Chris, "Obama's five rules for covert drone strikes," Bureau of Investigative Journalism, September 6, 2012.

62 Robinson, Linda, *Tell me how this ends: General David Petraeus and the search for a way out of Iraq* (New York, NY: PublicAffairs, 2008).

63 icasualties, "Iraq Coalition casualties: Military fatalities," as of February 11 2012.

64 Wikipedia, "Casualties of the Iraq War."

65 Kurtzleben, Danielle, "What did the Iraq War cost? More than you think," *U.S. News*, December 15, 2011.

66 Chicago Council on Global Affairs, "Foreign policy in the new millennium: Results of the 2012 Chicago Council survey of American public opinion and US foreign policy," 2012.

14

Predator Effect

A Phenomenon Unique to the War on Terror

MEGAN BRAUN

1. DRONES AND THE CIA: A MODEL FOR FUTURE WARS?

The widespread deployment of robotic systems in combat is one of the most significant technical advancements of the post-9/11 era. The technology that has attracted by far the most attention is the Predator, an armed drone used by the United States for reconnaissance and to conduct precision missile strikes on targets in many parts of the world.[1] The US military has used Predators in the wars in Afghanistan and Iraq, as part of NATO operations in Libya, and for more than 400 air strikes on terrorist targets in Yemen, Pakistan, Somalia, and the Philippines. The Predator has become a poster-child for the war on terror and some government officials have lauded it as the "the only game in town" for disrupting al-Qaeda. In light of the Predator's widespread deployment and significant impact, it has become fairly common to hear that drones represent a revolutionary technology and herald a new era of warfare. Michael O'Hanlon, a defense policy expert at the Brookings Institution, has gone so far as to declare that "the era of manned airplanes should be seen as over."[2]

Despite the obvious novelty of drone use, these claims are both overly broad and excessively narrow. Arguments predicting a drone revolution are too broad, in part because commentators refer to drones as a single class of technology when in fact that there are many types of drones that are used in a variety of ways. While the US military has dozens of different types of drones (and other militaries have many additional versions), a significant amount of commentary focuses on armed Predator drones. Yet even discussions on the Predator are often too narrow because they focus on the transformative impact of the technology without considering the impact of the organizations and policies controlling drone operations, which may represent the predominant drivers of change.

Labeling drones "revolutionary" is a bold claim. Revolutionary military technologies are those that represent a technical breakthrough and lead to a transformation in military doctrine, fundamentally altering the conduct of warfare.[3] In this sense, nuclear weapons qualify as a revolutionary technology. One bomb, dropped from a single airplane, can unleash more destruction in an instant than waves of conventional bombers operating for a week.

At its core, the Predator is an airplane capable of launching a precision missile. This is something that countries around the world have been capable of doing for decades. The Predator's unique features are that it erases the risk borne by pilots, can loiter in one place for hours on end, and offers real-time surveillance with the capability for immediate surgical strikes. But on most battlefields these are only incremental improvements over existing military aircraft. What makes the Predator revolutionary, then, is not what it can do, but how it has been used. The war on terror and the vision of the CIA created a unique set of circumstances in which the niche capabilities of the Predator could be optimized. It is this process that has led drones to become so significant within current conflicts.

More so than prior military engagements, the war on terror is intelligence driven and oriented toward individual targets. This stems from the unorthodox nature of the adversary. The United States is fighting diffuse sub-state organizations whose membership is bound together by a common ideology and scattered across more than a dozen countries. Al-Qaeda does not have a centralized command center or military fortifications, so there are few conventional military targets. And the real threat posed by the group stems from individuals plotting attacks on US interests. As a result, the war effort has relied heavily on intelligence agencies, particularly the CIA. Despite ongoing counterinsurgency operations in Afghanistan, the heart of the war effort is found in the anarchic tribal regions in Pakistan and Yemen.

In response to these circumstances, the US government, in large part as a result of CIA initiatives, has developed a national security strategy focused on the targeted killing of al-Qaeda operatives. In this sense, the transformative agents for the shifts in warfare that define the current conflict are al-Qaeda and its affiliates, and the CIA and its partners. Al-Qaeda initiated the conflict that heightened the significance of targeting individuals and elevated the importance of intelligence. In response, the CIA outlined a vision for addressing the global war against terrorism and pioneered the policy of targeted killing. While the Predator has been indispensable to the CIA's efforts, it is a technical enabler, not a revolutionary weapons system.

To understand this issue, it is necessary to situate the Predator's development and use within its historical context. The CIA's unique vision for a global war on terror was a response to the specific threats posed by al-Qaeda. It is within this strategy that the particular capabilities of the Predator have proved to be especially useful. Two themes emerge when tracing the history of the CIA's Predator drone operations from initial reconnaissance flights in the 1990s, through the development of the armed Predator in 2001, to its current use in various parts of the world. The first is the extent to which the CIA has been the driving force behind the development and implementation of the targeted killing program. The second is the degree to which the widespread use of armed drones by the United States is related to a particular historic, strategic, and political context. This suggests that the current Predator program is unlikely to be replicated in the near future and does not represent a general, transformative shift in national security strategy.

2. PROOF OF CONCEPT

One clue that the Predator's transformative impact may be unique to the war on terror comes from the contentious debates regarding the development of unmanned armed vehicles. The concept of an armed drone was initially met with skepticism, and neither the US military nor the intelligence community was willing to deploy the technology. Even the CIA, a major champion of surveillance drones, was reluctant to take command of the armed Predator. In fact, it was not until after 9/11, when facing the specific threat presented by al-Qaeda, that missile-equipped surveillance drones were gradually understood to be indispensable tools for protecting national security. It was only then that the weaponized Predator took flight.

Much of the credit for the technology's development belongs to the CIA. While unmanned aircraft have existed since the 1960s, current surveillance and weaponized drones are a relatively new creation. During the 1980s, the Pentagon experimented with various types of unmanned reconnaissance vehicles, but it was the CIA that first deployed a long-range surveillance drone.

The aircraft, known as the Gnat-750, was capable of loitering mid-air for hours on end while relaying real-time, high-resolution video back to intelligence analysts watching from thousands of miles away. It was purchased in 1993 by the CIA under Director James Woolsey, who was looking for a long-range surveillance system for reconnaissance operations in Bosnia, where dense cloud cover obstructed satellite and U-2 imagery.[4] After the CIA successfully deployed the Gnat-750, the military realized the value of the technology and commissioned an improved version for battlefield surveillance.[5] The result was the Predator, which debuted in 1995 and was quickly deployed on reconnaissance missions in the Balkans, Kosovo, and Iraq.[6]

Just as the Predator came into existence, terrorism was becoming an increasingly significant security threat for the United States. In 1993, Islamic extremists bombed the World Trade Center, and in 1998 al-Qaeda attacked the US embassies in Kenya and Tanzania. By 2000, the Clinton administration was looking for innovative ways to combat this new enemy.

In March 2000, Richard Clarke, the National Security Council (NSC) counterterrorism adviser, prepared a memo for President Clinton outlining US covert action efforts to locate Osama bin Laden. Clinton was unimpressed. He sent the memo back with a note scrawled in the corner saying, "This is disappointing. Need to do better."[7] Clarke responded by asking Vice Admiral Scott Frye, the Joint Chief of Staff's director of operations, to work with Charles Allen, the CIA's assistant director for collection, to develop a joint effort between the Pentagon and the CIA. One proposal was using the Predator to conduct real-time aerial surveillance over Afghanistan to locate bin Laden.[8]

While Clarke was supportive of the idea, many at the Pentagon were opposed to using battlefield surveillance technology to support an intelligence operation.[9] CIA managers were similarly reluctant, arguing that the project was a "distraction" that would divert personnel and resources away from other more important global operations.[10] Unenthusiastic about the new program, the CIA and Pentagon fought for several months about who would pay for it, with the CIA ultimately agreeing to spend $2 million in operation costs for two months of trial flights, while the Pentagon funded the initial $2.4 million to jump start the program.[11]

In fall 2000, President Clinton approved their proposal for a sixty-day "proof of concept" mission called Operation Afghan Eyes to determine whether the Predator could produce actionable intelligence about bin Laden's location.[12] After the first test flight on September 7, Clarke described the imagery as "truly astonishing."[13] Ten out of the Predator's fifteen trial missions were rated a success. On one flight, the video of Tarnak Farms, a known bin Laden hideout near Kandahar, showed a tall man in flowing white robes surrounded by a security detail. CIA analysts could not guarantee that this was bin Laden, but they concluded that he was the "highest probability person."[14] The CIA notified the Pentagon, but it would have taken at least six hours for cruise missiles from US Navy ships in the Indian Ocean to reach the target. It was determined that the risk of bin Laden moving in the intervening period was too high and the strike was called off.[15]

By early October, high winds and freezing temperatures proved too much for the fragile Predator airframe and Operation Afghan Eyes was called to a close.[16] The bin Laden sighting had indicated the potential for an armed

Predator and Air Force developers set to work.[17] However, by the time spring brought improved weather, the newly inaugurated George W. Bush administration had tabled discussions about drone operations while they conducted a comprehensive review of Middle East policy. At the time, the CIA and the Pentagon were embroiled in an ongoing debate about which agency would bear the costs of the program, whether the missile system would work, and whether the CIA should operate an armed Predator.[18]

Money for the project was a major obstacle. The air force was willing to loan its Predators to the CIA, but their policy was, "You break it, you buy it." The CIA disagreed. A Predator cost about $3 million, small change for the Department of Defense, but a hefty price for the fledgling Counter Terrorism Center (CTC), the CIA agency tasked with funding and operating the new program. While the senior management saw costs as a significant hurdle, Allen considered the "quibbling" over financing "ridiculous."[19] Roger Cressey, a member of the NSC staff, was more cynical. He told his colleagues that "it was going to take body bags" before the administration got serious about countering al-Qaeda.[20]

While the deputies debated the costs, George Tenet, then-director of the CIA, questioned whether the agency should operate an armed Predator. He raised a series of thorny questions: What would be the chain of command? Who would actually fire the shot? Would American leaders be comfortable with the CIA performing this task outside of normal military command and control? While some at the CIA, such as Allen, said they would have no problem with agency responsibility for armed attacks, Tenet was appalled and declared that neither they nor he had any such authority.[21] The CIA had been strongly censured by Congress for its role in political assassinations in Cuba and South America during the 1960s, and had since become wary of covert targeting operations.[22] Tenet accepted the established convention that the CIA should not exercise lethal force and was reticent to become embroiled in what might become another public scandal.

Amid this strife, the military had yet to certify the armed Predator as ready for operations. The Air Force had, to its credit, expedited the development of the drone, taking a project that ordinarily would have required three years and completing it in a matter of months.[23] While the Hellfire anti-tank missile system they affixed to the Predator performed well in initial tests, it needed to be redesigned to hit smaller, more mobile human targets. By mid-2001, the military was insisting on additional testing, arguing that the first shot at bin Laden would likely be the best one they would ever get.[24]

On September 4, 2001, the Principals Committee, the senior interagency forum for national security issues, gathered for their first meeting on al-Qaeda.

When it came time to discuss the armed Predator, opinion was mixed. The Defense Department argued for attacking bin Laden as part of a much larger air strike using conventional weapons that would cripple al-Qaeda's training infrastructure.[25] General Myers, the vice chairman of the Joint Chiefs of Staff, indicated that if the military was tasked with the mission, they would use cruise missiles; and if the operation needed to be covert, then it should be run by the intelligence community. However, Tenet remained adamantly opposed to CIA drone strikes, arguing that it would be a terrible mistake for the CIA to fire such a weapon.[26] Ostensibly, he believed that the CIA lacked the appropriate legal authority, but it is also likely Tenet sensed that the political fallout from a failed strike would seriously damage the reputation of the agency.

When the meeting concluded, the summary compiled by National Security Advisor Condoleezza Rice reflected a series of intermediate operational guidelines rather than an action plan. The committee agreed that the Predator was a promising tool but felt it was not yet ready for deployment.[27] Without a consensus on which agency would operate the armed Predator, it remained unclear what drones would be used for. They were viewed as a potential option for the military in the future that could be considered alongside other operation proposals. Meanwhile, the CIA considered flying drones on reconnaissance-only missions to gather actionable intelligence on bin Laden's whereabouts.[28]

One week later, on September 11, 2001, 19 men armed with box cutters hijacked four commercial airliners and killed 2,973 people.[29] It was the single largest loss of life from an enemy attack on American soil. The United States, a country that spends $354 billion a year on defense, homeland security, and international affairs, was caught totally unaware.[30] Overnight the political context was completely transformed, and US national security entered a new era.

3. THE OPENING SHOT

Following 9/11, the security context was completely transformed. The United States was under attack, but from a wholly different sort of enemy – a diffuse organization bound by ideological fervor with members operating in multiple countries. The United States possessed the world's most formidable military, yet there were no conventional al-Qaeda targets against which the United States could direct its extraordinary arsenal. This unique adversary required an innovative response based on extensive intelligence gathering and focused on attacks that targeted individuals rather than armies, two functions for which Predator drones were ideally suited.

On September 15, President Bush and his War Cabinet met at Camp David to develop a response plan. Tenet proposed offering full US financial and military support to the Northern Alliance, which had been waging an insurgency against the Taliban regime for years. CIA paramilitary teams and US Special Forces would work alongside the Northern Alliance to topple the Taliban and kill or capture the al-Qaeda leadership. At the same time, the United States would engage Afghanistan's neighbors to seal off the borders, and develop a coalition of countries to freeze al-Qaeda's financial assets and pursue their affiliates in sites around the globe. The armed Predator was to be a key component of Tenet's plan to locate and kill bin Laden and his top lieutenants.[31]

This was an abrupt about-face on his stance from barely a week earlier. Tenet later explained: "Now that we had been thrown onto a war footing, issues that had seemed intractable just days earlier suddenly seemed far less set in concrete."[32]

Prior to 9/11, the political blowback from a drone crashing or being shot down over Afghanistan in the midst of a lethal operation would have been significant.[33] However, as Richard Clarke noted: "There was no reputational risk to the Agency of acting in Afghanistan after the al Qaeda attacks in America. The only risk to the U.S. intelligence institution after September 11 was if it did not act."[34]

The CIA was also newly empowered by an expansive set of legal authorities. The Authorization for the Use of Military Force, approved by Congress on September 14, empowered the president to use "all necessary and appropriate force" against the perpetrators of the attacks.[35] Three days later President Bush signed a secret Memorandum of Notification authorizing the CIA to use lethal covert action against al-Qaeda operatives around the world.[36] That week, Tenet sent a memo titled "We're at War" to top officials at the CIA, exhorting them to take initiative. He wrote, "There can be no bureaucratic impediments to success. All the rules have changed."[37]

While the CIA's initial legal and political concerns about the use of the armed Predator had been mitigated by the transformative effect of 9/11, the military leadership still preferred conventional weapons and there is no evidence that they made a bid for operational control of the Predator in September or October 2001.[38] As General Myers comments at the September 4 NSC meeting indicated, if the military was tasked with destroying a target, they preferred to use cruise missiles or heavy bombers rather than the diminutive and unproven Predator. In the early months of Operation Enduring Freedom, the military continued to rely primarily on conventional weapons to topple the Taliban government. As the military sought to secure control over the country of Afghanistan, the CIA pursued a separate but parallel mission that focused on killing or capturing high-value al-Qaeda targets. The Predator proved to be the ideal tool for the job.[39]

After the War Cabinet approved Tenet's plans, Cofer Black, the prickly and profane chief of the CIA's CTC, tapped Hank Crumpton, a twenty-year veteran of the Clandestine Service, to lead the Afghanistan campaign. Under Crumpton's direction, the CTC/Special Operations command created a designated targeting division and assumed control of the CIA's fifty-officer drone unit.[40]

The Predator quickly proved to be a low-cost, low-risk, high-performance asset that could be used to provide sustained surveillance of suspected terrorists, battlefield reconnaissance, close scouting for ground patrols, combat air support, and precision strikes. And at a cost of around $3 million apiece, politicians loved the drones. At one point, while the CIA was briefing the president on an operation, complete with vivid video imagery provided by the Predator, Bush exclaimed, "We ought to have 50 of these things."[41] The persistent stare of the Predator loitering overhead gave ground forces unprecedented battlefield awareness and real-time feedback, which proved indispensable to a campaign that was often identifying targets on the fly.

One of the major advantages of the Predator was its ability to take risks that would have been inconceivable for a manned aircraft. In early October, just days before the air assault began, a reconnaissance flight brought one of the CIA's two Predators within range of a Soviet-era radar system. Crumpton and his team watched as the radar antennae slowly swiveled toward the drone. When the team leader instructed the pilot to evade, Crumpton counter-manded and ordered the pilot to keep going.

As a MiG recently launched from a nearby airfield quickly began to intercept the oncoming Predator, someone asked, "What if they shoot us down?" "The value of the intelligence is greater than the cost of our UAV," Crumpton instructed "Fly it right at them." Moments later the MiG zipped by. The Taliban pilot's approach was too fast. He turned around for another pass, followed by another. But he could not intercept the slow-flying Predator. The video from the engagement was quickly passed to the military for analysis.[42]

The Predator also endeared itself to soldiers by providing critical combat air-support. On October 20, the CIA's sole-armed Predator assisted in a Joint Special Operations Command (JSOC) attack on the compound of Mullah Omar, the most senior Taliban leader. The Predator provided aerial surveillance as 200 Army Rangers parachuted in and secured the area deep in the heart of Taliban territory. As they did so, a Chinook helicopter launched from a carrier in the Indian Ocean flew in a JSOC commando team to seize control of the compound.

As the drone monitored the area, an analyst spotted an anti-aircraft gun in the flight path of the oncoming helicopter. The CIA relayed the information to JSOC command, who replied, "Take it out." The team at CTC headquarters watched as one of the Predator's two Hellfire missiles flew wide of the mark. The helicopter was just minutes away as the Predator operator carefully took aim. A burst of smoke filled the video screen as the second missile scored a direct hit. This was the first time the Predator had provided air-to-ground fire support for a combat operation. Minutes later, JSOC forces swooped into the compound and video of US forces easily penetrating the Taliban's safe haven was quickly broadcast around the world.[43]

Crumpton insists the Predator was so precise it could shoot a Hellfire missile straight through a window or take out a lone enemy combatant from miles away.[44] Throughout the fall it successfully targeted a number of bin Laden's top subordinates. In November 2001, a CIA drone strike killed Mohammed Atef, al-Qaeda's military chief and third in command, along with seven other al-Qaeda members.[45] Then in mid-December a Taliban prisoner revealed the location of several al-Qaeda and Taliban command posts along the Pakistan border. As US military aircraft leveled the enemy sites, the Predator identified one individual fleeing on foot. He leapt on a motorbike and took off down the road, only to be incinerated moments later by a Hellfire missile. The man was Qari Amadullah, chief of Taliban Intelligence.[46]

By spring 2002, the CIA-operated drones had proven the immense military value of the Predator. As the CTC/Special Operations division's role at the front lines drew to a close, the Pentagon assumed primary control of combat drone operations. Under the military, drone operations were confined to combat zones in Afghanistan, Iraq, and later Libya, where they targeted suspected terrorists and provided combat air support to ground units in full compliance with the Law of Armed Conflict (LOAC) and pursuant to rigorous oversight from military lawyers.

Meanwhile, without clear guidance from policymakers, the CIA became increasingly unsure of its future mission, and by extension the future of its drone program.[47] The Predator had proven itself as a useful addition to the war-fighting capabilities of the United States and had enabled the CIA to have unique access to the battlefield. However, in the context of the ensuing ground war in Afghanistan, drones became one of many surveillance and air assault systems available to the US military.

4. THE BIRTH OF TARGETED KILLING

It was not until a year after the war on terror had begun that the unique strategic value of the Predator was fully appreciated. By 2002 hostilities in Afghanistan had achieved a level of stasis, as it became increasingly clear that the fight against al-Qaeda would lack the decisive and cathartic conclusion that America desired. Toppling the Taliban was just the beginning. Like the opening shot in a game of billiards, the US invasion had sent bin Laden and his affiliates ricocheting throughout the region while their radical ideology echoed around the world.

With no major military targets left for the United States to attack, the war against al-Qaeda became first and foremost an intelligence operation. It fell to the CIA to identify and track the dozens of top al-Qaeda leaders who had escaped across the borders of Afghanistan and to expose their subordinate networks around the world.

In the face of a diffuse al-Qaeda network, the CIA began to view the Predator as key for an offensive campaign against their global infrastructure.[48] The new war would not just have different battlefields; it would require radically different tactics. Drones would prove an indispensable tool for managing threats in countries where governments were unable or unwilling to deal with the presence of terrorists and their threats. One such country was Yemen, which had repeatedly failed to capture some of the highest priority targets from a US-generated list of wanted al-Qaeda associates. So, the United States took matters into its own hands.

On November 4, 2002, the *New York Times* reported: "The Central Intelligence Agency, using a missile fired by an unmanned Predator aircraft, killed a senior leader of Al Qaeda and five low-level associates traveling by car in Yemen on Sunday."[49]

The attack targeted Qaed Salim Sinan al-Harethi, also known as Abu Ali, who was initially described as "the senior Qaeda operative in Yemen and perhaps one of the top dozen or so Qaeda figures in the world."[50]

The manhunt that led to the drone strike was a massive inter-agency affair that involved FBI agents, the US Army's covert "Gray Fox" surveillance unit, a Special Operations team from CENTCOM, the NSA, the CIA, and State Department diplomats. The Gray Fox team specialized in using advanced equipment to intercept communications. When al-Harethi activated one of his cell phones, the NSA notified the Gray Fox team on the ground, which tracked the call and fed the coordinates to a CIA-operated Predator. The drone was deployed to al-Harethi's location in Marib and monitored the location as he and his group prepared to leave.[51]

After the Predators were deployed to Marib, Tenet called his counterpart at CENTCOM, Lieutenant General Michael DeLong, and informed him that al-Harethi had been located. The Predator continued to watch as the cars sped off down an empty road in a desolate area, minimizing the chance for collateral damage.[52] DeLong was coordinating the operation. DeLong recalled: "[Tenet] goes, 'You going to make the call?' And I said, 'I'll make the call." He says, 'This SUV over here is the one that has Ali in it.' I said, "OK, fine." You know, "Shoot him."[53]

The drone pilot lined it up and took the shot. At the time, the identities of the other victims were unknown. Later reports indicated that four other Yemenis, as well as US citizen and alleged terrorist Kamal Derwish, also died in the blast.[54]

Al-Harethi's death, which came in the first direct strike on an al-Qaeda target outside of Afghanistan since September 11, marked the culmination of a protracted debate about the legality of targeted killing. As one former agency official noted, "There was discussion about this for years in the CIA. The discussion is now over, and the operations have begun."[55] In the weeks following the strike it was reported that President Bush had approved a list of about two dozen suspected terrorist leaders that the CIA was authorized to kill. According to sources, Bush was not required to approve additions to the list, and the CIA did need to seek approval prior to carrying out specific strikes.[56]

The Senate Intelligence Committee, which is responsible for overseeing covert operations conducted by the CIA, defended the policy. The committee chairman, Senator Robert Graham, argued: "Having defined this as an act against a military adversary and applying the standards of international law, this was within the legal rights of a nation at war."[57]

This opinion was echoed by others in the administration. "I can assure you that no constitutional questions are raised here," stated Rice, in an interview shortly after the incident. "[The President is] well within the bounds of accepted practice and the letter of his constitutional authority."[58]

However, the unilateral announcement of the attack on the eve of the US elections severely damaged the relationship the United States had with Yemen. Although CIA and Pentagon officials refused to comment on the incident, within forty-eight hours, Deputy Secretary of Defense Paul Wolfowitz appeared on CNN and seemed to confirm US involvement.[59] When asked about the CIA strike in Yemen, Wolfowitz characterized it as "a very successful tactical operation" and noted the effective cooperation of the Yemeni government.[60] Official reports in Yemen claimed that the explosion had been caused by a car bomb, so the CIA was reportedly furious with the Department of Defense for leaking the story.[61] Yemen's Deputy Secretary General, General Yahya M. Al Mutawakel, broke the government's official silence, complaining: "This is why it is so difficult to make deals with the United States. This is why we are reluctant to work closely with them. They don't consider the internal circumstances in Yemen. In security matters, you don't want to alert the enemy."[62]

The United States had lost the trust of President Saleh and learned a tough lesson about the importance of maintaining plausible deniability. It would be eight years before Yemen would allow another drone strike on its soil.

Despite the loss of Yemen's good graces, the attack on al-Harethi was a major coup for the CIA. It demonstrated the viability of using drones to locate, track, and kill terrorist leaders abroad. Over the next several years, the CIA would gradually build up a network of informants throughout the Middle East and Southeast Asia, as well as information-sharing arrangements with intelligence agencies around the world – sources that would later provide the basis for the development of a massive targeted killing operation heavily reliant on drones.

5. THE THIRD FRONT

The 2002 strike on al-Harethi was a watershed moment in US targeted killing operations, but the policy implications were slow to emerge. Over the next two years, drones continued to make headlines as the Air Force announced plans to develop fifteen new squadrons and used the Predator with great effectiveness in Iraq. Nevertheless, at this time, the CIA's drone operations went quiet.[63] Much of the reduced activity may be attributable to a general reduction in the level of intelligence resources dedicated to al-Qaeda. "In March 2002, John McLaughlin", deputy director of the CIA, announced that the agency was scaling back operations in Afghanistan. Over the next year the intelligence community's center of gravity would shift from bin Laden and his affiliates to Iraq.[64]

The next drone attack came on June 18, 2004, in Pakistan. In early 2004, after months of pressure from the CIA, the Pakistani intelligence service had accepted a deal. The CIA offered to kill Nek Muhammad, a tribal militant who had recently humiliated the government by killing sixty soldiers and then reneging on a negotiated peace, if Pakistan would agree to allow the CIA to conduct regular drone flights over the Federally Administered Tribal Areas.[65] Pakistan agreed. Muhammad was killed while eating dinner with four other men and speaking on a satellite phone.[66] Two young boys, aged sixteen and ten, the sons of Muhammad's host, were also killed.[67]

In many respects, public engagement with this operation played out in a very different manner than the al-Harethi attack. The strike generated little media attention and no US officials spoke about it on the record. *Dawn*, a local Pakistani paper, reported that Muhammad was killed in a missile strike launched by Pakistani security forces and a military spokesman publically accepted responsibility.[68] CNN and the *Washington Post* published similar stories.[69] Only the *New York Times*, which included quotes from local residents claiming the attack was carried out by an American drone, noted any US participation. But Pakistani General Shaukat Sultan denounced reports of American involvement as "absolutely absurd."[70] The following day, US military spokesman Lieutenant Colonel Tucker Mansager told a news conference in Kabul, "The coalition ... congratulates Pakistan for their success in eliminating the former Taliban fighter Nek Muhammad."[71]

After another hiatus, the next strike occurred in May 2005, when a CIA drone took out senior al-Qaeda operative Haitham al-Yemeni and his driver in Northern Waziristan. The US media reported that the CIA had kept al-Yemeni under surveillance for weeks with the hope that he would lead them to bin Laden. However, after capturing another high-level al-Qaeda leader in Pakistan, they began to fear that al-Yemeni would go into hiding and decided to kill him instead. Following the attack, the Pakistani military denied reports of a drone strike and one of the local papers indicated that two people had been killed by a car bomb.[72]

Subsequent attacks continued to be shrouded in ambiguity, with persistent silence from the CIA and ongoing government denials in Pakistan. On November 5, 2005, articles by the Associated Press and the *Daily Times*, citing Pakistani army officials, reported that eight people, including a woman and three children, were killed while suspected militants were making explosives.[73] Later reports confirmed that a US Predator had in fact killed the wife and daughter of Hamza Rabia, al-Qaeda's third in command, along with six others, while a wounded Rabia escaped, only to be killed a month later in another drone strike on December 1.[74] Residents who witnessed the December explosion said they saw a drone fire a missile on the house. Pakistani officials vehemently denied this and Pakistani Information Minister Sheikh Rashid Ahmed claimed that Rabia died while working with explosives.[75]

Throughout 2007 and 2008 Pakistani authorities continued to claim that many of the attacks were results of explosive mishaps by bomb makers, a cover story that quickly wore thin.[76] In fact, it was widely believed that these incidents were US drone strikes carried out with the secret consent of the Pakistani government.

On October 31, 2006, the Pakistani government initially took responsibility for a missile strike that they claimed killed eighty militants hiding in a madrassa. However, locals said that US drones were on scene at the time of the strike and Pakistani helicopters arrived only later. Media reports quickly confirmed that the dead were mostly children. *The News*, a prominent Pakistani paper, listed the names of seventy-nine victims, and only three were over the age of twenty.[77] The Pakistani government quickly amended its story and blamed the CIA. An aide to President Pervez Musharraf told the *Sunday Times*: "We thought it would be less damaging if we said we did it rather than the US. But there was a lot of collateral damage and we've requested the Americans not to do it again."[78]

However, rather than scaling back, the CTC urged stepping up the drone strikes, insisting that attacks against al-Qaeda needed to occur "at a pace they could not absorb."[79]

By spring 2008, after five long years in Iraq, the Bush administration began shifting resources back to Afghanistan. Steve Kappes, the deputy director of the CIA, and Michael Leiter, the head of the National Counterterrorism Center, formed a task force to begin reorienting the intelligence community's attention toward bin Laden. The result was an increase in the number of drones over the tribal areas, more case officers, and more frequent cross border raids.[80] After averaging less than three drone attacks per year, the rate of strikes increased to almost one per month from January through July 2008.[81]

The Bush administration had consistently maintained close ties with President Musharraf. However, by early 2008, in the wake of a series of foiled terrorist plots with ties to Pakistan, there was a growing recognition that the situation in the country's tribal areas was untenable. Despite ongoing wars in Iraq and Afghanistan, the most immediate threat to the United States came from Pakistan, where al-Qaeda and other extremist groups had established 150 training camps. While the Inter-Service Intelligence (ISI), the Pakistani spy agency, accepted payments from the United States in exchange for intelligence cooperation, they also secretly funneled money to extremist groups.[82] By 2008 President Bush explained that he had enough. "We're going to stop playing the game," he said. "These sons of bitches are killing Americans."[83]

When Musharraf was forced to resign in mid-August, the Bush administration took the political transition as an opportunity to revise its drone policy and abandoned the practice of seeking permission from the Pakistanis prior to launching individual strikes. As a result, the period from when a target was identified until it was attacked dropped from many hours to forty-five minutes and the CIA carried out nine strikes in under a month.[84]

Bush's national security team had long believed that the al-Qaeda leadership was the organization's keystone, and if they could decimate the senior ranks the entire organization would collapse. The CTC maintained a list of the two dozen or so leaders at the top of the organization and focused their attention tracking these so-called "high-value targets." In October 2004, the *Washington Post* acquired a list of twenty-eight of these named individuals. By their tally, eight had been killed or captured by the end of 2002, five more in 2003, and one in 2004. Notably, bin Laden and his top deputy, Ayman Zawahiri, remained at large.[85] Around the time of that publication, drones became a key component in the hunt for terrorist leaders. From June 2004 to July 2008, the Bush administration conducted sixteen drone strikes in Pakistan that killed eight high-ranking al-Qaeda and Taliban commanders.[86]

Despite these successes, in summer 2008, senior officials at the CTC told President Bush that "personality strikes" against high-value targets were not doing enough to erode al-Qaeda's capabilities. They persuaded the president to authorize a major expansion that would allow the CIA to target groups of suspected militants believed to be associated with terrorism without necessarily knowing their identity. These "signature strikes" were based on monitoring patterns of activity to identify signatures, such as possession of explosives, travel to al-Qaeda compounds, or association with known militants.[87] In the words of one former intelligence official, "It's always more dramatic to take the bishop, and, if you can find them, the king and queen," but "pawns matter."[88]

Then-CIA Director Michael Hayden justified the policy in November 2008, saying that the CIA was depriving terrorists of a safe haven, making them "doubt their allies; question their methods, their plans, even their priorities."[89] During the last five months of Bush's term, there were thirty drone strikes in Pakistan. The CIA had quietly opened up a third front in the war on terror. Although public attention remained focused on the ongoing wars in Iraq and Afghanistan, drone strikes were becoming the central means for degrading the al-Qaeda network.

6. OBAMA'S WEAPON OF CHOICE

In 2009 the CIA braced for major policy shifts associated with the first new president since the start of America's war on terror. However, Barack Obama surprised critics and supporters alike with his enthusiastic embrace of clandestine operations and the use of limited deadly force, leading one commentator to label him "the covert commander in chief."[90]

Although the subsequent proliferation of drone strikes has been widely attributed to President Obama's initiative, much of the activity is a result of the sustained implementation of policies adopted by the Bush administration in late 2008. Obama reaffirmed the CIA's authority to operate without seeking individual approval from the Pakistanis and continued the controversial policy of signature strikes. However, during 2009, Obama's first year in office, the rate of CIA drone strikes in Pakistan actually fell to 4.5 per month, down from 6 per month during the waning days of the Bush era.[91]

The Obama administration soon became much more proactive. The airline-bombing attempt on Christmas Day 2009, the first close call of Obama's term, demonstrated the severity of the ongoing threat posed by al-Qaeda. In addition, a December 31, 2009, suicide attack on a CIA base in Afghanistan reenergized the agency. President Obama expanded the CIA program to fourteen around-the-clock orbits, each with three drones that alternated for constant surveillance of Pakistan's tribal areas.[92] By then about 20 percent of the CIA's analysts worked as "targeters," whose primary function was to scan data to identify individuals to be recruited, captured, or killed by drone strike.[93]

Meanwhile, over the course of the summer, the security landscape in Afghanistan changed dramatically as the 30,000 surge troops ordered by President Obama the previous December began to arrive. In September 2010, the US military launched a major offensive in Kandahar, a southern province of Afghanistan experiencing a resurgence of Taliban influence. As militants fled across the porous border into Pakistan, there was a simultaneous spike in drone activity with twenty-four strikes in September alone, as compared to five in August and fifty-four in all of 2009. The intensity continued throughout the rest of the fighting season, with fifteen strikes in October, fourteen in November, and twelve in December. By the end of 2010, it had become the deadliest year on record for drones. Between 611 and 1,028 people died during 122 attacks, a rate of one strike every three days.[94]

However, the intensity proved unsustainable. Beginning in January 2011, a series of diplomatic incidents severely taxed US relations with Pakistan, and the CIA repeatedly suspended or curtailed drone operations to allow for political reconciliation. On January 27, Raymond Davis, a CIA contractor, shot and killed two young men in the middle of Lahore. In the midst of the ensuing diplomatic furor, drone strikes were suspended for almost four weeks as the United States sought to negotiate Davis's release.[95] Public outcry further hampered the CIA's relations with Pakistan and the agency came under considerable pressure to reduce the number of operatives working in Pakistan.[96]

Barely a month after Davis was returned to the United States, a team of US Navy SEALs breached Pakistani airspace and swooped into Abbottabad, where they shot and killed Osama bin Laden. Pakistan was incensed by the unauthorized intrusion and became even more outspoken in its condemnation of drone operations, calling them "illegal" and a "violation of national sovereignty."[97] The most damaging blow came on November 26, 2011, when twenty-four Pakistani troops were killed in a cross-border raid by NATO forces.[98] An outraged Pakistani government evicted CIA drones from Shamsi Air Base in the Balochistan Province, closed down NATO supply routes, and demanded an end to air assaults within Pakistan's borders.[99]

Following the closure of Shamsi Air Base, the CIA moved their drone fleet to Afghanistan and ceded additional control to the US military, which shifted its drone orbits closer to the Pakistan–Afghan border, to reduce the number of strikes on Pakistani soil, and so the CIA could hand off targets once they moved into Afghanistan.[100] After a seven-week hiatus following the deadly cross-border raid, drone strikes resumed in January 2012, but continued to be sporadic as the United States negotiated for the reopening of NATO supply routes.

In part due to this string of diplomatic incidents, by the end of 2011 the CIA had carried out just seventy-two strikes, a 40 percent decrease from the 2010 peak.[101] The vicissitudes of US–Pakistani political relations were a critical factor in the waxing and waning of CIA drone activity, as were a series of key policy developments that contributed to the reduction in strikes.

As drones became the centerpiece of US counterterrorism efforts, Congress began to ask questions. In April 2010, the House Committee on Oversight and Government Reform convened a panel of legal experts for a hearing titled "Rise of the drones: Unmanned systems and the future of war." They asked witnesses to testify regarding the legality of using unmanned weapons to target individuals. Opinion was mixed. While several lawyers supported the emerging practice of targeted killing, Mary Ellen O'Connell, of the University of Notre Dame Law School, argued that drone strikes outside of combat zones violated international law and CIA drone operators were illegal combatants.[102] No policy changes were introduced as a result of the hearing, but it marked the beginning of a robust public debate regarding drones.

In the midst of this controversy, Senator Dianne Feinstein, who took over as chair of the Senate Intelligence Committee in January 2009, pushed for closer scrutiny of CIA drone operations. The CIA had traditionally submitted reports to the intelligence committees within 24 hours of each strike, detailing the target, location, and result.[103] Feinstein instituted a policy whereby staff members from the House and Senate Intelligence Committees held meetings at the CIA once a month to review drone strike records and assess their legality, precision, and effectiveness. However, when interviewed, congressional staffers could not point to any restrictions they had imposed on the CIA or policy changes that were made as a result of increased oversight.[104] The agency continued to operate with near complete autonomy.

The CIA continued to authorize risky operations, and intelligence failures repeatedly generated significant civilian casualties. In spring 2011, the US Ambassador to Pakistan, Cameron Munter, furious about a March strike that killed more than thirty-five people, forced a discussion regarding the drone program and demanded greater consultation with the State Department.[105] At the June 2011 meeting, Munter requested the authority to veto specific strikes. Panetta cut Munter off mid-speech and stated flatly, "I don't work for you."[106]

During the summer, the Obama administration conducted a comprehensive review of drone operations. Although support for the CIA program was ultimately confirmed, operating standards were tightened. In the words of one senior official: "The bar has been raised. Inside CIA, there is a recognition you need to be damn sure it's worth it."[107] Following the review, Pakistani officials were given advance notice of more strikes, attacks were to be suspended when Pakistani diplomats visited the United States, and the State Department was given increased input on targeting decisions.[108]

Shortly after the review, CIA Director Leon Panetta was tapped to become the next Secretary of Defense, and General David Petraeus became the agency's third director in three years. As the former commander of US forces and the International Security Assistance Force in Afghanistan, Petraeus was intimately familiar with the CIA drone program and sought to impose military discipline on the intelligence agency. According to senior officials, Petraeus immediately voiced "caution against strikes on large groups of fighters" and urged the CIA to focus on smaller, high-value targets.[109] While urging caution in signature strikes, Petraeus also reoriented the CIA's focus toward high-value targets. Successful attacks on leaders accounted for only 8 percent of all 2010 strikes; by 2012 that number had increased twofold to 14 percent. The six top commanders killed in 2012 included Abu Yahya al-Libi, al-Qaeda's second-in-command, and Badar Mansoor, al-Qaeda's most senior leader in Pakistan.[110]

Meanwhile, in the months leading up to the 2012 presidential election, the Obama administration began to voice previously unprecedented acknowledgment of US drone strikes and worked to convince the public of their legitimacy. In January 2012, Obama made his first official acknowledgment of drone operations during an online Google hangout session, a twenty-first-century version of Franklin Roosevelt's fireside chats.[111] In April of that year, John Brennan, Obama's deputy national security advisor, delivered a speech on the ethics of counterterrorism, in which he presented the administration's case to the public, arguing that drone strikes are a legal, ethical, and appropriate policy for minimizing the risk to civilians and mitigating the threat of terrorism.[112]

Over the course of Obama's presidency, Brennan had quietly become the president's key advisor on counterterrorism operations. Both men shared an appreciation for the tactical utility of drones, coupled with a deep-seated reservation about their potential to facilitate the executive branch's capacity to use force unilaterally. Following the rapid expansion of CIA drone operations in 2010, Brennan began to draft a set of standards by which drone strikes should be approved. He called it the "playbook." In his words: "What we're trying to do right now is to have a set of standards, a set of criteria, and have a decision-making process that will govern our counterterrorism actions."[113] In short, the playbook would provide a framework to guide the Obama administration's expanded use of drones and establish sustainable constraints on future presidents.

The playbook would formalize the ad hoc process that had evolved over the course of Obama's first term in office. The most important change was instituting a centralized process to streamline disparate approaches to targeting. In weekly meetings, almost one hundred officials, representing over a dozen agencies, would meet to review terrorist biographies and determine who should be nominated for inclusion on the Pentagon target list. These nominations would then be reviewed and approved by President Obama, with the help of Brennan.

The target list has since expanded into a broader "disposition matrix." This matrix contains the names of terrorist suspects and synthesizes the array of information and resources being used to find them, including indictments, maps of known sightings, and plans for special operations or drone strikes.[114] The CIA maintains a similar, though less inclusive, process for deliberations and, although Obama is frequently consulted, presidential approval is not required for each target.[115] However, as the administration struggled to restore their relationship with Pakistan, Obama began to insist that if the agency could not practically guarantee that there would be no collateral damage, he wanted to personally approve operations.[116]

NATO supply routes were eventually reopened in July 2012 and US–Pakistani relations appeared to normalize as drone activity remained subdued, with an average of just four drone strikes per month in 2012.[117] While drone strikes in Pakistan are expected to continue to decline, they are unlikely to cease entirely, as the Pentagon has begun to signal that after more than ten years of violence, the United States has likely only reached the midpoint in its war against al-Qaeda.[118] Although targeted killings in Pakistan are waning, lethal operations in Yemen are on the rise.

7. AN EMERGING THREAT

While concerted CIA attention from 2008 to 2012 did much to erode al-Qaeda's operational ability in Pakistan, by 2010 the United States had become particularly concerned with threats emanating from Yemen. There was particular concern related to Anwar al-Awlaki, a US citizen and radical Muslim cleric who urged his followers to kill Americans. Major Nidal Malik Hasan, the US Army psychiatrist who killed thirteen people at Fort Hood, Texas, in November 2009, exchanged ten to twenty emails with al-Awlaki in the months leading up to his rampage, but the US government initially saw no cause for alarm.[119] When the investigation of Umar Farouk Abdulmutallab, the Nigerian citizen arrested for trying to blow up an airliner with a bomb hidden in his underwear on Christmas Day 2009, revealed al-Awlaki's intensive involvement with the plot, the US government determined that al-Awlaki had evolved from a propagandist to an operational terrorist.[120] He was also linked to inventive plots to put ink toner cartridges filled with explosives on cargo planes headed to the United States and to surgically implant bombs in people's bodies.[121] In early 2010, the White House added al-Awlaki to its kill-or-capture list and reoriented its attention toward Yemen.[122]

Although CIA drone operations in Yemen were suspended after the 2002 strike on al-Harethi, in 2010 President Obama authorized the Pentagon to expand a clandestine air war over Yemen that allowed American jets and bombers to enter Yemen for specific missions. In May 2011, with the election of a new Yemeni president, JSOC began flying armed drones over Yemeni airspace.[123] The CIA had spent years building up a network of informants in Yemen, but US drones flew surveillance missions for the better part of the year without sufficient actionable intelligence to warrant an attack.[124]

Drone strikes outside of conventional battlefields had largely been under the exclusive purview of the CIA since the killing of al-Harethi in 2002. However, in 2011 the traditional boundaries began to blur as the military took the lead in operations in Yemen. While the military became a proponent of drone use following the 2002 invasion of Afghanistan, for years they were content to leave targeted killings to the CIA. Opinions were mixed, but some officers questioned the legality of expansive strikes outside of clearly defined combat zones and felt that these operations were inconsistent with the military's mission.[125]

However, over time Special Forces teams acting under JSOC began to carry out raids further afield, and soon were advocating for a drone unit of their own.[126] The CIA pioneered the use of armed drones and established a precedent for targeted killing. JSOC, the intelligence-driven, counterterrorism-focused division of the military that most closely mirrors the insular, adaptable CTC, has been the organization within the armed services that has most closely emulated the CIA's approach to drones.

The intensive counterterrorism campaign in Yemen began as part of a broader military collaboration between the United States and Yemen. JSOC played an advisory role for Yemeni soldiers and the US-provided munitions, while conducting cruise missile strikes and air strikes as necessary. The US military launches many of its operations in Yemen from an overcrowded airfield in the tiny country of Djibouti.

In September 2011, the CIA opened a new drone base in Saudi Arabia, which gave it easier access to Yemen.[127] JSOC's array of capabilities and the CIA's superior drone access gave rise to a close partnership. By 2012, the CIA routinely borrowed aircraft from the military's much larger fleet of Predators, military pilots flew the agency's drones and military Special Forces were increasingly becoming engaged in espionage activities.[128] This unprecedented level of cooperation led one reporter to label Yemen the "crucible of convergence."[129] Ten years after the first strike in Yemen, the CIA and the military were pursuing the same mission, using the same technology, in the same place.

On May 5, 2011, a missile fired from a US military drone killed two al-Qaeda operatives in Yemen in a strike intended for al-Awlaki.[130] Since al-Awlaki was a US citizen, authorization for the strike was one of the bolder legal decisions of Obama's presidency. After extensive interagency deliberation, a secret memo produced by the Justice Department in summer 2010 determined that killing al-Awlaki would be legal if it was concluded that capture was impossible.[131]

Four months after the May attempt, the government had another opportunity. On September 30, al-Awlaki was killed in Yemen, along with a fellow US citizen, this time in a strike carried out by the CIA.[132] While there had been speculation that the CIA was selected to improve the secrecy of the mission, insiders reported that it was purely pragmatic. After the CIA opened its base in Saudi Arabia, the military transferred several drones to the agency so that they could widen the search.[133]

Although the initial focus of the drone campaign in Yemen had been al-Awlaki, throughout 2011 a deteriorating political and security environment prompted greater US involvement. In the midst of political turmoil, al-Qaeda in the Arabian Peninsula (AQAP) began seizing control of southern cities such as Jaar and Zinjibar. The Obama administration responded by strengthening its partnership with the vulnerable Yemeni government. Working with the US military, which provided extensive air support delivered by drones, helicopters, and bombers, the Yemenis staged a military offensive to regain control of southern territory.[134]

Although JSOC initially conducted the majority of these strikes, by 2012 the CIA's list of high-value targets in Pakistan had fallen from two dozen to fewer than ten, and they began reorienting their attention and their resources toward Yemen, where the United States was pursuing about fifteen terrorist leaders at any given time.[135] As a result of combined attacks by the military and the CIA, the number of drone strikes in Yemen during 2012 soared to thirty-nine, up from ten in the previous year.[136]

President Obama acknowledged in an open letter to Congress in June 2012 that the US military conducts operations in Yemen and Somalia against members of al-Qaeda and al-Shabaab.[137] Obama is said to be heavily involved in the targeting decisions and has resisted mission creep or conflict escalation, keeping the operations on what has been described as a "very tight leash."[138] While operations in Afghanistan and Pakistan are constantly seeking to catch up with al-Qaeda, Yemen is viewed as a place where the United States has been able to get ahead of the curve in combating terrorism.[139]

Nevertheless, the complicated dynamics among Yemen's political parties often blur the line between terrorists and political dissidents. Reports indicate that a growing number of attacks targeting and killing low-level militants suspected of association with terrorism may in fact be on leaders of factions within Yemen's internal political struggle. One former US intelligence official noted, "There were times when we were intentionally misled, presumably by [former President] Saleh, to get rid of people he wanted to get rid of."[140] In May 2010, US aircraft took out what was believed to be a high-value target. The individual, who had been identified by Yemeni security forces, was actually a local deputy governor who had been working against AQAP, but was a political rival of Saleh.[141]

In stark contrast to degenerating diplomatic relations in Pakistan in 2012, Yemen's new president, Abdu Rabbu Mansour Hadi, proved to be an enthusiastic supporter of drone strikes and has repeatedly praised their capacity for discrimination. "They pinpoint the target and have zero margin of error, if you know what target you're aiming at."[142] Perhaps in part because of his receptiveness to the program, Mr. Hadi is said to personally approve each strike that is carried out in Yemen.[143] Meanwhile, public outrage is growing and it is unclear how much longer the government will be able to publically endorse drone use.

Pundits and security scholars have voiced concerns about the blowback effect, the theory that drone casualties incite more acts of violence against the United States. Nevertheless, evidence of this phenomenon is sparse and often contradictory. According to a report by the *Washington Post*, following a drone strike in Radda, Yemen, which killed twelve civilians on September 2,

2012, al-Qaeda fighters used the attack as a recruitment event, setting up a tent and handing out flyers blaming the United States and urging residents to take up arms against the government. Many did.[144]

Since the US bombing campaign began in 2009, AQAP has swelled from between 200 and 300 fighters to more than a thousand. Gregory Johnsen, a leading scholar on Yemen, views this as evidence that drones are "exacerbating and expanding the threat" more than "disrupting, dismantling and defeating it."[145] However, national security expert Christopher Swift disagrees. Based on interviews conducted in June 2012 with forty tribal leaders, politicians, and clerics from across Yemen, Swift concluded that drone strikes were not aiding al-Qaeda recruitment, but rather young men were driven into the insurgency for economic reasons.[146] While the rapid growth of AQAP is undoubtedly multicausal, the blame attributable to drones is difficult to assess. The same is true of their value.

Eliminating potential terrorists has obvious advantages for US national security, and the Obama administration places a premium on the number of terrorist leaders killed. However, the long-term consequences to US soft power, while not easily quantified, may prove equally important. The effects of drones are not merely the lives they take, but also the conditions they leave in their wake. An October 2012 report by Stanford University and New York University law schools documented the social harms of drone strikes, including elevated rates of post-traumatic stress disorder, lost family earning power, and community mistrust.[147] Recent evidence also points to the emergence of a "paranoid shadow conflict" between al-Qaeda and Taliban militants and local residents accused of spying for the CIA. Dozens of suspected spies have been captured, tortured, and executed, fueling distrust that further destabilizes vulnerable tribal societies.[148]

According to a June 2012 study by the Pew Research Center, in seventeen out of twenty countries, more than half of those surveyed opposed drone strikes, while 94 percent of Pakistanis believed that drone strikes kill too many innocent people.[149] As Peter Bergen, a national security expert and vice president of New America observed, "If the price of the drone campaign that increasingly kills only low-level Taliban is alienating 180 million Pakistanis that is too high a price to pay."[150]

8. CHANGING OF THE GUARD

In his second term, President Obama is recalibrating his counterterrorism strategy, and the future of US drone operations appears to be at a crossroads. There are many signs that the drone program is poised for continued growth.

While CIA drone strikes have largely been localized to Pakistan and Yemen, drone bases are proliferating and the reach of the program appears poised to expand.[151] There have been reports of two strikes on leaders of a militant Somali organization affiliated with al-Qaeda.[152] The strikes, which occurred in June 2011 and January 2012, are rare drone attacks in a larger US counter-terrorism effort in Somalia that has been going on since 2003, but which intensified in 2007 shortly after Ethiopian forces invaded Somalia.[153] There is also evidence that US drones may have been used to provide surveillance for an airstrike in the Philippines in 2006 that killed fifteen militants associated with Abu Sayyaf and Jemaah Islamiyah, groups that are suspected to have ties to al-Qaeda.[154]

The increasing reach of the program has been matched by a growing infrastructure. In October 2012, the CIA submitted a request for an additional ten drones to supplement its existing fleet of approximately thirty to thirty-five Predators and Reapers (the larger, faster, more heavily armed version of the Predator that the CIA began acquiring in 2004).[155] The proposed expansion suggests that armed drones will continue to play a critical role as the war against al-Qaeda marches into its twelfth year. Meanwhile the military's Defense Intelligence Agency has requested funding for hundreds of new spies, a bold step into the intelligence functions traditionally performed by the CIA.

As the United States braces for another decade of conflict, there is a growing sense that the tactics used against terrorism must become both more sustain-able and tightly regulated, and that the strategic priorities of the US intelli-gence community must be reevaluated. Senator Feinstein stated, "I think this is the time for transition." Counterterrorism will remain the CIA's top priority, but the agency needs to begin focusing on cyber security and other vulner-abilities. "We have to strengthen human intelligence in key areas," Feinstein said, "and transition from the kind of Pakistan–Afghanistan intelligence gathering" that has overtaken the agency's agenda in recent years.[156]

Terrorism is likely to be a security threat for many years to come, but so are cyber-attacks, nuclear proliferation, and the emergence of China as a potential rival in the Pacific, and these issues require increased attention. Brennan, the current CIA director, agrees. In the midst of what could be a major redistribution of power within the US national security community, he has argued that the CIA should focus on intelligence collection and that lethal operations are the proper purview of the military, leading to efforts to transfer the CIA's drone responsibilities to the Pentagon.[157] Thus, after eleven years of CIA drone operations, close to four hundred strikes, and thousands of casualties, it is unclear whether targeted killing will remain a core function of the CIA.

9. TOMORROW'S DRONES

The decision about which institution should operate armed drones going forward raises important questions about the value and efficacy of the Predator in future conflicts. Under the control of the CIA, the Predator performs a special mission, tracking and killing suspected terrorists linked with al-Qaeda and other groups in places far removed from the battlefields where American troops are stationed. The prospective transfer suggests that drone use may soon be integrated into the military's larger security mission and operate alongside other military weapons systems and according to the military's rules of engagement.

Perhaps more significant than the question of what will happen to the Predator without the CIA is what will happen to the Predator with al-Qaeda. When the war on terror eventually draws to a close, will the Predator continue to play a key role in national security or will it fade away? Has the Predator ushered in a sustained transformation in warfare or will the United States return to earlier modes of conflict? The answer to both questions likely lies somewhere in the middle.

The Predator has been transformational in the war on terror, but this is largely because it was so ideally suited to the post-9/11 vision of the CIA. In many respects, the Predator is the perfect weapon for targeted killing. However, it is likely that this tactic will remain largely confined to unconventional wars against non-state enemies like al-Qaeda. America's war on terror, a global conflict against a sub-state organization, is without precedent in US history. And it is by no means certain that this type of war will recur in the future.

Without al-Qaeda, the Predator is likely to become just another aircraft in the US military's arsenal. In this context it will remain a prized reconnaissance asset and at times a very useful form of air support. But its utility is limited by its extreme vulnerability to air defense systems. It can only be used in what the military calls "permissive" environments, places where the local government is incapable of shooting it down or lacks the desire to do so.[158] Thus, the Predator's transformative effect will likely remain confined to a very narrow set of circumstances: particular types of conflicts (limited wars), specific military contexts (permissive environments), and against a unique class of foes (non-state actors).

Despite the Predator's limitations, other forms of unmanned aircraft have immense potential. As Peter Singer, one of the leading experts on evolving military technology, has argued, this is merely the first generation of drones. The Predator is the drone version of Ford's Model T.[159] Surveillance drones, such as the Sentinel, which the CIA used to spy on the bin Laden compound in Abbottabad and continues to use to monitor Iran's nuclear program, come in all shapes and sizes.

Unmanned systems will not simply replace vehicles once controlled by people: They will perform novel functions that even science fiction authors have yet to imagine. For example, developers are already working on insect-sized drones equipped with cameras and microphones that can go places too dangerous for soldiers or spies.[160] One can only speculate on the impact of these new forms of technology, but these too will need to be considered on an individual basis and in the particular context in which they are deployed. The Predator's transformation of warfare is likely to be localized to its current context, but future forms of drones may yet qualify as revolutionary.

NOTES

1 The US operates two types of armed drones, the MQ-1 Predator and the MQ-9 Reaper, also known as Predator B. Colloquially the terms Predator and Reaper are used to refer to these different airframes. However, because reports on drone strikes rarely disclose whether a Predator or Reaper was used, and because both are a variant of the same technology, for the purposes of this chapter, the term Predator can refer to either type of airframe.

2 Fahey, Jonathan, "A golden decade for defense companies is ending," Associated Press, August 12, 2011.

3 McKitrick, Jeffrey, James Blackwell, Fred Littlepage, George Kraus, Richard Blanchfield, and Dale Hill, "The revolution in military affairs" in Barry R. Schneider and Lawrence E. Grinter (eds.), *Battlefield of the future: 21st Century warfare issues* (Maxwell Air Force Base, AL: Air University Press, 1995), pp. 65–97.

4 Author interview with Abraham Karem, August 31, 2012.

5 Author interview with James Woolsey, August 8, 2012.

6 Cantwell, Houston R., "Beyond butterflies: Predator and the evolution of unmanned aerial vehicle in air force culture (BiblioScholar, 2012).

7 Benjamin, Daniel, and Steven Simon, *The age of sacred terror: Radical Islam's war against America* (New York, NY: Random House Trade Paperbacks, 2003), p. 321.

8 9/11 Commission, *Final report of the National Commission on terrorist attacks upon the United States* (New York, NY: W. W. Norton & Company, 2010), p. 189 [hereafter *Final report*].

9 Benjamin and Simon, *The age of sacred terror*, p. 321.

10 9/11 Commission, *Final report*, p. 506 n112.

11 Ibid., p. 506 n113.

12 Ibid., p. 189.

13 Ibid., pp. 189–190.

14 Ibid., p. 190.

15 Crumpton, Henry A., *The art of intelligence: Lessons from a life in the CIA's clandestine service* (New York, NY: Penguin Press, 2012), p. 154.

16 Coll, Steve, *Ghost Wars: The secret history of the CIA, Afghanistan, and Bin Laden, from the Soviet invasion to September 10, 2001* (New York, NY: Penguin 2004), p. 534.

17 Author telephone interview with John Jumper, April 8, 2013.

18 9/11 Commission, *Final report*, p. 211.

19 Ibid., pp. 211, 513 n240.

20 Clarke, Richard A., *Against all enemies: Inside America's war on terror* (New York, NY: Free Press, 2004), p. 222.

21 9/11 Commission, *Final report*, p. 211.

22 Hearings before the Select Committee to study governmental operations with respect to intelligence activities of the United States Senate, Vol 7: "Covert action, December 4–5, 1975" (Washington, DC: US Government Printing Office 1976).

23 Author interview with John Jumper.

24 9/11 Commission, *Final report*, p. 211. Benjamin and Simon, *The age of sacred terror*, pp. 337, 345.

25 9/11 Commission, *Final report*, pp. 213–214.

26 Benjamin and Simon, *The age of sacred terror*, pp. 345–346.

27 9/11 Commission, *Final report*, p. 214.

28 Ibid.

29 Ibid., p. 311.

30 Ibid., p. 361.

31 Tenet, George, *At the center of the storm: The CIA during America's time of crisis* (New York, NY: Harper Perennial, 2008), pp. 177–178.

32 Ibid., p. 179.

33 Author interview with Roger Cressey, member of the NSC staff, August 14, 2012.

34 Clarke, *Against all enemies*, p. 277.

35 *Authorization for the Use of Military Force*, Pub. L. No. 107-40, 115 Stat. 224 (2001).

36 Woodward, Bob, *Bush at war* (London: Simon & Schuster, 2003), p. 101; Risen, James, and David Johnston, "Threats and responses: Hunt for Al Qaeda; Bush has widened authority of CIA to kill terrorists," *New York Times*, December 15, 2002.

37 Tenet, *At the center of the storm*, p. 179.

38 Author interview with Henry Crumpton, former member of the CIA's Clandestine Service, April 15, 2013. Author interview with John Jumper.

39 Author interview with Henry Crumpton.

40 Crumpton, *The art of intelligence*, pp. 189, 200.

41 Woodward, *Bush at War*, p. 223.

42 Crumpton, *The art of intelligence*, pp. 219–220.

43 Ibid., p. 221.

44 Ibid., p. 220.

45 Johnston, David, and David E. Sanger, "Threats and responses: Hunt for suspects; Fatal strike in Yemen was based on rules set out by Bush," *New York Times*,

November 6, 2002. CNN, "Reports suggest Al Qaeda military chief killed," November 17, 2001.

46 Crumpton, *The art of intelligence*, pp. 253–255.

47 Ibid., p. 282.

48 Author interview with Roger Cressey.

49 Risen, James, and Judith Miller, "Threats and Responses: Hunt for Suspects; CIA is reported to kill a leader of Al Qaeda in Yemen," *New York Times*, November 5, 2002.

50 Ibid.

51 Zenko, Micah, *Between threats and war: U.S. discrete military operations in the post-cold war world* (Stanford University Press, 2010), pp. 85–86; Mark Mazzetti, *The way of the knife: The CIA, a secret army, and a war at the ends of the Earth* (New York, NY: Penguin Press, 2013), pp. 86–87.

52 McManus, Doyle, "A U.S. license to kill," *Los Angeles Times*, January 11, 2003.

53 Kirk, Michael, "Top secret America," PBS, *Frontline*, September 6, 2011.

54 Priest, Dana, "CIA killed U.S. citizen in Yemen missile strike," *Washington Post*, November 8, 2002.

55 Miller, Greg, "Despite apparent success in Yemen, risks remain," *Los Angeles Times*, November 6, 2002.

56 Risen and Johnston, "Threats and responses: Hunt for Al Qaeda; Bush has widened authority of CIA to kill terrorists."

57 McManus, "A U.S. license to kill."

58 Witt, Howard, "United States: Killing of Al Qaeda suspects was lawful," *Daily Times*, November 25, 2002.

59 CNN, "Sources: U.S. kills Cole suspect," November 4, 2002.

60 US Department of Defense, news transcript, "Deputy Secretary Wolfowitz interview with CNN international," November 5, 2002.

61 Hosenball, Mark, and Evan Thomas, "The opening shot," *Newsweek*, November 18, 2002.

62 Smucker, Philip, "The intrigue behind the drone strike," *Christian Science Monitor*, November 12, 2002.

63 *Washington Post*, "Air force to build up drone squadrons," Reuters, March 19, 2005.

64 Gellman, Barton, and Dafna Linzer, "Afghanistan, Iraq: Two wars collide," *Washington Post*, October 22, 2004.

65 Rohde, David, and Mohammed Khan, "Ex-fighter for Taliban dies in strike in Pakistan," *New York Times*, June 19, 2004. Mazzetti, *The way of the knife*, pp. 108–109.

66 Rohde and Khan, "Ex-fighter for Taliban dies in strike in Pakistan."

67 Khan, Ismail, and Dilawar Khan Wazir, "Night raid kills Nek, four other militants: Wana operation," *Dawn*, June 19, 2004. Khattak, Iqbai, "Nek killed in missile strike," *Daily Times*, June 19, 2004.

68 Khan and Khan Wazir, "Night raid kills Nek, four other militants."

69 CNN, "Pakistan kills tribal leader," June 18, 2004. Lancaster, John, "High-profile attacks force Pakistan to confront extremists," *Washington Post*, June 19, 2004.

70 Rohde and Khan, "Ex-fighter for Taliban dies in strike in Pakistan."

71 *Daily Times*, "US Army, Afghan govt welcome Nek's killing," June 20, 2004.

72 Priest, Dana, "Surveillance operation in Pakistan located and killed Al Qaeda official," *Washington Post*, May 15, 2005.

73 *Gulfnews*, "Accidental blast while assembling bombs kills eight," Associated Press, November 6, 2005. *Daily Times*, "8 killed in blast at militant compound," November 7, 2005.

74 Zenko, Micah, "The courage of Pakistani journalists," *Atlantic*, September 20, 2011. Khan, Ismail, "Senior Al Qaeda commander killed," *Dawn*, December 3, 2005.

75 CNN, "Al Qaeda no. 3 dead, but how?" December 4, 2005.

76 *Daily Times*, "3 killed in mysterious explosion in North Waziristan: Tribesmen warn of ending peace deal," April 28, 2007; *Agence France-Presse*, "Missile strike on Pakistan militant hideout kills 13: Officials," February 28, 2008.

77 Ali, Yousaf, "Most Bajaur victims were under 20," *News International*, November 5, 2006.

78 Woods, Chris, "The day 69 children died," *Express Tribune*, August 12, 2011.

79 Miller, Greg, "At CIA, a convert to Islam leads the terrorism hunt," *Washington Post*, March 24, 2012.

80 Bergen, Peter L. *Manhunt: The ten-year search for Bin Laden–from 9/11 to Abbottabad* (New York, NY: Crown, 2012), pp. 71–72.

81 New America, "The year of the drone: Leaders killed." http://securitydata .newamerica.net/drones/pakistan/leaders-killed.

82 Woodward, Bob, *Obama's wars* (New York, NY: Simon & Schuster, 2011), p. 3.

83 Ibid., pp. 4–5.

84 Bergen, L. Peter, *The longest war: The enduring conflict between America and Al-Qaeda* (New York, NY: Free Press, 2011), p. 345; New America, "The year of the drone: Leaders killed."

85 Gellman and Linzer, "Afghanistan, Iraq: Two wars collide."

86 New America, "The year of the drone: Leaders killed."

87 Miller, Greg, "Increased U.S. drone strikes in Pakistan killing few high-value militants," *Washington Post*, February 21, 2011.

88 Ibid.

89 Bergen, *The longest war*, p. 346.

90 Ignatius, David, "The covert commander in chief," *Washington Post*, September 10, 2011.

91 New America, "The year of the drone: Leaders killed."

92 Shachtman, Noah, "Drone war's rules: Shoot first, ask permission later," *Wired*, March 23, 2009.

93 Miller, Greg, and Julie Tate, "CIA shifts focus to killing targets," *Washington Post*, September 1, 2011.

94 New America, "The year of the drone: Leaders killed."

95 Ibid. Mazzetti, *The way of the knife*, pp. 272–276.

96 McCarthy, Julie, "U.S. relations with Pakistan sour," NPR, April 14, 2011.

97 BBC, "US defends Pakistan drone strikes," June 6, 2012.

98 Georgy, Michael, and Emma Graham-Harrison, "Rage grips Pakistan over NATO attack," Reuters, November 27, 2011.

99 Masood, Salman, "C.I.A. leaves Pakistan base used for drone strikes," *New York Times*, December 11, 2011.

100 Entous, Adam, Siobhan Gorman, and Julian E. Barnes, "U.S. tightens drone rules," *Wall Street Journal*, November 4, 2011.

101 New America, "The year of the drone."

102 House Committee on Oversight and Government Reform, *Rise of the drones II: Examining the legality of unmanned targeting: Hearing before the Subcommittee on National Security and Foreign Affairs*, 111th Cong., 2nd sess., April 28, 2010 (Washington, DC: US Government Printing Office 2011).

103 Miller, Greg, "Under Obama, an emerging global apparatus for drone killing," *Washington Post*, December 27, 2011.

104 Dilanian, Ken, "Congress zooms in on drone killings," *Los Angeles Times*, June 25, 2012.

105 Hastings, Michael, "The rise of the killer drones: How America goes to war in secret," *Rolling Stone*, April 16, 2012.

106 Mazzetti, *The way of the knife*, p. 292.

107 Entous et al., "U.S. tightens drone rules."

108 Ibid.

109 Ibid.

110 New America, "The year of the drone."

111 BBC, "Obama backs Pakistan drone raids," January 31, 2012.

112 John Brennan, "The ethics and efficacy of the president's counterterrorism strategy," speech given at the Woodrow Wilson International Center for Scholars, Washington, DC, April 30, 2012.

113 DeYoung, Karen, "A CIA veteran transforms U.S. counterterrorism policy," *Washington Post*, October 24, 2012.

114 Miller, Greg, "Plan for hunting terrorists signals U.S. intends to keep adding names to kill lists," *Washington Post*, October 23, 2012.

115 Becker, Jo, and Scott Shane, "Secret 'kill list' proves a test of Obama's principles and will," *New York Times*, May 29, 2012.

116 Ibid.

117 CNN, "Pakistan reopens NATO supply routes to Afghanistan," July 3, 2012.

118 Miller, "Plan for hunting terrorists signals U.S. intends to keep adding names to kill lists."

119 Johnston, David, and Scott Shane, "U.S. knew of suspect's tie to radical cleric," *New York Times*, November 9, 2009.

120 Savage, Charlie, "Christmas day bomb plot detailed in court filings," *New York Times*, February 10, 2012.

121 Klaidman, Daniel, *Kill or capture: The war on terror and the soul of the Obama presidency* (New York, NY: Houghton Mifflin Harcourt, 2012), p. 260.

122 Ibid., p. 215.

123 Mazzetti, *The way of the knife*, p. 229.

124 Boone, Jeb, and Greg Miller, "U.S. drone strike in Yemen is first since 2002," *Washington Post*, May 5, 2011.

125 Hersh, Seymour M., "Manhunt: The Bush administration's new strategy in the war against terrorism," *New Yorker*, December 23, 2002.

126 Mazzetti, *The way of the knife*, pp. 128–129, 311–312.

127 Ibid., p. 308.

128 Miller, Greg, "CIA seeks to expand drone fleet, officials say," *Washington Post*, October 18, 2012.

129 Miller, "Under Obama, an emerging global apparatus for drone killing."

130 Shah, Pir Zubair, "Drone strike said to kill at least 8 in Pakistan," *New York Times*, May 6, 2011. Boone and Miller, "U.S. drone strike in Yemen is first since 2002."

131 Shane, Scott, "Coming soon: The drone arms race," *New York Times*, October 8, 2011.

132 BBC, "Islamist cleric Anwar al-Awlaki killed in Yemen," September 30, 2011.

133 Klaidman, *Kill or capture*, pp. 261–262. Worth, Robert F., Mark Mazzetti, and Scott Shane, "Drone strikes' risks to get rare moment in the pubic eye," *New York Times*, February 5, 2013.

134 Miller, Greg, "Yemeni president acknowledges approving U.S. drone strikes," *Washington Post*, September 29, 2012.

135 Miller, "Plan for hunting terrorists signals U.S. intends to keep adding names to kill lists."

136 New America, "The year of the drone."

137 Entous, Adam, "U.S. acknowledges its drone strikes," *Wall Street Journal*, June 15, 2012.

138 Becker and Shane, "Secret 'kill list' proves a test of Obama's principles and will."

139 DeYoung, "A CIA veteran transforms U.S. counterterrorism policy."

140 Miller, Greg, "U.S. drone targets in Yemen raise questions," *Washington Post*, June 2, 2012.

141 Klaidman, *Kill or capture*, p. 255.

142 Shane, Scott, "Yemen's leader, President Hadi, praises U.S. drone strikes," *New York Times*, September 29, 2012.

143 Miller, "Yemeni president acknowledges approving U.S. drone strikes."

144 Raghavan, Sudarsan, "When U.S. drones kill civilians, Yemen's government tries to conceal it," *Washington Post*, December 24, 2012.

145 Baron, Adam, "Drone use surges in Yemen, the frontline against Al Qaeda," *Christian Science Monitor*, December 28, 2012.

146 Swift, Christopher, "The drone blowback fallacy," *Foreign Affairs*, July 1, 2012. Central Intelligence Agency, "CIA world factbook: Yemen," 2012.

147 International Human Rights and Conflict Resolution Clinic, Stanford Law School and Global Justice Clinic, New York University School of Law,

"Living under drones: Death, injury, and trauma to civilians from US drone practices in Pakistan," September 2012.

148 Walsh, Declan, "Drone war spurs Pakistan militants to deadly reprisals," *New York Times*, December 29, 2012.

149 Pew Research Center, "Pakistani public opinion ever more critical of U.S," *Global Attitudes Project*, June 27, 2012. Pew Research Center, "Global opinion of Obama slips, international policies faulted: Drones strikes widely opposed," *Global Attitudes Project*, June 13, 2012.

150 Bergen, Peter, and Megan Braun, "Drone is Obama's weapon of choice," CNN, September 19, 2012.

151 Zenko, Micah, and Emma Welch, "Where the drones are," *Foreign Policy*, May 29, 2012.

152 Jaffe, Greg, and Karen DeYoung, "U.S. drone targets two leaders of Somali group allied with al-Qaeda, official says," *Washington Post*, June 29, 2011. Leonard, Tom, "US accused of making insect spy robots," *Telegraph*, October 10, 2007.

153 Naylor, Sean D., "The secret war: How U.S. hunted AQ in Africa," *Army Times*, October 30, 2011. Zenko, *Between threats and war*, p. 145.

154 Zenn, Jacob, "US drones circle over the Philippines," *Asia Times*, February 29, 2012. Mazzetti, *The way of the knife*, pp. 133–134.

155 Schmitt, Eric, "U.S. drones crowd Iraq's skies to fight insurgents," *New York Times*, April 5, 2005. Miller, "CIA seeks to expand drone fleet, officials say."

156 Miller, Greg, "Obama's pick for CIA could affect drone program," *Washington Post*, November 24, 2012.

157 DeYoung, "A CIA veteran transforms U.S. counterterrorism policy."

158 Reed, John, "Predator drones 'useless' in most wars, top air force general says," *Foreign Policy*, September 19, 2013.

159 Singer, P. W., *Wired for war: The robotics revolution and conflict in the 21st century* (New York, NY: Penguin Press, 2009), p. 62.

160 Leonard, "US accused of making insect spy robots."

15

Disciplining Drone Strikes

Just War in the Context of Counterterrorism

DAVID TRUE

1. DRONES, ETHICS, AND JUST WAR

During the Obama administration, drones have become a key weapon in the fight against al-Qaeda and other terrorist groups. Indeed, drones mark a substantive shift in war fighting. Gone is George W. Bush's era of talk of a "global war on terror" and full-scale conventional invasions. In their place, we now hear references to asymmetrical war, Special Forces, and drones. Mr. Bush's "long wars" have become Mr. Obama "drone wars."

The change in policy is not simply that of one administration versus another. Rather, it helps explain the recent, brief history of drone strikes. As early as the 2008 presidential campaign, candidate Obama vowed to step up the fight against al-Qaeda by making greater use of drones, especially in Pakistan. True to his word, Obama's first term saw a marked increase in the deployment of drones, especially in the Pakistani tribal areas.[1] The policy, of course, has proven controversial in Pakistan, with traditional allies, and with segments of the US population, although sizable majorities of Americans continue to support Obama's aggressive use of drones overseas.[2] Even as critics questioned Obama's reliance on drone strikes, the administration was dramatically reducing the number of strikes, tightening the requirements for a strike to be authorized, and shifting control from the CIA to the Pentagon.

If the recent past is any indicator, there is good reason to suspect that US drone use will continue to evolve and expand. To some extent, this is typical of high-tech warfare, especially when the technology in question is relatively inexpensive and widely available, as is the case with drones. Drone deployment is also linked to our evolving international political context, for in an age of global terrorism, we are likely to see continued unconventional and asymmetrical conflicts. While in these situations it is difficult to distinguish between combatants and non-combatants, drones, it is said, enable us to do just that. Drones give us new capabilities and powers, so it makes sense that the demand for drones will increase and widen. However, it is important to note that we are nearing the end of a period in which drones have been almost exclusively the weapons of the United States.

Within the next several years, militarized drone use is expected to proliferate. As more countries gain access to drone technology, it is possible that we will see emerging international movements to regulate their use. If so, the United States would be well served to be at the forefront of that effort. However, managing this evolving technology should not focus solely on an assessment of past or current drone capacities, but must envision the drone policies and practices of tomorrow. This is not simply an issue for policy, but also a matter of morality. Engaging drones in this manner requires understanding how this powerful new weapon can be used responsibly. Assuming that ethical drone strikes are possible, what should be the moral criteria for their use?

To examine these issues, it is useful to draw on what are often considered conflicting perspectives: the just war tradition and the realism of Reinhold Niebuhr. Just war theory is centuries old and provides a framework of principles and criteria for evaluating whether or not war and its conduct are ethically justified. Niebuhr was a twentieth-century Christian theologian and public intellectual who articulated a framework he characterized as biblical or Christian realism.

Niebuhr was suspicious of the just war thinking of his day because it appeared to him inflexible and ahistorical. He was keenly aware that moral ideals like "just cause" or "probability of success" could mask self-interested abdications of responsibility, as well as imperialistic ambitions. In place of an inflexible just war theory or a narrowly interested realism, Niebuhr advanced a critical approach to power that understood war as both the failure of politics and an instrument of politics. War, for Niebuhr, was always tragic but at times necessary, in that there are moments in history in which the goods at stake define war as a responsible choice.

At the time, others voiced concerns that the just war tradition was overly permissive. For example, Christian pacifists claimed that categories such as "just cause" to legitimize some armed conflicts and "last resort" suggesting accepting war after other options have been tried often fail to clarify the actual nature of war. Such ideas may express a set of concerns that are significant yet seldom judged sufficient to prevent war, and may serve to legitimize armed conflict at the expense of other pressing moral concerns.[3]

In fact, today's drone strikes provide a clear example of how the permissiveness of just war thinking impacts policy. It is this very permissiveness that helps explain both the dramatic increase in drone strikes under the Obama administration and why US drone attacks abroad have failed to generate a significant domestic public debate. This presents our nation with a situation of great peril, especially as drone deployment expands to become ever more international.

To understand this dynamic, it is necessary to first assess a permissive interpretation of just war and then to consider why questions about the morality of drone strikes have failed to either generate substantive public debate in the United States or alter drone policy. One might suspect that this analysis would lead to an embrace of political realism, but the story is more complicated, involving as it does constitutional rights and democratic ideals. To make sense of this tension, it is useful to consider Niebuhr's critical appreciation of the power of the nation's self-interest. In this way, Niebuhr can be seen as something of a friendly critic of the just war tradition at a time when this body of critical thought risks being made irrelevant by new technologies. Just how this works is discussed below, but here it may be helpful to point out that just war thinking does not operate in a vacuum as its logic and assessments are informed by social context.

An ethical analysis of drone strikes needs then to take into account the larger moral landscape. It is precisely in this way that we can chart a more ethically engaged approach to the use of drones, now and into the future. The possibility of a moral management of drones requires a form of discipline and care that we have yet to see in US policy. The costs of this failure, especially as drones proliferate, are significant.

2. DRONES AS A MORAL MODEL

From the perspective of the just war tradition, the core concern in conducting war, *jus in bello*, involves distinguishing between combatants and non-combatants. This principle of distinction lies at the heart of the just war tradition's concern with disciplining – but not eliminating – war. So, while war involves killing, legal war ought not to involve careless or murderous killing.

Understood in this way, one might think that the principle of distinction might rule out anything but most exceptional use of drone strikes. However, this is not the case, and the principle has not provoked a sustained public debate over the potential killing of non-combatants. One might suspect that this has to do with a lack of public awareness, but the many media reports on non-combatants killed by drones cast doubt on such an explanation.[4]

The lack of public debate has less to do with an uninformed public than with the ways in which the American people have internalized assumptions of conventional just war thinking. The first of these assumptions is that non-combatants are inevitably killed in war. Such deaths are part of the tragic nature of war and morally permitted if the deaths are unintended. Critics may raise a principled position – the duty to discriminate between combatants and civilians – but this criticism fails to gain traction. This is because the principle itself acknowledges that in war civilian deaths are inevitable, even as they are tragic and to be avoided where possible. Civilians' deaths, then, do not break a rule so much as raise a concern and question: Were their deaths the result of either intentional targeting of civilians or the excessive and disproportional use of force? If either is true, there has been a violation of the just war principle.

If, however, the civilian deaths are unintended, then the issue becomes whether they were *foreseen*. The distinction between intention and foreknowledge is crucial because where non-combatant deaths are unintended but foreseen, the moral reasoning turns to one of weighing goods lost versus goods gained.

What started out as a prima facie duty, distinction then evolves into a process of calculating consequences. The just war tradition refers to this calculus as the principle of *proportionality*. What should be clear is that proportionality is not a moral principle applied in the abstract. Instead, it relies on human judgments as to the worth of competing goods. There is no agreed-upon formula that ranks combatants and non-combatants. Because of this, anyone might calculate how many civilian deaths are acceptable in relation to the killing of one, two, three, or any number of combatants, or for that matter, any particular known combatants, say the leader of an opposing force. In this way, proportionality operates more like a caution or warning against the casual disregard for taking innocent lives.

The irony is that advocates of targeted drone strikes claim that drones are justified precisely because of their capacity to enable particularly accurate adherence to the principle of distinction. Though drones are not perfect in discriminating between combatants and non-combatants, they nevertheless offer greater precision than more conventional weapon systems. They are capable of providing lengthy surveillance, helping to confirm a target's identity, and identifying those in the target's vicinity. This enhanced accuracy, coupled with the use of precision armaments, suggests that only the correctly identified combatants will be targeted and with a reasonable limitation on civilian deaths.[5]

The majority of Americans support drone strikes through what appears to be a moral calculus that justifies the small number of civilian deaths compared with more conventional weapons. This is not surprising as the public's appetite for war waxes and wanes. However, in the context of conducting war, Americans consistently display great interest in potential US casualties, yet little interest in considering the issue of proportionality with any sophistication and care. Nevertheless, public support might be altered if the number of non-combatants killed shocked the conscience, but there is nothing to indicate the likelihood of such a development with expanded drone operations. In fact, the greater precision of drone attacks compared to other forms of warfare would seem to support their widespread use.

If proportionality were going to be the subject of a public debate, it would likely require presidential leadership. Such a move would be a bold and imaginative act on the part of any president, but especially so considering the continuing threat of al-Qaeda. As it is, the president himself has shown a willingness to personally accept responsibility for the killing of non-combatants in return for the tactical gain of disrupting al-Qaeda's leadership or command structure.

3. CRITICISM OF JUST WAR – NATIONALISTIC IMBALANCE

Just war as justice in war tends to see the drone as a moral weapon because of its comparative advantage in distinguishing between combatants and non-combatants and delivering precision attacks. This might be the end of an ethical assessment, leading to the conclusion that drones are, in fact, a model, or at least moral, weapon. However, there are significant voices that have continued to speak out against the killing of non-combatants in drone strikes. In the United States there is strong, but limited, opposition to targeted drone attacks among human rights groups and others. However, in virtually all other nations, with the possible exception of the United Kingdom, solid majorities oppose the American government's lethal drone policy.[6] This discrepancy warrants further consideration. What accounts for this difference, and to what degree does it reveal a key moral component of US reliance on drones?

From a Niebuhrian perspective, the difference in support for US drone activity is one of nationality and the perspective and political positioning associated with citizenship.[7] Americans tend to view drones strikes as defending their nation's right of self-defense, a relatively straightforward exercise of national sovereignty. Other nations, even allies, see that the strikes occur within the territory of another sovereign state with which the United States is not at war.

In this light, it is easy to understand why Pakistanis protest strikes on their soil. They have heard repeated protests from some of their political and military leaders condemning strikes, mild admissions of acceptance from others, and live in a state of general uncertainty as to the legal status of US attacks within their country. The statements of Pakistani leaders may be political cover to ease criticisms of those in the United States, yet this is of little help to the people of Pakistan. They have understandably become suspicious of their political leaders who have secretly supported these acts, seeing them as duplicitous agents in the service to a foreign power.

Other nations, such as Yemen, may have political leaders who openly support US drone strikes. While this has legal significance for the legitimacy of such acts, the larger point holds: The attacks are highly unpopular and are commonly experienced as an affront to national pride and identity. It is not surprising that citizens of one nation protest another nation's bombing within its territory, especially outside of a formal state of war. There are cases, such as a civil war or foreign attack, in which a government or opposition force has called for and even welcomed military intervention. Such cases are clearly the exception. What we see in Pakistan, Yemen, and elsewhere is anger at the excess and hubris of US drone strikes, a position that echoes with national pride, as well as a sense of moral outrage.

Opposition to US drone strikes is intensified by contextual factors, the most obvious of which is the identification of a foreign power with a history of colonialism. In such cases a people's opposition often becomes animosity, which may seek and find an outlet in protest or even violent opposition. While drones may be able to reach areas politically or practically impossible for ground troops, Special Forces, and manned aircraft, drones are not without limits and costs. Like other forms of attack, drones tend to intensify nationalistic resentment and generate resistance. Indeed, other nations may see drones as giving the United States an unfair advantage. Certainly, US drone deployment presents an overall pattern that appears to many as a case in which an imperial power pursues its own interests with little to no regard for the sovereign rights of other nations, the well-being of foreign communities, and the lives of foreign nationals.

If one is tempted to think that nationality is an issue that only resonates for people in other countries, one might consider the case of Abdulrahman al-Awlaki, the sixteen-year-old son of Anwar al-Awlaki killed in October 2011 in Yemen by a US drone in what appears to be an unintended collateral death.[8] In every respect, this case appears to be like other civilian casualties, save one – nationality. Abdulrahman al-Awlaki was a US citizen, and because of this, his case generated much greater concern both in Washington and in the US media. To some degree, the same is true of the killing of Anwar al-Awlaki, except in his case the American government acknowledged targeting him because of his leadership role in planning attacks against the United States. There is much to consider in each case, yet what is clear is that the opposition to the strikes, or at least the concern they generated in the United States, confirms the importance of nationality in shaping how Americans view the value of the lives of potential drone strike victims.

Within the legal community, critics worried that the targeted killing of an American citizen violated core constitutional rights. Broadly speaking, concerns over due process are specified in the context of both domestic and international law. The latter form intends to stiffen the procedural requirements for identifying both Americans and foreign nationals as legal targets, treating both equally as people possessing core human rights. This is a laudable goal, but it has received little attention in US political debate that has focused, not surprisingly, on domestic law.

Arguments of a domestic nature tend to assume the existence of a radically expanded battlefield. Their focus is on protecting the citizen's legal rights within this expanded war zone.[9] One can see why an American politician and his or her constituents might be attracted to such a view. It holds out the possibility of a zone of maximum security for citizens, albeit with certain sacrifices demanded of non-citizens. In other words, great care must be taken with the lives of citizens, but a Pakistani villager may be knowingly sacrificed in order to kill a high-value target. The Pakistani villager, then, is an unfortunate consequence of a "moral" policy that protects our nation and its citizens.

The legal context may shape dramatically different goals and approaches to fighting terrorism and employing drone strikes. A domestic focus might well afford significant legal protections to US citizens in a context in which drone strikes and targeted killings become the norm. The focus on international rights and corresponding state obligations is more ambitious and might well make targeted killings the exception to the norm.

In legal terms, however, advocates of these positions should not feel confident of their standing in US courts. The judicial branch has tended to give the executive and legislative branches leeway when it comes to declaring and waging war, whether conventional or unconventional.

In fact, the legislative branch has shown some concern with the al-Awlaki killings. In spring 2013, concerns over due process led a bipartisan group of senators to delay and threaten to block Mr. Obama's nomination of John Brennan to serve as director of the CIA.[10] The senators also claimed that the administration had operated drones without sufficient transparency and congressional oversight. Under the pressure of a threatened filibuster, the administration made public an internal policy document. Rather than ending debate, however, the memorandum generated further criticism. Critics objected that the "White Paper" failed to describe the process by which a "kill list" is constructed.[11] Then in May 2013, the president gave a speech at the National Defense University. Occurring as it did three months after the memorandum was released, it appears to have been another attempt to quiet opposition.

The president's speech was billed as a pivot point that would spell out significant changes in US counterterrorism policy, especially regarding drones. Following the speech there was some debate over the extent of any such shift. Critics complained that the speech contained little that was new, especially in terms of drone policy. However, several commentators noted that the president's tone was different and that he appeared more open and interested in dialogue. Also, the president confirmed that drone strikes had peaked in frequency and that their decline would continue. He closed with an appeal to public debate about drone policy and counterterrorism more broadly. There was, in other words, some reason to hope that drones might now receive sustained public consideration.

Interestingly, soon after, the nation learned of the Snowden leaks and related concerns about state surveillance. These issues have since come to dominate domestic reviews of drone actions and capabilities. The media and public appear largely concerned with reports of the NSA's collecting and analyzing phone calls and the ways in which drones might be part of this set of actions. Here the moral issue is one of privacy and government intrusion: domestic drone surveillance rather than international drone strikes.

This situation makes clear the strong domestic support the president enjoys on drone strikes abroad, and also helps explain why this is the case. The prevalence of privacy concerns suggests a foreign policy failure at least in terms of our political culture. If President George W. Bush is rightly criticized for raising expectations with his talk of a "global war on terror," it appears that President Obama has failed to offer a compelling vision of the nation's role in the world. Instead, his administration is allegedly busy keeping America safe and secure without recourse to an overarching international justification for these acts.

This practical orientation might be appropriate if it were linked to a larger vision of the United States' role within a community of nations. However, the policies leave open the question: What is the goal of the United States in its continued policy of drone attacks other than degrading al-Qaeda's capacity? This leads to the larger question: Why are we fighting? While this issue extends beyond their deployment, drones are at the core of these questions and have come to stand for multiple issues associated with national security, a domain that seems today to be sadly disengaged from ethics.

4. DRONES AS AN EXCEPTION TO THE NORM

An assessment of the ethics of drone policy exposes a narrow range of competing goods. Specifically, the just war principle of proportionality requires that if non-combatants' deaths are foreseen, then those deaths must be outweighed by other goods. Further comparative analysis reveals that Americans are almost unique in thinking that the deaths of foreign civilians are largely insignificant in relation to national security concerns, such that this issue, even in the absence of a broad defining justification of these policies, stimulates little to no debate. In comparison to these deaths, due process and privacy issues, especially as they play out in a domestic context in relation to US citizens, are widely viewed as much weightier.

The principle of proportionality makes clear that just war thinking is not an objective or clinical analysis, but is instead a value-laden interpretation. Niebuhr's criticism of just war helps us go a step further. If, as he argued, just war theory is a historically conditioned form of moral reasoning, and thereby subject to the influence of national interests, then we should not be surprised to find the goods of due process and privacy being limited by national boundaries.

This Niebuhrian-informed critique leads to a revised account of just war that expands the range of goods or valuation. Throughout Niebuhr's work one sees a consistent emphasis on an expansive moral vision. For example, Niebuhr advocated supporting the Allies against Germany at a time when isolationist voices were winning the public debate. Some claimed that this was another European war, others that the war was already lost, and still others that war and violence were simply wrong. However, Niebuhr made the case that the war involved a conflict between civilization and barbarism and that, even though the outcome was far from clear, the risk must be taken on strategic and ethical terms.[12]

Niebuhr's critical approach also meant that he was attentive to new developments, whether "facts on the ground" or power dynamics at play behind the scenes. For instance, he initially supported the Kennedy administration's policies in Vietnam as a necessary limited action. He later criticized the escalation of the conflict because he thought that the Johnson administration's ideological framing of it was inconsistent with updates on the fighting and with the goods actually at stake. He recognized that the Vietnam War was not principally a war of democracy versus communism, but was instead a civil war that emerged out of a colonial history. Niebuhr's realism informed his work as a persistent critic of narrow self-interest and ideology. In their place, he advocated a practical wisdom that seeks to reconcile the responsible pursuit of justice with an enlightened sense of self-interest.[13]

Niebuhr confronted American nationalism and its internally focused parochialism with its tendency toward isolationism, by identifying *civilization* as the good at stake in the war against the Nazis. When commenting on the Vietnam War he remained a realist, but in this case he argued that the war and its conduct harmed our national interest. The reality that Niebuhr identified was that the nation's interests were part of larger geopolitical struggle with the Soviet Union, which was in large part an ideological struggle for the hearts and minds of developing nations. The war, he argued, was a military stalemate at best and an ideological loser. US participation played into the Marxist propaganda that capitalist nations were inherently imperialistic.[14]

Niebuhr's legacy prods us to identify the broader goods at stake in the struggle with al-Qaeda and inquire how drone strikes relate to these broader goals. In the struggle with al-Qaeda, the United States and allied nations confront an enemy convinced of its moral superiority. Al-Qaeda, associated groups, and other opponents resent what they believe is the imposition of an alien and domineering culture that spreads an individualistic ethic and rejects religion, morality, and community.

The proper response, says al-Qaeda, is a war that will drive the West from Muslim nations, allowing them to form an Islamic super-state. In the war against the West, there are no innocents. All are guilty and subject to punishment for the oppression and murder of Muslims. If this is al-Qaeda's vision of the West, who do we say we are or aspire to be? A common response from the West is that the conflict is waged in defense of freedom. However, if this is true, it is important to emphasize that the West understands freedom not as antagonistic with morality, but rather as bound to fundamental human rights and the idea that human beings are moral agents.

Freedom of conscience is at the core of our vision; but conscience also involves expression, association, and equal political participation. Freedom, understood more fully, deserves legal respect and judicial protection institutionalized in a system of rights. The West is not fighting for a freedom that makes us free to do whatever individuals please, but that individuals and families possess a dignity that demands respect for their freedom to follow their conscience. This view of humans as possessing an inherent dignity means, at a minimum, a nearly absolute respect for life and, more substantially, an impulse to cultivate a system of social security related to education, health, housing, and employment.

This set of ideas highlights a moral trajectory. Indeed, it represents a shared vision of human beings and the good life – one open to a plurality of interpretations, but still a competing vision to that offered by al-Qaeda and associated groups. This presents a competing story of the struggle and suggests a set of normative expectations. For example, in contrast to al-Qaeda, the West recognizes the dignity of all human beings, and with this idea comes a fundamental obligation, both legal and moral, to respect the right to life. However, these claims are undermined and mocked when a drone attacks a wedding party or kills innocent civilians.[15] This is true as well with the use of other weapons, but with drones there may well be a deeper insult. That is, how is it that innocent lives are taken with powerful unmanned machines when one of their primary and widely celebrated characteristics is their precision?

Drones allow for choices, but they also enable us to avoid tragic choices. Our vision or reason for fighting dictates that we avoid the tragic choice. This suggests a series of basic principles that express core ethical concerns.

The first principle is that drone strikes in unconventional conflicts should demonstrate a special respect for non-combatants. This is in keeping with who we say we are and what we say drones can do. In the case of drones, the just war principle of discrimination should be revised so that foreseen deaths are no longer permitted or excused. This change would heighten the military's responsibility, but such a change is in keeping with the greater capabilities of the weapon. Furthermore, this aspect of drone policy should be publicly presented and clearly enunciated to heighten the degree to which drone policy is openly presented as being in line with core moral precepts.

The second principle is that drones strikes should only be used in cases of formal conflict or when explicitly recognized by a sovereign state. Drones may be used in nations with which we are at war or in another form of recognized conflict. Where there is not a state of war, drones strikes should not be used in a nation unless the host nation explicitly authorizes the strike or strikes. The principle accords with the shared vision of a community of nations in which human dignity is respected at both the individual level and among nations.

At a minimum this means respect for international law, including respect for democratic processes. Citizens, like those in Pakistan, have a right to know the military agreements their leaders have made with other nations. One might also add that it is not in our long-term interest to undermine the legitimacy of an ally's political class. This suggests that our integrity and national self-interests may at times overlap, especially in the long-term. The same point is at work in terms of competing ideologies.

Clearly the struggle against al-Qaeda is in no small part an ideological battle. Drones are powerful weapons, but for all their technological capacities, they are not capable of winning a competition among ideologies. They can, however, severely damage US interests and seriously hinder efforts in this area.

If the ideological battle is lost, the United States and its allies will likely end up losing the war or possibly being drawn into actions that profoundly damage our society, as well as the places where we deploy our military. That is, if we lose the ideological struggle, it is likely that we will have become the tyrannical power our enemies claim we are. At the heart of tyranny is the arbitrary use of power. The danger of drones is that they will carry this symbolic message – that the United States possesses god-like power that it unleashes as it pleases with little regard for the humanity of those living in the places where it deploys its military might.

To his credit, President Obama seems to recognize the extraordinary responsibility that comes with targeted drone strikes. This is in keeping with the president's understanding of the burden and power of his office. When one considers his early morning trips to Andrews Air Force Base to honor soldiers killed in action or his detailed orders for the troop surge in Afghanistan, then his personal review of drone strike "kill lists" does not appear out of character. His overriding sense of responsibility was on full display in his speech at the Defense University. Speaking of the killing of al-Awlaki, President Obama conveys the weight of such decisions: "Alongside the decision to put our men and women in uniform in harm's way, the decision to use force against individuals or groups – even against a sworn enemy of the United States – is the hardest thing I do as President. But these decisions must be made, given my responsibility to protect the American people."[16] The president speaks in defense of his own moral seriousness, assuring his audience that he does not take these matters lightly.

This leads to a third key principle, which is to move these decisions out of the White House and back into the military chain of command. The irony here is that President Obama's reference to his responsibility, admirable as it may be, should raise concerns. Certainly Niebuhr would warn the president that none of us are capable of bearing the power of making life and death decisions alone.

Drone strikes should not be made independently. This is important not only to protect non-combatants but also to address the needs of those within the military who operate the drones. There are increasing reports that drone pilots and others are prone to psychological trauma because they have trouble coping with the power of killing from a distance while witnessing the impact of their actions. From their position thousands of miles away, they are able to observe a target for hours on end, perhaps watching a target interact with family members. Here again we find drones appearing to be make modern warfare more humane, but in reality generating new forms of violence and trauma.[17]

5. THE NIEBUHRIAN CHALLENGE, MORAL RESPONSIBILITY, AND DRONE DEPLOYMENT

There is a pressing ethical need to discipline drone strikes and revise just war thinking. In some sense this call should be expected. We are still coming to terms with the implications and significance of this powerful new weapon. Perhaps part of the problem is that we have become so accustomed to radical technological advances that drones and their innovation now appear normal. Nevertheless, as their presence and power become familiar, we struggle to appreciate the implications of their capacities. Drones enable an exceptional ability to accurately identify and attack targets so that a conventional reading of just war thinking finds them an exceptionally useful and justified weapon. Indeed, drones are thought by many to be the model of a morally justified weapon.

Conventional just war theory has come to accept – in fact, to expect – the inevitability of the tragic, the foreseen but unintended death of innocents. Yet this is just what drone strikes call into question. At a minimum, the awesome power of drones raises the question of new responsibilities. If drones are capable of identifying targets and then avoiding collateral deaths, are we not then responsible for using these capabilities?

Drones present us with the burden of power – that is, responsibility. The penetrating critique of Niebuhr's realism helps expose our self-interested avoidance of this burden. Rather than discipline this new power and perhaps modern war fighting and just war theory, America's political culture appears fixated on constitutional rights involving due process protections and privacy. The problem is not with these legal institutions but with the blinding power of self-interest grounded in the nation. Such pride, Niebuhr warned, is the undoing of great nations.

The power of self-interest is such that moral progress on drones is likely to require help. We might expect such help to come from President Obama. The irony is that Niebuhr is supposedly one of Obama's favorite thinkers. Indeed, it may well be that Mr. Obama reads Niebuhr as stressing the need for individuals to assume responsibility. Such a reading would be consistent with the President's taking responsibility for the list of drone targets. However, while this position is understandable and to some extent commendable, it also represents a misreading of Niebuhr with significant moral consequences. The Niebuhrian challenge in all cases is to discipline power, to limit power, and to find ways to check and balance power so that it may be used responsibly, and thus avoid the twin evils of tyranny and anarchy. Concentrating power is the problem, not the solution.

The president's well-intentioned assumption of responsibility discourages a sustained public debate. By concentrating and shuttering drone decisions within the White House, there is a lack of debate within the larger administration, in Congress, and among the American public. In large part this has to do with the lack of transparency. Government officials are reluctant to raise critical questions in public, questions that might also help foster debate in civil society. According to Niebuhr, democratic government is distinguished by its ability to balance and check power. One of the key forms of such balancing, he argued, is the critical spirit of democratic civil society.

Toward the end of his career, Niebuhr worried that democratic debate might itself fail, that the divisive nature of our culture was undermining the democratic process. However, the irony within the lack of a domestic drone debate regarding foreign targeting is not its divisiveness, but rather a type of unexplored consensus. Indeed, one might be tempted to call it a moral consensus, based on a conventional just war theory reading of drones as a model of morality in conducting war. The consensus is strengthened by the indiscriminate violence of al-Qaeda and legitimate concerns for US national security. In this context drones represent a moral hazard, tempting us to moral callousness even as we feel self-righteous pride in comparison with terrorist organizations. However, to give over to such a dynamic would be truly perilous not only in terms of the struggle against al-Qaeda but also in terms of our self-understanding. In this context, with these moral dilemmas, it is time to rethink just war theory. Perhaps we should be glad that the proliferation of drones is likely to push us to do just that.

NOTES

1 Dowd, Alan W., "Drone wars: Risks and warnings," *Parameters* (Winter–Spring 2013): 7–16.

2 Brown, Alyssa, and Frank Newport, "In U.S., 65% support drone attacks on terrorists abroad," Gallup, March 25, 2013.

3 Hauerwas, Stanley, *War and the American difference: Theological reflections on violence and national identity* (Grand Rapids, MI: Baker Academic, 2011).

4 Brainard, Curtis, "Drones and transparency," *Columbia Journalism Review*, February 20, 2013.

5 Byman, Daniel. "Why drones work," *Foreign Affairs* 92 (July 2013): 32–43.

6 Pew Research Center, "Global opinion of Obama slips, international policies faulted: Drones strikes widely opposed," *Global Attitudes Project*, June 13, 2012, p. 3.

7 The distorting power of a collective's self-interest, especially that of the modern nation-state, was a central concern of Niebuhr's. For a classic statement of this

concern, see Niebuhr, Reinhold, *Moral man and immoral society* (Louisville, KY: Westminster John Knox, 2001).

8 al-Awlaki, Nasser, "The drone that killed my grandson," *New York Times*, July 17, 2013. The letter laments that "attorney general, Eric H. Holder Jr., said only that Abdulrahman was not 'specifically targeted,' raising more questions than he answered."

9 The irony is that a seemingly liberal legal position takes on a communitarian perspective on the law.

10 Mazzetti, Mark, and Scott Shane, "Drones are focus as C.I.A. nominee goes before senators," *New York Times*, February 7, 2013.

11 Zenko, Micah, "Confront and confuse," *Foreign Policy*, May 28, 2013.

12 Niebuhr, Reinhold, "The will of God and the Van Zeeland report," in D. B. Robertson (ed.), *Love and justice: Selections from the shorter writings of Reinhold Niebuhr* (Louisville, KY: Westminster John Knox, 1992), pp. 168–171.

13 Niebuhr, Reinhold, "Reinhold Niebuhr discusses the war in Vietnam," *New Republic* 154 (January 24, 1966): 15–16.

14 Niebuhr, Reinhold, "The limits of military power" in D. B. Robertson (ed.), *Love and justice: Selections from the shorter writings of Reinhold Niebuhr*, pp. 191–193.

15 Worth, Robert F., and Scott Shane, "Questions on drone strike find only silence," *New York Times*, November 22, 2013.

16 Barack Obama, "Remarks by the president at the National Defense University," Fort McNair, Washington, DC, May 23, 2013.

17 Bumiller, Elisabeth, "A day job waiting for a kill shot a world away," *New York Times*, July 29, 2012.

16

World of Drones

The Global Proliferation of Drone Technology

PETER L. BERGEN AND JENNIFER ROWLAND

At the beginning of the "Global War on Terror," launched by President George W. Bush in 2001 following the attacks of 9/11, the United States had a virtual monopoly on drones. According to data compiled by New America, as of December 2013, 82 countries owned some type of drone, although only a small number of those nations possessed armed drone aircraft. The United States, United Kingdom, and Israel are the only nations that are confirmed to have used armed drones against their adversaries, although other members of NATO's International Security Assistance Force, such as Australia, have "borrowed" drones from Israel for use in Afghanistan.[1]

When the United States first invaded Afghanistan in October 2001, the Pentagon had fewer than 50 drones, and had never used armed drones in combat. By late 2012 it had around 7,500, and was launching regular drone strikes against suspected al-Qaeda militants in Afghanistan and Yemen. The first US armed drone attack, which appears to be the first such strike ever, took place in Afghanistan in mid-November 2001, which killed Mohammed Atef, the military commander of al-Qaeda. Since then, the CIA has used drones equipped with bombs and missiles hundreds of times to target suspected militants in Pakistan and Yemen.

And drone technology is proliferating rapidly.[2] Building drones, particularly armed drones, takes sophisticated technology and access to the specific weaponry that can be launched from an unmanned vehicle. Governments are increasingly willing to invest the necessary time and money either to buy or develop them because armed drones are increasingly seen as an integral part of modern warfare.

The Teal Group, a defense consulting firm in Virginia, estimated in 2012 that the global market for the research, development, and procurement of armed drones will nearly double in the next decade, from $6.6 billion to $11.4 billion, and that the United States will account for 62 percent of drone research and development, and 55 percent of drone procurement.[3] A 2011 study estimated that there were around

680 active drone development programs run by governments, companies, and research institutes around the world, compared with just 195 in 2005.

Israel is the world's largest exporter of drones and drone technology, and the state-owned Israeli Aerospace Industries (IAI) has sold to countries as varied as Nigeria, Russia, and Mexico. IAI has also reportedly sold a "loitering weapon" called the Harop to India, Turkey, France, and Germany. The Harop can circle over a target for hours before it is activated and sent to the ground as a single-use missile. Israel itself has used armed drones in the Palestinian territories.[4]

The United States trails Israel in the drone export race, but US-based drone development companies are rapidly expanding. In 2010 US-based General Atomics received export licenses to sell unarmed versions of the Predator drone to Saudi Arabia, Egypt, Morocco, and the United Arab Emirates.[5] In March 2012, the US government agreed to arm Italy's six Reaper drones but rejected a request from Turkey to purchase armed Predator drones.[6] (An official in Turkey's Defense Ministry then said in July 2012 that Turkey planned to arm its own domestically produced drone, the Anka,[7] anticipated to be ready for test flights by 2016.[8]) And in May 2012 NATO finalized a $1.7 billion contract with Northrup Grumman for five Global Hawk drones that will be based at a NATO airfield in Sicily.[9]

Sweden, Greece, Switzerland, Spain, Italy, and France are working on a joint project through state-owned aeronautical companies and are in the final stages of developing an advanced armed drone prototype called the Dassault nEUROn. France plans to manufacture armed drones for its air force using this technology.[10] And in February 2013, a regional Russian government posted online and then quickly removed photographs of two Russian-made armed drones. The two systems were reportedly scheduled to begin test flights in 2014.[11]

Pakistani authorities have long tried to persuade the United States to give them armed Predator drones, and though they continue to fail to acquire missile-equipped UAVs (unarmed aerial vehicles), they deployed their first domestically produced unarmed drone at the end of 2013. Neighbor and rival India owns an armed Israeli drone designed to detect and destroy enemy radar, and in August 2013 the scientific advisor to India's Defense Minister announced that a state military research firm would begin test-firing precision missiles from drones "in a couple months."[12]

In September 2012 China announced that it would use surveillance drones to monitor a group of uninhabited islands in the South China Sea that are controlled by Japan but claimed by China and Taiwan.[13] China had taken the United States by surprise in November 2010 at the Zhuhai Air Show, where it unveiled twenty-five drone models, some of which were outfitted with the capability to fire missiles.[14] Two years later, at the November 2012 Zhuhai Air Show, Chinese companies displayed full-size armed drones, the CH-4 and Li Yong.[15] Meanwhile, Taiwan has also been building indigenous drone capabilities, and Taiwanese authorities announced in December 2013 that they are developing an armed drone.[16]

In February 2013 a state-run newspaper reported that Chinese authorities had considered using armed drones to kill Naw Kham, a drug lord in Myanmar who was accused of murdering thirteen Chinese sailors. In the end, China decided to capture Naw Kham instead of launching a drone strike, but the report showed China's capacity to carry out armed drone attacks.[17]

In August 2010 Iran unveiled what it claimed was its first armed drone, the "Ambassador of Death."[18] This aircraft would essentially function as a kamikaze drone, crashing into its target and detonating its explosives upon impact, and did not appear to be much of a step up from the single-use drones Iran had years earlier. As early as 2006 during the Israeli–Lebanese War, the Lebanon-based militant group Hezbollah launched three Iranian-supplied Ababil drones, each carrying an 88-pound warhead, into Israeli airspace. The drones were easily shot down. However, during fall 2012 Iran's military chief, General Amir Ali Hajizadeh, disclosed details of a new long-range drone that he said could fly 2,000 kilometers (1,250 miles), which puts Tel Aviv easily in range.[19] A year later, Hajizadeh announced that Iran would begin mass-producing and exporting the drone, which he said is capable of carrying up to eight missiles.[20]

States are not alone in their quest for drones. Insurgent groups, too, are moving to acquire this technology. Libyan opposition forces trying to overthrow the dictator Moammar Gadhafi in 2011 bought a sophisticated surveillance drone from a Canadian company, for which they paid in the low six figures.[21] As drone technology becomes more widely accessible, it is only a matter of time before well-financed drug cartels acquire them.

Given the relatively low costs of drones – already far less expensive than the costs of a fighter jet and of training a fighter jet pilot[22] – armed drones will likely play a key role in future conflicts. In addition, there may be a lower threshold for the use of force when armed drones are an option, because they allow for combat in which personnel are not placed at risk. Still, it will be many years before other countries are able to build up the capacity that the United States has to carry out lethal drone strikes almost anywhere in the world. As of 2013, US drone bases are in at least eleven countries: Afghanistan, Djibouti, Ethiopia, Niger, Qatar, the Philippines, Saudi Arabia, the Seychelles, Turkey, the United Arab Emirates, and Yemen. And the drone base in Balochistan, Pakistan, from which many of the hundreds of CIA strikes were launched, was only shuttered in November 2011 after an errant NATO helicopter strike hit two Pakistani Army posts near the Afghan border, killing twenty-four Pakistani soldiers.

The United States has been able to improve the accuracy of its strikes by using high-tech, laser-guided missiles, something not all countries have been able to develop or obtain. And the many targets on the US government's kill lists are identified through extensive intelligence networks on the ground in multiple countries, in tandem with advanced geospatial intelligence equipment. It is hard to imagine that another country will catch up to the United States on either of these criteria anytime soon.

At the same time, the capacity of US companies to export the latest drone technology to other nations is limited by the country's membership in the 1987 Missile Technology Control Regime (MTCR), an international agreement designed to restrict the proliferation of ballistic missiles. The MTCR strongly urges that members should not transfer drones with a range greater than 300 kilometers and a capacity to carry 500 kilograms or larger payload, ruling out most long-range armed drones.[23]

And it is not as easy as some might believe for other nations to arm unarmed drones. Such weapons systems require specific electrical engineering; the wings must be reinforced in order for the aircraft to sustain the force of launching a missile; the drone must be equipped with fire control systems; and built-in mounting brackets are needed to attach munitions to the vehicle.

But even with these inherent limitations, the drone industry thrives and more companies, research institutes, and nations continue to jump on board the drone bandwagon. And the aggressive and secretive US drone campaign against al-Qaeda and its affiliates is setting a powerful international norm about the use of armed drones, which it uses for pre-emptive attacks against presumed terrorists in Pakistan and Yemen. These kinds of drone strikes are especially controversial because the use of drones in a conventional war is not much different, legally or morally, than the use of manned aircraft that drops bombs, uses cannons, or fires missiles.

There has been virtually no substantive public discussion about drone attacks among policymakers at the international level. Just as the US government justifies its drone strikes with the argument that it is at war with al-Qaeda and its affiliates, one could imagine that India in the not-too-distant future might launch such attacks against suspected terrorists in Kashmir, or China might strike Uighur separatists in western China, or Iran might attack Baluchi nationalists along its border with Pakistan.

Table 1 summarizes which countries currently possess drones and how they have come to acquire the drones, based on an analysis of thousands of news reports and government documents.

Table 1 classifies drones according to the US Air Force tier system. Tier I includes low-altitude, long-endurance drones like the Hermes 450; Tier II is comprised of medium-altitude, long-endurance (MALE) drones like the Predator; and Tier II+ applies to high-altitude, long-endurance (HALE) drones, like the Global Hawk. Mini- and micro-drones are not classified in the tier system.[24]

TABLE 1. *Drone Classification*

	Countries with Drones Used in Combat	Source of Technology	Tier I (Low altitude, long endurance)	Tier II MALE	Tier II+ HALE
1	Israel	Israel has domestic production of drones[25] and imports drone engines from the United Kingdom. Israel refuses to release the full list of countries to which it has sold military arms, totaling nearly $7 billion.[26] Israel is the largest exporter of drones in the world, responsible for 4 percent of all drones exported between 2001 and 2011, according to a database compiled by the Stockholm International Peace Research Institute.[27] Israel continues to lead the world in drone exports, exporting nearly $4.6 billion worth of systems between 2005 and 2012, as reported by US consulting firm Frost & Sullivan.[28]	Yes	Yes	Yes
2	United Kingdom	The United Kingdom has domestic production of drones, imports drones from United States, and has very limited imports (one drone) from Israel.[29]	Yes	Yes	No
3	United States	The United States has domestic production of drones and imports drones from Israel. The Pentagon asked Congress for nearly $5 billion for drones in 2012.[30]	Yes	Yes	Yes

	Countries with Armed Drones	Source of Technology	Tier I (Low altitude, long endurance)	Tier II MALE	Tier II+ HALE (endurance)
4	China	China has domestic production[31] of drones and limited imports from Israel.[32] There are also limited imports from Japan, and some reports indicate that Germany has provided the engines used in Chinese	Yes	Yes	Yes

304

TABLE 1. (*continued*)

Countries with Armed Drones	Source of Technology	Tier I (Low altitude, long endurance)	Tier II MALE	Tier II+ HALE endurance
	drones.[33] In August 2006 Japan's Yamaha Motor Company was accused of selling the RMAX helicopter drones to Beijing Technology Company, China, which has ties to the Chinese People's Liberation Army (PLA), in violation of Japan's Foreign Exchange and Foreign Trade Control Law.[34] Chinese authorities said in February 2013 that they had considered using a drone to kill a drug dealer in Myanmar responsible for the deaths of thirteen Chinese soldiers.[35] China recorded the successful flight of first stealth combat drones, the "Sharp Sword."[36] China also unveiled the CH-4 and Yilong drones equipped with Blue Arrow-7 anti-tank missiles, which have designs similar to that of the US Predator drones equipped with Hellfire missiles.[37] China's drone arsenal has grown large enough to compete with the United States.[38] Reports accuse China of hacking into US drone companies and accessing information needed to ramp up their drone technologies.[39]			
5 France	France has domestic production[40] of drones, and also imports from Israel[41] and Canada.[42] Collaboration with Britain,[43] Sweden, Spain, Greece, Germany, and Canada in producing drones. Imports from the United States include Reaper drones.[44] France deployed two of the recently purchased unarmed Reaper drones to Niger to support the mission in Mali.[45] France has joined with Germany, Greece, Italy, Netherlands, Poland, and Spain to create a "drone users club" intended to compete with Israeli and US drones markets.[46] Morocco is considering purchasing France's surplus Israeli drones.[47]	Yes	Yes	Yes

TABLE 1. (*continued*)

Countries with Armed Drones	Source of Technology	Tier I (Low altitude, long endurance)	Tier II MALE	Tier II+ HALE endurance)
6 Iran	Iran has domestic production of drones.[48] In August 2010 Iran unveiled the "Karar" drone, which President Mahmoud Ahmadinejad called an "ambassador of death," and which reportedly can carry up to four cruise missiles with a range of more than 600 miles. Hezbollah has used Iranian-made Ababil drones, which function more as cruise missiles. There is also domestic production of drones of short-range reconnaissance, such as the Yasseer drone[49] and Shahad-129 drone, capable of 1,700-km range carrying up to eight missiles.[50] In November 2013 they released Fotros drones with a 2,000-km range.[51] Officials claimed to have reproduced a US drone that was downed in Iran.[52]	Yes	Yes	?

Countries with Drones	Source of Technology	Tier I (Low altitude, long endurance)	Tier II MALE	Tier II+ HALE
7 Algeria	Algeria has domestic drone production,[53] and imported the medium-range Seeker II tactical drones from South Africa in 1998.[54] Reports suggest Algeria operates Denel Dynamics Seeker drones and is interested in obtaining Adcom Systems Yabhon United 40 Block 5 drones.[55] Algeria has possibly purchased	Yes	No, however they are interested in the Yabhon drones with MALE capabilities.	No

TABLE 1. (*continued*)

Countries with Drones	Source of Technology	Tier I (Low altitude, long endurance)	Tier II MALE	Tier II+ HALE
	military drones equipment from Israel, although what exactly was purchased is unknown. In 2009 Israel requested export-processing permits to Algeria to supply components for drones.[56] Algeria is reportedly in discussions with China to purchase the Xianglong HALE unmanned aerial vehicle.[57]			
8 Angola	Reports indicate that Angola imported Heron drones from Israel.[58] The company Aeronautics reports selling its Aerostar Tactical Unmanned Air Vehicle System to Angola.[59]	Possible	Yes	No
9 Argentina	Argentina has domestic drone production.[60] It is possible that there is cooperation between Israel and Argentina but reports are unconfirmed.[61]	Yes	Yes	No
10 Armenia	Armenia has domestic production of their Krunk drones, which is a close reconnaissance drone.[62] Armenia has also agreed to export their Krunk drones to Denmark.[63]			
11 Australia	Australia has domestic drone production and has also imported drones from the United States and Israel.[64] Plans moving forward include purchasing the Northrop Grumman MQ-4C Triton drones.[65]	Yes	No	No

307

TABLE 1. (*continued*)

	Countries with Drones	Source of Technology	Tier I (Low altitude, long endurance)	Tier II MALE	Tier II+ HALE
12	Austria	Austria has domestic drone production.[66] Reported plans include importing more drones, though it is unclear form where,[67] and there are recent purchases of Cassidian Tracker mini-drones from a UK-based company.[68]	Yes	Yes[69]	No
13	Azerbaijan	Azerbaijan has imported drones from Israel[70] and begun domestic production in partnership with Israeli firms.[71] Shipments of drones from Israel continued through 2013.[72]	Yes	Yes	No
14	Belarus	Belarus has imported drones from Russia.[73] Belarus President Alexander Lukashenko announced plans to begin production of drones in Turkmenistan,[74] and plans to export drones to Vietnam.[75]	Yes	No	No
15	Belgium	Belgium has domestic production of drones,[76] and is cooperating with a British company, an Israeli company, and a French company for production.	Yes	No	No
16	Botswana	There are reports of domestic production, but Botswana has also imported drones from Israel.[77] There are reports of requests from Botswana to purchase drones from the United States.[78]	Yes	No	No

TABLE 1. (*continued*)

Countries with Drones	Source of Technology	Tier I (Low altitude, long endurance)	Tier II MALE	Tier II+ HALE
17 Brazil	Brazil has domestic production of drones but has also imported from Israel.[79] Their production is in cooperation with Argentina[80] (both countries importing from Israel), with the possibility for a joint production venture with Turkey in the future.[81]	Yes	Yes[82]	No
18 Bulgaria	Bulgaria has domestic production of drones.[83] Bulgaria has signed on to be a member of NATO's Airborne Ground Surveillance Program.[84] Bulgaria is supposed to have HALE drones by 2017, to be a part of the Alliance Ground Surveillance.[85]	Yes	No	No
19 Burundi	Burundi has drones in the form of military aid from the United States.[86]	Yes	No	No
20 Canada	Canada produces drones domestically and in cooperation with the United States. They have also leased drones from Israel to use in Afghanistan, and imported drones from Israel. It is possible that they have imports from France and are considering imports from the United States.[87] Reports indicate Canada also plans to acquire lethal drones.[88]	Yes	No	No

TABLE 1. (*continued*)

Countries with Drones	Source of Technology	Tier I (Low altitude, long endurance)	Tier II MALE	Tier II+ HALE
21 Chile	Chile has domestic production of drones and has imported drones from Israel.[89] There are reports of drone purchases from Iran[90] and reports of Hermes 900 medium-sized drones purchased from Israel by the navy.[91] The air force is already operating Hermes 900 drones.[92]	Yes	Yes	No
22 Colombia	Colombia announced the launch of domestic production of a drone program meant to combat drug trafficking.[93] There are also imports from the United States.[94] The *Washington Post* reported that it was not clear from WikiLeaks documents whether the drones were flown by US military forces in Colombia or given to the Colombian armed forces as part of a multibillion-dollar military aid program.[95] There have been imports from Israel,[96] and Colombia is considering purchasing another Hermes 900 drones.[97] The country's first drone flight simulator for training operators of drones was successfully produced in 2013.[98]	Yes	Yes	No
23 Croatia	Croatia has domestic production of drones and has imported from Israel.[99]	Yes	No	No

TABLE 1. (*continued*)

Countries with Drones	Source of Technology	Tier I (Low altitude, long endurance)	Tier II MALE	Tier II+ HALE
24 Czech Republic	The Czech Republic has domestic production of drones. In February 2012 several European countries – Bulgaria, the Czech Republic, Estonia, Germany, Italy, Latvia, Lithuania, Luxembourg, Norway, Romania, Slovakia, and Slovenia – were considering purchasing drones from the United States.[100]	Yes	No	No
25 Denmark	Denmark has imported from France and possibly from the United States.[101] There is also domestic production of drones in cooperation with the Netherlands (which loaned out two sets of Raven drone systems)[102] and Sweden (which loaned the Puma AE for Tactical Unmanned Aerial System, known as Tac-UAS).[103] Small commercial UAS drones are imported from Armenia[104] and produced domestically.[105] Armenia also was exporting Krunk drones capable of close reconnaissance, transmission of real-time video data, and taking high-resolution still images (Armenia deploys Krunk drones for military purpose, but Denmark intends to use the drones for commercial agriculture purposes).[106] Military reconnaissance drones are	Yes	No	No

TABLE 1. (*continued*)

Countries with Drones	Source of Technology	Tier I (Low altitude, long endurance)	Tier II MALE	Tier II+ HALE
	produced domestically with no payload capacity, but the Huggin X1 drones can be linked with a Canadian-built (Colt Canada) network platform-mounted to a soldier's weapon and is designed to provide surveillance based on the direction and angle of the soldier's weapon.[107]			
26 Ecuador	Ecuador has imported drones from Israel (IAI Heron Machatz-1)[108] and has domestically produced some (UAV-2 Gavilan, or "Hawk").[109]	Yes	Yes	No
27 Egypt	General Atomics received export licenses to sell an unarmed export version of the Predator to Saudi Arabia, Egypt, United Arab Emirates, and Morocco in 2010.[110] They have domestically produced ASN-209 drones in cooperation with China.[111] There are also reports that Egypt is planning on importing Turkey's ANKA drones.[112]	Yes	Yes	No
AUS; 28 Estonia	Estonia has drones in the form of military aid from the United States for use in Afghanistan.[113] There are reports that Estonia plans to purchase surveillance drones, such as the RQ-4 Global Hawk UAV, within the	Yes	No	No

TABLE 1. (*continued*)

Countries with Drones	Source of Technology	Tier I (Low altitude, long endurance)	Tier II MALE	Tier II+ HALE
	next few years.[114] They have domestically produced UAS Swan III by ELI Military Simulations, which are also exported to Georgia.[115]			
29 Ethiopia	Ethiopia has domestically developed and produced drones but has also imported drones from Israel.[116] The United States is operating drones bases out of Ethiopia.[117]	Yes	Possible	No
30 Finland	Finland has domestic production of drones but has also imported from Israel.[118]	Yes	No	No
32 Georgia	Georgia has domestic production of drones,[119] and imported drones from Israel[120] and Estonia.[121]	Yes	No	No
31 Germany	Germany has domestic production[122] of drones but has also leased drones from Israel for use in Afghanistan,[123] and has imported from the United States.[124] They recently cancelled a $1.3 billion purchase from the United States.[125] Germany has joined with France, Greece, Italy, the Netherlands, Poland, and Spain to create a "drones users club" intended to compete with Israeli and US drones markets.[126]	Yes	Yes	Yes

TABLE 1. (continued)

#	Countries with Drones	Source of Technology	Tier I (Low altitude, long endurance)	Tier II MALE	Tier II+ HALE
33	Greece	Greece has domestic production of drones, and some reports indicate they import from France.[127] Greece is a member of the drones "club" with France, Germany, Italy, the Netherlands, Poland, and Spain for the joint production of MALE drones.[128]	Yes	No	No
34	Hungary	Hungary has domestic production of drones.[129] There are reports that Hungary has also imported drones from Israel (Elbit Skylark).[130]	Yes	No	No
35	India	India has domestic production of drones,[131] but has also imported drones from Israel (Searcher, Heron, and Harpy Killer UCAV),[132] and is working with Israel to import and develop the Rustom-1 and -2 MALE, Pawan, and Gagan.[133] The Defence Research and Development Organization, an agency of the Republic of India, is continuing development on the AURA drones, a combat designed drones set for release as late as 2020.[134] Officials announced that they would soon be equipping drones with precision-guided munitions.[135] There was a recent request for forty-nine hand-held mini-drones for troops.[136]	Yes	Yes (Rustom-1 MALE)	No

TABLE 1. (*continued*)

Countries with Drones	Source of Technology	Tier I (Low altitude, long endurance)	Tier II MALE	Tier II+ HALE
36 Indonesia	Indonesia has imported drones from Israel.[137] Officials announced that the domestically produced Wulung drones will be mass-produced.[138]	Yes	No	No
37 Iraq	Iraq has imported from the US Navy, and the Iraq Navy has purchased US drones to protect the country's oil platforms in the south, from where most of Iraq's oil is shipped.[139] Iraq imported ScanEagle drones from the United States for surveillance against terror fight.[140]	Yes	?	?
38 Italy	Italy has domestic production of drones[141] (Hammerhead drones produced by Piaggio Aero Company and Selex ES);[142] and imports from the United States, including the RQ-1B Reaper drones.[143] Reports indicate that the United States plans to arm Italy's drones;[144] however, this request from Rome has gone unfulfilled for nearly three years, leading Italy to proceed unilaterally with Black MALE drones production.[145] Italy has joined with France, Germany, the Netherlands, Poland, and Spain to create a "drone users club"	Yes	Yes	No

TABLE 1. (*continued*)

	Countries with Drones	Source of Technology	Tier I (Low altitude, long endurance)	Tier II MALE	Tier II+ HALE
		intended to compete with the Israeli and US drone markets.[146]			
39	Ivory Coast	The Ivory Coast has imported drones from Israel.[147] They have also sent a request to the United Nations for drones to monitor their border with Liberia.[148]	Yes	No	No
40	Japan	Japan has domestic production of drones.[149] Negotiations are underway to allow for the relocation of US Global Spy Hawk drones to territories within Japan, enabling Japan to share information with the United States.[150] The prime minister's Cabinet has approved the purchase of three drones in a push to build up the nation's defense.[151] Japan's Defense Ministry plans to deploy its first Global Hawk in 2015, which will be co-maintained with the US Air Force.[152]	Yes	No	No
41	Jordan	Jordan has domestic production of drones and co-production of drones with an Italian company.[153] The Jordan Falcon drone, produced as a result of a joint venture between the King Abdullah II Design and Development Bureau and Jordan Aerospace Industries, is an	Yes	Yes	No

316

TABLE 1. (*continued*)

Countries with Drones	Source of Technology	Tier I (Low altitude, long endurance)	Tier II MALE	Tier II+ HALE
42 Kazakhstan	unarmed drone capable of reconnaissance, surveillance, and target designation and tracking. Kazakhstan imported Orbiter drones from Israel in 2008,[154] and has also reportedly imported drone technology from Russia.[155] Kazakhstan is in talks with the Israeli companies Elbit and IAI to establish a tactical drones manufacturing facility in the country in 2013.[156] Kazakhstan also signed a deal with Sagem in 2010 to jointly produce drones within Kazakhstan; however, this agreement has yet to manifest.[157] The Kazakhstan Ministry of Defense purchased ten Irkut-10 unmanned reconnaissance aircraft systems from the Russian Irkut Corporation, and has plans to possibly purchase Irkut-3 drones.[158]	Yes	No	No
43 Latvia	Latvia has domestic production of drones.[159] The Drones Factory is a company within Latvia that is manufacturing drones capable of capturing real-time intelligence data.[160] Latvia's production comes from the Drones Factory, which produces the Penguin C, BE, and	Yes	Yes	No

TABLE 1. (*continued*)

	Countries with Drones	Source of Technology	Tier I (Low altitude, long endurance)	Tier II MALE	Tier II+ HALE
		B drones.[161] The Penguin B is touted as the current world record endurance holder, operating for a continuous 54.5 hours.[162]			No
44	Lebanon	Lebanon's drones were provided by the United States as part of a military aid package.[163]	Yes	No	No
45	Libya	Libya is implementing surveillance and reconnaissance drones to carry out operations and inspections within the Libyan Air Force.[164]	Yes	Possibly	
46	Lithuania	Lithuania contributed more than $6.5 million to NATO's Alliance Ground Surveillance (AGS) division developed by NATO, scheduled be put in place by 2015.[165] The NATO AGS is an alliance between fourteen nations, who will share five Global Hawk RQ-4B drones for high-altitude reconnaissance and surveillance over large areas of land.[166]	No	No	Yes (shared operational endeavors)
47	Malaysia	Malaysia has domestic production of drones in co-operation with US companies.[167] Three companies, Composites Technology Research Malaysia (CTRM), Systems Consultancy Sdn Bhd (SCS), and Ikramatic Sdn Bhn combined	Yes[170]	No Yes	No

318

TABLE 1. (*continued*)

Countries with Drones	Source of Technology	Tier I (Low altitude, long endurance)	Tier II MALE	Tier II+ HALE
	and formed the Unmanned Systems Technology Sdn Bhd (UST) to manufacture Malaysian drones.[168] The Malaysian firm Unmanned Systems Technology began producing low-altitude, long-endurance, and MALE unmanned aerial vehicles in 2010. The drones are a joint venture with Adcom Systems, a United Arab Emirates company.[169]			
48 Mexico	Mexico has domestic production of drones (Hydra Technologies, Mexican Navy Institute for Technology Innovation) and also has imported drones from Israel (Elbit Systems Hermes 450).	Yes	No	No
49 Morocco	The status of drones in Morocco is uncertain. General Atomics received an export license to sell unarmed Predator drones to Morocco, but it is unclear whether that deal has been completed.[171] The Royal Moroccan Armed Forces announced its pre-production search and development phase of drones for 2014–2015.[172] Reports from French sources indicate that Morocco has purchased at least three Israeli Harfang MALE drones.[173]	?	?	?

TABLE 1. (*continued*)

Countries with Drones	Source of Technology	Tier I (Low altitude, long endurance)	Tier II MALE	Tier II+ HALE
50 Netherlands	The Netherlands has domestic production of drones and possible imports of drones from France.[174] They have acquired four MQ-9 Reaper MALE drones under the United States Foreign Military Sales Program. The drones are expected to have full operational capability at the end of 2017.[175]	Yes	Yes	No
51 New Zealand	New Zealand has domestic production of drones (Hawkeye, by Skycam UAV NZ Ltd),[176] and imports drones from the United States (from General Atomics).	Yes	No	No
52 Niger	A status of force agreement was signed with the United States that allows US troops to be in the country and use drones in the area.[177]	Yes		
53 Nigeria	Nigeria has imported drones from Israel.[178] Domestic production of drones began at the end of 2013.[179] The Nigerian Air Force Institute of Technology (AFIT) produces Gulma drones, which barely meet the Tier II classification, flying at a maximum altitude of 10,000 feet, reaching a top speed of 86 knots and possessing an endurance of 5.8 hours.[180]	Yes	Yes	No

TABLE 1. (*continued*)

Countries with Drones	Source of Technology	Tier I (Low altitude, long endurance)	Tier II MALE	Tier II+ HALE
54 Norway	Norway has domestic production of drones (by Prox Dynamics).[181]	Yes	No	No
55 Pakistan	Pakistan has domestic production of drones and has imported drones from China[182] and the United States.[183] There has been reported co-production of drones with Italian manufacturers[184] and reported collaboration with China on armed drones.[185] The Pakistani military deployed its first domestically developed drones at the end of 2013. It is unclear whether or not the drones were armed.[186] Military officials claim that the drones are for surveillance only.[187]	Yes	No	No
56 Panama	Panama imported at least four drones from the United States.[188]	Yes	No	No
57 Peru	Peru has domestic production of drones.[189] The Peruvian Army implements drones for surveillance purposes and the air force (Fuerza Aérea del Perú).[190]	Yes	No	No
58 Philippines	The Philippines have domestic production of drones and have imported drones from Israel.[191] The Philippine Army acknowledged in	Yes	No	No

TABLE 1. (*continued*)

	Countries with Drones	Source of Technology	Tier I (Low altitude, long endurance)	Tier II MALE	Tier II+ HALE
		December 2013 that they were using drones to conduct reconnaissance missions.[192] The Department of National Defense (DND) announced in December 2013 that they acquired drones for the Marines. The DND invited companies from around the world to bid on the project.[193]			
59	Poland	Poland has domestic production of drones and imports drones from United States, and collaborates with Israel.[194] In August 2012 the Polish government announced that it would replace its aging fighter jets with thirty armed drones, which should be in use by 2018.	Yes	No	No
60	Portugal	Portugal has domestic production of drones.[195]	Yes	No	No
61	Romania	Romania joined a group of fourteen NATO members that will buy five drones to be used for ground surveillance and intelligence missions.[196]	Yes	No	Yes (in cooperation with fourteen NATO countries)
62	Russia	Russia has domestic production of drones,[197] imported drones from Israel,[198] and	Yes	No	No

TABLE 1. (continued)

Countries with Drones	Source of Technology	Tier I (Low altitude, long endurance)	Tier II MALE	Tier II+ HALE
	co-produced drones with Vietnam.[199] Russia is developing its first long-range drones that will be capable of conducting ground attack missions; the drone is scheduled for deployment by 2016.[200] NBC News reported that Russia is developing a 20-ton attack drone whose prototype could be ready by 2020.[201] Russia plans to conduct test flights of a drone aircraft from the United Arab Emirates at some point in the future. The drones will be capable of carrying Namrod air-to-surface guided missiles.[202]			
63 Serbia	Serbia has domestic production of drones.[203]	Yes	No	No
64 Singapore	Singapore has domestic production of drones and imports from Israel.[204]	Yes	Yes	No
65 Slovakia	Slovakia has domestic production of drones[205] and is believed to have imports from Israel.[206]	Yes	No	No
66 Slovenia	Slovenia has domestic production of drones.[207]	Yes	No	No
67 South Africa	South Africa has domestic production of drones and exports to Algeria and United Arab Emirates.[208] In April 2013 South Africa reportedly agreed to help Saudi Arabia develop armed drones.[209]	Yes	No	No

TABLE 1. (*continued*)

Countries with Drones	Source of Technology	Tier I (Low altitude, long endurance)	Tier II MALE	Tier II+ HALE
68	South Korea	South Korea has domestic production of drones[210] and imports from Israel.[211] They have imported drones and drone technology directly from the United States.[212] With a delivery date of between 2017 and 2019, Northrop Grumman plans to export four RQ-4 Block 30 Global Hawk surveillance drones to South Korea.[213]	Yes	No	Yes (set for delivery between 2017–2019)
69	Spain	Spain has domestic production of drones and uses Israeli drones in Afghanistan.[214] Spain joined with France, Germany, Greece, Italy, the Netherlands, and Poland to create a "drones users club" intended to compete with Israeli and US drones markets.[215]	Yes	No	No
70	Sri Lanka	Sri Lanka has imports from Israel.[216]	Yes	No	No
71	Sweden	Sweden has domestic production of drones in cooperation with companies in Australia, United States, United Arab Emirates, and others.[217] Sweden participates in the development of the nEUROn with France, Spain, Italy, Greece, and Switzerland. Sweden entered into an agreement with	Yes	No	No

TABLE 1. (continued)

Vietnam to provide drone technology and help in producing drones.[218]

	Countries with Drones	Source of Technology	Tier I (Low altitude, long endurance)	Tier II MALE	Tier II+ HALE
72	Switzerland	Switzerland has domestic production of drones.[219] Switzerland also produces drones domestically in cooperation with a German company, and with other European nations developing the nEUROn.[220] Switzerland is contemplating importing drones from Israel.[221]	Yes	No	No
73	Taiwan	Taiwan has domestic production of drones.[222] They are reportedly developing drones similar to the Predator MQ-9, as well armed drones.[223] Taiwan confirmed in December 2013 that they are developing an armed drone at a military-run research center.[224]	Yes	No	No
74	Thailand	Thailand imports drones from Germany and Israel.[225] Thailand's Royal Thai Air Force commander in chief announced plans to request funds to continue development of a drone developed domestically.[226]	Yes	Yes	No
75	Trinidad and Tobago	Reports indicate that Trinidad and Tobago are trying to acquire drones, primarily for surveillance purposes.[227]	No	No	No

TABLE 1. (*continued*)

	Countries with Drones	Source of Technology	Tier I (Low altitude, long endurance)	Tier II MALE	Tier II+ HALE
76	Tunisia	Tunisia has domestic production of drones (Tunisia Aero Technologies Industries S.A.).[228]	Yes	Yes	No
77	Turkey	Turkey has domestic production of drones (Turkish Aerospace Industries, Inc.) and has imported drones from Israel.[229] The Turkish government signed a contract to acquire ten drones from Turkish Aerospace Industries that were domestically designed and produced. The contract calls for delivery in 2016 of MALE drones capable of being armed.[230]	Yes	Yes	No
78	U.A.E	The United Arab Emirates (UAE) has domestic production of drones and imports drones from the United States.[231] UAE is reportedly in talks to export Adcom Systems Yabhon United 40 Block 5 drones to Algeria and Russia.[232]	Yes	No	No
79	Uganda	Uganda has drones as part of military aid package from the United States to combat al-Shabaab in Somalia.[233] Uganda also imports Orbiter 2 drones from Israel (Aeronautics Defense Systems).[234]	Yes	No	No
80	Ukraine	Ukraine has left-over Soviet-made drones still being used for surveillance.[235]	Yes	No	No

TABLE 1. (*continued*)

	Countries with Drones	Source of Technology	Tier I (Low altitude, long endurance)	Tier II MALE	Tier II+ HALE
81	Uruguay	Uruguay has domestic production of drones.[236]	Yes	No	No
82	Venezuela	Reported has domestic production of drones with the help of Iran, along with direct imports from Iran.[237] Venezuela also reportedly received help with its drones program from Russia and China, and plans to export drones in the near future.[238]	Yes	No	No

	Nascent and non-state actor drones programs	Source of Technology	Tier I Low altitude, long endurance	Tier II MALE	Tier II+ HALE
1	Vietnam	There are reports of mini-drones be constructed with the help of Russia,[239] and separately with Sweden.[240] Vietnam domestically built and tested six drones that were approved for civilian and military use, and has plans to purchase drones from Belarus.[241] Drone engines and propellers are imported from France and Japan.	Yes	?	?
2	Syria	European and US security officials say Iran provided surveillance drones to the Assad regime in Syria to control protestors.[242] There has also been speculation that the drones were domestically produced.[243] Syrian rebels claimed to have captured government surveillance drones.[244]	?	?	?

TABLE 1. (*continued*)

Nascent and non-state actor drones programs	Source of Technology	Tier I Low altitude, long endurance	Tier II MALE	Tier II+ HALE
3 Sudan	Rebels claim that the Sudanese government has imported drones from Iran,[245] which Sudanese officials deny. The UN said in 2009 that video surveillance equipment used in Sudanese drones was sold to Sudan by Iranian businessmen in violation of a UN arms embargo.[246] The UN Special Envoy to South Sudan has urged the UN to consider deploying surveillance drones in the region.[247]	?	?	?
4 Saudi Arabia	In 2010 General Atomics received export licenses to sell an unarmed export version of the Predator to Saudi Arabia, Egypt, the United Arab Emirates, and Morocco.[248] South Africa has also reportedly agreed to help Saudi Arabia develop armed drones.[249]	?	?	?
5 Hezbollah	Hezbollah acquired Iranian-built Ababil unmanned aerial vehicles (drones), capable of carrying an 88-pound warhead for up to 150 miles.[250] Israel says Hezbollah received at least twelve Drones from Iran.[251] Hezbollah claims it manufactured the drones domestically. Israeli and US intelligence sources told NBC News that Hezbollah obtained the drones from Iran and that Iranian soldiers are stationed just across the border to help operate them.[252]	?	?	?
6 Libyan Rebels	From a Canadian company, Libyan rebels bought a surveillance aircraft – essentially a tiny quadrotor with a dangling pod carrying a stabilized-image day- and night-vision camera.[253]	?	?	?

NOTES

1 Corcoran, Mark, "The kill chain: Australia's drone war," ABC *News* Online, June 27, 2012.

2 Gertler, Jeremiah, "U.S. unmanned aerial systems," Congressional Research Service, January 3, 2012.

3 PRNewswire, "Teal Group predicts worldwide UAV market will total $89 billion in its 2012 UAV market profile and forecast," April 11, 2012.

4 Human Rights Watch, "Israel: Gaza airstrikes violated laws of war," February 12, 2013.

5 Shalal-Esa, Andrea, "Airshow – General Atomics sees growing demand for drones," Reuters, July 20, 2010.

6 Entous, Adam, "U.S. plans to arm Italy's drones" *Wall Street Journal*, May 29, 2012.

7 Soncan, Emre, "Turkey to manufacture armed version of national drone," *Today's Zaman*, July 18, 2012.

8 *Turkish Weekly*, "Turkey prepares to launch first domestically made drones," January 15, 2014.

9 Brannen, Kate, "NATO signs $1.7B Global Hawk contract," Defense News, May 21, 2012.

10 Dassault Aviation. www.dassault-aviation.com/en/defense/neuron/introduction/.

11 Zudin, Alexander, "Pictures: Secret Russian UAV design revealed," Flight Global, February 13, 2013.

12 *Hindu*, "UAVs capable of launching weapons soon: DRDO," August 27, 2013.

13 *Independent*, "China to use drones in islands row," Associated Press, September 24, 2012.

14 Page, Jeremy, "China's new drones raise eyebrows," *Wall Street Journal*, November 18, 2010.

15 *Sky News*, "China air show: Drone and fighter jet unveiled," November 13, 2012.

16 *Want China Times*, "Taiwan developing weapons-capable drone," December 7, 2013.

17 Perlez, Jane, "Chinese plan to kill drug lord with drone highlights military advances," *New York Times*, February 20, 2013.

18 Karimi, Nasser, "Bomber drone unveiled by Iran called 'Ambassador of Death,'" *Christian Science Monitor*, August 23, 2010.

19 Associated Press, "Iran unveils new long-range drone," September 25, 2012.

20 Press TV, "Iran mass-produces indigenous Shahed 129 UAV," September 27, 2013.

21 Rozen, Laura, "How the Libyan rebels bought a miniature drone on the Internet," Yahoo News, August 25, 2011.

22 Boyle, Ashley, "The US and its UAVs: A cost-benefit analysis," American Security Project, July 24, 2012.

23 Missile Technology Control Regime, "MTCR guidelines and the equipment, software and technology annex." www.mtcr.info/english/guidelines.html.

24 *UAV Business Review*, "UAV platform categories."

25　Williams, Dan, "Buzz of Israel's drones resonates throughout region," Reuters, December 5, 2011. Wilson, Scott, "In Gaza, lives shaped by drones," *Washington Post*, December 3, 2011.

26　Benn, Aluf, "Who does Israel sell arms to? The defense ministry won't tell," *Haaretz*, January 9, 2014.

27　Morley, Jefferson. "Israel's drones dominance," *Salon*, May 15, 2012.

28　Goldenberg, Tia, "Israel is world's largest drones exporter," *Huffington Post*, July 5, 2013.

29　Entous, Adam, and Julian Barnes. "U.S. pursues sale of armed drones," *Wall Street Journal*, December 15, 2011.

30　Gertler, "U.S. unmanned aerial systems."

31　Singer, Peter W. "Inside China's secret arsenal," *Popular Science*, December 20, 2012.

32　Bhatt, Semu, "India's indigenous drones," *Himal*, October 2010. Page, "China's new drones raise eyebrows."

33　Lorenz, Andreas, Juliane von Mittelstaedt, and Gregor Peter Schmitz, "'Messengers of death': Are drones creating a new global arms race?" *Der Spiegel*, October 21, 2011.

34　Otsuka, Tomohiko, "Yamaha unmanned helicopters can easily be converted to military use; company oblivious about military value," *Tokyo Sankei Shimbun*, August 6, 2006. Miller, Patrick M., and Malinda K. Goodrich, "Mini, micro, and swarming unmanned aerial vehicles: A baseline study," report prepared by Federal Research Division Library of Congress, November 2006.

35　Perlez, "Chinese plan to kill drug lord with drone highlights military advances."

36　BBC, "China 'flies first stealth drones,'" November 22, 2013. Harress, Christopher, "The rise of China's drones fleet and why it may lead to increased tension in Asia," *International Business Times*, January 11, 2014. Doyle, Gerry, "Chinese stealth drones makes first flight," *New York Times*, November 22, 2013.

37　Gertz, Bill, "Game of drones: China stepping up drones deployment," *Washington Free Beacon*, March 26, 2013.

38　Koebler, Jason, "Report: Chinese drones 'swarms' designed to attack American aircraft carriers," *U.S. News*, March 14, 2013.

39　Pasternack, Alex, "Hackers are helping China build cheap clones of America's drones," *Vice: Motherboard*, October 15, 2013.

40　Fiddian, Paul, "Sperwer MkII drones for French army," *Armed Forces International*, June 14, 2012.

41　Pfeffer, Anshel, "France to buy Israeli-made drones, 42 years after it banned weapons sales to Israel," *Haaretz*, July 24, 2011. *World Tribune*, "France using Israeli drones in Mali," February 15, 2013.

42　United Press International, "French Air Force wants more drones," October 21, 2009.

43　Irish, John, and Emmanuel Jerry, "France, Britain agree drones cooperation," Reuters, February 17, 2012.

44 *Huffington Post*, "U.S. readies sale of reaper drones to France," *Agence France-Presse*, July 15, 2013. Franceschi-Bicchierai, Lorenzo, "France will use America drones to spy on al Qaeda," *Mashable*, December 20, 2013. Martin, Guy, "First French Reapers delivered to Niger," *DefenceWeb*, January 13, 2014.

45 Martin, "First French Reapers delivered to Niger."

46 Dahlburg, John-Thor, "Europeans form 'drones club' to compete with U.S.," *USA Today*, November 19, 2013.

47 Flight Global, "Morocco to acquire surplus French Harfangs," January 20, 2014.

48 Yong, William, and Robert F. Worth, "Iran's president unveils new long-range-drones aircraft," *New York Times*, August 22, 2010. Black, Ian, "Iran unveils bomber drones that aims to deliver peace and friendship," *Guardian*, August 22, 2010.

49 Ynetnews, "Iran unveils short-range reconnaissance drones," September 28, 2013.

50 Ynetnews, "Iran unveils new drones: 'World will be awestruck,'" September 27, 2013. Press TV, "Iran mass-produces indigenous Shahed 129 UAV.'"

51 RT, "Iran unveils 'biggest' attack drones with '2,000 kilometer range,'" November 19, 2013. Tempo, "Iran ready for drones war," November 22, 2013. BBC, "Iran unveils new 'biggest' drones," November 18, 2013.

52 Dehghan, Saeed Kamali, "Iran gives Russia copy of US ScanEagle drones as proof of mass production," *Guardian*, October 21, 2013. Powell, Stephen, "Iran says it has brought down a foreign spy drones," Reuters, February 23, 2013. Jaffe, Greg, and Thomas Erdbrink, "Iran says it downed U.S. stealth drones; Pentagon acknowledges aircraft downing," *Washington Post*, December 4, 2011. Press TV, "Iran researchers build new unmanned aerial vehicle," December 25, 2013.

53 Mzoudi, Anouar, "Algerian researchers manufacture Algeria's first unmanned plane," *Morocco News Tribune*, March 11, 2013. BBC, "U.S. reportedly refuses to sell drones to Algeria," April 12, 2010.

54 Institute for National Security Studies, *Military Balance Files*, "Algeria," p. 11.

55 Engelbrecht, Leon, "Denel develops new UAV," ITWeb Innovations, April 3, 2008. del Fresno, Daved, "Algeria shows interest in Yabhon," *Drones Actual*, November 19, 2013.

56 *Dawn*, "British report reveals Israel's arms exports to Pakistan," June 25, 2013.

57 DefenceWeb, "Algeria acquires Chinese artillery; evaluating drones," January 27, 2014.

58 Homeland Security Newswire, "Hezbollah drones represents changing technological landscape for Israel," October 19, 2012.

59 Aeronautics Ltd., "Aerostar drones." www.aeronautics-sys.com/aerostar_tactical_drones. Homeland Security Newswire, "Hezbollah drones represents changing technological landscape for Israel."

60 Cattan, Nacha, and Taylor Barnes, "Spread of drones programs in Latin America sparks call for code of conduct," *Christian Science Monitor*, May 20, 2011.

Glickhouse, Rachel, "Explainer: Drones in Latin America" (Argentina), Americas Society/Council of the America, August 28, 2013.

61 Serrano, Rodrigo Lara, "No man's air: Military and police drones proliferate in Latin America," Worldcrunch, December 2, 2012.

62 News AM, "Armenia-made drones operated during CSTO military drills," September 19, 2012.

63 PanARMENIAN.net, "Armenia to export drones to Denmark," October 3, 2013.

64 Ratnam. Gopal, "General Atomic wins approval to sell first Predator drones in Middle East," *Bloomberg*, July 20, 2010. Maj. Gaub, Darin L., *The children of Aphrodite: The proliferation and threat of unmanned aerial vehicles in the twenty-first century* (Fort Leavenworth, KS: School of Advanced Military Studies, US Army Command and General Staff College, 2011). Cox, Timothy H., Christopher J. Nagy, Mark A. Skoog, and Ivan A. Somers, *Civil drones capability assessment*, draft version prepared for NASA, December 2004. Corcoran, "The kill chain." Miller and Goodrich, "Mini, micro, and swarming unmanned aerial vehicles: A baseline study."

65 Rosenberg, Zach, "Australian interest in MQ-4C Triton moves forward," Flight Global, May 16, 2013. Corcoran, Mark, "Australia moves to buy $3b spy drones fleet," ABC *News*, September 4, 2012.

66 Cochrane, Joe, "At Asia air show, plenty of competition for sales of drones," *New York Times*, February 16, 2014.

67 *Huffington Post*, "Austria: Drones to be used for surveillance at home and abroad," Associated Press, June 4, 2012.

68 sUAS News, "Austrian army selects Cassidian Tracker mini UAVs," October 16, 2013.

69 Schiebel, "Camcopter S-100," www.schiebel.net/Products/Unmanned-Air-Systems/ CAMCOPTER-S-100/Introduction.aspx. Schiebel is an Austrian-based Company producing the Camcopter S-100 drones since 2003.

70 *Haaretz*, "Israel signs $1.6 billion arms deal with Azerbaijan," Associated Press, February 26, 2012. Clayton, Michael, "Drones violence along Armenian–Azerbaijani border could lead to war," Global Post, October 23, 2012.

71 Karabakh, "Azerbaijan steps up national drones production," September 22, 2011. United Press International, "Azeris get Israel drones built under license," October 7, 2011.

72 Israel's Homeland Security Home, "More Israeli mad UAS to Azerbaijan," June 20, 2013. United Press International, "Azeris get Israel drones built under license."

73 United Press International, "Russia to build mini drones," March 20, 2012.

74 Smith, Matthew, "Belarus to begin drones production in Turkmenistan," IHS Jane's 360, November 10, 2013. Adamowski, Jaroslaw, "Belarus, Turkmenistan to jointly produce drones," Defense News, November 6, 2013.

75 Thanh Nien News, "Vietnam to buy unmanned aerial vehicles from Belarus," May 17, 2013.

76 Trimble, "Trimble Acquires Gatewing to Expand its Survey Solutions to Include Aerial Mapping," April 6, 2012.

77 Cohen, Gili, "Israel reveals more than $7 billion in arms sales, but few names," *Haaretz*, January 9, 2014.

78 Hinshaw, Drew, "For African generals, drones are the latest thing," *Wall Street Journal*, September 27, 2013.

79 AEL Systems is a Brazilian company that manufactures drones. www.ael.com.br/ing/ael_sistemas.php. United Press International, "UAVs tested for Brazilian police," August 3, 2009. Liphshiz, Cnann, "Brazil under fire for spending $350 million on Israeli drones," *Haaretz*, January 6, 2010. Otis, John, "Brazil leads the way on global commercial drones boom," Global Post, January 6, 2013. Cattan and Barnes, "Spread of drones programs in Latin America sparks calls for code of conduct."

80 United Press International, "Argentina plans more defense manufacturing," April 18, 2012.

81 Aydin Albayrak, Ankara, "Turkey's homemade Corvette, drones attract Brazil's attention," *Today's Zaman*, August 20, 2012.

82 Otis, "Brazil leads the way on global commercial drones boom." Liphshiz, "Brazil under fire for spending $350 million on Israeli drones."

83 Dalamagkidis K., K. P. Valavanis, and L.A. Piegel, *On Integrating Unmanned Aircraft Systems into National Airspace System* (Heidelberg: Springer, 2012), p. 240.

84 Northrup Grumman, "NATO AGS." www.northropgrumman.com/Capabilities/NATOAGS/Pages/default.aspx.

85 North Atlantic Treaty Organization, "Alliance Ground Surveillance," www.nato.int/cps/en/natolive/topics_48892.htm. Army Recognition, "Bulgarian army would like to create first reconnaissance drones unit to join AGS NATO program," July 31, 2012.

86 BBC, "Uganda and Burundi to get US drones to fight Islamists," June 28, 2011. Baldor, Lolita C., "Pentagon sending $45M in equipment to Somalia," Associated Press, June 26, 2011.

87 Brewster, Murray, "Ottowa considers high altitude drones for Arctic surveillance, *Globe and Mail*, May 30, 2012.

88 CBC *News*, "See Canada to acquire attack drones: Air Chief," March 6, 2009.

89 Pugliese, David, "Chile's army orders SpyLite mini-drones system," *Ottawa Citizen*, April 6, 2013. Cattan and Barnes, "Spread of drones programs in Latin America sparks calls for code of conduct." Sanders, "An Israeli military innovation." United Press International, "Chile orders mini-UAVs," April 5, 2013.

90 McClatchyDC, "Increasing drones usage in Latin America," November 4, 2013. RT, "Latin American drones use on the rise and unregulated-report," November 5, 2013

91 Egozi, Arie, "Chilean Navy considers Hermes 900 deal," Flight Global, October 7, 2013.

92 Arancibia, Juan Carlos, "Report: Chile acquires Hermes 900 drones," Chile's Defense & Military, May 19, 2011. Cattan and Barnes, "Spread of drones programs in Latin America sparks calls for code of conduct." Sanders, "An Israeli Military Innovation."

93 Fox News Latino, "Colombia to develop its own drones program to combat drug-trafficking," October 26, 2012. Fox, Edward, "Colombia producing its own drones," *In Sight Crime*, October 26, 2012.

94 Cattan, Nacha, and Taylor Barnes, "Colombia mulls buying more Israeli Drones," United Press International, January 23, 2012.

95 DeYoung, Karen, "WikiLeaks: Colombia began using U.S. drones for counter-terrorism in 2006," *Washington Post*, March 23, 2011. Glickhouse, Rachel, "Explainer: Drones in Latin America" (Colombia), Americas Society/Council of the America, August 28, 2013.

96 Sanchez, W. Alejandro, "Latin America puts forward a mixed picture on the use of drones in the region," Council on Hemispheric Affairs, October 8, 2013. Fernandez, Belen, "The purity of drones," *Al Jazeera*, November 10, 2012.

97 Cattan and Barnes, "Colombia mulls buying more Israeli Drones."

98 Global Post, "Colombia rolls out flight simulator for drones," May 10, 2013. Robbins, Seth, "Colombia develops drones technology to fight drugs, rebels, illegal mining," Diálogo Global, August 1, 2013.

99 Drones Global, "Elbit Hermes 450."

100 Pawlak, Justyna, "NATO to buy U.S.-made unmanned drones aircraft." Reuters, February 15, 2012.

101 United Press International, "Denmark, Sweden eager to buy and sell arms," September 25, 2009.

102 Radio Netherlands Worldwide, "Denmark borrows Dutch Drones," April 12, 2012.

103 Rosenberg, Zach, "Denmark signs deal for handheld Puma drones," Flight Global, June 12, 2012. Eshel, Tamir, "Sweden, Denmark opt for PUMA AE, Wasp mini-UAVs," Defense-Update, June 12, 2012.

104 sUAS News, "Armenia to export UAS to Denmark," October 4, 2013.

105 ScandAsia, "Danish firm launches 'good drones' in Philippines typhoon cleanup," December 3, 2013.

106 PanARMENIAN Net, "Armenia to export drones to Denmark."

107 Army Recognition, "Sky-Watch Huginn X1 X2 drones unmanned aerial system." Pugliese, David, "Aim, fire – and fly a drone," Defense News, June 24, 2013.

108 Institute for National Security Studies, *Military Balance Files*, "Israel," p. 5. Cattan and Barnes, "Colombia mulls buying more Israeli Drones." Lorenz et al., "'Messengers of death.'"

109 Sanchez, "Latin America puts forward a mixed picture on the use of drones in the region.

110 Ratnam, "General Atomics wins approval to sell first Predator drones in Middle East."

111 Mortimer, Gary, "Egypt: Nation produces drones in cooperation with China," sUAS News, May 18, 2012. Strategy Page, "Warplanes: Egypt builds Chinese drones," May 24, 2012.

112 Ahram, "Egypt to import Turkish-made aerial drones: Report," November 21, 2012.

113 Embassy of Estonia to the United States, "New U.S. tool in Estonian NATO arsenal," October 25, 2010.

114 Army Recognition, "Estonia plans to purchase Global Hawk drones to increase its military reconnaissance capabilities," January 11, 2013.

115 ELI Military Simulations, "Unmanned aerial system SWAN III." Clayton, Nicholas, "How Russia and Georgia's 'little war' started a drones arms race," *MINNPost*, October 23, 2012.

116 Tesfa-Alem Tekle, "Ethiopia produces first military drones aircraft," allAfrica, February 14, 2013. Chute Systems, "Ethiopia buys UAVs." Solomon, D., "Ethiopian Army to get BlueBird drones," *Ethiopian News*, April 12, 2011. Whitlock, Craig, "U.S. drones base in Ehtiopia is operational," *Washington Post*, October 27, 2011.

117 BBC, "US flies drones from Ethiopia to fight Somali militants," October 28, 2011. Whitlock, "U.S. drones base in Ehtiopia is operational."

118 Jantti, Bruno, "Despite opposition, Finland proceeds with Israel arms deal," Electronic Intifada, July 20, 2011. Opall-Rome, Barbara, "Israeli company wins Finnish mini UAV Bid," Defense News, May 16, 2012.

119 Office of the President of Georgia, "The president of Georgia was introduced to the Georgian-made unmanned air system," press release, October 4, 2012. Kucera, Joshua, "Georgia shows off new drones," *Eurasianet*, April 10, 2012.

120 Chivers, C. J. "U.N. blames Russia for downed drones," *New York Times*, May 27, 2008. RIA Novosti, "Georgia to test first domestically designed drones," April 9, 2012. Mortimer, Gary, "Israel sold Georgian drones codes to Russia," sUAS News, Feb. 29, 2012.

121 ELI Military Simulations, "Unmanned aerial system SWAN III." Clayton, "How Russia and Georgia's 'little war' started a drones arms race."

122 Tarantola, Andrew, "The stealthy Barracuda UAV is Germany's future flying force," *Gizmodo*, October 17, 2013.

123 Silverstein, Richard (website), "Israeli drones leased to German Army in Afghanistan hacked and crashed," November 12, 2013. Andreas et al., "'Messengers of death.'"

124 Defense Industry Daily, "RQ-4 Euro Hawk drones readying for takeoff," October 13, 2011.

125 PressTV, "Germany cancels USD 1.3 billion purchase of US-made drones," May 15, 2013.

126 Wastson, Leon, "Europe forms a 'drones club' to develop unmanned aircraft to rival the US and Israel's military technology," *Daily Mail*, November 19, 2013.

127 Editor, "Greece orders two additional Sperwer drones systems from Sagem Defense," Defence Talk, June 19, 2006. Fiddian, Paul, "Sperwer MkII Drones for French Army," Armed Forces International, June 14, 2012. Army-Technology, "Sperwer tactical unmanned air vehicle, France."

128 Rettman, Andrew, "Seven EU states create military drones 'club,'" *euobserver*, November 20, 2013.

129 *Budapest Times*, "Hungarian drones create a buzz," November 12, 2012.

130 Military Factory, "The Israeli Elbit Systems Skylark drones series has taken hold in the inventories of several world powers," July 9, 2013.

131 Gormley, Dennis M., "New developments in unmanned air vehicles and land-attack cruise missiles" in *The Stockholm International Peace Institute Yearbook* (2003). Politics (All Hungary Media Group), "Drones for Hungarian military use in the making, report says," June 21, 2013. Hungarian Ambiance, "The all Hungarian made military drones will be deployed in Afghanistan this year," June 21, 2013.

132 *Pakistan Today*, "Indian armed forces building deadly drones arsenal," February 5, 2013.

133 Pandit, Rajat, "India lines up Israeli drones in race with Pak," *Times of India*, March 26, 2010. Dvorin, Tova, "India to buy 15 drones from Israel," Arutz Sheva, December 30, 2013. Space War, "Israel IAI wins $958M India drones deal," October 12, 2012.

134 Live Fist Defence, "Exclusive: First official impressions of India's AURA UCAV," June 12, 2012. Bhatt, "India's indigenous drones."

135 Keck, Zachary, "India eyes drones-launched smart bombs," Diplomat, August 29, 2013.

136 Sagar, Pradip R., "DNA exclusive: 49 drones to keep an eye on China and Pakistan borders," DNA India, September 30, 2013.

137 *Jerusalem Post*, "Indonesia to buy four Israeli spy drones," October 22, 2006.

138 Lamb, Kate, "Indonesia readies mass production of drones," *Voice of America*, April 30, 2013. *Jakarta Globe*, "Don't worry about drones' source, Indonesia defense ministry says," February 8, 2012. Malaysia Flying Herald, "Indonesia strives towards full squadron of Wulung drones," May 8, 2013.

139 Markey, Patrick, and Ahmed Rasheed, "Iraq turns to U.S. drones to protect oil platforms," Reuters, May 21, 2012.

140 Ratnam, Gopal, "U.S. providing drones and missiles to aid Iraq in terror fight," *Bloomberg*, December 26, 2013. Carey, Bill, "U.S. speeds delivery of drones, Hellfires to Iraq," AIN Online, January 10, 2014. American Forces Press Service, "DoD speeds delivery of surveillance assets to Iraq," US Department of Defense, January 7, 2014.

141 Kington, Tom, "UAE ups its stake in drones-maker Piaggio Aero," Defense News, November 15, 2013.

142 Govers, III, Francis X. "Hammerhead drones takes to the skies over Italy," Gizmag, November 21, 2013.

143 *Guardian*, "Drones by country: Who has all the drones?" August 3, 2012.

144 Schmitt, Eric. "U.S. proposal would arm Italy's drones," *New York Times*, May 29, 2012. Kelley, Michael, "The Italian drones fleet you didn't know about is getting Hellfire weapons from the US," *Business Insider*, May 30, 2012.

145 Butler, Amy, "Italy looking to develop black male drones," *Aviation Week*, May 20, 2013. Schmitt, "U.S. proposal would arm Italy's drones."

146 Watson, "Europe forms a 'drones club' to develop unmanned aircraft to rival the US and Israel's military technology." Schmitt, "U.S. proposal would arm Italy's drones." Butler, "Italy looking to develop black male drones."

147 O'Sullivan, Arieh, "Israel grapples with blowback from booming drones industry," Global Post, October 16, 2012.

148 Ibid. BBC, "Ivory Coast wants drones to monitor Liberia border," April 17, 2013.

149 Knapp, Alex. "Japanese defense ministry develops spherical flying drones," *Forbes*, November 3, 2011.

150 Ortega, Jaime, "Japan purchases U.S. drones," *Daily Journalist*, November 4, 2013.

151 Sekuguchi, Toko, "Japan to protect islands with drones and amphibious units," *Wall Street Journal*, December 17, 2013. BBC, "Japan boosts military forces to counter China," December 17, 2013.

152 *Japan Daily Press*, "Japan to launch unmanned Global Hawk surveillance drones in fiscal 2015," January 3, 2014.

153 United Press International, "Jordan works with Selex for drones," December 2, 2009. King Abdullah II Design and Development Bureau, "Drones production." Military Factory, "Jordan Falcon light reconnaissance aerial vehicle (drones)."

154 Institute for National Security Studies, *Military Balance Files*, "Israel," p. 6.

155 BNews, "Kazakhstan to buy Russian drones," September 28, 2012.

156 Kucera, Josh, "With Belarus venture, Turkmenistan to become newest Eurasian drones manufacturer," Security Assistance Monitor, November 6, 2013.

157 Sagem (Safran Group), "Sagem and Kazakhstan Engineering sign an agreement to create joint venture for drones," November 2, 2010.

158 Russian Aviation, "The Ministry of Defense of Kazakhstan will purchase drones from Irkut Corporation," October 3, 2012.

159 Blyenburgh and Co., "UAS: The global perspective" in *2010–2011 UAS Yearbook*, 8th ed. (June 2010, online).

160 Airforce Technology, "Penguin V unmanned aerial vehicle (drones), Latvia."

161 UAV Factory, "Unmanned platforms and subsystems."

162 Airforce Technology, "Penguin V unmanned aerial vehicle (drones), Latvia."

163 United Press International, "Lebanon gets Raven mini drones from U.S.," March 23, 2009.

164 *Libya Herald*, "Libyan drones take to skies for the first time," March 17, 2013. Libyan Embassy–London, "Radar project agreed," April 15, 2013.

165 15min.lt, "Lithuania to contribute 4.8 million euros to NATO's unmanned aircraft program," May 23, 2012.

166 Ibid. North Atlantic Treaty Organization, "Alliance Ground Surveillance."

167 Musa, Zazali. "CTRM eyes regional market for its Drones," Star Online, June 21, 2012.

168 Tan, Marsha, "Najib: Army set to use made-in-Malaysia drones," Star Online, May 16, 2007.

169 Brahmand, "Malaysia to produce indigenous drones is 2010," December 3, 2009.

170 Composites Technology Research Malaysia, *ALUDRA SR-08*. www.ctrm.com.my/ps_alu_sr.php.

171 Ratnam, "General Atomics wins approval to sell first Predator drones in Middle East."

172 Royal Moroccan Armed Forces, "Industry: First Moroccan-made drones," January 17, 2014.

173 World Tribune, "Morocco said to buy Israeli-designed drones from France," January 20, 2014. Rojkes Dombe, Ami, "Morocco acquired IAI's Heron," Israel Defense.

174 DutchNews, "Use of drone aircraft by police is increasingly secretive," March 28, 2013.

175 Fiorenza, Nicholas, "Reaper goes Dutch," *Aviation Week*, November 21, 2013.

176 Hawkeye Drones. www.hawkeyeuav.com/.

177 *Chicago Tribune*, "Obama deploys 100 US troops to Niger to set up drones base," Reuters, February 22, 2013.

178 O'Sullivan, "Israel grapples with blowback from booming drone industry."

179 Atherton, Kelsey D., "Nigeria shows off its first drones," *Popular Science*, December 18, 2013.

180 Nikala, Oscar, "Nigerian commissions new drones," Defence Web, December 19, 2013.

181 *Military & Aerospace*, "Army asks Norwegian company to design Black Hornet pocket drones helicopter for foot soldiers," 2013.

182 Cox et al., "Civil drones capability assessment."

183 Stewart, Phil, "US to supply Pakistan with 85 mini-drones," Reuters, April 21, 2011.

184 United Press International, "Pakistan to make its own drones," August 31, 2009.

185 O'Sullivan, "Israel grapples with blowback from booming drone industry."

186 *New York Times*, "Pakistan: domestic drones ready," November 25, 2013.

187 Craig, Tim, and Haq Nawaz Khan, "Pakistan unveils its own military drones, as protests continue against U.S. attacks," *Washington Post*, November 25, 2013.

188 Cordova, Rogelio, "Panama boost investments in security," Dialogo, June 30, 2011. Newsroom Panama, "Panama looking at $93 million a year for surveillance drones," February 8, 2011.

189 Glickhouse, Rachel, "Explainer: Drones in Latin America" (Peru), Americas Society/Council of the America, August 28, 2013.

190 Sanchez, "COHA Report: Drones in Latin America."

191 Magdirila, Phoebe, "In the Philippines, drones are used for news reporting and rescue operations," Techinasia, January 22, 2014.

192 Felongco, Gilbert P., "Philippines admits use of drones against anti-government forces," Gulfnews, December 21, 2013.

193 Romero, Alexis, "Philippine military to acquire drones," *Philippine Star*, December 13, 2013.

194 Egozi, Arie, "Will the real drones revolution begin in Poland?" Israel Defense, August 27, 2012.

195 Uavision. www.uavision.com/.

196 Ibid.

197 Bogdanov, Konstantin, "A Russian drone with a complicated history," Ria Novosti, August 11, 2011.

198 United Press International, "Israel sells drones to Russia, on condition," June 26, 2009. *Haaretz*, "Russia in talks to buy Israeli-made spy drones," Reuters, December 8, 2009.

199 United Press International, "Russia to build mini drones."

200 Gertz, Bill, "Russia to deploy long-range attack drones by 2016," *Washington Free Beacon*, November 13, 2013.

201 Chow, Denise, "20-ton attack drones under development in Russia," NBC *News*, October 7, 2013.

202 Defence Talk, "Russia to test UAE-Made drones next year," December 5, 2013.

203 Balkan Monitor, "Drones: Serbian drones solution 'Sparrow,'" January 29, 2010.

204 Lucey, Danielle, "Singapore airshow 2012: American companies stand their ground, Asia-Pacific and Israel stand up new drones," Association for Unmanned Vehicle Systems International, February 16, 2012. Warwick, Graham, "Singapore's Skyblade drones operational," *Aviation Week*.

205 Etair-Drones. www.etair-uav.com/.

206 Pravda, "Army bought drones, tried to hide it," November 7, 2009.

207 Mining-Technology, *Pushing the limits of mine-mapping technology: Drones over the Andes*, September 24, 2012.

208 Roelf, Wendell, "S. Africa targets bigger share of missile industry," Reuters, September 22, 2010.

209 United Press International, "Saudis 'turn to South Africa for UAVs,'" April 16, 2013.

210 Barrie, Allison, "South Korea developing 'kamikaze' drones," Fox *News*, October 9, 2012.

211 Andreas et al., "'Messengers of death.'"

212 Wolf, Jim. "Exclusive: Obama moves to sell Northrop drones to South Korea" Reuters, August 31, 2011.

213 Perrett, Bradley, "South Korean Global Hawks set for 2017–2019 delivery," sUAS News, November 11, 2013.

214 Lorenz et al., "'Messengers of death.'"

215 Watson, "Europe forms a 'drones club' to develop unmanned aircraft to rival the US and Israel's military technology."

216 Martin, Guy. "Asian Region UAV Capability on the Rise." *Defence Review Asia*, December 20, 2012. Lorenz et al., "'Messengers of death.'"

217 Nylander, Johan, "Combat jetmaker Saab plans to build drones," Swedish Wire, November 24, 2013.

218 Yahoo News, "Sweden to provide drones technology to Vietnam," November 21, 2012.

219 Jaberg, Samuel, "Successful takeoff for Swiss commercial drones," Swissinfo, May 20, 2013.

220 Cenciiotti, David, "New image of Neuron European stealth killer drone's flight trials emerges," Aviationist, December 7, 2013.

221 Egozi, Arie, "Switzerland seeking new drones," Israel Defense, May 3, 2012.

222 UMS Group. www.swiss-uav.com/.

223 Waldron, Greg, "Taiwan looks to develop advanced unmanned systems," Flight Global, August 12, 2011.

224 *Want China Times*, "Taiwan developing weapons-capable drone," December 7, 2013.

225 United Press International, "Thailand signs up for drones mine-hunters," December 15, 2011.

226 Thai Intel Diplomacy News, "Thai intel: Thailand to develop advance drones to be ASEAN's 'droneshub,'" July 2, 2013.

227 Kowlessar, Geisha, "Drones go into action next year," Guardian Media, September 12, 2013. McClatchyDC, "Increasing drones usage in Latin America."

228 Tunisia Aero Technologies Industries S.A. http://tati-uas.com/.

229 Institute for National Security Studies, *Military Balance Files*, "Israel," p 7.

230 Journal of the Turkish Weekly, "Turkey prepares to launch first domestically made drones," January 15, 2014.

231 Trimble, Stephen. "Dubai 09: UAE-designed drones almost ready to fly," Flight Global, November 17, 2009. Associated Press, "UAE to acquire $200 million worth of US drones," Times of Israel, February 18, 2013.

232 North Africa Post, "Algeria: Reinforcing aerial defense," November 19, 2013. Awad, Mustafa, "Russia to conduct test flights of Emirati Drones," Defense News, December 9, 2013.

233 BBC, "Uganda and Burundi to get US drones to fight Islamists." Baldor, "Pentagon sending $45M in equipment to Somalia."

234 Egozi, Arie, "Uganda Army to acquire Orbiter drones," Flight Global, February 2011.

235 Niiler, Eric, "Ukraine Reviving Retro Drones to Spy on Rebels," Discovery, August 8, 2014.

236 Glickhouse, Rachel, "Explainer: Drones in Latin America" (Uruguay), Americas Society/Council of the America, August 28, 2013.

237 Ellsworth, Brian. "Venezuela says building drones with Iran's help," Reuters, June 14, 2012. Paraszczuk, Joanna, "Iran admits exporting drones tech to Venezuela," *Jerusalem Post*, December 12, 2012.

238 Langlois, Jill, "Venezuela building drones with Iran, Russia, China," Global Post, June 15, 2012.

239 United Press International, "Russia to build mini drones."

240 Yahoo News, "Sweden to provide drones technology to Vietnam." Voice of Vietnam, "Sweden helps Vietnam manufacture Drones," November 20, 2012.

241 Wadhwaney, Rohit, "Vietnam builds six drones," Asia Pacific Defense Forum, June 6, 2013. Keck, Zachary, "OK drones: Vietnam enters the drones market," Diplomat, May 21, 2013.

242 Hosenball, Mark, "Iran helping Assad to put down protests: Officials," Reuters, March 23, 2012.

243 Ben-Yishai, Ron, "Syrian-made drones spy on rebel strongholds," Ynet News, March 7, 2012.

244 Arnott, David R., "Syrian rebels claim they captured government drones, reveal images found inside," NBC *News*, November 13, 2013.

245 United Press International, "Iranian-made drones downed in South Sudan" March 14, 2012.

246 Charbonneau, Louis, "Iranians linked to banned drones videos in Darfur–UN," Reuters, November 6, 2009.

247 Nichols, Michell, "U.N. urged to consider drones, gunships for South Sudan mission," Reuters, July 8, 2013.

248 Ratnam, "General Atomic wins approval to sell first Predator drones in Middle East."

249 United Press International, "Saudis 'turn to South Africa for Drones.'"

250 La Franchi, Peter, "Iranian-made Ababil-T Hezbollah drones shot down by Israeli fighter in Lebanon crisis," Flight Global, August 15, 2006.

251 "Hizbullah's worrisome weapon," *Newsweek*, September 10, 2006.

252 Myers, Lisa, "Hezbollah drones threatens Israel," NBC *News*, April 12, 2005.

253 Austen, Ian, "Libyan rebels reportedly used tiny Canadian surveillance drone," *New York Times*, August 24, 2011.

PART IV

DRONES AND THE FUTURE OF WAR

17

No One Feels Safe

"ADAM KHAN"[*]

I am thirty-seven. I run a medical supply store in the Miran Shah bazaar in North Waziristan. I have been going to this bazaar almost all my adult life. From my village, Datta Khel, west of the capital, I often travel by pickup truck to the bazaar, sometimes hanging on with dozens of others.

Along with the noise of daily life in the bazaar, I have now grown accustomed to another sound.

A steady humming. This is the sound of CIA drones.

The drones have been hovering above the skies of Waziristan for several years. Their presence is a constant element of our lives. And everyone knows that they frequently fire missiles.

Personally I am not afraid of the drones.

I am neither a Taliban nor an al-Qaeda.

But, I fear becoming part of the "collateral damage" when missiles from the drones hit a car in the bazaar, a mosque, or a school.

I don't want to be at the wrong place, at the wrong time, or find myself with the wrong people.

What if I am standing near a car with tinted glass in the bazaar on my way to the shop and a missile hits the occupants of the car with some target inside?

That is my worst fear.

In 2006, I was a government contractor building a small road in my village. I remember that was when the United States had increased their flights over Waziristan and we started to see and hear the drones.

In the last few years the number of drones in the air and the number of attacks on the ground seem to be increasing. Many of the attacks focus on the

---

[*] This interview was conducted, edited, and prepared for publication by Pir Zubair Shah.

tribal area of North Waziristan in the area of Datta Khel, which is where my village is located.

This is the home of the Waziri tribes of Waziristan.

There, the most powerful political leader is Hafiz Gul Bahadur, a Taliban commander. You could even say that he rules the area.

After the fall of the Taliban regime in Afghanistan in 2001, many of the al-Qaeda and Afghan Taliban commanders moved to the region where I live. Some like the Haqqanis were already here. They had a house on the outskirts of Miran Shah, the capital of North Waziristan, and ran a religious school and a training center in the middle of town.

The drones have killed a lot of high-value al-Qaeda and Haqqani Network commanders. And they say the drones have also killed most of the top Pakistani Taliban leadership.

I don't object to this program.

I like the technology. It is precise and effective. There are many people that support drones because of their precision.

Also, what is the alternative? Military operations? They are bad too. How many people would be killed then?

Some say that control over drones should be handed to the Pakistani government. I am not sure. Then, Pakistan would kill only its enemies, and not necessarily the enemies of the Americans. But then again, Pakistan has been complaining that this is what the Americans are doing now. However, just because the drones are effective in killing targets doesn't mean that there are not real problems with these strikes.

One of the biggest issues with drones in North Waziristan is when innocent people are killed.

When this happens their families do not get any compensation from anybody. At least with other types of attacks that kill civilians, the families receive some compensation from the government.

So why is that not the case with the victims of drone strikes?

What if the sole breadwinner of the family is among those killed? Then it is difficult for the family to live without any type of support. They suffer for no fault of their own.

Another problem is the retaliation from militants who are attacked by drones. They often accuse locals of spying against them. They have abducted and killed many people. Many of those killed include prominent tribal elders and their deaths have a deep impact on the families and tribes.

In many cases, individuals accused of spying for a drone target are picked up a few days after an attack. And sometimes the militants kill someone for a different reason and then use a drone attack as an excuse.

But drones are not the only problem. There are many other problems that affect our lives. For example, the Pakistani military imposes a curfew in our area every Saturday and Sunday. And there are specific curfews that are sometimes imposed during the week. When this happens, the roads are closed to any type of movement.

Then, from dusk until dawn you can't even drive a pregnant woman to the hospital. The curfews affect local businesses and schools. They increase unemployment.

Perhaps the biggest difficulty of all is that we live in an environment of constant fear.

No one feels safe, whether he is a driver, a student, or a shopkeeper like me.

That is why people have been leaving the region.

There is so much uncertainty.

The only certain thing is death.

And, here, death comes in so many different ways.

18

"Drones" Now and What to Expect Over the Next Ten Years

WERNER J. A. DAHM

1. REMOTELY PILOTED AIRCRAFT AND THE CHANGING NATURE OF WARFARE

There is a great deal of discussion these days about the use of remotely piloted aircraft (RPAs) and how they are changing the nature of warfare. However, much of the public debate on these issues reflects a lack of awareness about how the systems are actually operated, as well as how they will become more transformative over the next decade and beyond. This is partly a reflection of a larger problem encountered with the introduction of new technologies; namely, that the rates of innovation and implementation often outpace the general public's understanding of what is being developed and for what purposes these technologies may be used.

Many current concerns regarding what are often colloquially referred to as "drones" involve the idea that these vehicles are "unmanned," though this is, in fact, inaccurate. While it is true that these systems do not have pilots in the vehicle, most of these systems today are anything but unmanned. In fact, the manpower burdens that they have created, albeit with tremendous improvements in capabilities, are quite substantial.[1] This is true with regard to the ground-based pilots that fly these aircraft, as well as for the associated sensor operators, ground crews, and maintenance staff. This is especially true for those involved in the processing, exploration, and dissemination (PED) functions of managing the tremendous amounts of intelligence, surveillance, and reconnaissance (ISR) data that are produced by these systems. Altogether this produces a manpower footprint per system that is actually much larger than what it takes to keep an F-15 up in the air.[2]

So, the way that RPAs are staffed reflects substantive changes in military technology. In fact, the current platforms – such as the MQ-1 and the MQ-9 – are only the beginning of a future of innovation and technological advancement that will enable the United States to significantly expand its capabilities in the very near-term and, more importantly, over the next ten years.

2. HUMANS AND THE F2T2EA KILL CHAIN

The role of humans in what is called the "kill chain" is one of the most relevant issues in the development of emerging military technologies. Some descriptions of these systems suggest that drones are robots that can operate autonomously and kill without direct human interaction. This is not accurate; RPAs do not kill autonomously.

From my position as the former chief scientist of the US Air Force (USAF), there is nothing in our roadmap – and this plan extends twenty years into the future – that involves autonomous strikes. A human being will be in the kill chain for as far as we are looking into the future.[3]

That said, one might be concerned about potential adversaries that may not place the same cultural or legal burdens on themselves. Certainly, RPA development is well underway in many countries that have significant militaries. For instance, China has ramped up development of its own fleet of RPAs and there are indications that these may be deployed in foreign criminal operations.[4] Perhaps even more worrying is RPA use by non-state actors. For example, Hezbollah has already employed crude drone technology.[5] It is certain that in the coming years RPAs will become a ubiquitous presence in military arsenals across the globe, and it remains to be seen how they will be employed operationally.[6]

While other forces may explore autonomous RPAs that remove humans from the kill chain, nothing in the US military's plans suggest that we are taking the cultural step toward "full autonomy." More importantly, it is not only cultural resistance to fully autonomous lethal strikes that has led to this policy position; there are also purely technical reasons to avoid fully autonomous lethal strikes.

Understanding why this is so requires an engagement with what is known as the F2T2EA kill chain, which stands for "find, fix, track, target, engage, and assess." General Ronald R. Fogleman, USAF Chief of Staff, first coined this term in a 1996 speech before an Air Force Association symposium.[7] For some time it served only as an unofficial concept, until it was adopted as part of official USAF targeting policy in 2006.[8] The F2T2EA chain describes a sequential process that is followed when engaging potential targets and helps outline the current and potential roles of human operators, as well as autonomous capabilities in each step of the process.

The first step in this chain is the "find" phase, which entails using ISR to detect an entity of interest. Commanders may immediately identify some entities as targets because they have already been defined in the targeting process, while others may be clearly identified as not being targets and may be put on a "no strike" list. The remaining entities are deemed "emerging targets," which require additional ISR and analysis to determine whether or not they can be listed as targets. This review process continues until the entity is either cleared as not a target; designated a probable target but not one requiring dynamic targeting; or is designated a probable target that is also a "time-sensitive target" (TST), which necessitates continuing the F2T2EA process. This review process can occur in the span of a few minutes.[9]

The "fix" phase confirms an emerging target as worthy of potential engagement and establishes the location of the target. Fixing the potential target in this sense can often pose significant challenges. It requires ISR sufficient to identify the positions of either stationary or mobile targets at any time, under any weather conditions, and in any terrain to a degree of accuracy necessary to engage weapon systems. Additionally, a target may be identified as a TST during this stage, requiring a determination of the target's window of vulnerability. Under the most favorable circumstances, fixing a target can occur nearly simultaneously with finding it, particularly where detection of the target is achieved by the same system that will engage it.[10] Next, the target is "tracked" and its activity is observed until an engagement decision is finalized.[11]

As the target is "tracked," the "targeting" step finalizes the desired effect against the target. This last step is highly time consuming,[12] as it requires operations personnel to ensure an attack on the target complies with target restrictions (including collateral damage), military guidance, the laws of war, and the rules of engagement. Additionally, it matches available assets against the desired effect, a process involving assessment of the operational status of strike assets, support asset availability, weather conditions, target range, available fuel and munitions, target range, the accuracy of available targeting data, and risk. Once all this is accomplished, an appropriate weapon system is selected for engagement and engagement requirements are submitted.[13]

These requirements are relayed to those "engaging" the target, who must confirm receipt of the requirements and comprehension of their contents. Only then can the target be engaged, which refers to the actual delivery of the specified weapon on the specified target in the specified manner.[14] Afterward, the engagement is "assessed," which includes collecting information regarding the results of the attack and any potential need for a second engagement.[15]

This F2T2EA chain is followed regardless of whether there are RPAs involved in any of these steps. As we move toward RPAs with increasingly autonomous functions, it is worth asking if we may ever enable this chain to allow for fully autonomous lethal strikes. While there are legal and policy elements involved in this question, there are equally important technical reasons that, at a minimum, would greatly reduce whatever appeal there might seem to be for fully autonomous lethal strike capabilities.

To understand this, it is essential to note the time that is typically involved in completing each of the sequential steps in the F2T2EA chain. The find, track, and target steps generally take the longest time, followed by the assess and fix steps. By comparison, the "engage" piece of the chain – namely the decision that involves actually committing the weapon onto the target – is generally the simplest and least time-consuming step. As a consequence, in terms of the overall time required to strike a target, automating the engagement step provides little benefit from an operational point of view. There is simply very little to be gained by enabling that step in the chain to become autonomous. In other words, removing humans from the engage part of the F2T2EA process provides essentially no strategic gain.[16]

So it is not only that the USAF has a cultural resistance to fully autonomous strikes and that it lacks the legal and policy underpinnings to authorize such actions. The resistance to autonomous weapons that remove humans completely from the F2T2EA chain offers little in the way of operational benefit. Indeed, the technology for such fully autonomous strikes largely already exists, but operators are not asking for such strike capabilities because there is no sense that such a change would improve the strategic deployment of force.[17] The United States benefits enormously from the existing RPA-enabled strike capabilities, which are revolutionary in terms of their war-fighting impact, and these benefits are gained without having to engage in fully autonomous strikes.[18] In this sense, keeping humans in the loop is not holding us back at all. This is a very important point and an area where there is often significant misunderstanding of the nature of emerging military technologies.

During the time I was assigned to the Pentagon, I worked closely with the Chief of Staff. When we would meet to discuss the state of maturity of various technologies, his biggest concern was often whether the USAF would have the legal and policy underpinnings to be able to use those technologies in sufficiently unfettered ways to justify the investments being made to develop them. It is a fact that law and policy issues significantly impact real war-fighting capabilities. In the case of RPAs, it will likely soon be the case, if it is not already, that the legal, policy, and cultural aspects of such systems will prove more constraining than technological limitations.

For instance, several states and cities have already passed laws constraining the domestic use of drones.[19] Many others are considering such legislation, often in haste.[20] More relevantly, Congress has been considering new regulations on RPAs, both before[21] and in wake of the Senator Paul's highly publicized filibuster.[22] The United States is also presently engaging the international community in order to create global rules on the use of RPAs.[23] Such efforts could prove useful for placing new technologies on a firm legal footing, but they might also prove overly constraining if not appropriately coordinated with the reality of RPA technology and use. For instance, a proposed "drone court" could dramatically limit the USAF's ability to engage TSTs or other emerging targets.[24] Any efforts to update existing laws to deal with RPAs or to create new legal regimes to regulate them must be carried out responsibly.

3. THE FUTURE OF REMOTELY PILOTED AIRCRAFT

There are enormous and rapid changes underway in the world of RPAs, and their capabilities are growing to enable a far greater range of missions than how they are used today. The combined ISR-strike missions that are the focus of current deployments will continue, but there will be a variety of new platforms with much greater capabilities for performing those missions. For example, the Navy has been working on carrier-based RPAs, and there are various "sensorcraft" concepts that have been under substantive exploration for some time.

Many of these new RPAs are going to have far greater ISR capabilities, because of the clear value of these abilities in terms of warfighting impact. There will be long-endurance RPA systems that will be able to stay aloft for long periods of time. These will provide a continuous view of what is occurring on the ground that will be far more valuable than the relatively intermittent reviews using current systems. There is now tremendous emphasis on developing RPAs that can stay up in the air for weeks, months, or even years at a time.

There will also be entirely new roles for autonomous systems, including as airborne communication relays and airborne gateways, which are very important functions. Currently there are a tremendous number of disparate communications systems in theater. Many of them cannot talk to one another because they were developed in different times and use different technologies. As a consequence, a continual aerial communications relay that allows them to interact is critical. Also, ISR systems are increasingly extending beyond the current electro-optic and infrared video capabilities.

Low-observable traits are going to become very important, because the Unites States has been operating these remotely piloted systems in what is essentially fully permissive airspace. Many potential future conflicts are likely to occur in highly contested and even highly denied environments, so adding low-observable characteristics to these systems is critical. In addition, electronic warfare functions are going to have to be added to RPAs. These aircraft, especially if they are going to have low-observable capabilities, must be able to perform jamming and other types of electronic attacks or electronic support functions, which are not possible in today's RPAs.

The coupling of directed energy systems with RPAs is another area that will likely emerge over time. This includes high-powered laser strikes for near-zero collateral damage, as well as high-powered microwave strikes to enable defeat of an adversary's electronic systems with reasonably focused effects.

There are also likely to be significant advances in autonomous aerial refueling.[25] This is a very near-term technology that many people know little about. If these remote-piloted systems are going to stay aloft in theater for long periods of time, they need to be able to be refueled in the air. This will require adjustments to our existing airborne tanker fleet so they can refuel RPAs, together with manned systems. There are some challenging technical issues involved in this.

Aerial refueling of RPAs would require relative navigation based on GPS signals that can operate even when a tanker may obscure parts of the GPS constellation. The USAF has developed the software and the control laws to be able to do this even under conditions where there are wind gusts, where the tanker wake may interact with the trailing aircraft, and where both aircraft are going through steep banking maneuvers. For this to work, the RPA must be able to autonomously follow the tanker and remain in tanker contact position under such conditions.

Not only has the software for this been developed, but it has also been successfully tested and demonstrated on an autonomous Learjet platform as part of the development effort. This is a piloted test aircraft that is flown to about a mile behind a tanker in the air. At that point the pilot takes his hands off the controls and switches over to the software noted above, which then flies the RPA into the hold position off the tanker wingtip. From there the software autonomously brings the RPA into the contact position behind the tanker, and it stays in this contact position through a variety of complicated maneuvers.[26] The Air Force has collected an enormous amount of data from such flight tests; it turns out that the autonomous system's ability to stay in the contact position behind the tanker is better than that of piloted systems. That is just one instance where properly developed autonomous control technologies perform complex tasks better than humans.

There are also ultra-long-endurance RPAs in various stages of development and testing that can stay aloft for long periods of time, as compared to the tens of hours for today's systems. Most of these are still in the exploratory phase, but the technologies are moving along quite quickly. There are demonstration systems in the DARPA Vulture program in a USAF research laboratory program called MAGIC (which stands for medium-altitude global intelligence and communications platform), as well as systems being developed in other programs. Some of these systems are large enough to carry a useful communications and ISR payload.[27]

Large unmanned airships that can stay aloft for months or even years at a time and can carry potentially enormous payloads may also be developed.[28] There will be tremendous technical challenges to get them to work. They will require lightweight structures with the ability to generate and store energy and capacity to remain aloft in very harsh environments. Some of these systems will operate at altitudes around 60,000 feet, where the solar radiative environment is harsh and can cause materials, such as airship skins and photovoltaic arrays, to fail. However, many of these technologies have been advanced far enough that the USAF is seriously exploring such systems.

In fact, there are airship ISR systems going into theater. The army has its LEM-V, which is in testing, and depending on the outcome may be the first of these large unmanned airship systems to be deployed. An even larger DARPA system, called ISIS, is under development to further advance the needed technologies. These are enormous systems that have literally football field-sized radars in them that can provide substantial resolution and sensitivity for both airborne and ground target identification and tracking. Such systems could potentially be game changing for addressing the challenges the United States is likely to face over the next several decades.

Electro-optical infrared (EO/IR) camera systems, such as Gorgon Stare[29] and ARGUS-IS, also represent dramatic advances. Gorgon Stare, which is now fielded in theater, provides nearly full-motion video from twelve independently steered spots. ARGUS-IS is a 65-spot system that will be able to transmit individually steerable beams directly down to the warfighters on the ground, because they have a significant need to see what is going on around them, especially in complex environments.

These systems are being developed very rapidly and put into theater using a different and much faster acquisition process than what is traditionally used. In effect, these are demonstration systems that can provide such a dramatic increase in capability that the USAF cannot wait for them to be "perfected" and introduced through the normal acquisition process. This is somewhat controversial because these systems do not always perform exactly as the warfighter wants them to. However, rather than waiting years to perfect these systems, it makes more sense to bring their capabilities into theater quickly and then improve them based on how they perform. In fact, the Predator and Reaper RPAs were put through similar rapid development and fielding processes. Such rapid fielding and improvement is becoming increasingly important, because the technologies that both the United States and its potential adversaries have access to are advancing on a time scale far faster than the traditional acquisition process can accommodate.

Another sensor field that is advancing rapidly is wide-area airborne surveillance (WAAS). These systems use multiple cameras to provide a high-resolution view across a very large area. The resulting stitched video stream is saved, so that if an event such as an improvised explosive device strike occurs within the field of view, it is possible to zoom in at high resolution and play back the video to see what led up to the event. Such a TiVo-like capability allows us to understand how our adversaries operate and then take appropriate follow-up actions. Additionally, RPAs will increasingly make use of sensor modalities beyond EO/IR cameras, including LIDAR, which has been in use elsewhere for some time. LIDAR is somewhat similar to radar but uses the extremely short wavelengths of laser light to achieve tremendous depth resolution. It allows 3-dimensional terrain mapping with enormous accuracy, even in a complex urban environment. This can produce a picture of the terrain in which every pixel has target-quality 3D mensurated coordinates associated with it.

4. UNDERSTANDING THE VALUE OF EMERGING TECHNOLOGIES

RPAs, with their sensors and other capabilities, are among the most publicly debated examples of emerging military technologies that are transforming warfare. To ensure that these systems can be developed and deployed in the most effective ways possible, it is essential for the public to have an appropriate understanding of what these technologies can do and what capabilities they can provide. The benefits derived from them typically appear first in the military domain, but in many cases there are enormously useful applications in broader civil society. Emergency response, civilian law enforcement, and natural resource management are a few of the areas where RPAs and their sensor technologies are already finding significant public-sector applications. As future RPAs will draw on entirely new types of platforms, sensors, and missions, it is expected that their potential military and civilian applications will continue to rapidly expand.

At the same time, military-derived technologies often reflexively instill fears regarding their potential misuse in the public domain. In many cases these fears are grounded in fundamental misconceptions about the technologies themselves. For example, there are widespread public misconceptions about autonomous lethal strikes by the military. As noted, the military does not conduct fully autonomous lethal strikes with RPAs because there is no operational benefit to removing human operators from the F2T2EA kill chain. Although it may be technically possible to do this, there is no demand from within the military for doing so.

Future platforms, sensors, and mission payloads are likely to represent increasingly important capabilities for meeting the nation's military and civilian sector needs. However, as other nations also develop similar technologies, the United States must be mindful of the precedents it is setting.[30] Appropriate laws and policies to govern RPA use will become increasingly important as the underlying technologies lead to the advance of evermore capable systems. Meanwhile, the United States cannot allow the current novelty of RPAs to lead it to set up inappropriate rules and restrictions that respond more to public misconceptions about these platforms than to realities.[31]

In the military domain, the coupling of ISR and strike capabilities on current-generation RPAs has enabled substantial shortening of the F2T2EA chain and allowed targeting with significantly reduced collateral damage.[32] Such systems have been especially well suited to recent decentralized conflicts.[33] Future potential conflicts involving more capable adversaries are likely to require RPAs with substantially different attributes. In the civilian sector, other types of RPAs are likely to evolve that will meet the needs of other applications.

In both domains, ensuring that society gains benefits from these systems will require an appropriate framework of supporting laws, policies, and regulations. Achieving such an effective framework will demand greater attention to education and debate in the public sector as to the true capabilities and potential uses of these systems. As impressive as current RPAs may seem today, within a relatively short time frame, probably within the coming decade, we will witness substantial innovations of a transformative nature in these systems and in the benefits that they can bring to society.

NOTES

1 The substantial manpower needs for operation of RPAs has often created significant staffing shortfalls. Thompson, Mark, "Manning unmanned systems," *Time*, September 10, 2012.

2 Operating each drone can be a manpower-intensive endeavor that requires pilots, maintenance crews, sensor operators, mission coordinators, and administrative personnel. One 24-hour combat air patrol, for example, requires 174 service members and 4 drones. Hoffman, Michael, "Army, air force answer critics of UAV progress," *Army Times*, June 19, 2010.

3 US Department of Defense, *Autonomy in Weapon Systems* 7 (November 21, 2012), which describes that present policy requires any system design to "incorporate the necessary capabilities to allow commanders and operators to exercise appropriate levels of human judgment in the use of force."

4 Perlez, Jane, "Chinese plan to kill drug lord with drone highlights military advances," *New York Times*, February 20, 2013.

5 Ashley, Fantz, "Hezbollah claims it sent drone over Israel, but expert calls it 'rinky-dink,'" CNN, October 12, 2012.

6 Presently between 75 and 87 countries have used RPAs in their militaries. To date, only three have actually deployed them operationally: the United States, United Kingdom, and Israel. Only the United States has deployed it non-domestically. Nonetheless, the technology is quickly proliferating. Singer, P. W., "The global swarm," *Foreign Policy*, March 11, 2013.

7 Tirpak, John A., "Find, fix, track, target, engage, assess," *Air Force Magazine* (July 2000): In October 1996, General Fogleman gave a speech predicting that "[i]n the first quarter of the 21st century, it will become possible to find, fix, or track, and target anything that moves on the surface of the Earth." The comment was subsequently amended to include engagement and assessment.

8 US Air Force, "Targeting: Air force doctrine (Document 2-1.9), June 8, 2006, p. 46.

9 Ibid., p 50. Department of the Army, "The targeting process 97–98," November 26, 2010.

10 US Air Force, "Targeting: Air force doctrine (Document 2-1.9), p. 51. Department of the Army, "The targeting process 97–98," pp. 98–99.

11 H. S. Lo, Edward, and T. Andrew Au, "Improving the kill chain for prosecution of time sensitive targets" in Alisson V. Brito (ed.), *Dynamic modelling* (Vukovar, Croatia: Intech, 2010), pp. 93–110.

12 Ibid.

13 Department of the Army, "The targeting process 97–98," p. 100.

14 Ibid.

15 Ibid.

16 I have previously explained that there is no operational gain from removing humans from the engagement element of the targeting process. See Dahm, Werner J. A., "Killer drones are science fiction," *Wall Street Journal*, February 15, 2012.

17 Ibid.

18 The gains from autonomy will primarily be in the ability to rapidly assess incoming ISR in order to provide commanders with the appropriate information to determine whether to engage or not. Cheater, Julian C., "Accelerating the kill chain via future unmanned aircraft," Center for Strategy and Technology, Air War College (April 2007): 1–81, pp. 6–7.

19 For instance, Charlottesville, Virginia, was the first city to pass a moratorium on the use of unmanned aircraft in the city. Hennigan, W. J., "City in Virginia passes anti-drone resolution," *Los Angeles Times*, February 6, 2013. Similarly, Virginia, among other states, has passed drone regulations. Koebler, Jason, "Virginia becomes first state to pass drone regulations," *U.S. News*, February 5, 2013.

20 McNeal, Gregory S., "North Carolina's poorly worded drone killing privacy bill," *Forbes*, March 31, 2013.

21 Jakes, Lara, "Congress considers putting limits on drone strikes," Associated Press, February 5, 2013.

22 Rogin, Josh, "Corker calls for more congressional oversight of drone strikes," *Foreign Policy*, March 20, 2013.

23 Zakaria, Tabassum, "As drone monopoly frays, Obama seeks global rules," Reuters, March 17, 2013.

24 Wittes, Benjamin, "Jeh Johnson speech on a 'drone court': Some pros and cons," *Lawfare*, March 18, 2013.

25 Skillings, Jonathan, "Global Hawk closer to autonomous aerial refuelling," *CBS News*, March 10, 2011.

26 Reed, John, "Navy getting very close to UAV aerial refueling," Defense Tech, January 26, 2012.

27 Mortimer, Gary, "Orion selected by AFRL for the first stage of medium-altitude global ISR and communications," sUAS News, September 30, 2010.

28 Boyle, Alan, "Airship groomed for flight to edge of space," *Today*, May 21, 2004.

29 Gray, Mel, *Gorgon Stare will deploy in March, USAF general says*, Defense News, February 17, 2011.

30 Conan, Neal, *John Brennan delivers speech on drone ethics*, NPR, May 1, 2012: CIA Director John Brennan observed that RPAs will be soon be widespread technologies and that the United States must be aware of the precedent it sets.

31 Bell, David, "In defense of drones: A historical argument," *New Republic*, January 27, 2012: David Bell contends that the futuristic nature of drones provokes undeserved criticism of the systems. He emphasizes that drones are simply another technological step forward in the longstanding race for technological advantage.

32 Under even the least favorable estimations, RPAs have a far lower rate of collateral damage than other systems. Shane, Scott, "The moral case for drones," *New York Times*, July 14, 2012. Saletan, William, "In defense of drones," *Slate*, February 19, 2013.

33 Young, Alex, "A defense of drones," *Harvard International Review*, February 25, 2013.

19

From Orville Wright to September 11

What the History of Drone Technology Says About Its Future

KONSTANTIN KAKAES

1. REFLECTING ON THE PAST TO UNDERSTAND THE FUTURE

Even before they worked well, drones changed the course of American history. On the evening of August 12, 1944, Colonel Elliot Roosevelt, FDR's son, was flying high above the English countryside, just south of Halesworth, a few miles from the coast where Suffolk meets the North Sea.[1] Roosevelt was part of a large delegation of high-ranking officers, including General Jimmy Doolittle, the commander of the 8th Air Force, who had come to watch the first mission of Operation Anvil,[2] a US Navy effort to use drones to attack German targets that had proven tough to destroy by dropping bombs.

Anvil relied on B-24 Liberator bombers that had been converted to fly by remote control. Although the planes could be flown remotely, the Anvil drones needed pilots to get them off the ground. Joseph Kennedy Jr., brother to the future president, had just taken off and was sitting in the cockpit at the pilot's controls of the first Anvil drone. A related Army Air Force program called Aphrodite used converted B-17s. Aphrodite's first three missions, which had taken place over the previous week, had not gone well. But the Navy had a more sophisticated control system than the Army – an early version of the television camera in the B-24 drone sent pictures to the mother ship control planes, which could be as far as fifty miles away.

Flying below Roosevelt in the fading light, Kennedy's plane, *Zootsuit Black*, was loaded with 24,240 pounds of Torpex, a new high-powered explosive. This was three times more explosives than B-24s normally carried, and the idea was that, unlike bombs at the time that lacked precision, *Zootsuit Black* could be guided directly at its target – a Nazi super gun dug into a chalk hill on the French coast. (It would be a few months until the Japanese kamikazes would adopt a similar technique with manned craft.)

Kennedy and his engineer, Wilford Willy, were supposed to jump out of the plane while it was still over England. But just before they could jump to safety, the plane exploded, incinerating both Kennedy and Willy. Kennedy's father, Joseph Kennedy Sr., had considered running for president himself, and was widely thought to be grooming his eldest son to run. That mantle now passed to the next oldest: John.

By the time of Joseph Kennedy Jr.'s death, the American military already had nearly thirty years of experience with unmanned aircraft. They were called robot planes and pilotless planes, and, at least since the mid-1930s, drones. They had been used as weapons, as targets, and for reconnaissance. They had not, for the most part, worked well. Guidance and communications were difficult problems that would take decades to solve. In general, figuring out how to use drones effectively was a challenge.

There are many strands of technological development that have gone into the development of drones – flight control surfaces, imaging sensors, propeller engines and jet engines, navigation and stability, communications and radar. They are all efforts to accomplish the same goal: trying to make the aircraft as independent as possible from the men who made it. As early as 1922, the *New York Times* proclaimed, "Automatic control device called more dependable than human aviator."[3] In fact, the technological history of drones is littered with similar predictions by military leaders, the heads of the aviation industries, and journalists, all promising that revolutionary change was just around the corner.

Reality has been slower than these predictions. The world is big, windy, and uncertain. Robots do best in controlled environments. The airspace relevant to military conflict is filled with dangers and difficulties. Each incremental step in the march toward autonomy has been hard won through the labor of thousands of engineers working for thousands of hours.

Every success was preceded by many costly failures, and followed by more. The heavy veil of secrecy that hung over drone development for much of the Cold War served – and continues to serve – as a protective blanket for industry, allowing it to fail and to learn. It also has been a license for private industry to profit from public subsidies given without sufficient scrutiny and to overextend ambitions beyond what the technology of the time could support, resulting in the delayed production of multiple costly and ineffective systems.

During wartime, the pressing needs of the moment repeatedly broke through this aspirational logjam and led to widespread deployment of the best technologies of the day. By the end of the Vietnam War, drones flew 12 percent of America's reconnaissance flights.[4] Further improvement came in Israel's wars – in the 1973 Yom Kippur War and in Lebanon in the 1980s. The United

States honed its drone tactics in the 1991 Gulf War and over the Balkans in the 1990s, many years before drone use began its rapid growth following the 2001 terrorist attacks.

This chapter could not possibly describe every American drone made between 1915 and 2001. There are simply too many. An incomplete list includes: the Kettering Bug and Bull Goose, the McDonnell Quail and Buck Duck, the Martin Matador and Marin Mace, the Falconer, Overseer, Sky Spy, Swallow and Osprey, the Kaman Drone and Gyrodyne DASH, the Snark, the Firebee, the Lightning Bug, Tagboard, Compass Cope, Compass Arrow and Compass Dwell, Amber, Gnat and Condor, DarkStar, Pointer, Pioneer, Chukar, Aquila, SkyEye, Shadow, Hunter, and, of course, the widely known Predator and Reaper.

The history of drone research, invention, testing, and deployment illustrates just how rocky the path has been to get to a present where drones have become a key component of military strategy. A reflection on this past suggests that substantive advances will continue to be difficult and will likely be less grand or rapid than drone proponents believe.

Neither the inflated hopes of the unmanned aircraft industry nor the aggrandized fears of civil libertarians and privacy advocates regarding the might of drones will come to pass imminently. The lessons of the long history of drone development suggest that there are multiple engineering challenges that stand in the way of revolutionary change. The endurance, acuity, reliability, and capacity for violence of today's drones have allowed them to change the world in ways that were not fully anticipated by anyone until the capabilities were already well in hand. While further technical improvements will no doubt bring about similarly unforeseen changes in the nature of what drones can do in the world, how this will come to pass is impossible to predict with any confidence.

Still, a reflection on the past may shed light on the future. Some technical challenges remain as conceptually difficult today as they did generations ago. Managing the flow of information in a chaotic environment has always been difficult and, as the volume of data has increased by a factor of millions, this issue remains a serious impediment to many promised advances. While taking off and landing an airplane is easier and safer today than it was in the mid-1940s, it is far more challenging than flying in middle altitudes, just as it was at the time of Joseph Kennedy Jr.'s death and in the days of Wilbur and Orville Wright.

2. WORLD WAR I

From the very beginning, the American military's development of drones was characterized by inter-service rivalry. Elmer Sperry, a prolific inventor working with his son Lawrence, approached the Army in the summer of 1916. World War I was well underway in Europe, but the United States had not yet entered the war. Sperry proposed an unmanned "flying bomb" or "aerial torpedo."[5] When Sperry did not hear back, he went to the Navy.

Over the next several years, Sperry performed more than one hundred flight tests on Curtiss seaplanes, which flew with a safety pilot and automatic controls. Sperry stabilized the seaplanes with a gyroscope he designed. He had first demonstrated this in 1914, when he took his hands off the controls of an airplane at an airshow.[6] Though his 1917 tests were somewhat successful, pilots had trouble getting the plane off the ground. Sperry tried different contraptions for getting the airplane into the air without a pilot aboard before settling on a flywheel catapult. Sperry would test the aerodynamics of his "flying bomb" by driving down the Long Island Motor Parkway in a car with the drone fastened to the roof, in effect a "moving, open-air wind tunnel."[7]

Sperry guided his flying bombs by using the gyroscope to steady the direction (subject to being blown off course by winds) and then counting the number of spins of the propeller to estimate the distance (which also varied with the wind). The plane would dive on its target after a preset number of propeller revolutions. Sperry's longest test flight, in October 1918, was a failure in that the N-9 drone did not dive after 14,000 yards, but kept on flying "straight and level eastward over the ocean."[8]

In the meantime, Charles Kettering, a rival and sometime-collaborator of Sperry's, convinced the Army to develop its own unmanned system. Kettering had invented the automobile starter (obviating the need to crank a car by hand to get it going) and would go on to become vice president of General Motors. Kettering's and Sperry's machines were broadly similar, though Kettering's plane was smaller. While its official name was the *Liberty Eagle*, it was usually called the *Bug*. The *Bug*'s airframe was designed and built by Orville Wright and its control system was built by a player piano company.

Army officials talked about ordering between 10,000 and 100,000 of the unmanned craft, but only twenty of the *Bugs* were built. As historian Kenneth Werrell writes: "[A] few mechanically gifted visionaries, equipped with limited knowledge and resources, were unable to transform the 'flying bomb' idea into reality. Despite their best efforts and a few successes, the theory remained more advanced than the technology of the day."[9]

Werrell points out that limited knowledge of aerodynamics made it hard for the designers to build stable craft and guidance systems failed to perform as designed, so many aircraft were destroyed in tests. In this way, its development was essentially a process of trial and error, which made progress difficult.

Test failures in the closing days of World War I ended both the Army's and Navy's programs. Nevertheless, some aviators remained enthusiastic. Major General Mason Patrick, the head of the Army Air Forces, told an audience in Boston in January 1923: "[E]ven now it would be possible to send a pilotless plane with a cargo of bombs from Boston to New York at a given altitude and on a set course at a prearranged speed."[10] This was wildly overstating the technological capabilities of the day.

Experiments continued in the 1920s. The Army started to build pilotless planes that could be controlled by radio, rather than simply flying on their own in a straight line.[11] Still, there were many questions regarding what to do with unmanned planes. One *New York Times* article suggested that they might be used to disperse sleeping gas.[12] While in retrospect it is easy to view this idea more like a silly thriller plot than a serious military use, but at the time this appeared as reasonable a use for unmanned aircraft as taking pictures.

It took some time for the idea of unmanned reconnaissance to take hold. Hugo Gernsback, a science fiction pioneer, had mentioned the idea in 1924.[13] At the time, even manned aircraft were not widely used for photographic reconnaissance. In 1940, the *New York Times* reported: "[T]he bridges across the East River were particularly sharp as televiewed from the air . . . it was such 'shots' that lead observers to discuss the military value of the winged 'eye' . . . There could be no doubt that a teleplane would be of inestimable value in surveys and aerial photography in map making, bombing and in sighting targets."[14]

The *New York Times* described the airplane's transmitter as "vest-pocket" sized – it weighed sixty-five pounds. "The winged cyclops pulled back the curtain that opens the way to new vistas," the *New York Times* concluded.[15]

In fact, it took years for photographic reconnaissance capabilities to be integrated into air operations. The United States entered World War I without a significant Air Force, but by the end of the war, the country had deployed 8,000 observation aircraft.[16] However, at the time, the emphasis was on direct visual observation by pilots who then reported what they saw.

3. WORLD WAR II

As World War II unfolded, pilotless aircraft came to play a major role. Though their utility for reconnaissance was still a couple of decades away, Sperry's and Kettering's visions of aerial torpedoes had become a reality.

In June 1944, the *New York Times* reported: "For the last twenty-four hours parts of England south of a line drawn from Bristol to The Wash have been bombarded intermittently by robots."[17] Over the next several weeks, reports of the V-1 strikes would dominate the news. In response to the V-1 attacks, Harry Truman, then a senator, would hold hearings on American development of pilotless planes.[18]

However, the V-1 episode was a curious piece of history. By all accounts, even reports at the time, it was clear that if one side in a conflict wanted to inflict widespread damage on the enemy with any degree of accuracy, the V-1 was poorly suited for the task. The Nazis launched 10,492 V-1s against Britain and a comparable number against targets on the continent after the Allied invasion.[19] Of those aimed across the English Channel, about one-fifth of the V-1s crashed shortly after taking off, about three-fifths were intercepted by defenses in flight, and only about one-fifth reached London. The V-1s that landed killed 6,184 civilians, which was far fewer than the 51,509 killed by German bombing from manned aircraft.[20] The V-1's ineffectiveness as a weapon of war showed the limitations of a guidance system that relied on pointing a pilotless plane in a straight line and programming it to travel a preset distance – the same basic mechanism that Kettering and Sperry had created thirty years earlier.

Indeed, as Werrell writes, the improvement in performance from World War I to World War II was marginal. The main technological improvement was a shift from "pre-set guidance to radio-control."[21] Nevertheless, Werrell continues: "[W]hile radio-control efforts worked in theory and in tests, they did not work well in combat. Mechanical problems with missile, explosive, and guidance systems precluded adequate testing of both the equipment and the concept."[22]

In the early 1940s, both the US Army and Navy experimented with drones that were basically similar to the V-1. However, they made incremental improvements, such as the Navy's early testing of a radar altimeter on a drone in 1941.[23] Some in the Naval Bureau of Aeronautics wanted to ramp up production, but John Towers, the bureau's head, resisted the move until drones could prove superior to conventional aircraft.[24] Even though the V-1 was a tactical failure, it led the Allies to divert thousands of bombers to attacking V-1 launch sites instead of striking other targets. As such, it was an illustration of the fact that a new technology, even an immature one, can divert the course of a war effort.

The Allies also spent considerable resources on anti-V-1 efforts. The V-1 was vulnerable in flight. As one American pilot said, using one of its many nicknames: "[D]oodle-bug hunting is fun; they cannot shoot back."[25] This remains true of drones today and for the immediate future – and it represents a key weakness.

Aphrodite and Anvil – the ill-fated efforts that led to the death of Joseph Kennedy Jr. – were but one example of the Allies' focus on countering the V-1 and the V-2. Although, as a rocket the V-2 now seems to represent a fundamentally different category, at the time the two seemed more alike than different: they were both robots that differed in their propulsion mechanisms. Though Aphrodite was a failure – none of the nineteen raids with pilotless B-17s and B-24s succeeded in destroying their targets – American unmanned efforts were about to turn the corner.

The next stage of drone advances was marked by a growing distinction between cruise missiles that are destroyed when they attack a target and drones that can be recovered or returned following a mission. The technological commonalities meant that there would continue to be cross-fertilization in navigation and propulsion technologies, but the early years in which there was "no distinction between UAVs and missiles"[26] were coming to a close. Military planners saw the limitations of pilotless planes in World War II as temporary. The V-1 and Aphrodite were premature deployments of technology whose moment, they thought, was about to arrive.

By the time the United States entered World War II observation capabilities had actually atrophied. The Air Force had focused on building faster airplanes that would, in theory, be better able to evade the enemy, but which in practice flew too fast for useful observation.[27] During the course of the war, the Army Air Force rebuilt its capacity for tactical observation with light Piper Grasshoppers that could take off and land on roads next to troops. Their primary mission was to act as spotters for artillery, although they took on other tasks as well, such as using "smoke grenades to mark targets for heavy bombers."[28] By the end of the war, there were 1,380 American light reconnaissance planes in the European theater.

Even though unmanned reconnaissance was not a factor to speak of in World War II, this represented the first time in history that manned reconnaissance flights were a major component of military strategy. Despite their significance, these systems were limited by their own success in gathering data. "One of the major obstacles in regard to aerial photography was not flying the missions, but processing and distributing the results."[29] Immediately after the war, the Army worried that doctrine required an 18-foot high stack of photographs every day to cover sixty miles of front.[30] Getting enough developing chemicals alone represented a logistical challenge, to say nothing of the time required to review and evaluate the photos. While advances in technology can solve some problems – developing chemicals are no longer an issue – the larger question of efficiently and effectively evaluating imagery has become an even greater problem as both manned and unmanned aircraft produce ever-greater quantities of images, video, and other forms of data.

4. THE COLD WAR

After the bombing of Nagasaki on August 9, 1945 (following the bombing of Hiroshima three days earlier), it was almost a full year until another atomic bomb would explode. On July 1, 1946, the fourth atomic bomb in history was detonated 520 feet above Bikini atoll, in the middle of the Pacific Ocean. While drone planes had been ineffective in the war, here was a mission for which they were particularly suited – sampling the radioactive cloud that posed health risks to human pilots. Hanson Baldwin of the *New York Times* explained:

> The extensive use of drone planes in the two tests – pilotless planes equipped with television equipment in the nose as well as in the instrument panels and controlled by radio from mother planes – gave the Air Force's extensive experience with this new and developing tactic of war. The drones were far more successfully controlled than those actually used during the past war.[31]

The B-17s were flown from mother planes that were twenty-five miles away, but Baldwin said that a range of seventy-five to one hundred miles was possible. Operators even managed to hand off control from a mother plane with failing instruments to a "replacement mother ship."[32]

Communications were still difficult because "the radio and television transmitting and receiving apparatus is heavy and fairly bulky."[33] Launching was also complicated as the Navy experimented in Maryland with a new catapult called *Zebra*.[34] Still, these deployments revealed that the moment of reconnaissance drones had arrived. In fact, Baldwin speculated about "infra-red 'eyes'"[35] to see in the dark, and high- and low-level photoreconnaissance flights.

Doctrine was also still evolving. Speculation continued about the use of swarms of drones to overcome enemy air defenses[36] – though the United States would not launch such swarms until the cruise missile strikes at the start of the first Gulf War. Other ideas have yet to come to pass. Drone planes were to be used as mail carriers,[37] to replace test pilots,[38] and to play propaganda to enemy troops over a loudspeaker.[39]

Target drones developed rapidly in the late 1940s. Truman, now president, watched them in action on board the USS *Missouri* in September 1947.[40]

By 1954, the weak link in the chain that had killed Joseph Kennedy Jr. had been strengthened. The problem of explosives had been "virtually resolved."[41]

In the late 1940s, chemists working at America's Los Alamos nuclear laboratory in New Mexico had developed so-called "plastic-bonded explosives" (PBX), which were both powerful and stable, unlike the Torpex that killed Kennedy by exploding prematurely.[42] Navy chemists at the Naval Ordnance Test Station in China Lake, California, further developed PBX in the 1950s, testing various PBXs on rockets and aircraft.[43]

The chief remaining challenge was guidance: "[P]robably the greatest problem of them all, perhaps never to be completely solved – of sending electronic impulses through the air to guide the missile in flight ... of constructing robot brains to direct the bird toward the target – the problem of radar, of radio, of infra-red, of heat-seeking, target-seeking, celestial navigation."[44]

In March 1948, Goodyear began developing a system that would use radar to match terrain.[45] The Air Force began experimenting with using the stars for guidance in the late 1940s.[46] The cruise missile programs of the time (the Air Force Matador, Mace, and Snark, and Navy programs such as Gorgon, Regulus, Rigel, and Triton) were all beset by navigational errors. The Navy launched six F6F-5K assault drones off the deck of the USS *Boxer* in August 1952, but only one hit its target.[47]

The Air Force cruise missiles of the 1950s and 1960s were costly failures. Some in the Air Force had great strategic ambitions for cruise missiles, which they saw as capable of changing the balance of power with the Soviet Union. Ballistic missiles, however, proved far more important strategically. The Army, on the other hand, only sought some small tactical advantage – the ability to scout out enemy positions.

As the Air Force and Navy focused on developing cruise missiles, the Army began developing a reconnaissance drone called the RP-71, at Fort Huachuca in Arizona.[48] The RP-71 Falconer was first tested in 1955 and its descendants – Overseer, Sky Spy, Swallow, and Osprey – were never used in combat. All of these programs were eventually cancelled because of cost before they matured to the point where they led to a usable combat system, though some were provisionally deployed to Germany.

In 1957 the *New York Times* reported: "New Army camera flies alone at night for low-level glimpse of foe 'over hill.'"[49] The Army drone system resembled, in clunky fashion, that of modern-day drones. An operator sat in a mobile "radar and tracking cabin"[50] during the mission, triggering the camera when the drone was over its target. He would then fly the drone back over friendly lines and order it to pull a parachute for recovery. By 1964, the Army even had a system for real-time transmission of images from a drone, although it weighed 125 pounds.[51]

The Army cancelled its program in 1970, having decided it was too expensive. The Marines also had a short-lived flirtation with drones in the 1960s, commissioning a 60-pound drone called the Bikini, which could be launched from the back of a jeep using compressed air from the same type of unit already used for flame-throwers. This program was cancelled in 1967.[52] The technical challenge of drones lay as much with integrating them into the force structure as with the devices themselves. However, the Air Force would have greater success with linking these innovative technologies with their service.

5. THE VIETNAM WAR

By the end of the Vietnam War, US Air Force drones had flown more than 3,400 reconnaissance missions.[53] While the early versions of these drones were built in the late 1940s, it took more than a decade, until 1959, for Ryan Aeronautical to bring its XQ-2 target drone into full-scale production.[54] In 1962, two of the Firebees, as the XQ-2 came to be called, were converted into use as photo-reconnaissance drones.[55] The Q-2C, the first reconnaissance model, could fly just slower than the speed of sound and as high as 60,000 feet, and had an 800-mile range.[56] The early flights of the Q-2C convinced the Air Force of the value of reconnaissance drones, and it ordered more and larger models from Ryan. The Q-2C and its descendants solved the takeoff problem by being dropped off the wings of a C-130 in flight. In July 1963 the 4080th Strategic Reconnaissance Wing would become the first operational Air Force unit dedicated to drones.[57]

In October 1962, at the height of the Cuban missile crisis, Joseph Charyk, the undersecretary of the Air Force, planned a mission in which Teledyne–Ryan Fire Fly drones would fly over Cuba. The C-130 carrying the drones was taxiing to the end of the runway at Tyndall Air Force base, getting ready to launch the drones, when the mission was dramatically aborted by Air Force Chief of Staff Curtis LeMay, who did not want to risk revealing the secretive drones to the Soviet Union. At the time, the Air Force had only two reconnaissance drones.[58]

Almost two years later, on August 4, 1964, Lyndon Johnson claimed that North Korean boats fired on the USS *Maddox* in international waters in what came to be known as the Gulf of Tonkin incident. The Strategic Air Command Lighting Bug unit (the Fire Fly's successor) deployed to Kadena Air Force Base in Japan that same day.[59]

The Lighting Bugs flew their first mission two weeks later. They were sent over China rather than Vietnam. Ryan employees were forward-deployed to run the drones, which used flight plans developed weeks in advance and were based on estimations of conditions, such as wind.[60] The Lighting Bugs did not work very well, as Army analyst John David Blom explained: "[S]ome crashed, some made mysterious turns while in flight and never returned, one failed to switch to remote control for landing ... and even when everything did go right the Lightning Bugs often sustained considerable damage on the landings."[61]

The damage on landings led the Air Force to switch to mid-air recovery by helicopter. The helicopter recovery system had already been used to gather film from Corona spy satellites.[62] However, this approach did not work much better and half the drones were lost.[63] By the late 1960s, the Air Force improved its ability to recover drones in the air, and by 1973 they had more than a 90 percent success rate.[64]

Still, while many fewer drones were lost to accidents, they still were not very good at finding their targets. Leading up to the 1973 ceasefire in Vietnam, less than half of the flights overflew the planned reconnaissance targets.[65] The Lighting Bugs used a Doppler navigation system that depended on knowing the location of the C-130 control plane from which they were launched.[66] At first, the drones were flown at 50,000 feet, which meant that if they were six to nine miles off course – the typical drift – they could still recover usable images.[67] However, as the program advanced, they were flying at lower altitudes to gain tactical information, which made drift a big problem.[68]

By 1969, the Air Force was spending at least $1.34 billion (in 2010 dollars) annually on Lightning Bug operations.[69] Part of the reason they were so expensive was the overhead of the mid-air recovery system, which depended on having many helicopters available to recover the drones. By the end of 1972 the Air Force used drones almost exclusively during bad weather to examine the effects of bombings.[70] At the time, drones flew 12 percent of all reconnaissance missions. As Thomas Ehrhard writes, the drones were sent on the hardest missions: "The reality is that manned reconnaissance aircraft simply would not have been sent into the areas (like Hanoi during Linebacker II) covered by the drones ... the payback was reconnaissance effectiveness, not lives saved."[71]

John Dale, an engineer who worked on Vietnam-era drones, explained: "The only pictures briefed to Congress on how we didn't hit any bad targets during Linebacker II came from drones."[72] Of the 1,000 drones involved in Buffalo Hunter, as the Vietnamese reconnaissance effort was called, 200 were lost, with a total cost of nearly $6 billion in 2010 dollars.[73]

By the end of the war some Lightning Bugs were equipped with Maverick missiles, presaging the Predator–Hellfire combination that was to rise to prominence thirty years later.[74] During the war drones had been improved in many small ways through better cameras, better controls, better data links, and, eventually, improvements in navigation using Loran, a precursor to GPS.[75] By June 1972 the newest Lighting Bugs had working video data links that allowed a controller, sitting in the belly of a C-130, to see what the drone was seeing.[76]

Throughout the Vietnam War, drones were still not as capable as manned aircraft for most missions. As the American military shifted its attention to the European theater, drones failed to make the transition because they "simply cost too much for the limited capability they provided in that environment."[77] The convoluted launch and recovery operations meant they could not fly as often as manned aircraft.[78] It took twenty-four hours to turn a drone around versus three hours for a manned airplane. The C-130 control ships were vulnerable to Russian anti-aircraft systems, and the uncertain, cold weather in Europe presented other challenges to their deployment.[79] The Strategic Arms Limitations Talks also limited drones, like the Lightning Bug–Maverick combination, which carried weapons, because, in the legal language of the treaty, they were indistinguishable from the cruise missiles that had been evolving in parallel.

During and after the Vietnam War, the US government spent billions on a nearly totally separate track of drone development for strategic reconnaissance over China. From the early 1960s through the present, efforts to develop highly sophisticated drones for these purposes was constantly plagued by technological challenges leading to cost overruns. Eager intelligence and Air Force personnel, egged on by the contractors building the drones, would chase after gold-plated systems that inevitably failed to perform as advertised.

For much of the 1960s and 1970s it was unclear that drones were technically capable of accomplishing strategic reconnaissance in a way superior to satellites. Furthermore, in the 1970s the main advances in reconnaissance involved satellites. However, this did not stop the US government from continuing to spend billions of dollars on secret drone development.

One failed program, the D-21 Tagboard, looked like a mini-SR-71 spy plane. Eventually the Air Force built thirty-three of them at a cost of about $1.7 billion (in 2010 dollars).[80] They were built at Lockheed's "Skunk Works" facility, but kept secret even from the engineers working on the secret SR-71 in the same building. Kelly Johnson, who ran Skunk Works, tried to cancel Tagboard after a drone crashed into its SR-71 mother ship on the fourth test, killing one of the two-person SR-71 crew.[81] The National Reconnaissance Office (NRO), however, wanted to have the capacity to fly over China, particularly to monitor a nuclear test site at Lop Nor near the Mongolian border. To do this, it had Lockheed modify the D-21 to be launched by a rocket dropped from a B-52 bomber. The modifications meant that launching a D-21 cost a "bloody for-tune," according to one of its builders.[82] In March 1971 Senior Bowl, the code name for D-21 missions over China, ended. This decision came after four operational failures: a guidance failure on the first mission, a failed parachute on the second, a frigate running over the drone instead of picking it up on the third, and a loss over a "heavily defended area" in China on the fourth.[83]

Tagboard was not the only failure. Other early attempts at "High Altitude Long Endurance" (HALE) UAVs ended badly, including Compass Arrow, a stealth design from Ryan, and other efforts by LTV Electrosystems and Martin Marietta. However, some of these efforts yielded technological advances. For example, in July 1972 the XWM-93, a Martin Marietta drone, flew for twenty-seven hours and fifty-five minutes.[84] This set a record and proved extended drone flight was possible. However, it was very expensive and eventually the Air Force cancelled the program.[85] There were twenty Compass Arrows built (about the same size as the Tagboard program) at a cost of $1.7 billion.[86] As Ehrhard explained: "It was built to do the job right, but the price was too high, even for the NRO . . . [it] proved that the most advanced aerospace nation in the world was not up to the engineering challenge of long distance, high altitude, unmanned operation within feasible limits of time and money."[87]

6. ISRAEL'S DRONE USE

In 1971 Israel bought a number of Lighting Bugs. The Israeli military used drones in combat in the 1970s and 1980s and in so doing developed tactics for their use that the United States would later adopt. The technical question of how to build drones was still overshadowed by the equally tough question of what to do with them. In 1973 E. J. Kellerstrass, an Air Force Lieutenant Colonel in charge of planning for a special drone program office explained: "How RPVs [remotely piloted vehicles] are used and the methods employed will be as important to achieving operational success as the capability that is built into the vehicle."[88]

He knew what he did not know, yet he believed that a primary use for drones would be as agile dogfighters in the air, a task for which even present-day technology is poorly suited.

Kellerstrass thought "the unmanned craft complements manned aircraft by providing relatively low-cost systems to be deployed in large numbers."[89] But as he was writing, the NRO and Air Force were developing precisely the opposite: high-cost systems to be deployed in small numbers. They were, by and large, failures.

In mid-1973 the Israeli military tried to gain access to some of the capable but pricey Compass Arrow drones. However, rather than export the sensitive technology, Richard Nixon ordered the drones destroyed.[90] Nevertheless, Israel would later manage to successfully use domestically produced drones that were simpler than those developed by the United States.

Cruise missiles – essentially drones that exploded – had been used in World War II by the Germans. In the decades that followed, the Soviet Union put more effort into cruise missile development than the United States.[91] Nevertheless, the Air Force spent many millions on cruise missile design and development from the 1950s on, with little success. For example, the Snark cruise missile was a complete failure: "The average miss distance was over 1,000 miles. At least one came down in the wrong hemisphere, disappearing somewhere in the interior of Brazil."[92]

However, the skeptical attitude of the American military toward cruise missiles changed on October 22, 1967, when the Egyptian Navy sank the Israeli destroyer *Eilat* with a volley of four Soviet-made Styx cruise missiles.[93]

From then on, military strategists, especially those in the Navy, realized that the various technologies needed for cruise missiles had matured and that this technology had come of age, as they had "small efficient turbofan engines, microminiaturized electronics, high-energy propellants, small high-yield nuclear and conventional warheads, more accurate mapping data, and less radar-reflective airframes."[94]

Over time, the terrain-matching and inertial guidance systems that had been under development since the 1950s[95] were beginning to actually be accurate enough to be useful. One of the first effective terrain-matching systems, TERCOM, worked by assigning average elevations to each cell in a grid, a radar altimeter in the missile then estimated the elevations, and "voted" on how well the measured map correlated with the stored map.[96]

In the 1960s, engineers tried to put the system into Hound Dog missiles, which did not work. By the 1970s, electronics had gotten small enough to make such a system effective when combined with TAINS, an inertial guidance system that kept track of how far the cruise missile thought it had travelled.[97]

The turbofan engines used for the first successful cruise missiles in the 1970s had, in fact, first been developed for target drones.[98] As usual, though, the missile's proponents were overly enthusiastic about their capabilities. In 1977 two foreign policy analysts argued that "as few as four cruise missiles could search out and destroy up to 200 enemy tanks."[99] While in principle it might be technically possible to fashion a sophisticated cruise missile that could destroy fifty tanks, such a large and complicated missile would not be cost effective, reliable, or robust as compared to simpler, less capable missiles.

The idea that four missiles might be used to destroy 200 tanks exemplifies the type of flawed analysis common in considering the capabilities of an emerging military technology. In fact, these sorts of claims tend to obscure the more relevant questions of how well innovations function in comparison with existing alternatives.

In the Cold War era, much of the research and development on cruise missiles occurred, logically enough, within in the context of the US–Soviet military conflict. In this way, cruise missiles were compared to ballistic missiles and strategic bombers. However, a cruise missile is essentially a small airplane with some degree of autonomy that carries a warhead. Typically it is propelled by a jet engine, not a rocket. This means that cruise missiles travel more slowly than ballistic missiles, which are boosted by rockets to high altitudes before descending. The comparative efficiency of jet power gives cruise missiles a greater range than non-ballistic rocket-powered missiles, which travel with great speed but can only cover limited distances.

Translating these distinct capabilities into a tactical and strategic calculus is not straightforward. Nuclear-armed cruise missiles never proved as important as nuclear ballistic missiles for a variety of reasons, including the fact that cruise missiles are easier to shoot down. However, the fact that cruise missiles look and act somewhat like airplanes meant that they were useful in contexts when other missiles could not be deployed. For example, they could be used against targets – as in the 1998 bombing of Sudan – where there were significant political costs associated with using either manned aircraft or ballistic missiles.

Technological evolution, then as now, was constrained by politics. The Navy and Air Force were skeptical of cruise missiles because "more capable missiles limited importance of platforms and they wanted new platforms which were sexy."[100] In other words, the military was less interested in an effective missile that could be launched from an old-fashioned airplane like a B-52. For the leadership, what was more appealing were arms whose development could be used to justify the purchase of new, more glamorous airplanes.

The desire for new and more advanced airplanes was greater among Navy and Air Force officers than among the civilian brass at the Pentagon. As a result, the Department of Defense "took an opposite view to that of the military [services]. It saw cruise missiles as cost-effective and flexible weapons with great promise."[101] These debates went on interminably in times of relative peace. Ultimately, the tradeoffs were complicated and could not be resolved without being subject to the harsh reality of use within actual conflicts.

Israel was the first nation to prove the utility of unmanned aircraft. In the 1973 Yom Kippur War, US-made Chukar target drones led the successful Israeli counterattack to the Egyptian invasion. The Israeli Air Force launched the Chukars as decoys to provoke Egyptian radars into giving away their positions, allowing the Israelis to find the sites and bomb them.[102] Israel had also been flying US drones made by Ryan over Cairo to take surveillance photographs prior to the war.[103]

In the 1982 invasion of Lebanon, the Israeli Air Force revisited these tactics using domestically produced drones. The Stealthy Scout and Mastiff drones were sent to loiter over the Bekaa Valley[104] and then Sampson decoy drones were sent in. The refinement of adding the loitering spotter drones enabled the Israelis to destroy Syrian air defenses.[105] It is important to note that for more than a year prior to the invasion, Israel had been flying reconnaissance drones over Lebanon and Syria.[106]

Two days after the 1983 bombing of the US Marine Corps barracks in Beirut, which killed 241 (several thousand American servicemen had been deployed in Lebanon for about 18 months), Paul Kelley, the head of the Marine Corps, secretly flew to Beirut to see the carnage firsthand. As recounted in a *Popular Science* article: "Across the border, Israeli intelligence officers watched live television images of Kelley arriving and inspecting the barracks. They even zoomed the picture in tight, placing cross hairs directly on his head."[107]

The Israelis showed Kelley the footage hours later in Tel Aviv. Within months, Kelley persuaded the Pentagon to buy an Israeli Mastiff for testing.[108] The United States then bought several of a newer Israeli system, the Pioneer.

7. DRONES COME INTO THEIR OWN

Technology evolves incrementally. Over the decades, from Wright brothers to Sperry's and Kettering's first drones to the present, a great deal has changed. Improvements in aerodynamics resulted in more efficient and stable wings. Improvements in chemistry made explosives more reliable. Range and duration improved. Guidance became more precise. As these technologies matured, drones became steadily more capable and useful for actual deployment.

However, whether drones were taking pictures as in Vietnam, or dropping explosives as with the V-1, up until the early 1980s their targets had always been either infrastructure or masses of people, but never specific individuals. It was with Israel's deployment of drones in Lebanon that the various constituent technologies of drones had matured to the point that it became possible to watch a particular person from the sky, and then to target and kill that person. This capability was not an evolution of previous capabilities but, in fact, something fundamentally new. This capability made drones more akin to a preternaturally capable sniper than to any previous airplane, manned or unmanned.

This is the moment when drones came into their own. This is when the machines that what we understand today as "drones" became a transformative military technology.

It was the Israelis who first realized this change, at a time when the United States was spending hundreds of millions of dollars annually on drone research while struggling for results. While the NRO worked on top-secret drones that competed with satellites for strategic intelligence collection, work on smaller drones for battlefield intelligence proceeded quite openly. In the mid-1970s the Army's focus was on a project known as SkyEye, built by Developmental Sciences Incorporated (DSI).

By the mid-1970s the second version of SkyEye could stay aloft for up to nine hours, flying 150 miles per hour. It was controlled by a crew of six: a commander, planner, pilot, payload operator, electronics technician, and mechanic.[109] It could fly on autopilot on a pre-planned course or be piloted remotely. Operators could swap out sensor payloads – video feeds, infrared sensors, or still cameras. DSI built a model that could fire rockets, though the US Army chose not to buy the weaponized version. However, in 1982 the Thai Air Force purchased a squadron of weaponized SkyEye drones.[110]

The United States eventually bought two squadrons of SkyEyes. One squadron was sent to El Salvador in 1985 with a secret US Army unit that was supporting the authoritarian government in its fight against a leftist insurgency. Salvadoran rebels made fun of the Americans for flying "toy airplanes"[111] after a SkyEye crashed in the mountains (it may or may not have been shot down). By the mid-1980s the Soviets were equipping the Syrian Army with drones. In 1985 a US engineer expressed his fears to *Newsweek*: "In two to three years [the Soviets will] flood the Warsaw Pact with mini-RPVs."[112]

Throughout the 1970s and 1980s, the same technological competition with the Soviets – both real and imagined – that drove runaway spending on manned aircraft and *Star Wars* – type space systems also drove up the costs of drone research and development. The US Army was not satisfied with SkyEye's capabilities: they wanted more. In 1975, they began a dozen-year long debacle known as Aquila.[113] Initially, it was meant to be a more capable rival to SkyEye that could both take pictures and shine lasers at targets to guide artillery rounds. However, engineers had trouble fitting both the communications link and payload onto Aquila:[114] "[Its] complexity grew steadily from the beginning as it took on requirements for laser target illumination, for secure data links so the enemy could not jam or take over control, for the ability to return home automatically if communications were lost, and for evasive-maneuver capabilities to avoid anti-aircraft fire."[115]

Aquila was finally cancelled in 1987, after the Army had spent more than $750 million (about $2 billion in 2013 dollars).[116] Aquila accomplished its mission on only 7 out of 105 test flights.[117] According to a Government Accountability Office (GAO) report chronicling Aquila's demise, its major problems resulted from the fact that the Army had not adequately accounted for survivability in its testing, as well as "launch, detection, recognition, and location of enemy targets, reliability and maintenance, and human engineering."[118]

As the Army ran into problems with Aquila, the Navy had troubles of its own. The Navy had figured that it would be fairly easy to adapt the Pioneers it had bought from Israel – and which had been designed to be based on land – to operate from ships. But when they deployed Pioneers to the Persian Gulf aboard the USS *Iowa*, the drones kept crashing – three had engine failures, one was lost during a storm,[119] and three more crashed into the ship when trying to land.[120] Then, as now, the United States wanted to be able to spy on Iran. As John Cushman of the *New York Times* wrote in 1987: "Military leaders, in planning how American forces in the Persian Gulf region might be used, have been concerned about the possibility of a pilot falling into Iranian hands. The drone aircraft will help alleviate this concern."[121]

8. FIRST GULF WAR AND THE BALKANS

The first step of Operation Desert Storm – the 1991 Gulf War – was the destruction of Iraqi air defenses. The Coalition forces modeled their tactics on Israeli strategy used between 1973 and 1982, sending Chukar target drones (the Air Force had renamed the drones "Scathe Mean") to provoke Iraqi radar.[122] The thirty-eight target drones were flown by a secret unit that "was kept so small that even medical technicians were pressed into service as missile mechanics."[123] In addition, the United States fired 288 Tomahawk missiles, which also played an important role in the war and were the only weapons to be used against Baghdad during the day.[124]

The Iraqis had been testing drones of their own in preparing for the war, potentially for dispersing anthrax.[125] As the bombardment of Iraq continued in February 1991, the Navy used Pioneers to guide more than one million pounds of artillery fire from the USS *Missouri* alone.[126] A group of Iraqi soldiers waved a white flag to a Pioneer flying over Faylaka Island, marking the first recorded surrender to a drone.[127] The Army and Marines also flew the Pioneer in the Gulf War, although each service used a different video format,[128] making it difficult to share information. Two of the Pioneers were lost to electromagnetic interference[129] and one to enemy action.[130]

The Marines also flew the 45-pound hand-launched Pointer drone and the 90-pound Exdrone in the Gulf War.[131] The Exdrone had originally been intended to jam enemy communications, but was modified to transmit live video. It could loiter for up to two hours, and was flown over Kuwait City, scouting for the US Marines who were the first allied forces to enter the city.[132]

While drones had limited use in the First Gulf War, their performance alerted military planners to both their shortcomings and their increasing utility.

Even as the Navy used the Israeli-made Pioneers in the war, it was also developing a larger, secret drone of its own. The first version of this new drone, called Amber, was tested in November 1986.[133] Amber weighed 750 pounds fully loaded.[134] It was designed to carry the same cameras as the Pioneer, plus either a sophisticated radio relay system that would extend its effective range or a system for monitoring enemy communications.[135] However, the development of Amber "was cancelled after having demonstrated successful canister and runway launch and endurance of some 40 hours at 25,000 feet."[136] Even though it was technically promising, Amber became "yet another example of how a weak, divided constituency combined with Congressional scrutiny kept a promising system from reaching the field."[137]

Even after the Navy withdrew its support and DARPA funding ended, Amber eventually made it to the field. It had been designed to launch with a rocket booster from a canister. Its designer, Abraham Karem, an Israeli who had moved to California, also made a smaller version called the Gnat, which he wanted to sell commercially abroad.[138] With the outbreak of hostilities in the Balkans, another customer came calling: the CIA. In early 1993 the CIA deployed a Gnat-750 to Bosnia.

The United States learned how to use medium-endurance drones over the Balkans in the 1990s. The CIA led the way because the Pentagon's acquisition bureaucracy was too plodding.[139] In late 1993 the CIA was preparing to deploy two Gnat-750s to an Albanian base from which they were to fly over Bosnia. One of them crashed in California when a software glitch made the drone think it had landed while it was still in the air, vindicating Air Force critics who thought the CIA was moving too quickly.[140]

That first CIA deployment was limited. The Gnat "completed only 12 out of 30 missions attempted because of bad weather and data link problems."[141]

The Gnat drones had to send their data via a manual relay aircraft that could stay in the air for only two hours, and the infrared sensor they used was not very effective.[142]

At the same time, the CIA and Pentagon were both involved in developing a more advanced version of the drone, the Gnat 750-45, which would later become better known by another name: Predator. New synthetic aperture radars under development had better resolution, but the focus was on "stiff-arming" attempts to "complicate the program with add-on require-ments."[143] It was only the pressing need to deploy to Bosnia that prevented the Predator from going the way of Aquila, to be lost in a death spiral of cost overruns.

The Predator has a convoluted history. It had been conceived in the mid-1980s as a DARPA/Navy program, and at one point looked to be going to the Army until the secretary of defense designated the Air Force as the lead military service for the Predator in April 1996.[144] The new Predator squadron – the 11th Reconnaissance Squadron – was the first Air Force drone unit since 1979.

The CIA's Gnats shepherded UN convoys and scouted out Serbian artillery and anti-aircraft weapons. The Gnats redeployed to Croatia in summer 1994, but were still limited by their data links.[145] In July 1995, Air Force Predators deployed to Bosnia for the first time. The deployment was not without problems. Two of the three Predators deployed were lost; one was shot down and the other had an engine malfunction.[146] These early Predator drones had limited satellite connectivity. The next generation, which deployed from Hungary in March 1996, had better radar, de-icing equipment, and, for the first time, could broadcast video to multiple users.[147]

The deployment of the Predator in the mid-1990s also marked the first operational use by a drone of the almost brand-new Global Positioning System (GPS) for navigation.[148] With this innovation the problem of navigation was, for all intents and purposes, solved. However the early satellite control of the Predator was, in part, improvised – using commercial communications satel-lites not only to transmit images, but also for control signals.[149]

The older Israeli Pioneers were also deployed in Bosnia, although "the systems experienced numerous mechanical failures. Five vehicles crashed as a result of engine, generator, rocket-assisted takeoff, or computer failure. Add-itionally, the mountainous terrain proved to be a major hindrance to the Pioneers [sic] data link."[150]

At the time, the Predators were equipped with radios that let their pilots talk to air traffic controllers; this was a crucial technology for sharing airspace with manned aircraft.[151]

From March 1996 onward, Predators flew constantly over Bosnia, gaining experience. More than six hundred Predator missions were flown over the next two years and four months.[152] That experience not only tested and improved their capacity to communicate with air traffic controllers, but also a revealed a wide-ranging set of lessons in how to use this new tool. Steven Hampton, the commander of the 11th Reconnaissance Squadron, told *Air Force Magazine*:

> At first, we fell into the trap of "reporting the news" ... we were on the "scene of the crime," showing what was happening. [But] our job is to ignore that, go over the horizon, and find out what's not happening yet ... We were showing the warfighters what they wanted to see, rather than what they needed to see.[153]

By the time the conflict in the Balkans heated up again in Kosovo, drones had come to play a much larger role. By June 1999 the *New York Times* reported that "drones are crisscrossing the skies over Kosovo, acting as electronic scouts, finding and filming elusive targets, especially Serbian troops hidden in bunkers or woods, and sending those images immediately to fighter jets overhead."[154]

The paper described how at least twenty-one drones were lost over Kosovo for a variety of reasons, indicating the feverish operational tempo of their deployment. By June 2001, real-time video from an Army Hunter drone was able to guide a column of US soldiers out of an ambush.[155] (7,000 Americans and 50,000 NATO troops had deployed to Kosovo.) The Hunter would later be criticized for its ineffectiveness. Its "limited vision made it difficult to find small groups of enemy forces over large geographical areas."[156] Nevertheless, it was a start, as American soldiers were soon to find themselves in a mission that, although it resembled peacekeeping in its tactical challenges, was far different.

9. REFLECTING ON DECADES OF DRONE DEVELOPMENT

While whoever is building the latest strategic drone has almost always claimed that it will be cheaper to operate than what it is replacing, this has seldom, if ever, been true. The tactical use of drones in wartime has led to advances in technology because there is more tangible evidence of what drones can accomplish. Strategic drones, from the 1960s to the present, persistently overpromise performance and overrun budgets. In 2004, the Air Force said the Global Hawk would cost $6.3 billion,[157] less than half of what it currently estimates as the cost, and a number that is likely to grow in the future. Much of the accounting is done in secrecy and much money is spent on improving the sensor payloads, which are counted separately. The intelligence product that is eventually produced is shrouded in secrecy, so it is difficult to evaluate whether the tens of billions of dollars spent are in any sense "worth it."

The Predator's success (as well as the earlier successes of the Gnat and Amber drones) in the Balkans was paralleled by costly and failed strategic UAV programs in the 1990s, much as the Lightning Bug's success in Vietnam was paralleled by the failures of Tagboard and Compass Arrow in the 1960s and 1970s.

There were two major strategic UAVs being evaluated in the 1990s. The more successful version evolved into the Global Hawk, which continues to fly today. The other, Dark Star, was cancelled after between $250 million and $300 million was spent.[158] This is a useful example of how program secrecy makes it very difficult to evaluate whether or not the hundreds of millions of dollars spent were wasted or enabled productive advances that have enabled present-day UAV capabilities.

Lockheed Martin later built the RQ-170 Sentinel drone, about which little is known in the public domain. It has been pictured in Kandahar,[159] and a Sentinel either crashed or was brought down over Iran in December 2011.[160] The Sentinel and the Dark Star look very similar, and it appears that Lockheed Martin's work on the earlier drone, and the hundreds of millions spent, clearly informed the design of the Sentinel.

Similarly, each Global Hawk, manufactured by Northrop Grumman (which in 1999 acquired Teledyne Ryan, the Lightning Bug maker)[161] cost more than $12 billion to build.[162] The Air Force has only twenty Global Hawks,[163] and has been steadily cutting the number planned, from an initial seventy-seven. The same sort of problems that plagued Tagboard in the 1960s trouble the Global Hawk today: "Pentagon tests also suggested last fall that the new Air Force model was not reliable enough to provide sustained surveillance. Parts failed frequently."[164]

Takeoff and landing continue to be challenges, just as they were in the days when Orville Wright was designing the Army's first drone. The Predators, Reapers, and Global Hawks of today can be operated via satellite once they are in the air, but must be launched and landed by forward-deployed pilots who can see the runway. Part of the reason for this is the delay inherent in bouncing a signal up to a satellite and back. Another factor is the difficulty of "situational awareness." Even if a drone's operator can see high-fidelity images of what is going on below on the ground, that does not mean the operator has a full 3-dimensional sense of what is going on around the drone, the way the pilot of a manned aircraft does. These limitations are why drones remain vulnerable to a technologically sophisticated enemy who want to shoot it down. As the World War II pilot said, the doodle-bugs do not shoot back.

On September 11, 2001, a Predator drone was lost flying over Iraq; it remains unclear if it was shot down or crashed. Another had been lost on August 27 and a third went down on October 10. These three loses represented a third of the fleet. By October 11, 2001, the Air Force was left with a total of six Predators. This number would soon grow dramatically. Drones were about to transcend their status as useful, specialized tools. From that point on, they became a central part of the US military machine.

Even though they are now crucial to US military operations, drones remain limited in two key ways. The first is their vulnerability. The second is that they have become too good at gathering information. Drone operators are in danger of drowning in data, and automated imagery analysis is, for now and the foreseeable future, limited in what it can do. It is easy to be awed by a new gadget – a drone with longer endurance, more stealth, or a higher resolution sensor. But the limitations of drones are the limitations of the system, and for now these limitations are in the analysis of information, not its collection. Also, the evolution of drones over the last decade has taken place within the environments in which they were deployed, which have involved uncontested US air superiority. It is wrong to assume that the United States will always have such dominance.

Taking in the full panorama of the technological history of drones – from Orville Wright's design of the Kettering bug, to the lives lost in Operations Anvil and Aphrodite in the 1940s, to the many debacles of Cold War drone development – shows that change has never come as quickly as drone proponents claimed it would. There is no good reason to believe today is different.

Setting aside projections of change, the drones of the present already have a profound effect on the ability of the United States to gather information and to deliver lethal force where and when its leaders choose.

It is difficult to understand and evaluate the transformative nature of the present-day technological capacity of drones. It is neither clear how the capacity of drones affects US interactions with its allies and adversaries, nor how the ability to see so much, strike so selectively, and so far away impacts national sovereignty or core issues of fundamental rights. Throughout the long history of aircraft – manned and unmanned – it has always been easier to look to the future than make sense of the present.

Until the change was seen in practice over Bosnia, no one in the US defense establishment fully appreciated the fundamental change in what drones could do once they could loiter indefinitely instead of make quick observing passes. There can be no doubt that the same is true of tomorrow's drones. If the century-long history of drones shows anything, it is that heralded revolutions have never come to pass as foretold. Change has snuck up, escaping notice and understanding until after it has already happened.

NOTES

1 Miller, Donald, *Masters of the air: America's bomber boys who fought the air war against Nazi Germany* (New York, NY: Simon and Schuster, 2007), p. 302.

2 Ross, Stewart Halsey, *Strategic bombing by the United States in World War II: The myths and the facts* (Jefferson, NC: McFarland & Company, 2003), p. 115.

3 *New York Times*, "Pilotless plane flies ninety miles," November, 15, 1922.

4 Ehrhard, Thomas P., *Air force UAVs: The secret history* (Arlington, VA: The Mitchell Institute for Airpower Studies, 2010), p. 28.

5 Werrell, Kenneth, *The evolution of the cruise missile* (Maxwell Air Force Base, AL: Air University Press, 1985), p. 8.

6 Blom, John David, "Unmanned aerial systems: A historical perspective," Occasional Paper 37 (Fort Leavenworth, KS: Combat Studies Institute Press, 2010), p. 45.

7 Werrell, *The evolution of the cruise missile*, p. 11.

8 Ibid.

9 Ibid., p. 17.

10 *New York Times*, "Pilotless plane flies ninety miles."

11 *New York Times*, "Big bomber sets record at air meet," October 6, 1923.

12 *New York Times*, "The worst menace of another war," November 23, 1924.

13 Kellerstrass, E. J., "Drone remotely piloted vehicles and aerospace power," *Air University Review*, September–October 1973.

14 Dunlap, Orrin, "Sightseeing with a birdman," *New York Times*, March 10, 1940.

15 Ibid.

16 Blom, "Unmanned aerial systems," p. 8.

17 Daniell, Raymond, "Winged 1-Ton bomb bared; German weapon is erratic," *New York Times*, June 17, 1944.

18 *New York Times*, "US robot plane action under Senate's inquiry," June 18, 1944.

19 Werrell, *The evolution of the cruise missile*, p. 60.

20 Ibid.

21 Ibid., p. 35.

22 Ibid.

23 Ibid.

24 Ibid., p. 24.

25 *New York Times*, "Quotations," June 25, 1944.

26 Sullivan, Jeffery, "Evolution or revolution? Rise of UAVs," *IEEE Technology and Society* 25 (2006): 43–49.

27 Ibid., p. 14.

28 Ibid., p. 17.

29 Ibid., p. 21.

30 Ibid.

31 Baldwin, Hanson, "Lessons learned in Bikini tests," *New York Times*, August 1, 1946.

32 Ibid.

33 Hanson Baldwin, "The 'drone': Portent of a Push-Button War," *New York Times*, August 25, 1946.

34 *New York Times*, "Navy air device shown: Pilotless planes and missiles are launched by 'Zebra,'" October 4, 1946.

35 Baldwin, "Lessons learned in Bikini tests."

36 Baldwin, "The 'drone': Portent of a push-button war."

37 *New York Times*, "Robot mail planes proposed," June 24, 1944.

38 *New York Times*, "Test flying opposed," October 1, 1946.

39 *New York Times*, "Guided-missile use seen in psychological warfare," June 3, 1951.

40 Trussell, C. P., "Truman watches attack by drones," *New York Times*, September 17, 1947.

41 Baldwin, Hanson, "Awesome era of fantastic missiles," *New York Times*, August 29, 1954.

42 Lundberg, Anders, "High explosives in stockpile surveillance indicate constancy," *Science & Technology Review* December (1996): 13–17.

43 Babcock, Elizabeth, *Magnificent mavericks: Transition of the naval ordnance test station from rocket station to research, development, test, and evaluation center, 1948–58* (Washington, DC: Government Printing Office, 2008), p. 326.

44 Baldwin, "Awesome era of fantastic missiles."

45 Werrell, *The evolution of the cruise missile*, p. 110.

46 *New York Times*, "Stars seen guiding pilotless planes," June 10, 1949.

47 Werrell, *The evolution of the cruise missile*, p. 115.

48 Blom, "Unmanned aerial systems," p. 50.

49 *New York Times*, "New army camera flies alone at night for low-level glimpse of foe 'over hill,'" December 28, 1957.

50 Blom, "Unmanned aerial systems," p. 50.

51 Ibid., p. 51.

52 Ibid.

53 Werrell, *The evolution of the cruise missile*, p. 142.

54 Kellerstrass, "Drone remotely piloted vehicles and aerospace power."

55 Ibid.

56 Blom, "Unmanned aerial systems," p. 55.

57 Ibid., p. 56.

58 Ehrhard, "Air force UAVs," p. 8.

59 Ibid.
60 Blom, "Unmanned aerial systems," p. 58.
61 Ibid.
62 Ehrhard, "Air force UAVs," p. 24.
63 Kellerstrass, "Drone remotely piloted vehicles and aerospace power."
64 Ibid.
65 Ehrhard, "Air force UAVs," p 9.
66 Ibid.
67 Ibid.
68 Ibid.
69 Ibid., p 24.
70 Ibid., p 29.
71 Ibid., p. 28.
72 Ibid., p. 70.
73 Ibid., p. 28.
74 Ibid., p. 34.
75 Ibid., p. 26.
76 Ibid., p. 26.
77 Ibid., p. 29.
78 Ibid., p. 35.
79 Ibid.
80 Ibid., p. 10.
81 Ibid.
82 Ibid.
83 Ibid.
84 Blom, "Unmanned aerial systems," p. 65.
85 Ibid.
86 Ehrhard, "Air force UAVs," p. 12.
87 Ibid.
88 Kellerstrass, "Drone remotely piloted vehicles and aerospace power."
89 Ibid.
90 Ehrhard, "Air force UAVs," p. 12.
91 Signor, Philip W. "Cruise missiles for the U.S. Navy: An exemplar of innovation in a military organization," Naval War College, 1994.
92 Betts, Richard, Cruise missiles: Technology, strategy, politics, *Washington Quarterly* 4 (1981): 66–80.
93 Signor, "Cruise missiles for the U.S. Navy: An exemplar of innovation in a military organization," p. 4.
94 Betts, Cruise missiles: Technology, strategy, politics.
95 Ibid.
96 Werrell, *The evolution of the cruise missile*, p. 135.
97 Ibid., p. 136.
98 Ibid., p. 141.

99 Pfaltzgraff, Robert L. Jr., and Jacquelyn K. Davis, *The cruise missile: Bargaining chip or defense bargain?* (Cambridge, MA: Institute for Foreign Policy Analysis, 1977), p. 21.

100 Werrell, *The evolution of the cruise missile*, p. 190.

101 Ibid., p. 190.

102 Ehrhard, "Air force UAVs," p. 25.

103 Blom, "Unmanned aerial systems," p. 72.

104 Schefter, Jim, "Stealthy robot planes," *Popular Science*, October 1987.

105 Ibid.

106 *New York Times*, "Israel derides Syrian photos," May 14, 1981. Shipler, David, "Habib and Begin talk after Syria downs a drone," *New York Times*, May 15, 1981. Shipler, David, "Missiles from Syria down Israeli drone: Begin makes offer," *New York Times*, May 25, 1981. Kifner, John, "Syrian soldiers are jubilant as missile brings down Israeli drone," *New York Times*, May 15, 1981. Farrell, William, "Syrian SAM missile downs Israel drone over East Lebanon," *New York Times*, May 23, 1981.

107 Schefter, "Stealthy robot planes."

108 Blom, "Unmanned aerial systems," p. 72.

109 Ibid., p. 68.

110 Ibid., p. 67.

111 Marbach, William, Peter Maclevey, John Berry, "Homing in with drones," *Newsweek*, September 16, 1985.

112 Ibid.

113 Schefter, "Stealthy robot planes."

114 Blom, "Unmanned aerial systems," p. 69.

115 Schefter, "Stealthy robot planes," p. 68.

116 Cushman, John, "Flaws force new delay in army drone," *New York Times*, October 6, 1987. An estimated $750 million was spent on the project from 1975 to 1987. When 1981 dollars are converted to 2013 dollars, the total is around $1.92 billion.

117 Government Accountability Office, "Aquila remotely piloted vehicle: Its potential battlefield contribution still in doubt," October 1987.

118 Ibid.

119 Cushman, John, "A warship's 'eyes' scan Gulf region," *New York Times*, December 20, 1987.

120 *New York Times*, "Navy giving up drone planes on losing 4 of 5, Officials Say," February 17, 1987.

121 Cushman, "A warship's 'eyes' scan Gulf region."

122 *Aviation Week & Space Technology*, "BQM-74 drones operated by former GLCM unit played key role in deceiving Iraqi military," April 27, 1992.

123 Ibid.

124 Nicholls, David J., "Cruise missiles and modern war: Strategic and technological implications," Occasional Paper No. 13, Center for Strategy and Technology, Air War College, May 2000.

125 Broad, William, and Judith Miller, "The deal on Iraq: Secret arsenal," *New York Times*, February 26, 1998.
126 Blom, "Unmanned aerial systems," p. 89.
127 Ibid., p. 90.
128 Ibid.
129 Ibid., p. 84.
130 Ibid., p. 90.
131 Ibid.
132 Ibid., p. 91.
133 Morocco, John, "Navy plans operational trials for Amber RPV in 1989," *Aviation Week and Space Technology*, December 12, 1987.
134 Ibid.
135 Ibid.
136 Ehrhard, "Air force UAVs," p. 21.
137 Ibid
138 Ibid.
139 Fulghum, David, and John Morrocco, "CIA to deploy UAVs in Albania," *Aviation Week and Space Technology*, January 31, 1994.
140 Ibid.
141 Asker, James, "Spying on Bosnia," *Aviation Week and Space Technology*, June 6, 1994.
142 Fulghum, David, "CIA to fly missions from inside Croatia," *Aviation Week and Space Technology*, July 11, 1994.
143 Asker, "Spying on Bosnia."
144 Ehrhard, "Air force UAVs," p. 51.
145 Blom, "Unmanned aerial systems," p. 94.
146 Ibid., p. 93.
147 Ibid.
148 Ehrhard, "Air force UAVs," p. 49.
149 Ibid.
150 Blom, "Unmanned aerial systems," p. 94.
151 Sweetman, Bill, "US UAVs stick to their guns," *Interavia Business* and *Technology*, July 1, 1998.
152 Ibid.
153 Tirpak, John A., "The robotic Air Force," *Air Force Magazine*, September 1997.
154 Becker, Elizabeth, "They're unmanned, they fly low, and they get the picture," *New York Times*, June 3, 1999.
155 Gordon, Michael, "For G.I.'s, a Balkan road of neither war nor peace," *New York Times*, July 17, 2001.
156 Blom, "Unmanned aerial systems," p. 110.
157 Government Accountability Office, "Changes in Global Hawk's acquisition strategy are needed to reduce program risks," November 2004.

158 Fulghum, David, "Long-term stealth project gets the ax," *Aviation Week and Space Technology*, May 24, 1999.

159 Sweetman, Bill, "The beast is back," *Aviation Week and Space Technology*, January 25, 2011.

160 Reynolds, James, "Iran shows film of captured US Drone," BBC, December 8, 2011.

161 Northrop Grumman. www.northropgrumman.com/heritage/index.html.

162 Drew, Christopher, "Costly drone is poised to replace U-2 spy plane," *New York Times*, August 2, 2011.

163 "RQ-4 Global Hawk," USAF Fact Sheet, January 27, 2012.

164 Drew, "Costly drone is poised to replace U-2 spy plane."

20

Drones and the Dilemma of Modern Warfare

SAMUEL ISSACHAROFF AND RICHARD PILDES

1. THE LEGAL TRANSFORMATION OF WAR

The morality and legitimacy of the practices of war – or, at least, the use of military force – are undergoing a fundamental transformation. This transformation is not yet directly or fully reflected in the formal laws of war, but as these changes embed themselves in the practices of states, especially dominant states, in practice they might eventually come to be embodied in the legal frameworks that regulate the use of force. The fundamental transformation is this: Whereas the traditional practices and laws of war defined "the enemy" in terms of categorical, group-based judgments that turned on *status* – a person was an enemy not because of any specific actions he himself engaged in, but because he was a member of an opposing army – we are now moving toward a world that implicitly or explicitly requires *the individuation of personal responsibility* of specific "enemy" persons before the use of military force is considered justified, at least as a moral and political matter. This shift applies not to any one particular type of military force, such as lethal force, but to all exertions of military power over enemies, including the ways in which they are captured, detained, incapacitated, or tried.

To a limited but significant extent thus far, this transformation is reflected in the domestic law of some countries. Some of these issues have been addressed, for example, in evolving US constitutional jurisprudence resulting from recent decisions of the United States Supreme Court, as well in interpretations of international law by different domestic courts, including the Israeli Supreme Court.[1] However, this quiet, subtle, and inadequately appreciated transformation has been taking place far more as a matter of slowly accepted practices than as settled legal development.[2] The process of legal transformation in turn shapes arguments about the proper uses of military force in the context of fighting terrorism, yielding a debate that often comes across as polarized or confused or simply unable to engage with diverse positions, however reasonable. Precisely because we are in the midst of this transformation, we do not have clear prior legal frameworks, either domestically or internationally, to draw on to provide determinate legal guidance for addressing the transformed and transforming nature of modern warfare.

2. INDIVIDUATING ENEMY RESPONSIBILITY

Three principal sets of factors are driving this transformation in the morality and practices of modern uses of military force. First, the unique structure of modern terrorism inherently creates a need for responsive states to be able to identify correctly the specific individuals who are, in fact, terrorists. Second, modern technological developments, which make terrorism more potentially threatening, also enable dominant states to respond in more discriminating ways; the capacity to do so is likely to generate pressure toward an obligation to do so (if "ought" implies "can," as theorists have long debated, "can" sometimes implies "ought"). Third, the post–World War II rise of the more general concern for human rights, as a legal and cultural matter, has created pressure for dominant states seeking legitimacy for their actions to incorporate a more general humanitarian concern into their actions, including with respect to the rights of enemies during wartime.

The key to the traditional, status-based regime of the laws of war was that conventional soldiers fought openly as members of an organized military under state control. In particular, they wore uniforms (except for covert operatives), displayed weapons, and fought under an organized command structure. As a result, it was accepted, legally and morally, that the opposing side could treat them on the basis of their status, as simply members of the opposing fighting force.[3] As an initial matter, little dispute typically existed about their identity as a member of the enemy – the open carrying of weapons and wearing of uniforms resolved that issue.[4]

In addition, there was no need to determine whether such a soldier had committed any specific identifiable act that would legitimately make him a target for the use of military force. Whether a soldier had fired at the opposing side, or planted a bomb, or engaged in any specific act, or even just handled clerical duties, was irrelevant: group membership in the opposing army was sufficient.[5] Thus on the front end of the use of force – capture, detention, even uses of lethal force – there was no need to differentiate among soldiers or attempt to individuate personal responsibility for participation in the enemy's war machinery. Only if someone was going to be tried for acts outside the permissible scope of the laws of war – for war crimes – was there a need to determine individual levels of responsibility.[6] Finally, the same status-based, group-membership principles applied on the backend of the use of force; how long an enemy soldier would be detained was not a function of his own individual responsibility for specific acts, but of his membership in the group. Prisoners of war were released collectively, as part of a group, at the war's end or as part of mutually agreed-upon prisoner exchanges.[7]

Terrorism inherently changes all of this. Among the distinct features of terrorism are two that remove it clearly from conventional warfare and that pose significant challenges for states forced into combat. Both turn on the strategic centrality of placing civilian populations at risk, a clear violation of the evolved laws of war. The first factor is that terrorists, as a matter of practice, target civilians as civilians, and not because of proximity to conventional military objectives. Targeting civilians breaks down any traditional understanding of the battlefield or even of the potential zone of engagement. A nightclub in Indonesia is interchangeable with a commuter train in Madrid or the Boston Marathon. This places great pressure on states responding to terrorism to become proactive and to respond anticipatorily to perceived terrorists. In turn, the need to act swiftly outside any confined battlefield leads to the second complicating feature of terrorism. Because terrorists do not wear uniforms, attributions of status based on group membership are far more uncertain and complex. Terrorists (and some guerrilla forces in civil wars) violate the cardinal principle of "distinction" by which combatants can be clearly differentiated from the civilian population.

Moreover, even apart from the issue of uniforms, the ability to know that an individual is part of a terrorist organization, based on anything other than his own individual acts of terrorism, is also difficult. Terrorists typically do not "join" the organization in some formally visible way equivalent to the wearing of uniforms.[8] While some terrorists do swear oaths of affiliation to signify their membership in an organization, many do not; in addition, even if such an oath has been taken, obtaining proof of it is far more difficult than proof that a solider was wearing a uniform. Indeed, it might be easier to prove that an individual committed a specific act of terrorism than it is to prove that he or she took an oath of affiliation.[9] Attributions of status through group membership alone are therefore extremely difficult to establish. Most terrorists against whom military force is used, therefore, are not identified on the basis of membership, per se, but because of the specific acts in which they have engaged. Perversely, the act defines their status.

As a result of the nature of modern terrorism, therefore, these structural features inevitably and unavoidably propel the use of military force to be directed against specific individuals based on the specific *acts* those individuals are believed to have committed, as opposed to their status. That is why the use of military force against terrorists *necessarily* must shift, and has shifted, away from the traditional group-based membership attributions of responsibility and toward individuated judgments of responsibility.[10] And this individuation – or the pressure to maintain this individuation – applies to every stage of the use of military force.

First, the initial threshold issue of identification becomes far more complex and consequential: Is this actually the specific person believed to have committed specific acts? A whole new regime (whatever its precise contours) to ensure the *accuracy* of the initial identification question becomes necessary – something virtually irrelevant in the traditional war context. Second, the *degree and type* of the appropriate use of military force up front might suddenly become relevant in a way that they are not in the traditional context. In traditional war contexts, one did not distinguish among soldiers and officers based on any sense of specific responsibility; if a barracks could be bombed or artillery directed at an advancing force, these things were done without any attempt to differentiate the different levels of responsibility or culpability of individual soldiers or officers. Today, however, it might well be that uses of lethal force, in the form of targeted killings of specific individuals through measure like drone attacks, are more appropriate and justified against high-level commanders than low-level foot soldiers.[11] Similarly, on the backend of the use of military force, when it comes to matters like detention of enemy terrorists, it might also be proper – as a moral and political matter, at least – to individuate responsibility. We might hold the architects of 9/11 indefinitely, but it might not be appropriate similarly to hold low-level couriers or others indefinitely. In traditional wars, of course, these distinctions were mostly irrelevant; all members of the enemy, based on their status, were released as part of group-based releases.[12]

The central focus of this chapter is on the effects of the altered battlefront on the conduct of war. There is a great, but unrecognized, paradox underlying the emerging individuation of responsibility. This paradox accounts for a good deal of the polarized positions that have circulated since 9/11 about the legitimate uses of military force. As the fundamental transformation in the practice of the uses of military force moves, even implicitly, toward an individuated model of responsibility, military force inevitably begins to look justified in similar terms to the uses of punishment in the criminal justice system. That is, to the extent that someone can be targeted for the use of military force (capture, detention, killing) only because of the precise, specific acts in which he or she as an individual participated, military force now begins to look more and more like an implicit "adjudication" of individual responsibility. A tremendous premium immediately comes to be placed on what we might call "adjudicative facts" – is this the person who did X? – rather than "legislative facts" – is this person a solider in the opposing army? As soon as military force must be tied to individuated judgments of responsibility, it is easy to understand why, for some critics of the use of force, questions will arise regarding why it is the military and not the judicial system that is making these individualized, adjudicative judgments. These kind of individuated judgments have not traditionally been the province of the military, after all. And there is an understandable impulse to conclude that if we are in the world of individualized, adjudicative-like judgments, the institution most traditionally designed for that function is the judicial system.[13]

Thus, as the unavoidable structural forces that drive uses of military force against modern terrorism come to depend on individuated judgments of responsibility, it is also inevitable that the boundaries between the military system and the judicial system will become more permeable than in the past. The two systems are unlikely to exist in hermetic isolation from each other. The considerations that have traditionally informed one will spill over into the other – and vice versa. That is the fundamental reason that the debates over the appropriate uses of military force have been, or are likely to remain for some time, unresolved, uncertain, confused, and polarized.

In our view, the principal task of the modern morality and, eventually, the laws of war – the task this chapter sets for itself – is to come to terms with the transformed legal and military environments of modern warfare and with the emerging imperative to individuate responsibility when using lethal force against terrorism. We believe it is a serious mistake to conclude from this inevitable individuation that the traditional civil and criminal judicial system should, as a result, fully supplant and displace the uses of military force altogether. For this reason, the use of military force must be adapted – as it already is in the midst of doing under both internal and external pressures – to embrace and to take fully into account the reality that "enemy" responsibility in this era must be individuated.

The military, for example, is already in the process of trying to generate procedural protections, analogous to those used in more traditional adjudicative settings but adapted to the unique context of military force, that provide sufficient accuracy and legitimacy to ensure that these individuated attributions of responsibility are being made through credible processes and structures to make them as accurate and fair as possible.[14] That is true whether the military force at issue involves detention or targeted killings. To the extent the US government as a whole succeeds in generating the novel structures, institutions, and processes necessary to legitimate the use of military force in an age of individuated enemy responsibility, these uses of force will be more widely accepted. Our aim is to contribute to that project.

We structure our inquiry around the key issue of the individuation of proper targets in modern war settings, whether for purposes of long-term detention or – more dramatically – for purposes of targeted killing. Although our discussion here is limited to the consequences of the projection of lethal force, targeted killing shares with the detention of irregular combatants the critical features of targeted warfare. Both turn on proper and legally justifiable decisions about the nature of the individuals selected for coercive action, either through capture or physical elimination. To the extent that the object-ive is not prospective punishment but incapacitation of a military threat, both detention and targeted killing fall within the historic domain of military conduct. Yet the requirement of certainty as to individual complicity in threatening activities lends legalization to the individual-specific determin-ations and begins to bleed into the civilian law concepts of criminal proof and due process. However, even the individual-specific determinations mask the fundamentally different objectives of the criminal versus military deter-minations. In its pure form, the criminal law justifies ongoing detention by a retrospective examination of the severity of the proven crime. Military decisions, whether through detention or targeted attack, are prospective assessments of the future dangerousness of the enemy combatant,[15] a decision for which past conduct may be the most important evidentiary consideration, yet one that may not be determinative – as we shall set out further.

3. TARGETED KILLINGS AND DRONES

The general legal concerns over lawful and appropriate uses of military force in today's circumstances were acutely brought to light when the US government killed Anwar al-Awlaki, an American-born radical Islamist cleric, on September 30, 2011, while he was traveling between Marib and Jawf Provinces in northern Yemen.[16] The targeted killing was carried out by Joint Special Operations Command (JSOC) in apparent cooperation with the CIA.[17] The mission involved two Predator drones flown from a secret American base in the Arabian Peninsula, which fired Hellfire missiles at a car that was carrying al-Awlaki and other alleged operatives from al-Qaeda's branch in Yemen.[18] The Obama administration explicitly authorized the targeted killing of al-Awlaki early in 2010, placing him on lists of terrorists approved for capture or killing[19] – lists that are maintained and made operational by the CIA and the military.[20]

Such targeted killings highlight the reality that the modern practice of military force in asymmetric conflicts cannot be carried forward without a kind of individuation of enemy responsibility that was largely unknown to the traditional laws of war. As a result, analogous kinds of novel ex ante and ex post processes and institutional issues inevitably emerge concerning when specific individuals can properly be targeted for lethal military force. Targeting a particular enemy combatant may be viewed as the antithesis to the general, indiscriminate bombing of civilian centers during World War II, or the general strafing of enemy armies. Indeed, as practiced, the most sophisticated targeted killing programs make fine-grained distinctions among and between enemy "soldiers" as only those exceptionally high up in the command and operational structures singled out for personalized targeting. Thus, as with detention, there is a tremendous premium on making sure the initial identification decision is accurate, unlike in conventional wars when battlefield armies and uniforms inherently resolve the identification and accuracy issues. What processes should suffice to ensure sufficient accuracy in the critical initial determination that the specific acts of a particular individual rise to the level appropriate to trigger the use of lethal force? Which institutions in the government, and how many branches of the government, should be required to participate in that decision and in what form?

Similarly, ex post process and accountability issues arise concerning how to assess whether the individuated judgments of enemy responsibility were indeed accurate and how proportionate the effects of a targeted killing were to the legitimate military objectives. Retrospective refinement of the criteria and processes used for decision making emerges as critical to all targeted warfare decisions. The ex post issues differ between detention and targeted killings in certain obvious ways. In detention the issue is how to determine appropriately whether someone represents a continuing threat, while in targeted killings the issue is retrospective analysis of the initial targeting judgments. The fact that individualized judgments of responsibility are involved creates similar pressures for ex post assessment to ensure the justification of subsequent military action.

Finally, the recurring paradox associated with individuation arises just as much with targeted killings as with detention. If the government is making such adjudicative-like judgments of individual responsibility before using military force, should it be required to use the more traditional institutions and processes through which similar ascriptions of individual moral and legal responsibility are traditionally made – namely, the criminal law?[21] The al-Awlaki case provides a useful introduction: "Unlike detention, for which litigation has produced detailed public elaboration of the government's legal standards, the drone program is shrouded in secrecy, though presumably targeting decisions are based on similar law of armed conflict standards in assessing who is or is not an enemy fighter."[22]

Targeting critical enemy leaders is a longstanding, if delicate, facet of warfare. Whether the means involve training the long rifles of the post–Civil War-era on opposing field commanders, or deploying snipers, or shooting down the airplane of Admiral Yamamoto during World War II, warring armies have always recognized that all soldiers may be soldiers, but some pose a more lethal threat than others, or at least may be subjected to specific targeting. While new forms of targeting allow warfare to be conducted from distances far removed from the exchanges of fire on the battlefield, it is important to note that the history of military technology has always focused on the ability to deliver lethal force from a distance. The current debate over drones and targeted killings, then, is in one sense a mere technological update of earlier efforts to degrade the military ability of the enemy.

In an important sense, however, modern targeting and the use of drones is a more central part of contemporary warfare. What may have originated as a tactical response now emerges as a central strategy for attacking enemy forces. The specific forms of targeting are a reflection of the particular geo-political context in which we live, the military technology now available, and weak or failed states that cannot or will not control the threat these groups pose to citizens and residents of other countries.

Military attacks conducted from a distance involve either static or dynamic targeting. Static targeting, in which the aim is to take out a particular fixed facility, is essentially no different than the bombing runs of World War II, save for the technology. By contrast, the new technology, as with cruise missiles, offers the ability to engage in dynamic targeting that responds to momentary windows of opportunity against specific individuals or activities, rather than the more examined decision to take out fixed structures.[23]

Drones present the question of dynamic targeting most clearly, but do so in at least two different contexts, according to public accounts. In the first context, the government might be aware, for example, that a certain house is used by Taliban-associated forces for bomb making. When drone surveillance detects a group of militants entering the house carrying weapons and materials used to make bombs, and the drone operators launch a missile strike at the house, they might not know the names of any of the individuals involved. In the second context, intelligence actors might have been tracking the whereabouts of the Taliban's chief bomb-making expert, and when he enters the house, the drones are ordered to strike – in this context, military decision makers know the name of the figure involved.

Traditionally, the laws of war grew out of the intersection between the Law of Armed Conflict (LOAC), developed by militaries to govern the rights of combatants, and international humanitarian law (IHL), which was largely developed to govern the treatment of civilian non-combatants and combatants *hors de combat* (soldiers who are placed out of combat when they surrender or are injured, later becoming prisoners of war).[24] For soldiers bound to follow LOAC, the use of lethal force is limited to military objectives, usually defined territorially by the need to take a particular hill, base, strategic site, or equivalent objective.

The first formal international gathering on war practices, the Saint Petersburg Conference of 1868, issued a series of limitations on the application of lethal force. For example, the Saint Petersburg Declaration prohibited the use expanding bullets that would not so much disable enemy forces as guarantee subsequent death. Similarly, later military conventions banned serrated bayonets on the grounds that a straightedge bayonet disabled an enemy combatant, whereas a serrated edge ensured subsequent death from an infected wound that could not heal. This logic took hold even in the worst of direct combat, when French troops in World War I had a standing order to shoot immediately any German prisoner captured with a serrated bayonet – a consequence that was quickly internalized by the German forces, which abandoned the prohibited weapon.[25] Thus, even in traditional wars against conventional enemies, the LOAC contained incipient, if not highly developed, principles against the infliction of gratuitous or excessive violence against enemy soldiers outside the need to disable the enemy's military capacity.

In our view, there are four myths about the modern use of drones to target specific, identifiable individuals for lethal force. The first myth is that targeting specific individuals for death is a modern innovation in military practice. In fact, targeted killings have long been a part of military practice; the invention of the long rifle, for example, gave snipers the ability to pick off opposing field officers. The modern practice, however, begins with the discrete act of seeking out military enemies outside normal wartime engagements based on an individualized assessment of the threat they present. The use of lethal force is not incidental to a battlefield objective of capturing a particular piece of territory, but becomes a distinct response to the generalized threat posed by a particular individual. Killing is not secondary to a distinct military objective, but becomes the objective itself because of a specific determination about the threat posed by the continued operation of an individual. At a more fundamental level, as Professor Eyal Benvenisti argues, the laws of war had two major premises that fail in modern asymmetric conflict. First, it was possible to distinguish military and civilian objectives; second, battle could be directed to military objectives, as with the capturing of territory or overtaking a military installation. Neither premise necessarily characterizes military engagements in asymmetric war – or put another way, the military objective becomes killing itself.[26]

The object of the targeted attack changes as well, in a way that seems morally defensible. Drones enable military planners to focus on high-level targets. There is a further morality in that, and we should appreciate a technology that can discriminate between low-level and high-level combatants because doing so can minimize the larger loss of life to foot soldiers of the other side by concentrating fire on selected leaders. Precision-targeted killings should be seen as a substantial humanitarian advance in warfare, assuming that use of force is justified in the first place. Whereas traditional LOAC placed foot soldiers at the greatest risk of being killed in combat, the new targeted-killing regime initially redirects the focus of lethal force to the enemy's command structure.

In our view, it is a mistake to focus exclusively on the level of force being used without also understanding that the targets (if accurately identified) bear a moral culpability for unlawful warfare completely distinct from anything that could be attributed to conventional soldiers in a state-authorized war, especially in the case of conscript armies. As the technology has improved, most notably with drones, targeting can expand from the command structure to operational centers, as with attacks on remote sites where enemy combatants assemble or are trained.

A second myth concerning targeted killings as a new form of warfare is that the ability to project force from a distance itself raises new legal issues. But this view is simply an exercise at drawing a technological line that, in our view, has little moral or legal force in and of itself. Drones present the same *legal* issues as any other weapons system involving the delivery of lethal force. Advances in military technology have often been about the ability to project force from a distance. Ancient technological innovations, such as catapults and longbows, involved the delivery of force from a distance and represented advances over hand-to-hand personal combat.

Drones are a relatively new military technological development, but this does not change the core legal issues, under either domestic or international law, relevant to deciding whether particular uses of force are justified. In technologically advanced countries, militaries have long been in the business of delivering lethal force at great distances from their targets. The US Navy has engaged enemy personnel by firing cruise missiles from ships in the Mediterranean into Libya, Iraq, and Sudan. And US Air Force pilots frequently take off from bases hundreds and even thousands of miles from the actual theater of conflict and drop their bombs based on computer-generated targeting information from far above the ground. For example, the bombing campaign over Serbia during the Kosovo War involved pilots taking off from the Midwest in the United States and returning there.

The US drone operations reportedly follow the same rules of engagement and use the same procedures as manned aircraft that use weapons to support ground troops.[27] The military's use of drones operates within the same military chain of command, subject to civilian oversight, as do all other uses of military force.[28] One can view the technological advances that make drone warfare possible with horror or with fascination, but the idea of projected force beyond hand-to-hand warfare does not by itself present radically new legal issues. As the philosopher David Luban rightly concludes: "[Targeted killings] are no different in principle from other wartime killings, and they have to be judged by the same standards of necessity and proportionality applied to warfare in general: sometimes they are justified, sometimes not."[29]

A third myth, or prevalent misconception, is that drones and targeted killing pose a major threat to the humanitarian purposes and aims of the laws of war. The key concepts of the laws of war are the principles of necessity, distinction, and proportionality – which define core commitments that force should intentionally be used only against military targets and that the damage to civilians and non-military targets should be minimized and proportionate to legitimate strategic objectives. The technological and informational sophistication of drones, as compared to many other tools of military force, better realize these principles than any other technology currently available. Indeed, they allow for *the most discriminating uses of force in the history of military technology and warfare*, in contexts in which the use of force is otherwise justified. If the alternative is sending US ground forces into Yemen or the frontier regions of Pakistan, the result would be far greater loss of both civilian and combatant lives than with the deployment of drones.

A fourth myth arises from a more subtle concern that perhaps underlies the humanitarian critique of targeted killings: drone warfare might make the use of force "too easy." As powerful states do not have to put their own pilots or soldiers directly at risk, will they resort to force and violence more easily? This is a serious issue, but some historical perspective might help put this concern in a broader framework.

Throughout the modern history of warfare, there has been concern that humanitarian developments in the way war is conducted will, perversely, make it more likely that states will go to war. The argument is essentially that there is a Faustian tradeoff between the laws of war and the initial decision to go to war. This is an enduring moral issue that has attended virtually every effort in the paradoxically sounding project of making warfare more humane; pacifists in the nineteenth century objected to the formation of the International Committee of the Red Cross and its efforts to mitigate the horrors of war.[30] Moreover, the same paradox surrounds even purely humanitarian aid during wartime; in some contexts, access to such aid has become a strong economic incentive to continue the war, for the very purpose of extracting more of this financial assistance.[31]

A more complicated picture emerges if we shift from the perspective of the civilian leaders who authorize the use of force to those who actually deliver that force. One of the consequences created by individuating the responsibility of specific enemies, combined with drone technology, is the possibility of a much greater sense of personal responsibility and accountability on the part of drone operators for lethal uses of force than that exhibited by prior generations of fighters. At least some drone operators report exactly this kind of experience of personal responsibility for their actions, including their mistakes, which were much less likely in earlier generations when "the enemy" was faceless and undifferentiated in most circumstances.[32]

Of course, if such a perverse tradeoff does end up driving state practice, the same concern could be applied to the use of force for humanitarian purposes, as in Libya. Did the use of drones in the Libya operation make humanitarian interventions "too easy"? The right question, it seems to us, should focus on whether the use of force is justified in the first place. Moreover, one should be careful not to romanticize traditional combat and the pressures toward excessive violence it nearly always unleashes. To the extent the humanitarian critique of the use of drones is that sending in ground troops acts as a restraint on the use of force, compared to the use of force from remote locations, such as with drones technology, this idea might have matters backward, at least once the decision to use force at all has been made (and made, hopefully, for appropriate and lawful reasons).

Dramatic overuse of force is more likely when young soldiers who may be inexperienced, frightened, and lacking in accurate information come under attack on an active battlefield and respond with massive uses of force directed at only vaguely identified targets. Remoteness from the immediate battlefield – with operators able to see much more of what is going on – almost surely enables much more deliberate responses. One Air Force combat officer who became a drone operator supports this conclusion. He commented that compared to conventional combat, both in the air and on the ground, the distance involved with drones enable operations to be "deliberate instead of reactionary – that compared to manned combat flights, he experienced drones as affording "the ability to think clearly at zero knots and one G"; and he observed that other "methods of warfare could be, and often were, much more destructive."[33] Indeed, he went so far as to comment that when marines were sent into operations, they "broke things and killed people," while drones enabled US military force to be "less brutal."[34]

Whether one accepts this particular self-reported drone operator's experience, a realistic appraisal of all the costs and benefits of the use of drones must confront the "compared to what?" question. Perhaps in some contexts, if drones were not available, no force would be used; but in many cases, it seems likely that much greater force would be used instead. Put another way, powerful nation-states are unlikely to remain passive in the face of significant risks to the physical security of their citizens and property that emanate from other nations that are unwilling or unable to control these threats. It is not clear why states should be understood to have a moral obligation to permit their citizens and territory to be attacked. If states have the capacity to do so, they will neutralize these threats through killing or capture; at times, the humanitarian costs of capture, in terms of harm to and loss of innocent life will be great, and at other times, capture might not be practicable for any number of reasons. As a result, any general humanitarian critique of the targeted killing has a moral obligation to offer a credible, practical alternative that a state can realistically employ to protect the lives of its citizens and that better serves the humanitarian aims of the laws of war.

4. LEGAL JUSTIFICATIONS: THE NOVEL ROLE OF INDIVIDUATION

The government's legal justifications under domestic and international law for targeted killings, including of American citizens overseas in certain contexts, has been laid out in broad outline through a series of speeches by key legal and counterterrorism officials, including the Obama administration's National Security Advisor John Brennan,[35] State Department Legal Advisor Harold Koh,[36] and, in the most important speech, Attorney General Eric Holder.[37] We do not want to tarry long on these already much-discussed general legal principles, or on the puzzles presented about applying them properly at the borders (such as whether the same principles appropriate for the conventional battlefield of Afghanistan can properly be extended to targeted killings in places like Yemen and Somalia).[38] Neither do we want to spend much time on whether the same principles that justify targeted killings of al-Qaeda operatives can properly be extended to individuals working for groups loosely affiliated with al-Qaeda or generally aligned in aim, such as al-Shabaab (which indeed became formally affiliated with al-Qaeda in 2012). Instead, we want to focus on the ways in which these legal justifications reflect our central theme, which is the increasing individuation of enemy responsibility under both the practice of modern military uses of force against alleged terrorists and the legal understandings (or at least, the perceived legal understandings of the United States) of what the law permits and requires with respect to targeted killings. Some aspects of this individuation are well recognized by specialists in this area, while others are subtler.

In the Obama's administration's first major articulation of its legal justification for the targeted-killing program, Legal Adviser Koh concluded that the United States was engaged in an ongoing armed conflict under international law with al-Qaeda, the Taliban, and associated forces, and that a state that is "engaged in an armed conflict or in legitimate self-defense" has the right to use lethal force and is not legally required to provide those targets with any kind of legal process before targeting them.[39] This use of lethal force also had to meet the IHL requirements of distinction and proportionality as well.

In a later and more detailed speech that specifically addressed the application of these principles to the intentional targeted killing of American citizens who are overseas and allegedly involved in terrorism (of which there has been one at the time of this writing), Attorney General Holder asserted that such targeting was permitted at least when the citizen targeted (1) is located overseas; (2) has a senior operational role; (3) is with an al-Qaeda or al-Qaeda–associated force; (4) is involved in plots that aim at harm or death of Americans; and when (5) the threat is "imminent," though the precise boundaries of this concept remain to be given more specific content;[40] (6) there is no feasible option of capture without undue risk; and (7) the attack complies with IHL principles of necessity, distinction, and proportionality.

And in a more recent, important elaboration of the legal, ethical, and prudential principles that inform the administration's targeted killing decisions, National Security Adviser Brennan asserted that lethal force was used only when capture was "not feasible." He described this principle as an "unqualified preference," which suggests ambiguity about whether the administration regards the principle as a legal constraint or an ethical and prudential one; he also appeared to limit the infeasibility of capture as a constraint that applied to those targeted away from the "hot battlefield" of Afghanistan – which suggests this constraint might not apply to targeted killings on more conventional battlefields.[41]

What emerges is a new American doctrine governing the use of lethal force outside the traditional battlefield context. The result does not yet have the form of hard law, but provides legal-style guidance. Within this general framework, the emergence of individuated enemy responsibility as an essential predicate to the use of military against that individual force – as in the detention context – arises at two points, at least.

First, all these accounts of the legal framework employed make clear that lethal force outside the conventional battlefield context is not employed against any "member" of the enemy. As Brennan put it, "We do not engage in lethal action in order to eliminate every single member of al-Qaida in the world." Targeted killings are limited to those who pose a "significant threat" to US interests. Brennan offered illustrative examples, such as an individual identified as an operational leader of al-Qaeda or associated forces; an operative, in the midst of training for or planning to carry out attacks against US interests; or someone with "unique operational skills that are being leveraged in a planned attack."[42] In his remarks, Koh used the language of "high-level al Qaeda leaders who are planning attacks"[43] to refer to the individuals who were being targeted, without any further specification of how far the legal or ethical justifications for targeted killings extended. And Holder referred to targeting "senior operation leaders of al Qaeda and associated forces."[44] In addition, credible journalistic accounts report highly focused internal deliberations and even debates about whether specific individuals, based on extremely specific facts about their alleged role, can or should be targeted.[45]

It is important not to lose sight of the profound transformation these developments reflect. The crucial point is that, even as the US government asserts that it is at war and has the power to use lethal force against its enemies, it is not adhering to the traditional law of war principle that lethal force can be directed against any member of the enemy armed forces, whether high-level commander or low-level foot soldier. Instead, the government is individuating the responsibility of specific enemies and targeting only those engaged in specific acts or employed in specific roles.

The government is making what has all the appearance (and reality) of adjudicative-like judgments based on highly specific facts about the alleged actions of particular individuals (and not their membership per se in the opposing side). And here too, as with detention, this individuation of enemy responsibility is undoubtedly part of what fuels the demand in some quarters that the criminal justice system, rather than unilateral executive direction of military force, should be used instead: If the government is using force only after such fact-bound determinations of responsibility are made, is not that the traditional province of the criminal law? Of course, this criticism does not address the fundamental underlying problem, which is that the government cannot feasibly capture these individuals in the first place.

What motivates this change in practice in the perceived legitimate use of military force? The short answer is that the lines between law, morality, and prudence become blurred here; the categories spill over into each other in the context of unconventional war and technological change in the conduct of war. It is not clear whether the Obama administration believes that some or all of this individuation is already legally required by international law or whether this individuation is thought necessary as a matter of morality and sound strategy. Because courts play so little role in adjudicating these questions, particularly in the targeted killing area, the line between law, morality, and prudence is likely to remain blurred for some time to come.

Much greater technological capacity at refining the use of force undoubtedly also plays a role in driving the law, morality, and prudence of these uses of force in a more individuated direction. As Jack Goldsmith nicely notes: "[T]echnological developments that in once sense enhance the United States' military authority also end up constraining it because once there is capacity to be precise in targeting, the moral or political (and, soon, legal) duty to do so soon follows, regardless of what the law previously required."[46]

That dynamic is part of what is fueling the transformation of the law of war into the more individuated framework of enemy responsibility.

The "preference" for capture over killing is a second, subtler outcropping of the emerging norm of individuation. Again, the departure from the traditional laws of war is striking; no such preference, let alone legal requirement, exists during the traditional laws of war. Enemy soldiers can be killed, even if they could be captured, except in the limited circumstance in which they have engaged in extremely clear manifestations of surrender or are considered *hors de combat* as a result of wounds. There is no obligation to differentiate between soldiers whose threat can be neutralized by capture versus those who can be neutralized only by killing. To be sure, there is ambiguity in the emerging American practice about whether what we might call the "least restrictive alternative requirement" of "capture over killing" is a legal requirement necessary to justify targeted killings or merely a policy preference rooted in strategic calculations (capture enables mining for intelligence) or moral considerations (killing is gratuitous when capture is possible). John Brennan's statement suggests a policy preference, not a legal requirement.

In Israel, the legal understanding of the constraints under which targeted killings can permissibly take place does appear to make this "least restrictive alternative" constraint an actual legal requirement.[47] Thus, even before the Israeli High Court adjudicated the legality of these killings, the internal executive branch guidelines developed between 2000 and 2002 specified a set of six requirements, including that "arrest is impossible" and that such operations were to be limited to areas not under Israeli control (presumably because in those areas, capture is feasible).[48] Moreover, in the most important judicial decision thus far on the legality of targeted killing, in 2005 the Israeli High Court specifically seemed to hold that Israeli law precludes a targeted killing "if a less harmful means can be employed."[49] As a matter of Israeli domestic law, Justice Aharon Barak concluded for the High Court that Israeli law includes a proportionality requirement, which entails the constraint that, among available military measures, the military "must choose the means whose harms to the human rights of the harmed person is smallest."[50]

If this principle actually becomes embedded in Israeli law, it would constitute in two respects an even more radical reconceptualization of the legal constraints on the use of military force during wartime. Moreover, this appears to be an example in which the emerging legal rules of warfare concerning terrorism might be spilling over into more conventional war contexts; nothing in the Israeli High Court decision suggests that this principle of "minimal force required" is limited to the asymmetric warfare settings as opposed to being a general legal principle applicable to all war contexts. That would constitute a remarkable move toward construing law (either domestic or international) in ways that highly individualize both the nature of the specific individual actions involved and the contexts in which force can be applied against particular persons.

Within American domestic law, the requirement that capture not be feasible before killing is justified does appear to be a *constitutional* requirement with respect to American citizens, at least in the understanding of Attorney General Holder and the Obama administration. Thus, whether this "least restrictive alternative" requirement applies to targeted killings in general, as reflected in the uncertainties construed in John Brennan's statement, the targeted killing of American citizens overseas does specifically require that capture not be feasible.

A host of questions arise, of course, about precisely what it means for capture not to be "feasible." It appears that the term feasible in this context derives from the military risk involved in capture, rather than any sense of impossibility. What remains most essential to notice about this requirement is that, at least with respect to American citizens, we are seeing further recognition within the executive branch, without judicial compulsion, of a more individuated approach to uses of military force.

As this move toward individuating enemy responsibility continues to develop, one question it will confront is whether law itself (as opposed to morality or political prudence) will require or permit different treatment of a country's own citizens who pose terrorist threats from that of non-citizens who pose the identical threat. Currently, American legal understandings are that there is a significant difference, as reflected in the differences and tensions between the Brennan and Holder speeches. American citizens overseas who pose identical threats as non-citizen have greater substantive protection than non-citizens; force must be the only feasible option for the former but not the latter.

Differentiating the treatment of threats coming from citizens as opposed to non-citizens is a deeply controversial matter, both in theory and in international law. Particularly when force can be used only once, the enemy "target" is highly individuated in terms of his specific actions. It is not at all clear why, in principle, an American citizen in the same overseas location who poses the identical threat as a non-American should have greater legal protection. As a matter of domestic politics, perhaps, one can understand why political leaders would want to ensure their own citizens that they receive special protection against the exceptional circumstance of their own government using lethal force against them. But as a matter of law, why should governments have the power to kill non-citizens who could otherwise be captured, but not kill citizens in that circumstance? As a matter of morality, David Luban argues, "the nationality of casualties is irrelevant . . . To focus on the lives of Americans is parochial in a way that the morality of war is not."[51]

Further, as a matter of international law and the domestic law of some countries, providing greater protections to one's own citizens in the terrorism context can be a reason to *condemn*, not praise, the practices by which a country metes out its use of military force. Political process theory suggests that the only protections non-citizens would likely have in these and similar contexts would arise where the country's own citizens must live under the same legal regime. Indeed, United Kingdom's House of Lords held British anti-terrorist detention policy illegal precisely because it imposed greater restrictions on non-nationals than on British citizens.[52]

And, finally, despite the apparent distinctions suggested by Attorney General Holder's speech between targeting citizens and non-citizens, Daniel Klaidman, in describing President Obama's decision to authorize the killing of al-Awlaki, writes that after the president reviewed the intelligence, he was left with no doubt that al-Awlaki posed a major and imminent threat to American security. The fact that al-Awlaki was an American, President Obama believed, "was immaterial."[53] Perhaps there is journalistic license in that summary statement, but whether the emerging individuation of the *laws* of war, both domestic and international, requires or permits the further individuation and differentiation of citizens and non-citizens remains a difficult and unresolved question. Indeed, President Obama stated after the attorney general's speech that the United States will apply the same substantive principles to the targeting of both citizens and non-citizens.[54]

5. PROCEDURAL SAFEGUARDS

As with all use of lethal force, there must be procedures in place to maximize the likelihood of correct identification and minimize risk to innocents. In the absence of formal legal processes, sophisticated institutional entities engaged in repeated, sensitive actions – including the military – will gravitate toward their own internal analogues to legal process, even without the compulsion or shadow of formal judicial review. This is the role of bureaucratic legalism[55] in developing sustained institutional practices, even with the dim shadow of unclear legal commands.

These forms of self-regulation are generated by programmatic needs to enable the entity's own aims to be accomplished effectively; at times, that necessity will share an overlapping convergence with humanitarian concerns to generate internal protocols or process-like protections that minimize the use of force and its collateral consequences, in contexts in which the use of force itself is otherwise justified. But because these process-oriented protections are not codified in statute or reflected in judicial decisions, they typically are too invisible to draw the eye of constitutional law scholars who survey these issues from much higher levels of generality.

In theory, such review procedures could be fashioned alternatively as a matter of judicial review or accountability to legislative oversight (using the processes of select committee reporting), or the institutionalization of friction points within the executive branch (as with review by multiple agencies). Each could serve as a check on the development of unilateral excesses by the executive branch. And, presumably, each could guarantee that internal processes are adhered to such that mechanisms of accountability could prevent inappropriate application of force.

The centrality of dynamic targeting in the active theaters of war, such as the border areas between Afghanistan and Pakistan, make it difficult to integrate legislative or judicial review mechanisms. Conceivably, the decision to place an individual on a list for targeting could be a moment for review outside the boundaries of the executive branch, although even this has its drawback. Any court engaged in the ex parte review of the decision to execute someone outside the formal mechanisms of crime and punishment risks appearing as a modern variant of the Star Chamber. Similarly, there are difficulties in forcing a polarized Congress as a whole to assume collective responsibility for decisions of life and death, and the incentives have not turned out to be well aligned to get a subset of Congress, such as the intelligence committees, to play this role effectively.[56] Perhaps the executive branch (or Congress, if capable of acting in this area) could create an independent, after-action review process that would be able, credibly, to provide some public assessment of the accuracy and error-rate of these strikes, without compromising confidential intelligence.

Under President Obama the choice has been a far more formalized process of executive oversight, drawing on multiple agencies to cross-check targeting decisions. The recent work of Professor Gregory McNeal sets out the detailed formal procedures that exist ex ante, and the mechanisms of accountability that exist ex post, for evaluating pre-planned targeted strikes by the military, including targeted killings in Afghanistan by military-controlled drones. (It is important to keep in mind that this analysis covers only military strikes, not those that the CIA, for example, might engage in.[57]) Any evidence on these questions at this stage of experience must, of course, be viewed as highly uncertain, given that these attacks take place by definition in areas in which it is very difficult to get reliable reports on the numbers and identities of those killed or wounded. Moreover, we must stress that McNeal's account involves only operations the military conducts. There is a fair amount of public information now available, as in McNeal's work and that of journalists, about the extensive interagency processes involved in targeting decisions involving the military. By contrast, there is at this stage virtually no public-record information about the ex ante and ex post processes used for targeting operations that the CIA allegedly conducts.[58] Thus, there might well be significant differences in many of the key elements – how accurate the identifications are or what the ratio of combatant to civilian deaths or injuries are – between targeted strikes conducted by the military and those conducted by the CIA.

Professor McNeal's reports present two striking findings. First, civilian casualties reportedly occurred in less than 1 percent of pre-planned strikes (and other strikes, when time and combat circumstances make it possible)[59] that followed the protocol the military now employs, called Collateral Damage Mitigation assessment (CDM). Second, under internally self-generated guidelines, a senior commander (typically an officer who holds the rank of general), the president, or the secretary of defense is required to approve in advance any pre-planned military strike in Afghanistan in which one or more collateral civilian casualties is projected. To be sure, as the first analysis to open up these issues, McNeal's work has yet to be tested; the empirical facts on matters such as these are likely to be much debated. But as the first actual descriptive account of the processes and protocols that the military uses in pre-planned targeted strikes, McNeal's work advances public knowledge considerably.[60]

As McNeal describes, even *before* military planners and their lawyers turn their attention to laws of war and international legal requirements, such as proportionality analysis, they engage in CDM, which is designed to generate a less than 10 percent probability that a pre-planned strike will produce any "collateral damage." In any targeted strike, a first and essential stage is implementing the law of distinction, of course, which means correctly identifying the person who is properly treated as a legitimate target of lethal military force. Both legally, with respect to who can be made a lawful target, and factually, with respect to the accuracy of these initial determinations, this subject is one of those most often discussed in academic literature and public debate.

But McNeal describes a far less familiar second ex ante stage, in which military planners first identify the collateral damage concerns, to persons or the environment, within the radius likely to be affected by the strike. These planners then implement a series of "mitigation techniques" designed to minimize the probability and amount of damage or injury to collateral individuals and property. These techniques, based on empirical data and computer analyses, involve "progressively refined analysis of available intelligence, weapon type and effect, the physical environment, target characteristics and delivery scenarios keyed to risk thresholds established by the Secretary of Defense and the President of the United States."[61]

These measures aim to ensure less than a 10 percent probability of serious or lethal wounds to non-combatants and percentage probability of damage to collateral structures.[62] These techniques *precede* legal analysis of the proportionality issue.

These protocols also build in heightened procedural mechanisms and enhanced executive branch accountability when the analysis suggests substantial collateral damage. The rules of engagement contain a non-combatant casualty cutoff value, established by the president and secretary of defense. For estimates below this level, a senior commander (such as a major general) may authorize the operation; for estimates above, the target must be approved by an entity called the National Command Authority,[63] and military commanders must go through a special "sensitive target approval and review process."[64] According to McNeal, for pre-planned strikes in Afghanistan, the current cutoff is one, which reflects the strategic importance in counterinsurgency operations of minimizing civilian casualties.

Thus, if a targeted strike operation is expected to result in one civilian casualty, the National Command Authority must approve it. The reported results, no doubt still subject to confirmation, reveal low levels of unintended casualties,[65] certainly light years removed from the carpet bombing of the aerial wars of the twentieth century. Independent of the accuracy of reported numbers of such casualties,[66] though, is the point that the CDM and related processes reveal the internal development of "lawlike" institutional procedures and protocols that the military and executive branch can develop to discipline their discretion, without the direct intervention of courts (and where even the shadow of judicial oversight is small).

With respect to alleged CIA targeted killings in Pakistan, one important source of independent evidence is New America, which uses multiple Western and Pakistani media sources to compile statistics on remote killings in Pakistan.[67] In several articles, Peter Bergen and Jennifer Rowland, of New America, have argued that the data suggests that these formal procedures may well be effective, given the precipitous decline in civilian casualties from drone strikes, falling from a high of 12 percent of drone strike casualties in 2009 to "at or close to zero percent" by 2012.[68] Bergen and Rowland attribute this rapid improvement to the use of smaller munitions, improved drone flight technology, increased congressional oversight, and stricter executive branch guidelines regarding the use of drones.[69] Regardless, tallies of civilian deaths remain an inexact science and Bergen and Rowland's reports have been met with some criticism.[70] But it is noteworthy that even the London-based Bureau of Investigative Journalism (BIJ), which is generally more skeptical of the strikes, in addition to being skeptical of Bergen and Rowland's claim that close to zero percent civilians were killed during the first seven months of 2012, recorded a similar dramatic decline by 2012.[71]

In addition, as of the end of 2013, civilian casualties from drone strikes are at their lowest level. That is partly the result of a sharply reduced number of drone strikes in Pakistan and partly the result of more precise targeting. According to data collected by New America, three to five civilians and three to four "unknown" individuals – where it is not clear if the victims were civilians or militants – were killed in drone strikes in 2013. Two other organizations that track the CIA drone program in Pakistan, the Bureau of Investigative Journalism and the *Long War Journal*, report zero to four civilian deaths and fourteen civilian deaths, respectively, for the same time period.

Even a procedurally regulated use of targeted weaponry will remain highly dependent, of course, on military intelligence about the enemy. The fewer the resources on the ground, the more likely mistakes are going to be made, including terrible losses of civilian life. To the extent that drones or air strikes are used as the primary form of engagement, as for example in Yemen, the greater the risk of error appears to be.[72]

What emerges overall is the beginning of institutional practices rooted in the hazy intersection of the laws of war, the moral obligations of democratic states, and evolving military capabilities. As a substantive matter, there are many myths, confusions, and misunderstandings in public debates about drones and targeted killings. However, the technology and techniques of drones do not raise exceptional legal issues; the question is whether the use of force is justified regardless of whether the delivery of force is through a drone, manned plane, or cruise missile. As a procedural matter, though, it is extremely important that first, the legal justifications for this power be articulated fully, publicly, and as transparently as possible; second, that the processes and institutional structures for making targeting decisions be as accurate as possible at the identification stage and are designed to minimize civilian casualties; and third, that there be post-attack reviews and mechanisms of accountability. That such processes are likely to be internal to the executive branch does not remove the importance of formalizing legal safeguards.

6. THE FUTURE OF WARFARE

The United States is at the early stages of a profound but partial transformation regarding the legitimate use of military force. An emerging imperative increasingly requires adjudicative-like individualized judgments about the particular responsibility of specific individual "enemies" before military force can legitimately be used against them. This is a transformation from the traditional status-based or group-based justifications for use of force against "the enemy" to a more act-based or individuated justification for when force is legitimate.

This change is being propelled by a combination of the inherent structural differences between the nature of insurgent, guerrilla, and terrorist groups today (the principal targets of military force by democratic forces in today's world) and the conventional armies of the past; by technological changes that enable far more discriminating deployments of force; and by the post–World War II emergence of a more general humanitarian sensibility, at least among Western democracies.

This change is already beginning to be reflected in the evolving military practices of dominant states. Military practice and moral arguments about this change will move far quicker than legal change, but to this extent, this transformation is also beginning to be reflected in the domestic laws of some states and in arguments about obligations under international law. Military practices, perceptions of morality, and legal obligations will mutually influence each other as this transformation unfolds.

The ramifications of this emerging imperative to individuate enemy responsibility are wide-ranging. Military forces will inevitably have to develop analogues appropriate to the military context for the procedural protections (hearings, evidence-based assessments, and the like) designed to ensure accuracy of adjudicative-like judgments of individual responsibility when coercive state power is deployed domestically. The United States military in its evolving post–9/11 self-understanding has been doing that, and these types of procedural protections will have to be credible if military force will be sustainable over the long run in these contexts.

Similarly, it is also probably inevitable that courts will step in to play a somewhat more significant role to assess the use of at least certain exercises of military force (perhaps more in the context of detention than military operations themselves) than they have in the past. As the justification for force becomes more closely tied to ascriptions of individualized responsibility, the courts will instinctively experience certain of these issue as closer to the kinds of questions with which courts deal traditionally. Once the United States recognizes that it is moving toward a regime of individuating enemy responsibility, at least to some extent, it is also perhaps inevitable that pressure will arise from some quarters to insist that only the most traditional model for how to assign those judgments – the criminal justice system – is fit for this task.

But a central theme of this chapter is that the existing legal frameworks, both domestic and international, do not provide a direct answer to the critical legal question this transformed military context spawns. The question is not whether terrorism is more "like" war or crime. Neither the legal regimes for regulating war (primarily, international law) nor for regulating crime (primarily, domestic law) were designed to reflect the emerging individuation of responsibility toward which practice and morality are moving. The question is how best to adapt either international law or domestic law or both to come to terms with the perceived imperative to individuate responsibility while also recognizing the functional and practical constraints under which military power must inevitably be deployed.

While we seek to capture one important emerging strand in the practice of warfare in certain modern contexts, we do not suggest that our account offers a comprehensive descriptive or normative perspective on all forms of modern military practice. Surely there will continue to be contexts in which traditional armies of nation-states confront each other on conventional battlefields, as in the two recent wars the United States fought against Iraq. In addition, even outside this traditional warring of nation-state armies, there will be many contexts in non-conventional wars in which military force will continue to be directed against groups of individuals believed to consist of enemy forces (or against military objects, such as training camps, where such groups of individuals are thought to be present). In these contexts, the traditional status-based distinctions and justifications for the use of military force will continue to characterize its use. But how might the emerging individuation of enemy responsibility affect these more traditional contexts?[73]

In one projection of the future path of the morality and law of the use of military force, we might envision two distinct regimes that co-exist side-by-side: a regime of status-based uses of force in more "traditional" contexts alongside the more individuated regime of enemy responsibility we described here. However, we might also ask whether it is plausible that two such distinct regimes could be sustained in stark "acoustic separation" from each other.[74]

In a different projection of that future, therefore, we might imagine that the emergence of the more individuated regime will have moral or legal ramifications that spill back, to some extent, into the more traditional regime. Professor Gabriella Blum, for example, speaks of the "changing nature of the battlefield" that is creating a military environment that "is increasingly dependent on case-by-case judgments."[75] To the extent technologies of intelligence and military force enable more discriminating judgments even in more traditional contexts between those enemy "soldiers" who pose a serious threat and those who do not (by virtue of their specific role, for example, in the enemy's army), perhaps pressure will arise to refine traditional status-based attacks to more individuated, threat-based attacks.

We are not arguing that the use of military force in all contexts is moving from a status-based to act-based regime; there are and will continue to be many contexts in which the traditional status-based approach will continue to be justified and legitimate, both morally and legally. But we have only dimly seen that the fundamental imperative driving policy and argument on these issues is the need to individuate enemy responsibility in a credible and justifiable way. The more we grasp that fundamental transformation, the more clarity we can bring to the creative act of deciding how to design military and legal regimes that will appropriately reflect this transformed military, moral, and legal environment.

NOTES

1 See, e.g., *Hamdi* v. *Rumsfeld* 542 US 507 (2004): American citizens held in the United States as enemy combatants are entitled to habeas petition to challenge factual basis of detention. *Boumediene* v. *Bush* 553 US 723 (2011): held the congressional act suspending habeas review for detainees at Guantanamo unconstitutional, given the inadequate protections of Combatant Status Review Tribunals as then-constituted. HCJ 769/02 Pub. Comm. Against Torture in *Israel* v. *Government of Israel (PCATI)* [2005] (Isr.): restricted conditions under which the Israeli military could select militants for targeted killing and mandated that all such killings be followed by ex post independent inquiry to determine their appropriateness.

2 Becker, Jo and Scott Shane, "Secret 'kill list' proves a test of Obama's principles and will," *New York Times*, May 29, 2012: The Obama administration developed a set of elaborate protocols for making the determination of whether and under what circumstances to place enemy combatants on the "kill list" used for targeted killing determinations.

3 The Supreme Court addressed the significance of uniforms to military identity in *Ex Parte Quirin* 317 U.S. 1 (1942): "The spy who secretly and without uniform passes the military lines of a belligerent in time of war, seeking to gather military information and communicate it to the enemy, or an enemy combatant who without uniform comes secretly through the lines for the purpose of waging war by destruction of life or property, are familiar examples of belligerents who are generally deemed not to be entitled to the status of prisoners of war, but to be offenders against the law of war subject to trial and punishment by military tribunals." The emphasis on recognized membership in an armed force was later codified in the Geneva Conventions. Geneva Convention Relative to the Treatment of Prisoners of War, art. 4, August 12, 1949, 6 U.S.T. 3316, 75 U.N.T.S. 135 [hereinafter Geneva III]: prisoner of war protections for militia or volunteer forces is made contingent upon their "carrying arms openly" and "having a fixed distinctive sign recognizable at a distance."

4 Geneva III art. 4.

5 For example, in discussing the general power to detain someone in wartime, the Supreme Court in *Hamdi* cited authority to the effect that: "The time has long passed when 'no quarter' was the rule on the battlefield . . . It is now recognized that 'Captivity is neither a punishment nor an act of vengeance,' but 'merely a temporary detention which is devoid of all penal character' . . . 'A prisoner of war is no convict; his imprisonment is a simple war measure.'" *Hamdi* v. *Rumsfeld*, at 518 (quoting Winthrop, William, *Military Law and Precedents*, 2nd ed. (Washington, DC: War Department, 1920), p. 788.

6 Winthrop, *Military Law and Precedents*: "The capture and detention of lawful combatants and the capture, detention, *and trial* of unlawful combatants, by 'universal agreement and practice,' are 'important incidents of war'" (quoting Ex Parte Quirin, at 28, 30).

7 Geneva III art. 118: "Prisoners of war shall be released and repatriated without delay after the cessation of active hostilities."

8 Waxman, Matthew C., "Detention as targeting: Standards of certainty and detention of suspected terrorists," *Columbia Law Review* 108 (2008): 1365–1430, pp. 1382–1383: "Al Qaida and other terrorist organizations do not generally identify their membership. They do just the opposite, operating in the shadows, blending in with local populations . . . In these respects, terrorist networks take the identification problems long posed by guerrilla warfare to new heights." Bradley, Curtis A., and Jack L. Goldsmith, "Congressional authorization and the war on terrorism," *Harvard Law Review* 118 (2005): 2047–2133, p. 2113, which explains the difficulty of identification.

9 Chesney, Robert, and Jack Goldsmith, "Terrorism and the convergence of criminal and military detention models," *Stanford Law Review* 60 (2008): 1079–1134, p. 1099:

"[A]ssociational status as a detention trigger is difficult to apply to an amorphous clandestine network such as al Qaeda. Beyond the leadership core, it is difficult to determine what degree of association with al Qaeda suffices to warrant status-based detention even if the facts can accurately be determined."

10 In the detention context, Afghan detainees now routinely have the appropriateness of their detention evaluated on an individual basis. See generally Lt. Col. Jeff A. Bovarnick, "Detainee review boards in Afghanistan: From strategic liability to legitimacy," *Army Lawyer* June (2010): 9–49; see pp. 9, 15–20, and 22, which describe the evolution and structure of detainee review procedures in Afghanistan. With respect to targeted killings, evaluation of the threat posed by specific *individuals* dictates their inclusion or exclusion from the Obama administration's "kill list." Becker, Jo, and Scott Shane, "Secret 'kill list' proves a test of Obama's principles and will," *New York Times*, May 29, 2012: "Given the contentious discussions, it can take five or six sessions for a name to be approved, and names go off the list if a suspect no longer appears to pose an imminent threat."

11 Officials associated with the targeted killing program in the United States have apparently determined that strikes against individuals are, in fact, most appropriately directed at terrorist leaders rather than foot soldiers. Becker and Shane, "Secret 'kill list' proves a test of Obama's principles and will": "William M. Daley, Mr. Obama's chief of staff in 2011, said the president and his advisers understood that they could not keep adding new names to a kill list, from ever lower on the Qaeda totem pole."

12 Geneva III art. 118.

13 Among the critiques that Daphne Eviatar of the NGO Human Rights First advances with respect to the current Detention Review Board system for detainees in Afghanistan, for instance, is the fact that, fundamentally, military tribunals conduct adjudicative proceedings and without the sufficient trappings of the civilian justice system. Eviatar, Daphne, "Detained and denied in Afghanistan: How to make U.S. detention comply with the law" (Washington, DC: Human Rights First 2011), which argues for the importance of providing legal counsel to detainees and claims that the current system of "personal representatives" for detainees (who need not be lawyers) is insufficient as a substitute.

14 Bovarnick, "Detainee review boards in Afghanistan," p. 38: aware of the importance of perceived legitimacy and credibility, the military in Afghanistan has begun to allow NGOs to observe the non-classified portions of proceedings in Detainee Review Board adjudications.

15 Becker and Shane, "Secret 'kill list' proves a test of Obama's principles and will," which reports that "names go off the list if a suspect no longer appears to pose an imminent threat." Bovarnick, "Detainee review boards in Afghanistan," p. 29: "the board must determine whether the detainee meets the criteria for internment and, if so, whether continued internment is necessary to mitigate the threat the detainee poses."

16 Mazzetti, Mark, Eric Schmitt, and Robert F. Worth, "Two-year manhunt led to killing of Awlaki in Yemen," *New York Times*, September 30, 2011. "Awlaki hit misses al-Qaeda bombmaker, Yemen says," *Washington Post*, September 30, 2011.

17 Griffin, Jennifer, and Justin Fishel, *Two U.S.-born terrorists killed in CIA-led drone strike*, Fox News, September 30, 2011.

18 Mazzetti et al., "Two-year manhunt led to killing of Awlaki in Yemen."

19 Shane, Scott, "U.S. approves targeted killing of American cleric," *New York Times*, April 6, 2010. Fox News, "American-born cleric added to capture-or-kill list, called 'terrorist no. 1," April 6, 2010,

20 The US Treasury Department also added al-Awlaki to its list of Specially Designated Global Terrorists on July 16, 2010. This froze any US bank account he may have possessed, forbade Americans from doing business with him, and banned him from traveling in the United States. See "U.S.-born radical cleric added to terror blacklist," Fox News, July 16, 2010.

21 Others have also explored the potential relationship between detention and targeted killings. Matthew Waxman, for example, has asserted that the more tolerant standard of "reasonable care" that attaches to targeting decisions should govern, at least initially, the decision to detain. Waxman, "Detention as targeting," pp. 1401–1404. See also Hakimi, Monica, "A functional approach to targeting and detention," *Michigan Law Review* 110 (2012): 1365–1420, p. 1366, which argues against the utility of the binary combatant/non-combatant and civilian/non-civilian division and in favor of proportionality test applied in individualized decision framework.

22 Waxman, Matthew C., "The structure of terrorism threats and the laws of war," *Duke Journal of Comparative and International Law* 20 (2010): 429–455, p. 450.

23 Our thanks to Maj. Andrew Gillman, USAF, for addressing this distinction.

24 The terms "international humanitarian law," "law of war," and "law of armed conflict" are all used to describe the legal regime governing the battlefield, with some disputation about whether they are fully synonymous or evolutions of one from the other. See Geiss, Robin, *European Journal of International Law* 24 (2013): 722–729: book review of Claire Finkelstein, Jens David Ohlin, and Andrew Altman (eds.), *Targeted killings: Law and morality in an asymmetrical world* (Oxford University Press, 2012); book review of Roland Otto, *Targeted killings and international law* (Heidelberg: Springer, 2012); book review of William H. Boothby, *The law of targeting* (Oxford University Press, 2012). For our purposes, the terms are used interchangeably.

25 Gross, Michael L., *Moral Dilemmas of Modern War: Torture, Assassination, and Blackmail in an Age of Asymmetric Conflict* (Cambridge University Press, 2010).

26 Benvenisti, Eyal, "The Legal battle to define the law on transnational asymmetric warfare," *Duke Journal of Comparative & International Law* 20 (2010): 339–359, p. 341.

27 Martin, Matt J., with Charles W. Sasser, *Predator: The remote-control air war over Iraq and Afghanistan: A pilot's story* (Minneapolis, MN: Zenith Press, 2010), p. 104:

"To us, the Predator is a longer-duration, lightly armed (and much less survivable) version of an F-16."

28 Ibid.

29 Luban, David, "What would Augustine do: The president, drones, and just war theory," *Boston Review*, June 6, 2012.

30 Finkelstein, Claire, Jens David Ohlin, and Andrew Altman (eds.), *Targeted killings: Law and morality in an asymmetrical world* (Oxford University Press, 2012), p. 389: for some perspective, this was exactly the argument that led Florence Nightingale initially to oppose the development of the International Committee of the Red Cross (ICRC) to monitor treatment of prisoners; as she wrote to the founder of the ICRC in rejecting the organization: "Such a society would relieve governments of responsibilities which really belong to them which they only can properly discharge ... and being relieved of which would make war more easy." She eventually changed her mind, of course. For an excellent account of the moral ambiguities and complexities of these issues, see Anderson, Kenneth, "First in the field: The unique mission and legitimacy of the Red Cross in a culture of legality," *New York Times*, Literary Supplement, July 31, 1998 (review of Caroline Morehead, *Dunant's Dream: Switzerland and the History of the Red Cross*, [New York, NY: Carroll & Graf Publishers, 1999]).

31 Nzelibe, Jide, "Courting genocide: The unintended effects of humanitarian intervention," *California Law Review* 97 (2009): 1171–1218, pp. 1197–1204, which discusses the factors that led rebel factions in Darfur to behave intransigently at peace talks in order to exploit the possibility that outside intervention could force a favorable settlement to the conflict. Ryle, John, and Justin Willis, "Introduction: Many Sudans" in John Ryle, Justin Willis, Suliman Baldo, and Jok Madut Jok (eds.), *The Sudan Handbook* (Suffolk, UK: James Currey, 2011), pp. 27, 29, which similarly addresses disequilibrium created by foreign humanitarian intervention.

32 Klaidman, Daniel, "Daniel Klaidman on the mind of a drone strike operator," *Daily Beast*, June 8, 2012: as an example, consider the following account of an exchange between a drone operator and Harold Koh, Legal Adviser to the State Department, when Koh commented that he had heard drone operators had a "PlayStation" mentality: "The lead operator lit into Koh. 'I used to fly my own air missions,' he started, defensively. 'I dropped bombs, hit my target load, but had no idea who I hit. Here I can look at their faces. I watch them for hours, see these guys playing with their kids and wives. When I get them alone, I have no compunction about blowing them to bits, but I wouldn't touch them with civilians around. After the strike, I see the bodies being carried out of the house. I see the women weeping and in positions of mourning. That's not PlayStation; that's real. My job is to watch after the strike too. I count the bodies and watch the funerals. I don't let others clean up the mess.'" Martin, *Predator*, p. 53, where similarly, as Martin puts it: "I doubted whether B-17 and B-20 pilots and bombardiers of World War II agonized over dropping bombs over Dresden or Berlin as much as I did over taking out one

measly perp in a car." See Klaidman, Daniel, *Kill or Capture: The war on terror and the soul of the Obama presidency* (New York, NY: Houghton Mifflin Harcourt, 2012).

33 Martin, *Predator*, p. 104.

34 Ibid., p. 108.

35 John Brennan, "The ethics and efficacy of the president's counterterrorism strategy," speech given at the Woodrow Wilson International Center for Scholars, Washington, DC, April 30, 2012.

36 Harold Koh, "The Obama administration and international law," keynote address at the annual meeting of the American Society of International Law, Washington, DC, March 25, 2010.

37 Eric Holder, address at Northwestern University School of Law, Chicago, IL, March 5, 2012.

38 For a significant article on legal issues concerning the proper geographic scope of detention and targeted killings outside conventional "hot battlefield" settings, from a former Human Rights Watch lawyer and national-security lawyer in the Obama administration, see Daskal, Jennifer C., "The geography of the battlefield: A framework for detention and targeting outside the 'hot' conflict zone," *University of Pennsylvania Law Review* 161 (2012): 1165–1234. For a critical response to Daskal's attempt to resolve these issues, see Anderson, Kenneth, "Jennifer C. Daskal, The geography of the battlefield: A framework for detention and targeting outside the 'hot' conflict zone," *Lawfare*, May 5, 2012.

39 Koh, "The Obama administration and international law": "[A] state that is engaged in an armed conflict or in legitimate self-defense is not required to provide targets with legal process before the state may use lethal force. Our procedures and practices for identifying lawful targets are extremely robust, and advanced technologies have helped to make our targeting even more precise. In my experience, the principles of distinction and proportionality that the United States applies are not just recited at meetings. They are implemented rigorously throughout the planning and execution of lethal operations to ensure that such operations are conducted in accordance with all applicable law."

40 Klaidman, *Kill or Capture*, p. 220: Harold Koh argued for a legal theory called "elongated imminence," which Koh analogized to the battered wife syndrome defense – if alleged terrorists showed a consistent pattern of violence, that should be understood to meet the "imminence" standard, even if they were not about to engage in any specific strike at the moment at which they were targeted. While this "elongated imminence" legal theory might be appropriate for the context of terrorism, whether it is consistent with prior understandings of imminent threat under international law doctrines might be the subject of continuing debate. Holder himself appeared to reject strict notions of temporal imminence for what he instead called the "last window of opportunity" to stop an attack. Consider also this striking passage on how the administration defines "imminence" from a speech by John Brennan: "This Administration's counterterrorism efforts outside of

Afghanistan and Iraq are focused on those individuals who are a threat to the United States, whose removal would cause a significant – even if only temporary – disruption of the plans and capabilities of al-Qaida and its associated forces. Practically speaking, then, the question turns principally on how you define 'imminence.' We are finding increasing recognition in the international community that a more flexible understanding of 'imminence' may be appropriate when dealing with terrorist groups, in part because threats posed by non-state actors do not present themselves in the ways that evidenced imminence in more traditional conflicts." John Brennan, "Strengthening our security by adhering to our values and laws," speech given at the Harvard Law School Program on Law and Security, Cambridge, MA, September 16, 2011.

41 Brennan, "Strengthening our security by adhering to our values and laws."

42 Ibid.

43 Koh, "The Obama administration and international law."

44 Holder, address at Northwestern University School of Law.

45 Savage, Charlie, "At White House, weighting limits of terror fight," *New York Times*, September 15, 2011.

46 Goldsmith, Jack, "Thoughts on the latest round of Johnson v. Koh," *Lawfare*, September 16, 2011. See also Blum, Gabriella, "The dispensable lives of soldiers," *Journal of Legal Analysis* 2 (2010): 69–124, p. 74: changing a form of warfare "requires states to invest in military technologies that enable them to tell combatants apart from civilians and target the former without harming the latter. To do this, they must often engage in individual-based determinations of the identity and role of their target."

47 The emerging American doctrine has striking parallels to the decision of the Israeli Supreme Court on the lawfulness of targeted killing. Israel accepts a much greater judicial role in overseeing military operations, thus leading to an earlier hardening of the legal categories. Per the decision by President Aharon Barak, there are four requirements: (1) "Information which has been most thoroughly verified is needed regarding the identity and activity of the civilian who is allegedly taking part in the hostilities"; (2) "Second, a civilian taking a direct part in hostilities cannot be attacked at such time as he is doing so, if a less harmful means can be employed"; (3) "Third, after an attack on a civilian suspected of taking an active part, at such time, in hostilities, a thorough investigation regarding the precision of the identification of the target and the circumstances of the attack upon him is to be performed (retroactively). That investigation must be independent"; and (4) "Last, if the harm is not only to a civilian directly participating in the hostilities, rather also to innocent civilians nearby, the harm to them is collateral damage. That damage must withstand the proportionality test." HCJ 769/02 Pub. Comm. Against Torture in *Israel* v. *Government of Israel (PCATI)* [2005], slip op. para. 40.

48 Blumenfeld, Laura, "In Israel, a divisive struggle over targeted killing," *Washington Post*, August 27, 2006, which describes the internal executive branch processes for targeted killings by Israeli forces.

49 HCJ 769/02 Pub. Comm. Against Torture in *Israel* v. *Government of Israel*, slip op. para. 40.

50 Ibid.

51 Luban, "What would Augustine do," para. 40: "From the point of view of just war theory … If they are enemy belligerents, they can be targeted, regardless of their nationality."

52 *A v Secretary of State for the Home Department*, [2004] UKHL 56, p. 68 (HL) (the "A Case").

53 Klaidman, *Kill or Capture*, p. 265.

54 Barack Obama, "Remarks by the president at the National Defense University," Fort McNair, Washington DC, May 23, 2013.

55 We borrow the term from John Witt. Witt, John Fabian, "Bureaucratic legalism, American style: Private bureaucratic legalism and the governance of the tort system," *DePaul Law Review* 56 (2007): 261–292.

56 See Zegart, Amy B., *Eyes on spies: Congress and the United States intelligence community* (Palo Alto, CA: Hoover Institution Press, 2011).

57 McNeal, Gregory S.,"Targeted killing and accountability," *Georgetown Law Journal* 102 (2014): 681–794. Given that the US government has not acknowledged any drone program the CIA might control, there is, needless to say, no comparable information on any such program, assuming from news accounts that one does exist.

58 For the most extensive analysis of the CIA's targeted killing program, see Mazzetti, Mark, *The way of the knife: The CIA, a secret army, and a war at the ends of the Earth* (New York, NY: Penguin Press, 2013).

59 McNeal reports that since June 2009, pre-planned operations constituted all air-to-ground operations in Afghanistan, other than emergency situations in which close air support was called in. See McNeal,"Targeted Killing and Accountability."

60 Recent disclosures confirm the high-level authorization requirement. Becker and Shane, "Secret 'kill list' proves a test of Obama's principles and will": "In Pakistan, Mr. Obama had approved not only 'personality' strikes aimed at named, high-value terrorists, but 'signature' strikes that targeted training camps and suspicious compounds in areas controlled by militants."

61 Ibid.

62 Ibid.

63 This authority is apparently delegated to the commander of US and ISAF forces, which had been General Petraeus, and as of this writing is General Allen.

64 General Counsel, "Joint Targeting Cycle and Collateral Damage Estimation Methodology (CDM)," November 10, 2009.

65 Woods, Chris, "Analysis: CNN expert's civilian drone death numbers don't add up," Bureau of Investigative Journalism, July 17, 2012.

66 Becker and Shane, "Secret 'kill list' proves a test of Obama's principles and will."

67 See, generally, New America, "Drone Wars Pakistan: Analysis." http://securitydata. newamerica.net/drones/pakistan/analysis. Woods, "Analysis: CNN expert's civilian

drone death numbers don't add up," where it is noted that New America's data is "the most frequent source of statistics for the US media, including CNN itself. So the accuracy of its material is important."

68 New America, "Drone wars Pakistan: Analysis."

69 Bergen, Peter, and Jennifer Rowland, "Civilian casualties plummet in drone strikes," CNN, July 14, 2012.

70 The London-based Bureau of Investigative Journalism, in addition to being skeptical of Bergen and Rowland's claim that "at or close to zero percent" civilians were killed during the first seven months of 2012, is generally more skeptical of the strikes. Nevertheless, it recorded a similar dramatic decline in 2012 in its own comprehensive database. Woods, Chris, and Jack Serle, "June update: US covert actions in Pakistan, Yemen and Somalia," Bureau of Investigative Journalism, July 2, 2012, in which they report "fewer civilians are being killed in CIA drone strikes in Pakistan than at any time in the Obama presidency." Shane, Scott, "The moral case for drones," *New York Times*, July 14, 2012, in which he reports that "[t]he bureau has documented a notable drop in the civilian proportion of drone casualties, to 16 percent of those killed in 2011 from 28 percent in 2008. This year, by the bureau's count, just three of the 152 people killed in drone strikes through July 7 were civilians." *Express Tribune*, "Pakistan civilian deaths from US drones 'lowest since 2008,'" July 2, 2012. Friedersdorf, Conor, "CNN's bogus drone-deaths graphic," *Atlantic*, July 6, 2012.

71 Woods and Serle, "June update: US covert actions in Pakistan, Yemen and Somalia." Shane, "The moral case for drones." *Express Tribune*, "Pakistan civilian deaths from US drones 'lowest since 2008." Friedersdorf, "CNN's bogus drone-deaths graphic."

72 Sudarsan, Raghavan, "When U.S. drones kill civilians, Yemen's government tries to conceal it," *Washington Post*, December 24, 2012. Sudarsan has written a remarkable piece of reporting on a recent strike in Yemen that appears to have rested on faulty intelligence, with major loss of innocent lives and serious counterproductive strategic consequences, if the article is accurate.

73 We are particularly indebted to Marty Lederman for pressing this point with us.

74 Dan-Cohen, Meir, "Decision rules and conduct rules: On acoustic separation in criminal law," *Harvard Law Review*, 97 (1984): 625–677.

75 Blum, "The dispensable lives of soldiers," p. 74.

21

How to Manage Drones

Transformative Technologies, the Evolving Nature of Conflict,
and the Inadequacy of Current Systems of Law

BRAD ALLENBY

1. DRONES, LAW, AND EMERGING TECHNOLOGIES

Drones lie on the difficult border of three different conceptual domains: emerging technologies, the evolving nature of conflict, and the laws of war. The first two are characterized by extraordinary and growing complexity and the third is a reasonably well-understood and fairly carefully defined policy and legal framework. Within the domain of the laws of war, also known as international humanitarian law, drones do not engage issues of complexity within the system, but rather raise questions as to whether this important discourse and practice is still viable. That is, to what degree do drones lead us to a radical reconceptualization of the laws of war given foundational changes in technology and the nature of conflict? Rather than consider drones as a specific element of war, which is how they are usually addressed, we should consider them through a lens through which the future can be glimpsed, presenting us with ideas and challenges that extend beyond the demands of a single technology system.

Technological innovation, military operations and practice, and their broader social and cultural impacts, have been co-evolving throughout history. This process is often obvious: stirrups and composite bows privileged horse warriors such as those from the Eurasian steppes; corned gunpowder, developed by Europeans in the late fourteenth century, offered far better performance than black powder; cast cannons mounted on ships favored European navies during their global imperialist expansion; nuclear weapons made some kinds of war too awful to rationally contemplate but provided certain strategic advantages to nations that controlled them. However, most military technologies with transformative power have also had profound cultural implications. Gunpowder and cannon technology, for example, not only shifted the power relationship between infantry and heavy cavalry (knights), but, also, because of the logistic and administrative scale required to mount a campaign using them, privileged larger political and economic powers over smaller entities.

In considering military technology, especially in a US context, it is important to walk a fine line between appreciating the potentially revolutionary impact of some technologies and avoiding the pitfalls of technological determinism. In this regard, it is important to bear in mind the words of Qiao Liang and Wang Xiansui of the Chinese People's Liberation Army, who note in their 1999 classic strategic analysis of how a country such as China should compete militarily with the United States: "Observing, considering, and resolving problems from the point of view of technology is typical American thinking. Its advantages and disadvantages are both very apparent, just like the characters of Americans."[1]

In short, while it is important to consider the strategic, tactical, and operational implications of new military technologies such as drones, and while new technologies are an excellent lens to view a complex and rapidly changing geopolitical and strategic space, it is also a fundamental mistake to fixate on any technology as a military and social competence.

Perhaps this point is best made by considering a few of the implications of a technology system that today appears mundane and even banal: the railroad. Because in many ways the world as it is now co-evolved with the railroad, it is difficult for us to understand how profoundly this technology changed life for those in Western Europe or the United States in the 1840s and 1850s who directly experienced its rapid expansion.

One might begin with a review of the way modernity has structured the experience of time. Prior to the introduction of railroad technology, local times were uncoordinated and varied unpredictably. In the United Kingdom, London time differed from that in Reading by four minutes, and from that in Bridgewater by fourteen. The United States, meanwhile, had more than two hundred local time zones even as late as the 1850s. This situation, however, was not dysfunctional. Travel between towns was by existing modes of transportation – by horse, walking, or canal – that did not require uniform coordinated time communication. And those activities that required coordination, such as daily religious observance, were local such that differences of minutes between communities were not relevant and went largely unnoticed. Indeed, early railroad routes tended to be simple replacements for roads (from a mine to a port, for example), and involved very few daily trains traveling long distances with multiple stops. However, when railroads began to integrate into regional networks, the lack of a uniform and precise time system became increasingly problematic.

If looked at historically, the railroad case study also illustrates the process of cultural, social, economic, institutional, and cultural adaptations that such changes require. For example, in the United States, developing uniform time zones began with the actions of individual firms, largely because shared track infrastructure was rare. Thus, time would be uniform for a particular company but differ between companies.

At one point, for example, Buffalo, New York, was served by three railroad companies, each running on its own time, while Pittsburgh, Pennsylvania, a larger station, had six companies on six different running times serving firms (and each firm also had its own station, so in many cases "changing in Pittsburgh" would mean taking a tram or taxi from one company's station to another's).[2] Simply put, no one really knew what a global time system would look like, so it had to be invented. And that process itself took time. By 1883 US railroad companies managed to standardize to four time zones, but it was only in 1918 that the United States created a legally mandated set of standard regional time zones. Analogously, rapid and increasingly complex transportation networks required similar evolution in communication technology, so railroads created significant incentives for the development of telegraph technology, which in turn stimulated other developments that connected previously disparate communities. Over time, the secondary social, institutional, and cultural implications of the railroads and telegraph were transformative.

Just as cannon and gunpowder created economies of scale that privileged the power of the Renaissance princes of Europe and enabled the evolution of the financial and administrative sinews of the nation-state model of international governance, so too did railroad technology generate its own institutional changes.[3] This was because, as railroads grew into transportation networks, they became by far and away the most complex structures for the development of new financial and administrative systems that capitalism had yet produced. Modern managerial capitalism, with the idea of division of labor extended from the factory floor to white-collar administrative and managerial levels, became an operating necessity once the railroads were a core part of the economy. Capital-intensive physical infrastructure created a huge demand for liquid finance, which not only changed financial institutions and instruments, but also led to the development of innovative fraud schemes on the part of budding magnates. At regional and national levels, railroads created economies of scale that ushered in an age of monopolies and trusts (and, eventually, regulatory responses such as anti-trust law).

Because railroads dramatically lowered the price of bulk goods and increased their speed of transport, prices for commodities first converged in national markets and then internationally. The increase in agricultural demand that railroads enabled, combined with the bulk commodity capability of railroads, helped make industrial agriculture economically feasible. This, in turn, transformed vast regions of the world, such as the American Midwest, which went from swamp to breadbasket with all the ecological and social challenges that this implied.

These changes were not limited to institutional, economic, and physical realms of society. Railroads were also psychologically disconcerting to many. Many critics saw them as obliterating the "natural" sense of place and rhythm that slower and less aggressive transportation technologies represented. In addition, they were viewed as commodifying people, who complained of being treated like so many packages rather than as unique individuals. Railroads were the first mass transportation technology and, as such, they led to a set of critiques that have subsequently been applied to many other significant technological innovations.

Railroads had substantial military and security implications as well. Most people are familiar with the contribution that a strong railroad infrastructure provided to the war effort of the North in the American Civil War, but an equally if perhaps less well-known case is provided by the Prussian experience. When in 1848 unrest broke out across Europe in reaction to the conservative absolutism that leading states had attempted to reimpose following the trauma of the Napoleonic Wars, Prussia was able to maintain order in part by using its railroad network to rush troops to where they were most needed. This gave the Prussian leadership experience in rail-mediated conflict management, as well as a healthy respect for the military and security advantages a good rail network could provide. Thus, the Prussians established the Prussian Railway Fund to support construction of lines that might not be commercially viable but were militarily valuable, and they designed their commercial railroad cars so that in times of conflict they could easily be repurposed to carry soldiers, horses, and military equipment. Prussian mobilization plans were based on railroad technology, with each regiment assigned to a specific rail station that was designed to allow for both commercial traffic and the efficient loading of military trains.

However, powerful technologies are always disruptive. Accordingly, while Prussia seized a technological opportunity, many regions and countries explicitly rejected it, with significant consequences for their future military prowess. The French and the US South, for example, were lukewarm on railroads for fear they might shift power between social classes. In Russia and Austria, the ruling elites deliberately stifled the spread of railroad technology because they feared destabilization of their feudal economic and class structures. However, rejecting a new technology only works where one's cultural and geopolitical competitors do the same. The South lost the Civil War in part because of its failure to industrialize and adopt modern technologies, especially the railroad. And the Austrian Empire was stunned when in 1866 it lost the battle of Koniggratz to Prussia, still a relatively minor state. In these and other instances (e.g., the Franco–Prussian War of 1870), rail technology was not the only factor – among other things, the Prussians had the advanced needle gun, a militarized society, and brilliant military leadership, exemplified by the Prussian General Staff – but it was certainly a major element of the outcome of the conflict. Still, it is worth noting that the Prussian mobilization for the Franco–Prussian War was characteristically flawless, and their railroad-centric plan worked to perfection, while the French mobilization was confused, chaotic, inefficient, and, in the end, ineffectual.[4]

The railroad example illustrates the fundamental point that all but the most specialized military or security technology systems will impact civil society and, similarly, virtually any serious technological innovation will have military and security implications. The categories that we use to think about such things – bins labeled "military," "security," "civilian," "technology," and many others – are both useful and adequate, but they can lead to a failure to acknowledge underlying connections that are critical for rational strategy and policy development.

Economic historians have developed the idea of "long waves" of innovation, sometimes called "Kondratiev waves" (after the Russian economic historian Nikolai Kondratiev) to address the fact that major technology systems co-evolve with other technologies, institutions, economic trends, and social and cultural patterns. These waves are characterized by decadal patterns of economic growth and retrenchment linked with a core transformative technology or set of technologies. Although the existence of such waves is debated and there is room for differing interpretations as to which changes constitute long waves, key examples include the textile manufacturing technology cluster initiated the Industrial Revolution around 1750 in the United Kingdom; the rail and steam innovations created a long wave that extended from around 1840 to 1890; the cluster of new materials and related energy advances, including the development of steel and harnessing of electricity that ran from about 1890 to 1930; and the links between petroleum processing, the automobile and aircraft, and associated mass consumption and mass transportation, which served as catalysts for a wave from around 1930 to 1990.

There are several points about transformative technology systems that are critical for a reflection on drones. First, regardless of how one chooses to define and analyze each of these examples, the general idea of technology clusters is useful for understanding historical patterns. Second, powerful technology systems destabilize and restructure human systems and institutions at multiple scales and are likely to also change natural systems. Railroads, for example, opened up continental interiors to industrialized agriculture, which in turn supported a greatly increased global human population. Automobiles not only enabled a complementary built environment but also profoundly impacted the atmosphere and the climate. In this way, each modern technology cluster or long wave of innovation has played a role in transforming people's connections to the world and even the natural environment.

Third, each of these processes has been accompanied by ever-increasing levels of complexity; especially as global human-built and natural systems become more integrated with each other, as well as evermore interdependent, such that changes in any single system create wider and more profound changes across other systems. As a result, changes in technologies with potential military and security implications, such as cyber or geoengineering (e.g., deliberate manipulation of solar insulation) not only have immediate implications for operations, tactics, strategy, and policy, but also rapidly and unpredictably affect civil systems at regional and global scales. This phenomenon is of great significance in that it increasingly blurs the boundaries that have been applied to categories such as "military" or "civilian."

Such implications are of particular concern given that we now face rapid and accelerating evolution of not just one but five powerful foundational technology systems. These technology systems, sometimes called the "Five Horsemen," include nanotechnology, biotechnology, robotics, information and communication technology, and applied cognitive science. Taken together, they are generating fundamental and unpredictable shifts in both single sectors and across the entire technology frontier. They can be understood as the next evolutionary step in an ongoing process through which humans have sought to gain mastery over the Earth and its natural, human, and built environments.

Nanotechnology extends human design to the atomic level. Synthetic biology extends it to the smallest functional elements of life. Information and communication technology creates social networks of unprecedented complexity and scale and gives every individual the accumulated memory of civilization via powerful search engines, thereby enabling evermore-potent virtual and synthetic realities that encourage the integration of the physical and informational worlds. Robotics link applied cognitive science and biotechnology, connecting living and non-living domains in ways that are obvious (e.g., robots that expand on existing human activities) and less obvious (e.g., research to enable humans to be directly wired into weapons systems via sophisticated computer–brain interfaces). Applied cognitive science informs the accelerating diffusion of cognition across integrated techno–human networks, and provides the theoretical and experiential support for development of increasingly autonomous robotic systems. While we may not be able to know what world these emerging technologies will help create, it is certain that they will be transformative in ways that will profoundly shift current ideas of social order, in ways analogous to prior revolutionary technologies, and in ways that defy current understanding.[5]

2. THE CHANGING CONTEXT OF CONFLICT

No military technology can be understood outside of cultural, social, economic, and institutional contexts, which impact the nature of conflict. From the perspective of those responsible for military and security domains in today's world, the effects of these changes add important additional layers of uncertainty and complexity to the management of armed conflict. To understand these challenges, it is useful to consider four basic observations with associated strategic implications, which should be recognized for viable long-term military and security technology policies.

First, developed countries generally, and the United States specifically, are becoming less tolerant of combat fatalities and engage in warfare in a manner that leads to significantly lower death rates for members of their armed forces. In World War I, single battles sometimes killed more than half a million men. For example, more than 500,000 were killed in the First Battle of the Marne; 800,000 were killed at Verdun; and more than 1.1 million were killed in the Battle of the Somme. In comparison, around 58,000 US soldiers were killed in the entire Vietnam conflict. And, from the initial invasion of Afghanistan in 2001 and the invasion of Iraq in 2003 through the end of 2013, there have been less than 6,800 US military deaths. In general, civilian deaths in conflict zones have also been significantly reduced and there are increasing pressures to further reduce what has come to be known as collateral damage.

The strategic implication of drones and related technologies, as well as more advanced future systems that involve computer–brain interfaces that connect a remote human to a weapons platform, are critical because they remove humans from the line of fire. This may reduce military casualties even more while greater accuracy may potentially limit civilian deaths during conflict.

However, a subtler strategic implication of this shift is that the successful implementation of new technologies that reduce combat deaths may lower the threshold for initiating conflicts. This may lead to more violent interactions and more warfare, and all of the resulting implications.

Second, militaries in industrialized nations are faced with unfavorable long-term demographic trends in that as societies age, there are fewer physically active individuals available for military service. Moreover, as that pool shrinks, the military will be competing with industry, raising the possibility that recruitment cohorts will become less educated and less technologically sophisticated over time. Added to this challenge is the fact that in many of the more chaotic regions of the world, such as sub-Saharan Africa and the Middle East, there is the opposite problem: very young populations in which growing numbers of men are entering stressed economies that offer few job prospects and limited opportunities.

One of the strategic implications of this trend is that autonomous technologies will become far more common. This translates to a military environment that will mirror a trend that has dominated economic development from the beginning of the Industrial Revolution in which capital substituted for labor.

The subtler strategic implications of this shift is that non-traditional populations, such as women in some cultures, will be increasingly recruited into full combat roles, and countries that are culturally able to tolerate high levels of immigration may link military service with legal immigration and perhaps citizenship to ensure fully staffed armed forces. More speculatively, identifying potential military roles for seniors could help allocate younger soldiers to appropriate positions.

Third, the increasing complexity and information density of the combat environment itself means that the cognitive function of the warrior will be extended across technological networks. Furthermore, cognition within the military will be understood and designed as a network function, rather than as a collection of isolated individuals operating in tandem. That is, the linkages between military personnel will evolve in relation to new technologies, and machines and humans are likely to be intimately connected through modes of networking that redefine the relationship between individual soldiers, larger units, and various missions. The strategic implication of these changes is that far more cognitive processing power must be designed into emerging military technologies, with the human component of the system performing those functions that it is best at (e.g., pattern recognition). This will also drive development and deployment of increased, albeit bounded, autonomy for technological systems.

The subtler strategic implications of these shifts include vast transformations of military cultures and the laws of war, which are currently premised on individual liability and traditional assumptions of human responsibility leading to accountability. In a sufficiently complex augmented cognition network, such assumptions need to be revisited. While individual responsibility may still apply in many circumstances, it would be naive to assume that these ideas will define the only modes of human accountability without explicit and ongoing analysis.

Fourth, militaries are increasingly aware of the high and rapidly accelerating levels of complexity, both technological and geopolitical, within which they must operate and provide security. The challenges posed by increasing complexity range from unpredictable technology developments in domains, such as cyber or biotech, to understanding and managing the implications of major non-traditional opponents. Different and more complex practices will be needed if traditional forms of conflict are augmented by non-state, non-geographically situated, amorphous extremist movements. This is highlighted by particular strategies such as the use of suicide bombers, who are generally understood as non-combatants and may become combatants only for short periods of time that can be difficult or impossible to predict.

The strategic implication of these shifts places increasing pressure on militaries – especially those active against non-traditional opponents – to engage in a deep and reflective study of the assumptions underlying their activities. This is important not just to maintain and enhance operational effectiveness, but also to discuss and negotiate new international agreements without inappropriately undermining operational effectiveness and security. As regards the use of drones, for example, is it the technology that so many critics focus on that represents the main problem, or is it the changing geopolitical shifts to which the military must respond? If it is the former, critics and their military targets may be able to achieve some accommodation. However, if it is the latter, it is likely that the military, because of its operational experience, will perceive and understand the shifts far better than critics with limited knowledge of managing the actual projection of force and no responsibility for the civilian and military damage resulting from breakdowns in security. In this context, a mutually satisfying solution may not be possible because addressing critics may pose unacceptable costs regarding mission effectiveness and national security.

Subtler strategic implications include the fact that militaries need to avoid focusing too much on emerging technologies, because major elements of their missions, especially those dealing with non-traditional opponents, cannot be addressed through purely technological responses. In an era of cyber conflict, new versions of asymmetric warfare involving non-traditional globally organized opponents will force militaries to focus not only on protecting their states and societies from unrestricted warfare, but also on complex and integrated visions of long-term security. That is, many elements of the larger social structure, such as areas of economic vulnerability, may pose the greatest risks.[6]

Consider some of the ways in which conflict has become more complex over the several decades. Most obviously, the sorts of wars that countries currently fight are not traditional military-to-military conflicts in the classic European sense. That is, conflicts in the Afghanistan–Pakistan region (AfPak), Iraq and the surrounding region, the former Yugoslavia, former French African colonies, and even Vietnam are very different than state contests that defined the Napoleonic Wars or the First or Second World Wars. Recent European and American conflicts have not been for the conquest or control of territory or for the establishment of colonies, but to achieve ideological aims, defeat disfavored elites, and support greater global integration in line with national security objectives. This is certainly the case for most Cold War–era conflicts and arguably true for post–Cold War conflicts as well.

Armies do not congregate and meet each other on the field of battle as used to be the norm; indeed, one reason drones are being used as they are by the US troops is that, in the very real conflict between established states and Islamic *jihad*, there is no geographically defined "field of battle." An even more abstract battle space is found in cyber conflict and in other emerging threats, especially if cyber conflict is understood to include criminal harassment and hacking or disrupting civilian systems.

These four key points and their strategic implications and impact on the growing complexity of conflict are illustrated in Figure 6. This visual description reinforces an important point: many of the assumptions and conceptual frameworks that have been stable over the past centuries are increasingly contingent. Some more obvious examples include a growing acceptance that some of the internal activities of states, such as institutionalized violence and discrimination based on race or religion, are unacceptable and even illegal and, at times, may lead to intervention by the international community. Similarly significant, and widely recognized, is the growing importance and power of non-state actors. These developments should not be understood as suggesting, as some simplistic formulations claim, that the nation-state is obsolete. Rather they undermine the assumption that the nation-state is the only key relevant actor within modern international law in general and within the laws of armed conflict more specifically.

Moreover, the moving parts of this complex system are all interconnected. As the missions and goals of conflict change, and the geographic certainty that used to bound combat becomes increasingly questionable, technologies such as drones, autonomous robotic systems, and cyber are used in ways not encompassed by existing norms and legal agreements.

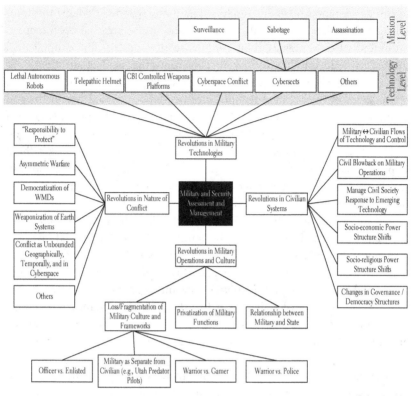

FIGURE 6. Mission-level and technology level flow chart
Note: CBI: Computer brain interface
WMDs: Weapons of mass destruction
Source: Allenby, Braden R., *The theory and practice of sustainable engineering* (Upper Saddle River, NJ: Prentice-Hall, 2012), p. 294. Used by permission

Figure 6 illustrates the four major domains of rapid change that are affecting military and security operations, tactics, strategy, and policy. These four domains are described here as "revolutions" to highlight their profoundly transformative nature. They are: Revolutions in Military Technologies, Revolutions in Nature of Conflict, Revolutions in Civilian Systems, and Revolutions in Military Operations and Culture. Note that the figure suggests that these domains are independent; however, that is for purposes of exposition only, because in reality they co-evolve, which is one reason they create so much unpredictability, uncertainty, and complexity.

The first of the four major domains identified, Revolutions in Military Technology (RMT), is perhaps the most immediately relevant to drones and to the development of increasingly autonomous systems. Perhaps the most salient observation is that while most attention in this area has been focused on individual technologies, their cumulative effects across the technological frontier has tended to be overlooked. This means that inadequate attention is focused on the larger implications of these changes and the significance of entire suites of inter-related technologies (e.g., the designed warrior or grid computer linked robotic systems across time and space). This presents some of the most significant real operational, tactical, strategic, and policy challenges. This is especially true because the complexity of these systems makes them unpredictable, and their management requires not targeted interventions or responses, but the development of a core competence of agility and adaptability in the face of fundamental uncertainty.

Revolutions in the Nature of Conflict (RNC) have been part of warfare for thousands of years. Here, as with the transformative technological changes, substantive shifts in conflict are not sudden and discontinuous, but rather are a confluence of trends that create accelerating and unpredictable evolution. This destabilizes existing foundations of law, morals, policy, and strategy. One way this occurs is by dislodging the nation-state (which is premised on respect for a vision of sovereignty once understood to mean that states had the absolute right to do what they wanted inside their borders) as the primary or sole actor within international affairs.

Over the past sixty years, with growing intensity and specificity, traditional ideas of sovereignty have been eroded through the creation of a broad human rights framework. More recently, the transformative nature of this idea is seen in the "responsibility to protect" (R2P). This principle places an obligation on countries not directly involved in particular conflicts or situations to intervene in the affairs of other countries under circumstances where the state is responsible for profound human suffering or unable to address the situation. While the sorts of incidents that have led to the development of this principle are not new, such as the severe repression directed toward local populations in the Balkans, Rwanda, and other regions and countries, the 2005 UN initiative to establish R2P represents an emerging and contentious extension of existing humanitarian law (and this shift is opposed by many countries, including China and Russia, which have difficult internal conflicts and oppose this idea, possibly fearing Western intervention). Such shifts in the primacy of the nation-state and traditional commitments to sovereignty represent profound challenges to existing worldviews and dominant legal structures and may lead to a reconceptualization of how legal force is understood.

On a more mundane level, the structure of conflict has also become more complex. Much strategic thinking and an intricate body of humanitarian law developed as a result of the traditional battles that characterized European warfare during the eighteenth, nineteenth, and twentieth centuries. Starting in the middle of the twentieth century, counterinsurgency (COIN) conflicts have became more common. This challenge is still evolving; and there is still no adequate consensus regarding the proper way to manage conflicts between nation-states and non-state actors, such as guerrilla organizations operating within a nation and, more recently, with global terrorism groups spreading over multiple locations. Such conflicts are not as defined by time and space as more traditional conflicts and raise specific operational, tactical, strategic, and policy questions.

Perhaps the most interesting recent evolution of these challenges is found in cyber conflict, which raises extremely difficult questions of attribution, nation-state control over global botnet assets (a "bot net" or "zombie army" is a large group of computers that have been surreptitiously captured by illegal software so that they can be used to, for example, launch spam or denial of service attacks on targeted websites), and, indeed, what constitutes conflict to begin with (at least for purposes of enabling a legal armed response).

From a technological and sociocultural perspective, a significant source of additional complexity is the increasing intermixing of police functions with traditional military combat operations. This situation, common in places such as Afghanistan and Iraq, creates substantial stress, as these are very different activities with very different psychological and legal frameworks. This radically expanded mission increases complexity and also affects technology choice. For example, a weapon like an Active Denial System (ADS) that generates strong but non-lethal pain through microwaves or other means, thereby dispersing mobs and crowds without causing them permanent damage, is not particularly effective in a combat situation but could be quite useful in a policing situation. Equally confusing is that where police and military missions are intermixed, there may be confusion as to the correct body of law to be applied. The laws of war forbid targeting non-combatants, so in a military situation, the ADS could not be used to specifically target civilians, whereas in a policing situation, where other laws apply, it could be used, especially if the alternative were lethal force.

Revolutions in Civilian Systems (RCS) is a large category reflecting the many changes in social and civilian systems that affect technology and warfare. For example, the continuing rise of what the analyst Samuel Huntington has called civilizational non-state actors, such as Islamic fundamentalist movements and activist groups such as Aum Shinrikyo, represents a complex intermingling of civilian and security challenges and cultures. Equally challenging is the increasingly rapid transfer of technologies designed for military and security missions into civilian life, where their impact is much different. For example, a quadrotor, a pilotless helicopter-like vehicle that is commercially available, which nicely supports COIN operations, raises much different implications when used in the domestic environment by a local police force, a divorce lawyer, or a political party. It does not take much imagination to see that the set of technologies conceptually linked to drones – including ground robots, GPS, data mining, and radio frequency identification, which are effective in mixed-conflict situations – may have complex, troubling, and possibly illegal results when used in peacetime settings. This may well be true whether they are deployed by a government seeking to maintain high security standards or by civilians with various interests.

Finally, there are Revolutions in Military Operations and Culture (RMOC), which have a broader impact than many people realize. After all, an internal military culture, backed by substantial training, is a major reason that modern militaries, from the United States to European states to China, maintain their norms and compliance standards. In addition, the structure and social norms of a country's military is also a major determinant of the potential for coups, political instability, and military intervention in domestic governance. The internal military culture is rapidly changing as conditions of conflict are transformed. For example, the military model in most developed countries is to create a volunteer, professional, and highly trained military core force around which additional forces (e.g., National Guards) can be assembled when necessary. But when part of the core mission is to protect civilians and the built environment and to minimize violence, as in many of the deployments in AfPak or Bosnia, these efforts begin to look a lot more like policing, an activity to which only specialized parts of the military culture are adapted, such as the US Military Police.

Drones, of course, create and reflect similar cultural and institutional issues. If they are used in a policing environment, lethality is a last resort, and generally the domestic law of the state where the operation occurs applies. If drones are used in a war zone by military forces, they are under tight operational control and must meet the requirements of applicable law (one may argue about the correct choice of law and interpretation of law, but not whether US forces are committed to following the law as determined by the government). However, if drones are used by covert and intelligence forces the applicable law and restrictions on operations are both less clear and less transparent.

Technologies often change cultures. One of the major questions posed is to what extent will the psychology and culture of military organizations like the US Air Force be changed by drone technology. Many initial critical analyses of drone technology have focused on the superficial similarity between drone operations and gaming, arguing that drones may trivialize killing by turning war into a video game. However, actual research on drone operators has shown that the stresses and psychological effects of operating a drone are far more complex than initially believed.

This conceptual mapping illustrates the complexity of the issues surrounding emerging military/security technology systems such as drones. The scope, degree, and depth of these transformations require new understandings as outlined in this typology: RMT, RNC, RCS, and RMOC. What is most important here as regards the debate over drones is the suggestion that the usual dialogue around emerging technologies is overly simplistic and superficial. A more substantive and engaged review of drones and their integration into a rapidly changing environment raises questions as to whether the current laws of war are adequate to meet the challenges of emerging technologies and their transformative nature.

3. THE LAWS OF WAR

The laws of war can be defined as:

> [T]he customary and written laws and regulations, and associated practices, that generally govern the initiation of, and conduct during, and after, conflict situations, including but not limited to, LOAC/IHL [Laws of Armed Conflict/International Humanitarian Law].[7]

Traditionally, the laws of war have covered three separable but inter-related domains: *jus ad bellum*, the rules covering the legality of engaging in war; *jus in bello*, the rules covering how a war is legally fought and managed; and, less traditional but increasingly of interest, *jus post bellum*, or the rules associated with legal occupation and the management of post-conflict societies.

Like all systems that regulate human behavior, the laws of war rely on a number of basic assumptions, many of which are implicit and exist on an unconscious level. Technological evolution, especially at current scale and speed, is highly destabilizing and is augmenting rather than reducing the complexity of conflict and its regulation. As such, current laws of war may be inadequate in whole or in part for addressing emerging issues regarding conflict.

Consider, for example, how two of the primary assumptions underlying the laws of war – that nation-states are the primary parties to a conflict and that there exists clarity as to the geographical site of conflict and acts of war – are inapplicable to at least two of the major threats in the world today: the challenges posed by a global fundamentalist Islam movement and the challenges of cyber conflict, whether between states or involving states and non-state actors of various types. A global Islamic *jihadist* movement is a powerful ideological and, in places, physical force, and yet it has no geographic center. When challenged in Asia, the movement may well reappear in Africa or somewhere else. Dominant methods of physical attack, such as terrorist bombings, can be deployed virtually anywhere with relatively limited logistical and bureaucratic structures. Cyber conflict poses different difficulties. For example, in cyber conflict it may be extremely difficult to know the identity of what force is behind an attack and whether the force is that of a state, a non-state actor, or some combination of the two.

Both of these cases also illustrate how the physical nature of warfare is changing. The laws of war are ill-suited to conflict where the same individual shifts from being a civilian to a combatant and back again, and travels in either status around the world to launch attacks. The solution within traditional laws of war is that if a person is in a geographical space defined as a battlefield and is a combatant, he or she can be attacked; if not a combatant, he or she cannot be attacked. However, if the person is a criminal, arrest should be made regardless of location (though he or she may be extradited to where charges originated) and then processed through the criminal justice system. This system, however, has become obsolete. In many cases, there are simply no definable battlefields. Indeed, the idea that there is still a condition called "war" that is separable from other conditions of conflict and conflict management may, in fact, be naive. If the conflicts of the future – whether between nation-states, superpowers, or nation-states and non-state actors – are to involve unrestricted warfare, such as where the use of financial instruments may be as "weaponized" in their destructive powers as missiles, then the laws of war have indeed been destabilized.

However, it is also legitimate to note that many of these observations, while exacerbated by current geopolitical trends, are not new. In fact, what the future holds may not involve the substitution of "traditional combat" by unrestricted warfare, cyber conflict, and complex non-state actor conflicts, but rather an augmentation of a set of existing issues. In this way, the portfolio of conflict conditions is expanding such that operations, tactics, strategies, and policies must evolve to cover a broader and more complex set of challenges that extend beyond traditional understandings. In other words, just as Newtonian physics was augmented, but not replaced, by quantum mechanics and relativity, so the forms of combat to which the laws of war apply may come to be understood as a particular element of a larger and more complex and multidimensional understanding of conflict.

The most important observation to be drawn from this reflection is that it is unlikely that the evolution of military technology, conflict, and related social and political transformations have rendered the laws of war irrelevant. On the one hand, the pervasive and accelerating change hinted at above is clearly challenging the doctrines and principles created and refined under different and significantly less complex conditions. On the other hand, it is also clear that few human systems change completely and discontinuously; even fundamental changes in economics, institutions, technologies, and geopolitics have deep roots in past events, and develop gradually, although they sometimes appear to be completely new. Moreover, the laws of war and, more generally, the study of war have developed over millennia and reflect the wisdom of many cultures. It is worth remembering how many military strategists around the world, not to mention business students, continue to read Sun Tzu's *The Art of War*.[8] To assume that such a robust tradition would become completely irrelevant to current conditions is a strong claim indeed.

The more appropriate questions are first, how do we redefine the domains of the laws of conflict and strategy to recognize the challenges raised by new and emerging technologies, new forms of conflict, and a rapidly changing geopolitical context? Second, how do we know when the traditional laws of war apply and when they require augmentation or replacement? Third, how do we work out the new operational implications, tactics, strategies, policies, laws, and norms that are appropriate for current and future challenges?

Answering these questions effectively is neither easy nor trivial for a number of reasons. To begin, much of the analytical framing of conflict, especially among those who are deeply engaged with immediate challenges of security, military operations, and associated human rights issues, is imbued with potentially obsolete assumptions and institutional pressures and structures. Because of this, developing the ability to clearly perceive and analyze new conditions and non-traditional warfare will be difficult. Additionally, all dimensions of the relevant space are evolving, usually at rapidly accelerating rates, creating a difficult analytical challenge, even if perception and awareness were clear. Moreover, as in AfPak or Iraq, the traditional and non-traditional overlap in ways that make many analyses overly simplistic: policing, crowd control, COIN, and combat overlap in confusing ways, sometimes in the same battle zones, and cyber elements have already become central to many military operations. The element of complexity and the associated increases in unpredictability and uncertainty have always been troubling to military and security strategists and policymakers. Today the challenges are truly daunting; nonetheless, there is no choice. It is our world that has forced this enhanced complexity upon us.

4. OBSERVATIONS ABOUT DRONES

It can now be seen that much of the public discussion concerning drones is superficial in that it assumes that the existing laws and norms governing conflict are appropriate and adequate. This seems particularly true of some of the less analytically sophisticated critics of US policy, many of whom fail to appreciate the differences between the world of traditional combat between nations and the current environment, which is much more complex. However, those responsible for the military and security activities of the United States neither have the luxury of clinging to outmoded perspectives on the world, nor can afford to fail to understand that the nature of national security challenges have changed and will continue to change in dramatic and difficult ways.

This is not to suggest that those managing US security interests have done everything right, or that well-founded criticism is not important and necessary. After all, understanding and acknowledging fundamental shifts in the operating environment means that the specific responses selected are more likely to be correct and responsibly managed. Nevertheless, good analyses, strategies, and policies require a clear understanding of underlying conditions. Although we do not have a complete understanding of how conflict is changing, pretending that past assumptions are still fully viable is increasingly inadequate, and, indeed, dysfunctional.

However, one point is clear: it is not a particular technology system – drones – that is, itself, a problem. Rather what is at issue is the complex ways in which drones are currently being used and the implications of these actions. Thus, for example, a drone deployed by the US military in an attack within an established war zone operates under existing law of armed conflict and its targeting and attack activities are strictly controlled and monitored to ensure such compliance. A similar drone operated by an intelligence agency may use different procedures because the laws of war do not fully govern espionage activities. If a drone on a targeting mission were to be piloted by private entities, such as mercenaries, there would be still different laws governing their use. Moreover, drones used for policing activities would be used differently and, again, would operate under another set of rules than those being used in support of combat operations in a defined theater of war.

Increasingly, drones are being used domestically by civilians (there are already some effective and inexpensive quadrotors with cameras available on amazon.com), as well as by military and government entities. This raises many issues of privacy and safety. Nevertheless, to date there has not been a reported case of a drone or quadrotor being used as an attack platform in the United

States, although it is probably only a matter of time before such an incident occurs. When a private individual uses one of these machines in this way within the United States, it will be a criminal matter. When a government agency uses drones to project force, the usual legal standards will likely apply. However, the politics of this issue might become quite complex; it is doubtful that libertarians will appreciate fleets of domestic surveillance drones, but one wonders if the National Rifle Association would view armed drones as simply another expression of the US Constitution's Second Amendment.

Major technological change has always tended to destabilize existing psychological, institutional, social, cultural, and economic frameworks, especially institutions such as national and international law that are intended to support social stability. It is desirable that regulatory systems, such as the laws of war, are difficult to change because this supports their coherence and validity. However, when rapid, transformative change occurs, the strengths of such essentially conservative institutions can rapidly become weaknesses.

Technologies such as drones are often identified as "the problem" in part because the underlying complexity is often daunting, and those seeking rigid and ideologically pure solutions will not find them within a shifting state of messy ambiguity. However, engaging the difficult reality of these changes is far better that acting as if they did not exist. In fact, we need to understand the dialogues and disagreements about such technologies as a means of perceiving when the cycle time of institutional change lags behind, or even decouples from, the underlying strategic, policy, and geopolitical environments. In this way, we can help develop more sophisticated and appropriate governance systems.

Accordingly, the best way to think about drones at this point is not as a unitary technology, but as a portfolio of potential responses to specific conditions and challenges. Using drones in a geographically distinct COIN environment is different than using drones as part of a global response against globally diffuse non-traditional, non-state actors. And both are different than using drones in traditional combat environments. This is true as a matter of law and policy even if the equipment is exactly the same in all cases. It is not drones that are an issue, and more arguments about drones themselves will not compensate for the fundamental weakness in the existing debate.

It is not the technology per se that should be the focus of our attention if we seek a deeper understanding of the challenges we face and desire a more rational strategy and set of policy guidelines. What is needed is greater understanding of the context and the complexity within which the technology is deployed. If we gain a better understanding of these complexities – of revolutions in military technologies, revolutions in the nature of conflict, revolutions in civilian systems, and revolutions in military operations and culture – and their interactions, and we combine this understanding with a more sophisticated engagement with how technology interacts with social, cultural, military, and security institutions, we will begin to be able to appropriately manage drones.

NOTES

1 Liang, Qiao, and Wang Xiansui *Unrestricted Warfare* (Los Angeles, CA: Pan American Publishing Company, 2002), p. 60.

2 Wolmar, Christian, *The great railroad revolution: The history of trains in America* (New York, NY: Perseus Books Group, 2012).

3 Schivelbusch, Wolfgang, *The railway journey: The industrialization of time and space in the 19th century* (University of California Press, 1977).

4 Boot, Max, *War made new* (New York, NY: Gotham, 2007).

5 Allenby, Brad, *The theory and practice of sustainable engineering* (Upper Saddle River, NJ: Pearson Prentice/Hall, 2011).

6 For example, Adm. Mike Mullen, Chairman of the US Joint Chiefs of Staff, warned policymakers that "[o]ur national debt is our biggest national security threat."

7 Mattick, Carolyn S., Braden R. Allenby, and George R. Lucas Jr., 2012 *Chautauqua Council Final Report: Implications of Emerging Military/Security Technologies for the Laws of War* (Arizona State University, Lincoln Center for Applied Ethics, 2012).

8 Tzu, Sun, *The art of war* (Oxford University Press, 1971).

22

Drones and the Emergence of Data-Driven Warfare

DANIEL ROTHENBERG

1. DRONES AND THE PROMISE OF LEGAL WAR

Drones both embody and threaten the promise of legal war. On the one hand, drones offer the possibility of realizing one of the core objectives of the laws of war: to direct lethal force only against combatants while, at the same time, protecting civilians. On the other hand, for those living in areas where drones are deployed, their use suggests a profound sense of vulnerability; an emerging reality in which distant powers act with impunity, watching those they choose and then projecting deadly force against targets selected based on hidden criteria. This challenges the broad moral and legal vision of the laws of war to create a mutually reinforcing sense of order among multiple parties to a conflict with the goal of jointly limiting the brutality and destruction of warfare.

Discussions about the ethics and legality of drone deployment are often criticisms of larger US policies rather than reflections on the particular challenges raised by this emerging technology. For example, critics commonly focus on the numbers of civilians killed by drones. However, the serious legal and moral issues of mistaken targeting or collateral damage are no more significant whether attacks are conducted by drones or a manned aircraft (and there is evidence that drone use minimizes this harm). Others focus on the illegality of drone deployment outside of clearly defined war zones, such as in Northern Pakistan, Yemen, and Somalia. Again, this important legal and strategic question is the same regardless of whether the attacks are conducted by drones, fighter jets, missiles, bombers, or other military technologies. Where public discussion fails to engage the unique challenges posed by drones, it draws attention away from the debates that we need now, while this emerging military technology is in its early stages of development and deployment.

This chapter argues that drones symbolize a shift in the nature of warfare with significant legal and policy implications. Drones gather data through 24-hour surveillance, link this data with multiple forms of coordinated intelligence and direct precision attacks from thousands of miles away. They project lethal force based on a scope and breadth of information gathering and analysis never before possible. In this way, drone deployment pre-figures a new era of data-driven warfare whose implications are only now emerging. Supporting the protective vision and moral promise of legal war requires seriously engaging the ways in which today's drone wars challenge existing understandings of the rules regulating conflict.

This chapter begins with a discussion of the technological and strategic innovations of drone technology. It proceeds with a brief review of distinction, the key principle through which the laws of war regulate targeting. It reviews the special challenges related to targeting in non-international armed conflicts, which represent the majority of contexts where the United States deploys militarized drones. The chapter then suggests that "signature strikes" present a useful illustration of the particular innovation of drones and how they signal significant shifts in the practice of war. In these actions, US forces identify individuals and groups to be killed not based on knowledge of their identity as specific insurgent leaders – their clear status as members of al-Qaeda, the Taliban, or associated groups, or through their direct engagement with the conflict – all modes of targeting that comply with the laws of war – but instead justify lethal drone strikes based on patterns discerned from the collection and analysis of multiple data sources.

Even if today's signature strikes comply with the principles of legal targeting, they illustrate a newly invasive form of projecting lethal force that links substantive advances in the coordination of data collection, analysis, and remote killing. In changing the process of targeting, it is likely that there will be a steady expansion of the types of individuals that will be subjected to precision attacks. In this way, drones are the iconic representation of a transformation in the nature of conflict toward data-driven warfare. Facing this challenge requires rethinking the laws of war and developing, sooner rather than later, new rules for regulating conflict.

2. DRONE INNOVATION

On their own, drones are not revolutionary. Technically, they are platforms onto which different technologies are attached, including video and communication systems, targeting mechanisms, and missiles.[1] They extend various known capabilities (long flight times of light vehicles, aerial surveillance technologies, the capacity to launch precision missile attacks) and offer multiple advances (low unit cost, the strategic benefits of unmanned vehicles) that are, in many ways, similar in nature, or at least closely related to, existing military technologies.

What makes drones significant is not so much what they are as how they are deployed. Drones gather and analyze information, record activity as it occurs on the ground, and send this data around the world for immediate review and permanent storage. This data is integrated with multiple other forms of information and is used to target and kill opponents with striking precision. In this way, drones help define an emerging mode of warfare in which enormous amounts of information are collected and correlated as an integral element of a military strategy that is of special relevance when facing complexly organized, non-state armed groups, such as al-Qaeda or the Taliban.

Within the military and among technologists, drones are usually referred to as unmanned aerial vehicles (UAVs). While drones themselves are unmanned, they are flown by teams comprising a pilot – who controls the aircraft – and a sensor operator – who manages the cameras, data collection instruments, lasers, and targeting systems. These teams communicate with commanders, intelligence analysts, and others who may be stationed in multiple sites around the world. Full drone deployment depends on many levels of interconnected professionals, including technicians and launch teams, and multiple levels of command and control. Their operations are processed through globally transmitted video feeds and communication networks involving multiple intelligence sources, methods, and personnel.

Drone innovation lies in the way they link – in a single platform – intelligence capabilities and the capacity to deliver precision attacks within a complex inter-connected system. The intelligence advances of drones can be understood to involve improvements in the immediacy, constancy, coordination, scope, and nature of data used to identify opponents.

Drones communicate what is occurring as it happens in the areas where they are deployed and over which they provide surveillance, enabling a heightened engagement with an immediacy of information. Drone pilots, sensor controllers, data analysts, and those managing targeting decisions can track the movement of potential insurgents, watching in real time what they do on the ground. By linking these intelligence capacities with the ability to target and attack opponents, drones enable a contextually sensitive mechanism of targeting. For example, drone surveillance allows those controlling them to delay attacks until a target distances himself from his family or other civilians by, for example, walking into a field alone or leaving a densely populated area to enter an isolated building or vehicle. This capacity is notably different from other modes of precision killing, such as the use of cruise missiles, which once launched cannot shift the timing of their impact in relation to observed changes on the ground. Even fighter jets or other planes that can adjust their attacks while in the air are nevertheless unable to fly over targets for long periods of time and cannot be used to carefully watch those below, waiting to strike in a manner that minimizes civilian casualties.

Drones are outfitted with on-board computers that calculate trajectory, distance, speed, and other variables, and have laser-targeting systems that mark sites for missile attacks. While these technologies are used by other military platforms, such as fighter jets, the capacity of drones to stay aloft for many hours allows these calculations to be adjusted for greater accuracy, potentially enabling a more discerning process of attack that strikes only those that can be legally targeted.

Drones also allow for significant advances in the constancy of data. A fully loaded Predator drone can stay in the air for nearly 24 hours. By using a small group of drones that alternate missions, teams can provide complete surveillance over days, and even weeks. And, in the not-so-distant future, it will be possible to provide full, live data collection and surveillance over ever-larger areas for ever-increasing periods of time. In this way, drones are distinct from other surveillance mechanisms that have limited capacity to provide constant intelligence. Satellites cannot provide ongoing data collection because their orbits take them in and out of areas of review. And, their surveillance abilities are marred by weather conditions and multiple other obstacles. While manned aircraft can carry much heavier and more sophisticated intelligence equipment, they lack the flexibility of drones and cannot provide continual data collection. In contrast, not only can drones stay aloft for many hours, they are outfitted with cameras that adjust to shifting conditions, such as infrared for nighttime surveillance and synthetic aperture radar systems to see through smoke or clouds.

Woven into drone deployment is an ever-expanding system of data coordination. In this way, the true innovation of drones lies not in what they can do on their own, but in their operation as part of a networked system that is complexly and multiply linked to other sources of data collection and analysis. The coordination of information gathered from drones with multiple other sources defines a substantive increase in the scope of data used for targeting and other military operations. As the quality and depth of this data increases, information analysis will play an increasingly significant role in managing conflict and defining strategy, at least for the empowered and technologically advanced forces that control drones and related technologies.

In more traditional understandings of war, the information relevant to attacks generally related to the location of opponents' forces and their movements. While these issues remain salient, drones radically increase the nature of data collected, allowing this information to be linked with phone intercepts, human intelligence, and other sources of information that, taken together, enable ever more complex mapping of the social reality of opposing forces.

These innovations are linked to a shift in the very nature of the data collected and analyzed. Drone video feeds, images, and all of the other interconnected sources of intelligence are digital or are digitized for storage and review. Records of people's actions on the ground – visiting families, attending meetings, moving armaments, driving vehicles, praying – are stores in ways that can be endlessly reviewed. This data can be linked with human and signal intelligence of various types and then categorized in multiple ways. As such, drone deployment is a key element of the creation of permanent records of adversaries, potential adversaries, and their communities, which can be repeatedly searched and analyzed for various purposes.

In addition, digital data can be stored indefinitely in a manner that allows for access, at least in theory, from almost any location. Over time, this means that data collected by drones on particular places or people become part of a permanent digital record, which can be multiply referenced for various purposes. The implications of this form of data collection have yet to fully emerge, but all the material now gathered by drones – as well as all the other digital information from the mass biometrical data of detainees, to scanned documents, and to electronic records of financial transactions – represents a body of information that can be correlated and subjected to coordinated analysis during current conflicts and on into the future.

While these shifts are profound, they are also relatively new, and their transformative nature remains unknown. At present, drones are plagued by multiple limitations. They have no defensive capabilities and cannot maneuver well to avoid attack. They can be severely affected by bad weather. Their communication systems routinely experience problems, delays, and difficulties. There are limited numbers of drones and limited skilled teams to manage them. Each new drone requires multiple professionals that need to be trained, including pilots, sensor analysts, maintenance staff, and others.

Perhaps the most significant issue regarding the data-gathering capacity of drones and related technologies is that the collection of massive amounts of information creates its own problems. In general, data analysis requires far more resources than data collection. So, where significantly more data is gathered, more experts and review systems are needed to process the information. There is already far more digital information gathered by drones and other systems than can be fully analyzed, especially where the review must correlate multiple and distinct sources of data. These problems will only increase as data collection continues to grow through an expansion in the number and capacities of drones, as well as the related deployment of new and emerging technologies. One reason this is significant as regards the implications of the shift toward data-drive warfare is that more information will require more comprehensive automated systems to render sensible what is being gathered and stored. This is not to suggest that suddenly war will be about data alone, but rather that these shifts are transformative and that drones provide a window into their significance.

3. TARGETING AND THE LAWS OF WAR

Within the laws of war, the principle of distinction provides guidance as to who can be legally targeted. Distinction involves three key obligations that apply to all parties involved in conflicts: they must distinguish between combatants and civilians, they must direct attacks only against combatants, and they must take precautions to minimize collateral civilian casualties.[2] In this way, the principle of distinction plays a central role in minimizing the potentially indiscriminate and broadly destructive nature of war.

The laws of war involve a balancing process between the strategic demands of projecting force, known as military necessity, and core legal commitments to protecting civilians.[3] Distinction is essential to the protective vision of the laws of war in that civilians are never to be purposefully targeted, while combatants are legitimate targets at all times. That is, any party to a conflict can legally kill opposing combatants whether they are engaged in battle, advancing toward an attack, or sleeping at a base far from the front line.

Targeting under the laws of war varies based on whether the conflict is an international armed conflict involving two or more states; or a non-international armed conflict, in which government forces face non-state armed groups; or where the struggle is between multiple non-state armed groups. While the principle of distinction applies to both types of conflict, the justification and specificity of legal obligations differ, with significant implications for drone deployment.

International armed conflicts are regulated by international treaties – most notably the four Geneva Conventions of 1949 and Additional Protocol I – while non-international conflicts are regulated by customary law (and by Additional Protocol II).

Within international armed conflicts, parties engage the principle of distinction by indicating combatant status through clearly displayed uniforms and insignia. Armies identify members of the military, as well as military vehicles, planes, ships, and installations, in ways that are readily discernable. They similarly clearly designate those that cannot be legally targeted, such as medics and health personnel. This allows all parties in a conflict to know who and what can be legally targeted while also making it easier to protect civilians. In addition, clear markings of status help civilians protect themselves by keeping physically apart from combatants, particularly in the midst of conflict.

Combatants are protected from targeting only when they no longer present a possible threat, known as *hors de combat*, such as when they are wounded or surrender.[4] In those cases, there are stringent rules regarding how combatants brought under the control of an opposing force as prisoners of war should be treated. They must be detained in humane conditions, provided with appropriate medical care, and safely housed until the end of the conflict, at which time they are repatriated. These rules express a vision of war in which the legitimate projection of lethal force cannot be used to punish opponents, but only to achieve set strategic ends.

However, the contexts in which drones are currently deployed are best understood as non-international rather than international conflicts. Within non-international armed conflicts, the principle of distinction remains in effect, but its application is more complex. Legally, non-state forces cannot be parties to international treaties and are not bound by the specific provisions of the regulations, making the mechanisms and processes of targeting less clear. In part, this is because in civil wars and armed insurgencies – as well as the situations in which the United States and its allies face al-Qaeda and related forces – non-state forces rarely distinguish themselves in a clearly identifiable manner. These groups generally do not wear uniforms or display insignia and their military strategies often rely on their close links and integration with civilian populations. As such, members of such groups often appear indistinguishable from civilians. Furthermore, non-state armed groups may attack from within civilian populations or may hide among civilians following attacks. This makes it difficult to accurately distinguish members of armed groups from civilians and heightens the possibility that attacks will kill civilians. In addition, since these groups are not professional state militaries, they often rely on individuals that participate in conflicts on an intermittent basis, mixing their lives as civilians with their engagement with military activities.

Because non-international armed conflicts are less formally regulated, there exists significant debate and discussion regarding the rules that apply.

Nevertheless, there is widespread agreement that the principle of distinction operates in these situations. The International Committee of the Red Cross (ICRC), the global authority on interpreting the laws of war, suggests that in non-international armed conflicts it is essential to differentiate between individuals that are members of non-state armed groups and civilians who participate only partially in conflicts. Members of armed groups are those defined by a "continuous combat function" and can be legally targeted at any time, a situation analogous to that of combatants within conventional armed forces.[5] Those who are occasionally or intermittently involved in the armed actions[6] are generally classified as civilians and are "entitled to protection against direct attack unless and for such time as they take direct part in hostilities."[7]

Civilians that participate in these groups can only be targeted when they are acting in a way that satisfies set criteria linking them to military elements of the conflict. That is, the acts must "adversely affect military operations or military capacity" in a direct, causal manner that supports one party in opposition to another.[8] Some argue that these definitions are too broad and others suggest that they are too narrow.[9] The key point in this interpretation of the laws of war is that members of organized armed groups may be targeted at all times during a conflict based on their status, while civilians that support these groups can be targeted only when they are directly engaged in military actions. As the ICRC explains, "This illustrates that the notion of direct participation in hostilities does not refer to a person's status, function, or affiliation, but to his or her engagement in specific hostile acts."[10]

In this way, civilians are protected, and force cannot be legally used against the array of individuals, families, and communities that live with and among members of organized armed groups, even if they provide various types of non-military support. While these ideas have a technical nature, they support the overall legal vision of the principle of distinction, namely, to ensure that lethal force is directed only against those involved in the conflict while civilians are protected from harm.

Non-international conflicts present special challenges because of the difficulties of identifying members of armed groups. So, within these contexts, targeting is always a question of gathering intelligence, whether the data comes from informants on the ground, satellite imagery, or intercepted communications. In theory, the uncertainties of distinction within non-international conflicts could be fully addressed through perfect intelligence. That is, if one were to gain access to data that allowed members of non-state armed groups to be located and identified in a completely accurate manner, then targeting decisions against these groups would be similar in nature to those against formal militaries that publicly indicate their status as described above. And if this data were coupled with precision strikes, one could imagine a situation in which the projection of force in non-international conflicts would be directed only against those that can be legally targeted.

Some claim that drones and other emerging military technologies are moving warfare in precisely this direction, even suggesting that these capabilities create a moral "duty to use drones."[11] To the degree that linking massive data collection with precision attacks provides greater legal clarity for targeting in non-international conflicts, this may well be true. That is, if the constant surveillance of drones coupled with multiple forms of other intelligence leading to precision strikes allows the United States to kill only members of al-Qaeda and related groups while protecting civilians living in conflict regions from harm, these acts would support the moral vision and key obligations of the laws of war. Even where the process is marred by imperfect data and related problems, drone strikes may well minimize civilian casualties, especially as compared to other means of projecting lethal force. In fact, some researchers suggest that locals living in the parts of northeastern Pakistan where drones are deployed support these strikes precisely because of the discriminate nature of their targeting.[12]

If, in fact, drones enable a level of lethal accuracy directed only against members of non-state armed groups, they could insert into non-international conflicts an adherence to the principle of distinction never before possible. That is, the link between broad surveillance and complex, integrated data analysis might allow far more accurate determinations of who is and is not a member of a non-state armed group while identifying which civilians are directly participating in hostilities and at what times. As such, drones and the future systems they inspire could enable the application of a level of rigor and certitude analogous to what is found in international armed conflicts, where uniforms and other markers of status are required and provide clarity of distinction. Where such information is linked with precision killing, one could imagine drone deployment as embodying the promise of legal war, to direct lethal force only against legitimate targets – combatants and military installations – while protecting civilians.

This vision assumes that drones' link of substantially improved intelligence with precision attacks clearly maps onto accepted legal means of targeting. Yet, what if the advances in data collection and analysis associated with current drone deployment do not simply improve the quality of intelligence available for targeting under existing norms, but rather expand the scope of those subjected to lethal force? What if the newly invasive nature of data collection – constant 24-hour digital review, ever-increasing areas of surveillance, intercepted communications, Internet data trails, satellite imagery, electronically tracked movement and transactions – all of which are permanently stored, collated, and cross-referenced – shifts the practice of targeting beyond what is currently envisioned by the laws of war? In fact, radically increased capacities of knowing more about those on the ground than was previously possible has already changed the process of targeting and may also have expanded who is targeted. To date, this shift in targeting is most clearly exemplified in the use of drones by US forces to conduct "signature strikes."

4. THE IMPLICATION OF SIGNATURE STRIKES

"Signature strikes" are forms of targeting based on the analysis of data gathered about individuals and groups that reveal suspicious patterns. They represent the most useful illustration of how drones' management of intelligence gathering, analysis, and precision targeting redefines how drones project lethal force. Signature strikes are distinct from the use of drones for "personality strikes," where an attack is directed against a particular individual on the basis of his identity and known role within al-Qaeda, the Taliban, or associated groups. Signature strikes are also distinct from attacks by drones or other platforms conducted within international armed conflicts, where targeting is guided by clear indications of combatant status through uniforms, insignia, and other means. There is evidence that signature strikes have been used often and are a key element of today's drone wars.[13] In fact, some reports suggest that most drone strikes in recent years, especially those directed by the CIA, have been signature strikes.[14]

Drones play a key role in these strikes by contributing essential data used in the analysis that enables targeting decisions, while also delivering the precision attacks and engaging in post-mission review. Drones collect information in all the ways described above – circling above homes and villages, following people from place to place – sending this data for review, collation, and comparison with other forms of intelligence. This allows analysts and commanders to make determinations regarding who can be targeted. When the individual or group is at a location set apart from civilians, or where a decision is made that military necessity allows for an attack at a site where there are civilians, drone pilots initiate a strike using precision munitions, a process that is viewed live in multiple locations.

After the missiles have done their damage, drones continue to fly above the area, sending video feeds of the aftermath of the attack. Sometimes they remain overhead for hours, or the surveillance is continued for even longer periods of time by newly arriving drones. This allows for an ongoing review of the impact of an attack, viewing how families and communities react, and even surveilling the subsequent funerals and mourning rituals. This entire process is something new within warfare: an intimate link between surveillance, the projection of lethal force, and a vastly increased engagement with data collection and analysis.

Signature strikes are a response to the particular targeting demands of non-international armed conflicts. That is, in the absence of clearly defined combatant status – with uniforms, insignia, etc. – targeting has to be based on information gathered and processed by the applicable laws of war. For signature strikes to be legal, they must be based on reasonable interpretations of the principle of distinction, targeting only those that are clearly defined members of organized armed groups (based on their "continuous combat function") or civilians while they are directly engaged in hostilities. The high bar on targeting civilians cuts to the heart of the moral vision of the laws of war, which allows lethal force to be directed only against those that clearly present a strategic threat. Underlying this issue is the question of what defines "direct participation" and what information is used to make this determination.

The US government's position is that all drone attacks, including signature strikes, fully comply with the law. These claims tend to be made in general terms as when President Obama stated, partly responding to concerns about expanded drone strikes, "America's actions are legal ... Under domestic law, and international law."[15] Similar claims have been made by other high-ranking US officials: "There is no question that we are abiding by international law and the law of war ... And anyone who suggests that somehow we're employing other tactics that somehow violate international law are dead wrong."[16]

Many critics disagree. Some argue that as a result of the program's secrecy, especially with signature strikes, drone attacks cannot be legal, and that "the total absence of any forms of credible transparency or verifiable accountability" means "the United States cannot possibly satisfy its obligations under international law to ensure accountability for its use of lethal force."[17] Others situate this lack of transparency within a larger context of military actions that express limited adherence to international norms, arguing that "the legality of so-called 'signature strikes' is highly suspect."[18]

In fact, the administration has revealed very little about the ways in which signature strikes are authorized. There is not enough publicly available data to allow for a serious review of whether signature strikes comply with the laws of war. Some suggest that legal safeguards are substantial and the problem lies in the secrecy of the targeting procedures. As a legal expert and former George W. Bush administration official has written, "The major challenge to legitimating the shadow war against terrorists is that the Executive branch is hand-tied by its own rules, and cannot disclose what it is doing to permit Congress and the American people to judge whether it approves."[19] Others have used the available information from press reports and official statements to piece together the criteria used for signature strikes, suggesting that some, but not all, of these attacks are legal.[20] Not surprisingly, many interested parties – from human rights groups to members of Congress – have asked the US administration to provide more information about signature strikes so that the issue of their legality can be discussed with greater rigor and specificity.[21]

Even if all the rules, procedures, and analytic mechanisms used in current signature strikes were to be made public, and even if all of the drone attacks to date have complied with the laws of war, signature strikes raise troubling issues about how today's drone wars are transforming the process of targeting. This is because drones enable distinct and particularly intrusive forms of projecting power that redefine the conditions under which individuals and groups are identified and, in some cases, killed.

The newly emerging vision of war identifies individuals and groups not through specific hostile acts, but rather through an amalgamation of distinct data points. An individual might be known based on recorded Internet usage, cell phone calls, placement in a social network, commercial transactions, travel records – all of which provide a representation of actions among people whose identities remain unknown. In fact, the very point of signature strikes is to gather data about participation in conflict in the absence of clear indications of status.

The increases in data collection, analysis, and information management that come with today's drone wars do not simply define an increase in the amount of intelligence used to make targeting decisions; rather they signal a transformation of the role of data in guiding warfare. Drones enable newly intrusive projections of power such that the lives of those under review are subjected to 24-hour-a-day video recording that is coupled with data mining, conversation intercepts, human intelligence, satellite imagery, and other information collected by a series of rapidly expanding tools and methods.

It is important to note that the process of data collection is not focused solely on those that can be targeted – as in battlefield surveillance of combatants or in personality strikes – but is rather a means of determining targets from a review of the lives and activities of a designated population. The open-ended nature and full scope of this analytic process remains unknown. While at present these capacities are constrained by the technical limitations of drones and related surveillance systems, the expansion of these capabilities is inevitable and may be extremely rapid. Signature strikes evoke a vision of data–driven warfare that will expand as technological capabilities increase. The greater the immediacy, constancy, coordination, scope, and breadth of information that can be gathered, the more likely these capacities will be deployed to broadly surveil territory to determine suspicious patterns and reveal potential targets. The significance of this shift is clear if one imagines a steady advance in the capacities that drones have already brought to those that manage them.

For example, the most significant sign of the constancy of data derived from drone deployment lies in the ongoing surveillance provided when groups of drones take turns circling above areas of interest to the United States. This form of data collection is, in many ways, an early sign of far more advanced future technologies. Imagine if these capacities were to be expanded ten, a hundred, or a thousand times through new types of drones, improved sensors, or still other modes of data collection that might be deployed permanently or in ways that we have yet to understand.

What we see in current drone deployment is a mode of intelligence gathering that is not only more significant in terms of the quantity of information collected, but also involves a set of capabilities that are far more invasive than possible in earlier times. Today, people's ordinary activities – walking through a village, farming, meeting with neighbors, praying – can be reviewed and permanently recorded, with ever-expanding capabilities of coverage. The daily world of those living under the surveillance of a party to a conflict that manages drones becomes a legitimate space for militarized intrusion. People with no connection to hostilities who are disengaged from the conflict are likely to become subject to a significantly intrusive projection of power.

In many ways this is a rational response to the fact that in non-international armed conflicts, it is often difficult to identify adversaries. They may appear generally indistinguishable from civilians and may be complexly integrated into civilian social life. It is in the interest of those projecting force to gather the maximum amount of information possible about the areas where adversaries operate. They may record conversations, seek to know the identities and relations of those in a community, and otherwise engage in activities that help with the development of full profiles regarding opponents or whoever might pose a military threat. The expanding nature of this process is likely as emerging capabilities extend the traditional meaning of intelligence used for targeting and as mass data collection and analysis techniques are directed toward ever-larger areas and populations. While the initial stated goal may be to identify members of organized armed groups or civilians directly partici-pating in hostilities in line with the laws of war, the process will inevitably yield a level of intrusive knowledge of everyone surveilled that will become a core component of the management of conflict.

The use of drones and other intelligence sources is collated to reveal what are known as "patterns of life" through which repeated observations of suspi-cious behavior are identified and used for targeting. Some of these acts, such as engaging in direct attacks or laying improvised explosive devices along a road meet accepted legal standards for targeting and show how drone deploy-ment can aid military goals and even increase adherence to the laws of war. Yet, what of other patterns in people's lives that might raise suspicion, even as they have little direct link to accepted understandings of distinction? Given that many organized armed groups and their civilian supporters are deeply integrated into local life, it is likely that many patterns of life of legitimate targets are profoundly entwined with ordinary civilian life such that the principle of distinction and its core limitations within the laws of war will be breached in favor of ever-expanding uses of intelligence. Viewed from above, any meeting of men might appear suspicious, even if it is little more than a family gathering, a collection of community leaders managing a civil dispute, or a social or religious ceremony. As individuals visit known combatants who are relatives, or meet with local leaders or clerics who play a variety of functions within a community, their activities may be recorded, analyzed, and potentially used for targeting decisions.

In the not-so-distant future, drones will provide far expanded range of surveillance such that the patterns of life of many people, perhaps entire communities, will be permanently recorded and available for review and possible use for targeting. This will be linked with whatever other data sources are available from intercepted communications that might pick up on key words and phrases, or other indications of political association, whether clearly linked to an organized armed group or not. This data might further be correlated with social network analyses linking individuals by tribal, neighbor-hood, familial, and commercial ties. As reviewing traces of actions and mapping patterns of behavior of as broad a group as possible expands – with today's drones only the first step – a new vision of targeting will likely emerge and with it a new understanding of the nature of war.

As mentioned above, accurate analysis is one of the most significant problems of mass data collection. The more information gathered from multiple sources, the more inherently complex the challenge of proper analysis becomes. If there is a steady increase in the number of sources of data, such as drones, coupled with an increase in the amount that can be gathered by each source, the scope of what will be gathered even in a single day will quickly overwhelm the reviewing capacity of human teams.

In fact, to some degree this is already true, as far more data is currently collected than can be effectively processed. For mass amounts of data to be rendered sensible, there will be a need for various modes of expanded automated review. As a result, the patterns drawn from the data gathered will be determined using algorithms and other tools that can rapidly assess and review enormous amounts of diverse digital information. A reliance on these automated methods will provide guidance for attacks, and may even be used to identify differences between civilians, who must be protected, and those who can be legally targeted. In this sense, the issue of automation with new technologies may have less to do with machines that operate on their own and more to do with analytic frameworks used to process data.

In this way, there are signs that war, or at least some aspects of war, is shifting to become a process through which individuals are targeted based on an amalgam of data, multiply collected, and complexly reviewed, possibly by teams located around the world. Drones and related emerging military systems may increasingly engage in attacks where targeting is not based on status or actions "directly related to hostilities" but on intricate automated reviews of data that reveal patterns understood to be indications of who represents a threat and can be legitimately targeted. This is what is presaged in today's signature strikes.

To the degree the data used for targeting is limited in its focus and serves to provide greater clarity for the projection of force in a manner that adheres to the laws of war, drones and related technologies present no significant threat to the principle of distinction. Yet, like so many advanced technologies, it is likely that newly emerging capabilities and innovations will begin, if this has not already begun, to drive targeting.

Certainly, the temptations are there, and it is difficult to imagine that targeting will not expand the understanding of "direct participation in hostilities" to cover an ever-increasing array of actions that support adversaries. For example, linking drone surveillance with electronic reviews of financial transactions and money transfers may lead to the determination that a banker who has assisted an organized armed group in moving money is a legitimate target. The same may occur for an ideological figure, such as writer or cleric, whose claims are viewed to be motivating conflict, determined perhaps though cross-referenced data on who listens to his speeches, quotes his writings, attends his lectures, etc. Similarly, information gathered on local leaders, regionally significant business professionals, or any number of others who can be traced in multiple ways and through possible relationships to organized armed groups might lead to their designation as legitimate targets.

The point is that, at present, there are limited accepted mechanisms, tests, or clear guidelines to manage the way that data-driven warfare should be regulated. While the key principles of the laws of war are well established, how these should be used to guide action within a world defined by ever more complex and invasive data collection and analysis remains an open question. What, then, are the rules needed to address the transformation of warfare evidenced by today's drone strikes? And who will define and establish new understandings of the laws of war?

5. WHY DRONES? PREPARING FOR DATA-DRIVEN WARFARE

After nearly a decade and a half of war, drones are the only military technology that has captured America's, and possibly the world's, popular imagination. Some of this fascination is born of misconceptions about what drones do, yet the special role played by drones in the world touches on an intuition, largely correct, that there is something innovative and newly disturbing about these unmanned military machines.

Drones, as they currently operate and as they will likely develop in the future, signal a fundamental transformation of warfare. Increasingly, and in ways we can only begin to understand now, war will be defined by radical expansions in the gathering and analyzing of information for military purposes. As with signature strikes, this process will reconfigure the projection of force in ways that no longer rest on status but exist as a correlation of data points drawn from multiple sources and analyzed in ever more complex ways. In this sense, drones not only represent the enormous asymmetries of technological capacity between those who control them and those living where they are deployed, but also involve fundamentally distinct means of projecting power.

Drones are the iconic representation of an emerging set of new military technologies with extraordinarily invasive capacities to gather data, enable complex analyses, and deliver precision attacks. These capabilities allow those controlling drones to more effectively target specific individuals and groups while minimizing harm to civilians. This enables improved adherence to the principle of distinction in a manner that is technically far more precise than what was previously possible. Yet a growing reliance on significant increases in the scope and nature of data collected on potential adversaries suggests a broadening of those that will be targeted, especially within non-international armed conflicts where status distinctions are unclear and where conflicts are highly asymmetrical.

The challenges posed by today's drone wars require a reflection on the very purpose and logic of the laws of war. This set of rules has evolved over centuries in recognition of the constancy (and perhaps inevitability) of war, as well as the ethical and practical demands of minimizing the potential devastation of conflict. The field is defined by the profound and vexing challenge of creating systems that enable opposing forces to commit the most violent acts against each other – shooting, bombing, maiming, and killing – while accepting basic rules limiting their actions. While there are countless historical cases of its failings, the laws of war have helped restructure conflict to become more orderly and rule-based. Of special significance is the way in which these laws have, with increasing rigor and specificity, defined the principle of distinction such that parties to conflicts aim to protect civilians.

The laws of war are not simply a set of abstract rules to be mechanistically applied to conflict. Rather, they are a social achievement whose vibrancy and value is vulnerable to political shifts and repeated challenges by significant technological innovation. Grasping the value of the laws of war requires understanding that the rules regulating conflict, like all legal systems, are mechanisms for defining and enabling mutually reinforcing norms. Developing meaningful law within the context of the rapid change in the nature of conflict is a genuine and complex challenge for which there is no simple answer. Yet for the laws of war to function, they must have at their core terms that can be adopted by opposing forces as a means of limiting the destruction of war and as the expression of common moral understandings.

As abstract as this idea may appear, the value of broadly accepted rules is apparent when the lack of regulation presents real and present threats. One of the problems with today's drone debate is that it is largely premised on the idea that the technology will continue to be controlled by the United States. This cannot possibly be true, and there are many signs that point to the broad global diffusion of militarized drones. The importance of drone regulation, or at least greater clarity as to the rules for targeting within data-driven warfare, becomes clear when one broadens the discussion to engage the proliferation of drone deployment by multiple state and non-state actors.

Consider the powerful divide in public opinion on US drone deployment abroad and within the country. Polls suggest that the American people largely support US drone policy in multiple sites around the world (even as those in other countries largely oppose these policies).[22] There are likely many explanations for this, ranging from profound fear regarding the threats from existing elements of al-Qaeda or other groups, to a basic trust of the US government in managing foreign military operations, to a marked lack of concern for those living in the regions where drones are deployed. Within the United States, there is significant debate and discussion, as well as outrage and vocal opposition, to the possibility of domestic drone deployment.[23] While there are many ways to interpret this difference, it should be instructive for policymakers that the broad public support for the United States use of armed drones abroad is likely a sign of a failure to engage the implications of a broader global drone deployment.

Many countries currently possess drones and are developing their own military programs. No doubt, over time non-state actors will gain access to various forms of drone technology. As this process proceeds, the world will increasingly face the expansion of data-driven warfare. As drones are more widely used by multiple actors around the world, the targeting questions raised by drone deployment will be become a global policy issue. Trust in the appropriate use of force alone will prove a poor substitute for accepted principles and clear legal restrictions. Even where rules regulating warfare are violated in some cases, as always occurs, their existence provides a much-needed reference point and significant check on abuses within a dangerous and rapidly changing world. Some similarly rigorous set of rules for militarized drones is needed.

It is not difficult to imagine cases in which forces not allied with the United States might adopt drone strategies similar in structure to those currently used by the US government. The advanced Russian or Chinese militaries (and many others) might deploy drones and related military surveillance and attack technologies against armed insurgents within their territory, just across their borders, or in sites located around the world. Their legal justifications and the secrecy of the targeting process used might well mirror that of the US government. As data-driven warfare expands, the fundamentally invasive nature of mass surveillance and cross-referenced data sources might enable the creation of enormous digital files on large populations whose accuracy, specificity, and efficiency could redefine the nature of a security state. Where these capacities are coupled with precision killing and operate in a context unchecked by clear legal rules, the situation might well present serious challenges to the very real accomplishments of the laws of war.

Drones signify a significant shift in the very nature of warfare. Their mode of targeting, especially signature strikes, signals a substantive advance in how data collection and analysis are linked to precision attacks, defining a new set of strategic and legal issues. By reflecting on today's drone wars, at this early stage in the transformative process, we can take meaningful steps to prepare for the challenges of data-driven warfare.

NOTES

1 "Predator incorporates numerous payloads, including Electro-optical/Infrared (EO/IR) video cameras, laser designators, and Hellfire missiles. Additionally, the aircraft may be equipped with GA-ASI's Lynx® Multi-mode Radar, a highly sophisticated all-weather radar that displays photographic quality imagery of targets." General Atomics Aeronautical website. www.ga-asi.com/products/aircraft/predator.php.

2 International Committee of the Red Cross (ICRC), *Customary International Humanitarian Law*: "Rule 1. The Principle of Distinction between Civilians and Combatants ... The parties to the conflict must at all times distinguish between civilians and combatants. Attacks may only be directed against combatants. Attacks must not be directed against civilians."

3 The principle of distinction is widely accepted as a core element of the laws of war, requiring a distinction between combatants, defined in Article 4 of the Third Geneva Convention, and civilians, defined in Additional Protocol I to the Geneva Conventions. While the United States is not a party to the Additional Protocol I, it regards key elements of the text as customary law. There is often debate as to the exact definition of civilian between the International Committee of the Red Cross and the US government, and to some degree the challenges of drone deployment highlight the need for greater international consensus on the issue.

4 According to the Geneva Conventions Common Article 3 (called this because it is included with the identical language in all four conventions), "each Party to the conflict" must provide protection to "persons taking no active part in hostilities, including members of armed forces who have laid down their arms and those placed *hors de combat*."

5 ICRC, "Direct participation in hostilities: Questions & answers." www.icrc.org/eng/resources/documents/faq/direct-participation-ihl-faq-020609.htm.

6 Melzer, Nils, "Interpretive guidance on the notion of direct participation in hostilities under international humanitarian law" (ICRC, May 2009).

7 Ibid., p. 16.

8 The ICRC terms these the "threshold of harm," "direct causation," and "belligerent nexus": "Acts amounting to direct participation in hostilities must meet three cumulative requirements: (1) a threshold regarding the harm likely to result from the act, (2) a relationship of direct causation between the act and the expected harm, and (3) a belligerent nexus between the act and the hostilities conducted between the parties to an armed conflict." Ibid., p. 46.

9 "Targeting operations with drone technology: Humanitarian law implications," Background note for the American Society of International Law Meeting, Human Rights Institute, at Columbia Law School, New York, on March 25, 2011.

10 Melzer, "Interpretive guidance on the notion of direct participation in hostilities under international humanitarian law," p. 44.

11 Gross, Oren, "The new way of war: Is there a duty to use drones?" Minnesota Legal Studies Research Paper No. 14-14 (2014).

12 For example, see "Drones over Pakistan, drop the pilot: A surprising number of Pakistanis are in favour of drone strikes," *Economist*, October 19, 2013.

13 See Currier, Cora, and Justin Elliott, "The drone war doctrine we still know nothing about," *ProPublica*, February 26, 2013: "The first public reference to a signature strike appears to have been in February 2008, when the *New York Times* reported a change in drone strike policy, negotiated between the U.S. and Pakistan ... Over the next few years, they became the majority of strikes conducted in Pakistan, according to media reports citing unnamed officials."

14 Cloud, David S., "CIA drones have broader list of targets: The agency since 2008 has been secretly allowed to kill unnamed suspects in Pakistan"; *Los Angeles Times*, May 5, 2010: "Of more than 500 people who U.S. officials say have been killed since the pace of strikes intensified, the vast majority have been individuals whose names were unknown, or about whom the agency had only fragmentary information. In some cases, the CIA discovered only after an attack that the casualties included a suspected terrorist whom it had been seeking."

15 Barack Obama, "Remarks by the president at the National Defense University," Fort McNair, Washington, DC, May 23, 2013.

16 CIA Director Leon Panetta, interview on ABC's *This Week*, June 27, 2010.

17 Alston, Philip, "The CIA and targeted killings beyond borders," *Harvard National Security Law Journal* 2 (2011): 283–446.

18 International Human Rights and Conflict Resolution Clinic, Stanford Law School and Global Justice Clinic, New York University School of Law, "Living under drones: Death, injury, and trauma to civilians from US drone practices in Pakistan," September 2012, p. 103.

19 Jack Goldsmith, "The intersection of vague disclosure and reduced drone strike," *Lawfare*, May 27, 2013.

20 Heller, Kevin, "'One hell of a killing machine': Signature strikes and international law," Melbourne Legal Studies Research Paper No. 634, Melbourne Law School.

21 In 2012 and 2013 various members of Congress sent the Obama administration a number of letters seeking clarification on key aspects of US drone policy, including additional information on how signature strikes are managed. See Letter from Bob Goodlatte et al. to President Barack Obama, February 8, 2013; Letter from John McCain to John O. Brennan, Assistant to the President for Homeland Security and Counterterrorism, February 6, 2013; Letter from John Conyers et al. to Eric H. Holder, Jr., US Attorney General December 4, 2012 and May 21, 2012.

22 Gallup, "In U.S., 65% support drone attacks on terrorists abroad," March 25, 2013: "Nearly two-thirds of Americans (65%) think the U.S. government should use drones to launch airstrikes in other countries against suspected terrorists." Drake, Bruce, "Report questions drone use, widely unpopular globally, but not in the U.S," Pew Research Center, October 23, 2013: "[D]rone operations are widely unpopular in the rest of the world. In 31 of 39 countries surveyed last spring, at least half of the publics disapproved of the attacks. At least three-in-four held this view in 15 of the

countries. Aside from the U.S., the only countries where majorities supported the drone strikes were Israel (64%) and Kenya (56%). In Pakistan, they were opposed by 68% of the public."

23 Gallup, "In U.S., 65% support drone attacks on terrorists abroad": "66% opposed drone strikes within the U.S. against suspected terrorists, and 79% said drone strikes should not be used within the U.S. against American citizens suspected of being terrorists."

Index